SAILING TRAWLERS

By the same author :-

SPRITSAIL BARGES OF THAMES AND MEDWAY

SAILING DRIFTERS

MEMORIES   " Sometimes I sits and thinks "

TRAWL BASIN, LOWESTOFT

SAILING TRAWLERS

by

Edgar J. March,

Associate of the Royal Institution of Naval Architects

★

THE STORY OF DEEP-SEA FISHING
WITH LONG LINE AND TRAWL

★

A New Impression

DAVID & CHARLES

NEWTON ABBOT   LONDON   NORTH POMFRET (VT)

British Library Cataloguing in Publication Data

March, Edgar J.
  Sailing trawlers. – 2nd ed.
    1. Trawls and trawling – England – History
    I. Title
  623.8'28   SH344.6.T7

  ISBN 0–7153–4711–X

This book was first published by Percival Marshall & Company Limited
in 1953

This edition first published 1970
Second impression 1978
Third impression 1981

Printed in Great Britain by
Redwood Burn Limited Trowbridge and Esher
for David & Charles (Publishers) Limited
Brunel House Newton Abbot
Devon

Published in the United States of America
by David & Charles Inc
North Pomfret Vermont 05053 USA

INTRODUCTION TO THE 1970 IMPRESSION

As it is many a long year since sailing trawlers worked around our coasts I was indeed fortunate to find a few smacksmen who could speak at first hand of the time when sail was supreme before steam became a serious rival. To write such a story today would be impossible. Few written records were made, men carried their knowledge in their heads. All the information a craftsman required to build a smack was a half-model and this was not always essential as his eye often gave sweetness of line. Luckily I was able to rescue much data from oblivion, but by far the most valuable contribution came from the men who had trawled all their working lives on the wild wastes of the North Sea and elswhere. Men I count it a privilege to have known.

What characters many of them were, fearless and independent. Recently I heard from the grand-daughter of W. W. Dawson who, as related on page 24, defiantly built a smack too big to enter the Grimsby Fish Dock. "My grandfather had been campaigning for some time for the Grimsby Fish Dock lock to be enlarged and the building of the *Tubal Cain* was just his obstinate way of forcing the issue. The lock was widened as a result!"

In January 1966 Mr. Nicholas Prior sent me a list of smacks which he copied for me from a recent Danish Shipping Register lent by my friend J. Woodhouse of Caister. Of the forty vessels listed nine were built in Hull by W. & J. McCann, G. W. Brown and Hunt, Fowler & Co. Of the nine from Rye yards six built by J. C. Hoad included the cod smack *William Martin*, built 1883, and similar to the model whose plans appear on pages 312-314, three were from the yard of G. & T. Smith, and one is simply listed as built at Rye.

Eight built at Grimsby came from the yards of Smith Bros., F. & G. Collinson & Co., Smith, Stephenson & Son, and Furner, Leaver & Co. Sam Dewdney & Son built two, J. W. & A. Upham one of the three hailing from Brixham. From Burton Stather two were built by J. Wray & Son, one by J. Garside with one builder unknown. Two smacks were simply "built in England", and one came from each of the following yards: Cottingham Bros., Goole; H. Fellows & Son, Southtown; H. Britten, Great Yarmouth; J. E. Wilkins, Wivenhoe, and W. A. Gibbs, Galmpton.

Eighteen firms in different counties were responsible for such conscientious work that their vessels have survived the storms and hazards of eighty to ninety years. The oldest was built by McCann at Hull in 1874 and with the exception of *Briton's Pride* built by Upham at Brixham in 1895, the remainder were all built in the late 1870s and early 1880s, a wonderful tribute to the skill of shipwrights long dead and forgotten. Those stout timber hulls have withstood the vibration of motors, unknown when the smacks were built, as well as the tempestuous seas around Iceland and the Faroes, and can still earn their owners a living.

It gave me great pleasure to hear that *Sailing Trawlers* is constantly consulted by Scandinavian owners, being considered "their bible" in this sphere.

Green Acre,   EDGAR J. MARCH
Colwell Bay,
Freshwater, Isle of Wight.

To

The memory of Smacksmen in the days of sail

whose last haul has been made

PREFACE

THE passing of the fishing smack is the end of an era. The culmination of centuries of trial and error to harness to man's needs those unstable elements, wind and water, coincided with the arrival of forces no longer dependent on nature. Many of the crews were men of a breed which is passing from the earth, prime seamen nurtured in a hard school which formed character and taught self-reliance, so that they gained that quiet confidence typical of many of those it has been my pleasure to meet.

Some of these men have reached calm anchorages where they can relax and enjoy the fruits of their labours, others only just weather the rocks of adversity, while there are those who have sought shelter in some haven of refuge after buffeting on life's stormy seas, but I have found none who bewail their fate or decry the life they knew. Smack hulls were built by craftsmen who took a pride in their job and the fact that so many vessels survived fifty and more years hard use tells of the conscientious work put into tasks often hidden from the eye. Youth to-day, with advantages undreamed of years ago, might do well to ponder over the lives of such men.

In trying to tell the story of the sailing trawler I am fully aware of the many gaps which can now never be bridged, as over sixty years—a lifetime—have passed since steam began to oust sail from the fishing fleets. In some ports it brought a decline as swift as the meteoric rise the preceding years had seen, in others sail held its own until a crippling blow was dealt in the first world war when about one-third of the smacks afloat were sunk by enemy action. In the years between the wars a few lingered on at Brixham and Lowestoft, but they ceased working a decade or so ago and to-day not one deep-sea trawler is fishing under sail.

My chief endeavour has been to find men, now in the evening of their days, who knew sail in its prime and could speak at first-hand of their experiences. I succeeded beyond my most fervent hopes and without the valued co-operation of those mentioned in the text my history of trawling would, of necessity, have been more academic. For facts beyond their time I have consulted such scanty written records as are available, Government Blue Books and Reports of Commissions, where amidst a verbiage of statistics I have sometimes made an unexpected haul. I myself have been making notes over the years and a long time ago I was fortunate enough to obtain a copy of *Fisherman's Seamanship*, by O. T. Olsen, c 1885, annotated by an old skipper. I have also consulted *Deep-sea Fishing and Fishing Boats*, by Edmund W. H. Holdsworth, c 1874.

Everything has been checked over by the men themselves, or is their own written story, so accuracy should be ensured, and the supreme test has been the passing of my typescript by Skipper J. T. Crouch of Lowestoft, whose knowledge of the practical side of trawling goes back to 1886. It has been a great pleasure to meet and correspond with such men.

In presenting these facts I have endeavoured to hold the balance fairly, but limitations of space have of necessity curtailed the fullest account of every aspect of the life, and rigid selection has been needed to keep this already lengthy volume within bounds.

I am also indebted to Mr. R. M. Hewett and his son Capt. R. S. Hewett, M.C., who not only gave me whole-hearted assistance, but were good enough to read over the chapters dealing with Barking and the Short Blue Fleet, whilst those on construction and Brixham have been approved by Mr. P. A. Upham, whose firm has been building smacks for over a century. Messrs. Elliott & Garrood, the Royal National Lifeboat Institution and the Royal National Mission to Deep Sea Fishermen also supplied me with information. Mr. J. J. Hackett put me in touch with certain Ramsgate smacksmen and loaned me a few photographs to copy.

Few plans were ever made of fishing vessels so I was fortunate when I met Mr. W. S. Parker who kindly let me have some of his designs for Lowestoft smacks of forty and more years ago. I have had the privilege of taking off the lines of contemporary models, over one hundred years old, of Barking and Brixham cutters, as well as the famous *Ibex*, B.M.27. Thanks to the courtesy of Mr. G. Claxton of Ramsgate I was able to measure up *Master Hand*, L.T.1203, one of the last to be built at Rye, which enables a comparison to be made of design over a very long period, and I hope the many detailed drawings, probably available for the first time, will encourage enthusiasts to make really authentic models. The work of the late Mr. P. J. Oke on behalf of the Coastal Craft Sub-Committee of the Society for Nautical Research, has preserved the lines of other types.

As I, and fortunately my publishers, believe no work of this nature can have too many illustrations—one picture being worth pages of description—I have spared no trouble or expense in collecting every available photograph, no easy job. For instance, few seem to exist of Grimsby and Hull trawlers, and these I found amongst Mr. F. W. Beken's superb collection of yacht studies at Cowes. Mr. Jenkin's cellar at Lowestoft was a veritable treasure house and Mr. Yallop's permission to search through thousands of old plates about to be scrapped at Gorleston, enabled my wife and I to bring to light a few very fine pictures of old Yarmouth. Others came from Mr. John Lang, Capt. F. C. Poyser of the Nautical Photo Agency, Mr. R. Stimson and those mentioned elsewhere. Once again I wish to express my appreciation of the generous co-operation of my friend and fellow S.N.R. member Commander H. Oliver Hill, who placed his excellent photos of Brixham trawlers at my disposal, as well as his researches into casualties.

Many of my discoveries were not captioned and as I think a vessel without a name loses much of its interest, their indentification from registration numbers was a lengthy business. It involved the copying out of thousands of names from a 1910 *Olsen's Almanack* loaned me by Mr. J. Woodhouse and an earlier one of 1906 borrowed from Mr. J. Giles, and thanks to Mr. P. Kershaw, who allowed me the use of an 1885 M.N. List, it has been possible to add tonnage, date and place of building of some of the earlier vessels missing from my registers.

The selection of the most appropriate photographs from among the thousands in my collection has been guided mainly by the presence of some feature which illustrates remarks in the text.

My wife has been a real helpmate with her unfailing interest and encouragement, not to mention the reading aloud of every word, time and time again.

To everyone who has helped me in any way I offer my warmest thanks. Each scrap of information has added one more link in the chain of evidence to carry some record of past achievements into a future where it seems sail will be used only for pleasure.

Westgate-on-Sea, Kent.   EDGAR J. MARCH.
Colwell Bay, Isle of Wight.

POSTSCRIPT

May 1953. Since this book has gone to press I have learned with sincere regret of the passing of the following who gave me such wonderful co-operation:—Skippers Crouch and Moxey, Harry George, R. M. Hewett and Wm. S. Parker. I fear others have slipped their moorings without my knowledge.

CONTENTS

CONTENTS

CONTENTS

SKETCHES BY AUTHOR

NOTE. Sketches 20 to 50 are scale drawings, *Master Hand*, L.T.1203.

SCALE PLANS—*Pages* 311-347

PLANS

The following photostats are by courtesy of the Director, Science Museum, South Kensington and the Coastal Craft Sub-Committee of the Society for Nautical Research.

3, 7, 12, 17.

CHAPTER ONE

HISTORICAL

THE fishing smack is no more—she has joined the vanished fleet of brigs, topsail schooners, brigantines, ketches, luggers and other sailing craft which, not so long ago, made many a small harbour a thriving place and added a picturesqueness to a seascape that no power-driven vessel can hope to rival.

The cod smack dates back beyond the Middle Ages and hooking with long lines is of time immemorial, but the development of the sailing trawler in the 19th century is practically spanned by the lifetime of a man. Hooking and trawling are the two methods used for catching demersal fish which swim at or near the bottom of the sea.

Little is known of the design and build of the early vessels used for catching cod, but we shall not be far wrong in assuming they carried the single mast with a square sail, typical of the period. Then came the introduction of two and even three masts, the fore and aft rig, and finally wells in which the fish could be brought back alive.

In mediaeval times fish was a staple article of diet, both on account of the expense and scarcity of meat, and the ordinances of the Holy Roman Church which required the eating of fish on Fridays and certain fast days. Such a constant demand stimulated the fishing industry and developed the stockfish trade to northern waters. Salting was then the only method known for preserving perishable foodstuffs and the fish pre-eminently suitable for this purpose is the cod, which can be split open, salted and dried in the sun, either on rocks or impaled on stakes or stocks, hence the name stockfish.

Prolific and widely distributed in temperate and northern seas, cod live close to the bottom in depths from 25 to 50 fathom. Spawning in the spring, a female lays eggs numbered in millions which float on the surface. After spawning, the fish are in very bad condition and unfit for food, with huge heads and emaciated bodies, which is not surprising as a cod roe will weigh anything up to 8 lbs. The young, about one inch long by the beginning of the summer, are fit for market at the end of the second year, becoming mature twelve months later to average 12 to 20 lbs. in weight and up to 3 ft. long. The fish is in the finest condition from October to December, to quote an old saying " at its best as soon as it has had a bit of snow in its mouth ".

I

The flesh is of high food value, from the liver medicinal oil is extracted, the glutinous substance known as isinglass is prepared from the swimming bladder, while the gills are sometimes used as bait. Cod roe is a delicacy, tons once being sent to India and Australia in a salted state and enormous quantities were sold to the French, under the name of " rogue ", to be used for bait in the sardine fisheries.

Silvery-green in colour, cod move in vast shoals of approximately the same age and size, working southward in summer, north in winter. They are voracious feeders and Frank Buckland reported that a 48 pounder, 4 ft. 4 in. long, which he opened in February 1867, contained 4 whiting weighing 8 lb. in all, the largest being 2 lb. 14 ozs. In May 1878, Mr. Reid of Wick found 32 small herring in a medium sized cod, and in the November, Mr. Pulman discovered 13 large sized herring in the stomach of another. Fishermen, knowing cod are very fond of herring spawn, drop a greased lead on a likely ground and if spawn adheres know they will soon catch cod. Average size ranges from 2 to 4 ft. in length, weight from 20 to 50 lbs., a 70 pounder being the largest recorded. Cod are abundant all over the North Sea, but less numerous on the southern and western shores of the British Isles and are very susceptible to changes in temperature. The fish may be biting well and suddenly vanish, possibly influenced by a cold current.

When new grounds were first worked over truly enormous cod were frequently caught, but these monster fish, 5 to 6 ft. long, soon disappeared. The patriarchs of the finny world, they had survived marine perils and assault by other fish until the attraction of a well-baited hook lured them to extinction.

Cod favour certain banks, the most prolific being off Newfoundland, where the deep waters of the North Atlantic give place to the shallower shelf off the American continent. These grounds, discovered by Cabot in 1497, have been fished since Tudor days, when vessels fitted out at Dartmouth and other West Country ports. To the south-south-west of the Faroe Islands lies an oblong plateau, 40 miles by 30 miles, with an average depth of 60 fathom, known as the Faroe Bank ; the waters round Iceland teem with fish, and the Foula Bank, between Foula and the mainland of Zetland, was another favourite spot for the shoals. 300 miles west of the Hebrides in 57° 36′ N., 13° 42′ W., lies Rockall, an isolated bank, marked above water by a small, solitary conical rock about 30 ft. high. Soundings of 20 fathom lie all round with the 50 fathom line never more than a mile away. Here the bank gradually slopes away for about 20 miles in a direction E. of North and 35 miles W. of South before the 100 fathom line is passed, its width varying from 20 to 25 miles. Fishing was usually carried on in waters not exceeding 50 fathom in depth and it can readily be imagined how difficult it was for sailing smacks to work this ground. First it had to be found, and navigation was primitive in those days, then any bad weather made it dangerous to remain near the rock, with the subsequent problem of finding it again when the gale moderated, for the depths made it impossible to check positions by sounding. At times the shoals were so dense in the vicinity of these banks that it was a job to obtain a true cast of the lead. Nearer our coasts and worked by the Dutch early in the 16th century, is the famous Dogger Bank which has yielded a rich harvest for generations, until intensive steam trawling ruined the fishing to a very great extent. South of this plateau lie the many banks and gutters off the Norfolk coast, once teeming with young cod.

The history of the first vessels to visit Icelandic waters is somewhat obscure, but according to the Dunwich historian Gardner, who wrote in 1754, that ancient port, now under the sea, sent a fleet of 20 ships annually to the Iceland and North Sea fishing during the reign of Edward I, 1272-1307. There was an Iceland Company at King's Lynn and their first ships sailed to northern seas in 1412, when five men from one crew landed on the island. The following year 30 vessels went north accompanied by a cargo ship freighted with goods for barter, but owing to the behaviour of the fishermen these visits were not exactly popular with the inhabitants. In spite of this opposition 5 laden ships arrived in 1414 and 6 in the following year to trade for stockfish caught by the local men. The Danish King, who had sovereignty over Iceland, complained to Henry V about the conduct of his subjects and an edict was issued prohibiting any fishing in Icelandic waters, but the English king's mention of " anciente custom " suggests some ground for a greater antiquity for this fishing than the 3 years mentioned. In spite of their misdemeanours one must admire the courage and hardihood of those fearless men who faced stormy seas in tiny vessels, scarcely more than half-open boats, with the lack of fresh meat and vegetables making scurvy a constant menace.

In 1425 merchants from the port of Bristol sent " great ships " to trade with the Icelanders and bring back stockfish and by 1436 Scarborough fishermen were visiting the waters in search of cod and ling. In 1490 a treaty was made with Denmark by which our men obtained the right to fish off Iceland on payment of customs and under licence and it is known that 16 or more vessels fitted out at Southwold in the latter part of the 15th century.

During Tudor times there was a fairly extensive cod fishery on the East Coast and in 1528 no less than 149 ships went to Iceland and 80 to the Shetland fishing, ling being much sought after. 32 of these vessels sailed from Dunwich, Southwold and Walberswick, ports which have long since lost all their importance. The accounts of one ship, the *Mary Walsingham* of Dunwich and owned by Henry Tooley of Ipswich, are still in existence and tell that in 1538 dry cod were worth 34s. 4d. a hundred and ling 90s. per hundred. The crew were paid by " doles ", of which the Master took 8, three other officers 12 between them, and the rest of the crew one apiece.

The fleet sailed in March and returned in August, being generally " wafted " by one or more King's ships for protection against pirates and enemies. The trip from King's Lynn to Iceland took about 14 days, or some 70 miles a day, which does not compare unfavourably with that taken by Grimsby cod smacks 350 years later.

The late Mr. Ernest R. Cooper, F.S.A., wrote a most valuable article in the

"Mariner's Mirror" for April 1939, compiled from an unpublished manuscript belonging to Mrs. More-Molyneux of Losely Park, Surrey and I am indebted to his widow for permission to quote the following facts concerning "The Cargis of a good schyppe Callyd the *Jayms* of Syr Thomas Darssys knyght for a viage be the grace of god to be mayd yn ysland begonne the fyrst day of Dessember anno 1545 mayster vnder god for thes present viage long Sander of Dunwhyche & marchant Jeffrey Smythe. Hier after fowllowthe al manner of chargis for the provicion of the schep.

Impms delueryd to forsayd schype xv wey & a

          hauf of Salt at xxxvjs viijd the wey   xxviij viij iiij "

which I make out to mean that 15½ weys of salt were delivered to the ship at a price of 36s. 8d. the wey, and as the wey was a measure containing 40 bushels it makes the price of salt 11d. a bushel.

The document was of course written in Old English which was transcribed by Miss Lilian Redstone.

The next item must have been to quench the thirst engendered by salt provisions as it is for 44 "butz of bier" at 13s. 4d. the "but" and is the most expensive item in the whole account.

"Itm iij Last iiij Barrel of Caske at viij ye Last" amounting to j. vj. viij, defeats me unless it refers to the number of staves to be made up into barrels, but I am on surer ground with "bakons xxvj flyttchys at ijs vjd the flytche" as this can be none other than 26 flitches of bacon at 2s. 6d. a flitch. Two barrels of white herring cost £1 12s. od., "byskyt" £2, and Hammon the "myller" was paid 15s. 5d. for grinding the flour and "a mans chargis at the mille when the meelle was a paykyng (? baking) for ye space of viij days" came to 5s. 4d.

I cannot make even a guess at some of the entries which only amount to a few shillings each, but a bushel and a half of oatmeal was 2s. 6d., a barrel of pitch 12s., a barrel of "taerre" 5s., 6 gutting knives 1s., 3 splitting knives 1s. 4d. and 2 heading knives 10d. Half a cwt of cod was £1. 6s. 6d., a firkin of honey 9s., 3 firkins of salt butter £1 4s. 9d., a "wey and haulf of cheys wt chargis" £1 13s. 4d., 43 shillings worth of "Reyd heyrryng."

"Itm for strynges to the nomber of xl dossyn at vjs viijd the dossyn wythe chargis xiij. vj. viij" appears to be 40 dozen lines for fishing at 6s. 8d. a dozen, but "for tares vij dossyns at ixs viij the dossyn. iij.vs.od.," is a puzzler. 2 lanterns cost 1s., 2 "boet compassys" 2s. 8d., 15,000 hooks at 6s. a 1,000 amounted to £4 10s., and the same number of "snoythes" (snoods) at 4s. 8d. a thousand was £3 10s., 3 dozen boat oars cost £2 12s. and 8 lb. of whipping twine 4s. 8d. Then come various items for nails, "rufe & clynche", part charge for a "post from london & sendyng to London for schyps provicion" £1 1s. 4d. suggests that some of the stores were purchased in London. Two flaskets, cost 8d., were the big withy baskets used for carrying cod right down to the last days of the live cod fishery. A padlock cost 5d., and 2 boat hooks 8d.

" Jahn Chapman " was paid £2 15s. for 60 stone of beef at 11d. the stone, Mrs. Samson 3s. 4d. for a barrel of beer, threepence purchased 3 dozen spoons, fivepence a dozen dishes, tenpence 6 tankards, and a shilling provided a dozen platters.

A hint of the dues charged in Iceland can be seen in the entry " for Costum dew In ysland " £3 6s. 8d. and the merchant " Geffrey Smythe " had with him goods to the value of £38 4s. 1d., including 3 barrels of fresh butter, marking irons, copper kettles, linen of all sorts, 2 tuns of wine, wax, cloth, broadcloth, whetstones, coverlets, shirts and 2 " paer of Buets of Store viijs ". He received £6 for his services.

Then follows the wages paid for the voyage. Sanders the master received £11 for himself and his servant, " Jahn payne maister maet & stuard " £5 13s. 4d., Harry Gray " a skave maester " £8, and William Gray, a similar rank, £6 10s. The boatswain's wages were £3 6s. 8d., the carpenter's £5, the cooper 48s. 4d., the cook 46s. 8d., the " souldier " 40s., the gunner 43s. 4d., the 20 men making up the rest of the crew received from 45s. to 36s. 8d.

The " Somme tottallys of al manner of Chargys Outward amont to ccxxxij. xix. viij " or £232 19s. 8d.

I have only picked out items throwing some light on the cost of fitting out a vessel for the Icelandic fishing, and the endorsement on this most interesting document reads " A Raconyng of A Vyage into Eyeslond 1545 ".

The efforts of bluff King Hal to destroy the great Abbeys and the Roman Catholic Faith had far-reaching effects on the fishing community, as the demand for salt fish declined after the abolition of compulsory eating of fish on fast days, and in 1553 only 43 ships went to Iceland and 10 to the Shetlands. In an endeavour to revive the industry an attempt was made during the reign of Queen Elizabeth to compel the people to eat fish on Wednesdays, but having acquired a taste for meat they were not keen to go back to salt fish, and who can blame them.

In 1593 Dunwich and Walberswick only fitted out a couple of ships each and Southwold 4, but the fishery declined more and more owing to the competition of the Dutch and in 1665 Southwold was the last of the ports to fit out 3 ships.

The Hollanders excelled in the catching of cod and ling as well as the drift-net fishery for herring. Hundreds of vessels fished in Shetland waters, over 200 " fly boats " working for ling which were split and salted, upwards of 5,000 men being engaged in the salt fish trade. Stockfish fetched about £12 a last in the 1580's the price rising to £20 ten years later, while salted ling cost from £3 to £5 5s. per cwt. The continued decline of the English fisheries caused much concern to the authorities in Stuart times as this meant less skilled seamen were available for service in the Royal Navy and various schemes were suggested from time to time to combat the menace of Dutch competition.

The smaller Dutch boats fished with hand lines, using herring or lamprey for bait and the cod were either salted or brought alive in welled smacks to the London market. These vessels were known as " doggers ", a name in use as far back as the reign of Edward III, but whether they gave the name to the famous bank in the North Sea or vice versa is a moot point. Unfortunately little pictorial evidence is available about these craft, as fishing boats were far too humble to attract the attention of the few marine artists of those days and historians were more concerned with charters than details of boats and gear. Undoubtedly they were the one or two-masted vessels, typical of the times and having square sails on each mast. By the middle of the 18th century a dogger had a bluff-bowed hull, long bowsprit with jib, a square-rigged mainmast stepped nearly amidships and a small mizzen with a " smack sail " fitted with brails and bent to a lateen yard similar to that used in the larger vessels.

In the Privy Council Register dated 3rd June 1668 is an entry which suggests a praiseworthy attempt to break the Dutch monopoly :—" Michael Mewe Alderman of the town of Yarmouth . . . praying licence to buy two well boats or pinkes in Holland, to bring them over and to employ them in fishing for bringing live and Barell Codd of their own taking . . . by which means such vessels may be (by those patterns) built here to the great advancement of the fisheries of this kingdom and the increase of seamen and Navigation."

It would seem as if this application for a licence was pigeon-holed, or perhaps the continual wars claimed priority, as 44 years lapsed before the first well smacks were constructed at Harwich, only 3 being built by 1715. 5 years later the number had risen to 12, but it was not until 1735 that as many as 30 were engaged in fishing for cod, and six of these were owned by Nathaniel Saunders. He visited the Scottish coast using 4 of his smacks to convey goods to and from the then isolated northern harbours and line fishing between-whiles. In 1745 these vessels were hired by the Government to convey across the Moray Firth the loyal troops subsequently engaged in the Battle of Culloden.

In an old guide to the Isle of Thanet, published in 1775 and loaned me by Mr. J. H. Clarke, there is an extract from Camden's writings of 1594 :—" Common people are a sort of amphibious animal, who get their living both by sea and land, as having to do with both elements, being fishermen and husbandmen, and equally skilled in holding helm or plough, according to the season of the year. They knit nets, catch cods, herring, mackerel, etc., go voyages and export merchantdize." Another paragraph reads :—" Broadstairs. A few years since several ships went annually from this place to the Iceland Cod Fishery and it was deemed a lucrative employment, but they have lately been discouraged by want of success and that branch of trade has fallen almost to nothing."

In 1749, just after the close of the War of the Austrian Succession, in the King's Speech an appeal was made to the patriotism of the wealthier classes to come to the help of the fishing industry, not only on the general ground that it was one of the great schools of seamanship, but also with the more specialized object of taking the herring and cod fisheries from the Dutch. The House of Commons thereupon appointed a Committee to go into the matter with the result that the Free British

Fishery was incorporated with a capital of £500,000 and their activities are fully described in my book " Sailing Drifters ".

In the " Mariner's Mirror " of January 1932 there was a most interesting article by Mr. Michael Lewis concerning a number of original manuscripts which came into his possesion on the death of a great-aunt, who was a great grand-daughter of a certain John Turner, a wealthy London merchant in the mid-18th century.   I am indebted to the author, now Professor M. A. Lewis, for permission to quote from these documents, which concern a scheme to combine patriotism with philanthropy and both with profit.

Upwards of 80 citizens of Westminster petitioned Parliament to allow the opening of a free fish market at some convenient part of Westminster, with the object of increasing employment among fishermen, reducing the price of fish and removing the monopoly of Billingsgate.   This petition having received favourable consideration, the citizens wasted no time and at a Meeting held at the Sun Tavern, King Street, Westminster, on the 2nd July 1750, the subscribers put up the sum of £3,000 to encourage fishermen to fit out cod and other fishing vessels to catch and bring fish to Westminster Fish Market.   They proposed to advance money, not exceeding three-quarters of the value of the vessel, which had to be made over to the Society as a security and the men had to give bonds to carry out their obligations.

The next step was taken at a meeting at the Bridge Street Coffee House on the 9th August, when authority was given to publish " advertizements " in the " Daily Advertizer " and the " London Evening Post " for six successive days and that 500 handbills be printed offering to advance money to fishermen desirous of purchasing their boats, on condition that they agreed to supply the new market with all fish caught.   There was an immediate response and several fishermen offered to put up £125 towards the £500 required to build and equip a vessel, others could only find smaller amounts, one being as low as £10.   These cases were considered at a meeting held on Monday, 24th September.   Samuel Foster of Westminster proposed to advance £125 if the Society would put up the balance of £375 to build a " Cod Vessell " of about 60 tons.   He agreed to assign vessel and tackle to the subscribers, to pay 5 per cent interest and to pay off £5 per cent per annum of the principal, and to vend at Westminster Fish Market all fish caught.

The secretary then presented the bill for the advertisement of about 140 words which had appeared in two newspapers for six successive days, together with the printing of 500 handbills and it amounted to £1 19s. !

This reasonable sum met with such approval that authority was given for a further advertisement to be published for eight successive days.

On Monday, 8th October, all the original proposals were approved and on the 6th December, 1750 a document relating to an agreement with Henry Shurgall or Shergold of Barking was duly signed and sealed for the building of a fishing vessel of about 30 tons, to be named *Henry and Mary*.

On behalf of the subscribers, Thomas Smith and John Feary agreed to pay three-quarters of the price of the vessel and her equipment in the following proportions. First payment when stem and sternpost were raised, second, when smack was timbered and " wails wrought ", third, when smack was " plankt up to her heigth without Board, and Sealed to her Beams, within Board, and her Beams in the Round " and the fourth and last payment when the vessel was completely finished and launched.

On his part Shurgall bound himself to execute and deliver a Bill of Sale to Smith and Feary, handing over to them the actual possession of the vessel, and he further agreed to repay the money advanced at the rate of 5 per cent per annum, plus 5 per cent interest and covenanted to sell all his fish at Westminster Market.

In February the bills began to come in, but it would appear that they were not paid until 4th June, 1751, when Shurgall signed his article to supply the market and £318 was advanced to him. These bills are most valuable evidence of the expense of building and fitting out a 30-ton cod smack, ready for sea, in that year of Our Lord, 1751.

The hull cost £231, sails £54 2s. 4½d., cordage, cables, etc. £62 18s. 0d., blacksmith's work £11 15s. 7d., spars and blocks £23 1s. 11d., ironwork for capstan 18s. 9d., small boat £7 5s. 0d., a total of £391 1s. 7½d., while nets, lines, " chopsticks " and other necessaries added another £45 making the total cost of building and fitting out ready for sea £436 1s. 7½d.

The gear mentioned shows that line fishing as well as trawling was to be carried on, chopsticks being the spreaders to carry snoods and hooks and the equivalent of the sprawl wires used a century later.

Five of the original bills still survive. Little did those unlettered tradesmen dream that their accounts would arouse interest 200 years later. On the 28th February, 1751, Messrs. Eade & Bolton rendered their account for making a suit of sails which I give in the original spelling.

Capn: Henry Shurgall & Owners for the New Sloop....................Dr.

To Eade and Bolton

Feby 28th To a New Mainsail wt:ps: & bands 207½ yds: best Engn duck Wrought at /17d.	14 13	11½
To a New foresail wt:ps: & bands 52½ yds do at /17d	3 14	4½
To a New Middle Jibb wt:ps......57 yds do at /17d	4 —	9
To a New Storm Jibb wt:ps:......21¾ yds do at /17d	1 10	9¾
To a New Trysail wt:ps: Band....82¾ yds do at /17d	5 17	2¾
To a New Great Jibb wt:ps:.....100 yds do at /16d	6 13	4

To a New Crosjack 12 yds: 13 Clos: wt:ps: & Band 164 yds at /13d	8	17	8
To a Droge sail 8 yds Clos: wt:ps:..67 New Broad duck tar'd & Drest at 2/-	6	14	
To a New Tarpawling 3¼ yds: do at 2/-		6	6
To fixing ye Above wt: spunyr: housling & hambro Lines		11	6
To 34 Iron Thimbles & Labour	1	2	3

£54 02 4½

Receivd ye 4th of June 1751 the Sum of thirty two pound in Cash & Mr Surgalls Note of hand for twenty two pound when paid which is in full of this Bill for Mr Eade & Bolton
p me Robt Guy.

Evidently the odd 2s. 4½d. was pocketed by Shurgall as a discount, but history does not relate if he honoured his I.O.U.

Mr. Wm. Smith supplied the cordage and was paid in cash by Mr. " Shirgall " on the 4th June.   His account reads :—

		cwts	qs	lbs
Mr Henry Shurgall.......................Dr				
1750/51	To Willm Smith			
Feby 25	To shrouds, stays etc.	7	0	6
	To spunyarn & Worning	0	2	22
1751				
Aprile	To one Cablett 120 fatham 7 inch	12	0	15
	To one do	12	1	13
	To one trawl Rope 4½ inch	4	2	6
	To one Wharp 2½ do	2	0	17
	To 2 Coiles 2 inch & 2 do 1½ inch 3 ratlines of sizes	6	3	8
	To one Coile 3½ inch grown Rope & Guy	2	2	12

Cwt 48   1   15   at 26/-
£62.18.-

Recd June the 4 1751 of Mr Shirgall the full Contents of this Bill in Cash and note which when paide is in full of all demand
pr me Wm Smith

This account with its mention of a 4½ inch trawl rope is definite evidence that the smack went both trawling and line fishing, and that she rode to 120 fathom of 7 inch cable, chain not being used for this purpose until well into the 19th century.

The rope supplied for shrouds, etc., would be hemp as manilla was not available for the running gear of smacks until after the 1850's, when the first ropewalk was built at Grimsby by a Captain Harris to make rope from fibre he had discovered in Manila Is.

Mr. Richard Jackson evidently did himself out of 1s. in his bill of £11 15s. 7d. for smith's work, as the many items, too numerous to give in full, should total up to £11 16s. 7d., but it does not appear that his attention was drawn to the error ! Evidently Jackson's spelling was as shaky as his arithmetic, " a botte hook " supplied on 15th February is priced at 8d., and " 3 hoop for a bume & gassneack " on the following day came to 8s. 10d., whilst a " hoop for a bumme and a hook for a bould spitte " cost 2s. For a " fish hook & a takell hook & 2 thimble " weighing in all 10½ lbs he charged 3s. 6d., 4s. for an 8 lb. "laddenette "but a 13½ lb. "laddenette Nette " was only 6d. more. " A ring boult & a hoop for a scruggitt yard " amounted to 2s. 8d., but " 2 copp for 2 David Sheff " costing 5s. are a puzzle unless they refer to davit sheaves, a " prd of Troylheads ", weighing 1 cwt. 0 qt. 20 lb., cost £2 and a " gammon " 48½ lb. was 16s. 2d., while " a Doge & Kittell Guyes & tramelles & bars for ye Stoc & Cheakess for ye Stoc 36 lb." costing 12s. is anyone's guess, and " 6 rings for ye Katthetts " at 3s. is certainly an original way of spelling cat-heads.

Mr. Francis Gurton's account for supplying spars and blocks gives valuable data concerning the price of gear even if, to say the least of it, the spelling is erratic.

4 blocks 9 in. dubil @ 9s., 4 blocks 8 in. single @ 4s., 12 7 in. deadeyes @ 7s. and 2 12 in. @ 3s. are very reasonably priced, while a " pair of vain boards " at 1s. is a somewhat dubious item, 2 " ladnet starfts " were 1s. 4d. and " a boat hook staff " 8d.

For mast and spars, £3 10s. was charged for a " boom and bolsplit ", 18s. for a " garft and Croget yard ", £7 for a 55 ft. mast, 30s. for a " drove yard ", 2 pairs of "ours " 15 ft. long cost 8s. 3d. and 10 dozen of trucks 5s., were undoubtedly for parrels. Leathering the garft cost 2s. 6d., " wegging the mast " 1s., while the item " to parting the weell of " £1, taken in conjunction with the ladenets suggests to me that the vessel was a " welled smack".

Some more simplified spelling is seen in Richard Mason's bill for iron work for the capstan, made out to " Capt Henry Shurgall & Oners of ye new vessel cailed ye *Henrey & Mary*. John Paul, ears, Paule Bolte & 1 Dubbel forlock, jorn ribbs, 1 hope & 1 plate & 1 spindel for ye bottom of ye Cappstand " tell that the smith was happier with a sledge hammer in his hand.

But alack and alas ! After only 9 months in command of his new smack Henry Shurgall fell from grace by committing the heinous offence of selling his fish at Billings-gate, in spite of all the " whereas " and " in consideration of " which he had solemnly signed when he agreed to sell ALL at Westminster. Perhaps it was a dead calm and, fed up with trying to get up to Westminster, he succumbed to the temptations of the rival market. We shall never know, for the next we hear is a " very humble petition " signed by H. Shergold—no one seems to know how to spell his name—begging that the smack *Henry & Mary* be restored to him if only to save from ruin his wife and 3 children, as well as 3 servants who were no doubt the men employed as crew. He excuses his action " that of late could not by any means vend or dispose of his fish at the said Markett but was drove through meer necessity to dispose of them at Billingsgate ".

Just what was the result of his pleading is lost in the silence of a couple of centuries and it is strange to read these old parchments in days of atomic power, to ponder over the hopes and fears of men long dead and forgotten, save that they can speak to us through the medium of fading writing, preserved through all the upheavals of time and place. Most valuable for the light they throw on the cod fishing from Barking in the middle of the 18th century, and showing that trawling was the method used, probably in nearby waters, for it was not until 1766 that long lining was attempted on the Dogger Bank.

Plans of these small welled smacks appear in Chapman's *Architectura Navalis Mercatoria* published in 1768 and prints, c 1750, show them working off the Shetlands. Smack rig was carried, a gaff trysail with a small square topsail on fore side of mast with a square course below. The foresail is hanked or laced to the stay and a jib is run out on a traveller to the end of the bowsprit which is fitted with shrouds and bobstay.

Plate 2 shows a model now in the Science Museum at South Kensington. Length overall is 38 ft., breadth 13.5 ft. and depth in hold 7.5 ft. The auger holes allowing sea water to enter the well amidships are clearly visible on the round of the bilge.

In 1766 Mr. Orlibar of Harwich commenced fishing for cod with long lines on the Dogger Bank ; although unsuccessful at first he persevered in his efforts and by 1774, 40 of the 62 smacks owned at Harwich went to these fishing grounds. The number increased to 78 in 1778 and 96 ten years later, probably the maximum number to fish out of the Essex port, as about this time well smacks were being built at Barking, Greenwich and Gravesend. Gradually the fishery declined until by 1852 only 5 cod smacks belonged to Harwich, although the port continued to be used as a storing place for live cod in chests when the London vessels were forced to give up Gravesend owing to the increasing pollution of the river, which made it impossible to keep the fish alive for any length of time.

CHAPTER TWO

BARKING, GRIMSBY & SHETLAND COD SMACKS

ANYONE visiting Barking to-day and seeing the huge power station, the factories and miles of streets and houses, will find it difficult to realize that within living memory it was one of the principal fishing stations, having been an important centre when it was only an isolated village in the desolate Essex marshes, situated about 2 miles up the river Roding, later known as Barking Creek. An abbey with a nunnery adjoining was founded here in the very early days of Christianity in England, a fact which probably accounted for the development of the fishing industry.

As far back as 1320 Barking fishermen were summoned for using, contrary to regulations, 16 small mesh nets and these were publicly burnt by order of the Mayor and Corporation. In 1349 5 nets were confiscated and in 1406 rioting followed the seizure of 16 nets found in the river by Alexander Boner, sub-conservator of the Thames. As they did not comply with regulations he placed them in the custody of the constables of Barking, but the incensed owners rescued their gear the following day. Several were arrested, tried and found guilty, but they were pardoned on giving an undertaking to present their nets at the Guildhall for approval.

Barking men were among the first to make use of the trawl net and in 1631 complaints were made by certain fishermen in the Whitstable and Sandwich areas concerning the size of trawl used by the Barking boats. This, too, led to the arrest of a number of the offenders who had never heard of the prohibition. Many of them were bound over not to use the trawl again but they took little notice of such an instruction.

In 1722 Daniel Defoe, when making his tour of England, wrote of Barking as " a large market town, but chiefly inhabited by fishermen, whose smacks ride in the Thames, at the mouth of the River Roding, from whence their fish is sent up to London to the market at Billingsgate, by small boats". Barking Shelf formed a most convenient harbour inside which vessels could lie afloat at all states of the tide.

The fortunes of Barking as a fishing port are largely bound up with the name of Hewett and it is thanks to the courtesy of Mr. R. M. Hewett and his son Mr. R. S. Hewett, the present managing director of the firm, that I am able to give a very full account of these activities.

The earliest records that the family have with regard to the fisheries date from 1760 when Mr. R. M. Hewett's great-grandfather, Scrymgeour, came south from Scotland to look after some property belonging to his aunt. He was charmed with Barking, which he described as being the most beautiful little village he had ever seen, but I fear he would have cause to alter his opinion could he re-visit the scene to-day. He also fell in love with another beauty, the daughter of Mr. Whennell, a smack owner, eventually marrying her and starting in the fishing business. Dr. Alexander Hewett of Cupar, Fifeshire, was a man of means and financed his son's venture, which was later to become the well-known Short Blue Fleet, so called from the square house flag flown at the masthead of all their smacks. These vessels went long-lining for cod during part of the year and trawling for the remainder.

Scrymgeour's eldest son Fleming did not join the business, but his second son, Samuel, born in 1797, was of an adventurous disposition and ran away to sea in 1811, being subsequently apprenticed as a smack boy. He took charge of the firm soon after his return from the Napoleonic wars and his introduction of the use of ice as a preservative, followed by the change-over from wicker pads to wooden fish trunks when the fleeting system came into being, led to local fishing becoming a flourishing industry.

During the latter part of the 18th and the early years of the 19th century, Scrymgeour Hewett owned a Letter of Marque brig and one of his smacks *Fifeshire*, was pierced for guns. Other privateers were fitted out at Barking and largely manned by fishermen and Mr. R. M. Hewett told me that his maternal great-grandfather, Robert Muirhead, was captain and owner of the privateer *Essex*, Samuel marrying one of his daughters. Owing to the number of men at sea in the privateers and others who were " pressed " for the navy, there was such a scarcity of labour ashore that roads and lanes in the neighbourhood of Barking became so overgrown with trees and hedges that many were impassable.

Samuel Hewett was a far-seeing man and it is due to his initiative that Barking owed the great boom between 1830-70, but I shall confine my attention to the cod-smacks, leaving the trawlers to subsequent chapters.

It was the practice for the small welled smacks to land their catches at Gravesend where the live cod were stored in chests floating in the river, then pure enough to allow this to be done. To meet the demands of Billingsgate the fish were daily trans-ferred to wells in the " hatch-boats ", which left on the evening tide to convey them up-river to be sold alive in the market next morning, as in those days no Londoner would look at a dead cod. These hatch boats were beautiful, clinker-built craft, steered by a yoke and tiller ropes, and carrying a mainsail which brailed up to a standing gaff or half-sprit, with a topsail above. The foresail hanked to a stay and aft was a small sprit mizzen.

In his spirited etching, dated 1828, E. W. Cooke has drawn a hatch boat, double-reefed, beating down to Gravesend against a freshening easterly wind (Plate 1).

Another drawing depicts a hatch boat and oyster boats at Billingsgate, with a peter boat alongside, a type then used by fishermen working in the river, although salmon and other choice fish, once caught in abundance, were gradually deserting the sewage-laden water in the upper reaches.

When the Napoleonic Wars were over in 1815, the fishing trade revived and the Barking cod smacks went as far north as Iceland or fished on the Dogger Bank and their story was told me in May, 1946, by Mr. R. M. Hewett, who was born in 1860. It was fascinating to hear this fine old gentleman in reminiscent mood telling of events told him by his grandfather Samuel, born 1797, and to realize he was a living link with those now far-off days.

In 1820-30 there were two classes of smacks at Barking, the " new ", under 60 years old, and the " old ", vessels over that age, all built of English oak, much of which had seasoned for 20 years. The majority were built locally, all were rigged as cutters and many were " welled " smacks or as they are generally called " well smacks ". 40 to 50, carrying crews of 7 or 8 men, went line fishing for cod and haddock in the autumn and winter.

Built to face any conditions, there was no limit to a smack's life and none was ever lost through stress of weather. In heavy gales they always went to wind'ard and the only losses were by stranding or collision. In spite of their low freeboard of about 1 foot they rode the seas like eider ducks, taking very little water on board, even in the heaviest weather. Following London practice, the crews were on a weekly wage, the skipper alone having a part share in the catch.

The welled smacks were specially constructed for the purpose of bringing back choice cod alive, and the well was part of the vessel itself. Two caulked bulkheads were built athwartships across the hull from keelson to deck, thus enclosing a large watertight compartment amidships. This was called the " well " and a constant supply and free circulation of sea water flowed through large auger holes bored in the bottom at various distances below the waterline.

Access to the well was through a hatch on deck and in front and on either side of it was the well-deck, which narrowed the mouth of the well into a funnel, thus keeping the level of the water within certain limits when the smack was rolling or pressed down under sail. It also allowed passage along each side below the main deck. The watertight space was divided into two by a bulkhead, but many of the largest vessels often had three compartments. Well heads, decks and funnel were made of the best wood, exceeding in strength any other part of the smack, as they were subjected to tremendous strains in all weathers, and this work greatly increased the cost of a welled vessel, compared with a dry bottomed one, the difference often being as much as £300. Care had to be taken that the upper line of inlet holes was kept as low as possible for in a seaway a smack might heel excessively, and if even one or two holes came out of the water, air was admitted to the well and on the other roll a considerable quantity of water would be blown up the funnel, probably killing some of the fish. Round fish such as cod and haddock moved freely about the well, but halibut or plaice, being flat fish, tended to lie on the bottom or sides, choking the holes and preventing free movement of water. Halibut were usually secured by the tail with a length of line fastened to a wooden rod at the top of the well, but plaice had to be stowed in open-sided trunks or boxes, which were lowered into the well and stacked under the deck. The well was examined every day and any dead fish removed, split open and salted.

Mr. R. M. Hewett showed me some contemporary models which had survived the bombing of his house and he kindly offered me the loan of two so that I could take off the lines. Their transport was a bit of a headache as I had to face the rush hour traffic on the Underground with a large model tucked under each arm and was I popular when I joined the queue for a ticket to Victoria, while black looks were my portion when I succeeded in boarding a train. Great was my relief when I reached home with these precious relics intact and was able to feast my eyes on the beautiful lines of the carrier *Ranger*. The other was the builder's model of *Saucy Jack*, 51 tons, built Gravesend 1836, the last well smack to sail out of Barking, bringing back live cod from the Faroe Islands to Billingsgate in 1880. Fortunately Goering's bombs had only knocked off a few splinters and I was soon engaged in the pleasurable task of taking off the necessary measurements to enable me to draw up Plan 1, page 311.

The length overall was 60 ft., L.B.P. 54 ft., length of keel 48 ft. 6 in., extreme beam 16 ft. For'ard on deck was the usual handspike windlass, with the centre bitts supported by a long knee extending to the starboard bulwarks, next came the fore hatch and the mainmast, on the aft side of which stood the bitts carrying fiferail and belaying pins. Amidships was the grating over the well with hatches at either end, then a hand capstan and the companion leading down to the cabin. The tiller was beautifully carved with the conventional design and the stern boards were open below the taffrail, a feature typical of many of the early smacks. The hull had well-rounded bilges with hollow waterlines fore and aft and there was a heavy wale 18 in. below the covering board.

Mr. Hewett mentioned that the trips to Iceland lasted 14 weeks. Provisions, stores, beer and drinking water were taken in at Barking Creek, also the precious tinder box and " turbot bag ", a large bag of silver entrusted to the captain who was empowered to purchase choice fish from the inshore fishermen on the north and north-east coast. When the cod smack was homeward bound these men came off in their small boats to sell turbot caught in gill nets.

After taking in stores, the smacks went round to Whitstable to load bait, the common large whelk which, owing to its toughness, was not easily washed off the hooks. Bait was an expensive item, coming next on the list after wages, provisions and depreciation of vessel, and costing more than wear and tear of sails and rigging. As whelks are one of the greatest enemies of the oyster, the fact that they fetched 3s. a wash—a measure of 21 quarts and a pint of water—for use as cod bait was an added inducement to " flatsmen " to search assiduously for them, as their file-like weapon bores into the oyster shell to enable the pest to suck out the juiciest part. Curiously enough whelk shells generally have a right-hand twist, a left-hander being comparatively rare.

The whelks, stored in bags made of netting, were kept alive in the well of the smack until required, then the shells were broken and the fleshy part extracted and placed on the hooks, a long and uninteresting job for the crew before fishing could commence. Arriving in Icelandic waters, the smacks fished for cod with hand or long lines ; after being split and gutted the fish were salted and taken to the Shetlands, Orkneys or the northern ports on the west coast of Scotland, sometimes if a catch was made in a short time it was landed in the Faroe Islands. The smack then fished again, going wherever the wind was most favourable, landing the catch as before. The third voyage, completed in September or October, came to London, the finest cod and halibut being brought back alive in the well. Cod were landed at Billingsgate in long baskets called " flaskets " and realized high prices, 4 very big cod would fetch £4 to £4 4s. od. Cod's head and shoulder, served with oyster sauce, liver and roe, was considered a choice dish in the West End. Smaller and less good-looking cod came up 6, 8 or 12 to a flasket and sold at much lower prices, 5s. to 6s. each. Halibut, one of the largest of flat fish, frequently run up to 200-300 lbs. in weight, a big one being about 7 ft. 6 in. long and 3 ft. broad, even heavier specimens have been landed from time to time, one 8½ ft. long weighed 33 stone, but as a rule price realized is not high. A 700-pounder—over 6 cwt.—brought into Hull some 30 years ago only fetched 45s. or about ¾d. a lb.

This line fishing in Icelandic waters was carried on in the friendliest manner by all nationalities and it was not until trawling was introduced that the islanders' ire was roused. They considered it a most wasteful method of fishing, constant friction arose and irritating restrictions were brought in, culminating in complete prohibition in many areas. The coast line is one of the most rugged in the world, exposed to the full force of the heavy Atlantic gales ; the hinterland is desolate and weird, with hot springs emerging from frozen ground in many places, vegetation is sparse, communications poor, in those distant days the hardy ponies being the sole means of transport, while in winter there is daylight for barely 2 hours. Unlucky indeed was a vessel wrecked on such a shore, and even to-day, in spite of a splendid system of lighthouses, the toll continues and the news that a trawler has gone on the rocks strikes terror into the hearts of all concerned, as usually the only hope of escape is up the face of the precipitous cliffs and many heroic deeds of life-saving stand to the credit of the islanders. The warm ocean currents here meet the cold streams coming in from the Arctic, undoubtedly the cause of fluctuations in the fishing, as on some grounds huge catches were made in a short time, then the cod ceased biting and not one would be caught over the same area. Subsequent scientific investigations confirm the theory that cod prefer waters just above freezing point.

1 HATCH BOAT, c 1829
The hull is clench-built with pointed stern, steering is by yoke and lines, luff of mainsail is laced to mast and sail sheets to an iron horse.

2 WELL SMACK, c 1768
Note auger holes on round
of bilge.

3 LERWICK HARBOUR, 1872
Gossamer, L.K.55, 26 tons, built at Ipswich, 1834.

4   SHETLAND COD SMACK *PETREL*, L.K.141
Built at Southampton as a 52-ton cutter in 1826.
Wrecked 1888.

5   PADDLE TUG *TRIUMPH* AT SCARBOROUGH, c 1880.
Note otter boards and cobles under sail and oar.

6   GRIMSBY DOCKS, 1st AUGUST, 1901.
Scarborough yawls, smacks and steam trawlers laid up during the great
strike.

In the sixties it was common for a cod smack to fish with 15 to 20 dozen long lines, extending for a length of 10 to 12 miles, to which 9,000 to 12,000 hooks were attached, each of which had to be baited by hand. Cod roe found a ready sale in France where it was used as bait for the sardine fishery and this trade was worth about £80,000 a year.

By 1865 the cost of a welled smack had risen to about £1,500 and she carried a crew of from 9 to 11 men and boys, apprenticed at the age of 14. Hand-lining, a man might catch as many as 400 cod in a day and it has been known for 8 men to land some 80 score in a few hours. The codman's greatest enemy was the dogfish which attacked the fish struggling on the hooks, sometimes only skeletons remaining. Being taken from deep water, cod float helpless on their sides in shallow, owing to the dilation of the swimming bladder which had to be " pricked " to allow it to collapse and the fish regain its upright position before being put in the well.

After the middle of the 19th century the increasing pollution of the London river made it impossible to store live cod in chests at Gravesend, and many Barking smack owners began the practice of landing the fish at Harwich, once a centre for cod fishing, but declining in face of competition from Greenwich and Barking. In 1852, 46 Barking smacks were engaged in the cod fishery against 5 from Harwich, where the chests were moored in the tideway, the ends being rounded off to offer less resistance to the stream (Fig. 1, page 23).

But a revolutionary change was taking place which was to witness the rapid decline of Barking and the amazing development of the Humber as a fishing centre, due to the coming of railways and the enterprise of one of the companies, the Manchester, Sheffield and Lincolnshire railway.

The phenomenal rise of Grimsby as the greatest fishing port in the country, if not the world, will be described in subsequent pages, for the moment I will confine my attention to cod smacks and long-lining.

In the late 1840's, with commendable foresight, the Railway Co. continued its line to Grimsby, then a small village of 3,688 inhabitants, which required to use the prefix " Great " to distinguish it from that other Lincolnshire village of the same name. The company next acquired all the rights of the old Grimsby Haven Co. which had been formed in 1796, opening a dock accommodating 200 sail of ships 4 years later ; they also obtained powers to construct new docks. The railway was opened on the 1st March, 1848, and the Royal Dock was commenced in the following year and opened in 1852.

Many Thames smack owners now landed their catches for despatch by rail to London as the G.N.R. and the Midland had running powers into Grimsby, thereby providing a link with Billingsgate. In order to encourage more fishermen to emulate this example the enterprising company offered special facilities to men from Hull and elsewhere, having heard of the many complaints about the conditions then prevailing at the premier Humber port, even going so far as to agree to build a special dock for fishing boats only. Not content with these attractive suggestions, which might mean anything or nothing, to prove their *bona fides* the dock company together with the G.N.R. and M.R., promoted a joint enterprise named The Deep Sea Fish Co., and acquired or built a small fleet of vessels, 4 being trawlers, 1 a " liner " as smacks for long-line fishing were called, 2 steam liners and 2 auxiliary steam liners.

The favourable conditions soon attracted the attention of fishermen who wanted to make their homes nearer the fishing grounds and in 1854-55 Howard came north from the Thames with 8 line fishing smacks, whose names were *Howard*, *British Rover*, *Mary*, *Marquis*, *Laurel*, *Liberty*, *Success* and *Emma*. James Sweeney with 2 trawlers, and John Cooke with 1, left Hull and Robert Alward brought his 2 trawlers from Scarborough, then largely used by line and drift-net fishermen, who were violently hostile to the new practice of trawling, while the harbour was very exposed and the local Corporation indifferent to the opportunities offered by the fishing industry, preferring to rely on the increasing popularity of the town as a holiday resort.

Also based on Grimsby were two " whelkers ", small cutters engaged in collecting the vast quantity of bait required for line fishing. They were the *Abstainer* of 25 tons, built at Grimsby in 1853 and owned by Thomas Campbell, and the *Gulnare* of 24 tons, built at Hastings in 1827 and then owned by a man named Marshall, but in Mr. Campbell's possession by 1885.

In my search for data I was lucky enough to contact Mr. Ernest Campbell who wrote me in April 1946 :—

" My late father Thomas Campbell, and his uncle of the same name, were actively engaged in the shipbuilding and fishing industries all their lives. Thomas Campbell sen'r was the founder of the firm of that name at Grimsby which not only built vessels but ran them to the North Sea, Faroe, Rockall and Iceland fishing grounds, and also supplied all nets, lines, stores, etc., which were required from his own store at Grimsby. He was continuously engaged in this business from his early years until he died at the age of 91, after which my late father continued the business until such time as he could sell the remaining vessels as the advent of steam had some years prior to uncle's death made the working of sailing smacks obsolete.

Now I have been having a look through some old papers and the only reference I can find at the moment is the enclosed agreement dated 1853, to build the sailing smack *Abstainer*, G.Y.111. This may prove of interest to you and shows the size of vessels then."

The agreement, which was in excellent condition, reads :—

MEMORANDUM OF AGREEMENT FOR THE NEW SMACK *ABSTAINER*
Great Grimsby.   June 14th 1853.

MEMORANDUM

Of Agreement between Mr Thomas Campbell, smack owner of Great Grimsby in the County of Lincoln of one part and Robert Keetley Shipbuilder of the same place of the other part.

The said Robert Keetley agrees to build a smack of the following dimensions and constructed to the following specification, viz:—

Length on the Keel.	Forty three feet.
Breadth of Beam.	Thirteen feet six inches.
Depth.	Seven feet eight inches.

The keel to be Elm $9 \times 5\frac{1}{2}$ inches, stem and stern post English Oak sided six inches. The Frame timbers English Oak sided 5 inches, moulded at Keelson $5\frac{1}{2}$ inches, at head $3\frac{1}{2}$ inches. Keelson Oak 7 by 6 inches. The outside planking 2 inches Oak to lower edge of Binns and Two streaks under the Binns of Oak also Two Streaks Binns $4\frac{1}{2} \times 3$ in., remainder Elm.

One Oak Bilge plank each side 2 inches. Beams sided 5 inches Moulded in middle 5 inches, at ends 4 inches. Decks of Fir 2 inches.

The said smack to be Iron fastened and fitted with Rudder, Windlass, Hatchways, Companion, Cabin, Bulwark Rails and Iron work so far as connected with the Hull.

AND the said Thomas Campbell shall pay for the said vessel the sum of Two Hundred and Twenty pounds in manner following

THE SUM of One Hundred pounds when commenced, Sixty pounds when launched and remainder as may be agreed upon.

To be completed in 14 weeks.

        (Signed)   Thomas Campbell.

Witness. Edw Skelton.   Robt Keetley.

June 14/53

Received of Mr. Thomas Campbell the sum of One Hundred pounds on a/c as per agreement.

    £100   (signed) Robt Keetley.

Sept 23/53

Rec'd of Mr Thomas Campbell the sum of Sixty pounds being the second payment as per agreement.

                 for Robert Keetley

                 (signed) Edw Skelton.

Dec 8 1853

Rec'd of Mr Tho Campbell the Sum of £15 -0-0 on a/c of new smack as per agreement.

                        (signed) Robert Keetley.

July 3/54

Rec'd of Mr Thos Campbell the Sum of Twenty pounds on a/c of new smack.

    £20.0.0.   (signed) Robert Keetley

August 26/54

Rec'd from Mr Thos Campbell the Sum of Twelve pounds on a/c of this Agreement.

    £12.0.0.   for R. Keetley

                 (signed) E. Skelton.

September 20/54

Rec'd from Mr Thos Campbell the Sum of Thirteen pounds being the balance due to me as per Agreement.

£13.0.0   for Robert Keetley

                (signed) Edw Skelton

The Agreement was stamped with a 2s. 6d. stamp at Lincoln on 23.4.53.

It would seem that the smack was built to the satisfaction of both parties as pencil notes show sizes of timbers for another smack slightly larger.

Length on the Keel.	47½ ft
Breadth of Beam.	15½ ft
Depth.	Seven feet 9 inches

The Keel to be Elm 9 × 6 inches, stem and sternpost English oak sided six inches. The Frame timbers English Oak sided 5 in moulded at keels on 6 inches, at head 4 inches. Keelson Oak 7 by 6 inches. The outside planking 2½ oak to lower edge of Binns and Three of 2½ inches under the Binns of Oak also Two streaks Binns 4½ × 3 in, remainder Elm.

One Elm Bilge plank each side 2 inches, Beams sided 5½ inches, moulded in middle 5 inches, at ends 4 inches. Decks of Fir 2 inches.

Such a specification is most valuable as it shows how little costs had risen in 100 years, as the smack *Henry & Mary* of somewhat the same size cost £231 for hull alone, and she was probably built with a well.

If ever " Casting bread on the waters " met with a response there was a case when the Directors of the M.S.L. Rly. envisaged the changes likely to take place in the fishing trade when new markets were opened up in inland towns, but the luckless shareholders said the initials of the company stood for " Money Sunk & Lost " as few, if any dividends, were paid on the huge sums expended on building docks and other facilities. The company fulfilled one of its promises in 1856, when the Fish Dock with pontoon and fish market was opened and the following year 17 liners and 5 trawlers were registered at Grimsby, and many smacks from other ports made use of the facilities offered, nearly 3,500 tons of fish being sent off by rail alone. More and more owners of well smacks came north from the Thames and by 1863 there were 42 cod smacks registered, in 1870, 53 and 2 years later 82.

Contrary to trawler practice where the men are on the sharing system, the crews of cod smacks, numbering from 9 to 11 hands, were mostly on a weekly wage with the skipper alone having an interest in the catch as well, taking 9 per cent gross earnings, the mate received 22s. to 24s. a week, the men about 20s., the owner supplying all provisions, etc. As many as 4 or 5 apprentices were carried, generally lads of poor parentage, or from the Unions, but some were sons of owners or skippers. There was equal opportunity for all to rise in the world as subsequent stories will tell. The lads were paid £4 to £10 a year according to length of service, the owner generally found board and lodging and many boys lived in the homes of their employers to whom they were indentured, or were boarded out in private houses.

The procuring of whelk bait provided employment for some 40 cutters of 12 to 15 tons, which worked in Boston and Lynn Deeps, whilst huge quantities came from Harwich and along the Kentish shore. At Lynn whelks were caught in round withy basket pots about 1 ft. in diameter, with a hole at the top, baited with refuse fish and sunk in 5 to 30 fathom of water, or in shallow hoop nets, similarly baited and sunk. Around Harwich the method was by long lines called " trots ", with small crabs threaded on the snoods. The whelks seized this bait and held on so firmly that they could easily be hauled to the surface. Many of the Grimsby whelkers were fitted with wells as it was essential to keep the whelks alive and these cutters ran up to 30 tons and cost from £600 to £700 each. The importance of the fishing can be realized from the fact that 150,000 wash were needed annually, valued at some £22,000.

In the long-line season on the Dogger Bank or Cromer Knoll a cod smack would take to sea about 40 wash of whelks, but at the end of the season towards March, not more than 15 to 25 wash. These smacks were only at sea for a few days, seldom as long as a fortnight, the fish being kept alive in the wells. In April some of the smacks went north to the Faroe Is. and Iceland, fishing with hand-lines, and their catch was always salted ; the majority fished in home waters from July to October, from 10 to 30 miles out, seeking the cod which followed the herring shoals. A handline was about 45 fathom in length with a 5½ to 7 lb. lead weight which had an iron wire, the " sprawl wire ", fixed through the top of the sinker, with a 6 ft. snood and hook at the curved ends (Fig. 2).

Lamperns from the river Trent were also used as bait, being brought by train in casks, but the trouble was that the water had to be kept in constant motion, which the shaking in train or smack provided. At every stopping place on the journey to Grimsby, a man had to agitate the water in each cask, using a stick and a churn-like movement. Price was £4 to £10 a thousand.

When hand-lining was in progress the smack was hove-to and each man worked a line, keeping the bait a few inches from the bottom, unless herring were about, then the cod came very near the surface and a fathom or two of line sufficed. Cod bite more freely towards sunset when large hauls might be taken, the majority being half-grown fish, but size varied according to the distance from land, fish on the Dogger Bank being bigger than those caught 10 to 15 miles offshore.

In the 1860's a complete set of long lines was made up of about 15 dozen, or 180 lines, each 40 fathom in length, with 26 snoods 1½ fathom apart, with baited hooks attached. A " string ", made up of 180 lines, each fastened together, was about 7,200 fathom long, or over 7 nautical miles, say 8 statute ones, with 4,680 hooks, each baited with a whelk. Soon after dawn at about half-tide, the lines were shot across the tide to allow the snoods to drift clear of the main line, the smack being under easy sail, with the wind as free as possible so as to make a straight course while paying out (Fig. 3).

The lines, already baited, neatly coiled and laid in trays each containing 12 to 16 " pieces ", were paid out over the side. No corks or floats raised them off the ground, but the line was steadied at every 40 fathom by a very small anchor, and the two ends and every mile were marked by a hooped dan or buoy of conical shape, with a staff passed through it and carrying a small flag (Fig. 4). When all the lines were shot the smack hove-to in the vicinity until the tide was nearly done, then the foresail was lowered, the end buoy taken on board, and the vessel made short tacks along the course of the line which was hauled in and the fish taken off the hooks. Cod hooked in the lip, with no injury to throat or tongue, were dropped tail first into the well, if the fish went head first it was liable to strike the bottom and break its neck. Blemished fish were salted and packed in ice. Sometimes in calm weather the line was hauled into the smack's boat which was rowed along. She was about 18 ft. long, very beamy and fitted with a well in which the fish were kept alive until they could be transferred to the smack.

At all times a well smack had to be very carefully handled, no cracking-on indulged in, or hard driving into head seas, but a day or so of calm might prove fatal to the cargo owing to lack of circulation of sea water through the holes in hull. The well was inspected daily and any fish damaged by being knocked about were taken out, salted and packed in ice. An average trip would yield 20 to 25 score of live cod and about two-thirds that number in ice. A record cargo of 1,100 was once landed alive from *King Arthur*, an 83-ton ketch built at Scarborough in 1883, and in 1877 some 800 fish from *John Fildes*, 50 tons, built at Grimsby in 1865, realized £300.

As soon as a smack returned to Grimsby the live cod were swept out of the well with a long-handled landing net—the " laddenette " of the 1750 invoice—and stored in wooden chests, each 7 ft. long, 4 ft. wide and 2 ft. deep. The bottom and sides were made of 1¼ in. battens a few inches apart to allow free circulation of water as the boxes were kept floating in the dock. The top was planked over except for an oblong opening which was closed by a padlocked cover when the chest was in use, and two chain or rope handles made for ease in lifting (Fig. 5). Each chest held some 40 large or 100 small fish which would keep alive in good condition for about a fortnight. Only cod were so stored, unless a fine cargo of big live haddocks came in, but strangely enough this fish, so highly prized in Scotland, ranked as " offal " in England and in the early days was hardly worth bringing into port.

Most of the chests belonged to smack owners, others to mutual societies who used them for their own storage or hired them to anyone requiring extra accommodation, when a charge of 9d. apiece was made. In the early seventies there were some 400 chests, often all in use, and anything from 15 to 20 thousand live cod were stored until required, the boxes being examined every day and any dead fish removed.

To meet the demand of the London buyers sufficient chests were brought alongside a hulk moored near the fish market, then tackles were hooked in and a chest hoisted up by davits until nearly clear of the water which rapidly drained out, leaving

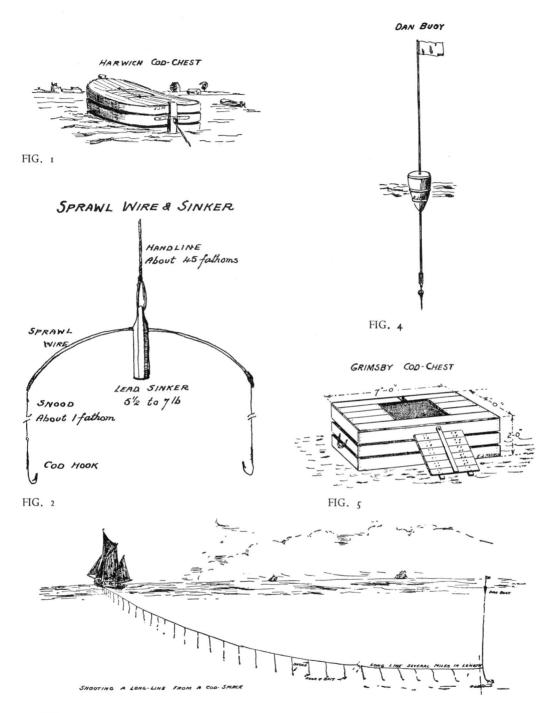

HARWICH COD-CHEST

FIG. 1

SPRAWL WIRE & SINKER

HANDLINE
About 45 fathoms

SPRAWL
WIRE

LEAD SINKER
5½ to 7 lb

SNOOD
About 1 fathom

COD HOOK

FIG. 2

DAN BUOY

FIG. 4

GRIMSBY COD-CHEST

7'-0"

4'-0"

2'-0"

FIG. 5

SHOOTING A LONG-LINE FROM A COD-SMACK

SNOOD

HOOK & BAIT

LONG LINE SEVERAL MILES IN LENGTH

DAN BUOY

FIG. 3

the fish high and dry. The cover was removed and a man got into the opening and seized a fish by its head and tail, stunned it with a short club, lifted it out and flung it up on to the deck of the hulk. This may sound simple but 40 or 50 cod lashing about in all directions made it no easy job. A man on deck now grabbed the fish tightly behind the head with his left hand, holding it firmly on deck, and with his right hand gave it a few sharp blows on the nose with a heavy club, killing it instantly. Hence the origin of the name " cod-bangers " by which Grimsbymen are often called to-day, long after such scenes have been forgotten, as live cod are now a very distant memory.

The dead fish were flung towards the bow of the hulk where they were caught by a man who threw them to another on the quay, whence they were loaded into trucks holding 12 score big fish or more smaller ones. Carefully man-handled, the fish were never allowed to fall and were sent direct to Billingsgate by express train, at a freight of 35s. a ton, arriving in good time for the early morning market, where the cod fetched a high price, being eagerly bought by West End fishmongers who often paid as much as 20s. apiece for choice specimens.

This method of storing in chests allowed for fluctuations in the market, due to erratic landings or demand, and ensured fish being supplied in the finest condition. I am none too sure that modern methods of selling fish caught and iced weeks before have much to recommend them.

In the late sixties and early seventies such scenes were a daily feature on the fish pontoon, and fine live ling, caught on the Great Fisher Bank, sold at 5s. to 6s. each direct from the smack's well, as these fish could not be kept alive in storage chests.

By 1865 the continual increase in the size of the smacks made the cutter rig very unhandy, the local name " long-boomers " tells of the enormous boom which made reefing exceedingly hazardous, and a change to ketch rig became essential.

In 1870 a herald of things to come appeared when the iron vessel *Tubal Cain* of 94 tons was built at Hull for W. W. Dawson of Grimsby, with a stern frame suitable for conversion into a steamer if the need arose. For the moment she was cutter-rigged with an iron mainmast which was not a conspicuous success, and later the ketch rig was adopted. Her design allowed for line fishing to be carried on by day, trawling by night, the former being the more successful venture. Her beam was greater than that of any other fishing vessel and the first lock of the fish dock was not wide enough to admit her. History does not mention if this fact was found out before or after she was built, maybe the idea was to force the authorities to increase the size of the locks. In later years the hull was lengthened and a steam engine installed, as by the eighties it was obvious to anyone but the most prejudiced believer in sail that the day of the wooden cod smack was over. Cod was being sold at $1\frac{1}{4}$d. to $1\frac{1}{2}$d. a lb. and even lower when there was a glut, as trawled fish could not be stored.

From October to Christmas the cod smack worked on the Great Fisher Bank and the Dogger, and the fishing outfit required was 16 dozen lines, each 30 fathom long, 2 lines or 60 fathom making a " piece ". 6,000 snoods, 2 ft. 6 in. long, the same number of hooks, which were distanced at 8 ft. 6 in. intervals if 52 to a piece, or 12 ft. if only 32 hooks were attached.

12 large and equal number of small anchors, 12 buoys with staff and flag, 12 buoy ropes, 16 trays and tray lashings. 60 whelk nets, each holding a wash, 1 sweeping-in and 1 sweeping-out net, 2 prickers and 2 tomahawks completed the inventory.

From Christmas to April the smacks fished along shore, using the same equipment, but only a small anchor with a buoy was placed between each shank to keep the line on the bottom.

From April to September the smacks went north to Iceland and the Faroe Banks and no long lines were carried. Hand lining required 4 dozen lines, each 35 fathom long, wound on reels or frames, 3 dozen cod leads, with the same number of cod wires to go through them and having an eye seized at each end to carry the snoods which were 10 to 12 ft. long, with hooks attached. 300 to 400 hooks of various sizes, 9 splitting knives, 2 heading knives, 6 gutting knives, 2 balls of gauging twine, 6 mops and brushes, 6 small brushes for cleaning fish, 3 files for sharpening hooks, 1 sharpening stone, 1 dozen tomboys, 1 dozen reels and 3 cod prickers made up the full equipment. In addition a cod smack required the same fitting-out as a big trawler, details of which will be found in the appendix.

Some of the largest smacks now carried a cook and steward whose duty it was to look after all provisions, do the cooking, clean the lamps, and keep fo'c'sle shipshape. He slept in all night. Usually a crew consisted of 6 boys, 4 men and the captain.

The cabin boy kept cabin and contents clean, saw all tools were in place and ready for use, lent a hand to work ship, steered when the gear was being hauled and obeyed all lawful commands.

In addition to his culinary duties the cook helped bait the lines, work ship and obeyed all orders.

Having learned the duties of cabin boy and cook a lad was an ordinary seaman and had to know how to splice, read the compass and steer by it, work ship, bait lines and know how to back them in, bend buoys and see them clear, gut fish for salting and learn how to handle a boat at sea. The oldest apprentice was in charge of all the boys and saw they performed their varied duties to the satisfaction of the master.

The men had to be able seamen as well as first-class fishermen, skilled in hauling lines, pricking fish, splitting for salting, and sweeping the well for fish. They had to know knotting, splicing and rattling down, and be fully experienced with rigging and unrigging a vessel, able to take soundings and well acquainted with the Rule of the Road.

In addition to an expert knowledge of everything expected of the men who were under him, the mate had to salt and ice the fish, know the character of lights, buoys, beacons, etc., the set of the tide and times of high water, and the soundings on the various fishing grounds. He had to examine and prick the well every morning and was supposed to be able to take a meridian altitude of the sun, find his latitude from it, and lay the ship's position off on a chart, but many of the older men were quite unable to use navigating instruments and read and wrote with the greatest difficulty. However they could find their way unerringly by lead-line and that sixth sense which seamen of less enlightened days so often had.

The master had to know everything connected with his calling, being responsible for stores and provisions and competent to handle his vessel in all weathers and conditions. He was expected to take his command out of dock and steer her until clear of all danger, note his departure, keep his dead reckoning, find his latitude by the sun, know everything connected with fishing grounds, nature of bottom, depths and set of tide. In addition he kept account of all bait that came on board and all fish taken out of the ship. Answerable to the owner for the safety of his ship and the proper use of everything on board, it was his duty to keep his place and keep his men in their proper places.

Before the smack arrived on the fishing ground the gear was prepared for shooting, hooks baited, buoy lines arranged in proper order, buoys examined to ensure water-tightness and flags put on staffs. When baiting, the lines were arranged on trays in tiers from left to right and coiled at the back of the trays. Then the lines were lashed up securely so that the trays could be handled in rough weather without risk of displacing the hooks.

When shooting lines on the Dogger or Fisher Bank the hands were roused about 5 a.m., and sails were trimmed to try and shoot N.E. or S.W. on account of the easterly current. First an anchor was let go with line and buoy attached, then 9 pieces were paid out, and another anchor and buoy went overboard, the process being repeated until all lines were out, the last being anchor buoy and codline with lead. The smack now lay-to for a couple of hours while the men got their breakfasts and the well was cleaned and pricked. Then came the long job of hauling the lines which were taken in over the gangway just abaft the rigging, the fish picked up in the sweeping-in net, and their bladders pricked before being placed in the well. After all the fish had been taken off the hooks the lines were paid overboard again and a boy—the backer-in—hauled them in over the stern and coiled them ready to be baited again if a second shoot was to be made, if not they were coiled away.

If the smacks were working the grounds along shore, as soon as the tide began to make, either the ebb or flood, the lines were shot by crossing the tide a little.

Most of the crews of the big cod smacks were on wages, which varied according to the season, the six winter months being from October to April, the remainder were the summer months. The smaller smacks were generally on the share system, out of the nett proceeds shares were divided into 8, 9 or 10 according to agreement, the captain taking $1\frac{3}{8}$, mate $1\frac{1}{8}$, men 1 share, boys $\frac{3}{4}$ and $\frac{1}{2}$ share according to age.

Working on the cod grounds in the depth of winter could be cruel work when fierce squalls drove icy blasts of sleet and hail against the faces of the men.   The smack would be snugged down, plunging and rearing like a frightened horse with dollops of freezing water swirling along the deck, so that the crew would soon be soaked through as they worked by the bulwarks, handling slippery fish freezing to the touch with hands so cold that all feeling had gone out of them.   A hard life indeed, and conditions aboard are graphically described by Mr. C. Alp who writes me :—

" When I was 13 years old I left school and got bound apprentice to a gentleman called Mr. Toogood who had 4 smacks.   I was signed up for one called *Lydia & Selina* (81 tons, built at Brixham in 1884).   My first voyage was what was called a salt fishing voyage, a 13 week trip to Iceland.   We used to fish with hand lines all along the ship's side and got 2d. a score for fish that measured 4 planks in ship's deck, smaller than that measurement did not count.   (Note : 4 planks would be about 2 ft.)   Well, it took us a fortnight to get to Iceland and nearly three weeks to get home again.   The men on board got 18s. a week and fourpence to the score, the mate got one pound a week and fourpence to score, and the skipper was on the share. I received 30s. for my voyage, I was only getting fourpence a week and when an apprentice earned any extra money it was put into the bank at the Board of Trade office for him.   The livers of fish were put in barrels holding about 40 gallons and they used to get about 10s. a barrel.

When I was a cook the skipper came and looked at all pots, pans, knives and forks and cupboards every night to see if things were in order.   I happened to leave a spoon out one night.   The skipper waited till I got asleep then he called me out to find out what was missing.   I overhauled everything but at last I found I was a spoon short, so I had to find it before I could go to bed again, and it took me a hour and a half to find it.   It was stuck into a strop made of rope at the masthead, so I never left things out of place any more after that, I think I got more good hidings than good dinners and they as a class of men were cruel to the boy apprentices.   One man as skipper was watching a boy cook frying fish for breakfast, looking through a trap door and the boy did not see him.   As he fried the first pan full he took it into his head to try a bit, but the skipper saw him and went in and put his hand into the frying pan in the boiling fat.   The lad was in that much pain that he jumped overboard and was lost.   The skipper got time in jail for it, there was a lot of such things done in those days that did not come to light, the skippers and mates were very cruel to the boys, but not all of them, there were some good ones and a lot of bad ones.

I have had a few rough times in the ships I have sailed in and have had more than my share, as you would not think I am writing this letter with a crippled right hand, with the little finger frozen off, and my mate dropped dead at my feet with exposure in a small boat, when our ship struck a ' blinder ', that is a rock submerged just under the water in Faxa Bay at Iceland.   I have been shipwrecked a few times, the latest was when I left home to go to sea at 2.30 a.m. on a Saturday morning and was in our house again at 11.30 p.m. the same day having lost ship and every stitch of clothing.   Old Jerry got us with a bomb in a convoy off Flamboro' Head and blew

the stern of the ship off.   I was the only one in the cabin aft and never got a scratch.
I often laugh at that, the fire and grate went under the table and soot all over everything, the clock, weather glass and looking glass over the fire grate, also the knives,
forks, and spoons in table drawer shot out and all the plates.   What a game I had.
I had just rolled into my bunk to have a nap when he got us.   I could not see way up
the cabin steps, but as soon as I saw a bit of clear I found them and was up in no time
with the water following my feet up, and we all had to jump for it.   Fancy jumping
for it in a freezing breeze in March and I never even got a cold.   The doctor wanted
me to go into hospital for observation as he said my age was against me.   I told him
I wanted to stop at home, but the doctor knew more than I did.   About a month
after I had a queer sensation and was ill, so off to the doctor I went and he laughed at
me and said ' You were so sure there was nothing wrong with yourself, but now you
are feeling the shock of the bombing, it had to come out sooner or later ! ' ''

Mr. Alp's writing is beautifully neat and easy to read, I only wish more of my
correspondents wrote as clearly.   What a contrast in conditions during the life of this
grand old seaman.   In his youth fishing for cod in the age-old way that dates back to
the Middle Ages and beyond, in his later days bombed by aircraft, which were not
dreamed of when he was a lad.   I shall be giving more of Mr. Alp's experiences when
I deal with trawlers and I was extremely fortunate to get into touch with one who
could describe the life in vessels now gone for ever.

Those fine fishermen, the Shetlanders, have long engaged in the cod fisheries
owing to the close proximity of grounds teeming with vast shoals.   Immense plateaus
lie within the 100 fathom line around the islands, their seaward slopes facing the warm
waters of the Gulf Stream which bring food and plankton to feed the ever hungry
hordes.   The waters around Iceland yielded immense catches, while Heglie's Bank,
accidentally discovered in 1889, proved a gold mine for many years.   250 miles to
the westward lies the Faroe Bank, one of the wildest spots in the North Atlantic.

Much of the offshore fishing was done from open boats—the sixerns—and will
be fully described in my book " INSHORE FISHING CRAFT ", but a number of
large smacks were owned and fitted out by firms of curers, the crews receiving half
the catch or its equivalent after all expenses had been paid, bread being the only
item provided by the owners.   In some cases the men were paid so much a score,
usually 6d. to 9d.   In 1872, 66 cod smacks, averaging 44 tons each, with crews up to
14 men, were engaged in the distant fisheries.

Fitting-out commenced in February when the vessels were cleaned and repainted
after the winter lay-up, stores, coal, salt, barrels and water for a 3 months voyage
were taken on board.   Bait was either whelks, locally known as buckies, or mussels
which were raked out of the sand to north of Lerwick harbour with broad, many
toothed grapnels.   The fleet usually sailed early in March but occasionally a few vessels
got away in February.   After taking in tobacco and spirits at Thorshaven, course
was shaped for the fishing ground where the smack was hove-to and the handlines

put over the side. If the cod were biting well it was not long before the deck was piled high with choice specimens, 40 pounders and over, each with its barbel cut off by its captor who retained it as a tally for his share of the catch. Meanwhile the splitting board was fixed up and all the paraphernalia of knives, tubs, etc., laid out ready for work as soon as the men ceased hauling. Then rows of cod were laid out, a man grabbed one, ripped it open and removed liver and roe, threw the offal overboard and flung the fish to the next man who chopped off the head before passing the carcase on to the splitter, who split the fish open from head to tail and removed the backbone.

After being washed clean of all slime, blood and offal the cod were passed below-deck to be salted and stacked away in tiers. Day after day the fishing continued until the ship had a full hold, anything from 20,000 upwards being considered a good trip, then sail was made for the home port where the fish was landed, washed clean and dried in the sun.

The first voyage generally ended about the second week in May and the crews spent 10 days ashore before sailing on the mid-Summer voyage, either to the Faroes or Rockall, returning again in mid-August to refit for the Fall voyage which was usually to Icelandic waters. On this trip the choicest cod were dropped alive into the well of the smacks so fitted and the catch was taken south to Grimsby for sale and the fleet was laid-up for the winter.

Many fast vessels, ex-yachts and fruit schooners, were engaged in the fishing during the sixties and seventies and could show their sterns to the heavily built smacks. They were much used to take the salted cod to Catholic countries in the Mediterranean, always one of the best markets for stockfish, but some were sent as far afield as Australia. When Hewett's built their new steam carriers in the mid-sixties some of the sailing cutters were sold to Shetland owners who found their speed an advantage in getting to and from the fishing grounds.

Plate 3 is a view of Lerwick harbour in 1872 and shows *Gossamer*, L.K.55, a 26-ton cutter built at Ipswich in 1834 and owned by M. Macrae in 1885. The top-sail schooner lying ahead of the Dutch auxiliary steam frigate may well be one of the many engaged in the cod fishing.

Plate 4 is *Petrel*, L.K.141, built at Southampton as a 52-ton cutter in 1826 and owned in 1885 by Peter Garriock of Lerwick. Later converted to a ketch she was driven into the harbour of Bremangerpol, near Bergen, Norway, in November, 1888, and became a total loss.

Thanks to Mr. H. Oliver Hill's researches into casualties to fishing craft I am able to give a few of the disasters to cod smacks.

On the 12th May, 1897, the 61-ton *Acacia* of London, built 1871, at Aldeburgh, was bound from Grimsby to the Faroe Is. with a crew of 7 when she stranded on Annet Bank at the entrance to Montrose harbour in a strong breeze and became a total loss.

On the 9th June, 1888, the 60-ton *Ana* of London, built at Ipswich in 1872, was fishing about 20 miles west of Rockall when her decks were swept in a westerly gale and one of the crew of 11 was washed overboard, 8 years later she stranded on Ringaroza Is. in a south-west gale and became a total loss.

The 50-ton *Hopeful*, built 1862, at Aldeburgh, stranded on the 10th October, 1884, in the harbour of Trangelsvig, Faroe Is. in a north-easter and was wrecked. *Sophia* of 46 tons, built in 1831, at Greenwich, stranded in Loch Eriboll, Sutherland-shire on the 2nd December, 1887, during a terrible W.S.W. gale. Another old smack *Adventure*, built in 1801, at Rochester, was fishing out of Grimsby on the 17th August, 1882, when she was in collision with the steamer *Woodstock* of Leith and sank 6 miles S.E. by S. of Flamboro' Head, and 6 of her crew of 10 were lost. As there was hardly a breadth of wind it would seem that the steamer was at fault. The 54-ton ketch *Emerald*, built in 1826, at Greenwich and still owned there on the 29th October, 1880, was homeward bound from north Faroe when she ran into that fearful N.N.E. gale which took such a terrific toll of shipping and was driven ashore at Bacton, Norfolk and lost with all hands. Then there was the *William & Lydia* of London, 48 tons, built in 1862, at Ipswich, she struck a floating wreck about 35 miles south of Noss Head, Caithnessshire when bound for Westra, Orkney with salted cod and became a total loss.

It will be noticed that all these losses occurred through stranding or collision, a fact which confirms Mr. R. M. Hewett's statement concerning the sea-keeping abilities of cod smacks, as I was unable to trace any case of foundering through stress of weather. The last of the cod smacks to work out of Grimsby finished up about 1904-6, but unfortunately a photograph I have of two survivors is too poor for repro-duction.

The design and build of well smacks reached culmination just at the time that steam trawlers were coming into use. Some of the finest were built in the old-world yards of J. C. Hoad, and G. & T. Smith at Rye, Sussex, names of high repute as builders of first-class vessels. Fortunately some evidence remains in the model of a smack built by Hoad in 1883. Constructed to a scale of ¾ in. to 1 ft., or 1 : 16, this fine example of craftsmanship was exhibited at the International Fisheries Exhibi-tion in 1883, Hoad being paid £50 for the model, a very high price for those days when full-size fishing boats were being built for £1 a foot.

I had long known of its existence as it was listed in the Science Museum hand-book, but was unable to find it on exhibition and an enquiry elicited that it was on loan to an East London Sea Cadet Corps. Some years later I again made enquiries and was informed that during its absence the model had sustained considerable damage. Eventually I was able to inspect it in store and found all spars and rigging on deck, but Mr. E. W. White most kindly offered me facilities to take off the lines and on the hottest day of the year 1948 I went up to take the necessary measurements. The model had been brought upstairs and placed on a revolving stand which was of the greatest assistance as it could be raised or lowered as required. Starting about 11 a.m. I worked non-stop until 5 p.m., recording some 600 measurements, not to mention innumerable sketches, and Plans 2, pages 312-314 are the result. On completion I sent the pencil draughts to Mr. White, who is a naval architect, and I was delighted to receive his comments. "I have examined your pencil drawings of the well smack with much interest and I must compliment you on the immense amount of detail you were able to record during such a short visit. It was nice of you to submit them for my criticism, but quite frankly, there is little to criticise, on the contrary I think the work is admirable." Coming from such an authority this commendation well repaid me for all the trouble taken to secure some record of these unique vessels.

As the model was the work of the builder of the original smack the workmanship was of the highest order. The registered tonnage was 88 tons, length 77.3 ft., breadth 20.3 ft., depth 12.2 ft., length of keel 70 ft., but unfortunately there is no hint of identification as the name is omitted. The port side is fully planked and shows the auger holes to admit water, spaced 1 ft. to 1 ft. 4 in., centre to centre, but on the starboard side the planking is broken amidships to show the construction and interior of the well which is divided into three compartments. One most interesting feature is the fact that the spacing of frames followed the peculiar Rye fashion which I found when measuring up the Lowestoft smack *Master Hand*. The timbers are set up in pairs, centred 2 ft. 5 in., being spaced 8 in. frame, 8 in. space, 8 in. frame, 5 in. space.

The well measures 20 ft. 9 in. inside bulkheads, centre compartment being 7 ft. and the others 6 ft. 3 in. long, 4 ft. 6 in. high to underside of well deck. The funnel is 2 ft. 3 in. wide athwartships, with the centre bulkheads carried up and sloping inwards, and fitted with sliding shutters to control the amount of water in the funnel, on deck is an open grating. The space between well deck and underside of main deck was used as a pound for storing salted or iced fish. Aft of well is a cabin larger than that found in a trawler, fitted with the usual bunks, stove, etc., and lit by a small skylight, for'ard is the sail locker and fore peak.

Deck fittings call for little comment, for'ard is the windlass with a stove chimney just aft, next the winch over the fore hatch and the chain pipe through which the anchor cable passed to locker at foot of mast—smacksmen always kept as much weight as possible out of the ends of the hull to keep them buoyant. Aft of the mainmast is the pump and on either side of hatch coaming are 4 ringbolts so that the boat could be lashed down on the opposite side to that on which fishing was carried on. To starboard of companion is stove chimney and another pump, aft the main sheet box and a belaying post, 8½ in. sq. and 2 ft. 1 in. high on either side of skylight. Generally speaking the deck arrangements closely follow trawler practice.

SPARS

As near as I could judge the mainmast measured 49 ft 8 in from deck to cap, with a 10 ft 6 in masthead, diameter at saddle 1 ft 5 in, head 12 in to 10½ in, at cheeks 1 ft 2½ in. Mast hoops are 18 in dia.

Topmast 38 ft 6 in heel to truck, 34 ft 4 in to hounds, heel 9 in sq for 1 ft 6 in, 6 in dia at head, with three fid holes 2 ft 6 in apart.

Mizzen 47 ft 8 in deck to truck, 12 in dia at deck, 10 in at hounds, 6 in at head. Mast hoops 15 in dia.

Bowsprit 38 ft 6 in overall, with a 9 ft heel 1 ft 1½ in sq. to 1 ft 1 in dia, 11 in dia at outer end. Traveller 1 ft 4 in dia.

Main gaff 32 ft to jaws, dia 9½ in to 7 in.

Main boom 43 ft 6 in to jaws, 11 in dia at jaw, 12 in at centre and 9 in at outer end, fitted with jaws which rest on a saddle near heel of mainmast.

Mizzen gaff 17 ft to jaws, dia 7½ in to 6 in.

Mizzen boom 21 ft overall, dia 6 in at gooseneck, 7½ in centre, 7 in at outer end.

Crosstrees. 18 ft overall, 5 in wide, 3 in deep.

SAILS

Mainsail	–	–	Head 29 ft. Foot 42 ft. Weather 30 ft. Lee 51 ft. Diagonal 54 ft.
Mizzen	–	–	Head 15 ft 9 in. Foot 19 ft. Weather 20 ft. Lee 29 ft. Diagonal 33 ft. Sail is diagonal cut.
Topsail	–	–	Yard 15 ft. Sail is diagonal cut. Head 14 ft 6 in. Foot 15 ft 6 in. Weather 12 ft. Lee 17 ft 6 in. Diagonal 25 ft 9 in.
Foresail	–	–	Weather 37 ft. Lee 29 ft. Foot 20 ft 6 in.
Jibs –	–	–	Not available.
Length of Keel	–	70 ft. Sided 12 in amidships, 9 in stem and stern.	
Rudder	–	7 in thick at after end.	
Deck planks	–	6 in wide.	

As a result of considerable research I find that several well smacks were built at Rye during the mid-eighties, each varying slightly in dimensions and tonnage, and 12 Rye-built vessels, fitted with auxiliary engines, were actively engaged in the Faroe Is. fisheries in 1950. Among them was the 76-ton *William Martin*, built in 1883 for W. Allenby of Grimsby. In 1894 she was sold to Nicholson & Co. of Scalloway, Shetland Is. and under Skipper J. Peterson never made a losing voyage until 1906. Two years later Evensen bought her and she was the last cod smack to work under sail; a 37 h.p. motor was installed and in 1950 she was still fishing, owned by D. P. Hejgaard of Ridevy. In 1896 Hay & Co. of Lerwick purchased the 76-ton *Buttercup*, built at Rye in 1884 for J. Leyman of Hull and she went cod fishing to 1904, then herring drifting until 1920 when she was sold to Faroe Is. owners and fitted with a motor.

Nearly 70 years have passed since Hoad built this model of a well smack and it is a far cry from such a vessel, whose master looked to wind'ard and the sky to foretell the weather, and the up-to-date steam and motor trawlers which now set out for Arctic waters, well equipped with radar, echo sounders, and the latest types of trawling gear. Their skippers can listen-in to the Meteorological Office reports, talk to each other and their owners on shore over the wireless telephone, but they still seek the shoals of cod.

7　A REEF AND TOPSAIL BREEZE ON THE DOGGER, 1892

Hibernia, G.Y.169, 83 tons, built at Dartmouth, 1877.　One reef is laced up in mainsail and mizzen, topmast is reefed, two of crew are gutting fish on port side of deck.　Note unusual lead of peak halyards on main gaff.

8   A FAROE ISLAND COD SMACK
An old Grimsby trawler, fitted with auxiliary
engine. Note lead of main peak halyards
and old-fashioned lead of topping lift.

9   ON THE HARD IN DOVER HARBOUR
D.R.74 *Forget-me-not*, 23 tons, built as a cutter at Dover,
1883. D.R.18 *Baron*, 22 tons, built as a lugger at
Newlyn, 1871.

Fishing Smack &c.

10 SOUTHAMPTON FISHING HOY, c 1829
Note clench-built hull, long boom and bowsprit, and reef
points in jib. To wind'ard is a dandy with lug mizzen.

11   BRIXHAM SLOOP D.H.60 AT RAMSGATE, 1857
Note bluff bows, winch, long masthead and boom, and open
transom.

CHAPTER THREE

HISTORY OF TRAWLING

ALTHOUGH the development of intensive trawling only dates to a century or so ago, the use of a trawl net to catch demersal fish probably goes back two thousand years and more. It is known that well-to-do Romans were very partial to the oyster, which, living on the bottom of the sea, can only be brought to the surface in a drag or " dredge ", a small bagnet with its mouth held open by a frame. It is not un-reasonable to suppose that fish were caught from time to time during dredging operations over the oyster beds, and the possibilities offered for catching demersal fish by this means must have been apparent.

That such a contrivance was destructive to fish life was realized in the reign of Edward III, when in 1376-77 a petition was presented to Parliament calling for the prohibition of a " subtlety contrived instrument called the wondyrchoum ". This consisted of a net 18 ft. long and 10 ft. wide " of so small a mesh, no manner of fish, however small, entering within it can pass out and is compelled to remain therein and be taken . . . by means of which instrument the fishermen aforesaid take so great abundance of small fish aforesaid, that they know not what to do with them, but feed and fatten the pigs with them, to the great damage of the whole commons of the kingdom, and the destruction of the fisheries in like places, for which they pray remedy ". *Responsia.* " Let Commission be made by qualified persons to inquire and certify on the truth of this allegation, and thereon let right be done in the Court of Chancery."

Thus was set up one of the first of the many Royal Commissions to enquire into the state of the fisheries and the allegation that trawl nets swept up undersized fish. The wondyrchoum had its head rope nailed to a beam having a frame at either end to raise it above the ground and the sole rope was weighted to keep it on the bottom.

It is obvious that trawling was known in the time of King James I, as on the 7th March, 1622, the Mayor of Hythe wrote to Lord Zouche complaining that fishermen of Rochester and Stroud were trawling off that port with illegal nets. They resisted his interference, but would answer any accusation at London. Then in 1630 Viscount Dorchester, one of the principal Secretaries of State, to whom the great fishery question was entrusted by Charles I, was inundated with petitions from fishermen on all parts of the coast complaining of the small size of mesh in nets used by some trawlers. A drawing of a trawl net with beam and head irons appears on the back of certain State papers dated 1635 and after the Restoration King Charles II regulated the mesh of trawl nets. From the reign of James II to the accession of Queen Anne similar Acts were enforced and there was a great increase in the numbers of trawlers around the coast.

I was very interested when reading through Act 1, George I. Sta. 2 Cap. XVIII to find that Article IV enacted that :

" From and after the twenty-fifth day of September one thousand seven hundred and sixteen, if any person or persons shall use at sea upon the coast of that part of Great Britain called England, any traul-net, drag-net or set-net whatsoever for the catching of any kind of fish (except herrings, pilchards, sprats or lavidnian) which hath any mesh or moke of less size than three inches and half at least from knot to knot, or which hath any false bottom or double bottom, cod or pouch, or shall put any net or nets, though of legal size and mesh, upon or behind the others, in order to catch and destroy the small fish which would have passed through any single net of three inches and half mesh, all and every such person and persons so offending shall forfeit all and singular such net or nets so used contrary to the true intent and meaning thereof, and also for every such offence the sum of twenty pounds of lawful money of Great Britain, to be recovered and levied in such a manner and form as the penalty above inflicted upon the master of any vessel, wherein fish shall be imported contrary to this Act, is above directed to be recovered and levied, and in default of payment of the said twenty pounds, or of sufficient distress, the offender to be imprisoned in like manner, during the space of twelve months."

In other words any one using a net having a mesh less than 3½ in. square was liable to a fine of £20 or 12 months, and have his nets confiscated and publicly burnt. The next Article says that all penalties and forfeitures in the Act were to be " disposed of in manner following, one moiety thereof to the informer, and the other moiety thereof to the poor of the parish where such offence shall be committed ".

Article VII specifies that no one was to sell or exchange for other goods any unsizeable fish and the minimum sizes are given " turbet 16 in., brill or pearl 14 in., sole 8 in., plaice or dab 8 in., whiting 6 in., etc., etc.", the length being measured from the eyes to the utmost extent of the tail. Any offender was liable to pay a fine of twenty shillings and if unable to do so was to be sent to a house of correction, or other common gaol or prison, " there to be severely whipped, and kept to hard labour for a space of six days and not longer than fourteen days ".

Dear me ! Some vendors of undersized fish would be a bit sore were such an Act still in force to-day ! The only hope of escaping the penalties was the fact that prosecution must be within one month of committing the offence.

This Act and several others were repealed when the Sea Fisheries Act of 1868 came into force.   Had it continued and been enforced it might have made a consider-able difference to the spoilation of grounds where young fry fed before moving into deeper water.   For example, millions and millions of small plaice were trawled up on the Eastern Grounds in subsequent years.   In his evidence before the Commis-sioners in 1878 James Pitcher of Yarmouth said that in one haul off the Dutch coast on the 18th June, 1877, he found 300 pairs of soles about 4 in. long.

This question was again argued in 1883 when smacksmen and others were getting seriously perturbed at the catching of immature fish, in spite of the bland assurances of certain scientists that there was little chance of overfishing in the North Sea.   A resolution was moved by John Helyer of Yarmouth, admiral of a fishing fleet for 10 years, and carried unanimously.   That was all that did move, for nothing much was done although for 2 years many of the trawling fleets voluntarily agreed to restrain from working on certain grounds at specified seasons, but this scheme broke down when single-boaters defied the ban.   To show the extreme variations, a box of plaice might contain as few as 50 or as many as 1,000 fish, the latter valued at the nominal price of 1s. in the market.

Nothing further was done for another half-century until discussions again took place just before the outbreak of war in 1939.   Still, one never knows, the question first arose in 1376 and Royal Commissions have been sitting on and off ever since.   It is a problem to tax the skill of the wisest statesmen as many other nationalities are concerned and it is useless to make laws restricting fishing to one lot of men, when all the rest go scot free and can do as they please.

Further evidence as to the antiquity of trawling has already been given in the 1750 accounts of the Barking cod smack, where the weight of a pair of " troylheads " is clearly given as 1 cwt. 0 qt. 20 lb., and the size of the trawl warp as 4½ in.   These figures suggest the use of a small beam, perhaps less than 20 ft. in length.

Working inshore in his local waters, a fisherman had his own special marks, such and such a clump of trees aligned with a church tower was the beginning of a good ground, a white house in line with a windmill marked a rocky patch, other leading marks told him he was in the vicinity of wrecks.   No such guides were available when he pushed out into unknown waters, as did the men from Barking and Brixham during the closing years of the Napoleonic wars and those following the declaration of peace.

Coming up Channel, the Devon men found banks a few miles off the coast in the Straits of Dover where such choice fish as soles, turbot and brill teemed at certain seasons.   Chief of these were the Varne and Ridge banks lying in the centre of the fairway midway between the English and French coasts.   Around the banks are depths of 14 to 18 fathom with the bottom sand, shingle and broken shells.   The Varne shoal is nearly 6 miles in extent, steep-to on either side, with depths of 15 fathom shoaling to as little as 1½ over the N.E. extremity, where the Keep of Dover Castle bears N. ½ E., distant 8½ miles.   The Ridge, 2 miles S.E. of the Varne, is nearly 10 miles in length, steep-to, with deeps of 11 to 15 fathom close by.   Here strong eddies run with very heavy seas breaking in bad weather.   Nearby is Rye Bay, famous for soles, and worked over by Rye and Hastings fishermen for generations. As time went on the Ramsgate men followed the example of the Brixham fishermen, who had made the Kentish harbour their station, and worked out into the North Sea, going across to the Dutch and Belgian coasts where prolific grounds were discovered.

In the 1830's the fishing industry in the Channel was in a bad way, and an official enquiry was held in 1833 to find the causes and suggest remedies.   The principal complaint was that 200 to 300 French boats came within a stone's throw of the houses, according to one witness, to catch bait for their long lines.   Having collected 4 to 5 bushels of 2 in. long fish, they ran out to sea, baited 1,600 to 1,800 hooks and shot the lines on the Ridge.   A few hours later 3 or 4 boats would bring in from 140 to 160 prime turbot and sell them on Dover beach or quay at 1s. 6d. to 2s. 6d. each, duty free.   What made the local men wild was that the French would not allow any fishing within 9 miles of their coast.

In 1831 Thomas Knight went on the Bassiere Bank, 8 or 9 miles west of Boulogne, and about 5 miles off the land.   Soon a big French lugger, armed with 4 guns and carrying a crew of 14, ran down, dropped anchor and sent off a boat manned by 5 men, one of whom, speaking good English, shouted to Knight :—" You must not fish here.   If you trawl within nine miles we'll take you into Boulogne, keep you there 3 months and make you pay £2 a month."   Knight retorted that 40 to 50 French boats were always working in Rye Bay, and he received the mocking reply. " Ah ! I know that, but the laws in France are not the laws in England."

Another grievance was that foreigners, short of provisions, could go to an English magistrate and obtain a licence to sell fish to buy food, whereas a boat driven into a French port by stress of weather was not allowed to sell fish, but the skipper had to go to the English Consul for relief.   In the herring season the heavy French boats, shooting a mile or more of nets, frequently drove down and cut away our men's gear, hauled the nets on board and sailed off, the fishermen, out-numbered by 3 or 4 to 1, being powerless to do anything to prevent this stealing of their property.

At Folkestone 33 small boats, of 5 to 8 tons, trawled for flat fish from April to September, working up to 3 miles out, but never going beyond Dungeness or much to the east of Folkestone.   Trawl beams measured from 16 to 18 ft., and net and warp were worth about six or seven guineas.   At Dover were 40 to 50 of the largest sized trawlers, many owned by Torbaymen who made the port their station.

John Lewis, a fisherman for 32 years, said they went away as far as Goree on the Dutch coast, about 200 miles from Dover, for the winter season, November to April, but the Dutch would not allow any fishing within 8 to 10 miles of Sceveland Bay, and threatened to cut away gear if they came inside that limit.   His smack registered 34 tons and had a crew of 5.   He also spoke of French interference, saying he never went within 16 to 17 miles of their coast, being afraid of molestation.   21 years before he could go out into the deeps and catch 7 or 8 bushels of soles and a few turbot, but now scarcely any were to be caught on the N. Foreland. Just after the Peace of 1815, his salesman at Billingsgate used to send him £1 1s. to £2 a pot for brill, soles and turbot, whereas now he only received 12s. to 16s. The fish was sent up by van from Dover.

Thomas Knight informed the Commissioners that in the first week of June, 1833, his turbot realized £4 for a half-pad, but the usual price was 18s. to £1 a pad, a basket measure.

A pad consisted of 3 " pots ", and the half-pad of 2 pots. This division was for the convenience of the salesmen, if 2 pads and 3 half-pads were to be sold, they were offered as 12 pots and fish were worth so much per pot that day. Fishermen also found this convenient, as if they had not enough prime fish at the end of their packing to fill a half-pad, they put it into a half-pad basket and called it a pot. A pot nominally weighed 40 lbs., but a half-pad subsequently came to weigh from 120 to 80 lb., the difference being caused by the fish being more or less piled up in the top of the basket.

The word pad comes from " ped ", a wicker basket used in Elizabethan days.

Many of the boats were prohibited from going out more than 4 leagues from the English coast and all had to hold a licence from the Customs, a precaution to try and prevent smuggling which was very prevalent among the Folkestone men at that time. Hollowed-out spars and oars were lined with tin and filled with brandy, when the boats came ashore the men picked up their gear and carried it up the beach under the noses of the Preventive men, who never tumbled to the ruse until a woman " blew the gaff ".

During the summer the London river hatch boats used to come as far down as the Foreland to collect fish, the crews were " boisterous, blustering men " to quote F. Tapley, a Billingsgate salesman, well able to drive a hard bargain. Their boats loaded from 50 to 60 bushels and many being fitted with wells could bring the fish in better condition to market than that sent up in vans during hot weather. Each boat paid a toll of one shilling at Billingsgate for the use of planks and ladders, and the dumb lighter to land the fish. At one time toll was a halfpenny a pad, but later it was levied on the van or boat, not the contents.

Mackerel had a ready sale in the London market and salesmen vied with each other to get the fish in the quickest time from the coast, a saving of one hour at Billingsgate might mean a gain of £20 to £30. If a hatch boat or van arrived with ten thousand mackerel at 5 a.m. the price would average 48s. to 50s. a long hundred, at 10 a.m. price dropped to 32s. to 36s. and by the afternoon it was only 24s. to 28s. Many of the Margate men would pay a steamboat £20 to get a tow up, as a catch worth £200 on the early market, kept until the next day would scarcely make £75, and more likely than not be worthless if the weather was very hot.

When the fish was sent up by road the vans were horsed by the posting masters and were exempt from post-horse duty, but they had to pay turnpike tolls, although an old act said all fish sent to London was toll free. From Hastings, William Breach used to send up as many as ten carriages a day in the height of the season, and in the years 1812 to 1816 he despatched 1,600 loads.

These post vans had a pair of horses and the rate was 1s. a mile, with an extra charge for the post boy of 1½d. a mile, 1s. for greasing the carriage and 6d to the ostler at every stage. A van would take 8 to 10 cwt. of fish, travel at an average of about 6 miles an hour with fresh relays every second hour, but if driven at a gallop, speed was of course much higher and the post boys did not mind as the passengers could not complain of the jolting !

Thus for 72 miles the charges would be :---

72 miles @ 1s. per mile	£3	12	0
Post boy @ 1½d per mile		9	0
Greasing carriage		1	0
Ostler @ 6d. a stage		3	0
	£4	5	0

exclusive of turnpike tolls, about 12 hours being taken for the journey. A load of Hastings mackerel would fetch £20 to £30, but the biggest price ever paid at Billingsgate was in May, 1807, when the first van from Brighton realized 40 guineas a long hundred, or about 7s. a fish, but the next load saw the price down to £13 13s. a 100. In February, 1834, one night's catch by a Hastings boat brought in £100. These fish were caught in drift nets, but I have used them as an example of the violent fluctuations of price in such a perishable article as fish and to show the vagaries of public taste.

The luggage vans, drawn by 4 or 6 horses, held three times the load of a pair-horse carriage. Tapley said he paid £4 17s. 6d. for 11 baskets of fish brought up from Portsmouth—72 miles—and occasionally £6 6s. for a load and a half. Most of the vans on the Dover Road had 4 horses, but he sometimes had 6 put in to ensure rapid delivery.

Fish were sold by various measures, only salmon and eels being sold by the lb. John Goldham, Yeoman of the Waterside and Clerk of the Market, stated that Dutch plaice went in " turns ", about 45 in a lot, soles by the bushel, turbot singly, mackerel and herring by the long hundred. There was no telling what the price would be as everything was sold by auction. The big West End buyers got away by 6.30 to 7 a.m., and he had seen the same sized turbot selling at 5s. which had made £1 a short time before, and a pot of soles sold for as little as 3s., on which carriage alone had been 4s.

Goldham said there was little sale for fish among the poor " The lower class entertains the notion that fish is not substantial food enough for them, they prefer meat, but at times will eat cheap herring or mackerel ''. He seems to have been a very hard-working, conscientious man as he remarked :—'' I have been there 18 hours out of the 24 and sleep at the market.''

As an example of delay caused by light weather I noticed that the smack *Sovereign*, Master F. Danson, with 687 turbot on board, arrived at the Nore on the 16th June, 1833, but was not at Billingsgate until two days later.

Although there is mention in the Report of the use of ice by fishmongers and the packing of Irish salmon in shallow boxes with ice, I could find no reference to its use at sea. Within the next decade Samuel Hewett of Barking made use of ice to preserve fish on board his smacks, enabling them to remain a week or more at sea, and this introduction, and wooden boxes instead of wicker baskets, led to the fleeting system. Here the daily catches were transferred to carriers for despatch to Billingsgate, for then, as now, London was the greatest market, taking approximately one-quarter of all the fish caught around the coasts. Barking smackowners were seeking new grounds further out in the North Sea, fishing off Yarmouth and the Lincolnshire shores and across in Dutch waters, but transport was still the greatest problem.

The development of Scarborough as a fashionable watering place induced the venturesome Devon and Ramsgate men to make use of the harbour during the season, as good prices could be obtained for choice fish from the wealthy visitors, the trawlers returning home for the winter months. It was the discovery of the Silver Pits, where prime soles gathered in abundance during severe winters, that led to the rapid rise of the Humber ports of Hull and Grimsby as fishing stations.

The coming of railways opened up new markets in towns where fish had been an almost unknown luxury, and soon hatch boats and posting vans became obsolete. In 1854, 635 hatch boats paid 1s. 6d. toll at Billingsgate, in 1857 only 305, four years later numbers had fallen to 115 and the 97 entries in 1863 showed the steady decline in water transport from Gravesend. 3,155 four-horse vans paid 1s. 6d. toll in 1855, but only 708 in 1858 with a further fall to 471 the following year. The numbers of two-horse vans rose from 7,959 in 1855 to 14,403 in 1859, an increase no doubt due to the need for transport from the railway termini to Billingsgate.

In the early sixties about 700 smacks were working in the North Sea and on fresh grounds as far away as the coasts of Schleswig, the vessels being now more powerful and better able to face the stormy waters around the Dogger Bank and the Great Fisher Bank. Within the next ten years the whole of the North Sea had been explored from shore to shore, Dutch, Belgian and Danish waters being visited at the appropriate seasons, while Heligoland, then a British possession, was an important fishing ground and base, quantities of haddock being smoked in the curing houses ashore.

It is well to remember that in the early days there were few charts and if any were available hardly a fisherman could read them, as some of the old men averred '' them there charts be alrite for them as knows the locality, but aren't a damn bit of use to them as don't ! '' The first chart of the North Sea was not made until 1847 and then the information was very imperfect from a fisherman's point of view. Depths, banks, gullies, rough grounds and the nature of the bottom were found by smacksmen using a lead armed with tallow which brought up a sample of the sea bed, sand, mud, small shells, etc. Torn nets were certain evidence of rough ground, best avoided if trips were to be successful. The experience of years enabled skippers to visualize the nature of the bottom to a certain limited extent and they could tell their position immediately after taking a cast of the lead, the colour of the water and run of tide being other unerring guides.

Few people realize the extent of the North Sea with its area of 152,000 sq. miles or thereabouts, nearly three times the size of England and Wales, with seas as turbulent as any in the world, due to the broken water caused by the extreme variations of the sea bed and the eternal contending of the tides. Fog and snow, prevalent in winter, made the risk of collision ever present when 200 and more sail of smacks were working in close proximity to each other, also there was the likelihood of being run down by sailing ships bound to and from Baltic and Scandinavian ports, often showing no lights to save a few miserable pennyworth of oil. Even more dangerous were the German liners, driving at full speed in thick weather, bent on record breaking in the keen competition for the passenger and emigrant trade to the Golden West, where riches untold were to be had for the asking, or so the story went.

All this pioneering of virgin fishing grounds was done by humble, often illiterate men, who owned or part-owned the small smacks in which they took great pride, and for a generation or two similar conditions prevailed, with crews frequently made up from one family and all sharing in the profits and losses. No man was better equipped than his neighbour, excepting in so far as superior knowledge of the movement of the shoals, the most likely grounds, and seamanship gave him an advantage.

In 1876 there were 3,142 first-class fishing vessels of over 15 tons registered in England and Wales, the numbers at the principal trawling stations being :—Hull 386, Grimsby 429, Scarborough 123, Yarmouth 552, Lowestoft 348, London 133, Ramsgate 157, Dover 20, Rye 33, Brixham 164, Plymouth 59, Liverpool 41 and Fleetwood 70. The figures for Yarmouth and Lowestoft include drifters as well as trawlers, but many of the herring boats were " converter " smacks.

Nearly all were owned by individuals, there being few joint stock companies engaged in the fishing industry at this time, the chief being the famous Short Blue Fleet belonging to Hewett & Co. of London. I analysed the list of Hull owners in 1877 from a small booklet kindly loaned me by Mr. A. M. Walker, and found that John Holmes owned 17 smacks, all named after stars and planets, excepting his latest vessel, the 81-ton *John Holmes*, built that year at Burton Stather. Next came A. W. Ansell with 11, Joseph Potter 8, James Evans 7, James Wood 6, Henry Toozes 5, C. Pickering 4, and Charles Hellyer 4. 93 men owned one smack apiece,

48 two, and 22 men owned three each. In September there were 390 smacks. The smallest registered 39 N.T., the largest 91, with only one smack of each size, the average was 56 to 80 tons, only 10 being over that tonnage.

Sufficient to say that individual efforts, financed by a small family circle, or friends and tradesmen, founded the immense industry known to-day. All honour to such men ; no subsidies assisted them, by their own efforts they sank or swam, and every smack sailed " on its own keel ". If a man was of good character he had no difficulty in obtaining credit from builders, sailmakers, etc., who knew they would be repaid unless disaster overwhelmed the vessel, and that affected the skipper, who would see that so far as possible his command was maintained in an efficient and seaworthy condition.

The first week in November, 1877, was the turning point in the history of trawling as steam was successful for about the first time in hauling the trawl. Owing to the decline in the numbers of deep-sea sailing ships visiting the N.E. coast ports, many of the old wooden, clinker-built tugs were laid up, but at times were employed to tow sailing smacks, then based at North Shields, out to the fishing grounds a few miles away. In some instances during calms they continued to tow the smack with her trawl down and it occurred to Mr. Wm. Purdy, part-owner of the tug *Messenger* that he might as well tow the trawl himself, without the smack. James Kelly, skipper of the largest smack *Zenith*, roundly denounced the notion of applying steam to trawling as being " absurdly newfangled and hopelessly impracticable " and he assured Mr. Purdy that he would lose his money. The tug owner replied that he had no money but wanted to make some and thought he had hit on a plan by which he could do so. " Go on then ", was the angry reply, " waste your money, you'll rue the day you spurned my advice ".

Messenger was a very ancient vessel, having being clench-built of wood at East Jarrow as far back as 1843, her dimensions being 71.5 by 15.7 by 8.3, 10 N.T., 55 G.T., and her engines were only 25 h.p. Mr. Purdy pushed ahead with the fitting-out, trawl nets were obtained from Grimsby at a cost of £10 10s., a pair of trawlheads were made by the local blacksmith for £5 10s. and a suitable length of timber for a beam was found lying on the South Dock and purchased for £3 10s. Many Job's comforters stood around watching the progress of the work and when Kelly saw the derrick, which was to hoist the cod out of the water, he announced " it was not strong enough to hang a man ".

Eventually the aged paddle-tug left the Fish Quay on 1st November with jeers and catcalls ringing in the ears of Captain Purdy, who had with him as fishermen a Scot named Alexander Fyall, and a Shieldsman, Thomas Tomlinson. The trip lasted 24 hours, the modest catch was sold for £7 10s. and in addition the tug picked up a lucky £5 for towing a ship into the harbour. A second successful trip saw other tug-boat owners falling over themselves to fit out their laid-up vessels, among them being *Pilot, Conquest, Helen, Alice, Stevenson* and others, until not one idle tug swung at moorings. During the winter 43 tugs were engaged in fishing, the number increased to 53 the following year and by the end of July about 900 tons of fish had been landed at N. Shields, as well as quantities at Sunderland and Newcastle. The largest take in one night was between 30 and 35 cwt., mostly choice fish, as the handy tugs were able to work over restricted grounds, often surrounded by rocks, over which the sailing vessels had been unable to trawl.

Joseph Gravels, for five years admiral of the fleet at Ramsgate before working for two seasons out of Grimsby, now became master of a trawling tug, working in 25 to 26 fathom and William Keble of the tug *Powerful*, a 34 h.p. wooden vessel built at Coble Dene in 1865, was fishing with a 44 ft. beam and a cod mesh of only one inch, shooting less than 8 miles from Tynemouth Pier and towing for a distance of 16 to 17 miles.

The most expensive tug working was *Patriot*, owned by John Robert Lawson and valued at £2,000. She had been built of iron at Low Walker in 1867, was 91 G.T., 18 N.T., on dimensions 86.4 by 17.6 by 9.3 and her engines developed 40 h.p. In 5 months trawling the gross takings were £12 to £56 a week, the expenses for coal, oil and tallow £5 a week and the remainder equally divided between owner and crew. Out of his half-share Mr. Lawson stood for the interest on capital and wear and tear of tug, the other half was further divided into six shares. The captain and first fisherman took 1¼ each, 3 men 1 share apiece, and the boy or sixth hand had ½ share.

Mr. Purdy's enterprise was promptly recognized by his fellow townsmen who assembled at the Sun Inn, Bell Street, and publicly presented him with a gold watch and chain, inscribed '' Presented to William Purdy by the Patrons of the Fish Trade for introducing steam trawling on the Tyne 1878 ''. I wonder if they asked Kelly for a subscription !

The family is still closely identified with the fish trade and I am indebted to Mr. George R. Purdy, grandson of the pioneer, for his courtesy in placing information at my disposal.

Many of these paddle-tugs worked from Scarborough, often landing their catches at Hull, and experiments were made with otter boards instead of the beam. One tug so fitted was the 50 h.p. *Triumph*, built of iron at Low Walker in 1867, her dimensions being 95.4 by 18.4 by 9.8, 14 N.T., 103 G.T. She was sold to Irish owners and registered at Londonderry in 1882. Plate 5 is from a photograph loaned me by Mr. Don Paterson, who found the original in an old guide book of Scarborough which was chucked away on a rubbish heap at Gibraltar during the recent war. A lucky find !

These small paddle-tugs were quite unsuitable for working deep-sea, and the smacksmen did not worry much about them as they had little or no interest in the confined grounds close inshore. Steam had been tried before and proved to be a failure, for they remembered *Corkscrew*, a 50 h.p. screw steamer, built of iron at

Blackwall in 1844, which had been fitted out at Grimsby in 1858 with a beam trawl on either side. Although fish were then plentiful she had been unable to earn her keep, and was sold to Bailey and Leetham, by whom she was lengthened and renamed *Jutland*, being registered at Hull in 1862. One or two hulls had been fitted with auxiliary steam power and, after vainly trying to earn a living, had been sold time and time again. There was nothing to worry about, engines were unreliable and ate up coal, then about 10s. a ton ! There was a use for steam in the carriers which brought in the daily catches of the smacks, but that was about all.

A few years later the blow fell when The Grimsby and North Sea Steam Trawling Co. had two iron screw vessels built, the *Aries* at Grimsby by T. Charlton in 1882, at a cost of £3,550, her dimensions being 95.4 by 20.3 by 10.2, 118 G.T., 67 N.T., with compound surface condensing engines developing 35 h.p., which gave a speed of under 10 knots. She was christened by Miss Moody, daughter of the chairman. *Zodiac* was built in 1881 at Hull by Earles Shipbuilding Co. at a cost of £3,500, 93 by 20.1 by 10.4, 114 G.T., 65 N.T., and she was christened by Miss Jeffs, daughter of C. Jeffs. The company had a capital of £50,000 and the subscribers included W. Moody, H. Mudd and J. Alward who were smack owners, others were interested in the M.S. & L. Railway. In 1883 four more steam trawlers were built to the order of the company, *Gemini* and *Taurus* at Hull, *Cancer* and *Leo* at Grimsby, all registering 128 G.T., 73 to 75 N.T. As well as being trawlers these vessels were used as carriers to bring in the catches of the Hull smacks working across on the Eastern grounds in the summer months. In 1923 *Aries* was Swedish and *Leo* French owned.

The further introduction of outside capital into the fishing industry was largely the outcome of the interest taken by the public in the 1883 International Fisheries Exhibition. Sail was still at its zenith, but the success of the few steam trawlers made it obvious that vessels dependent on the wind would soon be on the wane.

Many papers were read at the Conference of 1883 and it is interesting to see the reactions of scientific men, full of theories, and the practical fishermen who had spent all their working lives at sea. Discussing the question of starfish on the 26th July, Mr. Charles E. Fryer produced a typical head-in-the-clouds solution. " I have often seen the fishermen, when casting overboard his rubbish, tear a star fish in two and throw it away with a by no means complimentary valediction. What has such a man done ? Instead of casting back one starfish he had returned two to the water, for this creature has the power, if not of replacing its lost members, at least of living very comfortably minus one or two. . . . *A bucket of hot water would effectually close the career of such creatures* and fishermen should be instructed to absolutely destroy all kinds of vermin."

Well, the learned speaker may have known more than a fisherman about the capabilities of a starfish to exist when cut in two, but his remedy was ludicrous, can anyone imagine buckets of hot water being on tap in a smack ? Another scientist, Dr. Francis Day, seems to have known a little more about conditions at sea as he replied " I have been on fishing boats a good deal and think the fisherman would say that a far easier plan would be to put the heel of his boot on the top of the fish and crush it, as to carrying buckets of hot water about in trawlers to kill starfish, it was not a plan, which in my opinion, the fishermen would be likely to take to ".

Replying to a statement that cod ate twelve or more herring a day, John Hepton of Grimsby stated that he had gutted thousands and not more than 20 per cent contained any herring whatever, a very few had four or five in all stages of digestion. And so it went on, but I think the climax was reached by Professor Brown Goode. " The practical men, had," he confessed, " been rather an amusing feature of this exhibition. Some of them had stood on the platform and cried out against the views of men of science . . . it was quite unnecessary for some of the practical men to disclaim scientific knowledge, because the lack of such knowledge was quite evident from the tenour of their remarks."

But who caught the fish he no doubt enjoyed at dinner ? I should like to have seen some of those theorists out on the Dogger on a wild winter's night. They would soon have learned the truth that an ounce of practice was worth a ton of theory.

The coming of steam altered the entire outlook of all concerned with fishing. No longer dependent on the fickleness of the wind, a steam trawler could fight the elements and in calms continue fishing as in a breeze. Outside influences now frequently controlled the financial side of the business and individual ownership was being swallowed up by public companies, often directed by men who had not made fishing their livelihood. Gone for all time were the more happy-go-lucky days. The opportunity to own his own vessel practically disappeared, as few skippers could afford the thousands necessary to build, equip and run a steam trawler, while the men tended more and more to become deck hands and engineers, rather than fishermen.

On the Humber a few smacksmen, set in the ways of their youth, clung to sail and fought tenaciously to stem the tide of circumstances, but it was a losing battle. One by one they succumbed to the inevitable. It had required courage and supreme faith in the future of steam for hard-headed men to scrap almost brand-new smacks, built to Lloyd's requirements at a cost of £1,500 and more, and go in for the as yet untried steam trawler. Such however was the urge that the change-over took place practically overnight, so to speak, and in a little over a decade sail became almost a memory at Hull and Grimsby.

The tendency was now to abandon many small ports and harbours and concentrate in a few big centres, as the greatly increased landings necessitated new methods of marketing and distribution, while proximity to a coalfield was an added inducement in many instances. A large steam trawler would burn 10 to 11 tons a day, and the later vessels for the Icelandic fishing bunkered 220 to 250 tons. The spectacular increase in catches however did not lead to any great reductions in prices, but rather to supplies of fish being available in towns where it had hitherto been almost unobtainable, and this was all to the good from the public point of view.

In 1887 there were 448 first-class smacks registered at Hull, 839 at Grimsby, 90 at Scarborough, 627 at Yarmouth, 376 at Lowestoft, 105 at London, 140 at Ramsgate, 24 at Dover, 32 at Rye, 159 at Brixham, 89 at Plymouth, 34 at Hoylake and 43 at Fleetwood, the total for England and Wales being 3,006.

In 1889 Grimsby had 292 owners with one smack each, another 278 vessels divided amongst 93 men, one of whom owned no less than 45, and 7 companies owned 112 all told.

By 1893 the total of smacks had fallen to 2,037 and in 1899 it was only 1,133, but by 1903 the numbers had dwindled to NONE at Hull, 34 at Grimsby, 20 at Scarborough, 86 at Yarmouth, 356 at Lowestoft, 138 at Ramsgate, 193 at Brixham, 50 at Plymouth and 43 at Fleetwood, a grand total of 920 for the whole country.

The first steam trawlers used the beam trawl and their success was assured when it was found the catches were 3 to 4 times the landings of a smack, while the introduction of the otter trawl and improvements in design increased efficiency about eight-fold. For the moment the tide was fair, but by the turn of the century it was another story. Vessels were now costing anything up to £10,000 to build and £5,000 a year to run, and the North Sea grounds were rapidly showing signs of overfishing. Ten years had seen about 2,000 steam trawlers built and matters were not helped in July, 1901, when hundreds were laid up over a wage dispute. After three months idleness crews agreed to go to sea on the terms offered, pending arbitration, which, when given, was more than the one and less than the other demand. Mr. H. Fox of Grimsby kindly sent me some photos he took of vessels laid up, which give an idea of the small size of steam trawler then in use (Plate 6).

The early years of the 20th century saw the end of Yarmouth as a trawling station, the Short Blue Fleet ceasing to work in 1901-2, when hundreds of skilled men were forced to seek employment elsewhere. The sailing trawler was still able to hold her own in the Channel and at Lowestoft, and down to the outbreak of war in 1914 there were 193 at Brixham, 152 at Ramsgate and 265 at Lowestoft, or 610 at the 3 ports, and their landings of soles, the highest priced sea fish, were far in excess of the catches of steam trawlers.

The intensive submarine warfare played havoc with the helpless sailing smack and the end of hostilities saw their numbers seriously diminished. My analysis of war losses alone shows 127 sailing trawlers sunk in the North Sea, 62 on the South coast, and 60 on the West coast, a total of 249 with the loss of 53 lives. The method of sinking most favoured by U-boat captains was to order a crew to abandon ship and then sink her by placing a time bomb on board, 178 smacks were lost in this way. Gunfire accounted for 54, mines for 8, the balance were set on fire, scuttled or sunk by unrecorded means. In no case can I find a sinking by torpedo, the value of which far exceeded the worth of an obsolete sailing vessel. The submarine commanders reserved them for bigger game, but a few were fired at the decoy smacks.

Although mines were responsible for the loss of only 8 smacks, they took the heaviest toll of lives, 25, gunfire killed 14, bombs 5 and 2 smacks with 9 men were unaccounted for.

The coming of peace in November 1918 saw an attempt being made at Brixham and Lowestoft to replace war losses, about 17 being built for the Devon port and 33 for the Suffolk harbour, but it was a forlorn hope. The number ekeing out a living continued its downward trend. In 1923 Lowestoft had 136 and Brixham 90 big smacks, by 1938 there were only 20 and 6 remaining.

The outbreak of yet another war was the death knell of smacks. Some were used as obstructions to prevent seaplanes landing on inland waters, others flew balloons to protect harbours from air attack, the majority were just left to rot away. The sailing trawler was finished and not one is left to-day working on the old, familiar grounds. Some have been sold to Norway, others have been fitted with motors, but to my mind a smack shorn of the beauty of her tanned sails is like a seabird with clipped pinions.

Her history was brief, but glorious, its compass within the life span of a man, so far as the heyday was concerned.

CHAPTER FOUR

TRAWLING GROUNDS AND YIELDS

In the days of sail the principal trawling grounds lay in the North Sea with fishing stations at Barking, Lowestoft, Yarmouth, Grimsby, Hull and Scarborough, while in the Channel, Ramsgate, Brixham and Plymouth were the smack harbours and the grounds off the north-west coast were worked from Fleetwood and Liverpool. Cornish and Scottish fishermen would have nothing to do with trawling, holding it to be " unfair fishing ", as it undoubtedly is, since the net sweeps up everything in its path, be the fish large or small, edible or otherwise. They clung to the age-old line fishing, with catches landed in prime condition, not, as they alleged, crushed and bruised after being dragged along the bottom for hours, but there was no denying the fact that for every fish caught on a hook there were one hundred in a trawl. Strange to say Scotland leaped to the forefront when steam came in and Aberdeen, with its large fleet of trawlers, became one of the principal ports for the landing of white fish.

Of all these areas by far the most important grounds lay in the North Sea which has a length of roughly 600 miles from the Shetlands to the Straits of Dover, a width between Scotland and Norway of 360 miles, tapering to the bottleneck of 21 miles from Dover to Calais. Depth decreases in the same direction, the 100 fathom line lies off the Shetlands, between Scotland and Norway, the average soundings are 50 to 80 fathom, in the Long Forties 40 to 50, decreasing to 10 to 20 on the Dogger Bank, deepening again in the centre with a shallow shelf extending some 5 miles seaward from the coast north of Flamborough Head and widening to 10 miles or so south of that promontory. Seaward are sandbanks rising close to the surface, mostly long, narrow, steep-to ridges, lying parallel with one another and the shore. Between run channels known as " deeps " where soundings vary from 16 to 24 fathom off the Norfolk coast, shoaling rapidly to as little as 3 to 6 over some of the banks.

On the eastern side a similar shelf runs 5 to 10 miles seaward from the Danish coast, continuing round the German and Dutch shores, while the Flemish banks lie up to 30 miles from the French and Belgian coasts, where deeps of 15 to 18 fathom shoal rapidly to $1\frac{1}{2}$ to 3 on parts of the Outer Ruytingen.

As the tidal wave approaches our shores from the westward it divides into two main streams of different speeds. One travels northwards round the west coast of Scotland, through the Minch, then turns north-east to reach its maximum velocity as it pours through the narrow confines of Pentland Firth to flow up the North Sea. The other stream comes up the English Channel and races through the narrow Strait of Dover. These two tides meet twice a day a little to the nor'ard of the North Foreland and their contending and movements have considerable effect on fish life, while the constant inflow of water from rivers on both sides of the North Sea has a marked influence in the direction of currents, and the influx of cold water, following the melting of snow and ice in the Baltic, affects the feeding grounds of fish.

The eternal depositing of soil and debris borne in these streams brings continual alterations to shoals and sandbanks and the force and direction of the wind plays its part in the movement of the water. Thus a strong N.N.W. gale in the North Sea, combined with a low glass, will raise the surface 2 to 3 feet higher and cause the stream to flow half an hour longer than the predicted heights and times all along the coast from Duncansby Head to London. Strong easterly, S.E. and S.W. winds produce opposite effects, felt as far down Channel as Dungeness. I recall one stormy day during the war years when the water never left our bay which normally dries out for about half a mile at low tide.

The average length of a tidal day being 24 hours 48 minutes, the rise and fall of the tide varies from day to day, as does its height which depends on the phases of the moon, the range being greatest after new and full moon—'' springs ''—and least after the quarters—'' neaps.''

The movement of water in the centre of the North Sea is generally in an easterly direction, with comparatively little rise and fall of tide, in fact there is one place on the Dogger in 10 fathom where it is almost imperceptible.

In the North Sea practically every kind of demersal fish once abounded, cod, haddock, plaice, sole and turbot predominating, the choice flat fish mainly in the shallower southern area, cod, haddock and the coarser varieties in the deeper northern waters. The most famous ground was the Dogger Bank, in primeval days a vast forest judging by the fossilized remains of trees and huge bones of extinct mammoths which have been trawled up from time to time. The land gradually became submerged as mighty torrents of glacial water drained off the surrounding shores, bearing in their streams masses of silt which settled on the bottom and eventually formed the peculiar rise and fall of the sea-bed known to-day.

This vast submarine plateau, some 6,800 square miles in extent, has depths varying from a few fathom upwards, with places where the water shoals from 37 fathom to 9 in less than a mile. Roughly wedge-shaped, the western edge lies some 60 miles from the Yorkshire coast, and the bank extends N.E. for a distance of about 170 miles, with a maximum width of 65 miles, the general direction being from S.W. to N.E. The northern edge is very dangerous as in heavy weather the seas,

12   DANDY R.420 AT RAMSGATE
The sloop R.184 at the buoy is clench-built.   The snow
Dispatch is loading chalk ballast.

13 DOVER CUTTER *SURPRISE*, D.R.11
44 tons, built at Rye, 1869, converted to a ketch, 1882.

14 DOVER CUTTER CONVERTED TO KETCH RIG.

15   FELLING AN OAK TREE IN THE SUSSEX WEALD.

16   TIMBER " TUG " LEAVING THE WOODS.

17 MARKING OUT A BEAM
AT RYE
A wooden mould is laid on
a suitable piece of timber
and outlined with chalk.

18 SAW-PIT AT RYE
The top sawyer guides the
long saw, the bottom sawyer
pulls it down.

19 LAYING THE KEEL

Note rabbet cut to receive garboard strake, score on top of keel, frame on the right, also rough-lopped tree trunks to carry staging. In the background is hull of *Telesia*, built 1911, almost ready for launching.

20 SHIPYARD WORKERS AT RYE

Each man is holding the tool of his trade. In the background is a planked hull and another with frames erected amidships. Note pair of frames lying on planks, ready for erection and shores bolted to outside of frames.

21 THE RYE FASHION OF FRAMING

The frames, made from single timbers, are set up in pairs, spacing
6 in. frame, $7\frac{1}{2}$ in. space, $5\frac{1}{2}$ in. frame, 5 in. space. Note spalls and
shores to hold frames in shape, and scarphs in timbers.

22 ADZING STERN BOARDS

The stern timbers butt against the fashion frame, with filling timbers
between.

23 A SMACK IN FRAME AT RYE
Harpins bolted fore and aft, and ribbands amidships, maintain the shape
of the hull.

24 DUBBING OUT
Shipwrights adzing the inside of frames to make surfaces fair. Note
short and long arms of floors, bolts in keelson, stern timbers butting
against fashion frame, fairing batten on the right, spalls overhead and
cramps in foreground.

25 LAUNCH OF *IVANHOE*, L.T.720

61 tons, built at Rye, 1891. Lost with two of her crew on the 14th January, 1907, after a collision with S.S. *Tanfield* of London, 3 miles E. of Southwold in a light S.W. wind. Note stern framing in hull on the left, after cradle made up of planks, and groundways into the water.

26 *DEVON'S PRIDE*, B.M. 290

38 tons, built at Brixham, 1910. Note wire spans on gaff, lacing at head of sail, fish batten, reef pendants, main sheet and chock, dandy wink with spare beam, skylight and holes in rail for thole pins. Main sheet is left-handed rope.

27 *GODETIA*, L.T.394, JULY, 1934

25 tons, built at Galmpton, 1909. Masthead detail showing leader through grommet on luff of topsail, lantern halyards, peak halyards with short chain standing end, jib halyards, robands at head of mainsail, fore stay and foresail halyards, diagonal-cut sails, eyelets for reef lacing, and mast hoops.

rolling in from deep water, drive against the submerged cliffs, making a deadly, confused smother of broken water, which swirls around like a maelstrom. In winter this area was given a wide berth by sailing smacks as no skipper liked to be caught " on the Edge " with a no'therly gale coming on, although he would face any weather, given sea room and a true sea running. The significant name " The Cemetery " tells its own story of the many disasters which have taken place in that vicinity. In the summer these northern slopes are covered with a growth of scruff or " curly cabbage ".

The apex, jutting out to the N.E., is known as " The Tail of the Dogger ", the eastern edge, deepening into 16 fathom, is " The Hospital ", the southern edge, has depths of 7 to 9 fathom deepening into 16 fathom of rough ground. The S.E. side slopes more gradually but during gales the seas break heavily over the South West Patches, as here the water shoals rapidly to 7 to 8 fathom. Generally speaking, in deep water seas are longer, smoother and less steep than in shallow where they tend to break and become confused.

In smacksmen's vernacular " inside the Dawger " was south-east of the Bank, " below the Dawger ", beyond the north-west slope, and " the Sleeve " the waters of the Skager Rak. Contrary to what is generally supposed they never actually trawled on the bank, but in the waters around. To the south'ard lie many deeps, known as guts, pits or holes according to their configuration, with many patches of rough ground to trap the unwary.

One of the favourite fishing grounds was Botney Gut, lying some 100 miles east of the Humber, a narrow gap about 5 to 6 miles wide between foul ground, with depths varying from 29 to 35 fathom and the bottom mud, except at the S.W. end where the water is 21 to 24 fathom deep, the bottom sand and mud, and bordered by very foul ground. This ground opens out into the Outer Silver Pit which lies close to the southern edge of the Dogger and is some 60 miles in length and 8 in breadth with its western edge 70 miles E. by N. of the Humber. Here are depths of 38 fathom with the bottom mud, but further east is fine sand and sand, and soundings around 30 fathom, with one curious little hillock where the water shoals to 17 fathom.

The Silver Pit is a long narrow gut, 24 miles in length and only 1 to 2½ in width, running north and south, with its northern end some 25 miles from the Humber. In the centre are depths of 38 to 40 fathom, shoaling to 14 at the northern and 7 at the southern end, the whole surrounded by steep banks. In these pits soles once congregated in vast numbers in very severe winters and the discovery of these hiding places, c 1837 to 1840, led to the boom in trawling and the rise of the Humber ports of Hull and Grimsby as fishing stations.

The narrow, boomerang-shaped Sole Pit has depths of 28 fathom at the N.W. end, 43 to 50 at the elbow, 34 at the southern end and lies within the 50 mile radius of the Humber, being surrounded by water only 11 to 13 fathom deep. Then there is the tiny Coal Pit, 5 miles by 1 mile in extent with depths of 37 fathom in an area where soundings range from 11 to 12, with very rough ground lying just to the N.E., so awkward to work with a sailing vessel.

My friend Mr. Harry George, who first went to sea in 1887, has written me the story of the discovery of Markham's Hole, a ground some 14 miles in length and 6 in width with a bottom of mud and sand, lying in the midst of very foul ground where soundings are 16 to 20 fathom. At the N.W. end depth is 37 fathom, in the middle 45 and at the S.E. end 20 fathom. In his own words :—

" The most renowned of all the smack skippers sailing out of Yarmouth was Charlie Markham, who became famous after discovering a depression in the sea bottom a few miles south of the south side of the Silver Pits. There were only a very few square miles of it but the bottom was of mud, all around it for many miles was rough ground on which it was practically impossible to trawl without losing the gear or getting the net pulled to pieces. For a long time Charlie Markham was the only Yarmouth skipper who could find and work it, and it is marked on the fisherman's chart to this day as ' Markham's Hole '. It was very difficult to work with a smack, being very small and he had nothing to guide him except his leadline and perhaps a slight difference in the colour of the water, which in the North Sea turns darker when one comes to what we fishermen call a hole. He earned much money out of that hole which still bears his name, so much that his owner Mr. Robert Nichols built a new smack for him, Anaconda, Y.H.1007." (61 tons, built Southtown 1885.)

East'ard of the Tail the bottom is light gray sand with minute white shells, further east lies coffee-coloured soil, fine gray and speckled sand. Here was a favourite ground for haddock in September, but the strong easterly set of the tide meant that a four-hour trawl often called for a six-hour beat back against the prevailing westerly winds. Other bottoms yield shingle, evil-smelling mud, soft mud, rocky ground and even oyster beds which played havoc with the nets.

North-east of the Dogger lies the Great Fisher Bank, famous for cod, with depths of 36 to 40 fathom and the bottom of mud and speckled sand, the Little Fisher Bank has brown sand and shell with depths of 21 to 36 fathom. East'ard are the Clay Deeps another favourite ground, and Horns Reef off the Jutland coast, here depths vary from 15 to 16 fathom with a bottom of fine sand or speckled. Off the Dutch coast lie the Broad Fourteens where soil is fine sand and shell in depths of 12 to 14 fathom. Horns Reef and Broad Fourteens are two names which were to mean much in the 1914-18 war, as in September, 1914, the three armoured cruisers *Hogue*, *Aboukir* and *Cressy* were sunk early on the morning of the 22nd by torpedoes fired from the submarine U9, commanded by Leut. Weddigen who was subsequently rammed by *H.M.S. Dreadnought* when he attacked the Grand Fleet in U29. This serious disaster took place in the Broad Fourteens and involved the loss of nearly all the ships' companies. In 1916 the action known as the Battle of Jutland was fought in the waters around Horns Reef. In the more peaceful days of the late 19th century they were well-known grounds for flat fish which tended to be on the small size as the spawning grounds were in the neighbourhood.

About 50 miles from the Norfolk coast lies the Leman Ground where the bottom is fine gray sand and coarse sand and towards the shore are the narrow ridges named respectively Indefatigable, Swarte Bank, Broken Bank, Well Bank, Inner Bank, Ower Bank, Leman and Haddock Banks, Outer Dowsing and Cromer Knoll with a cluster of shoals inside.

Between Cromer and Yarmouth lie still more parallel ridges named Smith's Knoll, Hearty Knoll, Winterton Ridge, Hammond's Knoll and the Haisborough Sands, scene of many a shipwreck. Off Yarmouth and protected by the Scroby Sands are the famous Roads where once hundreds of sailing vessels sheltered in stormy weather, with the Cockle, Caister and Cross Sands in close proximity and parallel to the shore. The Cockle Gatway, only about half a mile wide, is the northern approach with the lightship of the same name as the leading mark.

To the south'ard of the entrance to Yarmouth Haven lie the Corton and Holm Sands with Hewett Channel the principal approach and having steep-to banks on either hand, subject to constant changes of depth, the St. Nicholas lightvessel being the leading mark.

South of Lowestoft are the Newcome and Barnard Sands with the changeable Stanford Channel the principal entrance to the harbour.

Thus in spite of the deceptive expanse of sea there is often only a fathom or less water over many of these banks, which are always on the move. For instance the Scroby rose from the sea about the early 1920's and dried out at low water. while the buoys guarding it had to be shifted again in 1934.

All these names and many more were as familiar to smacksmen as Piccadilly, Strand, Mansion House, etc., are to the average Londoner, and it will readily be understood how important it was for a trawlerman to know the sea-bed, probably even better than he did his own bed at home, which he was likely to use for only about six weeks in a year if he was working with one of the fleets.

Very different conditions prevailed in the West of England, where deep water is found right up to the iron-bound coast, hence the seas run truer than in the North Sea. There were many natural harbours to which a smack could run for shelter or bays where she could ride at anchor and according to the evidence given by the President of the Brixham Fishing Club before the Royal Commission of 1863, it was then the custom for the majority of the smacks to return to port *every night*, a very different state of affairs to that found in the North Sea.

What could be found further east ? Only artificial harbours. Dover, a place better out of than in during bad weather, Ramsgate, awkward to take with the strong tides setting across the mouth and the dreaded Goodwins and other sandbanks always awaiting a carelessly handled or unlucky vessel. Lowestoft has a narrow 130 ft. entrance between piers with the certainty of disaster to north and south if a skipper's judgment was faulty or his luck out.   Yarmouth, at one time one of the greatest trawling stations, was guarded by a bar on which the sea broke furiously under certain conditions, with numerous sandbanks in the vicinity.   Grimsby and Hull lay up a river, with the need to make a low lying coastline, beset by shoals and twisting channels. Nowhere the bold headlands of Cornwall and Devon, although the 306 ft. high hydraulic tower, which provided the power for working the Grimsby Dock system, made a fine leading mark, if the weather was clear enough to see it.

Many indeed were the dangers awaiting a smack homeward bound after perhaps weeks at sea and a skipper had to keep his wits about him and know how to handle his command if he was to avoid disaster and bring her safe into port, not once, but hundreds of times under every condition of wind, tide and weather, summer and winter, day or night.   This knowledge was second nature to the splendid seamen of the days of sail and is still found among the older skippers in steam trawlers, who learned their trade long before echo sounders, radar, etc., were thought of, let alone installed in fishing vessels.

The migratory movement of fish had to be understood so that the favourite grounds were worked over at the appropriate season.   Plaice, for instance, spawn in the southern part of the North Sea in December, January and February, the Sandettie Bank, Hinder and vicinity of Thames Estuary being a few well-known spots.   A female lays from a quarter to half a million eggs and a curious feature is that the young are round with an eye on each side of the head, but after about a month a gradual change takes place, the left eye moving upwards and forward until it reaches a position above and in front of the right eye, while the round form flattens out into the familiar shape seen on a fishmonger's slab.   The shoals work northward during spring and summer to feeding grounds in the middle of the North Sea, and the fish are mature at 5 to 6 years of age, but specimens have been known to live for a quarter of a century. The age of fish can be calculated by the rings in the earstones, just as the age of a tree can be found from its annular growth.   Soles spawn in deeper water off the Dutch and Belgian coasts during April to June and being nocturnal in habits more are caught by night than by day, haddock abound all over the North Sea, whiting are more plentiful in the Channel and hake on the Western seaboard.

In very cold weather fish go into deep water for warmth, but in summer prefer shallow, Mr. R. M. Hewett told me that he had frequently seen fine turbot swimming a few inches from the surface off the Dutch coast in the height of summer.

In the days before railways, only cod and plaice were sought on the more distant grounds, both being fish which could be kept alive in wells, all the rest were thrown away as local needs were supplied by the inshore fishermen and few, if any, smacks ventured far out into the turbulent waters of the North Sea.   When " fleeting " was introduced fish were divided for market purposes into two classes, prime and offal, in the first were the choice fish, soles, turbot, brill, cod, halibut and dorys, in the second, plaice, haddock, whiting, skate, etc.   Later cod tended to surrender its premier position as trawl-caught superseded line-hooked and plaice worked up from its lowly position as its value became more widely known.

Naturally the hauls varied according to ground worked over, season and the previous intensity of trawling in the same area. In the early years when virgin grounds were constantly being discovered tremendous catches were made. When giving his evidence before the Royal Commission of 1883, Mr. A. W. Ansell, smackowner of Hull, stated that William Sudds, a Ramsgate man, who claimed to have discovered the Silver Pits in 1837, told him that he once took 2,040 pairs of soles *in one haul* and weighing up to $12\frac{3}{4}$ lbs. a pair. During 1864 a smack caught $15\frac{1}{4}$ tons of soles and halibut, $51\frac{1}{2}$ tons of plaice, $36\frac{1}{4}$ tons of haddock, and $7\frac{3}{4}$ tons of mixed fish. In 1886 one Hull smack brought in 7 tons of soles which sold for £400, and in one night on the Eastern grounds a fleet took between 200 and 300 boxes of plaice and 200 to 250 of soles. It was not uncommon in the early days for a single smack to take 2 to 3 tons of fish in a 3-hour trawl, while 5 vessels once caught 17 tons between them in a night. During 1876 some 370 Hull smacks earned nearly half a million golden sovereigns.

Little wonder that the fishing industry boomed and in the short space of two decades the number of smacks at Grimsby alone increased more than twenty-two fold, with Hull and elsewhere showing similar figures. The golden years indeed.

Sometimes the trawl brought to the surface weird catches, ships' anchors, old cannon, Roman earthenware, bones of extinct mammoths, amber, coal—always useful to allow that extra shovelful on stove or boiler, but one of the most amusing was when a crew was hauling in the net on a black night and sighted an object glinting with phosphorescence and terrifying to look upon. Dropping everything, they rushed aft and yelled that the devil himself was in the net, horns and all. All hands battened themselves below out of reach of his satanic majesty and anxiously waited for dawn to break, when they crept on deck and found the cause of their alarm to be nothing worse than the head and part-carcase of a much decayed bullock ! ! I fear they must have been seeing things through over indulgence in the vile liquor bought from the copers.

Sad indeed were hauls which brought up the body of a smacksman, as in December, 1887, when 3 men were lost from the 63-ton Yarmouth cutter *Spark* of the Leleu fleet and all brought up in one trawl together.

Sometimes strange fish were caught in the trawl. In 1879 the 75-ton Grimsby smack *Kitty*, one of a number built at Elmshorn, near Hamburg, Germany in 1878, landed the largest sturgeon ever caught. Its length was 11 ft. 4 in., the head alone measuring 2 ft. 5 in., while the girth was 4 ft. 9 in. The "shackles" and armour plates were 10 in number and as large as saucers, and the weight was $44\frac{1}{2}$ stone. It was secured for a London museum by Frank Buckland, the well-known Fisheries Inspector.

There were two trawling seasons, winter and summer, the first being the principal when large fleets worked under the command of an experienced fisherman, the admiral. Each fleet had its own houseflag and admiral, whose smack was distinguished by one houseflag half-way up the topmast stay and another at the topmast head. This was used as the signal for the fleet to put to and haul their trawls at one and the same time, a very necessary arrangement as every night's catch was boxed and put aboard a carrier for despatch to market each morning. This practice continued in summer but many smacksmen then preferred to go " single-boating " and land their catches at a nearby port, rather than pay the high charges made by the carrier. Lo'stermen seldom worked to a fleet, but ten miles away the majority of the Yarmouth smacksmen did. Often catches were small owing to long periods of light weather and calms when little if any trawling could be done, not altogether a bad thing as the fish were not being disturbed continually and driven off their feeding grounds.

In the Channel the trawling grounds were more circumscribed, the Brixham smacks working over a stretch some 20 miles in length and of varying width, lying 3 to 8 miles offshore between Start Point and the N.E. of Torbay, while the Plymouth men trawled mostly to the west'ard of and inside the Eddystone over a similar length of ground with a maximum width of 9 miles, depths being around and below 30 fathom. These very limited areas were regularly fished over day in, day out, year after year and yielded a tolerable harvest until ruination was brought about by the innumerable wrecks which fouled the grounds during the 1914-18 war. Single-boating was the rule in these ports, only a few Brixham men went up into the North Sea and worked with the big fleets.

There was occasional trawling in the numerous bays in Devon and Cornwall, in the Bristol Channel, Carmarthen Bay, and various grounds in St. George's Channel and the Irish Sea, but fishing was never on the same scale as in the North Sea.

What of the prices realized for catches ? In his evidence before the Royal Commission of 1866 which I have before me, Mr. Henry Knott, smackowner, gave the following figures. In the 5 years 1860-64 the takings of one of his smacks amounted to 86 tons of prime fish, which sold for £1,971, or an average of £23 a ton, about 2½d. a lb. for the choicest sole, halibut, etc. Offal fish, including plaice, amounted to 357 tons, sold for £731, roughly £2 a ton or under a farthing a lb. The total catch, 443 tons, thus realized £2,702 or an average of £6 per ton, giving a price of under three farthings a lb. I have worked to the nearest rough figure, not going into the cwts. and qtrs. and the odd shillings and pence.

Even at such low prices the worst year's earnings came to £434 8s. 3d. and the best £632 13s. 6d., not bad money in those days.

The crews, being on shares, had an interest in prices, only in the London smacks were the men on a weekly wage, which had many drawbacks on both sides. Once out of sight of land there was no telling how much work was done. The end of the week, or rather trip, saw their money the same amount for good or bad catches, so why worry, and the attractions of the copers with almost unlimited quantities of cheap drink drew men like a magnet. The majority of the Londoners preferred it that way and it was not until they worked from stations using the share system that they were convinced of the merits of such a method of payment. A skipper might draw £30 in addition to his regular 14s. a week after an 8-week voyage, but with such a perishable article as fish, and the quantity landed dependent on the weather, prices naturally fluctuated wildly. There were always tons of offal fish to hundredweights of prime which, while realizing the highest individual prices, did not necessarily make the most money in the day's sales.

Only too often the smacksmen's toil brought little or no reward as catches might not realize enough at Billingsgate to pay for the cost of carriage by the cutter. If the weather was hot there was little sale, and as each day's market had to be cleared in readiness for the next, ridiculously low prices were sometimes bid by the coster-mongers who purchased by far the largest amount of the cheaper kinds of fish, haddock, etc., for hawking round the side streets. In 1886, 795 tons 6 cwt. 2 qrs. of fish were condemned, as if a salesman had any doubt about the freshness or otherwise of a trunk he sent for an official known as the " fish meter " and his judgment was final. Tainted fish went into the condemned cell in the hold of the landing stage, to be cleared by contractors who sold it for manure. The smacksmen therefore received nothing and might have to pay charges, while at times of heavy catches fine plaice and haddock only fetched 4s. a cwt.

How did these wholesale prices compare with retail charges ? In Manchester Fish Market during the first week in January, 1860, turbot was 1s. to 1s. 6d. a lb., in 1865, 8d. to 1s., sole 4d. to 6d. and 6d. to 8d., cod 6d. but only 3d. to 4d. in 1865, haddock 4d. to 6d. and 3d. to 4d., plaice 2d. to 3d. and 1½d. to 2d. a lb.

In 1886 the average price per lb. for all fish sold at the various ports during the year was: sole 9½d., turbot 6½d., cod 1¾d., and haddock ¾d., the highest prices being: sole 3s. 3d., turbot 1s., cod 1s., and haddock 2¼d. Average retail prices were: sole 1s. 3d., turbot 10d., cod 9d., and haddock 3d., and they included salesmen's commission, rail charges and fishmonger's overheads.

A few years after the introduction of steam the nearby fishing grounds began to suffer from over-fishing and hauls got smaller and smaller. In 1903 an average day's catch was just over 3 cwt., but 3 years later it was down to 2½ cwt. In the early 1920's catches in the North Sea rose enormously, due to the cessation of practically all fishing during the 1914-18 war, but it was a fleeting prosperity as in the thirties it was almost impossible for a sailing trawler to make a living, hauls chiefly consisting of masses of brash—rubbish—which had to be sorted over to find a few miserable specimens of fish. The enormous numbers of vessels sunk by U-boats on many a once clear ground led to constant loss of valuable gear and I remember quite a few Brixham smacks coming back " clean " with no beam and net stowed on the port rail. This state of affairs no doubt hastened the end of the sailing trawler.

CHAPTER FIVE

SMACK DESIGN AND HANDLING

THERE was a sense of power and purposefulness about a fishing smack which instantly appealed to the eye of a seaman. Built for her job, she would do it come what may and it needed more than a gale to overwhelm her. Seen in the quiet calm of harbour, hull and spars might look heavy, even clumsy, with rigging of inordinate strength, but they were not for the halycon days of summer and gentle zephyrs. A smack was seen at her best in the bitter gales of winter, riding the seas like a gull, facing weather that sent other vessels flying for shelter while she carried on her lawful occasions. Her mast was no gilguy, designed with a slide-rule and stayed by streamlined wires until it resembles a birdcage. It was a solid trunk, straight-grained and stepped right down on to the keelson, giving a little to the freshening wind which so often brings disaster to the scientist's dream of a perfect mast.

That splendid bow would shoulder the seas aside, seldom taking green water on board, the hull, buoyant as a cork, was framed of good English oak, wrought by eye and cunningly curved with a beauty of line that was a joy to see. Here was no product of a testing tank and intricate calculations, but the concentrated knowledge of generations of men who knew from practical experience what was best suited to their needs.

Those graceful curves came from the natural growth of timber, from age-old monarchs of the woods, that long had stood in summer sun and winter cold, gentle rain and perishing blizzard, living out their lives in God's free winds. Then, felled at the choice of men steeped in the lore of centuries of woodcraft, handed on from father to son—which fields and slopes provided trees most suitable for their requirements, as texture varies according to nourishment given by the soil—how long the logs should season in the rough before the slender saw ripped through the fibres and revealed the heart of oak, never before seen by mortal eyes, which started to form 120, 150, maybe 180 years before. As the keen blade cut its way through the baulk the very tang of the forest rose when the sweet-scented dust fell in a gentle shower on the bottom sawyer.

After due seasoning came the work of gnarled old shipwrights who erected the

and an ancient verti
the thick planks w
blocks on which tc
the scaffold staging
ever provided—con

The money we
stood in the woods.
of naval architectur
of a Royal Dockyar
his locality with pe
and appraised the p
catalogues of others
mistake which mig
faulty timber it was
be wasted labour to

I recall an age
methods :—'' In th
would have accepte
thirty years ago.''
into which I could i
the vessel, a mine-s
frames in order to s

Autres temps, au

Little wonder
50 years was nothin
Many an old-timer,
few being *Albert Vic*
1876, *Galatea*, 73 tc
Dartmouth 1878, *Su*
war in fish-carrying
Skibsliste are the nai
Humber, which are

Even more inte
built at Dover in 18
from Cape Town, S
held a master's certi
Aires, and on to Tri
On the 21st Septemb
in 40° 1′ S., 10° W.
In 1920 *Forget-me-not*
and since the recent

curved frames on the massive keel and clothed them with planking worked and bent to shape. No paper plans, only a rough half-model, gave sweetness of line, and the master builder's eye was the unerring arbiter, and his knowledge the safeguard that all would be well when the testing time came, as come it would, sooner or later.

Old England at her best, true craftsmanship, pride in one's job.

And what a proud day when the finished smack was handed over to her skipper who frequently had invested hard-won savings in a vessel and was now able to sign himself " master and owner ". Although probably ignorant of many of the things that pass for knowledge and education to-day, he was wise to signs of sky and cloud, sun and sea, able to take his command far out of sight of land, across the heaving wastes, to just that spot where he knew the trawl could be shot to glean the harvest of the sea.

Men of worth, whose sires had sailed with Drake and Frobisher, or fought with Nelson and Collingwood.

He and his band of brothers, for so often a crew was a family affair, spent all their working lives on the majestic, rolling waters which have remained the same since the Creation and they gazed out over an aspect of sea and sky, unchanging and yet ever changing, a view man has never been able to defile, do what he will on land.

The lines of the early smacks were the cod's head and mackerel tail design which gave sea-worthiness but not speed, and they culminated in the splendid ketches of the last days of the North Sea trawlers and the vessels built at Brixham after the 1914-18 war.

One peculiarity of trawling was the necessity for facing anything, as it was a certainty that a smack would frequently be caught out in bad weather with no harbour within reach. Where a drifter could cut and run as a last resort, a trawler had to ride it out or founder, but she had to be given speed so that her catch could reach market in as fresh a condition as possible, for not every port went in for fleeting. Hence the lines had to be fine and yacht-like, not too extreme or she would lose her valuable sea-keeping abilities which called for a deep heel, a straight keel and ballast properly stowed and secured to ensure an easy motion. This latter requirement was essential, both for prolonging the life of gear and the well-being of the crew. Ample displacement and a good draught made for a comfortable motion in a seaway, but care had to be taken that the forefoot and aft deadwood were not cut away too much in order to give easy steering, while too great a beam gave lively and uncomfortable motion. Insufficient draught brought excessive leeway, sharpness of bows did not necessarily denote speed as ends too fine meant a wet boat, but too full produced violent pitching and undue strain on gear.

The need for plenty of driving power called for a large mainsail, but forethought was required that this did not make the vessel hard-mouthed. Some time ago I was very interested to read that experiments made in wind tunnels had shown that a correctly bellied sail, carried in its natural form of an arched foot, developed about 50 per cent more pressure than a flattened sail laced to a boom, with nearly three-

quarters

design of

Desi

to work.

to a smac

mast well

generally

speed an

Channels.

The

was more

of the Nc

Yarn

speed was

stepping t

The

seas, maki

stern to t

breezes an

like a witc

to be the

called into

where and

Plate

owned by

the photo

crew are s

reefed mai

typical Hui

with the C

the weathe

was W. Ja

Little

ground fac

stores and

office, hen

a builder c

provided b

adapted to

razor edge

toes of a ca

Plate 9 shows her converted to ketch rig and hauled out on the hard in Dover harbour for hull cleaning and re-tarring.

These few examples of longevity show that building to last was not the monopoly of any one yard or district and are a splendid tribute to the work of men long since dead.

At the beginning of the 19th century fishing vessels were small bluff-bowed, beamy craft, usually clench-built. A plan of one appears in Steel's *Naval Architecture* of 1804 (Plan 3, page 315). She is described as a " Southampton Fishing Hoy ", length on the range of the deck 28 ft. 9 in., length of keel for tonnage 17 ft. 1 in., extreme breadth 11 ft. $9\frac{1}{2}$ in. and burthen in tons $13\frac{8}{94}$. The midship section has rounded bilges and stem and sternpost are well raked. Her rig was then called " smack ", probably derived from the Dutch word " smak ", a name given in the early 18th century to single-masted fore and aft rigged vessels. To-day she would be described as cutter-rigged with a small gaff topsail.

E. W. Cooke gives an etching of one of these vessels under sail in the Solent (Plate 10). The hull is clench-built with a square transom, the bowsprit is bowsed down with a bobstay to counteract the upward pull of the big jib and the mast is supported by three shrouds a side and a runner backstay. The masthead is long and topmast short, crosstrees are shown although they were seldom found in West Country smacks of this period. The loose-footed mainsail, fitted with three lines of reef points, has a long boom projecting well over the taffrail and both foresail and jib have one reef. Later practice was to set a smaller jib rather than take a reef in a larger one, thus avoiding a heavy bunch of wet canvas out on the bowsprit, where weight was certainly not wanted in a seaway. All the sails have a baggy cut.

Although probably a good sea-boat such a vessel was hardly likely to be fast, but speed was of little account until the coming of the railways opened up new markets inland and special trains had to be caught.

Plate 11 shows a typical Brixham sloop of the type which explored the new grounds in the North Sea and elsewhere, surely one of the earliest photographs of a fishing vessel, as it was taken at Ramsgate in 1857. Sturdy hull construction still prevails with bluff bows but the floors are sharper than those of *Charlie*, D.H.79, (Plan 6, pages 321-2.) The angle at which she is lying, due to the port leg sinking in the mud of the basin, gives an excellent view of the deck arrangements,with the winch used for hauling in the warp for'ard of the mast, and the pumphead aft of the main hatch, the open transom is typical of the period. To allow for an increase in the length of the trawl beam the head iron is berthed for'ard of the shrouds. In those days the Inner Basin almost dried out at low water and in the background is another smack with well-rounded bilges supported by legs.

A big mainsail is set, judging by the long boom, and such a sail was a job to handle when the wind piped up and reefing became necessary. The size of smacks kept increasing and this great length of boom, swanging about in a seaway, became a menace, so much so that during the early sixties it had to be shortened and a small mizzen mast was stepped inboard, carrying a standing lug or a gaff and boom sail.

This " dandy " rig had been used by Manx fishermen since the 1830's, when they saw the advantage a mizzen gave to the Cornish lugger when lying to her train of herring nets. They thereupon converted their cutters by fitting a jigger mast well aft and setting a small standing lug. This rig is seen in Plate 12 of R.420 lying in the basin at Ramsgate, ahead is a sloop R.363 and a clench-built cutter R.184. The snow is *Dispatch*, a real bluff-bowed old-timer, but I have been unable to trace her in my registers. There is a fine model of a dandy, *c* 1829, in the National Maritime Museum, Greenwich and Cooke shows one in his etching of a Fishing Hoy (Plate 10).

Plate 13 shows the Dover smack *Surprise*, D.R.11, 44 tons, built at Rye in 1869 as a cutter, converted to ketch rig in 1882 and afloat until 1906 when she was owned at King's Lynn. Plate 14 is a conversion to ketch rig, the mainsail has the same lengthed gaff but the boom has been shortened. The mizzen mast carries a gaff and boom sail. I have a photograph of *Surprise* in a similar rig, taken at Ramsgate *c* 1890, but unfortunately it is not clear enough to reproduce. The alteration is identical with the one chosen, but a boat gangway has been fitted.

The name " dandy " was still given by fishermen to the big ketch-rigged vessels built in the late sixties to fish with a longer beam of 46 to 50 ft. and to compete with them many of the cutters were hauled ashore, cut in two at the maximum beam, the stern half drawn away with tackles and an additional section built in. This lengthened the hull by as much as 15 ft. and these converted vessels, ketch rigged, often proved faster than in their original rig as cutters.

Brixham and Plymouth converted long after the North Sea trawlers had adopted the new rig, while at some ports, notably Ramsgate, the fastest cutters were retained to act as carriers as they could sail half a point nearer the wind. A converted cutter could always be distinguished from one built as a ketch by the mizzen mast being stepped further aft. This can clearly be seen in Plates 116, 146, 156.

In the mid-sixties a few smacks were composite built, with iron frames and beams but wooden planking, one being the 59-ton *Brunette*, built at Barking in 1865 for Hewett & Co. On the 6th December, 1893, she became badly strained during a heavy S.W. gale while fishing in the Clay Deeps and on her return to port was condemned and broken up.

Then followed the experiment of building hulls entirely of iron, possibly stronger but not so buoyant as wood, and thus rather unpopular among smacksmen, who valued sea-kindliness above all other qualities. They registered about 80 tons and appear to have been singularly unlucky as I find no less than 8 were sunk after collisions within a few years of being built.

BUILDING A SMACK

I CONSIDER it is most fortunate that I am able to describe and illustrate the building of a North Sea trawler at G. & T. Smith's yard at Rye, where so many fine hulls were launched, including *Master Hand*. This firm had a very high reputation and " Rye-built " was a hallmark second to none. A plentiful supply of excellent oak was available in the Weald, about 100 trees, of ages varying from 80 to 200 years, going to the construction of a smack.

In 1908 the stock of timber at the yard included 81 first-class quality trees, in the round, 3,366 cubic feet, valued @ 2s. 2d. a cub. ft., or £364 13s., 180 second-class, 4,110½ cub. ft. @ 2s., or £411 1s., and the 8 third-class, 76½ cub. ft. @ 1s. 10d., or £7 0s. 3d., speak eloquently of the standard of timber used. I find that the total value of all trees, planking, knees, etc., was £2,010 6s. 9½d.—a very considerable sum—iron bars, etc., in store were worth £205 12s. 4½d., blacksmith's tools £58 2s. 10d., nails £26 19s. 6d., moulds in loft £50, but the office equipment including a quantity of brass hinges, screws, small tools, etc., was only £38 13s. 9d., with a desk and two drawers valued at 7s., an office desk with rack at 30s., three stools 4s. 6d., one copying press and a copying book three-quarters used, valued at 8s. and 2s. 6d. Little was spent on writing materials, letters being written in ink ; pens, inkwells, and pencils being down at 3s. Overheads were obviously low and the other prices are given in the appendix. It is a salutory lesson to compare them with those ruling to-day, and the same office fittings survived in 1946 !

Trees were bought either standing in the woods, or in the round as they lay where they had been felled. Winter-cut oak was the best as the sapwood was almost as hard as the heart, but it was scarce as in those days bark had a high value for a variety of purposes. If trees were thrown in the spring the sap was running and the bark stripped off easily. When axe and saw were laid to the root of the tree (Plate 15) it soon came crashing down, branches and twigs were cut away before the trunk was measured for girth and cubic contents.

Next the trunks were hauled, butts for'ard, on to a timber " tug " and here was seen the perfect co-operation between the carter and his team, the willing horses instantly obeying his voice. Now came the job of taking the heavy load along the deeply rutted " rides " until the metalled road was reached and the straining horses had an easier pull (Plate 16). On arrival at the yard the logs were unloaded and lay in the rough to season before being rolled over the sawpit to be cut up into planks. These had to be stacked so that air circulated freely all round and the duration of seasoning varied with the thickness, one year to every inch being the minimum, but the longer the better and often a decade and more passed before the timber was considered fit to work. Hence there was always a large sum of money locked up in stock and the test of the buyer's judgment came when the wood was under adze and plane, any defects instantly showing up. No two trees build up their timber on precisely the same plan ; soil, exposure to prevailing wind, seasons of drought, etc., all affecting strength and quality.

In one corner lay piles of " crooks " ready to be fashioned into knees as the grain ran straight in both arms, and stacks of " thick stuff " cut from the curved branches would eventually be made into frames and beams. When that day came a light wooden mould was laid on a likely piece, which allowed the line of cut to follow the grain, and the outline was chalked in (Plate 17). This called for skilled judgment as the sawyer had to cut his coat according to his cloth, not vice versa, and build up his frames by making the best use of what was available, but every effort was made to cut port and starboard sides from the same piece of timber. This was now laid over the sawpit and the top sawyer, walking backwards, guided the long saw around the chalk line, while his mate below lifted it up and pulled down strongly, being constantly covered with a cloud of choking dust (Plate 18). The many and various patterns were made up in the mould loft, the shapes being taken from the half model, plans or blue prints were seldom, if ever, likely to be found in an old-world shipyard.

Although the construction and framing of the hull of a big smack followed a fairly general pattern, methods varied at different yards and much depended on the quantity and shape of timber available for conversion. I cannot emphasize this fact too strongly and sometimes it was a case of how much an owner wished to spend. One old man told me he went to enquire the price of a smack from a well-known firm and was asked " Do you want her ' made ' or ' built ' ? "

The elm keel, sided 8 in., moulded 12 in. and over, was laid on blocks given a fall of half an inch or so to the foot towards the water and was usually in two pieces, scarphed together, as it was becoming increasingly difficult, and very expensive, to find a tree from which a length of some 60 ft., without a flaw, could be cut, although in the old smacks the keel and keelson were often in one piece. At Lowestoft, Rye and Brixham the flat scarph was horizontal and about 4 ft. 9 in. long, bolted with eight $\frac{5}{8}$ in. bolts with a stopwater driven in below the rabbet to prevent water seeping behind the garboards. This was a plug of soft fir, driven tightly into a hole bored right through the joint and its expansion, when immersed, prevented any water creeping further up the scarph. At Ramsgate a vertical scarph was used and well-tarred " fearnought " cloth was placed between the faces and carried round the lips before the horizontal copper bolts were driven home and clenched. A $\frac{3}{4}$ in. score was made in the top of the join and a square stopwater driven in (Fig. 6). All the other keel bolts were galvanized but Mr. Moses told me that those for a scarph were always copper.

An inch and a half below the top of the keel was the base or " bearding " line, where the shipwrights began to adze away the wood to form the " rabbet ", the V shaped groove which took the inner edge of the garboard strakes. This can be seen in Fig. 6 and in Plate 19 where the master is lining up everything to his satisfaction. Next the position of the frame stations—the centre to centre of each frame, known as " the room and space "—was marked on upper side of keel and scores $\frac{3}{4}$ in. deep cut to receive a corresponding notch in the seating of the floors, thus letting them down the $1\frac{1}{2}$ in. to the base line. This was not done at Ramsgate where the full $1\frac{1}{2}$ in. was taken out of the floors only.

The oak stem and sternpost were now set up and morticed into the keel, the stem being joined by means of a curved timber which formed the rounded forefoot. The joint or scarph, called the " boxing ", was strengthened by through-bolting iron dovetail plates on either side. The sternpost was tenoned to the heel of the keel, which was usually left with a projecting piece, the " skeg ", to go under the heel of rudder post. The length of the tenon was one quarter the depth of keel, its thickness equal to one-third of its siding, and the width twice the thickness.

Framing commenced amidships and proceeded towards bow and stern alternately, the floors seating in the scores. Here again the practice differed. At most of the yards the frames were double (Fig. 6) which allowed for use of smaller sided timbers to those at Rye where the preference was for a single floor, butt-jointed and dowelled to futtock, which in turn was dowelled to the top timber. A double frame broke joint, the various pieces of oak being through-bolted with $\frac{5}{8}$ in. bolts with a wood plug—a trenail—at the head as a bolt might come in contact with the shelf fastenings. All the timbers held their siding or thickness in a fore and aft direction, usually 6 to 8 inches, but their moulding tapered from about 10 in. at throat of floors to $5\frac{1}{2}$ in. at the covering board. The length of floor arms depended on shape of tree and length available. The various scarphs used can be seen in Fig. 6.

Room and space varied. At Lowestoft and Brixham it was generally 6 in. floor, 6 in. space, at Ramsgate two $4\frac{1}{4}$ in. timbers made up an $8\frac{1}{2}$ in. double frame, with 17 in. centre to centre, but Rye had a fashion of its own. The frames were set up in pairs, 2 foot spacing, the siding of for'ard frame was 6 in., then a $7\frac{1}{2}$ in. space, next a $5\frac{1}{2}$ in. frame and a 5 in. space. With single frames this allowed some latitude in the siding of timbers and made for a slightly less expensive job. This style of framing can clearly be seen in Plates 20 and 21, which are also interesting because each man is holding the tool of his trade. Every floor was bolted to the keel and temporary chocks held the frames the correct distance apart.

The midship frame was " dead-flat ", i.e. had no bevel, and its position varied with the lines proposed, full or fine. It was usually a little for'ard of half the length and marked on the draughts with the symbol ⋊. All frames for'ard were bevelled on the forward edge, those aft on the after edge, the bevels being obtained from the bevel board if a yard had scientific leanings, by eye and the use of long battens placed round the frames if the more usual rule-of-thumb system prevailed.

To make certain that the midship frame was plumb and square to the keel it was first centred by a plumb bob from the middle of the cross spall—the temporary beam placed athwartship between top of frame—and then squared or " horned " by measuring with a long batten pivoted on a nail in the centre of keel and swung from port to starboard to see that the distance to either head was the same. Shores were then spiked or bolted to the outside of the frames to preserve the form while building by preventing the sides from falling outwards (Plate 20).

Towards the bow and stern it was not possible to obtain the requisite shape of

28 *SUNSTAR*,   B.M.314,   12th
AUGUST, 1935
23 tons, built at Galmpton, 1911.
Deck detail showing mast hoops
and seizings, bowsprit roller, boat
slide and cavil hook in deck.

29 *REVIVE*, B.M.134, 7th JULY,
1927
42 tons, built at Brixham, 1922.
End of main boom showing reef
pendants, first one has tackle
hooked in, clew shackled to end-
iron as well as lashed, main sheet
block with left-handed rope, mizzen mast hoops and seizings.

30 BENDING   THE   THROAT
CRINGLE, JULY, 1935
Winnie, B.M.125, 39 tons, built
at Brixham, 1904. Note jaws,
wooden shoe or tumbler, double
block shackled to iron tumbler in
slot.

31 *FRANK BUCKLAND*, G.Y.900

74 tons, built at Grimsby, 1883. L.O.A. 82 ft. Beam 20 ft. This superb model was awarded a diploma, highest prize and medal at Fisheries Exhibition, 1883, and is now in the Science Museum. Scale 1 in. to the ft. Note dandy line and wink, boat lashed with gripes, topmast stays shortened with sheepshanks, and topmast housed. The capstan is an early pattern as in fig. 14.

32 TAKING IN ICE AT
LOWESTOFT
Ice lighter alongside *Nancy*,
L.T.41, 59 tons, built at Lowestoft,
1904. Ahead is L.T.687 *Inverlyon*,
59 tons, built at Lowestoft, 1903,
and the stern of L.T.327 *John
Browne*, 57 tons, built at Lowestoft,
1890. Note cut and set of
Inverlyon's mizzen, and topsail
brailed in to topmast and left
aloft. The mizzen sheet upper
block is on a wire span.

33 REMOVING TYERS OF MAIN-
SAIL
Springflower, L.T.971, 59 tons,
built at Rye, 1903. Note rope and
wire guy on winch, bowsprit run
in, becket of lanyard for jib outhaul on starboard bitt, and ice
being taken aboard in baskets.
Sunk by U-boat on 6th March,
1916, 28 miles E. of Lowestoft.

34 CASTING OFF STERN WARP
Blencathra, L.T.1243, 39 tons, built at Lowestoft, 1921. The first reef lacing is rove off through a few eyelets and under foot of sail, note spare mast hoop and reef pendants, the round stern with vertical strakes of planking ; the smack alongside has a square stern.

35 GETTING UNDER WAY, TRAWL BASIN, LOWESTOFT
The three smacks under sail are from Ramsgate. R.206 *San Toy*, 24 tons, built at Rye, 1903. R.450 *Daisy*, 44 tons, built at Rye, 1880. R.389 *Lottie*, 42 tons, built at Sandwich, 1877.

36 HOISTING THE MAINSAIL
From left to right.　L.T.785 *Perseverando*, 38 tons, built at Brixham,
1897.　L.T.331 *Boy Willie*, 33 tons, built at Lowestoft, 1884. L.T.499
Myrtle, 55 tons, built at Lowestoft, 1891.

37 SHEETING HOME THE TOPSAIL
L.T.416 *Rose of Devon*, 25 tons, built at Galmpton, 1903. L.T.299
Olive, 57 tons, built at Lowestoft, 1901.　L.T.5 *Search*, 57 tons, built
at Rye, 1878. L.T.410 *Roma*, 46 tons, built at Brixham, 1906.
L.T.263 *Paradigm*, 61 tons, built at Galmpton, 1889.

38 A FAIR WIND
  To wind'ard is L.T.416 *Rose of Devon* with a square or transom stern,
  L.T.1012 *Successful*, 44 tons, built at Porthleven in 1906 has a round
  stern.

39 RUNNING OUT THE BOWSPRIT
  Susie, L.T.28, 60 tons, built at Yarmouth, 1878. Two of crew are
  about to hook jib to its traveller. The wherry *Belle* has a bonnet laced
  to the foot of her sail, with three lines of reef points above.

40 HEADING OUT TO SEA
    To wind'ard is L.T.252 *Picotee*, 27 tons, built Galmpton, 1908.
    L.T.359 is *Fern*, 56 tons, built Lowestoft, 1894.

41 SWEEPS OUT
    Girl Edna, L.T.1130, 25 tons, built at Lowestoft, 1920.

42 TRAWLERS BEING TOWED TO SEA

The tug may be *Powerful*, built at North Shields in 1856, as her sponsons differ from those in other twin funnel tugs.   She has the maximum tow allowed, five smacks. R.11 *Tara*, 52 tons, built at Ramsgate, 1887. L.T.323 *Maud of Scotland*, 64 tons, built 1886 at Bideford. L.T.88 *Brothers*, 61 tons, built at Rye, 1879. L.T.40 *Provider*, 48 tons, built at Lowestoft, 1885.

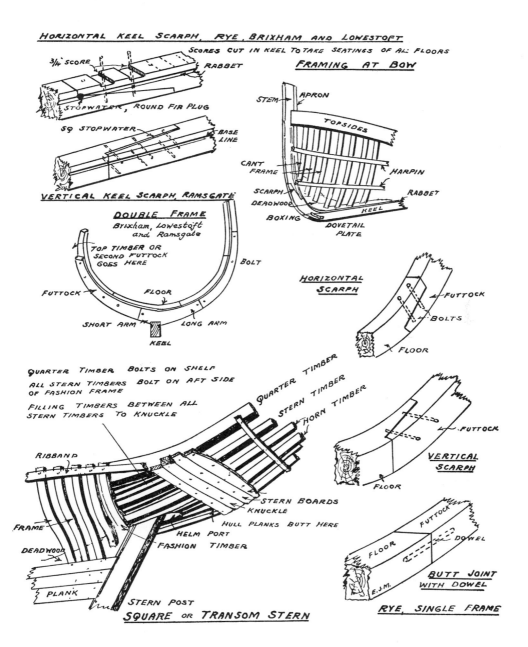

HORIZONTAL KEEL SCARPH, RYE, BRIXHAM AND LOWESTOFT

SCORES CUT IN KEEL TO TAKE SEATINGS OF ALL FLOORS

3/4 SCORE — RABBET

STOPWATER, ROUND FIR PLUG

SQ STOPWATER — BASE LINE

VERTICAL KEEL SCARPH, RAMSGATE

FRAMING AT BOW

STEM — APRON

TOPSIDES

CANT FRAME

HARPIN

SCARPH

DEADWOOD — RABBET

BOXING — KEEL

DOVETAIL PLATE

DOUBLE FRAME
Brixham, Lowestoft and Ramsgate

TOP TIMBER OR SECOND FUTTOCK GOES HERE

BOLT

FUTTOCK — FLOOR

SHORT ARM — LONG ARM

KEEL

HORIZONTAL SCARPH

FUTTOCK

BOLTS

FLOOR

QUARTER TIMBER BOLTS ON SHELF
ALL STERN TIMBERS BOLT ON AFT SIDE OF FASHION FRAME
FILLING TIMBERS BETWEEN ALL STERN TIMBERS TO KNUCKLE

QUARTER TIMBER

STERN TIMBER

HORN TIMBER

FUTTOCK

VERTICAL SCARPH

FLOOR

RIBBAND

FRAME

DEADWOOD

PLANK

STERN BOARDS

KNUCKLE

HULL PLANKS BUTT HERE

HELM PORT

FASHION TIMBER

STERN POST

SQUARE OR TRANSOM STERN

FLOOR

FUTTOCK

DOWEL

BUTT JOINT WITH DOWEL

E.J.M.

RYE, SINGLE FRAME

FIG. 6

the frames from natural-grown timber if the floors were to cross the keel, so the " deadwood "—blocks the same siding as the keel—was erected and kneed to stem and sternpost. The " cutting-down line ", or the height of upper side of frames, was marked off and half-frames erected with their heels faying against the deadwood and through-bolted.

The frame right aft was the " fashion timber " and here the bevel was usually not so excessive as to require the last few frames to be canted, but for'ard the first three or four were " cant " frames, set up on the deadwood at a slight angle to bring their faces more square to the outside planking. These frames were temporarily held together by nailing lengths of wood, sawn out to the desired curve and known as " harpins ", while the straighter lengths amidships had " ribbands ", whose flexibility allowed for the necessary bending (Fig. 6 and Plate 23).

The keelson scarphed into the fore and aft deadwood and was through-bolted to the keel with 1 in. bolts, through every floor at Brixham, elsewhere every other floor was usual practice, and clenched on rings let into the bottom of the keel. Inside the stem a timber of equal siding, known as the " apron ", was erected on the deadwood knee and through-bolted. A rabbet was cut in stem and sternpost to receive the hooding ends of the outside planking.

Next the stern timbers were erected and their arrangement varied according to whether the stern was to be square or transom, round or elliptical. In a transom stern the heels of the timbers butted against the aft side of the fashion timber to which they were bolted, the two centre ones on either side of the sternpost being the " horn " timbers, the outside ones the " quarter " timbers. Filling timbers extended from the fashion frame to the " knuckle " and a few stern boards were bolted across and adzed to shape and dimensions (Fig. 6 and 38, also Plate 22). The leading edge of the lower stern board took the butt ends of the upper strakes of planking. In a round stern the centre timbers were the " post " timbers and they were tabled to the sternpost, while the cants butted against the heels (Fig. 7). Some of this framing can also be seen in Plate 25.

The hull was now " in frame " (Plate 23) and the next job was to adze the inner faces of the frames so that the ceiling or lining would lie even, a process termed " dubbing out ", and done by the aid of fair and flexible battens, care being taken not to reduce the frames to less scantlings than those given. When the inside was fair a line was rased in on the timbers at the height of the underside of the beams and the shelf fastened with bolts (Plate 24). Note how short and long arm floors alternate, the bolt holes lie on either side of keelson, the deadwood aft rises up against sternpost with stern and filling timbers bolted to fashion frame and overhead are the cross spalls which preserve the shape of the hull until the beams are crossed.

It was no light job to bore out the long holes with an auger, getting through four or five feet of solid oak called for strength and skill if the bit was to keep true.

The inside planking—the " ceiling " or " lining "—was usually 1½ in. pitchpine,

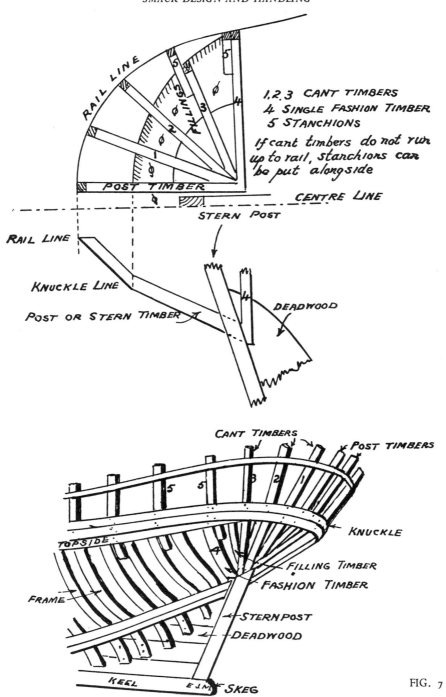

1,2,3 CANT TIMBERS
4 SINGLE FASHION TIMBER
5 STANCHIONS

If cant timbers do not run up to rail, stanchions can be put alongside

FIG. 7

ROUND STERN, LOWESTOFT SMACK

but 2 in. oak was the practice at Rye. Under the shelf were two strakes of thicker planking known as the " clamps ", Rye using 3 in. oak, Brixham 2½ in. pitchpine, between was a ¾ to 1 in. space to allow air to circulate round the frames. At the turn of the bilge, over the butts of floors and futtocks, were three strakes of thicker planking, known as the " stringers ", often 2½ to 3 in. oak, and the plank next the keelson was the " limber " strake, fitted so as to be easily removed if it was necessary to get at the bilges where the water collected and whose passage to the pump was through the limber holes cut in the seating of the floors. The outside was planked from topside to bilge and from garboard to bilge, the garboards being fastened with 7 in. by ⅝ in. galvanized dumps, the last plank fixed being about half-way up the frames. The oak topsides were three to four strakes 2½ to 3 in. thick, the planking 2 to 2½ in. with three strakes of 2½ in. to 3 in. at bilges. Some yards used elm but oak was preferred at Rye. A hull in this condition can be seen in Plate 20.

The heads of the frames were cut down to the required sheer and the framing of the deck begun. At the stem a strong oak breasthook rested on the shelf and was through-bolted to apron and frames (Fig. 20) half-way down stem was an iron one, bolted through ceiling to frames behind. The beams were placed athwartships with their ends bolted to the shelf. These were not necessarily spaced at even distances as a study of the plans of *Master Hand* will show, but they were always placed so that they formed the sides of hatches, the fore and aft sides being made by the " carlings ", short pieces of oak, some 5 in. wide and 3 in. deep, let down into the beams. If the hatch was to be smaller than the distance between beams a ledge was fitted between the carlings (Fig. 22, page 264).

All the beams were kneed with oak knees, for'ard of midships they were placed on the aft side of the beams, aft on the forward side, resting on the shelf and bolted to frames and beam. It was customary to knee both sides of beams in the way of masts, with iron hanging knees extending down ceiling to the bilge and through-bolted to frames behind (Fig, 26, page 270).

Heavy oak timbers—the " partners "—were placed between the carlings with angle chocks in the corners to form the octagonal holes through which the masts passed, wedges holding them secure. All these details can be seen in Figs. 20, 22, 24, 26, 32 and 33, which show Rye practice in the smack *Master Hand*, built for Lowestoft owners in 1920 and more fully described in chapter 13.

Coamings of 11 by 3 in. oak were dovetailed and bolted to carlings and beams round hatches ; windlass, winch, fair-leading post, towpost, companion, main sheet chock and skylight were framed up and erected, and heavy carlings fitted to take the weight of the capstan which was supplied by a specialist firm, Elliott & Garrood being the best-known makers. Full details are given in Figs. 21, 23, 25, 28, 29, 30 and 31.

The covering board of 12 by 2½ in. oak, was laid over the heads of the frames, stanchions fitted through mortices and bolted to shelf or frames, the deck planks were pitchpine, 5 by 2½ in., with a margin plank varying in width according to the beam of the hull. Planks had to be joggled into the covering board when the " snape " or diagonal cut across the width left a nib-end less than 2 in. wide, a sliver edge being impossible to caulk (Fig. 20, page 261).

Below deck the spalls were fixed athwartship and planks fastened on upper faces to form the platform, bulkheads were built up, and holds, sail lockers, ice room, cabin, etc., fitted out. Bulwarks, rails, chainplates, cavil rails, gangways and cleats were put in place and all deck and outside planking cleaned and caulked. After being painted and tarred the hull was ready for launching (Plate 19). Groundways were laid down the berth into the water and a rough cradle of planks and upright timbers built up on the sliding ways to take the weight of the hull. On the chosen day when the tide was suitable, the faces of the ways were well greased, the smack was christened by the wife or daughter of owner, or by a lady friend, the shores knocked away and the stern entered the water with a splash to the accompaniment of cheers from the small crowd (Plate 25).

In those days Rye was a busy place and the air rang with the sound of adze, saw and mallet. G. & T. Smith also built ketches and spritsail barges, but smacks were their mainstay, three usually being under construction at the same time. It is sad to see the yard to-day, as the place is well-nigh derelict.

FITTING OUT

IN few yards round the coast were cranes available, so it was necessary to use sheer legs for stepping the masts. The two spars for these were brought alongside, small ends aft, and parbuckled aboard. Two skids were placed over the side of the hull and the ends of a couple of ropes or chains made fast inboard, the spar was placed in the bights and by hauling on the upper part of the rope it was rolled on deck. The heads, resting on the taffrail or a strong trestle, were now crossed and secured with a figure-of-eight sheer lashing. The heels were drawn apart and the upper block of a three-fold tackle lashed under the cross and the tackle rove with the hauling part through the middle sheave to prevent chafing. Two for'ard and two aft guys, secured by cleats, were clove-hitched to the head of the sheers, then two tackles were made fast to the heels and led aft to haul them into position, oak shoes being placed to act as skids and to equalize the strain on the deck beams which were shored up from below. The lower block of the tackle was lashed for'ard, the fall taken to the capstan and the sheers raised by heaving. A preventer was set up in case the tackle carried away and care had to be taken that when the sheer legs were upright the main purchase hung plumb with the hole in the deck through which the mast had to pass. The heels were now lashed securely, guys and tackles belayed.

The mast was now brought alongside, head aft, canvas put round above its centre to prevent galling, the lower block lashed and a rope fastened to a cleat prevented it slipping. Then it was a case of " heave away " until the masthead was level with the rail, when the top rope was rove in the sheave, the fore halyards hooked on below the yoke and tarred canvas put round the bolsters to make a bed for the rigging. Then heaving continued until the mast was clear of the water, the heel was allowed to dry before being tarred and then the mast was hoisted high enough to permit the heel to enter the hole in deck. The fall was now eased until the tenon was placed into the mortice in the mast step on the upper part of the keelson.

The mizzen mast was stepped in a similar manner, using a smaller pair of sheer legs. Instead of using sheers the hull could be placed between two smacks in the dock and their main halyards secured to the mast, and with guys for steadying, the falls could be hauled on until the mast was high enough to step inboard.

In the days of hemp rigging, the shrouds were made of 4 strands and a heart, laid up right-handed, and for vessels using 3 shrouds a side the circumference was 7 in., for 4 shrouds 6 in., and for the mizzen rigging, 5 in.

When fixing rope rigging for three shrouds a side the foremost went on with a round turn at the masthead, one end leading to starboard, the other to port. The next went in pairs, but with four shrouds they were all in pairs, the first went to starboard, the second to port, the third to starboard and the fourth to port. The tackle strops went either in one piece with two strong seizings to form an eye, or each was fitted separately, one for each side, with the port one the stronger as it had to take the fish tackle.

With three wire shrouds, the eyes were spliced in the foremost shroud which went over singly, the middle and after in pairs, the tackle strops separately. If four shrouds they went in pairs as rope.

The measurement for eyes was once and a quarter round the masthead and before fixing rope rigging it was stretched, usually one inch for every foot. The eyes were wormed, parcelled and served, also a length about 8 ft. below them, likewise the ends, allowing about 4 ft. of service above the deadeyes. The after shrouds were served all over.

Deadeyes were one and a half the size of the shrouds, turned in left-handed if rope was cable laid, right-handed if hawser laid, in the former case the ends lay aft on the port and forward on the starboard side. A good throat seizing was put on and finished off by bending the end into place and securing with two snug seizings.

When rigging, the tackle strops were the first placed aloft, next the fore shrouds, first starboard, then port, then starboard pair, next port and finally the fore stay which had a long collar spliced in to go over masthead ; if of rope, lacing eyes were formed to go with a lashing at back of masthead. The fore stay, always set-up before the shrouds, bedded in a score on face of stemhead before passing inboard through hole, a heart was spliced in the inner end and a lanyard, passed between it and a hole in knee of windlass bitt, kept all taut (Fig. 20).

The eyes of all rigging were marked by a piece of spunyarn just under the parcelling and knotted, a starboard pair having one knot, a port, two. The size of the lanyards was half that of the shrouds and when reeving from a coil the ends of foremost shrouds were pointed aft and the end of lanyard rove through foremost hole of lower deadeye, up to corresponding one above, down and up and at hole nearest end of upper deadeye a Mathew Walker knot was formed. The drift between upper and lower deadeyes was about equal to the height of the bulwarks, 2 ft. to 2 ft. 3 in. The lanyards were then well greased and hauled taut by tackles, the knot lying for'ard on the starboard side and aft on the port, the end being usually hitched round lower end of shroud (Plate 133).

A sheer pole was now seized across the shrouds above the deadeyes to prevent any twisting before rattling-down commenced. Oars or handspikes were lashed across for the men to stand on and the ratlines were secured to the after shroud on the starboard side, on the fore shroud on the port side, so as to work with the sun. A small eye was spliced in each end, hitches passed round inner shrouds and heaved tight with a marline spike, the ends being seized to outer shrouds. Ratlines were usually 13 to 15 inches apart and kept parallel with the sheer pole.

Next the topmast was rigged, either the stays went with eyes over the head, or an iron band with eyes took hooks spliced in the ends of the stays, or thimbles were shackled. The mast was swayed aloft by the fore halyards with a strop just below the hounding and hoisted into the lower cap—the " yoke "—the mast or heel rope was now rove and the spar hoisted high enough to slip on the traveller of the leader, hook on the stays, reeve the topsail halyards, which go to starboard, put on the truck with flag halyards, then the mast was hoisted up and fidded.

The mizzen rigging was set up in a similar manner. Next the jaws of the gaff were placed in position and parrels secured, then the peak halyards were rove. First the wire strops were passed through the bullseyes, wormed, parcelled and served, eyes spliced, put on gaff and seized (Plate 26). The masthead blocks were hooked aloft and moused, then the halyards rove to starboard and a purchase block spliced in lower end. When steam capstans came in, the purchase was often omitted as the fall was taken to the capstan. The main halyards rove through a treble block on a saddle at masthead and a double one on an iron tongue working in a slot at end of gaff near jaws. The hauling part went to port.

Next a single block was spliced in one end of the topping lift and a thimble at the other to shackle on the boom end, the runner was spliced to a single block at masthead, rove through the first single block, back to the second and at the lower end was double block of luff tackle which was set up to starboard. The downhaul was fitted and the boom hung on its gooseneck.

The main sheet was always left-handed or cable-laid rope, and rove through two double blocks, the lower one working in a box bolted to the deck, the fall leading through a bullseye to a cleat on deck. The mizzen sheet belayed to a cleat on the stern horse, or transit rail as it was called at Lowestoft.

71

The jib was hoisted by the starboard part of the halyards, then sweated up on the luff tackle to port ; the foresail halyards rove through a single block hooked under port side of yoke (Plate 27). Two strops were fixed round booms, one for the guy, the other for reef tackle.

Grimsby smacks had a jump stay, either of rope or wire, Hull had none. An eye went over hounds of mizzen mast and one bullseye was seized in lower end, another at back of main sheet chock, a lanyard rove through both set the stay up taut.

Next the bowsprit was got on board and rigged with a traveller to which inhaul was seized, with chain in the nip of the sheave, the heel rope was rove, topmast stay led through bullseye on end-iron, and bobstay fixed with two single blocks and a length of chain, the uphaul secured, either a piece of small chain, or a small bullseye shackled to bobstay chain and a rope rove, one end being secured to an eyebolt at bow. Not all smacks were fitted with a bobstay.

The bag strop was lashed to the foremost shroud with a thimble in lower end, and main truss double block was seized to middle starboard shroud, topmast stays set up with luff tackles, they often had legs, equal to the housing length of the topmast, shackled in and taken away when the spar was reefed. The stays were then of a convenient length to secure close to the main shrouds, thus saving the difficulty of stowing away too much wire rope.

If the jib outhaul was chain it was long enough to come within about 2 ft. of the starboard bitt, with a bullseye shackled to its end. A becket in a lanyard slipped over the head of the bitt and the outhaul was set up by reeving the rope through the bullseye and belaying it back round the bitthead (Plate 92).

Jib sheets were 3 in. rope and fixed with a bullseye having two holes and a hook to go into clew of sail, or two separate bullseyes with a short length of chain and a toggle to go into clew. The fore sheet could go in a variety of ways. A piece of chain with a large link in lower end and a hook in other to go in sail, one bullseye shackled to chain, another to traveller on iron horse across deck for'ard of mast, with a rope fall connecting the bullseyes. At Lowestoft, deadeyes were used, at Brixham single blocks, the chain being served. Another method was a length of chain from horse and shackled direct to sail.

The hoops on the masts were parcelled in the centre with tarred canvas, marled down and seizings of small ratline put on ready for bending sail (Plate 28). Reef pendants were cut to length, wormed and stretched, then parcelled and served, a thimble spliced in one end or a stopper knot made (Plate 29). The parcelling was put on for about 6 ft. to take the nip on boom and in bullseye, the inner ends were served with two yarn, the outer ones with three yarn spunyarn. Paunch mats were fixed on each side of gaff to prevent chafe against rigging and topsail (Plate 133). The fore topsail tack could be done in two ways. One, a four-fathom length of 3 to 4 in. rope, with an eye 6 in. long spliced in upper end and a ratline lashing to fasten to topsail tack cringle, the lower end had a double block for the luff tackle spliced in.

This could be used with both topsails by simply taking lashing from one and putting it on the other sail. Another way was to splice a thimble in upper end and shackle to sail. If a runner and tackle purchase was preferred, a single block was spliced into lower end of pendant. The lower block of luff tackle hooked in a link on port side of gooseneck band. The mizzen topsail tack was often a gun tackle purchase, i.e. two single blocks. The mizzen halyards had two double blocks.

Topsail sheets usually had a short length of chain to take the nip in the sheave at gaff peak, as did the halyards.

BENDING SAIL

THE mainsail was laid fore and aft along deck, throat or nock cringle for'ard, peak aft. The throat shackled to eyebolt under the gaff (Plate 30) the peak was hauled out hand taut and an earing passed (Fig. 8). If too great a strain was put on the head of a new sail it tended to make a hollow leech. A stop was put in the middle of the gaff, the sail hoisted and all the mast hoops bent, then the clew was hauled out and sail left to hang with the weight of the boom taken by the topping lift. Plate 29 shows clew of sail shackled to end of boom, a later practice. After a time the sail was lowered, head pulled out slightly and bent to gaff with a lacing or robands. If a lacing was used a double hitch was put every four parts, so that should one chafe the rest would hold (Plate 26). Robands, made of sennit with eyes worked in the ends, passed through eyelets in head of sail and fastened off on top of gaff,

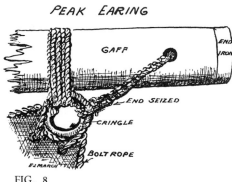

PEAK EARING

FIG. 8

care being taken to keep boltrope between sail and spar to save excessive chafing (Plate 27). The mizzen was bent in the same way.

The foresail was bent to hanks on the fore stay with rope or spun yarn, passing the seizing to and fro, then across between hank and luff to prevent the iron hank chafing the rope.

When bending the topsail it was essential not to stretch the head too much or the sail would never stand properly, several turns of the seizing were passed through the hole in fore part of yard. The luff ran on a " leader " (Plates 27 and 49).

No matter how well a suit of sails was cut, unless the utmost care was taken in bending and setting for the first time all the efforts of the sailmaker would be of no avail, as the canvas, once stretched badly, never stood well, and generally speaking any skipper worth his salt liked to see a well-fitting suit on his smack.

The foregoing is a typical fit-out for an 80-ton Grimsby smack in the eighties and practically every item can be distinguished in the superb model of *Frank Buckland* (Plate 31). Some differences were to be found in the various ports, while skipper's or owner's choice was often the deciding factor.

I have gone into details very fully so that anyone wishing to make a worthwhile model can do so with everything correct as in the full-sized smack. I shall itemize the lead of every rope when I deal with *Master Hand*, a Lowestoft trawler with which I was well acquainted and had the benefit of the skipper's advice for everything connected with her.

HANDLING A SMACK

BEFORE a smack set out on a fishing trip two to three tons of crushed ice were taken on board and shot down the bunker hole into the ice room below. Plate 32 shows the ice barge at Lowestoft going alongside *Nancy* L.T.41. Some of these lighters were self-propelled and I have a record of the cost of building one at Reynold's yard in November, 1900. The contract price was £315, which included £63 12s. 4½d. for wages, £40 for timber and £34 1s. 4d. for stores, fastenings, etc. Another built for the East Anglian Ice Co. in 1905, was 45 ft. L.O.A., 12 ft. beam and 4 ft. 6 in. deep. Here wages amounted to £42 11s. 11d., fastenings to £5 6s. 8d., but there is no record of any other costs or the contract price. The crushed ice was carried loose in the hold and loaded into the baskets seen on the hatch. Ahead is the *Inverlyon*, L.T.687, most interesting because she leaves her topsail aloft when mainsail is taken in, the sail being brailed in through a small block on the luff. When the gaff is hoisted the sheet is hauled out and the topsail set, thus saving a certain amount of time and effort. Only a few trawlers worked a topsail this way.

Both these smacks met with disaster. *Nancy* was lost in collision with the steam fish carrier *Brutus* of Hull, some 15 miles S.E. of Lowestoft, and *Inverlyon* was sunk by gunfire from a German submarine on the 1st February, 1917, while fishing 15 miles N. by W. from Trevose Head.

Whilst the ice was being taken in the crew of the smack were busy getting ready for sea. Plate 33 shows the tyers being cast off the mainsail aboard *Springflower*, L.T.971. Note the wire and rope guy made up on the winch and the heel of the bowsprit resting on the roller at foot of mast. Sail might be set before casting off, as in *Blencathra*, L.T.1243, 39 tons, built at Lowestoft in 1921, here the stern warp is about to be let go (Plate 34).

Working out of a crowded harbour under sail called for a high standard of seamanship, as dozens of smacks would be jammed together. Plate 35 shows a corner of the trawl basin at Lowestoft in the days when many Ramsgate smacks worked from the port, the three in foreground being *San Toy*, R.206, *Daisy* R.450, 44 tons, built at Rye in 1880, and *Lottie*, R.389, 42 tons, built at Sandwich in 1877. The ice lighter is between *Daisy* and *Lottie*.

Sail would be set to suit the direction of the wind and the prevailing conditions, sometimes the foresail would be hoisted first, at others the mainsail. Plate 36 shows *Persevarando*, L.T.785, 38 tons, built at Brixham in 1897, hoisting her mainsail. The main halyards were hauled down by steam to a proven mark, a piece of white twine stuck through the strands, while the gaff was kept as nearly square to the mast as possible. Then the halyards were belayed and the peak swigged up until the sail began to girt at the throat. Three men were needed at the peak halyards if the fall was not taken to the capstan. *Boy Willie*, L.T.331, 33 tons, built 1884, has mainsail, topsail and mizzen set, but the foresail is not yet sheeted home. The other smack is *Myrtle*, L.T.499, 55 tons, built 1891.

The topsail was hoisted chock-a-block and the tack well bowsed down before the sheet was hauled out to the gaff end. Plate 37 is of *Rose of Devon* sheeting her topsail home. She registered 28 tons and was built at Galmpton in 1912. The smack coming in is *Olive*, L.T.299, 57 tons, built at Lowestoft in 1901. L.T.5 with a gaff topsail set is *Search*, 57 tons, built at Rye in 1878. L.T.410 is *Roma*, L.T.263 *Paradigm*, all with sail up ready to come out of the basin.

The smacks would now head away for the harbour entrance, and Plate 38 shows *Rose of Devon*, L.T.416, to wind'ard of L.T.1012, *Successful*, 44 tons, built at Porthleven in 1906. Note also the difference between the round or elliptical stern of *Successful* and the square or transom one of *Rose of Devon*. The next job would be to run out the bowsprit, which is being done in *Susie*, L.T. 28, 60 tons, built at Yarmouth 1878 (Plate 39). Strictly speaking the spar should not have been heaved out until the smack was abreast of the pier heads in case another vessel was coming in. Outgoing craft had the right of way. The crew are about to bend the jib to its traveller, and the smack astern, with a cloud of steam coming from the capstan exhaust, is *Hesperus*, L.T.602, 57 tons, she was sunk by a time bomb placed on board from a German submarine on the 6th August, 1915, 37 miles E.N.E. of Lowestoft. The wherry *Belle* is one of the clinker-built traders peculiar to the Norfolk Broads. The only sail set was a mainsail which was hoisted by a single halyard, main and peak combined, the fall being led to the winch at the foot of the mast.

Once clear of the confines of the harbour the smacks headed boldly out to sea for the fishing grounds, making a fine sight as they heeled to the strong wind which filled the brown sails so that they stood out in lovely curves (Plate 40). The wisps of steam are from the capstan exhausts.

If the wind was foul, the smacks were towed out by one of the tugs owned by the Great Eastern Railway, five at a time being the maximum number allowed and the price charged was 5s. out, 7s. 6d. in (Plate 42). Two are Ramsgate smacks, R.11 being *Tara*, the others are *Maud of Scotland*, L.T.323, 64 tons, built 1886, *Provider*, L.T.40, 40 tons, built 1880 and *Brothers*, L.T.88, 61 tons, built at Rye in 1879. The tug looks like *Powerful*, built of wood at N. Shields in 1856, 84.2 ft. long, 18.1 ft. beam and 9.5 ft. deep, with 40 h.p. engines and owned by the G.E. Rly.

Maud of Scotland and *Brothers* have their big gaff topsails aloft. These were mainly used when passage making as most skippers preferred to trawl with a jib-headed top-sail set, the other was difficult to lower on the port tack as the yard was apt to foul the peak halyards.   *Maud of Scotland* was built for the Columbia fleet, sold to Leleu in 1889 and to Stocks of Lowestoft 1890.   If the wind was scant and a tug not handy a smack was sometimes rowed into and out of harbour (Plate 41).

When a smack was at anchor in a roadstead with a fair wind and a weather tide, the first job when getting under weigh was to muster all hands, see everything was clear, top main and mizzen booms by the topping lifts and have the sails ready for loosing, then heave short on the cable.

If the wind was light the mainsail would be set, in a smart breeze it was usual to heave right up and set the headsails to run the tide before hoisting the after canvas. In a crowded anchorage with a fine breeze and a lee tide the cable was shortened in and the smack allowed to dredge clear with the anchor just touching, until it was possible to cast on the right tack.   Then the anchor was got inboard as smartly as possible and all sail set.

When lying at anchor in an exposed anchorage it was advisable to take the following precautions.   Have the cable weather bitted and all chain ranged on deck with handspikes, chain stopper, winch handles, etc., handy for instant getting under weigh and the second anchor bent to the trawl rope ready to let go if an emergency arose.   At the turn of the tide the skipper came on deck to see that the smack sheered clear of her anchor.

Should a strong tide be running, just before it began to ease the vessel was sheered to leeward of her anchor, if necessary setting a piece of the foresail to keep her steady.   It was vital at all times to give a smack a steady sheer before the tide was done so that she did not fall back on her anchor and foul it by sweeping the stock.

The skipper had the helm until the smack was clear of all danger, then the gear was cleared up and the usual routine commenced.   Plate 43 shows a deck view taken on board *Boy Clifford* on her way to the fishing ground.   The boat was lashed down securely with gripes and the long cleat on the stanchions aft is where the sheet of the big tow foresail belayed.   The baskets are those in which the fish drained after being gutted and washed, prior to packing away in ice in the fish pounds below.   One of the crew is hauling out the reef tackle.

When making a passage with the wind abeam many smacks set a staysail between the masts and sheeting home at the taffrail and sometimes the tow foresail went up instead of the working one.   In the palmy days a jib topsail was often set with halyards leading to topmast head, the cause of many a broken mast if the skipper hung on to this big sail just too long.   Plate 44 shows *East Dean*, L.T.1233, 42 tons, built at Lowestoft in 1921, making a passage in July, 1935 and Plate 45 is a rather unusual sail plan in the big Mission smack *Alice Fisher*, L.O.77, 56 tons, built at Yarmouth in 1891.   She has a couple of staysails up, a tow foresail and a big jib as well, also her mizzen mast carries a fidded topmast and crosstrees.

Until well into the eighties the majority of smack sails were cut with vertical cloths although a few jibs were diagonal-cut with cloths parallel to leech and foot and meeting in a diagonal seam, the " angulated method " invented by Mathew Orr of Greenock, *c* 1830. Sails so made stood better but were rather more difficult to cut, as the art of sailmaking improved many owners had whole suits diagonal-cut. The sails were stronger but there was an added danger if a sea broke into the belly of a mainsail as the seams would not split so easily to spill out the water. The late Mr. H. L. Summers told me in 1939 that one of his smacks *Echo*, R.408, built at Rye in 1878, went over on her beam ends on one occasion when a sea broke into the mainsail and would undoubtedly have foundered if the vertical-cut cloths had not split and released the water. He was certain she would have gone down if the sail had been diagonal-cut.

If a vertical-cut cloth tore it usually split from head to foot and often left a considerable area which could still hold the wind, but when the cloths went from leech to luff the sail was in two portions which only flapped about. This difference can clearly be seen in Plate 46, of the 47-ton *Commander*, L.T.86, built at Brixham in 1899, with several cloths blown clean away, whereas in Plate 47 of *May*, L.T.573, 59 tons, built Porthleven 1904, the sail is useless. Two of the smacks shown fell victims to U-boat attack, *Commander* was sunk on the 16th February 1918, 8 miles S.W. of Beer Head, and L.T.97, *Emblem*, lying alongside *May* was lost on the 7th September, 1915, 44 miles E.S.E. of Lowestoft.

In October, 1946, I had a most interesting chat with Mr. Jeckells, sailmaker of Lowestoft and he showed me an oil painting of their *Queen Mab*, L.T.612, built at Lowestoft in 1894. She carried a suit of sails cut with the cloths parallel to the foot, the introduction of Mr. W. T. Jeckells and cut by him at a time when few, if any, yachts had cross-cut sails. *Queen Mab* was a total loss on the 2nd January, 1904, with 3 out of her crew of 5, following a collision with the German steamer *Alice*, 2 miles N.E. of the Corton Lightvessel, in a light W.S.W. wind. Her master was John Prior and his son told me that his father went skipper at the age of 19 and was 33 years with Mr. W. T. Jeckells, the longest service for one owner in Lowestoft annals, and when he left the sea after the sinking of *Queen Mab* Mr. Jeckells sold his other smack *Seabird* and gave up ownership.

When heaving-to, the helm was put down to bring the smack's head to the wind and the foresail sheet hauled a'weather to prevent her actually coming round, then the main sheet was eased until the required balance was effected (Plates 108 and 109). If a big swell was running after a gale Ramsgate men often rove off a guy from the end of the boom to the aft lee shroud, or to a ringbolt in the stanchions to save the boom from being unshipped or broken (Plate 74). Skipper Crouch tells me this was never Lowestoft custom, a boom guy, used only on the port tack, was done away with in his time and the practice was to take the topping lift well up and slack mainsheet out to ease the strain.

Although some vessels were fitted with reef points, the majority of smacksmen preferred lacings, the brass eyelets being stuck through the seams of vertical-cut sails, in the cloths if diagonal-cut, some makers sewing on reef bands for strengthening. Two pendants were always rove off ready for instant hauling down in an emergency, but the three main lacings, each consisting of seven fathom of 1½ in. rope, were stowed away below in the cabin locker to avoid any deterioration by weather, being laced up when required. A man stood in the belly of the sail, which was often full of water, to pass the lacing through each eyelet and under the foot, always working from aft for'ard and fastening off round the hoops thus holding them together. After a spell the sail would slacken and the lacing need pulling up again as can be seen in Plate 63. The first lacing in the mizzen was always kept in during the winter so that one man could reef if necessary (Plate 34). In *Master Hand* the first reef tackle was 12½ fathom of 1½ in. wire and rope combined, the double reef tackle 20 fathom of 2½ in. rope, the fall being clapped on to the capstan, but in the old days the reef pendants had to be hauled down by hand.

Reef lacing adjusts itself to the strain and so pulls evenly all along the row of eyelets and is thus less liable to tear the sail, but should one part chafe through the whole lot goes. A smack could only be luffed up into the wind before taking in a reef if the trawling gear was on board, when it was down luffing was impossible ; she was sailed full while the lacing was being passed.

Reefing is thus described by my friend Skipper J. T. Crouch :—

" To begin with the first reef. You pull up the topping lift to take the weight off the sail and to keep the boom up in place, then lower the main halyards down to required length. Next heave down the sail by the steam capstan with the reef tackle, then rack the tackle and make it fast on the boom. The main truss tackle from the starboard shrouds hauls up the cringle on the weather of the sail.

Now lace up the sail with the reef lacing as tight as you can get it to keep all the water out you can. Then pull your second pendant down tight, put a shackle in the end and it is all ready for use if you want it. The same methods are required, but you have to lower the main peak for the second reef and so on for the others if you require them, and that's that."

It was an awkward job to pass the third pendant, especially on a wild, dark night, as the man had to hang on to the leech with one hand and reeve the rope through the bullseye above his head, the smack sailing full so as not to shake him off the boom.

Close reefed, with the wind on the quarter, a smack made a fine sight as she boiled along with white water piling up under the lee bow and foaming crests running along the weather side. The bowsprit would be reefed and all sails straining at the boltropes, shrouds taut as iron bars to wind'ard, but sagging a little to leeward, and along the port rail was lashed the trawl beam with its rusty iron heads and dripping net, perhaps the sky inky-black, with the sun striking through in patches, and lighting up the angry sea, all broken water and creamy lacework.

It had to be blowing pretty hard before a second reef was hauled down and the topsail taken in.   Plate 48 shows *Elsie*, L.T.354, 68 tons, built 1886, taking a plunge in a fierce south-easter.   To require the third and fourth cringles to be lashed down meant very heavy weather indeed, a whole gale or storm with a wind force of 9 to 10, say 50 to 60 miles an hour, and then it was getting time to heave-to.

There were different methods of laying-to in a gale of wind.   Some skippers set a trysail instead of a reefed mainsail with its heavy weight of spars and soaked canvas, while a reefed foresail was hauled a'weather.   Others set a storm jib and a reefed mizzen.   Skipper Crouch writes :

" I have been with some skippers who used to lay-to with only the reefed mainsail and foresail, a method I did not approve of, I remember saying once, ' Don't you think she would lay much better with all four sails close reefed ? '   His reply was ' You can use your own ideas when you get skipper yourself ', which I did.   I liked to see all four sails set, even if they were close-reefed with storm jib.   I think that the vessel would scend the heavy seas much better with that small bit of mizzen up.   I always carried it out providing the masts held."

In a real snorter the net might even be unbent and the beam put overboard to act as a sea anchor, or the trawl would be left down.   One smack surviving a hard blow which overwhelmed several of her companions, found a good haul of haddock when she was able to haul her gear.

Concerning this, Skipper Crouch says :

" I have seen more heavy water shipped on deck when under sail than when trawl was down.   You see you are meeting it under sail, but with trawl down seas are meeting you.   It is all right shooting in bad weather, the ship is steady with trawl down, but the mischief is done in hauling, especially when the warp is getting short, say about 10 to 5 fathom out.   I have seen us have to surge out the warp when there is a big sea coming, then wait till the next smooth, then spur about and get the bridles on the capstan when it's not so bad.   I have seen a warp part in hauling when it got short, or else the trawl beam goes, for there is a terrible strain on everything.   There were uncomfortable moments when hauling in bad weather and we're all glad to get the beam alongside and the net aboard.   It's not all pleasure trawling in bad weather I can tell you.   It's more discreet to keep your trawl on the side if the skipper thinks it's too bad to shoot, as the catch rarely pays for the risk, about £90 of gear away if lost, and you lose a bit of time getting home for more, besides a black look from the owner as well, but some of them expect you to have a trip good or bad weather, so you see a skipper is between two fires."

If conditions allowed it was best to lay-to on the port tack as then the two ton weight of beam, etc., was on the windward side, whereas on the starboard tack it was down in the sea.

Caught in a sudden squall, a smack was either " luffed," i.e., brought to the wind to shake it out of her, or the jib was run in, topsail doused, booms topped and main and mizzen halyards lowered away. The advantage of setting a topsail over a single reefed mainsail was that it maintained the area of the after canvas, so keeping a balanced sail plan, and in a squall it could be quickly taken off and the fore staysail dropped, as this was a pressing sail.

If the rudder was lost at sea about 50 fathom of warp was veered away over the stern, then a spring was made fast and led in over each quarter and with this, and attention to the sails, the smack could be steered. Under such conditions vessels have been brought safely into port from considerable distances. If the weather was fine enough the boat could be used to assist in the steering.

There were two precautions always taken by thoughtful skippers, one was to have a sharp hatchet handy in case gear had to be cut away in a hurry and the other was to keep a tightly corked bottle, full of matches and dry lamp cotton, stowed in a drawer right up under the deck in the cabin. Then if lamps, stove or donkey boiler fire were extinguished by a sea finding its way below, it was possible to get them going again.

Smacksmen were never slow in going to the help of another vessel in distress and many a fine rescue was made in appalling weather conditions, disabled smacks towed into port and lives saved which would certainly have been lost but for the skill and courage of fishermen.

For one instance I am indebted to Mr. Charles Hillam of Grimsby, who wrote me :—" I was visiting two lady friends who for twenty years were our neighbours and the conversation turned on your prospective book. They recalled their mother's maiden name, Challis, and either a sister or niece of the said Capt. Challis mentioned. I think it will fit in, don't you ? There is one stipulation, please send it back to above address when you have copied same, as the sisters Burgess of Grimsby value same."

The papers referred to the foundering of the barque *A. B. Jones* in 1866 and the dreadful suffering of four of her crew who were exposed for upwards of thirty hours to the fury of a raging storm, without food or drink, before they were rescued by Captain Challis of the fishing smack *Gauntlet* of Sunderland, who within twelve years had rescued the crews of four ships in distress, three of which *Hutton*, *Phoenix* and *Thomas Wood* belonged to his home port, risking his own life to save those of others. I quote in full a letter from one of the survivors :

> 24, West Street,
> Barneswell,
> NEWPORT.
> March 13, 1866.

Dear Capt. Challis,

I sit down with very grateful remembrance of the kindness both you and your noble crew showed to us in our distress—kindness which I trust will never be removed from my heart. I speak not only on behalf of myself, dear captain, but of my three

43 DECK VIEW, LOOKING FOR'ARD
Boy Clifford, 41 tons, built at Lowestoft, 1920. One of the crew is
hauling out the reef tackle.

44 ALL SAIL SET
East Dean, 42 tons, built at Lowestoft, 1921. With the wind abeam,
the tow foresail and staysail have been set.

45 A MISSION SMACK
Alice Fisher, 56 tons, built at Yarmouth, 1891. Note fidded topmast on mizzen, topsails set a'weather, two staysails, tow foresail and big jib. Four reef cringles in mizzen and four shrouds a side show she could face any weather.

46 AFTER A HARD BLOW
  Commander, L.T.86, 47 tons, built at Brixham, 1899.   Note reefs in
foresail and mainsail, and the canvas dodger in mizzen rigging.   Sunk
by U-boat on the 16th February, 1918, eight miles S.W. of Beer Head.

47   A BADLY SPLIT MAINSAIL
  May, L.T.573, 59 tons, built at Porthleven, 1904.   *Nelson*, L.T.459,
56 tons, built at Lowestoft, 1905.   *Emblem*, L.T.97, 50 tons, built at
Brixham, 1899.

48 TWO REEFS DOWN
Elsie, L.T.354, 68 tons, built at Southtown, 1886.

49 TAKING IN THE TOPSAIL
Kestrel, L.T.1097, 44 tons, built at Oulton Broad, 1907. Note how grommets on luff run on the leader, which blows clear of mast as traveller on topmast drops on the cap.

companions also. I am sure that the name of your noble vessel and crew can never possibly be erased from our memory, no, not as long as we are permitted to dwell on earth, and though you desired nothing from us, but gave us freely all that we in our distress needed, yet I should have liked you only to have been here yesterday to have seen and heard the upliftings of the hearts of my dear family while I was telling them of your great kindness towards us, which even caused tears to roll down the cheeks of the most venerable of our circle of nearly sixty summers. I thought how well such a sight would repay you, for I am sure your noble heart would have been moved, as mine was, to tears. '' God Almighty bless and prosper them and their noble *Gauntlet* '' ejaculated from the mouths of friends when they heard our frightful tale. But, however, dear Captain, trusting that you will meet your reward hereafter, and that you may long be spared to save those who may unhappily fall into such a lot as ours was.

On behalf of myself and my companions, believe me,

Yours ever gratefully,

John Groves.

During the great March gale of 1883, the 68-ton Hull-smack *Cavalier*, built at Rye in 1873, was riding out the storm under bare poles when a tremendous sea struck her about 7.30 a.m. on the 4th March, tearing out the main and mizzen masts and making a clean breach of everything on deck, pump and all. For over thirty hours she lay on her side. The mate, up to his waist in water, started baling in the cabin, handing the full buckets to the cook on the ladder who emptied them through the companion. The skipper, third and fourth hands were on deck trying to get the anchor overboard, but were constantly drenched by the heavy seas coming on board which eventually smashed three of the beams supporting the deck. After a long struggle they succeeded in letting the anchor go and the battered hulk now rode more steadily. The men went below to assist in baling and after hours of work the weather side of the floor became visible. An attempt was made to light a fire but only two dry matches remained, one of which missed fire. When they succeeded in getting a fire going efforts were made to heat an iron bolt, hoping to pass it through a hand-spike and so make a rough and ready pump handle, but another huge sea broke on board, swept down below, filled the cabin once again and put out the precious fire. There was now nothing to be done but keep on baling all night and pray for dawn. Soon after 9 a.m. a steamer was sighted and during the next few hours several passed close by, but not one offered any assistance to the stricken *Cavalier*. About noon the Grimsby smack *Blanche*, 78 tons, built at Hamburg in 1868, was seen bearing down and hopes were raised as no smacksman willingly deserted another. Superbly handled by her skipper *Blanche* drew to wind'ard, threw out her boat, manned it and succeeded in getting alongside. All the crew were soon taken off, by now practically exhausted, having been soaked through and without food or drink for nearly a day and a half. Meanwhile the smack ran down to leeward and foot by foot the deep-laden boat worked towards her, now on the crest of a wave, now hidden in the hollow, frequently almost capsizing in the awful sea that was running, but at last she came alongside and all were safely hauled on board. *Cavalier* was later towed in.

Smacksmen thought little or nothing of such splendid acts of courage and frequently made no mention of them when they got ashore. At times they met with vessels in need of assistance and then there was always a chance of salvage money being earned and many a man risked his life boarding a waterlogged hulk in the hope of picking up a nice little packet. One such instance occurred in 1866 when *Welfare* of Ramsgate came across the Indiaman *Lucknow* ashore on the Galloper Sands, deep-laden with silks and goods from the Orient. At first her skipper refused assistance, thinking no doubt that the tiny smack could do little, but eventually he thought better of it and signalled for help. The smack worked to wind'ard in the teeth of the gale and threw out her boat, the mate jumped in alone and sculled towards the wreck. Springing on board he was put in charge and at once ordered all sails to be set to heel the vessel over. In a few moments she slipped off the sands into deep water and went off like a hound released from the slips, leaving some of her keel behind her. Eventually she made Yarmouth Roads and brought up with two anchors, but the little *Welfare* was three days beating up to Lowestoft. For this splendid feat of seamanship an award of £2,000 was given by the Admiralty Court to owner and crew.

January and February 1895 will always be remembered as two of the most severe months in that terrible winter. There was wild weather in the North Sea and the fleeters were covered in ice. The London docks were frozen for six weeks, great blocks of ice floating up and down on the tide, and spritsail barges were imprisoned in their berths for weeks.

On the 30th January the Norddeutscher Lloyd mail steamer *Elbe* sailed from Bremen bound for Southampton en route to America with 353 people on board. About 5 a.m. the next morning she collided with the small steamer *Crathie*, bound from Rotterdam to Aberdeen with a crew of 12, and sustained such damage that she sank within 20 minutes During those fleeting moments in the bitter blackness of a winter night frenzied efforts were made to launch the lifeboats, but all the tackles were frozen solid and had to be cut free with axes. When being lowered every boat except one capsized, and only one woman named Anna Bocker succeeded in getting clear and she swam about in the icy water until her cries attracted the attention of the only boat afloat, intended to hold 15 but actually carrying 19, and she was eventually hauled on board half-frozen.

The 50-ton Lowestoft smack *Wildflower*, built 1883, was fishing in the vicinity and some time elapsed before she was able to bear down and pick up the boat, then she made for home some 40 miles away with the only survivors from the proud liner crowded in her tiny cabin, where such help as was possible was freely given, and they reached port twelve hours after the *Elbe* had foundered. Skipper William Wright was afterwards presented with a new smack as a reward for his gallantry.

When a fishing trip was over the smack headed for home and outside the entrance to the harbour sails were taken in according to weather conditions. Sometimes all sail was carried until well inside the piers, at others topsail was dropped, jib and bowsprit taken in. Plate 49 shows the 44-ton *Kestrel*, L.T.1097, built at Oulton Broad 1907, approaching Lowestoft. The grommets on the luff of the topsail run on the " leader ", a chain and rope jackstay, the chain upper end fast to a ring sliding freely on the topmast and the rope belaying to cleat at foot of mast. The tack pendant can also be seen with its tackle hooked to the shackle in the iron band round the mast.

The usual practice at Lowestoft is thus described by Skipper Crouch :—

" If you have got a fresh breeze, say about S. to N., going round in the E. direction, coming from the nor'ard with a flood tide you work your way up to abreast of the harbour with a south breeze, then reduce all sail except the mainsail and foresail so that you can stop her for entering either dock. You always have the drogue ready, this is a large canvas bag shaped like a cone with a 5 fathom tow and a long line in the toe to pull it up and get the water out. If you are going to the inner harbour make sure that the signals are with you. If there is a green light at the signal mast and another one on the lock pit, they are against you, but if they are red it is safe to keep on your way, for a green light means less than 10 ft. of water at the bar and lock pit. So far, so good, but if the wind is shy you have to get in the best way you can."

With a southerly wind and ebb tide it was necessary to hug the weather pier head and with a northerly wind to carry sufficient after sail to luff up after passing the pier heads. By neglecting these precautions vessels have been driven to leeward and damaged against the piers.

Plate 50 shows *Our Merit*, L.T.535, 39 tons, built at Brixham in 1914, coming in with a pair of reefs down on the 15th January, 1939.

Once inside, the smack made for the trawl basin to discharge her catch. Plate 51 shows *May Queen*, L.T.128, 50 tons, built at Brixham in 1900, dropping main and mizzen sails, the foresail giving enough way to come alongside the quay, where the trawlers berthed head-on. The catch was landed, then the gear was made up, the strop round the cod end was hooked on to the after tackle and the net hoisted up to dry and another trip was over. Plate 52 of *Forget-me-not*, L.T.1252, lost with all hands in November, 1927, gives a good view of the roller gangway over which the warp was worked, the for'ard trawl iron with ground rope resting on beam and the net drying. Plate 53 is of the gear made up on deck.

Methods of working in and out of harbour naturally varied according to local conditions. At Brixham no tugs were available and the smacks generally brought up at moorings and the catches were landed in the punts. I chose Lowestoft as I was able to select appropriate photos from the many hundreds in my collection and Skipper Crouch could give me the benefit of his skill and knowledge.

CHAPTER SIX

TRAWLING GEAR

GENERALLY speaking the design of a beam trawl was the same all round the coast with local variations in the size and shape of head irons, whose weight differed according to depth of water and strength of tides on the fishing grounds. Otter boards were not favoured by sail trawlermen although I have seen them in use on a few Brixham smacks.

The beam, varying in length from 20 to 50 ft., was usually made of elm, ash, oak or beech, but in some instances it was suitable foreign timber, greenheart or lancewood. For the shorter beams it was not difficult to find a single length of naturally grown timber of the requisite thickness, requiring little if any trimming, beyond the removal of the bark, as the strength of a young tree was essential, being stronger and more elastic than any hewn from a larger trunk. Mr. Moses, smack builder of Ramsgate, tells me he used to go over to Ostend to buy trawl beams, as the Belgian elms yielded far more springy timber than any he could obtain elsewhere. For lengths exceeding 35 ft. it was necessary to scarph two or three pieces together, the joins being strengthened by iron bands. Up to the 1870's the length of beam was determined by the distance between the taffrail and after main shroud, one trawl head projecting just beyond the stern, where it was secured by a chain or rope stopper, the other resting between middle and aft shrouds, to which it was lashed in a seaway. Thus secured there was no danger of the heavy timber coming inboard as the smack rolled. In order to increase the length of beam the fore trawl head was sometimes berthed for'ard of the main shrouds. 50 to 52 ft. was the extreme reached and as the length of vessels had increased considerably, following the introduction of the ketch rig, the for'ard head now rested on the rail abaft the shrouds.

In order to raise the beam above the ground to allow fish to enter the mouth of the net, two wrought-iron frames, called the trawl heads or head irons, were driven on to the squared ends of the timber and secured by iron wedges. Weight varied according to depth of water worked in and size of net and beam, while the shape differed somewhat in various ports. Brixham men favoured the design seen in Fig. 9, with the socket above the top iron and the loop through which the ground rope passed was outside the heel of frame. A pair weighed from 230 to 360 lbs., the width was from 3 ft. to 4 ft. 6 in., and the shoe was double the thickness of the rest of the frame to withstand the constant abrasion of the ground. The ports of Ramsgate, Lowestoft, Grimsby and Hull, owed much to the influence of the Devon men and slight variations in design were to be seen, the chief being the bringing of the iron loop inside the frame (Fig. 10). This type was popular at Lowestoft and Ramsgate.

The Barking men used a stirrup shaped trawl head (Fig. 11) with socket and loop inside the frame and this form was generally adopted at Yarmouth following the London vessels making that port their station. Here again small differences were found, such as the placing of the socket above instead of below the head of the frame. A pair of these trawl irons weighed from 360 to 400 lbs. Another Yarmouth peculiarity was the use of a 36 to 38 ft. beam and a shorter ground rope to that seen in Grimsby and Brixham smacks, as the Barking men disliked working with wide-mouthed nets in the strong tides on the Dogger Bank, where heavy irons were needed to keep beam and net on the ground.

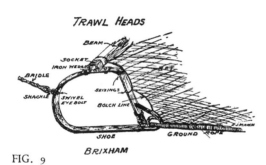

FIG. 9

The trawl was a triangular bag-shaped net, its length roughly twice the width of the mouth, the upper part was called the " back " and the front straight edge of the " square " was fastened to the beam and thus raised some 3 to 4 ft. above the ground. The lower part, the " belly ", extended from trawl-head to trawl-head, but was cut away in a semi-circle sweeping aft, with its centre or " bosom " at a depth equal to the length of the beam. A smack carrying

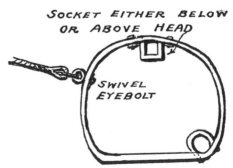

RAMSGATE & LOWESTOFT

FIG. 10

BARKING & YARMOUTH

FIG. 11

a 50 ft. beam would tow a trawl 100 ft. long, with a belly of 50 ft., thus there was a considerable area covered by the back of the net before fish lying on the bottom were disturbed by the under part whose curved sweep was fastened to the " ground rope", a length of old hawser rounded with lighter rope, a protection against chafing and an addition to its weight, as it was essential that the mouth of the net scraped the seabed. The ends were led in through the loop at the heel and made fast on each side by a few turns round the back of the frame. This ground rope was always old material with a breaking strain far less than the warp so that in the event of its becoming " fast " against rock or wreck, it would readily part and save the loss of all the gear. Otherwise there was the very serious danger that the smack would be anchored by her trawl, pooped by a following sea and possibly founder, while the least damage would be the breaking of the beam, necessitating a return to port if a spare one was not on board.

When working over ground for sole, a choice fish which tends to bury itself in the sand on the approach of danger, it was often the custom to fasten short lengths of chain, the " tickler ", the more to stir up the bottom and force the fish to rise and enter the net. Plate 54 shows the rounding to protect the ground rope and also the chain ticklers.

The narrow straight sides of net between back and ground rope, and extending from trawl heads nearly to the bosom, were called the " wings " or " gorings ". They were made of separate pieces of net and inserted when the whole trawl was laced up. From the bosom the net was a complete bag, its length equalling about two-thirds that of the trawl-beam, and tapering to the " cod " which was a narrow bag about one-seventh of the entire length of the trawl. This was the part where every fish which crossed over the ground rope eventually found its way, as once the beam had passed over the ground on which it was resting or feeding the only way of escape was by swimming forward under the beam, an unlikely event, as fish keep head to the stream and tend to dart forward if frightened, not turn round and go off in the opposite direction.

The extremity of the net, the " cod end ", was closed by a draw rope, the " cod line ", which gathered the end together and was secured with a special knot, easily released when the net was got inboard. The under part of the cod was protected from chafing against the ground by pieces of old net called " rubbing pieces ", or " false bellies ", which over-lapped each other across the bottom.

At the entrance to the cod were the " pockets ", one on each side of the net, and made by lacing together the back and belly for a distance of about 16 ft., the mouth being about 20 meshes wide and narrowing towards the end. The entrance to the cod was guarded by a piece of netting called the " flapper ", some 40 meshes in width, fastened to the back only so that the lower edge hung free and allowed fish to pass into, but not out of, the cod. Soles generally tended to work forward into the pockets, being helped by the back eddy of water, and were usually found there rather than in the actual cod.

In the early days of trawling the nets were generally made on board the smack, an operation known as " braiding ", the twine used for the belly was one size larger than that for the back, and was of hemp dipped in tar until the introduction of manilla. The mesh varied from 4 in. sq. in the back to 1½ in. in the cod and was measured by fingers, the smallest being two fingers braid, increasing to 3, 4 and 5 towards the mouth of the net. Usually the skipper braided the cod, the mate the belly, the third and fourth hands the bigger meshed portions and the boy the flapper. By the time he had finished his apprenticeship every mesh had passed through his fingers. This rough and ready method of measuring was good enough for nets made at sea, but when they had to be braided ashore, following the tremendous increase in trawling after the middle of the 19th century, a different gauge had to be found as women's fingers were not so thick as a man's. Pieces of hardwood, about 4 in. long, were shaped in sets to the sizes required, Grimsby using an oval spool, Barking a round one, the twine being knotted round it.

Trawl nets have always been made by hand, machinery never being successful in adapting itself to the peculiar shape and taper required. Strict accuracy not being essential, the girls and women could ply their wooden needles with lightning-like rapidity, the knot used being the sheet bend. These needles and the balls of twine can clearly be seen in Plate 54 of Lowestoft men repairing a trawl. Every smacksman had to know how to braid and mend a net.

At Grimsby a trawl net 42 ft. on the square was usually set up 200 to 220 meshes on the head, which was bent by clove hitches to the " bolch line ", this in turn was lashed to the beam at intervals of a few feet, the belly was 190 to 200 meshes. The " batings,". or diminishing pieces, joining the square, were 190 to 200 meshes braided down to 50, the cod was 10 to 12 ft. long and 4 ft. wide. The wings measured 43 ft. and were set up 190 or 200 meshes, braided down to 30 at the ends, with 55 in each wing, the remaining meshes forming the bosom. The ground part or belly was braided the same as the batings.

The ropes required were 20 fathom of bolch line, 16 fathom of ground rope, 3 fathom of codline, 9 fathom of headline, 1 long codline of 15 fathom, lashings for headline 1½ fathom each, 1 dandy bridle of 20 fathom, one pair of main bridles of 20 fathom each and a trawl warp 150 fathom in length. To complete the trawl gear were a dandy chain 3 fathom long with swivel and shackles, 2 trawl warp shackles, 2 main bridle shackles, 2 trawl warp and 4 bridle thimbles, 6 iron wedges for trawl heads, chafers for cod end and a flapper of 40 meshes.

The various pieces of netting were laid out on deck and the lower part of the square and the upper part of the batings were joined together, then the belly and wings. The net was now stretched along the deck with cod aft and the lower batings and belly joined together and pulled taut, the trawl being laced from the lower end upwards, wings and square stretched and laced from head downwards.   Next the turns were taken out of the bolch line and starting from the centre of the bosom the net was clove-hitched to the rope, making the spaces a little larger than the mesh.   Then the ground rope was stretched along the deck with bight aft and the for'ard ends were fastened to the bolch line, allowing 3 to 4 ft. for shrinking.   The flapper, 40 meshes in width, was now fastened to the back in line with the mouths of the pockets which were already laced up.

When the trawl was being towed the pressure of water expanded the net so that the mouths of the pockets were kept open, while the cod was greatly extended owing to its small mesh offering considerable resistance to the escape of water.

The trawl was towed by a 6 or 7 inch hemp or manilla rope, the "warp", 150 fathom long and made up of two lengths of 75 fathom spliced together.   One end was shackled to the mast in the warp room below deck, the other to the two spans or "bridles" which led to either end of the beam, where they were shackled to the swivel bolts in front of the trawl irons.   Their length varied according to the size of beam, being from 15 to 20 fathom each.   A smaller sized rope, the "dandy bridle", was made fast to that end of the beam which came astern when it was hoisted on board, the other end was hitched round the warp just above the shackle.   Fig. 12 shows a complete trawl net with all gear delineated, variations were to be found at the different fishing stations, and skipper's choice had considerable influence, but this tended to disappear when the nets were made ashore in a factory.

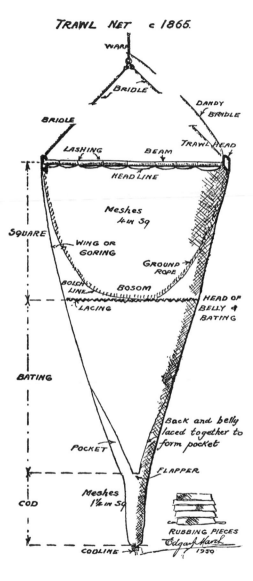

FIG. 12

In the 1870's a complete fit-out for a big smack cost from £70 to £80, and consisted of a double set of almost every part of the gear to provide against accidents.

A net lasted from 2 to 4 months according to nature of grounds worked over, with various parts renewed from time to time. The back, being exposed to the least wear, lasted the longest, the belly would need renewing twice, the cod 5 or 6 times before a net was finally condemned. A new hemp net cost about £9, manilla was more expensive, a net 50 ft. across the square running into about £16, but being stronger lasted longer. A trawl was dressed with coal tar, a better preservative than either tan or Stockholm tar.

There were two methods of working a trawl. In the West Country the warp was always hauled in over a roller at the bow, and led to a large geared winch for'ard of the mast. Astern was a smaller one, known as the " dandy wink ", stepped between head of companion and the port bulwark, and used for hoisting up the after end of the beam when the trawl was got on board (Fig. 13) also to be seen in Plate 26.

In the Barking and North Sea trawlers the warp was always worked on the port side and led in through a small gangway fitted with rollers, just abaft the main rigging, and the power was provided by a capstan. Amidships in all smacks was the pump head, usually known as the towpost or " dummy ", around which a couple of turns of warp were taken when the gear was being shot.

Generally speaking the cutter smacks of the early and mid-19th century were similar in design and build to the Barking well smack and the Brixham sloop (Plans 1 and 6). The majority were not fitted with wells, the fish being packed in baskets, " pads " or " flaskets ", and landed as early as possible after being caught. The exception was the " live plaice " trade where the choicest fish were kept in wells and sold alive in the London market. Icing and packing in wooden boxes or " trunks " were later introductions.

Smooth ground and a favourable tide of moderate strength were essential for trawling, as the gear was always towed in the same general direction but a little faster than the stream, both for ease of working, to keep the gear on the ground and check the net, which was lighter than the beam, from drifting forward and preventing the entrance of fish. The excess of speed of trawl over rate of tide varied from $\frac{1}{2}$ to $1\frac{1}{2}$ knots. When the smack arrived on her fishing ground trawling commenced just after the turn of the tide as she could then tow for 5 or 6 hours until the tide was done, during which time she might cover a distance of 12 to 15 miles. First the smack was put under easy sail in the direction she was going to tow, depending on wind suiting tide, so that a fairly straight course could be kept, hence the breeze had to be more or less abaft the beam.

All hands were on deck, the skipper aft to give his orders, see trawl all clear over the side, and attend to the after stopper and square the gear. The mate and third hand amidships streamed the trawl and veered the gear away, the fourth stood by to let go the fore-head, and the cook took the helm. These were the stations when shooting on the port tack, the more usual method as then the smack was already to leeward of her gear, but when shooting on the starboard tack the mate attended to the dandy bridle and the third hand the fore bridle, and all the gear had to be passed round the stern.

The bridles had already been shackled to the trawl heads and coiled down on deck, fore bridle for'ard, aft one just before the dandy winch. One end of the warp was fast to the mast, the other was taken up through the hatch, a couple of turns passed round the dummy, then led out through the gangway and in over the rail. The end was now shackled on the bridles which were then turned over clear for running.

At Brixham and Plymouth the warp passed out over a roller on port side of stem and the end was brought aft outside main rigging and then led in to be shackled to the bridles.

The dandy bridle was now run off the winch, the end passed round outside mizzen rigging, if smack was ketch rigged, and led for'ard to be made fast with a clove hitch to the warp just above the bridle shackle. The canting line was rove through the after trawl head and the cod end was tied up, a most essential point, otherwise no fish would be caught ! Some skippers preferred to keep the dandy bridle on the " wink ", slack away until beam was square and then run rope off the winch and lead it for'ard to be made fast to the warp. This method obviated the need for a canting line.

On the command " down trawl " the cod was thrown overboard, or " shot " as it was usually called, followed by the rest of the net until the whole trawl was clear and hanging from the beam, whose fore end was now lowered into the water and the fore bridle slacked away. The pressure of water brought the beam square to the stern, then the canting line, or dandy bridle, was let go and the gear slowly disappeared. More way was got on the smack and warp paid out to allow the trawl to sink to the bottom at some distance astern and to wind'ard of the vessel. Were the trawl allowed to sink nearly perpendicularly there was a considerable risk of the gear twisting and coming to rest on its back, an accident known as a " backfall ". Any irregular jerking of the warp as trawl was being towed along meant something was wrong, and the gear had to be heaved up and shot again.

Extra warp was now paid out according to the master's judgment, allowing for weather and tide, the nature of the ground and depth of water, and the kind of fish expected to be caught. Should the breeze freshen more warp was needed, in light weather less was out. When the required length was away and everything in order, the warp was made fast by a small rope, the " stopper ", of less breaking strain than the warp. A couple of turns of the stopper were taken round the dummy and the ends laid round the warp in opposite directions, so as to overlap and cross at each turn to ensure a good hold. The turns of the warp were now taken off the dummy and the whole strain of towing came on the stopper. If the trawl " became fast " the stopper would part and not the warp, thus saving the gear.

At Brixham the warp was already led in over the bow and secured to the winch, so that should the stopper part the loose warp flew overboard, the smack came up

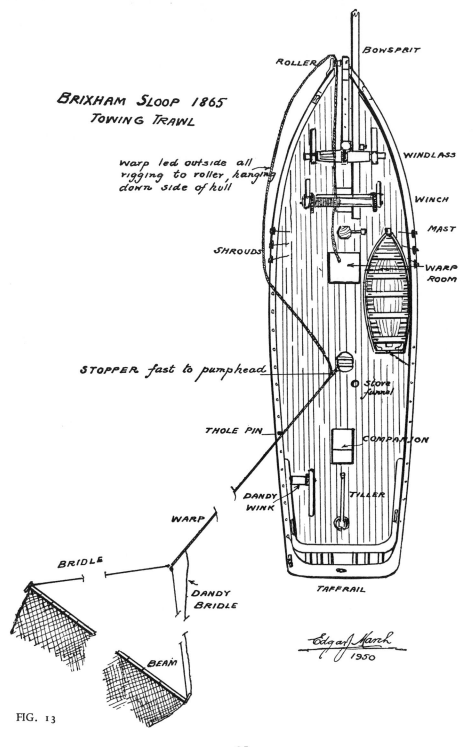

BOWSPRIT

ROLLER

BRIXHAM SLOOP 1865
TOWING TRAWL

*warp led outside all
rigging to roller, hanging
down side of hull*

WINDLASS

WINCH

MAST

SHROUDS

WARP
ROOM

STOPPER *fast to pumphead*

Store
funnel

THOLE PIN

COMPANION

DANDY
WINK

TILLER

WARP

BRIDLE

DANDY
BRIDLE

TAFFRAIL

BEAM

Edgar J March
1950

FIG. 13

into the wind and lost way. In the North Sea smacks, where the warp led in through a gangway on the port side, a bight of warp had to be taken for'ard outside the main rigging, hauled in over the roller at stem and secured to the windlass in order to attain the same result.

Owing to the large mainsail set for driving power smacks always had a tendency to fly up into the wind, and to avoid carrying excessive weather helm it was usual to make the trawl do the work, by keeping the warp at such an angle with the length of the vessel as to steer the course set. Should the wind be so fair that the smack could run nearly before it the warp was led over the stern, or more commonly, over the weather quarter close to the taffrail, and it was prevented from slipping for'ard by a stout thole pin inserted into one of the many holes bored in the rail. If the wind was on the beam the warp was carried farther for'ard and its position adjusted by rule of thumb and observation of course made, allowance being given for a good deal of leeway by heading the vessel nearer the wind—" making her look higher "— than her proper course. Should the pressure of the mainsail tend to swing the stern round it was opposed by the heavy drag of the trawl, which pulled it back and kept the smack straight on her course within the not very precise limits necessary for working with the tide over the fishing ground.

The resistance of the trawl was tremendous and made the vessel squat down on her stern, which was wide and flat to give maximum bearing surface. This can clearly be seen in Plate 55 of a Yarmouth smack towing a lee tide with the warp led out over the starboard quarter, when towing a weather tide it was kept well aft.

A speed of 8 to 9 knots free would be reduced to 1 to $1\frac{1}{2}$ knots when trawling, so plenty of wind was the smacksmen's prayer and winter the great trawling time. A " reef and topsail " breeze was the favourite amount, when a smack could carry a jib-headed topsail over a single-reefed mainsail.

Once the gear was down one man stayed on deck to look out for any change in the wind, trim sails, and feel the warp from time to time to see if the trawl was working properly. By placing a hand on the warp outside the rail vibrations were felt as the iron heads passed over ridges, etc., any irregular jerking meant rough ground or the gear not keeping steady on the bottom. It was the custom of some skippers to place their teeth on the warp, put a finger in each ear and feel the vibrations, which would give them a rough idea of the nature of the bottom. Such was a crude but effective method which enabled the pioneers to work over the as yet uncharted North Sea.

Whilst the trawl was down the rest of the crew turned in or occupied themselves in the hundred and one jobs necessary to keep a smack in first-class condition. When working for soles and other flat fish the usual rate of towing was $\frac{1}{2}$ to $1\frac{1}{2}$ knots faster than the tide, but in the West Country during the hake season it was necessary to keep the net almost clear of the ground and tow at a rate of 2 to $2\frac{1}{2}$ knots. To do this every stitch of canvas had to be carried, big tow foresail, and balloon jibs, even square sails being set on the weather side if the wind was well aft.   These can be seen in Plan 13 of the Plymouth cutter *Erycina* on page 333.

When the tide was done, or the limits of the fishing ground reached, the hands were called up from below, the stopper cast off and the slack of the warp went overboard, so that the smack soon swung round with her head to the trawl and then to the wind.   In the West of England, where the warp was got in over the bows, the foresail was dropped and any light sails taken in, the boy went below into the warp room just abaft the mast and two of the men commenced heaving in, a long and wearisome task, taking at least three-quarters of an hour in favourable weather, two to three hours in bad, with the smack rolling and pitching all the time.   As the warp came in dripping wet it was coiled away below by the lad who ran round and round, flaking it down ready for the next shooting.   When the shackles joining warp to main bridles came in, the end of the dandy bridle, which had been made fast just above the junction, was cast off, taken aft and brought in over the stern to the dandy wink, the men continuing heaving until the beam came to the surface.   Then it was swung alongside and the after end hoisted up astern by the dandy bridle and secured.   Next the heavy fish tackle, or the fore halyard, was hooked to the shackle of the fore side of for'ard trawl iron, and hauled upon until it could be brought in over the rail and made fast to the shrouds.   The net was now gathered in by hand and stowed on top of the beam and rail until only the cod was left in the water, and if luck was in it might contain anything from a half to three-quarters of a ton of fish. A selvagee strop was next passed round the upper part of the bag, the fish tackle hooked on to it and the fall taken to the winch which slowly hoisted the cod out of the water, two of the crew swung it in over the side and cast off the cod line, so releasing the catch which fell in a mass on the deck.

Unless the gear was good there was always the danger of such an accident as happened to the 39-ton *Thrive*, built in 1867 at Southtown.   On the 30th August, 1901, when fishing 40 miles E.N.E. of Leman Lightship, the block strop on the tackle carried away and one man was killed.   Another instance occurred on the 10th February, 1883, when the 43-ton *Fear Not* of Yarmouth was fishing 55 miles E.N.E. of Yarmouth in a S.S.W. gale and the warp broke and one man lost his life.

It was more than advisable to keep out of the bight of the warp when towing, even though it meant passing along the other side of the deck.   Failure to observe this precaution cost the life of one of the crew of the *Good Hope* when she was trawling on the 28th November, 1893, some 35 miles E. by S. of Lowestoft.   The stopper broke and the warp ran out, taking the man with it.   A similar case happened on board another Lowestoft smack the 49-ton *Sappho* in February, 1908.

A different method of hauling was employed in the North Sea smacks where the warp was led through a gangway in the port bulwarks to a round-about capstan amidships.   About the sixties an improved type of mechanical capstan was invented by Skipper Baley of Hull, two men faced aft and two for'ard and turned winch handles.

This was killing work in the iron cold of winter, at first the handles flew round but when the warp was up and down the strain was terrific, the men pushing and tugging, panting and heaving, slipping and cursing, as inch by inch the heavy gear came alongside in the pitch blackness of a rain-soaked night, in sleet and snow, or the sultry heat of a summer evening. Then the fish had to be gutted, washed, drained and packed in trunks ready for the carrier, should the smack be working with a fleet, or put away in ice in the fish hold if " single-boating ".

A hard life indeed, but not without its rewards as subsequent stories will tell, yet in too many instances there was little or nothing to show for a lifetime's toil on the heaving wastes of the North Sea or Channel. All had been swallowed up in living expenses, with dependence on one's children in old age, otherwise the almshouse or union.

The introduction of steam driven capstans in the late seventies lightened the heavy manual labour aboard as the warp was hauled, bowsprit run out, sails hoisted and even reefs pulled down by leading the fall of halyard or tackle to the capstan. Some of the first were designed and built by Smith, Stephenson & Co. of Grimsby, steam being raised at a pressure of 80 lbs. or thereabouts to drive a small reciprocating engine alongside, both below deck. The crankshaft turned a long shaft extending for'ard across the floor of the fish room to the bulkhead where a bevel wheel engaged in a horizontal geared wheel attached to a vertical spindle passing up through the deck. On its upper end was another small gear wheel which in turn drove gearing at the foot of capstan (Fig. 14). As might be supposed a lot of power was lost in the train of gears.

Similar capstans were built by Ransome, Sims of Ipswich, but it was not until 1884, when the late Mr. Wm. Garrood thought of the idea of taking the steam through the hollow spindle to an engine on top of the capstan, that a satisfactory result was achieved on half the consumption of coal. Soon practically every deep-sea smack was fitted with one and I am indebted to Messrs. Elliot and Garrood of Beccles, who kindly placed data and drawings at my disposal, and they tell me over 6,000 patent capstans have been supplied to the fishing fleets of the world (Fig. 15). Their HHI type, as fitted in sailing trawlers, only weighs 15 cwt., dia. of barrel is $19\frac{1}{2}$ in., height 3 ft. $6\frac{1}{4}$ in., a cylinder bore of $3\frac{7}{8}$ in. and stroke of $4\frac{1}{2}$ in., and it can haul any trawl up to 50 ft. beam, winding speed being $2\frac{3}{4}$ fathom a minute at 100 r.p.m., or 11 fathom at 400 r.p.m.

It was now the job of the man left on deck to do the stoking so that a good head of steam was available when the time came to haul the gear. Unfortunately several accidents occurred through tampering with the safety valves to get more steam pressure. The 36-ton *Fidget*, built at Yarmouth in 1872, was lost in this way on the 18th March 1893, when fishing 85 miles N.E. by E. of Yarmouth. The 53-ton *Ant* of Yarmouth had an engine installed in August, 1885, at a cost of £125 15s. 0d., and was burnt out less than 4 years later, involving the Insurance Society in a loss of over £600.

GRIMSBY STEAM CAPSTAN
C. 1876.

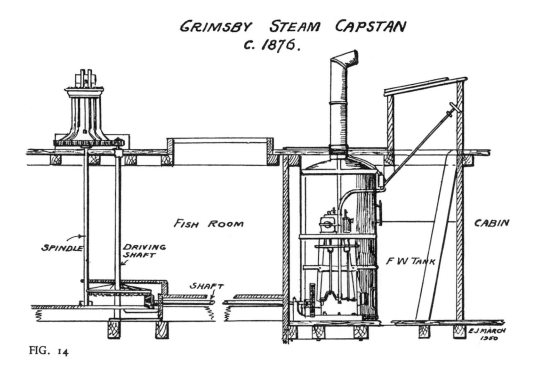

SPINDLE

DRIVING SHAFT

FISH ROOM

SHAFT

F W TANK

CABIN

E J MARCH 1950

FIG. 14

ELLIOTT & GARROOD'S STEAM CAPSTAN

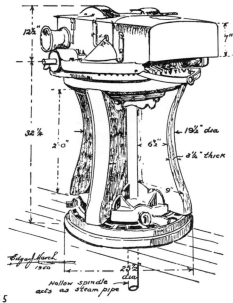

12½"

7"

32¼"

2'-0"

6½"

19½" dia

3½" thick

9"

Edgar March 1950

25½" dia

Hollow spindle acts as steam pipe

FIG. 15

When hauling was in progress on the 70-ton *Surf*, built at Yarmouth 1875, the capstan spindle broke owing to excessive strain and one of the crew was killed on the 15th January, 1896.

During the 1880's experiments were made with wire rope instead of manilla for the warp, which was becoming very unwieldy to handle and splice, often being 8 in. circ. in the largest smacks. Unfortunately wire is difficult to handle round a capstan and once kinked is almost impossible to straighten out. This trouble was overcome in steam trawlers by winding in on drums, but the sailing smack used rope to the end of her days, except in one or two rare instances. I recall that the big Mission smack, *Sir William Archibald*, used a wire trawl rope.

A new technique for working and hauling the trawl came in following the introduction of steam capstans and I give the practice at Lowestoft between the two wars as described to me by my good friend Skipper J. T. Crouch, who has been of invaluable assistance in giving me the benefit of his long years of experience.

His people were all fishermen and he first went to sea in February, 1886, at the age of 11 years and 11 months, signing on as cook in the 50-ton *John Frederick*, built at Lowestoft in 1877, and winner of the 1881 Smack Regatta, then in the 55-ton *Lance*, L.T.363, built at Brixham in 1868, followed by a turn in *Albatross*, L.T.546. All these smacks were well-known entries at the Lowestoft regattas, *Albatross* being a very fine vessel, sometimes used by her owner as a yacht. Registering 49 tons, she was built at Teignmouth in 1877, and was lost on the 27th August, 1897, after being in collision with the Norwegian barque *Grelle*, 25 miles east of Lowestoft, two of her crew being drowned.

Next followed spells in the 56-ton *Forester*, L.T.211, built in 1888, and *Olive Leaf*, L.T.648, of 50 tons, built at Lowestoft in 1874, before becoming deck-hand in *Skimmer of the Sea*, D.H.814, of 46 tons, built at Plymouth in 1871, and in *Blantyre*, D.H.63, both however owned at Lowestoft. *Blantyre* was a famous racing smack, winner of the 1879 race by a few seconds after one of the finest races seen as it was sailed in a strong E.S.E. wind. Built at Brixham in 1876, she registered 47 tons and was a total loss with her crew of five, following collision with the Norwegian barque *Dora* on the 8th September, 1894, about 45 miles N.E. by E. of Lowestoft. Before this disaster Mr. Crouch went as third hand in the 56-ton *Laurel*, L.T.26, built in 1892, then to *Lillie & Ethel*, 63 tons, built 1890, and in 1895 he became mate in *Counsellor*, L.T.267, which was sunk by U-Boat on the 27th July, 1918, 2½ miles N. of the Haisborough Lightvessel. Next he was in *Emblem*, L.T.97, also a victim to submarine attack as she was sunk on the 7th September, 1915, 44 miles E.S.E. of Lowestoft.

In 1900 Mr. Crouch became master of *Lily of Devon*, L.T.96, built that year at a cost of some £700. When attempting to make harbour she drove ashore on Lowestoft beach on the 21st November, 1927, in a full E. by S. gale with a very heavy sea running. Caught by the tide she missed the entrance and was carried into broken

50 MAKING FOR THE TRAWL
BASIN, 15th JANUARY, 1939
Our Merit, L.T.535, 39 tons, built
at Brixham, 1914. Two reefs are
down in main and mizzen and one
in the foresail, note how lacing is
passed round the hoops on mainmast.

51 TAKING IN SAIL
May Queen, L.T.128, 50 tons,
built at Brixham, 1900. She has
lost her trawling gear, only a
broken beam is on the port side.
Ahead is *Reliance*, L.T.422, 54
tons, built at Oulton Broad, 1903.

52 DRYING TRAWL NETS
Forget-me-not, L.T.1252, lost with all hands November, 1927.

53 GEAR MADE UP ON DECK
Forget-me-not, L.T.1252, 33 tons, built at Lowestoft, 1922. Note for'ard trawl head, ground rope with rounding, rope bridle, anchor, main halyard coil, and towpost just for'ard of hoodway.

54 MENDING A TRAWL NET
In foreground is the ground rope with its rounding and chain ticklers, one man is sitting on the spare beam, note wooden needles and ball of twine.

MENDING THE TRAWL NET

55 YARMOUTH SMACK TOWING A LEE TIDE
The tremendous drag of the trawl is making the stern squat down in the water, the topsail is set a'weather.

56　*LILY OF DEVON*, L.T.96
　　33 tons, built at Galmpton, 1900.
　　Ashore on South Sand, Lowestoft,
　　21st November, 1927.

57　SKIPPER J. T. CROUCH
　　At tiller of *Master Hand*, L.T.1203,
　　built at Rye, 1920.

shallow water where she bumped heavily on the sand (Plate 56). The crew of three took to the rigging, within two minutes the lifeboat *Agnes Cross* was launched and succeeded in veering down under the smack's stern but was badly damaged. The crew were taken off and with all hands hauling in the cable the lifeboat gradually worked clear of the surf. Her port washstrake was fractured, five ridge rope stanchions badly bent, handrail round engine room casing and motor starting handle broken, and the teakwood hatch casing smashed to pieces. Her coxswain, Albert Spurgeon, was awarded a silver medal and he and his crew received an additional monetary reward for their meritorious work.

To return to Skipper Crouch. From 1900 to 1915 he fitted out and sailed 7 new smacks, all for one owner, " not a bad record " as he proudly writes. During that time he had two rather nasty experiences. In 1911 when *Forget-me-not* was lying at anchor in Padstow Pool the anchor dragged in a gale and she drove ashore on the rocks, being high and dry at low water, but luckily escaping damage. Of 25 tons register, she was built at Galmpton in 1911, being one of the fleet belonging to Painter Bros. and named after flowers and shrubs, others being *Hawthorn*, *Acacia*, *Lily of Devon*, *Rose of Devon* and *Picotee*. I give the second incident in the skipper's own words :—

" In 1914 just after war broke out we were fishing off Lowestoft when we got a mine in our trawl, which exploded just before we got it on board. It gave us a shake-up I can tell you. It must have exploded downwards or else we should not have been here now. We got the remnants of the trawl on board and made for home. On arrival we found that the foremast had been unstepped and sprung in three places and we were leaking a bit, so after re-fitting we went to the West Coast to fish out of Padstow until April, 1915, when I came home to Lowestoft, but things were a bit grim, the Government were laying vessels up as the Germans were sinking a lot of them. I got fed-up with that and went straight to the Naval Base and joined up in the Navy as skipper, and went away in May the same year to Dover where I was stationed all through the war and had a few rough experiences. I dare say you remember the Channel raid with the *Broke* and *Swift*, and Evans of the *Broke*, well I was in that but came out all right. Another time we were laying mine nets off Ostend and got fired on from the shore but escaped once more, the next I was at Dunkerque and got injured in the knee during an air raid, so had to return to Dover and they sent me to Deal Hospital where I was nine weeks, that was Christmas, 1917. After coming out I got ten days sick leave, returned to Dover and got a light job ashore for a time, then off to sea again as mail boat and relief ship for the mine vessels that laid across the Channel from Folkestone to Cape Grisnez. That lasted until the end of the war, then back to Lowestoft in the November and two years fishing in smacks with one man. He sold out and I went to Rye to fit out *Master Hand* in 1920, had her for nine months and went back to Rye to fit out *Helping Hand* and 3½ years in her. Then I had three years of steam trawlers, and back to smacks again, finishing up in 1933, as I thought I had had enough of going to sea, so started as fish packer on the market until war broke out again, when I offered my services but was told I was too old. Now I am on the shelf at 73 and drawing the magnificent sum of 10s. a week O.A.P., and that is the end.''

Concerning other incidents the skipper writes :—

'' During the earlier times of my going to sea we were dismasted twice, once in *Olive Leaf* and once in *Counsellor* and we had to be towed home by another smack. I took part in saving two Norwegian crews in a gale of wind, we saved all of them, 20 in one crew, 25 in the other, without mishap owing to good skill and seamanship. They were sailors in those days and knew how to handle a boat in a gale of wind. Present day trawlermen don't know much about sailing vessels, they are all steam nowadays, more is the pity as I always found the sailing smack up to the mark, and I have had a go at both of them.''

Skipper Crouch told me that once he was setting the storm jib in *Helping Hand* when the cry came '' Look out, water ! '' and a big sea came over the port side, taking him overboard. Then he was washed back into the boat on the starboard side, out again to the mizzen rigging, where he clung to the light iron, grabbed the net and the next backwash brought him on board. In all his years as master he never lost a ship or a man.

Plate 57 shows the skipper at the tiller of *Master Hand*, L.T.1203, and is from a photo he kindly loaned me.

Describing a trip from Lowestoft he writes :—

'' If the wind is from S.E. to N.E., going round westwards, we can go from the harbour under our own sail, that is if you are to the east of the swing bridge, if not you have to tow out by the tug no matter how the wind is, that is the rule in sailing smacks. After getting clear of the sands we stow up all gear and proceed to the fishing grounds which may be perhaps 20 to 60 miles out. We start operations if the tide is favourable, should we be shooting the trawl off the port side, which is the easy way, we have to get good way on for what we call ' streaming the gear '. We put the net over first then the skipper shouts out ' Let go for'ard ' and he streams the gear fair across the stern with what we call the ' quarter strop ', then he lets go of the beam and the bridles run out until they come to the trawl warp, which has two turns round the towpost. When the trawl is all square the skipper says ' Wear away ' until we get the amount of warp out, which may be from 40 to 60 fathoms, it all depends what wind there is and the state of the tide, if a lee or weather one. The bridles were 22 fathom, rope or wire.

The other side of the picture is shooting round the stern. That means getting all the gear round to the starboard side, passing everything round outside rigging and mizzen sheet, bridles, dandy bridle and warp, which has two turns on the towpost or dummy as some call it. Then the net is payed out off the port side as before, brought square across the stern till everything comes tight to the trawl warp, but this time it is payed out to leeward out of the gangway until we get the required amount out. Then warp is legged up and turns taken off dummy and two turns put on the capstan ready for any emergency. We used a 110 fathom warp, all in one piece.''

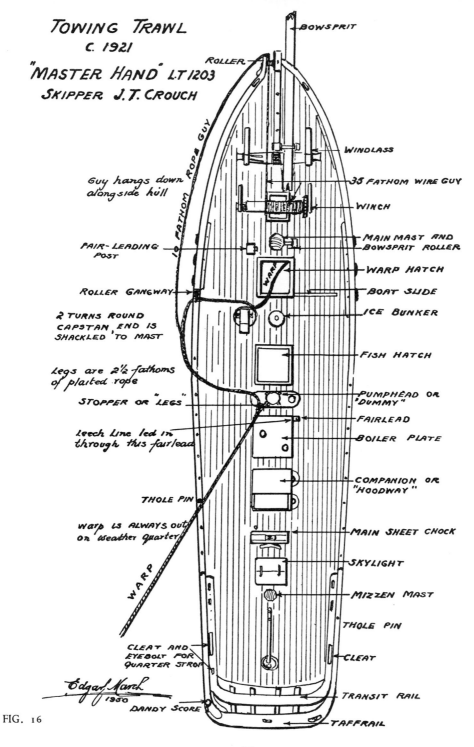

TOWING TRAWL
C. 1921
"MASTER HAND" L.T 1203
SKIPPER J.T. CROUCH

BOWSPRIT

ROLLER

WINDLASS

35 FATHOM WIRE GUY

Guy hangs down
alongside hull

WINCH

MAIN MAST AND
BOWSPRIT ROLLER

FAIR-LEADING
POST

WARP HATCH

BOAT SLIDE

ROLLER GANGWAY

ICE BUNKER

2 TURNS ROUND
CAPSTAN, END IS
SHACKLED TO MAST

FISH HATCH

Legs are 2½ fathoms
of plaited rope

PUMPHEAD OR
"DUMMY"

STOPPER OR "LEGS"

FAIRLEAD

Leech Line led in
through this fairlead

BOILER PLATE

COMPANION OR
"HOODWAY"

THOLE PIN

Warp is ALWAYS out
on weather quarter

MAIN SHEET CHOCK

SKYLIGHT

WARP

MIZZEN MAST

THOLE PIN

CLEAT AND
EYEBOLT FOR
QUARTER STROP

CLEAT

Edgar March
1950

TRANSIT RAIL

DANDY SCORE

FIG. 16

TAFFRAIL

10 FATHOM ROPA GUY

WARP

Plate 58 shows preparations being made for shooting gear on *Boy Clifford*, L.T. 1202. The fore bridle is coiled down on deck, ground rope is lying partly over rail and the fish tackle is still hooked to the eyebolt in deck. A fresh breeze is blowing and the smack is carrying a little weather helm, with a relieving tackle on the tiller.

In *Master Hand*, L.T.1203, the warp was secured to the dummy with two legs of $2\frac{1}{2}$ fathom of plaited rope, which gripped better than ordinary rope. It then led in through the gangway, twice round the capstan and down the main hatch where the end was shackled to the mast. The whole strain of towing was now on the stopper, but between the legs and the gangway a rope guy, 10 fathom in length, was made fast to the warp and led outside all rigging to the bows where it came in over the roller on port side of stem and was attached to 35 fathom of wire round the winch (Fig. 16). Should the stopper part, the warp flew overboard, but the strain was now on the rope guy which brought the smack up head to wind, then the guy was cast off and the warp brought in by the capstan.

Normally the smack was hove-to before hauling-in commenced, either by pulling the foresail sheet a'weather as can be seen in Plate 60, or the foresail was dropped and the halyards belayed to the second pin in the rail for'ard of the windlass.

Plate 60 is from a photograph taken on board *Boy Clifford* in July, 1930, and shows the splice in the warp about to come round the capstan, the " gate " over the roller gangway is open, the foresail is a'weather and in the right foreground is the head of the towpost or dummy, which takes the pump " brake " or handle.

The dandy line was 22 fathom of wire, and when the beam was alongside, the for'ard end of line was unbent from the warp, taken round the " dandy score " on port taffrail and led to the capstan which provided the power to hoist the beam up to the rail aft where it was secured with a rope stopper, the " quarter strop ", which belayed round the heavy cleat on the port cavil rail. Next the for'ard end of the beam was lifted up by hooking the fish tackle to the shackle on the head iron, then the ground rope was hauled inboard by the " leech line ", which consisted of $5\frac{1}{2}$ fathom of wire and rope, already fast to the centre of the ground rope with the other end secured round the beam near the for'ard trawl iron (Fig. 17). This line was now unbent, led through a sheave on the starboard side of boiler plate, and on through a snatch block to the capstan which did the work.

Plate 59 shows one of the crew of *Boy Clifford* leaning over the rail to unbend the leech line from the beam, the fish tackle is hooked into the shackle which also takes the thimble of the wire bridle.

The beam having been secured and ground rope brought inboard the next job for the men was to heave in the net with fingers clawing at the wet meshes, adapting their stance to the motion of the slippery deck (Plate 61). A vicious roll or a false step and a man might be overboard in two shakes of a jib sheet. When the cod came in sight a strop was put round the for'ard end and hooked to the fish tackle.

The fall led to the capstan which soon hoisted the bag high enough for the codline to be untied and so release the contents.

After the gear had been shot again the next job was to sort and clean the fish and I give this in the skipper's own words :—

" When you shoot the trawl for a lee tide you keep it down for about $5\frac{1}{2}$ hours if all goes well and then haul. If you are going to shoot again for the weather tide, that is if there is wind enough, you keep trawl down until the tide is just on the change again, so that you come round clear of your gear, that is of course according to which side you shot the gear for the lee tide. Well, between tides, you gut and wash your fish, put them in baskets to drain, then down into the fish hold and the skipper puts the fish into ice in the fish pounds, in tiers, with ice in between, the rough stuff, if any, for the bottom tier. In winter you put about four baskets to a tier, but in summer not more than three so that the fish keep in better condition for the market. In winter you need not be so particular in the icing, but you have to be in summer, as your trip may last 6 to 7 days, according to the amount of fish you get. If you got 40 or 50 boxes in winter that's not bad, for each box contains 7 to 8 stone of fish, but in summer perhaps they are smaller, unless you strike a lucky patch which sometimes happens in both seasons of the year."

I have thought it well to use the skipper's own words as much as possible to ensure authenticity.

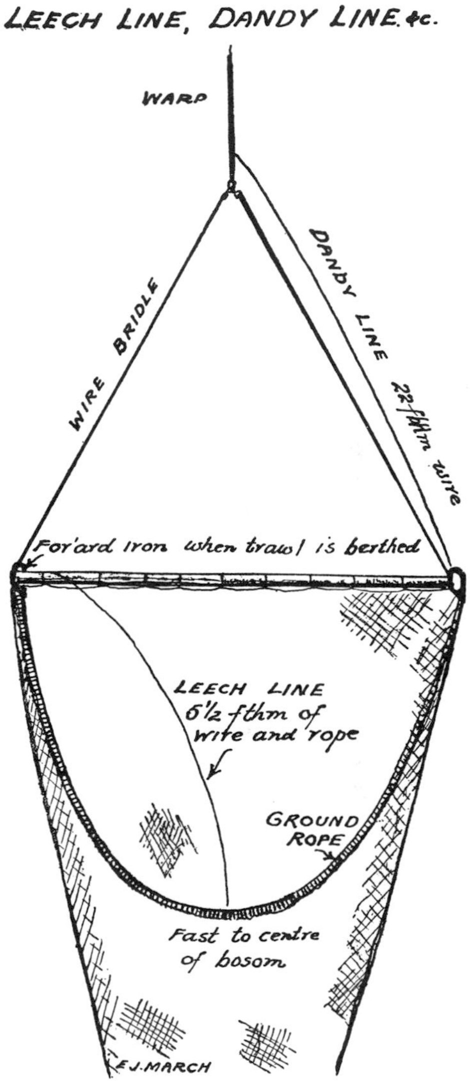

The photographs were taken in the sunshine of a summer day, but think of the job of hauling in the net in the blackness of a winter night, with snow clinging to the weather side of ropes and spars, lying in the folds of the sails, covering the deck,

FIG. 17

drifting into the small boat and piling up against the inside of the lee bulwarks, blocks all frozen so that the sheaves will not render, fierce squalls driving down, the heave of the sea hiding the lights of nearby smacks which presently reappear like stars twinkling on the horizon. The stiff oilskin cuffs lacerated the men's wrists which were often covered with ulcers and boils caused by the constant chafing, and fingers cut almost to the bone with salt water cracks. Then the job of gutting fish frozen as hard as if carved out of wood and this had to be done conscientiously with no scamping, or putrefaction would soon set in. The only light the fitful gleams of the moon or a feeble lantern as often as not likely to be blown out when most needed. The introduction of acetylene lamps brought about an improvement in deck illumination. Always there was the risk of serious injury as the smack rolled and pitched, sometimes a man would be flung against the winch or jammed under some of the gear lying on deck. The price paid for keeping the market supplied with fish was a high one in maimed and lost lives.

CHAPTER SEVEN

LIFE ON BOARD

Now to turn to the duties of a crew and the life on board a North Sea smack. The boy was supposed to be able to cook for the whole crew in a clean and proper manner, keep the cabin and utensils clean, especially the highly polished square copper kettle and see this was always full of boiling hot tea in winter, or cold drinking water in summer. Before galvanized tanks came into general use the fresh water was carried in barrels lashed near the tiller and fitted with a large bunghole to allow passage for a narrow tin tube—the '' didal ''—used to draw the water, another of the boy's jobs. He also saw that all tools, etc., reef lacings, fenders made from old rope and known as '' tiers '', and other small stuff were in their proper places and ready for use. He learned to braid and mend a net, the making of the flapper being his special duty, also reef points, usually called '' nettles '' or '' knittles ''. He learned how to box the compass and steer by it in fine weather, taking the helm when the trawl was shot, and he coiled away the warp when heaving-up. Then he was responsible for cleaning up the deck, removing the fish scales and getting rid of the '' brash '' or rubbish brought up in the trawl. With the help of the deck hand he trimmed and kept in their proper place all lights, flares, foghorn, spare pump gear and bell. Last, but not least, he obeyed all lawful commands although how a boy of 12 to 14 was to know whether they were lawful or not is not stated. He was hardly likely to carry a copy of Board of Trade regulations and look up section so-and-so, paragraph what-you-will, every time he was told to do anything, and he would have had short shift if he did not jump to it when an order was given.

In addition to being able to do everything expected of the cook, the fourth or deck hand had to steer and manage the smack in fine weather and take his watch whether fishing or sailing, and keep hold and fo'c'sle clean. He was expected to know how to handle a boat in fine weather, splice small ropes and whip them, make nettles, gaskets and sennet, braid a cod end and learn to mend small holes in the net. He had to know the marks on the lead line and be able to take soundings, tend the trawl in fine weather, keep sails in their proper places and know them by their marks —the pieces of twine with knots in the ends—so that he could find them in the dark. He made the thole pins for the rail and boat, helped to prepare fish for market and assisted the cook to trim the lights.

The third hand was supposed to know all the fourth hand had to do and be an ordinary seaman as well, competent to keep a watch of six or eight hours, manage the smack with the gear down, make himself acquainted with the set of the tide, and know the Rule of the Road. He had to be able to bend an anchor and let it go, fix a trawl, prepare gear for shooting, splice warps and bridles—these ran up to 8 in. circ. with hemp—and make stoppers. He had to be skilled at mending or braiding the net, attend to the rigging, especially looking out for chafes which he had to protect with chafing gear. He helped the fourth hand attend to the pump, hold and fo'c'sle, managed the boat when delivering fish to the cutter and did his share of gutting and icing the catch.

The mate had to be an able seaman as well as knowing all the duties of the third hand, he could set up, braid and fix a trawl net, bend and shoot the gear, and manage a boat in rough weather. He had to know the set of the tide on the various fishing grounds with the prevalent depth of water, be an expert leadsman, know how to trawl at all times and be well acquainted with the nature of the grounds. He was held responsible to the master for all stores which had to be ready for instant use, he took charge of the smack in the master's absence, either at sea or in port, had to know the various lighthouses, lightships, buoys and beacons, and the Rule of the Road, and like all the other members of the crew he obeyed the lawful commands of the master.

When he took charge of a smack it was the master's duty to overhaul rigging, sails, running gear, anchors, chain, pumps, side and masthead lights, see the compass was correct and order all provisions, ice and stores for the voyage. He had to know the duties of every man on board and see he did his duty, never forgetting that he was master and answerable to the owner.

Being able to handle his vessel skilfully at all times was not enough after the 1880's, the skipper had to know how to use a chart and find his position on it by the soundings taken, be able to find his latitude by meridian altitude of the sun, know the time of high water, know all the navigation marks and the nature of all his various fishing grounds, be an able seaman as well as a good fisherman, competent to handle his command in all weathers and pick up a boat in bad weather with safety. He had to see the warp was properly secured to the mast before fishing, inspect all lights and see they were trimmed, lit and in their places at sundown. He saw to the icing and cleaning of the fish and arranged for its sale in the market if necessary. When going to sea he had to navigate the smack himself until free of danger and above all, be ready at any moment, night or day, to come on deck when called and use his superior knowledge in all emergencies. It was his duty to see that his owner's property was used with the greatest care, no provisions wasted, acting as if everything was his own and not another man's property, see that the smack was kept clean and seaworthy, and ALWAYS KEEP A GOOD LOOK-OUT.

In other words, every member of the crew was expected to know his job and do it to the best of his ability.

Naturally life on board the old sailing smacks varied considerably, some writers have stressed the squalid side, the verminous cabins, uncouth men and sordid life. Such undoubtedly was the case in certain instances, just as slums are found in beautiful cities, but one would have to go a long way to find a finer type than the average smacksman, who at his best was a splendid seaman, taking a pride in his craft and calling. Granted, as the world to-day calls " educated " many were illiterate and unable to read or write, but that does not form character and to my mind better such a man whose word was his bond than some of the slick individuals masquerading in various walks of life to-day, who have misused years of free education and advantages undreamed of in the days of which I write.

I prefer however to let the men speak for themselves as to conditions prevailing in the heyday of sail, and who knew from personal experience what the life was like. Once again I turn to many letters written to me, some, alas, by men who have slipped their cables since they told me their reminiscences. My friend Mr. Harry George can speak at first-hand of the Yarmouth long-boomers, having sailed in *Lizzie*, 50 tons, built Ipswich, 1859.

" Well, my dear old dad was the skipper when I first went to sea and the year was 1887. His pay was 14s. for a 7 day week, 24 hours a day, and 1s. on the pound of the smack's earnings. I think we earned about £100 for the two months with the Columbia fleet, so he would lift another five pounds over and above his fourteen bob a week. A Yarmouth smack carried six hands, skipper, mate, third hand, fourth hand, deck hand and cook. The skipper's pay was one penny per hour, asleep or awake, and one shilling on the pound which was called poundage. They settled up about every two months and if the earnings of the smack amounted to £150 and the skipper drew £7 10s. he was very pleased with himself, but too often his takings after two month's trawling were perhaps £4 or £5. The mate got 18s. a week, the third hand 16s., fourth hand 14s., deck chap 12s. and the cook 10s. per week, sometimes 9s.

For dinner they had roast beef, suet pudding—" duff "—or perhaps Norfolk dumplings, that is if the beef was still fresh. After about a week they would have to fall back on salt beef, suet pudding and treacle and spuds, all boiled together in sea water. Believe me it was lovely grub, anyhow the crew were fat and strong, with hearts like lions. For breakfast they had fried fish, and what fish ! Cleaned and got ready on the day it was caught, not put in ice, for after a fish has been iced it loses about half its flavour. That is why the fish you get from shops is almost tasteless, it's been too long in ice.

Many of the skippers were uneducated, that is in the sense in which education is generally understood, some were absolutely illiterate, but they were Masters of Art at their job and their seamanship was superb. They were men who, had they received the necessary education and joined the Senior Service, and if promotion had gone by merit, could easily have become Captains, Commodores and Admirals in Her Britannic Majesty's Navy. They navigated by an old plain card compass, which if correct was more by accident than anything else, for it was hardly ever adjusted. The leadline was their main stay. They would sail from Yarmouth, shape a course for Smith's Knoll lightship, which in those days lay E.N.E. 21 miles, she is further south now, from there east-north-east 120 miles to Clay Deeps, trawl there for about nine or ten days and after keeping their reckoning with the lead line and apology for a compass would make a good landfall on the return journey. In those days there were lots of square-rigged ships knocking about the North Sea and if the weather was cloudy so that a captain could not get a sight of the sun to determine the ship's position, he would approach a smack and sing out 'Fisherman ahoy, how does the Smith's Knoll bear of you?' So sure of his position was the smack skipper that he would reply and give the bearing without a moment's hesitation.

I was never skipper of a smack but did a bit of trawling for a few years up to the age of 19, after that I went to sea in steam drifters and was skipper of *Puffin*, Y.H. 414, the second one to be registered at Yarmouth. However even now it would be very little trouble for me to take a sailing trawler to sea, so here goes.

We landed a trip of fish yesterday, after we had packed them in trunks, carted them to the Station and put them in trucks to be sent to Billingsgate, we washed out the fish lockers, swilled the decks down and then put on our go-ashore togs and made for home. Says the mate to the skipper 'what time in the morning?' The skipper replies '8 o'clock, I've ordered the tug and I shall be here at 10'. At 8 in the morning all hands were aboard and took in the ice, about 3 tons of it, water, coal for cabin and donkey boiler, stores, that is grub and anything which we required for another trip. At 10 the 'old man' would turn up, the tug being alongside. After shaking hands with the owner who sometimes saw us off, he stepped aboard, got hold of the tiller and sang out 'Let go aft'. The tug would start to move and next order would be 'let go for'rard', then away we went down the Yare towards the harbour mouth. On the way down the river 'Set the mainsail and mizzen, up tops'l, out bowsprit and big jib' (Plates 62 and 62a).

When out of harbour the skipper, having decided to try his luck in the Silver Pits, would go through the roads and make for the Cockle Lightship. From there we shape a course to Haisboro' Lightship, by this time it would be about 2 p.m. The mate and deckhand would take the watch, 'Keep her N.N.E.' says skipper 'and put the log over'. Dinner would be at 4 p.m. when we shifted watches. After dinner, the smack being then in the open sea, the skipper would decide on a nap. He was at all calls and took no regular watch. His orders were 'Let me know if there is any change of wind or weather and be sure to give me a call when the log says 60 miles'.

At 60 miles from the Haisboro' light, if skipper was still below, they would call him. First order 'Arm the lead and have a cast'. The smack would then be put head to wind until she had lost way, over would go the lead. '30 fathom, skipper.' 'Bring it aft, mud on the lead, we're in the pits. Up net and shackle on. Pay away. All ready for'rad? Lower away and let go.' Away would go the fore end of the trawl, the mate aft would hang on to the quarter strop until the trawl had squared itself across the stern. The trawl warp would then have the weight.

' Give her 80 fathom.' If that was not enough more would be slacked out until smack was towing at about 2 miles an hour.

We usually shot the trawl about 4 p.m., after about 6 hours we would begin to shoal the water, which meant we had now arrived at the Dogger side of the Silver Pits, so about 11.30 p.m. the cry would go forth ' Haul the trawl '. Then all hands would turn out. If the bag of fish was ordinary we used the mizzen tackle, if large, the fore fish tackle, which was stronger, but not so handy to work. ' Up net and round ropes,' the trawl, after tacking ship, was then on the leeside, so the bridles were passed around the stern, outside rigging, sheets, etc., the net payed away, trawl shot and it was then being towed from the weather side on its way back to the south side of the Silver Pits, which was known as the Well Bank side.

By the time the fish were packed up into boxes it would be about 1 a.m. Then crew went below for supper, which consisted of what was left over from dinner, hard tack, biscuits made from flour and water with a little salt. The third and fourth hands were now on watch, fourth keeping a look-out, whilst the third had his supper with the cook. After about half a hour the third hand went on deck and the fourth came down to his supper. The cook was not called again until 6 a.m.

After about another 6 hours we would again shoal the water and haul trawl, sometimes in a hurry, for the edge of pits are very rough ground and one can easily lose a trawl there. Then trim sails and beat to wind'ard to make up leeway which smack had made during night. That often took all day. When skipper wished to tack ship he sang out ' Look out, about ', sometimes just ' Shove her round '. Away for'ard would run one of crew, let go the lee sheet of the jib, hop over bowsprit and pull the other sheet in whilst smack was still up in the wind with all sails shaking. The stay foresail was left until the other sails were full on the other tack, then it was let go. When we were hove-to, we kept stay foresail a'weather. It acted as a brake and steadied the smack a lot.

After the catch was gutted, washed and iced it was about 10 a.m. and the cook called out ' Breakfast here-y-oh '. One man would be left on deck and the others went below to have a breakfast of fish.

Mat making was a favourite hobby of the smacksmen during the watch below when the weather was fine. They would visit the tailor's shop before they sailed and buy cloth clippings and a few yards of sacking. They cut the cloth into strips about half an inch wide and two inches long and threaded them into the sacking. The result was a lovely mat for the missus. Their favourite musical instrument was the accordion and some were great at playing it. Sometimes during the summer months there were several days and nights on end during which there was not enough wind to tow the trawl and the sea was as calm as a duck pond. When this happened we would lash the smacks alongside each other and go aboard each other's craft and in our own way enjoy ourselves. Then perhaps from another smack a mile or so away one could hear his accordion strike up an old-time song, such as ' Daisy, Daisy, give me your answer do ', there being no wind and nothing to obstruct the sound waves the music would carry a long way.

Well, it's the month of January. We've been trawling for a week and have a good trip on board and the 'old man' has decided to make for home. We hauled the trawl at 8 a.m., the weather is not too good, the dawn very red. The wind keeps freshening and is inclined to back, it looks like a breeze. (Smacksman's parlance for what is generally a gale.) After the fish have been gutted, washed and iced we have breakfast, the ' old man ' comes on deck, has a look round, goes below and has a look at the glass and says ' She's still falling '.

We already have two reefs in the mainsail, a six-cloth jib and a reefed mizzen, and are on the starboard tack, making about 5 knots or so. Up to now we have made about 20 miles, her head about S.W.$\frac{1}{2}$W. and so after allowing for leeway, making S.W. and about 100 miles from Smith's Knoll lightship which the skipper reckons bears S.W. The mate and deck hand had the morning watch and are asleep below, skipper, third and fourth hands on deck and the cook, busy looking after the dinner after scrubbing out cabin, trimming lights, etc., is pleased with himself because we are bound for home.

After sailing on the starboard tack for three more hours and still making a S.W. course, the wind backs and the old man, after looking at the compass, says ' She's broke off two points, I thought the wind would back, we're in for a hard blow. We'll reef her down and make all snug before it gets worse '. It is now 3 p.m. and will be dark a little after 4 o'clock. The skipper puts his head in the hoodway and sings out to the cook ' Call 'em out, boy '. When all hands are on deck the skipper orders ' Take another reef in and reeve the fourth down, settle the main a bit and slack the gaff haly'ds a little, sing out when you're ready and I'll shove her up into the wind '. When the mate calls out the skipper puts the tiller hard-a-lee and the smack comes head to wind, shakes her canvas and before she has time to pay off again and fill the sails the third reef is taken in the mainsail. Next order is ' Set the storm jib and reef stay foresail, let bowsprit in about 4 ft. before you pull storm jib out '. Next ' Reef the mizzen and wind the net round the capstan. Strike the topmast '' says the skipper, ' it's coming on a gale, glass is below 29 and still falling. Batten the hatches down and run life-line along '.

The life-line is then run from the capstan to mast so that crew have something to hold on should they have to go for'ard in the dark. By this time it is nearly dark, anyway the regulations say ' lights up from sundown to sunrise ', so it's ' Ship the sidelights up '. The boy lights them, hands them up and they are put in position and looked at often during the night to see they are burning bright. After the smack has been prepared for the storm the skipper tells the cook to take the dinner up, so off the stove comes the beef kettle, out of which cook takes the duff, a lump of salt beef and about half a stone of spuds with their jackets on, all having been boiled in salt water. The boy comes on deck and calls out ' Dinner here oh ', and all hands, except decky and cook go below for their dinner. After about 20 minutes the mate, whose watch it is until midnight, goes on deck and the others will have theirs. After dinner it is customary for watch below to have half a hour's yarn, the skipper joining in. Then he goes up for a look round and tells mate to let him know if it comes on any worse. ' If wind flies to nor'west as I think it will before long, keep her S.W. and call me at once. If it backs so she won't lay better than S.E. shove her round and tack again when you shift watches. Better try the pump when your chummy comes up, he is making a flare in case we should want one in a hurry.' ''

Plate 63 shows the nonchalance with which smacksmen faced a gale. I love the way they are enjoying a chat, not caring a damn for the big sea approaching. They know the smack will ride over it like a gull, scarcely taking a bucketful on board, other than spray, and for that they are well prepared in oilskins, sou'westers and long sea boots. The force of the wind can be judged by the way the mainsail is straining at the mast hoops. Two reefs are down, the lacing needs attention.

To continue Mr. George's story :—

" They were real sea dogs these smacksmen, some when ashore were hard drinkers, others were sober, God-fearing men. They hadn't much money, but a pound went a long way. They could go into a pub, lay down a sixpence, call for a pint and an ounce of their favourite shag and receive a penny change. Couldn't those chaps eat, nowadays if you went to a fishshop and bought what they used to eat for breakfast it would cost you a fortune. They were magnificent chaps, strong as donkeys and some equally headstrong ! Their ' bed ' was a large sack of straw, to undress to turn into their bunks was an unheard-of thing. They had a wash when they left home and another after ten days when they returned, for fresh water aboard a smack was very scarce. But when ashore they took great pride in their personal appearance, when you saw them out with the missus, wearing their leather Wellington boots, sealskin caps and blue pilot cloth trousers and jersey, they looked fine. Some of the skippers used to wear top hats and carry an umbrella or walking stick. They liked their beer, many liked it too well. They took great pride in their smacks, their cabins were very clean and they liked a sailing match with another smack and how they could handle their craft. Those men were made of the stuff which manned the *Victory's* guns at Trafalgar (Plate 64).

The last old-time skipper I saw in ' uniform ', that is top hat, walking stick and blue guernsey and trousers, was old Solly Brown. Each Sunday morning Solly would go to the House of God dressed like that. Some of the smack owners were queer characters. One of them, William Ball, after making a big fortune out of smacks and drifters, thought he would like to buy a farm. There was one to be sold at Potter Heigham, a village about eight miles from Yarmouth. Billy went to the auction dressed like a smack skipper who was down and out, and the auctioneer refused to take his bid. Says William ' If I buy the farm I can pay for it '. I heard he paid £10,000 for it.

On another occasion William was going to his farm from Yarmouth and although he would be dressed more or less like a tramp he often travelled first-class. He got into a first-class carriage in which was a young lady. She sang out ' Guard, come here and turn this fisherman out '. Along came the guard, looked at old Billy, then at the young lady and said ' I daren't turn him out, miss, he's one of our biggest share-holders ! ' Another time Billy got into a first in which was a chap who objected to William's presence. He too called the guard and said ' Look at his ticket '. William pulled out his first-class ticket and said to the guard, ' Now look at yon's. The guard did so and found the chap had only a third-class ticket.''

Plate 65 is from an old photograph taken at Yarmouth in 1860 and shows two smack skippers, bearded like the pard, wearing crumpled suits and hard hats, with rolled umbrellas, while the white-bearded old gentleman has a glossy topper. Do look at the young ladies—as no doubt the smacksmen are doing—and the dead-and-alive expression on the face of the young man wearing a round cap. The old grey horse evidently got fed up with waiting and shook his head just as the exposure was taken, for photography was a slow and serious business in those far-off days.   Y.H.238 is a cutter smack and the whole picture is a delightful one of days when trees grew on quay sides, and masts and spars lay alongside.

Plate 66 shows *Better Luck*, Y.H.1039, 69 tons, built Southtown 1885, off Gorleston with the clench-built paddle tug well astern and trying to catch up. The smack is snugged down with a small jib set, but bowsprit has not been reefed. Note how the boom is arched with the strain of the mainsail which has girt on the topping lift. Her side lights are carried on boards fastened to iron stanchions stepped in sockets abaft the mizzen rigging, the older smacks usually had theirs lashed in the main rigging as in Plate 69.

Mr. George thus describes the return home of a smack :—

" When nearing Yarmouth it was necessary for the skipper to give very few orders, the crew knew their job and were led by the mate and the working of the smack went like clockwork. About four miles from harbour the skipper would take the tiller, order all hands on deck and say to the mate ' Get anchor out and towrope ready '. When a mile or so from the harbour the tug would steam up alongside and throw his heaving line aboard. The third hand would make it fast to the towrope and the tug men would haul it aboard and hook on. The tug skipper would sometimes have a few words with ours and say ' What luck ? ' ' About 120 boxes and 20 of prime,' prime were soles, turbot and brill apart from the plaice the rest were called offal, which meant haddock, whiting, dabs, etc. ' How did you get on in the breeze ? ' ' We reefed her down, struck the topmast and battened down the hatches, she took a few lumps but everything held and we are all right.'

The tug would steam ahead, the towrope would come taut and our skipper would say ' Take the canvas in '. Then in would come the jib and bowsprit, after that, down topsail, then lower the mainsail, next go aft and take in and stow the mizzen. For'ard again and stow the mainsail and coil up the halyards. When nearing the bar the skipper would sometimes sing out ' Stand by here, somebody, in case I want a pull with the tiller going over the bar '. Safely over and round the bend the skipper would say to his helper ' All right now, hang the fenders over and get the mooring ropes ready. Bring the best one aft, there's a strong ebb and we'll swing her after we're alongside '. When abreast the fish wharf the skipper would hail the tug ' Let go '. The tugmen would then slip the towrope and the smack would have just enough way on her to get alongside the wharf. Next job was to get a good rope out aft, then let go the headrope and allow smack to swing round, as all fishing craft, when not moored end on, as they were when wharf was full of smacks, luggers, etc., must be moored with their heads towards the harbour mouth. When that is done she is made fast fore and aft and there she lies until she goes to sea again.

By this time the owner will come along and after shaking hands with the skipper will say 'What luck ?' 'About 120 and 20 of prime.' 'How many soles ?' 'Ten boxes, five of turbot, five of brill.' 'That's good.' says the owner, 'come and have a pint.' So off they go to the pub where the owner will tell what's doing amongst the other smacks, how many boxes of fish they had, what they made and generally all the news about things piscatorial.

The stocker buyer would go down to the smack and say to the mate 'Any stocker ?' 'Yes, about 20 boxes, most gurnets and small dabs.' 'How much for 'em ?' 'You can have the lot for three quid.' 'They're mine, here's the dough.' The mate then shares out ten bob each and the crew feel quite rich. Stocker is small unmarketable fish, which the crew save, mostly from the last few hauls and they are their perquisites.

Next job is to pack the catch in fish trunks, which are carted to the station, put in trucks and sent to Billingsgate to be sold, there being no trawl fish market at Yarmouth in the old days. Another night ashore and off we went again. Once in a while after about three month's trawling we would get a week ashore while the smack was undergoing a refit.

The soles would make about £5 per trunk, turbot perhaps £2 10s. per box, brill the same, haddock perhaps 10s. if we were lucky, plaice £1, cod 12s. Altogether a good trip, but it was not always like that, and if a skipper made too many bad trips he got the sack and had to look for another ship.

Prior to 1883 it was not necessary for a smack skipper or mate to hold a certificate. After then they had to pass an oral examination in rule of the road at sea, what course they would take to the different fishing grounds, what steps they would take to keep their trawls off the rough grounds, if in the Clay Deeps and decided to make for the Humber, what course they would shape, what light did the Smith's Knoll show, the Leman, Ower, Shipwash, Lowestoft lights, etc., and they had to know how to prick off a chart. Those who had already served as mate or master were given a ticket of servitude (Plate 102).

The examiners were owners who once went to sea as skippers. In later years smacksmen had to pass a much stiffer examination, find latitude by an observation of the sun, understand deviation and variation of the compass, rule of the road, seamanship, cross bearings, etc. These examinations were about equal to that for a skipper of a home-trade ship. To get all this and much more into their heads they had to attend a school of navigation for several weeks."

I have no doubt those practical men found it a good deal easier to do the job than write about it.

Mr. Harry George has written me a graphic story of the life he knew in his youth and I give it in his own words, but as it was told me in many long and interesting letters it has required a little editing to ensure continuity. Otherwise I have not altered a line.

Mr. George rose from skipper to owner, eventually having a fine fleet of steam drifters which alas went west in the economic blizzard of the 1930's. His brother rose from cabin boy in a sailing drifter to the command of a 10,000-ton merchant ship, *Empire Ruskin*, retiring with a D.S.C. to his credit.

I was told by one man that his father was apprenticed from the workhouse at the age of twelve, bought his first smack some years later and finished up with a fine fleet, having had no less than 59 vessels built for him, as well as many others purchased second-hand.

No one can say this lad was born with a silver spoon in his mouth, for he only had what he stood up in when he started his career, yet such was his ability and business acumen that he rose to affluence and died respected by all who knew him.

Another smack boy who made good was the late Mr. R. M. Crome who became Commodore-captain in the Ellerman Bucknell Line. He wrote me in the finest copperplate writing :—

" In the year 1886 I made two voyages in the converter smack *Fern*, Y.H.511 A converter smack was so called because about the month of September the whole foremast, together with topmast and crosstrees, was removed and the vessel fitted with a polemast and boomless mainsail for the herring drifting. Sailing smacks that did not belong to the large fleets but to small owners were known locally as ' single-boaters ' and were seldom away more than a fortnight. My step-father was a smacksman and as a boy I often listened to him recounting his experiences in the old sailing cutters on their way from the Dogger Bank or off the Texel, to Billingsgate and their difficulties in locating the fleet on the return passage.

In my time also, the cutter-rigged trawlers still survived with the old walk-around capstan for hauling the trawl. When at sea in the smack *Fern* one of these cutters was quite close to us and I heard the crew singing that old smacksmen's song ' Haul ! haul ! haul the trawl '. as they tramped around the capstan. The *Fern* was dandy-rigged which many confuse with the ketch. The dandy was really an elongated cutter with an additional mast stepped before the tiller. The ketch rigged vessel was a coaster, with a standing bowsprit which was also steeved and she carried as many as four or more headsails, whilst the dandy-rigged smack had a sliding horizontal bowsprit with only two headsails.

The *Fern* was furnished with a vertical boiler and a horizontal engine for working the capstan, both in the cabin. Incidentally when these were first installed in the fleeting smacks many of them arrived home with something in the cabin that resembled Lot's wife more than a vertical boiler, inasmuch it was a veritable pillar of salt ! There were several accidents from the same cause, for sea water was used in the boilers.

The pay of the boy cook was 10s. per week but in the smack *Fern*, which belonged to my uncle William Crome, the cook was quite an ancient mariner, insomuch he was the most elderly man on board, which was exceptional but would make no difference to his pay. But his age and experience would save him from making the mistake by a boy neighbour of mine, who as cook put the duff into a pot of cold water, so that when the expectant and hungry crew came down to their dinner all that the boy fished out of the pot was a steaming wet cloth. Probably after what he heard about himself, he remembered for ever afterwards that puddings and duffs must be put into boiling water.

58 PREPARING TO SHOOT THE TRAWL
Skipper John Smith is at helm, July,
1930. A relieving tackle is on tiller and
smack is carrying a little weather helm, fore
bridle is coiled down on deck and fish
tackle is hooked to eyebolt in deck.

59 UNBENDING THE LEECH LINE
Boy Clifford, 41 tons, built at
Lowestoft, 1920.
The lower block of fish tackle is
hooked into shackle which takes
thimble of bridle.

60 HAULING IN THE WARP
Boy Clifford, L.T.1202, July, 1930. The splice is passing round capstan,
and foresail is aback as smack is hove-to, note spare beam on deck, main
halyard coil, spare hoop at mainsail tack, the lanyards are spliced in
deadeyes, not knotted.

61 HAULING IN THE NET
The fish tackle is hooked in for'ard trawl head with its fall on sheave in fair-leading post, or " dummy " as it is often called by smacksmen, wire and rope guy is on winch, foresail is aback, topsail tack is on iron collar, and topsail sheet is on cleat on post.

62 YARMOUTH SMACKS BEING TOWED TO SEA
British Queen, Y.H.682, 38 tons, built at Cobholm Is., 1876. Ahead is Y.H. 289 *Teazer*, 44 tons, built at Yarmouth, 1860, one of Durrant's fleet. Y.H.194 has trawl beam to starboard, jib is being hoisted and topsail sheet hauled out. New reef bands have been sewn in mainsail of *British Queen* and lacing is in first four eyelets of mizzen. Note stirrup-shaped trawl irons.

62a SMALL CUTTER Y.H.729 LEAVING YARMOUTH
Note reef lacing rove through eyelets, reef pendants,
balance reef, pole mast, patent capstan and stirrup-
shaped trawl iron.

63 NORTH SEA WEATHER
The reef lacing is working loose and needs
pulling up, the chain locker is aft of mast as
shown by cable on deck.

64 SMACKSMEN ENJOYING A YARN

65 YARMOUTH QUAY, c 1860

When at sea in the *Fern* we encountered a dead calm which lasted for three days, during which three smacks were lashed together, bulwark to bulwark, the other two being *Clupedea* (50 tons, built at Yarmouth 1884, owner W. H. Crome) and the *Holmsdale* (38 tons, built Southtown 1878, owner Edward George). The crews played cards together and the cooks vied with each other as to who could turn out the best pancakes with the scanty ingredients to hand. During this period of calm the three skippers gazed with gloomy foreboding at a couple of old paddle tugs, converted to trawlers, which were raking and scraping the bottom and making enough noise with their paddles to scare all the fish out of the North Sea. Such forebodings were fully justified after a lapse of a few years, for with the advent of huge fleets of steam trawlers from Hull and elsewhere all trawl fish were scraped from the bottom of the North Sea, so much so that they had to go as far away as Iceland and the White Sea for the kind of fish that figured on the waybill of the smack *Fern* as offal. There were only two classifications on the waybill in the old carrier days, prime and offal. Soles, turbot, plaice, brill, mullet, etc., came under the heading prime, but cod, haddock, skate, roker, etc., was offal. It is many years since I saw or ate prime fish and the smell from the fishshop of to-day is nauseating enough.

My lowly beginning did not prevent me from attaining to the command of foreign-going cargo and passenger liners, due entirely to personal initiative. I am the third of a generation of seaman and my son a fourth, but I must not bore you to tears with too long a letter.''

Far from being bored I was only too delighted to get into touch with such a man as Mr. Crome and I have here worked in the gist of his letters, retaining his own words throughout. *Fern*, 32 tons, built 1871, was lost by fire in a calm on the 12th October, 1894, while fishing in Botney Gut.

Now a few lines from a man who served in sailing drifters as well as trawlers, Mr. A. Artis of Grimsby, who wrote me in a clear hand :—

" I am sending some of my experiences and two old pictures of the fishing fleet, the only ones I saved out of the book that was in our house when it was knocked down. I don't want them back. I was a fisherman for 46 years, but was mined in the Humber in September, 1940, there was four of us saved and eight killed. I went through the last war but got it in this. We lost everything in July, 1943, so I had to come to the old Fisherman's Alms Houses.

Some of the fleets that were sailing out of Yarmouth at the same time as Hewett's were the Leleu, Columbia and Durrant fleets. We used to call Durrant's the pawn ticket fleet because they had the red, white and blue painted on their bows. When the steam trawlers came the sailing fleets were broken up and sold to the foreigners. A lot went to the Faroes, the Dutch and also Norway. I saw some just before the war bringing fish to Grimsby and Aberdeen. I have seen them at the Iceland salt fishing and have known them go to Greenland. I was in the fleets, we used to stop out a month, sometimes six weeks. We would go to other fishing grounds, Smith's Knoll, Silver Pits, Goodwin Sands, across to the ' Skilling ' and Holland, and down the Belgian coast. They used to call us ' single-boaters ' when we were away for a week or ten days.   As a cook I was with my father, a skipper, I stopped with him for a time but he made life a bit hard for me so I went on my own in other smacks, till I left them to come to Grimsby in 1902 and went into steam trawlers.   The little one I was in was 33 years old, I've been to Iceland in her, we were away three weeks and only carried 94 tons of coal.   One of our warships asked us whether we stopped out all night !   I was always one for going to sea but none of my sons will, so that will be the last of my name.   I am lucky to finish my time in a house.   I think that the smack days were the best.   We had plenty of everything, they were wooden ships and iron men.   Well, goodbye to the old days, happy days. I am sorry I cannot tell you any more.   I have been in the Navy as an R.N.R., I was at Queen Victoria's funeral in 1901 at Spithead.   My father was an R.N.R. man, so was my brother who was lost in the last war.   My father was 84 when he died and his mother was 95 years old, not so bad.''

When intensive trawling developed and competition grew keener it became the practice for fleets of smacks to remain at sea, the routine being 8 weeks at sea and 1 in port, so arranged that the whole fleet was never in port at one and the same time. Instead of landing their catches individually, the smacks worked to a carrier so saving the waste of time going to and from market.   This practice was first introduced by Samuel Hewett with the Short Blue Fleet working out of Barking and fast sailing cutters took the catch to Billingsgate, in due course these vessels were superseded by steam carriers which however still retained the name of '' cutter ''.   They were among the hardest driven of all steamers as the loss of a tide meant failure to land in time for market, and as soon as they had taken in coal, ice and boxes they were off at full speed to pick up the fleet again, not always an easy job as it shifted about on the different grounds and no wireless was thought of in those days.   No sooner had they sighted the trawlers than the catches were ferried on board and back the carrier went to London, keeping almost railway time. (Plate 67.)

When the fleet was composed of smacks belonging to many owners another system was to make use of any fast trawler returning to port.   She hoisted a signal and the rest of the smacks gathered round and sent their catches on board in their small boats, obtaining a receipt from the skipper who was thus responsible for seeing that the fish was sold to mutual advantage and payment made to the respective owners. This was liable to abuse as it was not unknown for unscrupulous men to change over labels and sell choice fish as their own.   I shall describe these systems of fleeting, or trunking as it was sometimes called, when dealing with the fishing stations where they were practiced.

While fleeting ensured that the maximum use was made of a smack's catching capacity, it practically meant a life sentence on the dreary wastes of the North Sea for the crew, who could look forward only to 7 days ashore every 6 to 8 weeks, after the unremitting monotony of shooting and hauling the trawl, gutting, and washing fish, packing it away in boxes and taking full trunks to the cutter.   In the brief intervals snatching what sleep was possible in a bunk which could easily become vermin ridden. The small cabin reeked of unwashed humanity, stale smoke, fish, oilskins, cooking and bilgewater, an atmosphere likely enough to turn all but the strongest stomach, and to add to this variety of smells, should the vessel be a cod smack would be the overpowering stench from the barrel containing the putrifying livers, which were destined to be rendered down to make cod liver oil, a concoction much esteemed and recommended by the medical profession of those days. Smacksmen used to take it as a sovereign remedy should they feel out of sorts, and when first taken from the cod the liquid was clear as water.

Sanitary arrangements were non-existent, no facilities available for any form of relaxation and the cooking left to the tender mercies of a child, perhaps straight from the workhouse or reformatory, where one thing was certain, the learning of the culinary art had no place in the curriculum.

Is it to be wondered at that men sought forgetfulness in strong drink, an ever-present temptation as Dutch and German "copers" were always cruising in the vicinity of the Dogger and only required the signal—the "creagan"—an oilskin or bread bag hung on an oar over the stern, to bear down and await the arrival of the smack's boat. Once on board, an almost unlimited amount of cheap drink was available, spirits so strong that they would take the varnish off the spars, yet tasting agreeable to the healthy smacksmen, who drank them with gusto. Soon the devilish liquor took effect and men would collapse like logs, go berserk and even jump over-board in a fool-hardy attempt to swim back to their smacks. Dirty pictures added to the depravation of men who were far from the influence of their womenfolk, and some, when money was no longer available, sank to such depths as to sell the smack's gear to enable them to continue to purchase liquor, thereby endangering not only their own lives, but the rest of the crew. A smack with a drunken man at the tiller was a menace indeed, although it might seem impossible to imagine such an event far from land after weeks at sea. This was especially the case with vessels manned by East-end Londoners who had not the traditions of the sea in their blood.

Few indeed were the inducements for a man to choose such a life, yet great were the possibilities for a youth to become a skipper at an age when lads ashore were just out of their apprenticeship. Then to realize another ambition and become part-owner, with every possibility of having a fleet within a few years even retiring from the sea to conduct the business ashore. Could any mill hand or cotton opera-tive see a similar reward for his labours, and how many agricultural workers could aspire to own a farm ? Thus there were compensations for the hard life for those lucky ones on whom fate smiled, for the remainder, if the hurrying waters did not claim their toll, there might be little to show for toil and hardship.

Another of Mr. George's invaluable letters tells of fleeting in his day :—

" The bulk of the Yarmouth smacks worked with the trawler fleets, the most famous being the Short Blue, owned by Hewett & Co. of London. It was under the command of an admiral, a Frenchman whose name was Marco Polo Questo, and there was a vice-admiral who took command once every two months when his superior went home to refit. When the smacks put to sea on a new voyage which lasted eight weeks they shaped a course for the Smith's Knoll Lightship which in those days was stationed 21 miles E.N.E. from Great Yarmouth (Plate 68). From there they made for the Clay Deeps, another 120 miles E.N.E. On arrival at the fleet the first job, after delivering the parcels of good things which the womenfolk ashore had sent to their husbands and sons, was a visit to the Mission ship to lay in a stock of tobacco. They would sell us shag for one shilling and a penny a pound. It was lovely stuff, even now after all these years it almost makes my mouth water to think about it. Hard tobacco was tenpence per lb., woollen mufflers yards long, fourpence each, mittens, thigh boot stockings, Balaclava helmets for next to nothing. If you had a poisoned finger they dressed and made it well for nothing. If one of a smack's crew went sick, they would put a man on board to do his work whilst he was in the Mission ship's hospital, until he was well enough to return. The man's wife ashore would be drawing his money as usual and all free of charge.

When with the fleet we trawled all night, making two hauls, next morning we ferried our catch to the steam carrier which took the fish to Billingsgate. In the daytime the admiral carried one flag on his topmast stay, another at topmast head. When he hauled down his flag it meant shoot the trawls, if it was daylight and he hoisted his flag that meant haul the trawls. In the dark, green rockets, shoot trawls on starboard tack; red rockets, port tack; white, haul the trawls. The same signals applied if the weather was too bad to trawl and we had to heave-to, red, port tack, green, starboard. He had about 200 smacks under his command and his job was to keep them on the fishing grounds and clear of the rough sea bottom, for shooting there would mean a loss of hundreds of pounds worth of gear (Plate 108).

We always launched the boat from the lee-side, lifting her stern on to the smack's rail, then pushed her out until she just about balanced. The painter had been made fast for'ard on the lee bow, next we gave her a push when the smack rolled to leeward and on to the sea she went, it was about a three-minute job to launch a boat. Ferrying fish was a risky business at times but we were used to the job and took it as a matter of course, besides smacksmen were tough and had nerves of steel and hearts like lions. When hoisting in, we brought the boat close to the lee-side about amidships, hooked the fore fish tackle into an eyebolt in the boat's stem, and the after tackle, which came from the mizzen mast, into an eyebolt in the sternpost, hoisting her up level, then swung her aboard. That, too, took very little time."

Many smacks especially those from Brixham where most of the catches were landed in the punts, had a boat gangway on the starboard side just abaft the main rigging. This allowed the boat to be pushed out at deck level, but it left a wide gap in the bulwarks, a serious danger in the heavy weather experienced in a North Sea winter, hence the east-coasters preference for a solid rail (Plate 119).

Plate 69 is of *Little Wave*, Y.H.125, with a boat alongside the lee-quarter, the wind is very light but note that the topsail is set a'weather, its most efficient position, a contrast to latter day practice where it was usually set to port and left there. Her light boards are lashed across the main shrouds and the trawl beam is up at the rail. One reef is down and two more pendants are rove off ready and note how far the fourth cringle is up the leech. She was built at Grimsby in 1886 and owned there until 1897, when she was sold to Hewett & Co.

The moment the carrier was sighted all the fleet worked away to her windward side, ready for " putting out ", and lay so that the boats passing to and fro could be kept end on to the sea. (Plate 106.) Then each smack threw out her boat, two or three men jumped in and rowed down to the cutter, stroke facing for'ard, bow man aft, so that each could keep a sharp lookout for a breaking sea, a vicious cross sea being the greatest danger. The boats were sturdy, clinker-built craft, about 18 ft. long, 6 ft. 6 in. beam with flat floors and able to carry about 2 tons (Plate 70). Many were fitted with galvanized iron tanks under bow and stern sheets, of sufficient capacity to ensure buoyancy if the boat was swamped, and a line was secured along the keel to which the men could cling in the event of a capsize. A few had small oil tanks aft so that a trickle could spread out to smooth heavy seas coming up astern and prevent them breaking into the boat. North Sea fishermen rowed standing, pulling a rather curious stroke, and when three men were trunking, one steered with an oar over the transom.

Meanwhile the smack ran down to leeward of the cutter to pick up her boat which would be loaded with empty boxes, often piled high above the gunwale. (Plates 104 and 109.)

Plate 71 shows a smack's boat under way with a host of trawlers manoeuvring in close proximity to one another. The one with the well-patched sails is *Rescue*, Y.H.1068, 69 tons, built at Rye in 1886. Note how far for'ard the main mast is stepped.

Plate 72 shows the boats clustering round the steam cutter which is rolling heavily, although there does not appear to be much of a sea running, as somehow the camera never seems to give a true idea of weight and strength. But the way the wisp of smoke is cut off as soon as it leaves the funnel and the pitching of the smack to wind'ard tells the weather conditions. The cutter has a trysail aft and a reefed mainsail and foresail, as she welters in the short seas it was no job for a weakling to lift a heavy trunk of fish from the unsteady boat and land it safely on the deck of the carrier. A man had to judge to a split second just when the boat would be borne on the crest of a wave, too late would see an ever-widening distance.

I will now turn to one of Mr. W. G. Freeman's beautifully written letters to give a first-hand account of fleeting.

" I went to sea in a fishing smack from 1880 to 1884, then into merchant ships and in 1904 was licenced by the London Trinity House to pilot ships in and out of Yarmouth harbour. Messrs. Hewett's of London owned 100 smacks more or less and they all sailed from Yarmouth, their home port. They often carried six men and a boy cook, but the smacks belonging to Yarmouth which sometimes fished with the fleet for the first six months of the year were smaller vessels carrying five men and a boy. The fleet we attended worked to steam carriers which took the fish to Billingsgate and often the smacks had to deliver their catches in very rough weather. I will try and describe to you the dangers of ferrying the fish to the carrier. Each small boat carried three men and the carrier skipper was allowed to employ and pay two boats' crews, viz. six men, to help his crew to stow the boxes of fish away. These were called the ' icemen ' and were generally taken from the first two boats that arrived alongside the carrier. Some of the skippers hauled up their trawls about half a hour before the others so as to be first at the carrier as the few shillings received came in very acceptable, so that they were able to purchase tobacco and gin from the Dutch copers when they visited the fleet. They also received other privileges which you will see.

When the carriers left London they were loaded with empty fish boxes, as soon as they arrived at the fleet the small boats put out and went for the empty boxes, but it was an understood thing that all the best and new ones were reserved for the icemen. It was not always the same men who helped as when the eight weeks were up they went home and the crew were stood off for a week's holiday, so very likely none would go in the vessel again, as some of them would not suit the skipper and some the skipper would not suit.

In bad weather one winter's morning in 1884 with a strong wind and heavy sea, we were delivering fish into the carrier on the port side when a huge wave struck her on the starboard side and lifted a boat that was delivering fish on that side so that her port bilge struck the carrier gunwale, and holed it so that she sank immediately. The men had just time to scramble on board the carrier. The two icemen's boats were hanging astern of the carrier, bottom up, and now and again the keels showed above the water and they looked like the back of a large fish.''

Plate 73 shows empty trunks being thrown on to the deck from the carrier's hold.

'' Now for another episode. One fine morning the carrier arrived at the fleet and the smack boats put out. There was a certain skipper whose men assisted with the icing, he was a noisy individual and like to make his voice heard. I knew him by sight, he went under the sobriquet of ' Smasher Jackson '. He loaded up with the best boxes so that the men were unable to row, the trunks being a few tiers above the gunwale with Smasher perched on top. They left the carrier and let the boat drift so that the smack could pick her up. Another boat came past and Smasher called out ' That's the way to get good boxes ! ' One of the other men took his oar and struck the boxes which fell into the water and took Smasher with them but he managed to get into the boat again.''

So hazardous was the job of boating the fish to the carrier that Mr. Crome mentions that the two lowest ratings often preferred to remain so, as promotion meant they would have to be one of the boating men. One wild February morning the Great Northern fleet had seven men and Grimsby two men drowned. Clad in heavy seaboots and oilskins a man stood no chance, sinking like a stone and with the fatalistic outlook of so many seamen few would learn to swim.

During the year 1882, 12 men were lost ferrying, only 2 more than were drowned through overbalancing over the smacks' side when drawing up water. In 1887 the number lost rose to 24, the following years saw 18, 7, 11 drowned, but in 1891 only 2 men and in 1893, 5, probably due to the fitting of buoyancy tanks in boats, following Board of Trade enquiries, but many men refused to wear the heavy cork lifebelts which hampered their movements, others would not face the chaff and ridicule of those not wearing life preservers.

A moderate S.E. breeze was blowing on the 1st March, 1886, when the 71-ton *Fern* of London, built at Dartmouth in 1877, was trunking on the east side of the Dogger and her boat capsized with the loss of 3 men. In a fresh W.N.W. wind on the 6th October, 1885 the boat capsized from the 53-ton *Minx* of London, built 1873 at Dartmouth, while engaged in ferrying 11 miles east of the Dogger and 2 of the crew were drowned.

The 40-ton *Restless* of Yarmouth lost her boat and 1 man in a fresh W.S.W. breeze, some 35 miles N.E. of Yarmouth as did the 32-ton *Rose* from the same port while fleeting in Botney Gut in a S.W. blow.

Collisions were a grave danger, especially when a large number of smacks got bunched together round the carrier. On the 2nd May, 1892, the 71-ton *Henry Herbert* of Yarmouth, built 1877, was in collision with the steam carrier *Endeavour* of London, 120 miles E.N.E. of Spurn Point and sank with the loss of 5 hands. On 3rd July, 1895, *Rambler* of Yarmouth, 41 tons, built 1857, collided with the carrier *Jubilee* of Hull, about 90 miles E. by N. of Yarmouth and became a total loss with 5 out of her crew of 6. The 58-ton *Butterfly* of London, built at Bideford in 1878, seems to have been a rather unlucky vessel. On the 29th April, 1882, with a gentle breeze blowing, she ran down a boat belonging to *Spitfire* of London and 1 man was lost 20 miles off Borkum. A year later on the 6th September her own boat was swamped and 1 man drowned on the east side of the Dogger in a fresh westerly wind, and on the 3rd February, 1888, she herself collided with and sank the Yarmouth dandy *Rover* while fishing in the Clay Deeps.

Another total loss was the 34-ton London smack *Reindeer* built 1846 at Wivenhoe, following a collision with the dandy *Mary Gowland* of Yarmouth, 120 miles N.E. of that port on the 15th January, 1883. The 57-ton cutter *Transit* of London, built at Barking in 1853, ran foul of *Lily May* of Yarmouth in the Botney Gut on the 3rd January, 1884, and became a total loss.

The big iron smacks appear to have been very vulnerable to collision damage as I find that the 74-ton *Emperor*, built 1884 at Middlesbrough, sank on the 17th August, 1893, after an encounter with the Yarmouth smack *Alice and Ada*, *Iron Duke* of 80 tons, built 1877, was lost in the Silver Pits after collision with another Yarmouth vessel *Annie*. The 77-ton *Kaiser*, built in 1885, went down after colliding with

Progress of Yarmouth on the 12th May, 1888, *Topaz* built in 1885 was lost a year later on the 4th April in Botney Gut when she collided with the smack *Maa* in a strong S.W. breeze. *Turquoise*, a sister ship, collided with the steam carrier *Lord Alfred Paget* on the Dogger on a summer day in August 1890, and the 63 ton *Wild Duck*, built 1878, disappeared off the Dutch coast after a collision with *Wetherill* of London.

These instances, culled at random from records compiled by my friend Commander H. Oliver Hill, tell vividly of the hazards of a smacksman's life, summer and winter.

A lighter note is introduced from my correspondence with Mrs. Holtby, who sent me an excellent snap of her father, the late Mr. H. G. Harvey, who was born at Belton, Suffolk on the 15th November, 1867, went to sea at the age of 12 and was given his Certificate of Competency as skipper on the 3rd December, 1890, following the introduction of the new regulations of the Board of Trade. Mrs. Holtby was good enough to loan me this document, inscribed on white linen, now slightly stained with age. For 13 years Mr. Harvey was with Hewett's Short Blue Fleet, serving 4 years as mate and 9 as master in sailing smacks, then going as master in steam trawlers, only severing his connection with the firm when the business at Gorleston closed down in 1902. He then served 13 years with the Great Northern Steam Fishing Co. of Hull, saw service in the 1914-18 war and then sailed in the fleeters owned by Kelsall Bros. and Beeching Ltd. All his discharges testify to his capabilities as a seaman, his honesty, sobriety and industry.

Plate 75 shows him at the age of 26 at the tiller of his smack, with mate and crew, not forgetting the boy cook. Four of them wear the buttonless " oily frocks ", typical of that time and the skipper's physique justifies his nickname " Jumbo ". His first son was lost in the steam trawler *St. Sebastian* wrecked on Bear Is., September, 1938, his second boy was machine-gunned and killed in the bridge of his trawler *Arctic Trapper* in February, 1941, and he himself died the following year.

Writing to me in March, 1946, Mrs. Holtby tells something of the food and drink problems of men who were at sea 8 or 9 weeks at a stretch, and she throws an interesting sidelight on wives' reactions to their menfolk's smoking habits !

" Their meat supply was very salt beef, as the weeks went by it grew harder and harder. I have handled boxes made of it, you wouldn't know it from wood. Many men made intricately carved presents for their womenfolk. My father recalled running right out of the always meagre supply and they all had to produce their half-finished gifts, which, after having nails, rivets and locks removed, were softened with vinegar and used to vary the monotony of fish.

Also the 'bacca. No one smelling ' hard ' which was its only name, could ever forget it. Many are the stories about it, wives have left loved husbands, arguments have finished with fighting, when a man would not smoke it outside the living room. My two brothers were put off smoking thro' stealing little bits of Dad's to see if they were ' growed up ' Chewed into pellets it was a cure for toothache, it removed moths, many a time I would rather have walked about moth-eaten, than leaving behind the dreadful smell of ancient sea tobacco.

Then again there was a lot of humour among the fishermen. I remember nicknames, some quite unprintable, but one or two gems. There was always a Jumbo and a Lofty, but one of Dad's crews boasted an ' Onion ', due to his few sparse hairs, rather long and the colour of straw. This name stuck to him all his life, aye longer than his hair did. There was another with obnoxious breath who was always ' Jeyes '. All the old-timers I have met had a likeness for cats, any colour, sex or size. Most were superstitious. One friend knew how his crew resented the word ' pig ', never mentioned aboard, but as a nipper he had been given a tiny brass pig, which he grew to almost love. As a man he wore it round his neck at sea and in a little bag in his pocket ashore. He never lost a man or a ship tho' his pig was always with him. It was buried with him two years ago. Anyone who taxed him about his little bag was always told it was his first wife's wedding ring. His one and only widow told me this.

Might I tell you just a little about what I used to call smuggling ? From the age of 14 I began to carry off packets of shag for my father's old cronies. I found an outlet for my imagination and felt it was in good order as I was never paid for it. I would be helped across one or two trawlers by the same truly zealous young ' police-man ', who later would search Dad by feeling round his vast figure, which was obviously clothed in nothing more than fat. After the raising of his cap and pretended search of his very bald head—he was bald at 23, due to the wearing of the improperly cured sealskin caps of the times—he would say quite pleasantly ' Pass Jumbo ' and deliber-ately make eyes at me. This always made me laugh as I would have what he was after safely tucked into the space afterwards to be used by what we call a bust. It amuses me now to think of my home-made oilskin brassieres. My mother made them because one of my brothers brought off some 'bacca wrapped round himself in a napkin. Due to friction the wrapper burst and he broke out into a dreadful rash. I managed for years, tho' I can honestly say it was only for one thing, just the old fellows' shag. Father gave the lot away as he never changed from hard.

In 1932 my two brothers, one the skipper, the other mate, took Dad ' plea-suring ' for a trip. The old chap laughed heartily at the square white bath with a tap, and a beautifully polished wash basin, curtains drawn back by brass bands and lo and behold an electric fan for the bunk head, a chart room and a black and white tiled galley with new zinc buckets full of pure white dripping. He couldn't under-stand the need for such things, as he always kept himself clean with a sweat rag and a sluice down, and his skin was really lovely, tho' he never had what we call a real bath. I know because for his last two years I bathed and shaved him myself.''

This very human letter is another angle on a smacksman's life. I can confirm the story about salt beef as I once handled the hull of a ship model carved from a chunk which looked like mahogany. It came from a barrel of old naval stores which eventually found its way on to a Cape Horner.

Stores put on board a smack for an 8 week trip with the fleet included 200 lb.

of beef, 20 stone of flour, 1½ cwt. of hard biscuit, 25 lb. cheese, 28 lb. of treacle and same amount of cocoa, but only 6 lb. of tea. 16 tins of condensed milk, 40 lb. of lard, 8 lb. each of currants and raisins for duffs, 4 lb. baking powder and a lb. of carroway seed. To help down the salt beef was 4 lb. of mustard, ½ lb. of pepper and a dozen bottles of relish. Such vegetables as cabbage, carrots, onions, etc., and for the first few days there would be joints of fresh beef or mutton and newly baked loaves. Some bakers specialized in a loaf which went hard and dry after baking, but when well damped and placed in the oven came out crisp and sweet, even after several weeks. Meat in those days was about 4d. to 4½d. a lb. and home-killed, no frozen carcases. The small quantity of tea allowed may have been the reason for the strong brew beloved by smacksmen, who never allowed the boy to remove the old leaves until the kettle was full, and then only enough were taken out to make room for a handful of dry leaves. Three tanks of fresh water were carried and the men took with them such luxuries as they fancied and their wives could provide. When newcomers arrived on the fishing grounds they often brought out fresh vegetables, letters, etc., as did the steam carriers which arrived every day to take the previous night's catch to market.

When the smacks were fleeting it was essential that every skipper obeyed the admiral's signals implicitly, exemplified by one instance where lights were shown for going about on the other tack in anticipation of a gale coming on, some " know-alls " disobeyed and as a result several smacks ran into one another during the night.

Mr. J. Woodhouse kindly asked his grandfather to give me some of his experiences. He went to sea at the age of 11 and was married at 24 when earning 11s. a week. Later he was in the 46-ton *Boy Billy*, built in 1878 at Cobholm Is., Suffolk, and owned by W. J. Balls who had a fleet of six smacks. It seems that one March morning in 1897, *Boy Billy* was fishing off the Dutch coast and had her trawl down when the safety valve blew out of the boiler. The skipper, who was also admiral, cut a piece off the lead, ran it down and filled the hole up so that steam could be raised to get their gear. They had part of a trip on board so decided to return home to Yarmouth, the other smacks putting their catches on board as was the custom in small fleets not working to a carrier. The wind was S.W., a strong breeze, and just after leaving the fleet, sailing west on the port tack, they sighted a squall coming from the N.W., white along the water, so went about to head S.W. on the starboard tack. One of the heaviest gales known struck the smack and laid her down, and with the swell coming heavy from the south'ard on their lee side, things looked pretty bad. All hands were called to reef, while the skipper nailed the hatches down, headsails were lowered and all reefs pulled down in mainsail and mizzen and they let her lay like that. By luck the smack's boat was on the weather side and full of water, a fact probably responsible for saving the vessel. The gale came on about 2 p.m. and blew until 6 o'clock when it moderated. As the glass was rising the skipper ordered small jib and stay foresail to be set and kept on the one tack until they reached port next day. On the way an old ship was sighted, floating bottom up, and this was reported to Trinity House, eventually it drifted across into Dutch waters and was a big worry to smacksmen all that summer, especially at night, before it was sunk by the authorities.

In May the same year *Boy Billy* and her fleet were in Terschilling Bight, towing N.E. A strong nor'wester was blowing and John Brown, skipper and admiral, not thinking much of the weather, made signals for hauling. The rest of the fleet ignored him and kept on towing. When the gale struck, *Boy Billy* was got round on the starboard tack and allowed to draw through the water to keep her off Terschilling Point, instead of allowing her to lay-to until gale blew itself out as was the usual practice. The other smacks were not so well off as they had to haul in the gale, one man was washed overboard but was picked up by another smack. They got so close inshore that they were forced to lower away, anchor and ride out the storm in broken water, *Boy Billy* was on the starboard tack for 23 hours before the weather fined off. On one occasion Henry Brown of Caister was at the tiller for 36 hours in order to keep his smack off the coast of Holland.

When I visited Caister in October, 1946, old John Brown was sitting out in the sun and I had the pleasure of a short chat with him and he told me with pride that he had once been admiral of a North Sea fleet and knew the nature and soil on the grounds as well as he knew the back of his hand. Although nearly ninety his memory was as clear as ever it was and I was sorry to hear from Mr. Woodhouse that the old fellow died less than six months later.

John Cook, an admiral who never saw a man drowned while ferrying or lost a ship, mentions that his extra pay was 1s. 3d. on every 100 packages put aboard the carrier.

No story of a smacksman's life in the North Sea would be complete without some brief reference being made to the splendid work of the Royal National Mission to Deep Sea Fishermen, already referred to by Mr. George who has written me of their Christ-like work.

One of the greatest evils in the early days of fleeting was the presence of Dutch, Belgian and German vessels which cruised about, ostensibly engaged in fishing, but actually were floating grog shops where the vilest liquor could be bought at very low prices, gin was 1s., rum 1s. 6d., and raw brandy 2s. a bottle, while a further inducement were ample supplies of excellent tobacco, costing less than 1s. 6d. a lb. against the lowest price of 4s. 6d. a lb. ashore. These copers, as they were called, were a serious menace, as no law ruled on the high seas which are free to all once the International limit of territorial waters is passed.

Such were the opportunities to get rich quick that some Englishmen engaged in the nefarious traffic as it was easy to put into a port in the Low Countries, buy drink to the value of £500 and sell it at double the price and more on rejoining the fleet. *Annie*, *Dora* and *Angelina*, what innocent names, were some of the smacks so employed but the latter's halyards were cut when Hewett's asked the Insurance club to refuse to cover unless copering was given up. On the 21st May, 1888, *Angelina* foundered 10 miles N. by W. of Ameland.

Another grave matter was the total lack of any medical aid for the thousands of men always afloat, other than the crude surgical ability of a skipper who might suddenly be confronted with a badly fractured limb, a ghastly scalp wound if a man was brained by a block, and all the many and varied injuries likely to happen to men working in the dark under hazardous conditions.

In 1881 Mr. E. J. Mather paid a visit to the trawling fleets and was so impressed with what he saw that he talked matters over with two old skippers and the suggestion of a Mission smack was adopted. The 56-ton *Ensign*, one of the Short Blue Fleet, built at Southtown in 1877, was purchased for £1,000 and fitted out at bare cost by Mr. Harvey-George, Hewett's manager at Gorleston. A medical chest was placed on board, books and woollen comforts were collected and she sailed under Skipper Budd, an earnest, God-fearing man. Such a novel innovation was at first received with derision and scepticism, but when men saw that the preaching side was not unduly stressed, and real, practical help given, many who came to scoff remained to bless, and the fact that the crew were men of their own class, did much to convince waverers that there was " something in it ".

The question of combating the drink menace was another matter as when crews went on board a coper to buy 'bacca, they were tempted by the offer of a glass of schnapps, which meant much to men who had been weeks at sea. The coper knew full well that the taste for liquor would be encouraged by the sight of bottles galore. Mr. Mather realized he could do little if he was unable to sell tobacco at equivalent prices and so remove one of the attractions of the foreigner. But the Chancellor of the Exchequer refused to reduce the duty and the Customs would not allow the Mission to have it out of bond. However there are ways and means of getting round most regulations and it was found to be perfectly legal to send tobacco by rail to London from the factory at Bristol and export it duty free to Ostend, Mr. W. H. Wills agreeing to supply at cost and ship it abroad. At the Belgian port it was possible for the Mission smack to take the precious cargo on board, providing she had no fishing gear on board, and no duty was payable. The need for cheap tobacco was shown by the fact that over three tons, cut up into cake, was sold within two years. One minor incident of an amusing character was that after counting two collections of silver from the smacks, the bank at Yarmouth insisted on the money being boiled before it was paid in !

In due course common sense prevailed and in 1887 the Custom regulations were eased to permit the Mission smacks loading out of bonded warehouses in England. Meanwhile the venture was succeeding and within five years no less than seven Mission smacks were fitted out and equipped with dispensaries where free medical and surgical treatment was given to all. One of the young doctors was W. F. Grenfell, who later became famous as Grenfell of Labrador.

Books and magazines were distributed, a boon to men away from any form of recreation, and the needs of those unable to read were fulfilled in a certain measure by sending plenty of picture books, and innumerable woollen comforts were knitted by energetic lady helpers all over the country, a godsend to men exposed to the rigours of the North Sea in winter.

Conference after conference had failed to come to any agreement over the activities of the copers, the rock on which they always foundered being "interference with trading". But such was the success of the R.N.M.D.S.F. that within a few years the copers had been driven from the North Sea and their absence was ensured as a result of the International Convention of 1893, which prohibited the sale of spiritous liquors to men on board fishing vessels, or the exchange of gear, etc., for liquor, a law which came into force the following May.

Thus the efforts of Mr. Mather and his helpers were crowned with achievement in just over a decade. The Mission smacks were handled by practical men who did a certain amount of trawling to help with the expenses, and soon the conversion of existing vessels gave place to the building of craft designed for the job, one being *Queen Victoria*, 131 tons, built at Southtown in 1888 (Plate 74). The photograph was taken in 1892 when she was working with the Grimsby Ice Co's fleet on the Dogger. For many years she was in charge of W. H. Smedley, who was appointed skipper at the age of 25 and he thus described her in an interview with Mr. C. R. Chandler of Grimsby, who kindly sent me the particulars. Built and equipped for £3,500 she had 13 cots on board and carried a doctor. As to sailing qualities " she was a beautiful ship and like a kittiwake on the wing. The only time she ever shipped water was in the great May storm of 1895, when a fleet of over 100 was reduced to less than 40 effectives ". Steam as well as sailing trawlers were lost on that awful day with all hands, including the S.S *Bittern* with the admiral of the fleet, Henry Shackles, in command, but *Queen Victoria* stood the battering well, although her boat was smashed and the men in hospital thrown out of their cots.

Born in Sheffield, Mr. Smedley was apprenticed at the age of 14 after running away to sea, was once washed overboard and then swept back again, obtained his skipper's certificate at age of 18, his first command being *Flower of the Valley*, owned by Andrew Johnson, a Dane, who was grandfather of Amy Johnson, later Mrs. Mollison the famous airwoman, while her grandfather on the maternal side was Andrew Mudge, a Brixham man.

The Mission smacks were the first to attempt to alleviate the lot of men who toiled on the lonely wastes of the North Sea and the fact that they worked with the big fleets, facing the same storms and dangers, undoubtedly did much to ensure their success. I give one instance which happened to *Albert* in the same November gale in 1901, when the Caister lifeboat capsized. On the Tuesday it was quite calm, but the sky began to look dirty with heavy rain falling so Skipper Chown ordered sails to be reefed. The wind freshened and by 8 o'clock in the evening they had the foresail reefed and three reefs down in mainsail and mizzen. About 5 a.m. it came on to blow heavily so that the skipper thought it best to tack away from the fleet as the thick rain and mist made it almost impossible to see another boat's lights until right on top of them. Two hours later all hands were called to take the fourth reef in the mainsail and set the storm jib. At 10 a.m. they tacked ship with her head to the nor'ard and soon after she shipped a sea which split the stay foresail to pieces. Another was instantly bent and two reefs tied in it. At two o'clock they tacked the same way as the fleet was lying, head to south'ard and east'ard. A heavy sea broke on board, throwing the smack over on her side, smashing the boat in two, bursting the mainsail and second foresail and straining the deck so much that the hull was soon leaking badly. The big foresail was now set abaft the mast as a trysail and a seven cloth jib bent for a foresail. The decks were cleared up and the smack put before the wind, but the sea was so heavy that they were forced to heave-to at dusk. By Thursday morning the gale began to blow itself out and course was shaped for Yarmouth where a tug was picked up.

One of the last of the sailing Mission smacks was the 56-ton *Sir William Archibald*, built by Fellows at Yarmouth in 1927, and in common with other Mission vessels, fitted with a wheel instead of a tiller. When I saw her in October, 1946, she was laid up at Gorleston, but the splendid work of the R.N.M.D.S.F. is still carried on in up-to-date vessels. Mr. J. Mitchley of Lowestoft wrote me that he saw the *Sir William Archibald* on Overy's slipway for re-rigging early in 1947 and on the 5th May, Lloyds reported her sailing for Aakrehavn. Another Mission smack, the 99-ton *Clulow*, built by H. M. Restarick at Bideford in 1884 as *Edward Auriol*, was trading around the Danish coast in 1950, under the name *Bjorn Olafsson*, carrying 159 tons D.W. and fitted with a 20 h.p. motor.

CHAPTER EIGHT

DISASTERS IN PEACE AND WAR

DESPITE the magnificent sea-keeping abilities of the smacks and the high standard of seamanship of the crews, terrible disasters overtook the trawling fleets from time to time due to the turbulence of the North Sea, and the conditions of working, as the sudden onset of winter gales often caught them in the blackness of night with their gear down. Even more dreaded was snow, as the white flakes swirling down blotted out everything and with from 50 to 200 sail of smacks in company, collisions were inevitable and there was little hope of rescue when heavily clad men were hurled into the icy sea.

During the course of the year 1863, 132 smacks were lost, the great gale of 3rd December accounting for 24 which foundered with the loss of 144 lives, 84 widows and 192 children being left almost destitute.

When the storm was at its height *Fox* of Yarmouth came across the dismasted Swedish brig *Speculant* with all her boats stove in. The smack was close reefed and her skipper anxious to get sea room as the W.N.W. gale was driving them on to a lee shore, but without hesitation he managed to float a line down and get a towrope fast. After two hours the warp parted in pitch blackness and with the Texel light still in sight. Attempts were made to connect up again, but the Swedes were unable to secure the rope and asked to be taken off. *Fox* worked to wind'ard and threw out her own boat, the third, fourth and fifth hands got in and pulled down to the brig, whose crew of six lost no time in jumping in, but the captain refused to leave so the third hand did not stand on ceremony, he bundled him neck and crop into the deep-laden boat. Four days later the smack made Yarmouth, having had to fight every inch of the way home. This gallant rescue passed unnoticed by any authority in this country, but the Swedish Government sent £40 to the rescuers.

The year 1864 claimed 74 smacks and the following years saw losses of 98, 116, 188, 131, 153, 83, with 120 fishing vessels lost in 1871. On the 3rd March, 1877, 36 were lost, 215 men and boys drowned and 88 widows and 164 orphans left to mourn the breadwinner.

Tragic as was the toll of these years, it was far exceeded in the terrible nor'easter of October, 1880, when the wind force was officially recorded as eleven, a storm with a velocity of 70 miles an hour.   I have gone to the trouble of analysing out the majority of the smack losses from the excellent records loaned me by my friend and fellow S.N.R. member, Commander H. Oliver Hill.

First to deal with the Yarmouth losses.   The six-year old, 47-ton, *Ariel* was abandoned 120 miles W. by S. of Spurn Head, having lost 2 of her crew of 7, but she was later picked up and towed into Grimsby.   *Defiance*, 50 tons, master W. Childs, was sunk with all hands, *Dido*, 42 tons, built 1863, foundered 70 miles W.S.W. of her home port with the loss of 1 man.   The 35-ton *Expert*, built 1867, went missing with all hands, the 40-ton *Foam*, built 1847, was dismasted and half her crew drowned, while the 43-ton *Gleaner*, built 1854, foundered with all hands.   *Harbinger*, 45 tons, built 1861, lost her mizzen mast, boat and 1 man, the 40-ton *Luna*, built 1866, sank with all hands, as did the 39-ton *Mystery*, built 1867.   The 42-ton *Regalia*, built 1866, lost all her sails and half her crew while fishing in Botney Gut.   *Saucy Maid*, 26 tons, built 1846, collided with *Mary Ann Matilda*, 23 miles E. by S. of Yarmouth and sank with the loss of 3 of her crew.   The 31-ton *Yarborough*, built 1855, went missing with all hands.

The neighbouring port of Lowestoft lost the 48-ton *Albert and Alice*, built 1876, which went missing with all hands, *Alfred and Jane*, lost all her sails and 1 of the crew, the *Dowager Countess*, 42 tons, built 1873, went down with all hands, and the 47-ton *Ocean Queen*, built 1873, stranded on the Haisborough Sands and became a total loss.   *Harry* of London, built 1861, was last seen on the 27th October and the *Minx*, built 1873, lost her mizzen mast, boat and 1 man off the southern part of the Dogger.

The Hull smacks *Laurel*, 52 tons, built 1859, and *Sarah*, built 1858, with *Eliza*, built 1865, went missing with all hands, *Lurline*, built 1879, caught fire, *New Catherine*, built 1870, stranded near Hunstanton, *Alderman Ferries*, 73 tons, built 1876, went ashore near Saltfleet, and *Spray*, built 1844, ran on the main near Bridlington.

It will be noticed that disaster came to new and old smacks alike, and many others lost men overboard.   Take the case of the 54-ton *Willie*, of Yarmouth, built in 1873, which lost masts, gear and 3 of the crew off the S.E. part of the Dogger. Her skipper, John Mann, who had been 40 years at sea, said he had never experienced a worse time or seen a " snarlier sea ".   His smack was laying-to under close-reefed canvas when the fleet jibed round on the other tack just before midnight.   Two lads were on the lookout when a heavy sea came aboard, poured along the deck and down below.   The vessel rolled over on her beam ends and masts went by the board, but the boys were unhurt.   Everything on deck was swept away, the fishing gear went overboard on the weather side and the warp ran out.   The skipper's son and 2 men were missing, probably washed away when the bulwarks went.   The rest of the crew baled all night and at dawn John Mann found one of the pump boxes and tying a handspike across it, succeeded in pumping the smack free of water, but every scrap of food and water had been ruined.   After freezing in the icy wind for hours, the

66   COMING IN TO YARMOUTH HAVEN

Better Luck, Y.H.1039, 69 tons, built at Southtown, 1885.   Although a pair of reefs are down the main boom is bent with strain of mainsail which has girt on the topping lift.   The bowsprit is fitted with a bobstay.

67   STEAM CUTTER RACING TO MARKET

Gannet, G.Y.939, built of iron at Hull in 1884 for The Great Grimsby Ice Co. Ltd. 68 h.p., length 133.7 ft., beam 21.7 ft., depth 11 ft., 140 N.T., 244 G.T.

68 TRAWLERS PUTTING TO SEA
37 smacks are in sight.

69 *LITTLE WAVE*, Y.H.125
Built at Grimsby, 1886. The square blue flag of Hewett's Short Blue Fleet flies at main truck, topsail is set a'weather, and one reef is down in main and mizzen. The light-boards are lashed in the main rigging and a boat from another smack is alongside the lee quarter, her own boat is on deck.

70 SMACK BOAT LEAVING THE CARRIER

71 THE SHORT BLUE FLEET TRUNKING

Y.H.1068 *Rescue*, 69 tons, built at Rye, 1886. The admiral in stern sheets of the boat is holding a bundle of papers.

72 BOARDING FISH FOR BILLINGSGATE

The small boats keep end on to the short seas as they pass to and fro, always dropping down to leeward.

73 THROWING UP EMPTY TRUNK
FROM CARRIER'S HOLD

74 THE MISSION SMACK *QUEEN VICTORIA*
131 tons, built at Southtown by Fellows, 1888. Working with the
Grimsby Ice Co's fleet on the Dogger, 1892. Note boom guys rove off
to starboard, reef bands and four cringles.

crew sighted a Hull smack which bore down to the rescue, threw out a boat and supplied much needed food, water and firing. Next the warp was made fast and the *Willie* was towed for 3 days and nights until Grimsby was reached.

The toll taken of coasting craft was equally heavy, 11 brigs, 9 brigantines, 7 schooners, 7 ketches and 2 sloops were driven ashore all along the East Coast (Plate 76). Many of these vessels had survived the storms of over half a century, yet succumbed to the fury of that vicious nor'easter, but their names and history are outside the scope of this book.

The Wells lifeboat, *Eliza Adams*, capsized when going to the assistance of the brig *Ocean Queen* and 11 of her crew of 13 were drowned.

The fishing ports on the East Coast had scarcely recovered from the shock of this calamity when an even worse one overtook the fleets in March, 1883, and they mourned the loss of 255 men and boys.

For some days the trawlers had been working over the grounds to the nor'ard of the Dogger. There was a peculiar dullness of sea and sky with a lot of swell rolling on to the dreaded " Edge ", but there was little wind, in fact there had been almost four days of calm. The fleet shot their trawls about 11 p.m. and just before midnight a N.N.W. storm burst, the sea rose with amazing swiftness, and worst of all the Edge of the Dogger lay to leeward. In inky blackness some tried to haul, for no trawlerman likes to cut away valuable gear, but it was of little avail in many cases as the smacks pitched so violently that the thick warps parted as if made of cotton. Dawn broke over a roaring, foaming waste of water and revealed disabled craft in every direction. Men had been swept from their own smacks and washed aboard others, many had gone for ever, dismasted hulks with holds full of water, rolled sluggishly. One Grimsby vessel had a fishhold flagged with stone, which served as ballast and made a cool floor for the fish trunks. A huge sea struck her and *she rolled clean over*, the iron kentledge below the floors burst up and fish, flags and ballast were all mixed up together. Those vessels trying to run for it were like half-tide rocks as sea after sea filled the decks to the rails and the skippers hung on to their tillers for dear life.

Day after day the wind blew with appalling fury and when it took off the smacksmen tried to jury rig their sorely damaged craft, but food and water were the most serious problem as everything had been swamped. Those that could gave a friendly tow to others less fortunate, and slowly made for port where the docks rapidly filled with lame ducks. Harrowing scenes were witnessed as relatives met every newcomer, hoping against hope that a loved one had been picked up. As the days passed it was seen that the toll was to be a terrible one. 43 smacks were missing with all hands, 222 men, 7 had been abandoned with the loss of 4 men, 38 had been seriously damaged and 13 men drowned, while 51 had sustained some damage with the loss of 16 men. Many a man who survived had lost his nerve and never went to sea again.

I have thought it well that the names I have been able to trace should be recorded.

HULL LOSSES

Name of smack	Tons	Date and where built	Crew	Fate
Andrew Marvel	72	1877 Hull	5	Foundered
Ann Sims	62	1871 Brixham	5	Missing
Bernice	80	1878 Burton Stather	5	do
Bessie Lewis	83	1879 Goole	5	do
Brilliant	70	1875 Rye	5	do
Britannia	63	1872 Hull	5	do
Burton Stather	63	1867 Burton Stather	5	do
Clara	56	1870 Hull	5	do
Dart	84	1877 Dartmouth	5	do
Doncaster	69	1875 Sandwich	5	do
Dove	70	1876 Newhaven	5	do
Friend's Goodwill	65	1871 Hull	5	Missing
Harrier	65	1871 Burton Stather	5	Seen to founder E edge of Dogger
John Harker	73	1878 Hull	5	Missing
John Rogers	51	1866 Hull	5	do
Lily	71	1875 Dartmouth	5	do
Lively	61	1870 Hull		Sank after being abandoned 70 miles NE of Spurn Point
Lizzie Gale	56	1868 Whitby	5	Missing
Loch Long	75	1880 Goole	5	do
Mary Esther	82	1879 Dartmouth	5	do
North Sea	72	1875 Burton Stather	4	Sank 190 miles ENE of Spurn
Patriot	68	1875 Hull	5	Missing
Sunbeam	61	1871 Hull	5	do
The Boys	76	1878 Dartmouth	5	do
Uno	72	1870 New Holland	5	do
Vanguard	74	1877 Hull	5	do
Water Lily	76	1879 New Holland	5	do

It will be seen that these were fine, powerful smacks, the smallest registering 51 tons, the largest 84, the oldest was built 16 years before, the youngest 3, with the majority about 10 years old.

GRIMSBY LOSSES

Name of Smack	Tons	Date and where built	Crew	Fate
Cornellia	42	1879 Grimsby	5	Missing
Emu	56	1867 Burton Stather	5	do
Lark	76	1879 Burton Stather	5	do
Leader	64	1872 Hull	5	do
Olga	76	1880 Grimsby	6	do
Otter	61	1870 Brixham	5	Sank 25 miles E of Spurn
Rose	61	1867 Grimsby	5	Missing
William Gills	68	1877 Galmpton	5	do

YARMOUTH LOSSES

Name of Smack	Tons	Date built	Crew	Fate
Mascotte	28	1882	6	Last seen off Borkum
Mosquito	28	1848	5	do Winterton Shoal
Reaper	34	1877	6	do 20 miles off Yarmouth
Sea Flower	38	1868	6	Missing
Clarence	49	1876	7	Last seen in Silver Pits

LOWESTOFT LOSSES

Alacrity	39	1878	4	Missing
Red Rose	69	1878	5	do

COLCHESTER LOSSES

Conquest and *Express,* cutter smacks, missing all hands.

These were the major losses, dozens of smacks lost masts, sails, gear, etc., in varying proportions and one or more members of crews.

The 72-ton *North Sea* had been built of oak by John Wray & Son at Burton Stather in 1875, her dimensions being 72.6 by 19.9 by 10.1, and 70 to 80 tons of iron dross were carried as ballast. She was insured for £790, the largest sum allowed by rule 12 of the Hull & Grimsby Mutual Fishing Vessels Insurance Co., although valued at £1,200. None of her sails had been in use twelve months when she joined the Red Cross fleet in the Silver Pits on the 2nd February. On the 3rd March she boarded her fish at 11 a.m. and the admiral, Joseph Fern, skipper of the 69-ton *Smiling Morn*, built at Goole 1873, hoisted his flag that trawls were not to be shot. The fleet lay-to in a moderate breeze and by 1 a.m. it was blowing heavily, two reefs were down in the mainsail, three in the mizzen, one in the foresail and the storm jib was set. The sea continued to rise and at 9 a.m. while on the port tack the smack shipped a heavy sea, the masts went over the side, pulling the chain plates clean out and the deck was broken open. *North Sea* sank in 8 minutes, 3 men being picked up by the 78-ton *Dayspring*, built at Hull in 1876.

The 72-ton *John Harker*, insured for £850, was built by Hunt & Fowler at Hull in 1877 and measured 73.3 by 20.4 by 10, with oak planking from the bilge up, American elm below. Between her timbers was 5 to 6 tons of cement and ballast was 65 tons of iron dross. About 2 p.m. on the 6th March, during a thick snowstorm, William Rust, who was fleeting with the Great Northern fleet on the Edge of the Dogger, saw the *John Harker* 20 yards away with all sails blown away, fore gaff swinging about aloft, mizzen and boat gone with all the port bulwarks, and the hull level with the water. Her crew hailed to be taken off but this was impossible owing to the snow and an hour later when the squall cleared away there was no sign of the unfortunate smack.

The body of W. Nelson, master of the 72-ton *Andrew Marvel*, built by M'Cann at Hull in 1877, was hauled up in the trawl of the 79-ton *Emily Florence*, built Brixham 1881. *Olga*, built at Grimsby by James Hallett in 1879, was commanded by George Little, one of the most experienced men in the fishing trade, who had been admiral for many years, but was single-boating on this occasion and the lad, who was extra hand, was making his first trip to sea.

The Short Blue Fleet working on Swatch Bank to the south of the Dogger under admiral William Richard Skinley, sustained little damage. Most of the Yarmouth boats lost were small converter smacks. *Sea Flower*, built at Jersey by Joshua de la Laye in 1868, had been lengthened 6 ft. by Thomas Beeching in 1875, increasing her dimensions to 63.8 by 18.3 by 7.6. *Reaper*, built at Yarmouth in 1877 by Beeching, was only 55.8 by 17.7 by 7.7 and clench-built of 1⅛ in. American oak with copper fastenings to the lower plank of the topsides, which were 2½ in. English oak, carvel-built. Most of her sails were new when she left port to join Smith's fleet working off the Texel.

Mosquito was also clench-built and although given in the register as being built in 1848 had actually been constructed 20 years earlier, her dimensions being 49 by 13 by 6.4. In 1881 a new 2½ in. pitch-pine deck was fitted and a few minor repairs carried out by Beeching, who reported that the original timbers were still in very good condition.

Thomas & Florry, built at Barton-on-Humber by Frederickson & Fawcett in 1877, and insured for £880, was abandoned three-parts full of water, with hatches stove-in, after losing her boat and mizzen. The crew were picked up by the 75-ton Hull smack *Blessing*, built at Newhaven in 1876, but were later transferred to the Grimsby smack *Energy*, 68 tons, built at Galmpton 1881, and landed at Hull on the 9th March. As the starboard quarter of *Thomas & Florry* was open for 15 to 16 ft., the skipper of *Blessing* did not consider she was worth towing in, but the 73-ton Hull smack *Reynard*, built at Rye in 1877, picked her up later and towed the battered hulk into the Humber where she was surveyed by Mr. Tolley on the 12th March. The stern was much damaged, 40 ft. of the covering board and 6 stanchions had gone on the starboard side, and 5 stanchions on the port. 43 ft. of rails had gone on either side and bulwarks and washstrakes from aft to the main rigging, dandy winch, companion and skylight had disappeared, and the platform over the ballast had burst up. In spite of this damage the smack was worth repairing and in 1885 was owned by Mrs. Mary Ann Norris.

Some of the smacks which survived rode to their trawls, others to chain cables shackled to a stockless anchor, but the majority followed the usual smacksmen's practice of keeping under a considerable spread of canvas, a close-reefed main and mizzen, foresail and storm jib. Most skippers liked to keep steerage way, holding the belief that a smack rode more steadily, and was prevented from ranging about and falling into the trough of the seas.

The Court of Enquiry considered that it would perhaps have been safer to lay-to in such a gale as blew on that never-to-be-forgotten occasion, they found no case of loss having been caused by defects in spars, sails or rigging, but one or two vessels might have had structural weakness which came to light under such a severe test, while the ballast may have shifted in a few instances.

The consensus of opinion was that, in the main, crews were not so efficient as formerly, especially in the three inferior grades, due to the cessation of all control over apprentices following the 1880 Act.

This disaster was spectacular, but the 5 years 1876 to 1881 had claimed a toll of 425 fishing vessels and 866 lives. 1876-77 had seen 109 vessels and 313 lives lost, 1877-78 66 smacks and 82 lives, 1878-79 55 boats with 69 men drowned, 1879-80 70 vessels and 73 lives, while 1880-81 had taken 125 smacks and 329 lives.

The appalling figures include all types of fishing vessels working around the coasts of the United Kingdom and an analysis of the casualties shows that 172 strandings cost 55 lives; 105 collisions, 74 lives; 75 founderings, 117 lives; 81 missing vessels had 488 men and boys on board, and 16 " other causes " claimed 132 lives, a terrible toll to add to the price of fish.

In the years 1878-82 the Short Blue Fleet lost only 25 men, including 4 drowned while ferrying fish to the carriers.

Only nine months after the March 1883 gale another wicked nor'wester brought disaster, especially to the East Anglian smacks which were working with the Short Blue Fleet in the Botney Gut, and the names I can trace make a formidable list.

YARMOUTH LOSSES

Name of Smack	Tons	Built	Men lost	Fate
Adventure	47	1875	1	Lost mizzen, boat, bulwarks
Ann	47	1876	7	Collided with sch. *Cordellia* 2 m ENE of Corton Lightship
Cautious	55	1883	6	Last seen in Botney Gut
Dora	62	1883	7	do do
Evangaline	37	1871	1	Lost sails, 60 m NE of Yarmouth
Frances	54	1880	3	Foundered 10 m E of Silver Pits
Golden Fleece	44	1866	1	Lost bulwarks, etc
Hercules	53	1880	1	Lost sails, mizzen mast 40 m E of Yarmouth
Huntsman	48	1860	6	Missing
Jane	35	1853		Abandoned 45 m E of Yarmouth later towed in and condemned
Lothair	43	1872	6	Thrown on beam ends 38 m ENE Lowestoft, later drove ashore and broke up
Monarch	44	1865	1	Foundered in Clay Deeps

Name of Smack	Tons	Built	Men Lost	Fate
Scorpion	49	1861	6	Missing in Botney Gut
Selma	39	1871	6	do do
Spinaway	32	1883	1	Decks swept E side of Silver Pits

LOWESTOFT LOSSES

Champion	47	1862	5	Missing
Dewdrop	53	1873	5	do
Lizzie	60	1876	5	do
Topsy	50	1864	5	do
Nora Creina	47	1872	2	Lost masts, boat etc 70 m E of Lowestoft

LONDON LOSSES

Sincerity	58	1879	1	Dismasted in Silver Pits

HULL LOSSES

Name of Smack	Tons	Date & where built		Crew	Fate
Aerial	77	1881	Stoneham	5	Missing
Night Hawk	65	1886	Hull	5	do

GRIMSBY LOSSES

Baxter	74	1877	Grimsby	5	Missing
Conqueror	68	1870	Grimsby	5	do
Harriet	58	1869	Grimsby	5	Foundered 40 miles ENE of Spurn

These casualties were the highlights, but the number of men lost in the 5 years 1884 to 1888 amounted to the amazing total of 1,328, of whom 756 were lost by wreck, 572 in other ways. In 1889, 116 fishermen went missing in smacks never heard of again, but the following year not a man was lost in this way. In 3 years the lives lost included 108 men who fell or were washed overboard and 192 wrecked in 1884, 85 and 133 in 1885, and 93 and 85 in 1886, the average loss of life in 9 years being 268. The S.W. gale on the 25th June, 1890 claimed 42 lives.

In 1891 there was a rather extraordinary incident when two smacks were sunk by gunfire from H.M.S. *Plucky*, owing to the peculiar atmospheric conditions making for a serious error in the calculation of the distance the warship was from her target. In the southerly gale of the 11th November, 42 lives were lost, 16 smacks being overwhelmed. In 1893, 197 men were lost, but the following year was the blackest on record, no less than 492 men and boys being drowned in the course of that exceptionally stormy twelve months.

During the W.N.W. gale which raged from the 8th to the 12th of February, 1894, 43 lives were lost. The Hull smacks *Colin*, 78 tons, built 1879 at Hull, and the *James Colin Hoad*, 71 tons, built 1876 at Rye, went missing with all hands, and

Thomas Cook, 71 tons, built 1882 at Rye, stranded at Sondervig, Jutland. Grimsby lost the 75-ton *Rowland*, built at Hull in 1876, missing with all hands, while *Coventry*, 79 tons, built 1876 at Grimsby, foundered 115 miles N.E. by E. of Spurn, and *Dawn*, 66 tons, built 1871 at Grimsby, stranded on the Norwegian coast.

The Short Blue Fleet lost the 67-ton *Bluejacket*, built 1885, which foundered in Lat 55° 15′ N., 5° 25′ E., with loss of 6 men, *Lena*, 62 tons, built at Dover in 1873, sank after collision with *Ferret* in the Clay Deeps, and *Wildfire*, 73 tons, built 1878 at Dartmouth went missing with her crew of 6. All these were registered at Yarmouth. Of their London smacks *Ada*, 67 tons, built 1868 at Barking, sank after collision, *Majestic*, 60 tons, built 1882 at Dartmouth, foundered east of the Clay Deeps and *Mississippi*, 73 tons, built 1886 at Dartmouth, was never heard of again.

In the S.S.W. gale of the 10th to the 14th November, 1894, 20 lives were lost. One smack drove ashore on the Norfolk coast, was abandoned, refloated and was eventually picked up *in the Channel off Littlehampton*.

The worst disaster of the year was the W.N.W. blizzard of the 22nd December, when the Great Northern Fleet of Hull suffered a crippling blow, as they were caught on the port tack off the Edge of the Dogger and drove into shoal water. The other fleets, on the starboard tack, worked into deep water and rode out the gale successfully. That night Hull lost 106 men and 11 smacks, Grimsby 30 men and 1 smack, Yarmouth 30 men and 6 smacks, in all 229 lives were taken, and of these 163 went in vessels against whose names in the records is the laconic phrase " missing with all hands ".

Two years later 152 men were drowned and as steam supplanted sail the numbers were proportionally reduced, but by no means rendered nugatory, and the price paid in lives is still a high one.

I have spent many hours wading through dry-as-dust statistics hidden away in ancient blue books and other official records, and have endeavoured to translate cold figures into something more readable. Within the limits of such research, often done under hurried conditions in dusty offices, and taking tonnage as a fair guide, I have arrived at the following smack losses for the years 1879 to 1913.

Foundered 359. Lost in collision 355. Stranded 307. Lost by fire 45, a total of 1,066 vessels in 34 years, the majority being in the 19th century, the numbers from the various fishing stations will be given in the appropriate chapters dealing with each port, together with any special accidents or losses.

These casualties were brought about by Acts of God over which man could have little or no control, but in the four years following it fell to the Germans to descend to depths of infamy which at first seemed unbelievable to men who found their business in the great waters, as hitherto a fairly decent code of conduct had been adopted in naval warfare. But there was no plumbing the well of Hun Kulture as their U-boats began to make war on innocent, unarmed fishermen, who were striving to earn their bread upon the deep, and whose smack was their all, for even if compensation for loss came tardily, their means of livelihood had been ruthlessly taken from them.

Events moved swiftly following the declaration of war as on the 7th August, 1914, the 227-ton steam trawler *Tubal Cain* was captured by the armed merchant cruiser *Kaiser Wilhelm der Grosse*, 50 miles W.N.W. of Iceland. Three weeks later the Boston fleet lost 7 out of 8 in one day, the crews being taken prisoner. During the month 25 steam trawlers were sunk, chiefly by cruisers and destroyers, and by the end of May, 1915, no less than 91 had been sunk or captured.

It was not until the 18th November, 1914, that the first casualty occurred to a Lo'sterman, when the 60-ton *Speculator*, L.T.1050, struck a mine 12 miles E. by N.½E. from Smith's Knoll and sank with her crew of 5. On the 3rd June, 1915, the 60-ton *E. & C.*, L.T.563, was captured by a submarine 40 miles S.E. by E. of Lowestoft and sunk by a time bomb placed on board, while *Boy Horace*, L.T.943, was put down some 10 miles away, and the following day the 69-ton *Economy*, L.T.483, was sunk in the vicinity. On the 9th 4 smacks, *Edward*, L.T.951, *Qui Vive*, L.T.702, *Britannia*, L.T.592 and *Welfare*, L.T.555, were similarly destroyed on the same fishing ground.

June saw 9 smacks sunk and the attacks continued in July when 20 were captured and sunk off Lowestoft. August proved a black month, on the 11th no less than 10 vessels being sunk 17 to 48 miles off Cromer and the total sinkings rose to 29, falling to 7 in September. The first sinking in the English Channel was on the 30th of the month when *Albion*, B.M.160, was mined 8 miles S. by W. off Berry Head with the loss of the skipper and 2 men.

No further attacks took place in 1915, but the first month in the new year saw 7 lost off Lowestoft, 2 in February, 6 in March, only 1 in April and 4 in May, all on the East Anglian fishing grounds. June had no sinkings, but 7 boats were lost in July, 6 of them on the 17th near the N. Haisboro' lightship, in August losses fell to 2 and for the time being the scene of U-boat activity was transferred to the West Coast, where many Lowestoft and Ramsgate men had gone to fish. On the 9th September, 4 smacks were sunk about 20 miles S.S.E. of Start Point and only 1 in the North Sea off Smith's Knoll. October was free, but in November, 10 were sunk in the North Sea and English Channel. 2 of the 3 lost in December were put down 20 to 25 miles N.N.W. of Trevose Head, and 1 was mined off the Eddystone with the loss of 3 men. It was now evident that a submarine had found this area a happy hunting ground from her point of view, as in January, 1917, 6 were sunk by gunfire within 30 miles of land on the 30th of the month and 1 off Start Point, and the 1st February saw *Inverlyon*, L.T.687 (Plate 32) and *Ada* lost in the same area and only 1 out of the 10 sinkings was in the North Sea, where it was evident that the toll taken by the decoy smacks was having results.

March saw a sharp rise to 29, including 11 smacks sunk on the 12th off Trevose Head, and 9 on the 24th off the Eddystone, but only 3 were lost the following month, all off the south Devon coast. 6 sinkings took place in May, 4 being off the Stags, rising to 17 in June, 10 being off the Stags and Strumble Head.

In July the scene of submarine activity returned to the North Sea where 5 smacks were sunk, 2 being lost in August, but losses rose to 9 in October, including some Channel sinkings, falling to 3 in November and the same number in December.

January 1918, saw a rise to 9, all off South Devon, and the 8 lost in February were in the same vicinity, many being Lowestoft and Ramsgate vessels. March saw a U-boat working off the Isle of Man, probably indulging in target practice whilst lying in wait for the convoys heading for Liverpool, the month's total being 4. Only *Ruth*, L.T.1109, was lost in April near the South Cross Sand buoy, but the number rose to 12 in May, 3 being sunk near the Smith's Knoll Spar buoy, and 8 about 26 miles W.N.W. of the Calf of Man, whilst *Pretty Polly* was shelled off Round-stone Bay on the west coast of Ireland, with the loss of 7 lives. The 3 lost in June all fell victims to a submarine lurking in the vicinity of the Smith's Knoll Spar buoy, as did the 10 sunk in July, N.E. of the Haisboro' light vessel and these losses included the 44-ton *Francis Robert*, L.T.1024, which had the distinction of being the last sailing trawler to be sunk by a German U-boat, being destroyed by gunfire 8 miles N.E. from the Haisborough Lightship (Plate 78).

August, September and October were free from any smack losses and the last casualty occurred off Rye 3 days before the Armistice, when *Conster* struck a mine, fortunately without loss of life.

I am greatly indebted to Mr. James Giles of Skegness, who kindly loaned me his precious official record of merchant ship sinkings in the 1914-18 war. From this appalling list of 2,479 vessels sunk by enemy action I extracted the matter relevant to my story. A total of 675 fishing vessels, sail and steam, were sunk with the loss of 434 lives, 34 being destroyed by enemy cruisers, 578 by submarines, and 63 by mines.

A grim story, to which can be added the 136 fishing craft lost and the 60 damaged, with 814 casualties of the recent war. The fishermen of England have indeed played their part right nobly, and the tragedy is that such risks should be added to the already many marine perils, and by men who would willingly go to the help of each other in times of stress in peace time.

Among the many Lowestoft losses were some of the splendid smacks built at Reynolds yard, Lake Lothing, to the design of Mr. Wm. Parker, who kindly loaned me the data from which I drew up Plans 5, pages 318-20, and his signature thereon assures their accuracy. A few details of costs, etc., taken from his own notebook, may be of interest.

Crystal, L.T.325, sunk by time bomb placed on board by a U-boat on the 27th June, 1916, 25 miles E.S.E. of Southwold, was built in July, 1904, for Mr. H. R. Boardley. The contract price of £885 was for hull and spars, the nett costs being :—wages £167 3s. 11½d., timber £278 16s., stores and fastenings £55 5s. 4d., spars and blocks £81 15s., ironwork £82, small boat £7 10s. stones for placing under and round the stove £1 4s. 2d., stoves and funnels £7 15s. 9d., a total of £681 10s. 2½d., to which overheads and sawmill expenses had to be added, so there was not an excessive margin of profit.

Another loss was the 56-ton smack *Harold*, L.T.693, built for Mr. W. H. Podd in 1905, the sixty-fourth ship to be laid down in the yard. Wages here amounted to £205 8s. 9d., fastenings to £23 8s. 5d., and painters' labour and materials to £8 16s., but there is no record of contract price or total nett costs.

Henry Charles, laid down in July, 1906, cost £245 13s. 4d. for wages, and both these smacks measured 71 ft. 9 in. L.B.P., beam 18 ft. 9 in., depth 8 ft. 9 in., while *Francis Robert*, built in September had £258 12s. 10½d. expended on her in wages and £24 14s. 3d. in stores and fastenings. Other smacks lost were *Ivan*, *Ruth*, *Humphrey*, *Purple Heather* and *Arbor Vitae*, a pretty formidable list for the product of only one yard and it is possible that others may not have been entered in the book.

These losses of smacks actually engaged in fishing are outside the casualties to the decoys which started operations when sinkings rose to serious heights. The numbers sunk show how little the fearless smacksmen cared for this added peril to their daily existence, for it would have been easy for them to refuse to go to sea, but the meaning of the word "strike" was unknown to those splendid seamen, who fully realized the urgent need for their catches to augment the ever-decreasing meat ration as more and more refrigerated ships fell victims to submarines, which concentrated on these vessels and tankers as they did in the 1939-45 conflict.

Just one instance to show the spirit of these daring men. In January, 1916, the 22-ton *Acacia*, L.T.1087, was fishing when a U-boat surfaced and opened fire with a machine-gun, doing considerable damage to sails, rigging and main boom of the smack which had her trawl down. Then the submarine started to approach to leeward, but Skipper J. Crooks, who had lost his first smack the previous August, made up his mind that this should not happen again if he could help it. There was a fine, strong S.W. breeze blowing and when the enemy was about 200 yards away, Crooks ordered the warp to be chopped away with an axe. The smack leaped forward like a spurred horse and the skipper put the helm hard-up and tried to ram, unfortunately missing by only a few feet. The no-doubt astonished U-boat commander ordered a crash dive and the cowardly attacker was not seen again. *Acacia* escaped in the darkness and returned to Lowestoft to report. The Admiralty were graciously pleased to award the sum of £50 to the skipper and crew of 4, together with a letter of appreciation which no doubt became an heirloom.

Far from intimidating smacksmen this ruthless submarine warfare against helpless, unarmed vessels only aroused in them the urge to retaliate and I was fortunate enough to get into touch with Skipper F. W. Moxey who was one of the first to offer his vessel and services, saying "Give me a gun and I can sink a submarine" or shall we say, words to that effect.

Although such a novel suggestion fired the imagination of junior naval officers, it failed to convince the hierarchy until sinkings reached a very high level. Then the skipper was asked to report to the Naval Base at Lowestoft and 4 smacks were fitted out with 3-pounders and naval ratings supplied to work them. Within 48 hours of leaving harbour the U.B.4 was sent to the bottom on the 8th August, 1915, Skipper Moxey was at the tiller and Lieut.-Com. Hamond, D.S.C., R.N., in charge of the naval party. Just to make certain that the sailing smack was credited with the destruction of a submarine the German's flagstaff and naval ensign were produced.

The Admiralty now chartered additional fishing vessels, some being fitted with guns, others equipped with special mined nets in which it was hoped to enmesh the submerged raiders. Such decoy smacks were not altogether an unmixed blessing as the fact that a seemingly innocent craft might be an armed vessel, removed the last vestige of lack of justification for attacking without warning, as the U-boat captain could now never be certain he was not engaging a ship legitimately wearing the White Ensign. That was a minor matter as the sinkings would have gone on, decoys or no decoys.

First of all it would be as well to mention that the German U-boats of that day were not the big ocean-going submarines of the recent war, able to range far out into the Atlantic. Some were only glorified " cocoa tins ", about 90 ft. long and 10 ft. beam, with a surface speed of barely 6½ knots, reduced to 5 when running submerged. Armed with 2 torpedoes, and sometimes carrying mines, they had a small gun mounted close to the conning tower. Their thin hulls were easily pierced by shell fire and the mines carried were more than likely to detonate if the raider became entangled in the special nets.

Mr. Moxey wrote me that one of the first decoys fitted out was his smack *G. & E.*, built for him at Porthleven in 1906, at a total cost of £1,500, named after his two children Gladys and Edward, and the first smack to receive the official £1,000 prize money for a confirmed sinking. Other vessels were *Pet* and *Inverlyon*.

In September several engagements were fought and another of Mr. Moxey's smacks, *Telesia*, was commissioned and became the most famous of all the decoys, being credited with at least 5 and possibly 7 sinkings. At times it was difficult to obtain certain proof and the Admiralty were chary about allowing " possibles ".

On the 23rd March, 1916, under the command of Skipper W. S. Wharton, R.N.R., *Telesia* was in action with U.B.13 and succeeded in making two direct hits on the conning tower, bursting the submarine open. Her skipper was awarded the D.S.C. and two of the crew the D.S.M. In the following month her name was changed to *Hobby Hawk* and she was commissioned by Lieut. H. W. Harvey and in company with *Cheerio* put to sea to tow special nets attached to mines. These were shot on the usual fishing ground and later the hydrophone picked up the sound of a submarine's engines and soon after something caught up in the nets. Two explosions followed in rapid succession and when the gear was hauled fragments of steel were found enmeshed and a strong smell of oil was noticed.   That was all that remained of the minelayer U.C.3.

Further indecisive encounters took place, but another success was scored on the 19th May, 1916, when the U.77 was destroyed after she had sunk an unarmed Lowestoft smack a short time before.   On finding *Hobby Hawk* was armed, the men in the conning tower shrieked " Kamerad, kamerad " but it was of no avail.   Skipper Wharton now collected a bar to his D.S.C.

Another action with two submarines and the smacks *I'll Try* and *Boy Alfred* is best described in the skipper's own words :—

" One submarine was coming at us from the S.S.E. and the other from the S.E. The first opened fire on the *I'll Try*, Skipper T. A. Crisp, and then bore down on us. When 250 yards off her commander called out ' Leave your ship, I'm going to torpedo you '.   I left the tiller and walk for'ard and called out, ' What did you say ? ' He again called out, ' Leave your ship, I'm going to torpedo you.'   We launched our little boat to make him believe we were leaving our ship.   I then called to the gunner, ' Let go buffer.'   He fired and missed with the first shot, but got him square under the conning tower with the second and blew her right open—U.C.62—we could see the men in their black and white stocking caps.   As soon as we had sunk the first sub., the second one, U.B.36 submerged and we had to leave the pirates to their fate and try and sink the other one.   She came for *Boy Alfred* with only her periscope showing and got in between us and the *I'll Try*.   We fired six shots, but missed each time and we had to stop as we were in danger of hitting the *I'll Try*. This was part of the enemy's clever strategy.   We soon out-manoeuvred her and she fired a torpedo at us which missed.   At the same time *I'll Try* opened fire and the first shot hit her in the foredeck and burst her right open.   She sleeps with her kamerad in 28 fathoms of water 20 miles S.E. of Lowestoft.   When we went into action we sent a pigeon with a message to the Base at Lowestoft.   The Commodore sent a fast P-boat to our assistance.   We could see her coming up as fast as her engines would drive her, but it was all over when she arrived."

The *G. & E.* had been renamed *I'll Try* for reasons of concealment and this was again altered to *Nelson* when in August, 1916, in company with *Ethel & Millie*, they encountered one of the new U-boats mounting a 4.1 gun and so able to outrange the puny armament on the smacks.   *Nelson* was trawling on the port tack when Skipper Crisp sighted a submarine on the surface, and the engine was started up, as motors had been fitted into decoy smacks to increase their manoeuvreability.   The enemy opened fire at considerable range and soon began hitting, one shell completely dis-embowelling Skipper Crisp who, as he lay on the deck in his death agony, ordered his son to send off a pigeon with a message to Base, and then throw overboard all the confidential papers before abandoning ship.   When the boat was lowered the old man called to his boy to throw him overboard, but this they could not do, and within 15 minutes the gallant skipper went down with his command and the waters closed over her, apparently for ever.

The crew of the other smack had been taken prisoner and were last seen on deck as the submarine left the scene of the action. The survivors of *Nelson* rowed all night, hoping for rescue by some passing ship, but none came. At last they sighted a buoy and succeeded in making fast to it, being at length picked up and taken into port. H.M. King George V made a posthumous award of the V.C. to Skipper Crisp, while his son received the D.S.M.

Now comes the sequel. Two years after peace was proclaimed the stern portion of *Nelson*, ex *G. & E.* was trawled up where the action had been fought, 40 miles E.N.E. of Lowestoft. A seat was made from the timbers and I saw it when I was visiting Lowestoft in October, 1946, and Mr. Moxey kindly loaned me the photograph of the transit rail, with *G. & E.* deeply cut in it (Plate 77).

Telesia was present at the Silver Jubilee Review at Spithead and the late King George V came on board and Mr. F. W. Moxey was presented to him. She continued fishing up to the outbreak of the 1939-45 war, during which she was moored as an obstruction to prevent enemy seaplanes landing on the Broads. Later she was sold to Norway and sailed north in 1947.

Telesia was built at Rye by G. & T. Smith in 1911 and registered 46 tons. Plate 79 shows her hauled up on the slipway at Lowestoft for refit, and gives a good idea of the fine lines aft.

Another fishing smack which took part in the Spithead Review was *Boy Leslie*, L.O.392 (Plate 80) the last sailing vessel to fly the famous Short Blue flag, and I am indebted to Mr. R. Scott Hewett for some interesting facts about the crew which manned her on that historic occasion.

On board were Mr. R. Muirhead Hewett and his son Captain R. S. Hewett, managing director of the firm, his second son Lieut. G. S. Hewett, D.S.C., who served in the *Vindictive* in the 1914-18 war, and was aboard the smack as mate, also his grandson R. P. Hewett, a schoolboy.

Skipper F. Sutton commanded an armed smack during the war and when in the smack *Zircon*, L.T.134, 48 tons, was attacked by a German submarine 26 miles S.W. of the Smalls during a heavy gale on the 13th February, 1916. He and his crew, 5 in all, had to take to their boat without either food or water and they were rowing for 73 hours from Lundy Island before the wind, until they were picked up by the pilot cutter off Queenstown. Two of the men went insane and had to be shoved under the thwarts in the bottom of the boat where they were so frozen that they had to be wrapped in cotton wool for 3 days, suffering from frost-bite. The skipper was 16 weeks in hospital with frost-bitten feet, but this experience did not stop him as he next shipped in *Corona* and picked up a mine in his trawl. It exploded and practically sank the vessel, but by keeping 3 pumps going they were able to get into harbour. This happened in October, 1916. In 1917, in the same smack they were attacked by a German Zeppelin off Smith's Knoll, but although bombs dropped all round none succeeded in hitting the vessel.

The fishing mate, H. James, was blown up twice, once in March, 1916 in the 59-ton *Inter Nos*, L.T.647, 12 miles N.N.W. of Trevose Head, when a submarine came up alongside and blew them up by fastening a bomb on the rail. The crew were able to get into the boat and were later picked up by a patrol boat. Then in March, 1917, when in *Boy Clifford* off Lundy, a submarine ordered them to heave-to, but they refused to do so until she opened fire, then they took to the small boat and were picked up and taken to Milford Haven.

The third hand, S. J. Mills, was in the smack *Achieve* when she and 7 others were attacked and sunk by bombs placed on board. All the crews were able to take to their boats and were subsequently picked up by another smack and taken to Lowestoft. The cook, W. J. Hales, served in the navy throughout the 1914-18 war.

Such were the indomitable men who manned the North Sea and Channel smacks in peace and war.

CHAPTER NINE

EAST COAST TRAWLING STATIONS

BARKING

THE history of trawling at the Essex town dates back at least to Stuart days, if not beyond, as in the reign of Queen Elizabeth the local fishermen were granted immunity from the press gang, even when the Navy was desperately short of seamen. A similar protection was given by Cromwell and as warships of this period were manned largely by the sweepings of the streets and gaols the fact that such highly skilled seamen were exempt is certain evidence of the importance of the fishing industry as a producer of food for London markets. Barking ketches were considered sufficiently well built to be used as men-of-war by the Navy of the Commonwealth and King Charles II.

At one time the largest trawling station in the British Isles, if not the world, Barking owed its pre-eminence to the acumen of Samuel Hewett. In his evidence at the 1833 Enquiry he stated that the fishing from Barking had not been successful for several years. He had left the sea about eight years before and owned " six smacks of his own on shore and four others ", of the 120 then owned in the port, each of which averaged about 50 tons. Questioned as to foreign interference he said he had never found any opposition to fishing in Dutch waters but they seldom went within 7 miles of the coast. A friend had been forced to seek shelter in Texel when his smack broke her mast, and having no provisions or money, he sold a few fish and this cost him £9 10s. before he was permitted to leave harbour. Yet thirteen Dutch vessels were constantly landing turbot at Gravesend, making three or four voyages with about twenty score of fish in each boat. His smacks were licenced to carry a crew of nine and they made two to three voyages a month in winter, returning with fish " from half-seas across off Yarmouth ". They did no trawling off the Lincoln-shire coast as they fished there for cod with long lines, these cod voyages lasted about a month and after lining for three months the smacks returned to trawling. He reckoned if his fish was not at Billingsgate by 8 a.m. the market was over.

Christopher Spashat, for twenty-one years a fisherman, said he owned two welled smacks and fished off Norfolk for cod with long lines, but trawled for turbot off the Northumberland coast. The value of cod had fallen considerably in recent years, only fetching one-third of the price since the war. When in Dutch waters they fished eight or nine miles off Sceveland, but once when he had to go in for provisions it cost him £13 to sell 43s. worth of fish. The season was now over—1st July, only twenty trawlers were working off Sceveland with one or two carriers, but a month before there had been twenty to twenty-five carriers.

Thomas Harris, smackowner, informed the Commissioners that he had four vessels which worked in Sceveland Bay. Goree lying 30 miles one way and the Texel 90 miles the other. Turbot usually made £3 to £3 10s. a score at Billingsgate, some would weigh as little as 3 lb., others 14 to 16 lb. He had known 20 lb. fish to be sold for 5s. to 6s., and 6 or 7 pounders make the same price and more, if of prime quality.

Choice fish were then kept alive in welled smacks and the trawlers worked for soles and plaice on the grounds off Yarmouth. The live fish, packed in baskets called " pads ", were transhipped to the local clinker-built boats known as " cows " and landed on the beach, run across the sands in trawl carts and loaded into four-horse vans. These left Yarmouth at 5 p.m., the journey to Billingsgate being done at a gallop in about 10 mile stages, 48 horses were used and the same market was caught as the train does to-day (1946).

In his efforts to make his business more successful Samuel Hewett found that any fish could be preserved in ice, hitherto only used when sending salmon to market. Catches could now be landed in good condition, although losing some of the flavour, and smacks be away for a week or more at a time, yet their fish would be fresher than in vessels without ice, only two days out. This led to the decline of the welled smack.

New fishing grounds were constantly being discovered in the North Sea, further and further away from Billingsgate market, and Samuel thought out the idea of the fleet system, whereby smacks could remain at sea from four to eight weeks, putting their daily haul on board one of their number which brought the combined catches to London. By 1844 this method was sufficiently well developed to cause a strike in the November of that year, owing to the dissatisfaction of crews at being kept so long from home—always the greatest drawback of fleeting.

In those days there was no artificial ice and the only way supplies could be obtained was by collecting natural ice during the winter and storing it for use in summer. Local farmers collected the thin ice forming on the numerous ponds, streams and by flooding the marshes, and it is worth noting that the first supplies generally came in about 16th November. When plentiful the price was 3s. a load of 30 cwt., if scarce up to 6s. was paid. During hard frosts the ice would be from one to two inches thick and there were often rows of carts stretching right through the town, waiting to unload into the icehouses in Fisher Street.

These buildings, with brick walls 8 ft. thick, were 20 ft. underground with a thick roof which served as the floor of the sail-loft above. The thin sheets of ice soon solidified and approximately 12,500 tons were stored. Watchers were employed

75 SKIPPER JUMBO HARVEY,
1893

76 AFTER THE GREAT OCTOBER GALE, 1880
The brig *Lily* ashore near Scarborough.

77 TRANSIT RAIL OF *G. & E.*, L.T.649
Trawled up four years after smack was sunk as the decoy ship *Nelson*, in
which Skipper Crisp won a posthumous V.C., his son a D.S.M.

78 *FRANCIS ROBERT*, L.T.1024

44 tons, built at Oulton Broad, 1906. In tow of 30 h.p. iron paddle tug *Imperial*, built at Blackwell, 1879, for G.E. Rly. The last sailing trawler to be sunk by U-boat, 28th July, 1918, 8 miles N.E. of Haisboro' Light Vessel.

79 ON THE SLIPWAY
Telesia, 46 tons, built at Rye, 1911, by
G. & T. Smith.

80 *BOY LESLIE*, L.O.392
32 tons, built at Galmpton, 1911. The last smack to fly the famous Short Blue flag.

81 BARKING SMACK OFF GREENWICH, c 1829
The crew are hauling on the peak halyards, the topmast is housed and a big jib, with one line
of reef points, is set.

82 THE SHORT BLUE FLEET TRUNKING, c 1864
Fish trunks are being put aboard the 56-ton cutter
Don, built at Barking, 1860.

83 AN EARLY STEAM
TRAWLER *SWEETHEART*
Built of iron at Barking,
1885, 24 h.p. screw. The
paddle tug *Reaper* is towing
trawlers and drifters to sea.

84   THE SHORT BLUE FLEET LAID UP AT GORLESTON, 1902

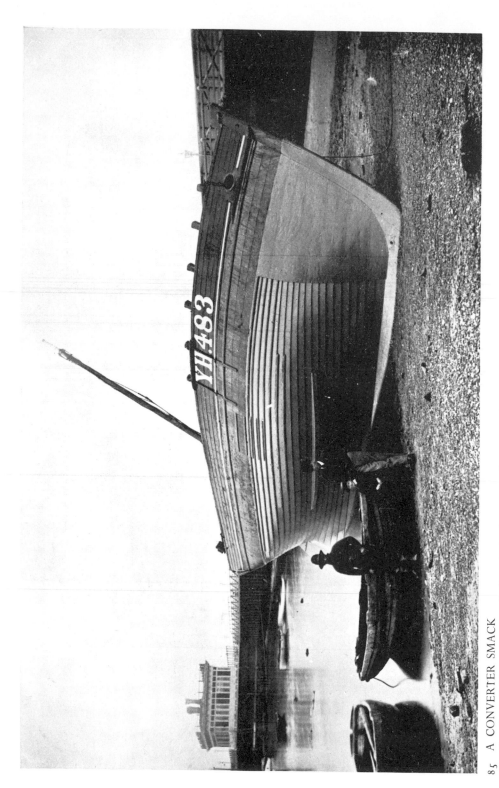

85 A CONVERTER SMACK

Dew Drop, Y.H.483, 40 tons, built at Surlingham, 1871 for W. Brighton. Hull is clench-built to the binns, carvel above. Copper sheathing at bows prevents anchor flukes catching up in lands of planking.

to see that as the ice formed on the marshes it was not ruined by skaters or people sliding. When local supplies were short, as in mild winters, ice was sometimes brought over from Norway in sailing ships. The best ice came from the lakes and towards the end of the winter the surface was scored with deep grooves by a horse plough. Then the blocks were cut out by men using saws with long teeth and it was possible to obtain large quantities in a very short time, the weight being from two to four cwt., and price about threepence a hundredweight. The blocks were placed on wooden runways and slid down by gravity to piers where they were loaded into the ship's hold and packed with layers of sawdust. Strange as it may sound ice was a dangerous cargo owing to risk of fire, due to an inflammable gas generated by the proximity of ice and sawdust, several ships being lost before the cause was discovered. Freights were low, but by the time the ice had been stored ashore, handled and re-handled its worth had risen to 4s. to 5s. a cwt. in later years just before artificial ice swept away the trade for ever, being cleaner, better looking and less liable to rapid melting.

When Mr. R. S. Hewett, the present managing director of the firm, took me to lunch with his father, Mr. Robert Muirhead Hewett, born 1860, he was good enough to bring his secretary so that a full account could be taken down of the old gentleman's reminiscences. It was a privilege to hear him talk of events told him by his grand-father, Samuel, as well as his father, Robert Hewett, born 1826, and I came away with a model under each arm and plenty of scribbled notes which I wrote up on my return home while everything was fresh in my mind, later I was able to add to them on receipt of the transcript of Miss Simon's shorthand notes.

Mr. R. M. Hewett was still living in his old country house, now surrounded by houses instead of fields, and considerably bomb damaged. One novel feature which instantly caught my eye was that the newel posts in the main staircase were tillers from old smacks, the carved oak black with age. Out in the garden were some of the big anchors slipped by the Dutch fleet before the Battle of Camperdown, 1797. These had been a constant cause of torn nets as they littered the trawling grounds, but all were brought to the surface eventually and landed at Barking.

In the old days the smacks sailed up to Barking, being tracked by men called "bobbers", who came out in their small boats and towed up those reaches in the river where sailing was impossible owing to the direction of the wind. The creek formed a natural dry dock where underwater repairs could be carried out.

In one of his delightful etchings of shipping in Greenwich Reach, E. W. Cooke has a small drawing of a typical Barking smack c 1829 (Plate 81). Many of the hulls were clinker-built, as this appears to be, the mast was stepped well for'ard giving a high, narrow stay foresail, and a big jib, with one line of reef points, was set on a reeving bowsprit. Three shrouds a side and a runner backstay supported the mast which had a long head and a short topmast on which a gaff topsail was set. The mainsail, fitted with a long boom projecting well over the taffrail, had three lines of reef points and a "balance reef" from the upper cringle on leech to the throat earing. This allowed the sail to be so reefed that either the peak or lower half could be set as a trysail for riding out a gale. The bobstay was set up by a gun tackle purchase with its lower block on a chain pendant shackled to an eyeplate in the stem at the waterline. One shroud a side gave lateral support to the bowsprit which rove through a gammon iron on the port side of stemhead. These smacks were practically identical with the cod smack already described, but not all were fitted with wells.

The smacks towed a 38 ft. elm beam, warp was 120 fathom of 6 in. rope, and the best depth for working was 20 to 30 fathom. The fish were packed in pads holding from 7 to 8 stone, and 12 to 14 pads was a good day's fishing.

In spring and summer the fishing grounds lay off the Dutch coast where flat fish were found in abundance, including very fine turbot, always in good demand for banquets and City dinners. Autumn and winter saw the fleet off the Lincolnshire shores, usually within sight of land—"land-dipping"—cod and haddock being the principal catch. It was rare for smacks to go trawling as far afield as the Dogger Bank, there being plenty of fish close inshore.

The custom of putting each day's catch on board one of the smacks working with the fleet soon gave place to the use of fast cutters, specially built for the purpose and Mr. R. M. Hewett courteously allowed me to take away the model of one so that I could take off the lines (Plan 4, page 316). It was the builder's model of the 52-ton *Ranger*, built 1864, probably at Barking. She had a short life as her name does not appear in the 1870 register.

Length overall was 74 ft. 3 in., L.B.P. 69 ft., length on keel 61 ft. 3 in., extreme beam 16 ft. 6 in. One interesting feature was that many of the sections closely corresponded to those of the well-smack *Saucy Jack*, but length of hull had been much increased. Floors were very sharp with hollow garboards, the lower waterlines hollow and the run long and easy.

The sail plan is on page 317. In summer rig the boom projected 14 ft. beyond the taffrail with foot ropes for the men to stand on when reefing down and such a sail needed handling when a gale began to blow up. The carriers were always hard driven, a mainsail seldom lasting more than one season. Not until the main boom dragged in the water was it considered necessary to pull down the first reef and in winter it was said the cutters took a dive on leaving the fleet and came up when they entered Sea Reach. The lee decks were seldom free of water and often the hatch coamings disappeared in the white smother. With such a perishable cargo as fish, minutes counted and the weather least desired was calm or light airs. The cutters could sail to wind'ard faster than any vessels then afloat. In the spring some of them used to make a trip to Spain and brought back the early fruit, oranges, etc., in competition with the famous Salcombe fruit schooners which they could always beat unless there happened to be a fair wind for the whole distance. If there was any thrashing to wind'ard the cutters were home first and the fruit fetched a high price in the London market.   The winning skipper received a present of £20 and his vessel was provided with a new suit of canvas.   As many as eighteen carriers were employed, and if it happened that more than one was with the fleet, trawling was carried on until it was her turn to load the night's catch.

After a cargo had been landed at Billingsgate the holds were packed with empty wooden fish boxes—" trunks "—and the carrier dropped down to Barking Creek where the specially built ice-lugs came alongside and put aboard 18 tons of ice.   Then cracking-on was indulged in so that the cutter could rejoin the fleet as soon as possible, often a difficult job as the smacks were constantly moving their ground, but the admiral generally dropped a mark boat to show he was working in the vicinity.

Immediately the fleet was sighted the cutter hoisted a flag at the gaff to show she was ready to load for market.   The smacks hauled their trawls, if they were fishing, stood out to wind'ard, threw out their boats and three men jumped in and rowed down to collect the empty boxes.   The smack meanwhile worked to leeward of the carrier to pick up her boat which was now loaded with trunks, piled higher than the gunwale. The boxes containing the night's catch were put in and the boat went back to the cutter, forcing a way alongside and the men flung the heavy trunks up on to the deck, obtaining a receipt for quantity and quality, i.e., prime or offal. As fast as one batch of boxes was stowed away in tiers, with ice between, two or three more followed, until from 500 to 1,000 packages had been handled, perhaps forty tons of fish for one night's catch.   The moment the last trunk was on board the cutter was off, topsail hoisted and sails sheeted home long before the hatches were battened down.

Mr. R. M. Hewett showed me a very fine oil painting by G. Earle of the 56-ton *Don*, built at Barking in 1860 (Plate 82).   The big gaff topsail has been dropped half-way down the topmast, but mainsail and jib are full as she is drawing slowly ahead with the wind abeam.   Dozens of deeply-laden boats are clustered alongside, whilst others are returning to their own vessels.   The admiral's smack, denoted by the long flag flying halfway up the topmast stay, lies to wind'ard of *Don*, and eight other trawlers are in close proximity.   It was usual for the second hand to go in charge of the boat and the admiral was generally the first to board for any orders sent out by head office, so if the weather was not too bad for him to go it was good enough for the rest of the fleet.

The skipper of the carrier received a percentage on the price obtained for the fish and as value depended on quick delivery it was up to him to make a fast passage. This averaged about three days but sometimes catches were on sale within twenty-four hours.   In summer supplies at Billingsgate often fluctuated considerably as days might pass without a single carrier being able to get up to the market, then Hewett's sent out tugs to pick up their cutters.   This sometimes meant a tow of upwards of one hundred miles.   In addition to a number of small owners, four other fleets belonging to Morgan, Reid, Forge and Shuckford then sailed out of the Thames.

In summer many Brixham and Yarmouth men joined the Short Blue Fleet, sending their catches to the cutter and paying a percentage for carriage and sale at market. The spring and early summer fishing was called the " Skilling " season and in the early years most of the haddock caught were thrown away, excepting those the apprentices strung up in the rigging as their perquisites, and these fish were known as " hazel haddocks ".

About 1854 the fishing side of the business was gradually transferred to Gorleston, a port nearer to the fishing grounds and now having rail communication with London. Building slips, ice houses, stores, sail lofts, etc., were built as well as houses for the men. All the smack repairs were done there but the carriers refitted at Barking.

When working on the Well Bank the trawlers frequently dredged up huge boulders which had been dropped from some glacier in the Ice Age. At first the men flung them overboard to be a further cause of torn nets, but Mr. Harvey-George, the manager at Gorleston, gave instructions that all were to be brought into port and many went into the foundations of his mansion which overlooked the entrance to Yarmouth Haven.

In the sixties the average number of men and boys employed by Hewett's was about five hundred, up to four apprentices, bound at the age of fourteen for seven years, sailing in each smack, with every opportunity of becoming a skipper when they came out of their time. The weekly wages bill amounted to over £700, only the skippers receiving a percentage on their catches, but soon after the completion of the removal to Gorleston new arrangements were made to bring the system in line with that adopted by the Brixham men. Hitherto Barking men would never work " on the lay ", i.e., for shares. Provisions were found and were on a far more generous scale than that prevailing in merchant ships, the lads were provided with clothing, food and lodging when on shore, as well as medical attention if required. Mr. R. M. Hewett's grandmother supervised the welfare of the 200 or so boys, only about twenty-five of whom were ashore at a time, and Samuel Hewett encouraged successful skippers to buy their own smacks. The firm still had the management of the vessels, kept them in repair, provided gear and stores, sold the catches and charged freight for carriage to Billingsgate. Many of these skippers based their ships at Grimsby, thereby helping in the development of that fishing station.

Pay was good for those days, 12s. a week in summer, 14s. in winter and all found, this being higher than wages ruling in many other trades. The daily allowance of food per man was 1 lb. of meat and 1 lb. of bread, with a limited amount of potatoes, sugar, tea, treacle, etc. Later sugar was almost unrestricted, but tea remained at 1 lb. a week for the crew, or about the same ration as was given to the public in recent years, 2 oz. per head.

The fishing fleet was victualled and watered for a period of six weeks, the average cruise, but if they remained at sea longer fresh supplies were brought out in the carriers. Now the smacks commenced trawling in the early spring off the

Dutch coast, working along from Camperdown to the Texel, taking quantities of soles, turbot and plaice, as well as numbers of haddock. Some time was spent off Vlieland Island and about 1st May the fleet went down to Schelling, the season finishing by the middle of July off the Island of Ameland. The smacks now worked their way into the middle of the North Sea to White Water Bank and Botney Gut, where they took soles, brill, haddock and large-sized plaice. The spots were scarcely visible on plaice caught near the Dogger, but those in the vicinity of Brown Bank had bright red spots. In 1864 about 33,600,000 plaice, averaging 1 lb. each, were sold at Billingsgate, nearly all to costermongers, whereas over 97,520,000 soles, about 12,000 tons, were disposed of to the West End fishmongers. These figures are of course the total sales, not the landings of the Short Blue Fleet. As winter advanced the fleet worked to the south'ard of the Dogger in the Silver Pits, where the water was too deep for the small trawlers to work, Hewett's smacks never worked on the northern Edge.

In 1864 Mr. Robert Hewett, son of Samuel, and father of Mr. R. M. Hewett, decided that the time had come to replace the cutters with steam carriers, which however retained the name of "cutter". A company was formed in which he held the majority of shares, other directors being G. Hewett, Lord Alfred Paget, M.P., and Admiral George Wellesley. Mr. Robert had a considerable say in the design of these steamers which were to carry three times the cargo of any sailing carrier and deliver it in one-third of the time. Four vessels were ordered, all to be built of iron at Stockton-on-Tees. They were undoubtedly the first steam trawlers, being fitted to do a certain amount of fishing to obtain exemption from the payment of heavy dues to the Port of London. ·

Lord Alfred Paget and *Wellesley* were delivered in 1865, each measuring 120.4 by 21 by 10.6, 133 N.T., 186 G.T., and the engines developed 50 h.p. In the following year the slightly larger *Frost* and *Hallett* went into service, each 130.6 by 21.1 by 10.6 and registering 142 N.T., 209 G.T., the increased length giving a little higher speed with the same horsepower. All had a capacity of 3,900 boxes packed in the hold in alternate layers of ice and boxes. This work was done by the crew of the carrier and one or two smacks' crews, engaged by previous arrangement.

When these steam carriers commenced running the majority of the cutters went fishing, but it was soon found that their big mainsails were unsuitable for trawling, so the booms were shortened, a mizzen mast with gaff sail was stepped ahead of the tiller and the ketch rig came into being. In the course of the next few years most of the smacks in the fleet were hauled out on the slips at Gorleston, cut in two, lengthened up to 15 ft. and converted to ketch rig.

James T. Morgan, who began life as a Barking fisherman, owned 35 smacks in 1865, but for 24 years he had also been a salesman at Billingsgate, handling about 350 baskets or 100 tons of fish a week, whereas Hewett & Co. were dealing with double that quantity as the Short Blue Fleet now numbered about 60 smacks. Morgan told the Commissioners that the cost of keeping one of his trawlers was £11 a week, but the cod smacks, fishing with long lines, averaged £16, and cod only paid because of the excessive price given by the wealthy classes for choice specimens.

Mr. R. M. Hewett went on to tell me that the majority of their smacks were built at Barking, when the yards there were full they went to Hoad or Smith of Rye, men who had a high reputation. Many of the smaller vessels were built at Wivenhoe and Gravesend and in the early sixties a big smack cost £700 to £800 ready for sea. His smack sails were always dressed with cutch which gave them a brown colour, whereas the Brixham cutters which worked with the Short Blue Fleet invariably had white canvas. In its heyday his fleet numbered 220 vessels, which was then, and probably still is, a record number to belong to one firm, though only a small tonnage as the average smack was about 75 ft. long and registered 50 N.T. Many had suits of sails cut and made by Ratsey of Cowes. At one time the late Mr. Tom Ratsey was very anxious to keep on some of his highly skilled sailmakers, but there was not enough yacht work in the winter months and he asked Mr. Hewett to give him some of his orders. These sails were superbly cut and stood beautifully and any skipper sporting a suit was the envy of the fleet. So far as Mr. Hewett could remember the mainsails cost £35 each, but he suggested I wrote to Ratsey and Lapthorn for further details. This I did and received a courteous reply from the chairman, Mr. T. C. Ratsey, who thanked me for a very interesting letter, but unfortunately all their records had been destroyed during the war and he was unable to add any more information.

In the seventies the Short Blue Fleet fished along the German coast and in later years off the Danish shores as far down as the Sleeve. During the autumn they worked in the Clay Deeps to the east of the Dogger and in winter over the Pits or the Shoal outside, always keeping well away from the South West Patches where the seas broke heavily in bad weather.

The smacks were deeply ballasted with a good proportion of kentledge, well secured against shifting and if hove down the vessels always righted. Trawling was in depths up to 40 fathom and over in the Silver Pits. A good day's catch was a ton per smack, consisting of about 3 cwt. of soles, half a ton of haddock, the rest plaice with some turbot, brill and whiting, but very few cod. One night's catch off Ameland in 1876 was over a thousand boxes from 151 smacks, each trunk containing about 70 haddock or 60 pairs of soles.

An interesting point mentioned by Mr. R. M. Hewett was that soles averaged about 1s. a lb., the price varying but little right down to recent times. The lowest he remembered was around 6d. a lb. in 1878.

Hewett's alone were now bringing more fish to London than the total of all landings at Billingsgate fifty years before. In 1874 another carrier, *Major*, was built of wood at Dartmouth, about the same size as the others but she proved to be too slow as her engines only developed 30 h.p. Later the first refrigeration plant was fitted in her but was not a success, any more than refrigeration is to-day, unless each fish is frozen separately. Whilst making experiments Mr. R. M. Hewett found that very low temperatures could be produced in the hold by a mixture of ice and salt, without any installation of expensive machinery and at very little cost.

In 1877 the cutter *Hewett* was built of iron at Stockton to practically the same dimensions as *Frost* and *Hallett* built eleven years before. Then followed *Progress* built at Port Glasgow in 1880, with engine power increased to 65 h.p. In 1881 the cutters made 286 trips bringing to market 376,426 trunks, about 15,000 tons, which sold for £182,772 or an average price of 9s. 8d. per box.

These steam carriers were probably among the hardest driven of all craft as they were only in the river long enough to unload, take in 30 tons of ice, 45 tons of coal and about 3,000 empty trunks. Once clear of traffic the engine room telegraphs rang for full speed ahead and the indicators remained in that position until the fleet was picked up, perhaps 300 miles away. Job enough in clear weather, but a nightmare in fog when smacks would suddenly emerge like wraiths to disappear into the clammy atmosphere. At night rockets shot up to tell of arrival and as soon as it was light the empty boxes were unloaded and the full trunks taken on board. The moment the icemen's boats were clear the carrier was on her way back, perhaps into the teeth of a sou'wester and shipping it green, or sliding over a long, oily swell with a sickening lurch and heave. The river pilot was taken at Gravesend and some 20 to 30 hours after leaving the fleet the cutter arrived at Billingsgate, and missing a tide might mean the loss of hundreds of pounds. Twice a week the carriers made the round voyage to the North Sea and back.

The moment the steamer was alongside the landing stage, gangways were run out and the full trunks carried ashore by licenced fish porters, who in 1880, made more money in less time than any other unskilled labourers in Europe according to a contemporary account. The licence cost 2s. 6d., including the official brass badge, and the men could earn 20s. a day, being finished by 10 a.m., a striking contrast to the toil and earnings of the men who caught the fish far away in the bitter North Sea.

Each porter wore a white apron, clogs and a curious leather hat with the inside packed with newspaper which became moulded to the individual shape of each man's head, hence no one could wear a pal's hat or the load would not balance properly. I wonder if this was the origin of the expression " if the cap fits, wear it ".

One stream of porters trotted down the springy gangway, each man picked up a full trunk, balanced it on his head and went up the other plank into the market to dump his load at the appropriate stand. It was Hewett's pride to put the first lot on sale before the last stroke of 5 a.m. had ceased to vibrate, the official opening of the day's market. Then arose a babel of sound from the 140 or so stands, trunks or heaps of fish being sold by auction; the winking of an eye, nod or whatever sign was used by a buyer seeing a lot change hands in a matter of seconds. To add to the din was the clatter of hoofs and the thunder of iron-tyred wheels as vans rumbled

about 100 sail belonging to the port, but they were solely engaged in drift-net fishing. "We do not trawl, there is no regular fishing for cod or turbot, and no trawlers go out of Yarmouth, but men come off our coast from Torbay. Our fishermen are different, our vessels luggers, in trawlers men are brought up as fishermen, ours are mostly in agriculture."

Such a method of fishing was entirely new to the Norfolk men and local trawling probably commenced on a small scale in the 1840's, as it was mentioned at the 1863 Enquiry that 17 to 18 years before there were only 4 or 5 trawlers belonging to the town, which suggests that it was not until Samuel Hewett made Gorleston the base for the Short Blue Fleet, c 1854, that the new idea really caught on. It is difficult to tell exactly how many vessels were engaged as the numbers registered include drifters as well as trawlers, likewise the quantities of fish despatched by rail were made up of herring as well as white fish. In 1863 there appears to have been 140 trawlers of from 50 to 60 tons, all cutter rigged. Four masters put in a signed document as evidence that in their experience fish were more plentiful than ever before. The youngest skipper had been trawling for 14 years and " within the last six weeks, while fishing on the Dogger Bank, we have frequently seen from 40 to 50 packages, weighing between 2 and 3 tons, taken by a single vessel for a three hours' trawl, the most of them being very fine haddock."

It would seem that the local men did not take seriously to trawling until the early seventies when the great change-over from lug to gaff rig took place on finding that a lugger was quite unsuitable for towing a trawl. Even then the majority of the boats were " converter " smacks, able to go herring drifting in autumn for about three months, and then changing over to a different rig for trawling. This delay in taking to a novel way of fishing is not surprising, as fishermen are often slow to adopt new methods until fully convinced of their merits and the tradition of catching fish in drift nets dated back for centuries.

This conservatism was also to be seen in the build of their smacks as boat-building practice was followed with hulls clench-built up to the binns and carvel above. Such a vessel is seen in Plate 85 of the 40-ton *Dew Drop*, Y.H.483, built at Surlingham in 1871 for Wm. Brighton. When fitting out for drift-net fishing a pole mast was stepped in a tabernacle and a boomless mainsail sheeted to an iron horse for'ard of the mizzen mast, but for trawling another fore mast was used, having a topmast and crosstrees, while a boom and gaff mainsail was set with the sheet block working in a box on deck.

A typical converter smack of this period was *Reaper* built in 1877 by T. Beeching, the well-known builder of Norfolk and Suffolk lifeboats. Her dimensions were 55.8 by 17.7 by 7.7, with net tonnage 33.71. The keel was American elm, frames English oak, lower clinker planking was 1⅛ in. American oak, copper fastened over rooves, the topsides were 2½ in. English oak, carvel-built and iron fastened. Deck was 2½ in. pitch pine, nailed with galvanized iron spikes.

The fore scuttle was 2 ft. sq., having a sliding hatch of 1 in. fir, with a hasp and staple, and coamings 6 in. high. The net room hatchway was 3 ft. 6 in. by 3 ft., with coamings 7 in. high and 3 in. thick, two hatches of 1¼ in. oak were secured by an iron bar to a hook at one end and a hasp at the other. The well hatch was similar to the net room, but the mastway hatch was 2 ft. by 1 ft. 3 in., with 2½ in. oak coamings 6½ in. high and one oak hatch. The warp room hatch was 2 ft. sq., coamings 7 in. by 3 in., with 1¼ in. oak covers. Companion of hoodway was 2 ft. 6 in. by 2 ft., 7 in. by 3 in. coamings, all carlings were oak and coamings secured by ⅝ in. iron bolts.

Twenty to twenty-five tons of ballast were carried, of which eleven tons were iron, the remainder shingle from the beach. The platform rested on four longitudinal bearers over which the planks were laid and nailed athwartships, but not secured to the sides of hull as there was a cant piece above at the wings. On the top of the planks were two fore-and-aft bearers, shored to deck beams by five or six shores a side. This was the usual method as alterations in ballast were made twice a year, when changing over for herring drifting and vice versa.

The sail plan consisted of a mainsail and topsail, stay and tow foresails, 5, 7, 9 and 11 cloth jibs, storm jib, mizzen sail and gaff topsail. A crew of six was carried when trawling, ten or eleven when herring fishing. Yarmouth boats were seldom fitted with skylights as the men liked to have the cabin as dark as possible for sleeping in the daytime, trawling being done at night, with two hauls, the first about 11.30 p.m., the second at daylight. It was usual to haul on both sides and the beam was frequently carried on the starboard rail as can be seen in many of the plates. Some of the smacks went single-boating, but the majority worked with one or other of the big fleets, putting their catches on the carriers. There was no local trawl-fish market as at Lowestoft, practically everything went to Billingsgate and water transport was far cheaper than rail, even though the latter was a fraction of the price paid for the posting vans forty years before.

The Great Eastern Railway charged 37s. 6d. a ton for prime, 26s. to 28s. for offal fish and this did not include icing for which a charge of 3d. a package or 5s. a ton was made, neither did the company collect or deliver free, a further 8s. 4d. was added for this service, so that by the time prime fish reached Billingsgate a sum of 50s. a ton had been paid for transport, about a farthing a lb. Small consignments went at package rate of 23s. 4d. a ton, cod 30s. a ton, but what seemed unfair to the fishermen was that beer was charged only 9s. a ton, including collecting and delivery. These figures were given by Vaughan of Yarmouth in 1883, and it was said such heavy charges made it almost impossible for single boats to earn a living, as local sales were negligible.

From time to time exceptional sized fish were caught by trawlers, in June, 1869, an 11 lb. gurnard, 2 ft. 1 in. long was landed, in May, 1868, a halibut 6 ft. 2 in. long, 3 ft. 4 in. wide and weighing 160 lb., followed another 6 ft. 6 in. long and 2 ft. 6 in.

wide caught two months before. In June, 1870, *Night Hawk* had a haul of 1,500 prime turbot in one night 40 miles from Heligoland, while a 16 lb. brill was another outstanding capture.

The small " half and half " boats were not powerful enough to tow a trawl in deep water, but they went across to Dutch waters in spring and early summer. Hauling was done by the conical capstan, three or four men tramping round and round to bring in the warp and gear. By the eighties the converter smacks were of bigger tonnage, carvel-built and better able to work during the winter months in Botney Gut and to the south of the Dogger.

Plate 86 is of *Fred Salmon*, Y.H.922, 49 tons, built at Cobholm Is. in 1884 for Frederick J. W. Salmon, who owned a small fleet which flew a square white flag with a red ball in the centre. The crew are seen sheeting home the topsail, the 10-cloth jib has been run out, but mizzen and foresail are not yet set. The mainsheet goes to a box bolted to the deck instead of to the iron horse athwartship, which can be seen for'ard of mizzen mast and must have been a bit of a nuisance as a man had to remember to duck his head everytime he went under it. The vertical conical capstan is visible just abaft the for'ard trawl iron which has the rope bridle made up round it, berthing pieces protecting the sides of the hull when it is hauled aboard.

I have already given a graphic description from my friend Mr. H. George concerning the life in the smaller smacks and he writes me :—

" The last smack to be laid down at Yarmouth was *Camellia*, a very fine vessel built by Alfred Castle, a famous shipbuilder who built her on spec. There were no buyers so he ran her himself, ' Chilley ' Hewett was her skipper. I remember seeing her being towed out of the harbour, with her tall spars, white canvas and great length she looked more like a yacht than a smack. (Built at Southtown 1893, 61 tons, not in 1905 register.)

Of all the smacks which sailed from Yarmouth the fastest was *Nell Morgan* (68 tons, built Lowestoft 1885, owners T. G. Morgan and F. Willett.) William Mitchel of Caister-on-Sea took her to sea new, she was a real clipper and the old men in this village talk about her to this day. She was to the fishing community what *Cutty Sark* was to the merchantmen. The best kept of all the Yarmouth smacks was *Bonnie Boys* (58 tons, built at Bideford 1878) and *Mississippi* (73 tons, built Dartmouth 1886) belonging to William Scott, who at one time was admiral of the Short Blue Fleet. He sailed in one of them himself and their sails fitted like a kid glove. He made some of them and if the topsails were not to his liking he would lower them on deck and alter them until they were correct. The most famous skipper sailing out of Yarmouth was Charlie Markham, who discovered the ground which still bears his name."

Many fine smacks were built for Yarmouth owners by T. Harvey & Son at Wivenhoe, up to 70 ft. in length, with keelsons all one piece of timber.

It was perhaps unfortunate that the International Fisheries Exhibition of 1883 gave a tremendous impetus to sail trawling just as steam was being introduced else-where. Outside capital was put into fleets which had little hope of being a financial success, close on 150 additional smacks being fitted out to compete with those already working. Many were soon running at a loss, others were laid up or sold to firms better able to keep them in commission and within a few years tens of thousands of pounds had been lost in ill-starred ventures.

The best known fleet sailing out of the port was Hewett & Co's Short Blue Fleet, which in 1882 numbered 82 trawlers of 55 to 65 tons, according to Mr. H. Harvey-George, the Gorleston manager. Many carried a crew of seven, and there were never less than six hands in their smacks. All the men were on shares, 570 being employed afloat and 107 ashore. The skipper was on wages and 1s. in the £, if the trip realized under £100, up to £150 he received 1s. on first £100 and a fifth on the extra, over £150 he had one fifth on the total. The mate was paid 14s. a week and 5d. in the £, over £100 he had 7d. on the extra, if over £150, 7d. in the £ on the total. The third hand got 14s. and 4d. in £, fourth hand 10s. and 3d. in £, fifth hand 9s. and 2d. in £, sixth hand 8s. and 2d. in £, cabin boy 7s. and 1d. in £ on the total earnings, no deductions being made as at Hull and Grimsby, a fact which drew surprised com-ment from the Commissioners at the 1882 Enquiry.

The average gross earnings of a smack for an eight week trip were approximately £160, and the capital invested in the firm amounted to about £100,000. New smacks cost £1,000 to £1,200 each, but those being fitted with steam capstans were consider-ably more. Mr. Harvey-George said he never had any difficulties with his men prior to 1880, but there had been terrible trouble since the passing of the 1880 Act, which repealed the one of 1854, giving deterrent punishment for desertion, " we have now no authority over the men and they know it." As a result in 24 months there were 550 cases of refusal to sail, often at the last moment which frequently held a smack up for days whilst casual labour was found, a most unsatisfactory method as the men were generally untrained and had to be supplied with clothing before sailing, yet earned more than clerks ashore. So bad had the situation become that he was forced to keep extra men on the pay-roll, standing about, to use as a reserve pool to save the serious loss occasioned by vessels being unable to sail.

He went on to give the expenses of an eight week trip. Wages came to £25, poundage £30, provisions £25, nets, etc. £40, or about £120, exclusive of insurance or any provision for serious damage or casualties.

621 first-class sail over 15 tons were divided amongst 298 owners, there being 333 trawlers of 25 to 70 tons, and 288 drifters, many of which were trawling out of the herring season. 420 second-class boats made up a total of 1,041 fishing vessels, 6,420 men were employed, but only 6 apprentices as nearly all the lads had broken their indentures since 1880.

Many of the big trawlers belonged to fleets owned or controlled by Billingsgate merchants and most of the fish caught went straight to the London market daily and never came to Yarmouth at all. The smacks came in after six or eight weeks at sea to settle up, give leave to crews and refit. In addition to the Short Blue Fleet there were 20 to 25 smacks owned by Frank Leleu of London, whose vessels flew a square flag with three red and three white vertical stripes. Among them were the three largest cutters sailing out of Yarmouth, the 59-ton *Flash*, built at Southtown in 1876, the 70-ton *Flame*, built at Southtown in 1877 and the 63-ton *Spark*, built at Yarmouth in 1875. These were used as carriers to take the catches to Billingsgate.

Then there was Morgan's fleet, once in charge of John Helyer, who stated in 1883 that he had been admiral for Flem Hewett and Morgan, but the high rail charges had brought about the break-up of both fleets. On one occasion his fleet of 180 sail each had about thirty trunks of large plaice, but no carrier was available, so all had to be thrown overboard as the fleeters carried no ice. One or two smacks went in to Yarmouth and sent up their fish by rail, the price realized being £6 and his share amounted to 24s.

Another big fleet of about 72 smacks belonged to the North Sea Trawling Co. Ltd., better known as the Columbia Fleet, a venture largely financed by the Baroness Burdett-Coutts, the philanthropist, born in 1814, the youngest daughter of Sir Francis Burdett and grand-daughter of Thomas Coutts, the banker, whose fortune she inherited in 1837. In 1881 she married W. L. Ashmead Bartlett who assumed the surname of his wife, and he is given in the registers as being owner of the fleet with an address in Stratton Street, Piccadilly, W., surely a strange place to find a smack owner ! The fleet flew a square blue flag with the letters C F in white in the centre and the flagship was the 66-ton *Sir Francis Burdett*, built at Southtown in 1884. The chief object of this fleet was to supply the London east-enders with cheap fish, a laudable idea, but not too practical, as a trawling firm, perhaps more than any business, needed skilled hands at the tiller. It was not likely that economical methods were used with almost unlimited money behind a management directed by a lady who was keen on good works. I find that in 1889 the flagship was owned by F. Leleu, but his fleet was losing money and in 1890 she joined the Hewett Short Blue Fleet. In its heyday two steam carriers worked to the Columbia fleet, *Speedwell* and *Resolute*, both built of iron at Stockton in 1884, length 120 ft., beam 21 ft., depth 10 ft., 80 N.T., 195 G.T., with engines of 75 h.p.

The Great Yarmouth Steam Carrying Co. Ltd., registered in London, also owned smacks and in 1884 had four steam carriers built at Middlesbrough, named *Endeavour*, *Energy*, *Industry* and *Perseverance*, but this venture soon failed and they came into the ownership of Hewett & Co. within a very few years.

I am greatly indebted to Mr. J. Combes, now living at Norwich, for sending me certain information concerning other fleets and their houseflags, and he kindly sent me a series of coloured drawings of many of the flags, a fine piece of research work I am pleased to record (Fig. 18). He wrote me :—

" Our house at the South Quay, Great Yarmouth, was unfortunately badly

HOUSE FLAGS OF YARMOUTH SMACK OWNERS

E. A. DURRANT
"THE RED, WHITE & BLUE FLEET"

Red, white, & blue stripes.

SAMUEL SMITH & SONS
"OLD COFFEE SMITH"

Red & white halves, brown letters

WILLIAM HARRISON

Red & white stripes

HEWETT & CO, L^{TD}
"THE SHORT BLUE FLEET"

Square blue.

FLEMING HEWETT
"FLAM HEWETT"

Red with white diamond

ROBERT WARNER

Blue & yellow halves

J. HECK L^{TD}

Red with white letters

H. FENNER L^{TD}

Green with white ball

FRED SALMON & SON

White with red ball

NORTH SEA TRAWLING CO L^{TD}
"THE COLUMBIA FLEET"

Blue with white letters

J. C. COX

Blue with white ball

H. F. EASTICK

Red & white chequers

LELEU & CO, L^{TD}

Red & white vertical stripes

JAMES PITCHERS

Oblong, blue with white letters

G^{T} YARMOUTH FISH SELLING CO, L^{TD}

Red with white diagonal stripe

BESSEY & PALMER L^{TD}
Red with white ball

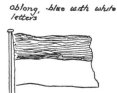

WILLIAM STANLEY
Oblong, blue & white halves

A. D. STONE
White with red & blue diamond

FIG. 18   DRAWN BY EDGAR J. MARCH   FROM DATA SUPPLIED BY M^R J COMBES. 1946

damaged in a fire blitz in April, 1941, and most of our stuff and records were lost, but fortunately I think I have enough here to supply ' copy ' for you. The largest private owned fleet was that of E. A. Durrant, who had 35 smacks and three paddle tugs. Starting in a very small way with one smack, by keen business enterprise old E. A. D. built up a big fleet. He also had a large bakery and shipstore business. When his fleet failed in 1902 most of his smacks were sold to foreigners or else broken up. My father bought much of old E. A. D's property and warehouses on the South Quay in 1903. The fleet was known as the ' Red, White and Blue ', his house flag being square with red, white and blue horizontal lines.

Samuel Smith & Sons had a fleet of 21 smacks and the presiding genius of this firm was old Samuel Smith, always known locally as ' Old Coffee Smith '. Tradition has it he was a great temperance advocate and no booze was allowed on any of his smacks, but a plentiful supply of black coffee was always carried. He appears to have been a man with many other interests, having shares in several of the fast clipper schooners which raced out to Grecian and Italian ports with cargoes of Yarmouth cured herrings. He also had large interests in the fish curing and export trade. This firm finally sold out in the early eighties and the smacks were all dispersed. The houseflag was square with red and white halves and the large letters S.S. in brown. The local wags used to say they stood for ' Silly Smith ', much to the old fellow's disgust.''

Smith certainly seems to have been a character as in 1882 he said he had been in business for 35 years and employed 200 men ashore and afloat, owning five carriers as well as smacks and drifters. He described himself as '' the last of the Mohicans, I still go by the last, happen to be one of the few left to do so. I do not belong to any Insurance Club ''. His reference is to the distribution of money by the last of herring, not by the share.

Mr. Combes continues :—

'' Apart from the large fleets a number of owners had a few smacks each, the best known were A. & R. Brown, W. H. de M. Bessey, J. Makepeace, W. Harrison, F. Utting, W. Brocklar, J. Heck Ltd., Saville King, A. D. Stone, Fred Salmon & Son, W. Prentice and Fleming Hewett, known locally as ' Old Flam Hewett ', a brother of Robert Hewett of the Short Blue Fleet. The best known single-boaters were no doubt Isaac and Randle Bridges, Wm.West, John Todd, W. Bowles, W. Brighton, John Smith and G. Grief. Owners who had no houseflag flew that of their ship agents and fish salesmen, the Great Yarmouth Fish Selling Co. Ltd., others flew the flag of their brokers or sail-makers.''

Speaking of the great changes brought about at the turn of the century Mr. Combes says ''When the great transfer of the Short Blue Fleet was made to Gorleston a large block of premises was built on the western side of the harbour, dry docks, engineering works, shipwrights' and carpenters' shops, stores, etc., were constructed and a big local industry sprang up, employing hundreds of tradesmen, such as blacksmiths, painters, riggers, block and spar makers, sail-makers and many others. Gorleston hospital was established by their manager Mr. Harvey-George for the benefit

THE CONVERTER SMACK *FRED SALMON*, Y.H.922
49 tons, built at Cobholm Is., 1884.   The jib is not yet sweated up or the topsail sheeted home.

87 LOWESTOFT SMACKS IN PORT
L.T.223 *Achilles*, 73 tons, built at Topsham, Devon, 1877. L.T.648 *Olive Leaf*,
tons, built at Lowestoft, 1874. L.T.20 *Dahlia*, 59 tons, built at Lowestoft, 18
The trawl basin is full and many smacks are in what is now the yacht basin.

88 THE LAST SMACK RACE AT LOWESTOFT REGATTA, 1896
The trawler to wind'ard with huge jib topsail is R.2. *Irex*, 61 tons, built at Whitstable,
1886. L.T.424 is *Resolute*, 53 tons, built at Lowestoft, 1891. All have staysails set
and topmast backstays set up right aft, L.T.357 in the lead has taken in her jib topsail
and set a balloon jib.

89 *SUNBEAM*, L.T.9

64 tons, built at Rye, 1884.   The mizzen mast has fidded topmast and crosstrees, the mast rope for main topmast is rove and the spar is a "ricker," the jib halyards are chain.   The mainsail is old and came from L.T.439, foresail has three lines of reef eyelets, windlass is the up-and-down or pump-brake pattern, not the usual handspike type.

90 *CHARLES HENRY, L.T.585*

53 tons, built at Brixham, 1872. The mizzen has a fidded topmast and a yard is fitted for carrying a square sail, the capstan is a patent one, worked with handles.

91 *HENRY STEPHENSON, L.T.611* The curved topsail yard is intended to make the sail
58 tons, built at Brixham, 1872. sit flat, the foresail has a bonnet, the mizzen a fidded topmast.

92 *GLADYS*, L.T.233

47 tons, built at Brixham, 1901. Topsail, mainsail and mizzen are diagonal-cut, the mizzen topsail has a short yard at clew with sheet fast to its centre, the jib outhaul is chain, belayed on starboard bitt. The mainsail came from G.Y.555, the mizzen from L.T.369.

93 *RESOLUTE*, L.T.42.
53 tons, built at Lowe stoft, 1891. Ashore o the North Beach, Lowe stoft, 14th January, 1902 One of crew is bein rescued in the breeche buoy. Note great lengt of gaffs.

94 *BOY RAMAH*, L.T.308
45 tons, built at Lowestoft, 1909. She has a round or elliptical stern and a boat gangway is fitted just aft of main shrouds, the topmast is a '' ricker '' and jib outhaul is chain.

95   *TRUE LOVE*, L.T.63
      49 tons, built at Rye, 1886.

96   *WAVE CREST* L.T.744
      46 tons, built at Rye, 1910.

of the crews. The advent of the steam trawler, with its wider radius of action, quicker and more steady supply of fish, was a serious competitor. The opening of ports nearer to the fishing grounds was also proving a menace and the ebb tide was running against the sailing craft. Up to 1899 Messrs. Hewett controlled the largest fishing fleet in Great Britain, but on a cold, windy day in 1901 the famous Short Blue flag fluttered down from the masthead of the admiral's flagship for the last time. The huge fleet of smacks lay moored at Gorleston Quay for a year or so, many were broken up, some were sold foreign, mostly to Dutch, Belgian or Norwegian owners, and a few of the best were converted into ketches for the coasting trade. This closing down was a bad job for Yarmouth and it caused a great deal of distress and trouble, a large number of the crews left and went to Hull and Grimsby.''

Conversions were far from satisfactory. Trading was a job for which smacks had never been designed and their sharp underwater lines meant they could only use deep water harbours, as taking the ground every tide was attended by considerable risk. In spite of this handicap many went into the coasting trade and several went deep sea in the hazardous cod fish trade from Newfoundland, facing the North Atlantic at its worst during the winter months. One of them was the little dandy *Challenger* built of wood at Yarmouth in 1872, and trawling from that station for many years, being owned by W. H. Makepeace. Her length was 79.9 ft., breadth 18.9 ft. and depth 8.95 ft., and in her fishing days she registered 53 tons. In 1901 she was purchased for £840, including certain repairs, by Mr. Thomas John Stephens and registered at Fowey and her net tonnage was now 56.53 after a deduction of 11.97 tons for crew space. In 1907, £180 was laid out on her at Scarborough and a new stem was fitted, following a collision. In May the next year she was dry docked and overhauled at Bristol. On the 11th December, 1908, *Challenger* sailed from St. John's, Newfoundland with a freeboard of only 15 inches, bound for Figueira with a cargo of dried cod, and manned by a crew of four. Her previous master, Capt. W. J. Osborne of Fowey, had frequently taken her to Fortune Bay and St. John's, but had to give up his command on account of ill health. Her new skipper held no certificate but was a man of great experience in the trade, having made many voyages to foreign ports and St. John's. On the 19th May, 1909 the vessel was posted at Lloyd's as missing and in due course an official enquiry was held at Falmouth and elicited the fact that the *Challenger* had been kept in splendid condition. At the time of her loss she was insured with the Newquay Club, Cornwall for £200, for total loss, with Lloyd's for £100 on the hull and £250 on the freight, her owner valuing her at £500, but the Court considered £450 would be nearer the mark.

Evidence was given by Ernest Bersin, boatswain of the topsail schooner *Little Secret*, built 25 years before at Portsmouth and a well-known Newfoundland trader. She sailed from St. John's on the 7th December, with a freeboard of 16 inches and when about 300 miles out encountered a heavy S.W. gale, hauling up to the N.W., and blowing with hurricane force for two days with frequent squalls of snow. Bersin considered that the *Challenger* had probably met the same gale soon after leaving port and the Court was likewise of the opinion that she might have foundered in it.

Two other small topsail schooners, *Isabella* and *Little Pet*, left Newfoundland about the same time as *Challenger* and arrived home safely.

In 1950 the 43-ton ketch *Daylight*, built at Gorleston in 1878 by H. A. Morris and owned by Hewett & Co., was trading on the Danish coast under the name *Svend Aage*, having had three other names since her original, and loading 100 tons D.W. on dimensions 80.3 by 18.5 by 7.4. A small auxiliary motor was fitted, developing about 7 h.p.

So far as I can trace 249 Yarmouth smacks were lost between 1879 and 1913. Of these, 98 foundered, 86 sank after collisions, 57 stranded and 8 were burnt out by fire. In 1910 the 40-ton *Cambria*, Y.H.444, built Yarmouth in 1869, was the last sailing trawler to go out across Yarmouth bar. Half a century had witnessed the rise of the port to become one of the premier trawling stations in England and its fall. In 1903 only 86 sail of 45 ft. keel belonged to the town which had seen over one thousand registered in local ownership. Dozens of fine schooners, brigs and brigantines carried on an extensive coasting trade, while deep water sailing ships brought in produce from far-off lands. To-day this huge fleet is nothing more than ancient history, carried in a few old heads, as many a written record was destroyed by enemy action during the recent war and to wander along the empty wharves and quays is to realize what a loss has come with the passing of sail.

LOWESTOFT

LOWESTOFT, like the neighbouring port of Yarmouth, had no trawling history until the middle of the 19th century, when many Ramsgate men began to make the harbour their rendezvous while fishing in the North Sea. In 1863 there were only eight trawlers, but numbers increased to 60 in 1870 and doubled within ten years, it is difficult to give exact figures as the registrations include drifters as well. The port was at its zenith at the turn of the century and in 1898 had 233 drifters and 247 trawlers, all sail, including twelve over 70 tons which were purchased from Hull owners when the break-up of the Humber fleets took place, but 45 to 50 tons were more suitable for local requirements. The oldest smack was the 56-ton *Precursor*, built at Grimsby in 1866 and only fourteen were under 40 tons. One of the Hull vessels was the 73-ton *Achilles*, L.T.223, built at Topsham, Devon in 1877, and seen in Plate 87, the photograph was probably taken when the majority of the fleet was in for Christmas, as all have winter topmasts up and no crosstrees.

I analysed these figures from an interesting booklet loaned me by Mr. E. J. Crews of Lowestoft, whose father, the late Mr. Jeremiah Crews, was the most famous skipper in the smack races which were a feature at the local regattas. Entering involved owners in the loss of about a fortnight's fishing and considerable expense was incurred in fitting out, but so keen was one man that when disappointed in a sail he telegraphed to London for nine bolts of canvas and the sailmakers worked all night to have it ready in time for the race next day.

In 1879 the course was round the S. Newcome Buoy to a flagboat anchored about six miles to the eastward, then round the Corton Float, returning same way but leaving buoys on other hand, approximately 42 miles, but the ground covered was probably nearer 55 miles when tacking was taken into account. The wind was strong E.S.E. when the five smacks made a flying start and at the flagboat *Blantyre* was a few seconds behind *Gem of the Ocean*, but when rounding the Corton Lightship her new jib sheets fouled and the sail could not be got over, all way on the smack was stopped and many lengths lost. *John Macey* went into a long lead and the beat back saw her well to wind'ard, but Skipper Crews judged his distance so fine that he just fetched the mark boat in *Blantyre* although a man could easily have jumped on board. On the run home *John Macey* was still in the lead with her rival to leeward, suddenly Crews surprised his men by ordering the mainsail to be hauled in and the jib dowsed. This checked the way on the smack and allowed the other to go to leeward in rounding the mark, while *Blantyre* got the wind, but *Gem of the Ocean* was so close that it was anyone's race until her jib topsail split. Slowly *Blantyre* edged up until it was possible to read the letters on *John Macey's* stern, then she drew level and went on to win the 35-guinea first prize by 40 seconds, having taken about four hours to cover the course, and only seven minutes separated first and last. The 47-ton *Blantyre*, built at Brixham in 1876, was the smallest smack in the race and Jerry Crews had never sailed in her before.

In 1880 he won in the 60-ton *Paramatta*, built at Rye in 1878, a model of her was purchased out of the Norwich Fisheries Exhibition for presentation to the children of the Prince of Wales. The following year six smacks crossed the line at 10.30 a.m., but the wind was so light that Skipper Crews in the *John Frederick* did not round the mark boat until 1.50 p.m. Then the breeze died right away and the vessels could make no headway against the strong ebb tide, at 5.17 p.m. *Havelock* with an enormous topsail drew up and seemed a likely winner, but fog came down " as thick as some people's heads " to quote the skipper, and the course lay through Pakefield Gat, dangerous enough at any time, but doubly so when it was impossible to pick out the buoys. One of the hands was sent for'ard to tell J. Crews how to steer, as it was too dense for him to see if the headsails were full or not. The lead was heaved continuously for five hours, the smack going about when in danger of " getting on the grit ", and so they groped their way through the treacherous sands until an anchored ship loomed up. Her crew was roused by shouts and said she was anchored halfway down the roads, so the skipper now knew where he was. Then a glimmer of a red light was seen on the starboard quarter and a hail told it was *John Macey*, whose master had been following the sounds aboard the other smack ! After 18 hours at the tiller Jerry Crews crossed the line 40 seconds ahead of his rival, some of the others anchored to wait for daylight before attempting to come through the Gat, concerning which the Pilot's Guide says '' this channel should not be attempted by vessels drawing over 10 ft., and then only at high water, with local knowledge '', and a smack draws 9 ft. 6 in. !

The 1882 race saw Capt. Crews at the helm of *Perseus*, 61 tons, built at Lowestoft in 1876. A strong W.S.W. wind was blowing and he soon found that if his command could not run she was good to wind'ard. A thick haze came down and *Havelock* lowered her topsail to the squall which struck *Perseus*, and with a report like a cannon the bowsprit, 36 in. circ, snapped off short, and all sails and gear went under the bows just as she was about to round the south mark boat. The skipper lashed the helm and ran for'ard to help clear things up and within half an hour the remains of the spar were stepped in the bitts and a smaller jib bent. Although first across the line *Perseus* lost the race by 2 mins. 21 secs., as the smacks were timed across at the start and allowance made for the various differences.

The next year Capt. Crews sailed *Gem of the Ocean*, a vessel he had frequently beaten, and two of the best smacks from Yarmouth were entered. At the start the wind was very light and one of the men was sent up to the crosstrees to boom out the staysail with his foot. The smack had a long lead after rounding the Gat Buoy on the last round, but turning to wind'ard was not her best point of sailing and *Elizabeth Jane* was coming up hand over fist in the freshening wind until her jib split, a new one was bent immediately and she sailed faster than ever, but *Gem of the Ocean* held on to win by 7 seconds.

Certainly smack racing was an exciting sport with Jerry Crews at the tiller.

In 1884, he was to have sailed *Gem of the Ocean* again, but *Sunbeam*, a brand-new boat, came in from fishing a day or two before the race and he asked if he could skipper her instead. She was a sister ship to *Paramatta*, both having been built at Rye for W. R. Jones (Plate 89). There was a fine westerly breeze and when running before the wind watersails were bent to the main and mizzen booms, and a large jib, set as a spinnaker, was held aloft by two men while a third hung on to the shrouds and had one leg on the boom to keep it from jumping as the smack rolled. After rounding the S.E. mark boat *Lance* kept trying to force *Sunbeam* to bear up and *Gem of the Ocean* worked out a lead of two miles. The wind was freshening and remembering his experience in *Perseus*, Skipper Crews gave special orders to watch the bowsprit, and he eased to every puff to save the topmast. *Gem of the Ocean* was being rapidly over-hauled, but shortly before reaching the mark both smacks went about, with the *Gem* to wind'ard. She tacked again and stood in for the buoy on the port tack as *Sunbeam* approached on the starboard, but Crews, having the right of way, held his course and his rival had to port helm and come under the lee of *Sunbeam* instead of heading her. When they rounded, her lead was only ten lengths, but with the wind abeam *Sunbeam* reached ahead to win by 2 mins. 34 secs.

The 1885 race saw a runaway victory for *Welfare* by 30 minutes and the following year *Wanderer* was first home by 4 mins. 39 secs., while in 1887 *Boy Ernest* was back in the trawl basin before any of the others had crossed the finishing line.

Skipper Jeremiah Crews died on the 9th December, 1891, at the age of 48, leaving a record never to be surpassed, 13 wins in 14 starts, always in a different smack, never in one of his own, but his good judgment, fine seamanship and skilled hand on the tiller made all the difference.

The last race was sailed in 1896 and Plate 88 shows them cracking on with staysails up, the leading smack has a tow foresail and big jib set, while the one immediately in her wake has a colossal jib topsail as well. Nerve was required to handle a vessel under such conditions, especially when all were bunched up at the mark boat.

Plate 90 is interesting because the 53-ton *Charles Henry*, L.T.585, built at Brixham in 1872, was owned by Jeremiah Crews, also it is the only photograph I have showing a yard for a square sail, with the fore braces leading to the end of the bowsprit and the after ones abreast the mizzen mast, which has a long masthead with a short fidded topmast. To judge from the new paintwork and the ladies on board it is probable that the smack has just come round new from the builders.

The 58-ton *Henry Stephenson*, L.T.611, also built at Brixham in 1872, is seen in Plate 91. The difference in the size of mizzen and topsails will be noticed, and it was then the fashion to cut topsails with a considerable round to the head to make them sit flat, the yard being bent as much as 15 inches. The position of the light boards in the main rigging was a source of danger when shipping the lamps in bad weather. I should imagine the man in the topper to be the owner, W. R. Jones, while the ladies' dresses are worth more than a passing glance.

When I was going through the building book of J. W. & A. Upham at Brixham in May, 1950, I came across some interesting details of smacks built for Lowestoft owners. Among them was *Forget-me-not*, L.T.30, built in 1883 to the order of W. Painter. The agreement was for £670, the cost of blocks being £16 2s. 6d. and extras included 8s. for the ornamental mizzen cap so typical of Lowestoft trawlers, and 13s. 8d. for the mizzen crosstrees. The total cost was £695 12s. 10d. for hull, boat and spars.

The hull was launched on the 21st June, the length of keel being 63 ft., and dimensions 70.6 by 19.3 by 9.6. Tonnage 59 $\frac{85}{100}$

The foremast was 37 ft. rig, topmast 32 ft. with 5 ft. pole. Boom 36 ft. 6 in. and gaff 32 ft.

The mizzen mast was 25 ft., with topmast 21 ft. and pole 3 ft. Boom 24 ft. Gaff 19 ft. Bowsprit 37 ft.

Distance of foremast from apron 23 ft. 6 in.

Centre foremast to centre mizzen 38 ft.

Mizzen mast from after part of post 9 ft. 2 in.

These particulars show how different was the spacing of masts at Lowestoft as compared to Brixham, where the ketches often had 26 ft. bows.

In 1886 *Samaritan*, L.T.89 was built by Upham for Mr. Lang and launched on the 30th December, dimensions being 66.6 by 18.5 by 9.1, tonnage 53 $\frac{15}{100}$.

The foremast had a 34 ft. 8 in. rig and a 9 ft. 6 in. masthead, while the topmast was 30 ft. long with a 5 ft. pole.

The main boom measured 34 ft., gaff 30 ft. The mizzen mast has a 25 ft. rig with a 17 ft. pole, gaff 17 ft. and boom 20 ft. 6 in., while the bowsprit was a 36 ft. spar.

Here the distance from apron to centre of mast was only 21 ft. 6 in. The total cost was £758 18s. 1d. and included an ice box, the details being :—

Platform and pound boards	730 ft. of 1½ by 11 in. pine.
Ice box	308 ft. of 1¼ by 7 in.
	100 ft. of 2½ by 5 in.
	350 ft. of 1½ in. sq. battens.
	1,200 nails.
	4 men, 4 days.

Plate 92 shows *Gladys*, L.T.233, 47 tons, built at Brixham 1901.

The elliptical or round stern was introduced at Lowestoft in the early 1870's, the credit being due to Fuller Bros., who had a yard on Lake Lothing. It was more sightly than the old-fashioned square transom and somewhat stronger, but the curved taffrail, etc., were a greater expense and more difficult to repair when damaged (Fig. 7). The difference can clearly be seen in Plate 38.

When I was at Lowestoft in October, 1946, I was fortunate enough to meet Mr. William Parker, who had been designer for H. Reynolds, a well-known smack builder whose yard was later owned by J. Chambers. From his notebook I give the nett costs for building trawlers, but sawmill charges, indirect wages and overheads have to be added and these were not given.

In June, 1900, a large smack was built for H. Holland at a contract price of £860 for hull and spars. The nett costs amounted to £760 17s. 3½d., being made up as follows :—

	£	s	d		£	s	d
Wages	231	3	5	Timber	279	5	5
Stores & Fastenings	48	8	11	Cartage	8	16	9
Two pumps	1	10	—	Cement	1	8	—
Castings for stem		5	7	Builder's plate		17	6
do deck gear	13	14	4	Spars & blocks	81	14	9
Ironwork	82	11	11	Small boat	9	16	2½
Funnelling	1	4	6				

The following year a small-sized smack of 37 tons, the *Magnolia* was built for W. Brown. The contract price was £650 and the nett costs £510 3s. od., the various items being :—

	£	s	d		£	s	d
Wages	157	7	11½	Timber	197	12	8
Stores, fastenings	26	18	1	Spars and blocks	52	19	9
Iron work, smithshop	52	10	—	Mainsheet chock	2	—	—
Deck castings	8	6	9	Stem casting		5	—
Stove and funnelling	3	13	9½	Small boat	7	7	4
Stove stones	1	1	8				

The stove stones were the flagstones put round and under the stove in the cabin. *Magnolia* was still fishing in the '30's.

A similar vessel, the 34-ton *Oleander*, was built for Painter Bros. and nett costs amounted to £509 2s. 11d. This smack was sunk by U-boat on the 21st February, 1916, while fishing 28 miles S.E. of Lowestoft. (Sail plan of small trawler on page 320.)

Mr. Parker told me that smacks cost more to build in winter than in summer owing to poorer daylight. Building usually took ten to twelve weeks, rigging out about a fortnight and ready for sea a smack cost from £1,000 to £1,200.

In February, 1904, *Seabird* was built for Wm. T. Jeckells at a contract price of £915, with nett costs £699 14s. 11d.

	£	s	d		£	s	d
Wages	187	8	8	Timber	278	16	—
Stores, fastenings	53	5	5½	Spars and blocks	81	15	—
Ironwork	82	—	—	Stoves and funnels	7	11	8
Stove stones	1	8	3	Small boat	7	9	10½

I met Mr. Jeckells, of Jeckells & Son, sail-makers, and he was good enough to send me full particulars of sails and boltropes, time taken to make, by hand and by machine, and the sizes of running and standing rigging, a most valuable record which will interest all sail lovers.

SAIL	TIME IN MAKING	
	Hand	Machine
Mainsail	5 weeks	3 weeks
Mizzen	2 do	1½ do
Foresail	1 do	5 days
No 1 jib	3 days	2½ days
No 2 jib	5 days	4 days
No 3 jib	1 week	5 days
Big jib	9 days	7 days
Main topsail	1 week	5 days
Mizzen topsail	4 days	3 days
Mizzen staysail	5 days	4 days

Tarred Ropes

SAIL	Head	Foot	Leech	Mast	Stay	Canvas No	Reefs	Quantity yards req'd
		inches						
Mainsail	2	2	4	$2\frac{1}{2}$		1	3	260
Mizzen	2	2	3	2		2	2	100
Foresail		2	$2\frac{1}{2}$-$3\frac{1}{2}$		$2\frac{1}{2}$	2	2	50
Jib. No 1		2	2		4	1		20
Jib. No 2		2	2		4	2		28
Jib. No 3		2	2		4	2		40
Big Jib		2	2-3		$3\frac{1}{2}$	6		80
Main topsail		2	2	$2\frac{3}{4}$		6 & 7		50
Mizzen topsail		2	2	2				20
Mizzen staysail		$1\frac{1}{2}$	$1\frac{1}{2}$		$2\frac{1}{2}$	7		50

Total 698

SIZES OF STANDING RIGGING

Fore stay	4 in circ.	64 feet	B.B. Wire
Shrouds, main.	3 in do	42 fathom	To make 6 shrouds
Fore sheet strop	$1\frac{1}{2}$ in do	3 ft 6 in	
Shrouds, mizzen	2 in do	98 ft	To make 4 shrouds

SIZES OF RUNNING GEAR

Main halyards	$3\frac{1}{2}$ in	27 fathom	
Peak halyards	$3\frac{1}{2}$	37 do	
Topsail halyards	3	21 do	
Topsail leader	3	47 feet, 8 ft chain and traveller	
Main sheet	$4\frac{1}{2}$	14 fathom	
Double reef tackle	$2\frac{1}{2}$	20 do	
1st reef tackle	$1\frac{1}{2}$	$12\frac{1}{2}$ do wire and rope combined	
Jib halyard	3	22 do	
do	$2\frac{1}{2}$	15 do	7 fthm each bow
Foresail	$2\frac{1}{4}$	20 do	
Fore sheet	$1\frac{1}{2}$	4 do	rove in sheet strop
Main reef lacing	$1\frac{1}{2}$	$7\frac{1}{2}$ do	Three required
Mizzen halyards, main	$2\frac{1}{4}$	19 do	
do do , peak	$2\frac{1}{4}$	26 do	
Mizzen sheet	$2\frac{1}{4}$	14 do	
Mizzen reef lacing	$1\frac{1}{4}$	$5\frac{1}{2}$ do	Three required
Mizzen topsail halyard	$2\frac{1}{2}$	18 do	
Mizzen reef tackle	2	8 do	
Mizzen boom brace	2	8 do	
Main boom brace	$2\frac{1}{2}$	12 do	

All for a smack with 36 ft rig, no fishing gear included.

Mr. James Breach wrote me that he was apprenticed in 1891 at the age of 14 to Mr. H. Summers of Ramsgate, whose sail loft was directly under the Tidal Ball on the West Cliff. Entry was from the top of the cliff, the lower part of building being used for stores and offices. Here three men and two apprentices found plenty of employment making and repairing the sails of the 41 smacks then owned by Mr. Summers. After serving seven years Mr. Breach returned to Lowestoft in 1898 and started on his own. The price of materials was :—

Hayward's No 1 flax canvas	1s 0½d per yard, in bolts of 40 yards, 24 inches wide, price falling ¼d per number.
American Cotton	8 oz, 5d per yard, 10 oz, 7d, 24 in wide.
Best hemp boltrope	8d per lb
White yacht manilla	10d per lb, (1950 price over 7s)
Labour	6d per hour for a 57 hour week.

Whilst on the subject of prices I came across some interesting figures in a small notebook kept by Commander S. Moriarty in 1862, when he was fitting out an armed sailing vessel for the Chinese Imperial Navy and for whom, no doubt, only the best and finest materials were good enough. This document, written in minute writing, was loaned me by Mrs. Kinloch, his grand-daughter.

In 1862 Ray & Son, timber and spar merchants of Millwall, could supply 4 in. oak plank @ 2s. 2½d. c. ft., 3½ in. @ 1s. 11½d., 3 in. @ 1s. 8½d., 2½ in. @ 1s. 5½d., and 2 in. @ 1s. 2½d. For elm prices were 4 in. @ 11d., 3½ in. @ 9¾d., 3 in. @ 8½d., 2½ in. @ 7¼d. and 2 in. @ 6½d. 4 in. Danzic fir plank was 9d., 3½ in. @ 8d., 3 in. @ 7d., 2½ in. @ 6d. and 2 in. @ 5d. per cub. ft.

A 10-hand—say 12½ in. dia.—mast of Danzic pine was £13, 9 hands £9, 8 hands £7, 7 hands £6 and 6 hands, say about 8 in. dia. £4. Girth measurement in hands of 4 inches.

Henry Hewetson & Co, Canvas makers, Old Fish St, E.C, quoted:

No 1 canvas	10½d to 19d per yard.
2 do	10d to 18½d do
	with a fall of ½d per number
Roping twine	8 lb balls. 8s to 12s 6d
Seaming twine	do 8s 6d to 13s.
Lead lines	25 fathom 4s 6d each
Deep sea	100 do 24s 6d each
Marline	3s 6d a bundle of 12 skeins of 12 fathom each.
Palms.	1s each.
Sail needles	assorted. 7s per 100

5% discount for cash.

Mr Bond, blockmaker, Limehouse gave his prices for brass-bushed single blocks: 5 inch 2s 3d. 6 inch 2s 6d. 7 inch 3s. 8 inch 3s 6d, 9 inch 4s 6d, 10 inch 6s, 12 inch 8s and 15 inch 13s 9d.

Double blocks, charged as two single.

Clump blocks, 6d extra up to 8 inch, 1s from 9 to 12 inch

The same price was quoted by Chas & Fred Ferguson, Mast House, Blackwall, who supplied 132 8 inch double blocks.

Harry Vane of Narrow Street, Limehouse quoted:—

10	inch elm deadeyes		15s	each
8	do	do	8s 2d	do
7	do	do	4s 8d	do
5	do	do	3s 2d	do

A dinner at Corsbies, St. James, Piccadilly, consisting of fried soles, roast beef, vegetables, apple tart, bread and cheese cost 2s., ale 4d., brandy 3d. and attendance 1d. I wonder what would happen to-day if you tipped a waiter one penny ! A glass of ale and a meat sandwich was 4d., and another dinner at 67 Cheapside, with a pencilled note " a good house ", was turbot and oyster sauce, roast mutton and vegetables 2s., a pint of ale 4d. Bass's draught beer was 4s. a gallon, brandy 2s. 8d. per pint., port 1s. 2d. per pint, bottles 2d. extra.

Single fare, first-class, from Paddington to Exeter was 16s., return 28s., the journey taking 8 hrs. 25 mins. From Waterloo the fare was 14s. 3½d. single, and Exeter to Plymouth 7s. 6d. and cab fare to Stoke 1s. The third-class fare from Paddington to Exeter was 6s. 9d. Second-class 11s.

These figures show that prices of gear, etc., had increased very little 46 years later, and they give some indication of what money would buy in the West End and City. When comparing wages in those far-off days with those paid now it is as well to remember purchasing power, the only true comparison.

In an advertisement of 1860, Hallet & Abbey, brewers of Brighton offer Brighton pale ale, B 9 gallons for 8s. 3d., BB cost 10s. 6d. India pale ale XXX was 1s. 8d. a gallon, Guinness 7s. a dozen quart bottles, Port and Sherry 36s. a dozen, Brandy 30s. to 36s. a gallon, Rum 14s. to 18s. a gallon, Whisky 18s. to 21s. a gallon.

In 1880 furniture prices were amazing. A dining room suite, covered in best roan leather, consisting of couch, six chairs and two easy chairs, was £18, superior quality £21 to £23. The same expenditure purchased a drawing-room suite of couch, two easy and six ordinary chairs, covered in cretonne, worsted rep or tapestry while bedroom suites were £9 to £20. Cloth trousers, ready made, 4s. 11d. to 9s. 11d., suits made to measure 30s.

But I must leave economics and get back to sail-making. Mr. Breach said there were different ideas among sail-makers with regard to the allowance for stretching of the canvas. Some used to sew their ropes on tight, putting in a lot of slack canvas, which made the sails baggy, but he did not believe in that. He allowed as much slack canvas as he thought the rope would stretch, on a 30 ft. gaff 1 ft. 9 in., on a 25 ft. one 1 ft. 6 in., 6 ft. on a big jib and so on.

The general rule for peak was half the length of gaff, plus one foot, thus if the gaff measured 32 ft., one half was 16 and 1 ft. added made 17 ft. for the peak gore.

For the cost of a suit of sails just after the 1914 war I turn to one of Skipper F. W. Moxey's letters. His smack *G. & E.*, built at Porthleven in 1906, cost ready for sea £1,500.

SAIL	YARDS	COST
Mainsail	256	£90
Mizzen	80	£45
Stay foresail	45	£20
Topsail	60	£35
Big jib	85	£40
Mizzen topsail	30	£15
Small jibs	35	£20
Big foresail, light canvas	60	£15
	Total	£280

Skipper J. T. Crouch told me that a good deck hand could tell each jib by the size of the boltrope. The storm jib was kept right for'ard in the pipe locker, then the five-cloth and seven-cloth ones and the spare stay foresail, all on the port side of the sail locker, the big sails to starboard so that there could be no mistake in finding the correct sail in the dark. Sometimes the storm jib was identified by a piece of twine with four knots in it.

Sails were dressed every year with a mixture of cutch and red ochre, a new mainsail was supplied every five years or so for winter use, the old one being carried in the summer months.

The Lowestoft-built smacks were fine sea boats and very well liked by the fishermen. Mr. Wm. Parker kindly let me have tracings and data from which I drew up Plans 5, pages 318-20. I sent them for his approval and he signed them as correct. The big smacks were 75 ft. L.O.A., 62 ft. 9 in. on keel, moulded breadth 18 ft. 8 in. moulded depth 9 ft. 4 in., displacement to L.W.L. 100.95 tons, centre of buoyancy from fore edge of stem 35.89 ft. There were usually slight modifications to owner's requirements, but the gross tonnage averaged 55 tons. Small trawlers were 52 ft. on the keel.

Plate 94 shows a typical Lowestoft-built trawler with a round stern, the 45-ton *Boy Ramah*, L.T.308, built 1909.

Generally speaking the smacks did not work on such distant grounds as the Humber fleets, and single-boating was the more usual practice, with trips lasting from six to ten days. Ice was supplied by the Lowestoft Ice Co. which sold 1,440 tons in 1875 and over 6,000 in 1882, the prices ranging from 21s. to 35s. a ton. Insurance in the various Mutual Societies cost 3¼ per cent to 3½ per cent in the '80's, the average value of a trawler being £550, and one society paid out £7,200 in five years.

The years 1879 to 1913 saw 163 smacks lost, so far as I can trace. Of these 59 foundered, 38 sank after collision, 58 stranded and 8 were burnt out by fire.

Many of the strandings were on the north or south beaches where smacks piled up if they missed the narrow 130 ft. entrance to the harbour. A few such casualties were the 53-ton *Mystery*, built 1901, lost on the N. pier 9th January, 1912, and the 45-ton *Peace*, built 1862, on the 29th January 1891, the 53-ton *Resolute*, built at Lowestoft in 1891, drove up on the N. Beach in an easterly gale and became a total loss on the 14th January, 1903. Plate 93 shows the coastguards rescuing one of the crew by means of the breeches buoy. A smack stood little chance under such conditions, the sea soon breaking her to pieces (Plate 95). Other losses were the 52-ton *Semper Fidelis*, built 1882 at Rye, wrecked in a southerly gale on the 17th March, 1903, near the south pier. *Sparkling Nellie*, 49 tons, built Bideford 1885, stranded outside the entrance in an E.N.E. gale on the 18th November, 1902. These are only a few examples of the many which met with disaster within sight of home and safety.

One of the most amazing incidents occurred on the 17th November, 1937. A S.E. gale was blowing and with a following wind and sea the 46-ton *Wave Crest*, L.T.744, built at Rye in 1910, tore for the narrow entrance (Plate 96). Just as she was making the north pier a huge sea lifted her and the bows drove up on to the wooden piles of the extension, snapping off the bowsprit. As the smack swung round, the mizzen boom broke off and she shot right across the harbour on to the concrete wall of the south pier and her stem mounted the landing steps. Here she pounded about for a time before sliding off and reaching safety. Such was her build that no serious damage resulted, although the smack had to go on the slipway for overhaul. In July, 1946, she was sold to Norwegian owners.

Losses by fire included the 36-ton *Verbena*, built at Lowestoft in 1886, and burnt out on the 6th November, 1902, in an E. by N. gale, while fishing 40 miles east by north of Lowestoft. On 2nd August, 1886, the 41-ton *Daring*, built at Yarmouth 1864, was destroyed by fire 12 miles E.N.E. of the Owers Lightship.

A heavy toll was claimed in peace and in war, as during the 1914-18 conflict 140 smacks were destroyed by enemy action and when peace was proclaimed only 180 were left on the register. Mrs. Gowring wrote that her uncle, Mr. W. H. Shipp, owned *Mayflower*, *Sunflower*, *Springflower* (Plate 33), *Fortuna* and *C.E.S.*, the best fitted-out smacks in the harbour, all of which fell victims to the German U-boats, a very high price for one man to pay. She herself braided the nets for awhile with the ship's husband, Old Joe, who had lost a leg at sea, while her grandfather, a one-time admiral, was stricken with palsy for 21 years following immersion in the sea when his smack was burnt out.

On the 26th November, 1932, *Kestrel*, L.T.1097 (Plate 49), skipper T. R. J. Damerall, was trawling about five miles N.E. of Smith's Knoll in a strong wind with a heavy sea running. J. Marjoram, aged 57, was unlucky enough to step into the bight of the warp just as the gear fouled a wreck at 1.55 p.m. The jerk broke the stopper and the warp ran out taking the deck-hand overboard. The third hand, Arthur Rose, at once threw a lifebuoy and the unfortunate man got his arm through it, but drifted astern too fast to be picked up from the smack. Hearing the shouts, the mate, J. Herrivan, jumped out of his bunk and rushed up on deck and with A. Rose launched the small boat into a boiling sea and both went to the rescue. It was half a hour before they sighted the lifebuoy and the man was dead. After considerable difficulty the body was got into the boat, which was now so far from *Kestrel* that the mate feared they would not be picked up before darkness fell and they had no means of burning a light. Meanwhile the smack had cut away her gear, went about and worked five to six miles before picking up the boat in a sea which the mate described as the worst he had ever been out on in a small boat during his 46 years' experience.

At the inquest the coroner recorded a verdict of accidental death, with no blame attached to anyone " on the contrary I feel that the other members of the crew are deserving of commendation, particularly the two who at once went off in the small boat with such a heavy sea running in an endeavour to rescue deceased. I feel they must have been in some jeopardy themselves and that their conduct in attempting to save the life of their comrade was most praiseworthy ".

The spirit of the old smacksmen lives on.

In the years immediately following the Armistice thirty-three new smacks were built, among them *Master Hand*, L.T.1203, which I measured up in 1946, and a full description of her is given in a later chapter. In 1930, 124 sail survived, sixteen being over thirty years old, one having been built in 1891, four in 1893, three in 1894, one in 1895, five in 1896 and two in 1898. Fifty-three registered 40 tons and over and eight were fitted with motors, but by 1939, only eight sail were working out of port. After the war some of the laid-up smacks were converted to full power, *Master Hand* for one. *Our Merit*, built by Upham at Brixham in 1914, was half-full of water when she was sold in 1945 and rigged out for the passage to Buckie, which took eight days in the light winds prevailing, but the final thirty-three miles were sailed in 2½ hours with a freshening N.E. wind on the quarter. Shorn of her canvas and fitted with a 160 h.p. Gleniffer engine, *Our Merit* is now engaged in seine fishing. *Crecy*, *Telesia*, *Helen May* and some others went to Norway, and now not one sailing trawler survives of all the brave fleet.

On Sunday the 13th October, 1946, I walked in drizzling rain round the banks of Lake Lothing. The graveyard was a depressing sight with gaunt ribs sticking up out of the mud where hulls had rotted away, others still bore some resemblance to smacks. I took several snaps, but none came out so clearly as the photo of *Seabird*, L.T.591, which I came across while hunting through Mr. Jenkins' cellar (Plate 97). She lies only a few yards from the slip where she was built in 1904, but the sheds were all falling to pieces and rank grass grew everywhere. I turned away more determined than ever to try and record something of the old sailing trawlers while it was still possible to find old men who knew them in their prime.

CHAPTER TEN

EAST COAST FISHING STATIONS

SCARBOROUGH

SCARBOROUGH was the first port on the east coast to begin trawling which commenced there in the early 1830's, when a few Brixham men came north to supply the needs of the wealthy visitors then flocking to the spa.   It was the custom to land catches in summer and early autumn from about four smacks of 30 to 34 tons, and as winter advanced they returned to Devonshire.   The local fishing was long-lining and drifting for herring and the men were very hostile to the newcomers, alleging that trawling was ruining their livelihood.   The harbour was very exposed to easterly gales and at times impossible to leave or approach, but prolific grounds on which choice fish were found lay in close proximity.   For some years the Devon men carried on in this unsatisfactory way, as frequently the family, goods and chattels were shipped to and fro, so that the men had one home in the south and another in Yorkshire.   When the Friendly Society of Fishermen was formed at Brixham c 1834, a special clause was inserted to allow owners and crews to convey furniture, etc., without invalidating the insurance which prohibited the carriage of cargoes in fishing smacks.

It is obvious from the Washington Report of 1849 that some of the local men were not opposed to trawling, as mention is made by John Edmond, foreman to R. Skelton, that the yawls commenced trawling in May, for which their lug-rig was far from suitable.   These vessels, built on the lines of the Yarmouth " punt ", measured 47 ft. 2 in. L.O.A., 43 ft. keel, 15 ft. moulded beam, and 6 ft. 6 in. depth of hold. 12 tons of ballast were carried and displacement to load draught was 30 tons, the hull accounting for 9.2 tons.   They were clench-built of American oak $\frac{5}{16}$ of an inch thick, copper fastened to the waterline, the timbers were English oak $5\frac{1}{2}$ in. by 4 in., floors $5\frac{1}{2}$ in. by $6\frac{1}{2}$ in., keel 5 in. by 9 in., fastened with fir trenails one inch dia., the wales 6 in. broad, 3 in. thick.   Rigged with jib, lug foresail and mizzen, they cost £310 ready for sea.

By the early fifties some of the Brixham men had decided to make their homes in the north, among them being the brothers G. & W. Alward, who brought two smacks, but later they moved to Grimsby.   At the 1863 Enquiry it was stated that

30 years before only two large trawlers belonged to the port against the 35 then fishing, but they still worked over the same local grounds, the name of one, " California," telling how profitable had been its yield.

The lug-rigged yawls soon gave place to cutters which closely followed Brixham design with full bows and fine runs, but by the seventies they were found to be too small and many were hauled up on the beach, ballast, mast and spars taken out and the empty hull pulled further up on the top of a spring tide. It was then cut in half at the point of greatest beam, a large block was chained to a bolt through the keel about 18 in. clear of the sternpost and another was shackled to a chain from an anchor well out in the bay. Then gangs of men sweated and heaved on the luff-on-luff tackles to draw the stern back for the distance required to insert a new midship section. The ends were jacked up and aligned, a new length of keel, already prepared, was scarphed on to the old, floors bolted across, frames fitted and new planking added. The beam in some cases was increased by boring out the old trenails, pushing the planking away and inserting several inches of packing on the frames. This work, which practically doubled the tonnage, had to be finished before the tides made again, then the lengthened hull was launched, the old mast stepped and a new mizzen added.

Plate 98 shows *Prize*, 58 tons, built at Sandwich, Kent, in 1866, dried out at low water which allows the lines to be seen, ahead is a clinker-built cutter with a " lute " stern, and the gaff, hoisted well up the mast, has its peak resting on the taffrail. By now most of the old luggers had converted to gaff rig and went trawling out of the herring season.

The skipper, first and second fishermen were on shares, but deck hand and boy had wages. In winter the smacks went single-boating, ice being taken if the trip was to be longer than three days. In summer they "went across" to join one of the fleets working on the Eastern grounds and catches were put aboard a carrier, but if numbers were sufficient the smacks fished together and put the united catches on one which took them to market.

In 1878 Samuel Randal told the Commissioners that 62 trawlers were fishing out of Scarborough. His smack, the 70-ton *Good Design*, had been built with a 70 ft. keel at Sandwich in 1877 and worked a 48 ft. beam, the cod mesh being 2 in. from knot to knot and he frequently kept the trawl down for 12 hours. From October he fished for soles, turbot, haddock and plaice 60 miles S.E. and N.N.E. of Scarborough, in March went across to the Dutch coast, then to Jutland, leaving in August for the inshore grounds off the Yorkshire coast. Quantities of small haddock, 6 in. long, sold at 6d. to 1s. 6d. a basket of three stone.

Taking the harbour in a gale was a dangerous job and if conditions were too bad, tar barrels were burnt at night to warn vessels not to attempt to enter. On the 1st February, 1884, the 44-ton yawl *Elizabeth & Susannah*, built 1872, stranded on the outer pier in a full E.N.E. gale and was a total loss with her crew of six. *Gauntlet*, a 44-ton dandy, built in 1867, stranded under Speeton Cliffs on the 29th October, 1880, in an E.N.E storm with the loss of five men. The day before, another yawl the 40-ton *Admiral Hope*, built 1859, stranded one mile north of Bridlington and was a total loss.

The summer visitors enjoyed eating fish fresh out of the sea, but the Corporation, who owned the harbour, was not keen on developing the trawling industry and did little to help fishermen, and this fact, allied to the amazing rise of the Humber ports, saw the decline of the sail fleet by the end of the century.

A few of the old smacks continued to earn a living in other ways. Plate 99 shows *Thomas & Ann* lying at Dover. Registering 38 tons she was built at Scarborough in 1858, and fished out of the harbour for many years, rigged as a yawl. In 1920 she was registered at Milford as a ketch of 29 tons and owned at Cardiff. Careful examination of the photograph shows the cut in rail and bulwark where the original boat gangway was, thus proving a link with the days when the Yorkshire town was a fishing station.

HULL

NEWS of the phenomenal catches of soles in the deep-water grounds south of the Dogger, now known as the Silver Pits, spread like wildfire amongst the fishing community. This accidental discovery has become a legend, conflicting reports telling how this man or that was responsible for the finding of the treasure store. There was a rush to the north by the Brixham and Ramsgate men, but lack of harbour facilities was the greatest drawback. Many smacksmen, finding Scarborough unsuitable, began fishing out of Hull where some of the local line-fishermen were already disposing of their catches as best they could. In 1845 about forty trawlers joined the two or three already working from the Humber, but they had to anchor in the roads and land their fish at any convenient jetty. There was no recognized market and it was every man for himself.

Several Brixham men, wearying of the annual move of leaving Devon in October and returning about Whitsun, decided to settle at Hull, among them being Robert Hellyer, a name not unknown in fishing circles to-day. Mr. J. W. Marshall of Bridlington wrote me in February, 1946 :—

" My maternal grandfather, whose name was Charles Vincent, of Ramsgate, Kent, brought his smacks from Ramsgate to Hull in 1852, and was one of the first pioneers. He brought the whole family, wife, one son and four daughters and one of his skippers was a man I personally knew, Henry Toozes, who eventually became an owner and rose to be Mayor of Hull in my young days. Unfortunately my grandfather was drowned at sea before my time. Three of mother's sisters eventually married and settled in Grimsby, all marrying fishermen and my mother and each of her sisters had a family of twelve children, so there are relatives galore in Hull and Grimsby. I was not satisfied with being the son of a Ramsgate smacksman's daughter

97 SMACK CEMETERY, LAKE LOTHING, LOWESTOFT
L.T.591 is *Sea Bird*, 57 tons, built at Lowestoft, 1904.

98 *PRIZE* of Scarborough
58 tons, built at Sandwich, Kent, 1866. Ahead is a clench-built cutter with a lute stern.

99   *THOMAS & ANN* AT DOVER
A 38-ton smack, built at Scarborough 1858, later converted to a trading ketch and still working in 1920.

100   A UNION INDENTURE, 1870

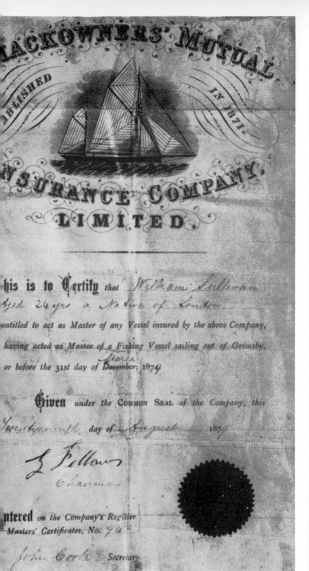

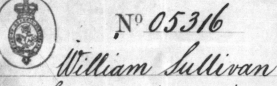

101 A MASTER'S CERTIFICATE, 1879

102 SKIPPER'S CERTIFICATE OF SERVICE, 1886

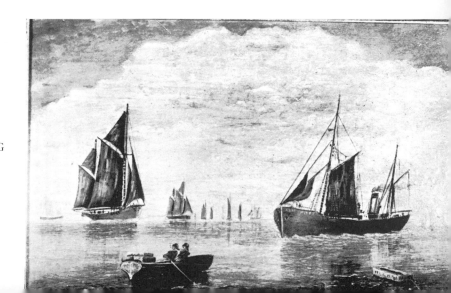

03 HULL TRAWLERS TRUNKING
FISH TO CARRIER *ASIA*

104 *SWAN*, H.182, C 1892
     86 tons, built at Brixham, 1891. One reef is down in
     main and mizzen and second jib is set. G.Y.354 has her
     jib aback and is about to pick up her boat which is to
     wind'ard of *Swan*.

105 STEAM CARRIER *GANNET*, G.Y.939
The flag at peak of gaff denotes that she is ready to receive
the trunks of fish from the trawlers.

106 STEAM CARRIER *PELICAN*, G.Y.938
Working with the Grimsby Ice Co's fleet, 1892. A long swell is running after a gale and the smacks
are seen working out to wind'ard, ready for "putting off". This "cutter" was built of iron at Hull
in 1884. Length 133.5 ft., beam 21.7 ft., depth 11 ft., 141 N.T., 244 G.T., 70 h.p. engine.

107 *FLOWER OF THE FOREST*, G.Y.983, c 1892
The gale has blown itself out and reef in mainsail has been shaken out, but lacing is still in first seven eyelets, and bonnet is off foot of foresail. Mizzen has one reef down.

108 GRIMSBY SMACKS HOVE-TO
G. I. C., G.Y.152, The admiral is flying his flag in the smack to wind'ard and both trawlers a̶ ready to put out their boats, being to wind'ard of the cutter waiting to take the fish trunks. All sa̶ are diagonal-cut and reef lacing is still in mainsail eyelets. A full head of steam is on the capstan, t̶ safety valve aft is lifting and one of the crew is easing capstan to allow steam to escape.

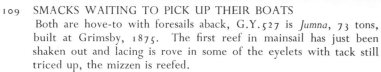

109 SMACKS WAITING TO PICK UP THEIR BOATS
Both are hove-to with foresails aback, G.Y.527 is *Jumna*, 73 tons, built at Grimsby, 1875. The first reef in mainsail has just been shaken out and lacing is rove in some of the eyelets with tack still triced up, the mizzen is reefed.

110 MAINMAST OF *SWAN*, G.Y.884
28 tons, built at Grimsby, 1883. Wrecked on the Wainfleet Sands, 17th July, 1915, mast still standing in September, 1948.

111
AFTER THE GREAT GALE AT
BRIXHAM, 1866.

112   BRIXHAM HARBOUR, c 1882
The brigantine is *Jane Wheaton* of Brixham, 187 tons, built at Rye, 1863.

113   MENDING A TRAWL NET ON A BRIXHAM SLOOP, c 1882
Note the dandy line on the dandy " wink," and the life buoy on fore
side of companion.

but I married the daughter of a Hull smacksman, Capt. John Dannatt, who in his young days sailed in the old whaler *Diana*. He was a very entertaining old gentleman, was born and died in Hull at the age of 81. I lost my dear wife on our Golden Wedding anniversary, 6th September, 1943, and we buried her sister last Saturday, she being the last of the old skipper's seventeen children. She was 74 years of age. He'd been a real smacksman hadn't he ? "

In 1845 there were 21 smacks sailing out of Hull, 10 years later 110, but no flags were hung to celebrate the arrival of an industry which in a few decades was to transform the mediaeval town into one of the greatest fishing ports. Indeed the authorities looked upon the fishermen as an intolerable nuisance, always seeking a place to dump their smelly fish baskets. The docks were for valuable merchandise and the two did not mix.

After some years the Dock Company allowed a shed to be used and rather ironically painted the name BILLINGSGATE thereon, but only four smacks at a time were allowed 'quay space. More and more owners were coming north and larger vessels being built, but no facilities were provided. The nearest railway station was a mile and a half away, dry docks were non-existent, smacks having to go on the hard to refit. The M.S.L. Rly. took prompt steps to offer inducement to owners to transfer their business to Grimsby on the other side of the river, twenty-five miles nearer the fishing grounds, and some did so.

In 1852 the number of pads landed was 8,159, five years later 80,194 and in 1864 no less than 119,489. Smackowners continued to press for improved facilities and in 1869 the Albert Dock was completed, ice houses, stores, etc., were erected by the trade after assurances had been given that the site was a permanent one, but within a few years the industry had again outgrown the accommodation and smacks often had to lie out in the river for several tides before being able to land their catches. In 1880 the then chairman of the Dock Co. said they would be glad to see the dock relieved of the strain put upon it by fishing smacks and offered the use of a " white elephant ", three miles further up the river, which had been designed for the shipping of coal, but traffic had not materialized. This meant the scrapping of all buildings and the erection of new ones on an inconvenient site. Steam was coming in and many owners shook the dust of Hull off their feet and moved lock, stock and barrel to other ports, but that is another story. In spite of these removals the fishing industry at Hull continued to thrive and it is still one of the premier ports for the landing of white fish.

My efforts to find authentic information concerning the sailing fleets have not been very successful. Mr. J. B. Fay, Director of the Municipal Museum, wrote that unfortunately all their literature and photographs had been lost during the enemy raids on Hull, but he kindly sent a small booklet from which I was able to glean a few particulars, otherwise nothing seems to remain as my appeals met with little or no response. Nearly seventy years is a long gap to span, salvage drives and family clearances of old photographs and documents have no doubt been responsible for the loss of much valuable material.

At the 1863 Enquiry it was stated that some £250,000 was invested in the 270 trawlers working from Hull, while the 1872 register contains 313 fishing vessels, averaging 55 N.T., and nearly all ketch rigged. In a publication of 1877, kindly loaned me by Mr. A. M. Walker, the number given is 390 smacks of 25,817 tons, or an average of 66 N.T., the largest being the 91-ton *Sirius* and *Eurus* followed by the 87-ton *Cyclops*, all built at Hull in 1877, fine powerful vessels, able to trawl in the deepest water in the North Sea.

The Humber fleets were built in various yards around the coast, a few well-known smack builders that I have been able to trace being John Wray & Son, and J. Garside at Burton Stather; Frederickson & Fawcett of Barton-on-Humber; Wm. M'Cann, Hunt & Fowler, Westermann of Hull; I. Masters of Sandwich, Kent; Smith Stevenson & Son, James Hallett, John Hadfield, Smith Bros., Thos. Campbell, and John Bell at Grimsby; W. Kelly, and Philip & Son of Dartmouth; W. A. Gibbs, and Calley of Galmpton; J. W. & A. Upham. R. Jackman, and S. Dewdney at Brixham; J. Hoad, and G. & T. Smith of Rye, Sussex.

By the early eighties these big smacks were being fitted with steam capstans, and cost from £1,500 to £1,700 ready for sea, and many built to Lloyd's survey survived marine perils for over 70 years.

Until the sixties the smacks fished in a fleet from September to April, staying out for six weeks, the fish was packed in baskets and taken to the vessel which had hoisted a flag to show that she was the carrier for that day, the price paid for this service being 1s. to 1s. 6d. a basket. Thus there was a constant succession of smacks joining and leaving the fleet. About Easter they refitted and went across to the Dutch coast to work with the Short Blue Fleet, whose cutters were supplied with English pond ice, but a charge of 20 per cent was made for their services and the sale of fish at Billingsgate. This was considered excessive by the Hull men, and in 1859 Robert Hellyer had the idea of importing ice from Norway. J. Westcott, H. Cousins and T. Halfyard joined him and each built a large cutter, swinging a 52 ft. boom. Having brought over two cargoes of ice these owners ran their own small fleet, taking the catches to Hull in the new carriers. This was the start of the Hull Mutual Ice Company, other owners combined to form the Hull Ice Co. The blocks were stored in sawdust in the cellars of a large warehouse and all went well until one morning when the store-keeper of the Dock Co. left a valve open and the premises flooded at high water, ruining all the precious contents. A new ice-house was built in Cambridge Street and the ice had to be taken through the streets in carts and the smacks supplied by the same means, a wasteful method in hot weather.

After the six weeks fishing the accounts were settled when the skipper, second and third hands met the fish salesman, who told them the proceeds of all sales. Of the nett sum realized the skipper received $\frac{11}{64}$ and each man $\frac{9}{64}$, from which was deducted one-fifth of the cost of the provisions, the two apprentices were provided for by the owner. The rest of the money went to the vessel, and as many skippers were part-owners they received this extra share.

When ice-boxes were fitted in each smack single-boating became usual and catches were landed at any convenient market, many boats going to Sunderland and Hartlepool. Then came the custom of working in fleets of 20 to 50 vessels from May to September, using about 20 cutters to carry the catches to Hull or London. The fleeters remained out 10 to 12 weeks and all returned together at the end of the season. In the winter each smack worked independently, taking 2 to 4 tons of ice to sea for a trip lasting 10 to 14 days, three trips constituting a " settling ". Fish was sold loose, by weight, and the buyer found the packages, small barrels holding 10 to 12 stone and called " kits ". In these the fish was packed with crushed ice between each layer, an extra quantity on top which was covered with straw and the lid fastened down, ready for despatch by rail all over the country.

By 1872 Hull was importing 16,000 to 20,000 tons of ice a year, mostly in foreign sailing ships, but the Ice Companies soon ran vessels of their own. In 1874 the 261-ton brigantine *Beagle* and in 1876 the 317-ton barquentine *Charlie Blackwood* were built at Prince Edward Is. for the Hull Ice Co., while the 274-ton barque *Fanny Bresiauer*, built at Stonehouse in 1871, belonged to the Albert Dock Ice Co., and by 1877 six ships were employed as well as several foreign vessels.

Undoubtedly the most interesting of these ice carriers was the 285-ton *Truelove*, built as a full-rigged ship at Philadelphia in 1764, and captured by the British during the American War of Independence. After a period as an armed ship she was sold by the Government to a Hull merchant and traded to Portugal. Four years later *Truelove* was converted into a whaler and made well over eighty voyages to the Arctic grounds. In her later years she was cut down to barque rig, making her last voyage in 1867-68, when the Hull whaling trade came to an end. Still capable of useful service the old barque was engaged in the ice trade from Norway before being broken up in 1887, after a working life of 123 years.

In 1880 the number of trawlers had increased to 420 and the question of manning the Humber fleets was becoming an acute problem as neither Hull nor Grimsby had any fishing traditions. Two of the five hands carried were apprentices, expected to be qualified to serve as skippers when out of their time and many in fact did so, often taking a part share in their command.

By some extraordinary looseness in the drafting of the Merchant Shipping Act of 1854 there was no obligation on a skipper to report a death at sea unless the vessel was damaged as well. While men shipping in deep-sea sailing ships had to have the articles they signed for a voyage explained to them by Board of Trade officials, there was nothing said about apprenticeship, especially applicable to fishing boats, no limit of age when a lad could be bound, nor was it imperative for a parent, guardian or any person to be a party to the indentures. This left a door wide open for advantage to be taken by unscrupulous individuals, and cases occurred where lads of 11 had bound themselves for 10 years without realizing what they were doing. No copy of the articles signed had to be supplied, there was no system for payment of adequate wages when a boy was of an age to be really useful, so that he frequently worked alongside a man well paid and less competent.

When the indenture was signed a boy was given three suits of clothes, value £7 to £10, provided with food, lodging and necessary clothing ashore as well as afloat during his time, generally living in his employer's house. Spending money was given and perquisites included "stockerbait", small fish then considered worthless in the wholesale market, such as dabs, lemon soles, whiting, etc. Many of the skippers and owners were men who had started life in very humble circumstances, but attributed their success to their apprenticeship. No doubt the system had its good points, especially when lads came from fisherman stock and were brought up in the environment of the sea, but it was now a case of finding boys anywhere and everywhere, and many came from the Unions, reformatories and training ships.

Section 246 of the 1854 Act gave the master, mate, owner, ship's husband or consignee, not to mention the police, the power to apprehend any deserter without warrant and take him on board or before a court, which could give up to a 12 week sentence for desertion or 10 weeks for disorderly conduct. Knowledge that this power existed had a deterrent effect on men deserting, but the repeal of this section in 1880 had far reaching results. Practically every apprentice broke his indentures with impunity and men walked off a smack when they liked, although now supposed to give 48 hours notice and nothing could be done by the skipper or owner unless he went to a magistrate for a warrant, by which time it was probably impossible to trace the man, while a summons was often a waste of time and money as the courts were no longer inclined to commit a man to prison, pending clarification of the new Act. Chaos resulted when hands jumped ashore as the smacks passed out through the dock gates and lads boasted of the number of times they had held up vessels through failing to join at an appointed time.

Casual labour, generally untrained, now took the place of semi-skilled lads, a practice held by many experienced men to be the prime cause of the ever-increasing losses in bad weather. Shipping only for the voyage many of these men were bad lots, the cause of mischief and trouble afloat.

When owners had a large number of apprentices in their employ it had become the custom to allow them 14s. a week to lodge out. Many of the bigger lads chose to go to places where they paid 4d. a night for lodging and no questions asked if they brought in girls as well, or their "chums" as they were euphemistically called. Chits of 15 or so met their "pals" coming ashore with perhaps £3 to £5 in their pockets and persuaded them to stay in their homes, while one police inspector testified that he sometimes went into brothels twice a week to fetch out lads at their mothers' request!

Things were brought to a head when two murders on Hull smacks drew public attention to the seriousness of the matter. One boy, Henry Papper, aged 14, tauntingly boasted in front of his skipper's wife of his sister's association with her husband and the irate man swore he would kill him when they got to sea. The sequel was that Osmand Brand, skipper and owner of *Rising Sun*, reported to the police that at 5.30 a.m. on the 1st January, 1882, when trawling 120 miles from Spurn, the cook William Pepper (sic) was knocked overboard by the big foresail sheet. The smack put about and every effort was made to effect a rescue, without avail, and the body was not recovered. Brand was so cool and collected that no suspicion crossed the mind of the inspector, W. Elliott who took the statement, which was subsequently read and passed by the Chief Constable. Such a report was by no means unusual. But murder will out and eventually Brand was hanged at Armley Gaol, Leeds, on 23rd May, 1882, the mate Wm. Dench, who was also implicated, went to prison and afterwards fled the country.

Rising Sun, 54 tons, built at Hull in 1866, stranded on the 10th January, 1883, at Dimlington, Yorks, in an E.S.E. gale and became a total loss.

On the 24th February, 1882, another entry in police records stated that Peter Hoye (also given as Hughes), age 16, was drawing up a bucket of water in the smack *Gleaner* when he fell overboard and was drowned. Again a likely mishap, as many a boy was dragged over the side through hanging on to the bucket rope when the smack was sailing fast. Here the mate was convicted of murder.

Then the skipper, mate and third hand of *Achievement* of Grimsby, were convicted for cruel, debasing and disgusting treatment of two lads.

These incidents, added to certain letters received by the Board of Trade concerning lads being apprenticed without their parent's knowledge, led to the appointment of a Commission of Enquiry, which found such cases as enumerated to be rare, but various suggestions were made and subsequently adopted. No allegations were made in other ports with fishing traditions where enquiries were held, rather the reverse in some cases. Several men came forward to speak of how their apprenticeship had helped them to rise in the world, many becoming skippers at the early age of 19.

Henry Toozes of Hull, who had 18 apprentices, but now only 3, said men made very poor masters unless they had served their time in smacks. " I always had very good lads, not more than 2 in prison. Forty years ago I served 7 years, was never beaten with a rope although deserved it."

Henry Smethurst of Grimsby, who owned 50 smacks with his son and son-in-law, stated he had 80 to 100 apprentices prior to 1880, three had been taken from Louth Union, one of whom was drowned but the other two became owners.

John Plastow put in a written statement that he was apprenticed from Hackney Union in 1854, to R. Hewett of Barking and served 7 years to 1861. A good man's wage was 14s. in summer, 16s. in winter and he saved £20 a year for two years, then came to Grimsby in 1863 and saved £65 in eight months, or a total of £105 in less than three years. He next took a smack to " work out ", putting £100 down and paid off the remaining £650, with interest, clear in three years. Again went to sea for two more years and saved £700, had another smack built and stayed on shore as a salesman. " I now own several smacks and represent 26 sailing out of the port. I believe every lad has same chance as I had, if he will save instead of spend. I had nothing given or left me, had to work hard for what I have."

In the years 1868 to 1877, 4,277 lads were bound to the fishing trade at Grimsby alone, in 1875, 199 were sent to Lindsey Prison for desertion, disorderly conduct, etc., 224 in 1876 and 246 in 1877, one boy being convicted no less than 26 times. Sentences ranged from 14 days to one month, most of them treated it " as an episode ", calling it " being sent to college " and a committal rather tended to make a boy " somebody " to his pals.

Somewhere between the two extremes quoted the truth lay, a lad either made good if he had it in him, or he remained a ne'er-do-well. Cases of cruelty to children by parents are not unknown even in these enlightened days, as many a court case shows.

Thanks to Mr. George W. Wilson, who loaned me some documents in his wife's possession, I am able to show a Union Indenture (Plate 100). William Sullivan, a poor boy aged about 16, was bound on the 19th September, 1870 by the Whitechapel Guardians to William Joys Skelton, owner of smack *Sir Henry Havelock* (56 tons, built at Galway in 1858). The lad, unable to write, made his mark in the presence of two magistrates that he was willing to serve for five years. It will be noticed that Union Apprentice Indentures ensured that the boy was made aware of the terms by disinterested parties, namely two J.P's. The parchment is endorsed by Geo. Jeff that W. Sullivan had served his apprenticeship satisfactorily and conducted himself with propriety and Sullivan agrees in the presence of a witness to take 12s. a week as deck boy and 14s. as third hand in lieu of board, washing, lodging and medical treatment.

Many of the Insurance Societies issued certificates of competency to skippers long before such papers were compulsory, one being the Smackowners Mutual Insurance Co. Ltd., established at Grimsby in 1871, and George Fellows, the president, testified that £320,000 was insured. " I went to sea in 1840, came to Hull when out of my time, 5 years 8 months, and from 1847 sailed as master. I left for Grimsby in 1864." A certificate cost 5s. with 2s. 6d. for renewal and William Sullivan was given one, No. 74, on the 29th August, 1879 (Plate 101).

One of the outcomes of the 1882 Enquiry was the issuing of certificates to skippers who had held command prior to the 1st September, 1883, when new regulations came into force, and William Sullivan, now able to sign his name, received his at Grimsby on the 17th July, 1886 (Plate 102).

It was most interesting to handle those old documents, still in excellent condition, especially as they dealt with the port of Grimsby. Mr. Wilson wrote that he himself had twice been shipwrecked in midwinter on the Icelandic coast, the first involving a five day trek across country on ponies, the second he was rescued just before the trawler broke up on the rocks.

Subsequent Acts of Parliament provided that no trawler of 25 tons or upwards could go to sea without a duly certificated skipper and second hand. A mate or second hand had to have served four years at sea and not be less than 19 years of age, and a skipper had to be over 21 and served 5 years at sea, including one as second hand. No boy under 13 could be bound apprentice and no one under 16 be taken to sea in a boat of 25 tons and more, to serve in any capacity, unless bound by an indenture. These conditions brought about the extinction of apprenticeship in most of the fishing ports, except at Ramsgate where it continued until the outbreak of war in 1914.

The first curing house was opened in 1847, by Self of Yarmouth, and a few years later a lad of ten, C. Pickering, started work there for 1s. a week and all found. After two years he went to another establishment and in 1867 commenced on his own as a fish merchant. Four years later he had the 72-ton *George Peabody*, built at Sandwich, Kent, others followed until he owned a fleet of twenty-one smacks. In the early eighties he ordered four steam trawlers and when they were delivered he disposed of all his sailing vessels. He was a generous benefactor to his native town.

According to Henry Toozes there were 420 smacks, 9 steam cutters and 6 ice vessels at Hull in 1882 and speaking of expenses he said :—

"In 1862, when I became owner, smacks cost £600 to £650, now £1,360 to £1,600 and steam capstans are £150 to £175 extra. Underwriters will not insure unless the vessel is built under Lloyd's certificate. The value of a steam carrier is £6,000 and an ice carrier £1,600 to £1,800. My smack *Progress* grossed £106. 8s. 6d. for an eight week trip. Dock dues, towing and watchman came to £3 13s. 6d., leaving £102 15s. od. An eighth share equals £12 16s. 5½d., the skipper gets £17 13s. 2d., out of which he bears his proportion of food, so received £12 13s. 3d. for the eight week trip, the mate £9 9s. The rest of crew are apprentices and found by the owner."

The figures for an average year's earnings for a smack were given as £800 for division among owner and crew. The skipper took £137 10s., less £20 for provisions equalled £117 10s. or £2 5s. a week, the second hand £112 10s. less £20 or £92 10s., £1 15s. 4d. a week.

	£
Provisions found by owner for three men	60
Wages at £1, 15s and 10s a week	117
Insurance. £900 at 3%	27
Repairs, sails etc.	250
Interest on £900 at 5%	45
Depreciation	50

Many of the trawlers belonging to Charles and Robert Hellyer were built at Brixham, the home they left about 1854. In 1882 Charles owned eight smacks and in that year had *Orlando* built by J. W. Upham for an agreement of £900 and total cost for hull, spars and small boat of £943 12s. 3d., her dimensions being 74.5 by 20.8 by 10.3, 81 $\frac{86}{100}$ tons. Then followed *Othello*, launched 9th June, 1884, at a total cost of £947 14s., her dimensions being 80.2 by 20.9 by 10.5, 88 $\frac{10}{100}$ tons, *Portia*, and *Rosalind* which was launched on 23rd September, 1885. Her total cost was £934 11s. 6d., keel 71 ft. and dimensions 80.6 by 21.65 by 10.65, 93 $\frac{28}{100}$ tons, 12 years A1 at Lloyd's.

When I was at Brixham in 1950 I found very full particulars of *Pelican*, built by J. W. Upham for Robert Hellyer and launched on the 28th September, 1886.

L.B.P. 79 ft. Beam 20.85 ft. Depth 10.75 ft. Tonnage 92 $\frac{41}{100}$

The agreement was £940 but total cost including certain extras was £990 15s. 10d. This fine trawler was classed A1 for twelve years at Lloyd's and it is interesting to compare her size with smacks built for Brixham owners.

Mainmast.	59 ft with 10 ft masthead.
Rig.	39 ft 6 in.
Topmast.	31 ft rig.
Main boom.	41 ft.
Main gaff.	32 ft.
Mizzenmast.	28 ft 6 in rig, with 19 ft pole.
Boom.	23 ft 6 in.
Gaff.	19 ft.
Bowsprit.	36 ft.

Sixty tons of stone ballast at 1s. 8d. a ton cost £5, and the chain for boat gripes, topsail halyards, topsail sheet, fore sheet and bobstay came to £2 5s. 6d.

For years I tried everywhere to find a photograph of a Hull trawler and it was not until May, 1950, that I succeeded, as among the thousands of plates in Mr. F. W. Beken's collection at Cowes was one of H.182, *Swan*, 86 tons, built at Brixham in 1891, and owned by John William Hellyer (Plate 104). Her foresail has just been allowed to draw as the boat has been picked up. Astern is G.Y.354, hove-to with jib a'weather and about to pick hers up, the boat being to wind'ard of *Swan*. Note the enormous length of the oars, and the men, standing to their work, are watching their vessel, ready to come alongside her lee side. Her stay foresail has been dropped and the main sheet is pinned in. A reef and topsail breeze is blowing as mainsails and mizzens have one reef down, and *Swan* has a reefed topmast and a small jib-headed topsail set. The bowsprit has not been reefed although a smaller jib is carried, the lightboards are in the mizzen rigging whereas the Grimsbyman's are on the main shrouds. Judging from the length of gaff showing I should think the main and mizzen sails are new, in fact it is quite likely that the smack is making her first trip to the Dogger as the photograph was taken in 1892.

Rail freights to London were 35s. a ton in a van, 25s. in a truck, with 5s. delivery charge, packages being at the rate of 30s. a ton.   Efforts to obtain a reduction having failed, The Hull Steam Fishing & Ice Co. had four iron steam carriers built locally in 1880, named *Asia*, *America*, *Africa* and *Europe*, with 60 h.p. engines.   The Great Northern Steam Fishing Co had *Onward* and *Vigilant* built at Port Glasgow with 65 h.p. engines, followed by *Eastward*, built at Hull in 1882 and *Colonel Smith* of 82 h.p., built at Blackwall in 1884.

These carriers were to run alternately to Hull and London, but so much trouble arose through skippers always sending their fish to Billingsgate, rather than to the Hull market that eventually everything went direct to the Metropolis.

I have been able to discover only one photograph of a Hull smack, but Mr. W. B. Duffill of Sutton-on-Hull saw my appeal in the local papers and kindly offered to have a photograph taken of an oil painting by C. Ward in his possession, showing S.S. *Asia* trunking (Plate 103).

In 1887 448 smacks were registered, but the next decade witnessed the virtual disappearance of sail at Hull and by 1903 not one was left.   I find that 191 smacks were lost after 1879, of which 89 foundered, 59 sank after collision, 36 stranded and 7 were burnt out.

A peculiar casualty occurred on the 15th May, 1896, when the 69-ton *Young Gregg*, built at Rye in 1875, was swept from her mooring in St. Andrews Dock owing to the gates of the new extension dock giving way, and became a total loss.

Some of the discarded smacks were sold for coasting and trouble overtook these traders from time to time.   On the 19th November, 1906, the 73-ton *Confidence*, built at Rye in 1877 for John Hill of Hull, later sold to Lowestoft and then to Plymouth owners, foundered in a S.S.E. gale off Brest, France, when bound for Aviles with a cargo of china clay from Par, her master, J. Shaw and the crew of four being lost.

The 90-ton *Alpha*, built at Beverley for F. Hellyer in 1884, stranded on the Knavestone Rocks, Farne Islands, on the 30th December, 1904, in a whole gale from the N.N.W. and became a total loss with her crew of 5, when bound for London with potatoes from Dundee.   On the 20th February, 1896 the 80-ton *Young Peter*, built 1876 at Hull, grounded at the entrance to Whitehills harbour, Banff, in a terrible southerly gale, when on her way to Sunderland from Balintore with a cargo of potatoes.

To-day Hull is one of the greatest fishing ports in the world, with steam and diesel engined trawlers working as far north as the Arctic Circle, equipped with all the latest navigational devices, wireless, telephony, etc.   The latest vessels cost anything from £45,000 to £125,000 to build and fit out with fishing gear, etc., while running expenses may amount to £225 a day.   Let it be remembered that this industry was built up on foundations laid by the old smacksmen seventy and more years ago.

GRIMSBY

THE rise of Grimsby as a fishing station was even more meteoric than that of Hull. A century ago it was a village of 956 houses, rated at £7,951, with one small vessel engaged in fishing. In 1861 the population was 11,067, ten years later 26,502, and by 1891 it was over 57,000 with 10,631 houses having a rateable value of £131,188, and 769 sail and 35 steam trawlers, while the first decade of the 20th century saw a further increase to 74,659, a development almost entirely due to the fishing industry and its ancillary trades.

When the M.S.L. Railway officials heard of the dissatisfaction among smack-owners at Hull, due to lack of facilities and little redress by the Dock Co., they sent agents to offer low dues and a special dock for fishing vessels, 25 miles nearer the North Sea grounds. Five owners came across the river and Mr. H. Monument, who played in the first football match for Grimsby Town in 1882, scoring the first goal, wrote me that one of the pioneers was his father-in-law, George Whiteway. He owned three smacks, *Shannon*, *Chesapeake* and *Two Brothers*, the last named after his two sons who were both drowned together some years later, the elder was cabin boy and the younger making a holiday trip when a sea broke amidships and washed both overboard, while the father was flung into the scuppers and sustained three fractured ribs. George Whiteway's wife was daughter of another Hull owner, Harry Cousins, one of the founders of the first ice company, and his brother, Philip Whiteway, all landed catches at the old herring slip until the docks were opened. "All Devonshire, of which they were never loth to boast."

George did not go to sea again after the tragic loss of his sons "he never cast a lead after that catastrophe . . . he spent his time braiding the cod-end with double twine, while his little daughter braided the 'belly' with her future husband filling her needles".

During 1858 catches landed amounted to 1,514 tons and the railway company now offered local merchants free tickets for the obtaining of orders in inland towns, an untapped market, and by 1863 the number of trawlers had increased to 70 with 42 cod smacks, seven years later to 263 smacks and 53 liners, and in 1877 a rise to 445 trawlers and 57 cod smacks. There were then 23 acres of docks for fishing vessels, a graving dock capable of holding eleven smacks, and a covered pontoon on which catches were landed and sold, with railway lines adjacent. In 1882 the 623 sailing vessels had two steam trawlers as rivals, and 1887 saw the maximum of 815 sail and only 15 steam, but the collapse was soon to begin as by 1893 there had been a drop to 665 for sail and increase to 143 steam, and ten years later 34 large sail and 476 steam.

Rail traffic had likewise increased by leaps and bounds, far exceeding the hopes of the companies. In 1854 only 453 tons had been despatched, rising to 13,468 in 1865, 36,794 tons in 1875, and 70,658 in 1885. During Easter week in 1894, landings from 97 steam and about 300 sailing trawlers amounted to 1,838 tons in over 30,000 packages. In seven and a half hours 617 tons 9 cwt. of fish were landed, sold, collected by the various buyers and packed into 10,708 packages of 28 lb. to 5 cwt., consigned to 2,665 persons all over the country, and another 40 tons were sent off in small parcels of 28 lb. downwards.

In 1858 James Sweeney was the first owner to take ice to sea in his 51-ton *Surprise*, built at Sandwich in 1855, the Dock Co. having erected an ice-house with a thatched roof to hold ice collected in the winter from nearby ponds and streams. In the course of time fleet fishing developed, but Grimsby men never took kindly to working under the directions of an admiral. Catches were sent to Grimsby for despatch by rail to London, later direct by water to avoid the heavy rail charges, plaice and haddock fetching only 4s. a hundredweight.

Mr. G. Alward gives the catches for his father's smack *Angelus*, 59 tons, built at Grimsby in 1866. 274 hauls were made during 1867, yielding 123 boxes of soles, 2,339 baskets of haddock, 1,900 baskets of plaice, 371 boxes of turbot, 180 of brill, 630 of cod, 14 of halibut, 53 of ling, with a quantity of small fish, dabs, whiting, slips, etc., making up about 96 tons in all.

Many smacks from other ports also brought their catches to Grimsby and in 1872 the average landings were 600 tons a week, or 31,193 tons in the year. Cod were sold by the score, and with ling and halibut were disposed of by auction to the highest bidder, but other trawl fish were sold by Dutch auction, the original price named by the salesman falling until a buyer was found. Wicker pads and pots had been replaced by wooden boxes called trunks, soles going 60 to 70 pairs, weighing about 100 lb., fresh haddock about forty to a box, but if for smoking they were sold by the barrel.

22,000 tons of ice were imported annually, chiefly from Norway, the Great Grimsby Ice Co. having been started in 1863, with a capital of £700. They owned, with the Co-Operative Ice Co., eight sailing ships, chiefly barques, among them being the 400-ton *Eddystone*, built at South Shields in 1860, and *Athenian*, 328 tons, built at Sunderland in 1862. Eventually these companies amalgamated and in 1880 imported 31,630 tons, rising two years later to 48,785 and in 1885 to 54,897 tons, then increasing yearly until in 1893, 62,378 tons of ice were brought over from Scandinavia.

The Grimsby Ice Co. purchased a large fleet of smacks, erected a £5,000 home for the accommodation of their lads when ashore, with separate cubicles for each boy, and a factory was started to manufacture their own boxes which were costing about £3,000 a year to buy. In 1884 four iron steam carriers were built at Hull, named *Albatross*, *Cormorant*, *Gannet* and *Pelican*, all varying slightly in size, the first three had 68 h.p. engines, *Pelican* 70 h.p. (Plates 105 & 106.) The flag at the peak of the gaff denotes that the carrier is ready to receive the trunks of fish caught the previous night and the beam lashed to the port side of *Gannet* shows that some trawling was done so as to avoid the payment of certain dues.

The 76-ton smack *Flower of the Forest*, G.Y.983, built at Elmshorn, Germany in 1884, was owned by the admiral, Henry Shackles (Plate 107). The weather having fined off, the first reef has been shaken out but the lacing is still in seven eyelets. The foresail is somewhat unusual as a bonnet has been taken off the foot, drifter rather than smack practice, and the big jib has been run out. Henry Shackles was drowned in S.S. *Bittern* during the great May gale of 1895, which reduced the fleet to such an extent as to bring about its break-up.

Plate 108 shows the admiral's smack to wind'ard of *G.I.C.*, G.Y.157, 85 tons, built at Grimsby in 1888. The foresail is a'weather as the crew are about to throw out the boat, being to wind'ard of the carrier, but in Plate 109 *Jumna*, G.Y.527, 73 tons, built at Grimsby in 1875, and another smack are to leeward of the cutter, with foresails aback, waiting to pick up their boats.

The German Government, anxious to develop a fishing industry, purchased a fine Grimsby trawler as a prototype, and built about fifteen smacks to sail out of the Elbe, but more time was spent in port than at sea. Eventually all were sold, many going to Grimsby owners, who had others built to order in yards at Elmshorn, Altona and elsewhere.

The ever-increasing number of smacks using the port called for a corresponding rise in ancillary trades, block and spar makers, building yards, rope makers, sail-makers, etc. In 1873 certain smackowners and others combined together to supply the fishing trade and the public generally with coal and salt. The practice of " barking " sails had only recently become universal on the Humber and The Grimsby Barking and Tanning Co. was purchased for £1,900. From such humble beginnings this venture, known as The Great Grimsby Coal, Salt and Tanning Co., soon became world-renowned as suppliers of all kinds of fishing gear and equipment; rope walks, net braiding rooms, ironmongery stores, outfitting departments for making fisher-men's clothing and oilskins, engine shops, trawl twine factories and others being added year by year. In 1878 four steam carriers were built *Celerity*, *Despatch*, *Precursor* and *Velocity*, the intention being to work to a large fleet of some 120 sail owned by the various shareholders. Some trips were to run to London, others to Grimsby, but differences soon arose, the carriers were laid up and eventually sold for £19,500 to Jack Emerson in 1881.

C. M. Mundahl, owner of twelve smacks, stated in 1882, that for the last five years the average gross earnings of each had only amounted to about £700, leaving a balance of £16 2s. 3d. on each for interest, etc. It was obvious from the remarks of Harrison Mudd that a number of owners had come to grief. " We have had 52 failures of owners of from one to twelve vessels, 114 smacks in all. One came 8 years ago, purchased three new vessels for £1,200 hard cash, has lost the lot and is glad to watch for 2s. 6d. a night."

A few were trying to get rich quick by " copering ". One man named Fisher had the 64-ton *Unity*, built at Rye in 1870, handed over to him to be " worked out ". He sailed at the end of April, went straight across to Geestemunde and laid in a stock of spirits, bacca, etc, working with various fleets from May to September. The unfortunate mortgagee had no news of his smack, except garbled reports of her nefarious activities, and no fish was sent in. Fisher, deeply in debt, as no doubt he was pocketing all his ill-gotten takings, pledged the credit of the vessel and eventually the tradesmen seized her in September and the owner had to send an agent over to pay off the balance of the accounts in order to obtain her release. On board were found a quantity of Yarmouth trawl nets, all marked and tallied, oilskins and fishing gear. One purchase out of many had been 100 lb. of shag @ 1s. a lb., 20 bottles of rum at 6d. each, 100 lb. of Rising Hope bacca, a favourite brand amongst smacksmen, @ 1s. 3d. a lb., 500 small bottles of rum for £7 10s., 36 bottles of brandy at 1s. each, Kummel @ 1s. 3d. a bottle, 2 cases of gin @ 8s. a case, 100 bottles of sherry @ 1s. each, 12 cases of scent @ 1s. a case, 10 cases of cigars @ 4s. a case, 24 doz. pipes for 6s., 104 pairs of wooden clumpers @ 1s. each, and 50 doz. eggs, 30s.

The eighties saw some of the finest smacks being built in the local yards and a complete inventory of one will be found in the appendix. Mr. John Bell kindly sent me a few launchings by the late John Bell, shipbuilder, Union Dock. *Frank Buckland* on the 5th September, 1883, 74 tons, L.O.A. 82 ft., beam 20 ft. A magnificent model to a scale of one inch to the foot was exhibited at the International Fisheries Exhibition in that year and awarded first prize of £25, a diploma and a medal. It is now in the Science Museum, South Kensington (Plate 31). Then followed five in 1884, *Professor Huxley* on 14th February, *Empress of India* 28th May, *Silent Wave* 26th July, *Salacia* 28th October and *Pandora* on the 20th December. During the next twelve months *Devonia* was launched on the 19th March, *Young Lizzie* on 30th June, *Richard Boston* on 10th October, while 1886 saw another five, *John Guzzwell* on 6th February, *Rainbow* on May 20th, *Mignonette* on 4th August, *Whimpbeck* on 16th October and *Young Herbert* on the 14th November. On the 24th December, 1889, the 101-ton *John Bull*, one of the largest to be built locally, went down the ways to be wrecked on the coast of Iceland fifty years later.

Mr. Bell goes on to say that the three last big smacks to sail out of Grimsby were *Britannia*, G.Y.297, *William Grant*, G.Y.1066 and *Henry Freeman*, 74 tons, built at Rye in 1877. They all finished up about 1906.

Mr. Ernest Campbell writes me that Thomas Campbell built the largest smack, the 104-ton *Ben Stark*, on Campbell's Jetty, Fish Docks in 1889. Length 79.3 ft., beam 20.6 ft., depth 11.6 ft., two others being the 89-ton *Maritana*, built 1886, 80 by 20.9 by 10.9, and the 80-ton *Alice Gertrude*, built 1884, 76 by 20.3 by 10.9. His father, Thomas Campbell, remained faithful to sail until his death in February, 1908, when his fleet was sold, five realizing only £215, the highest price being £60, the lowest £30 for vessels complete with all stores, sails and gear.   The oldest smack was built in 1884, and for some there were no bids.

I find that *Ben Stark* was still fishing in the Faroes in 1923, where so many fine smacks went towards the end of the 19th century when the great break-up of the Humber fleets took place.   Others still afloat in 1950 were *Agnes Louisa*, 101 tons, built 1886 by Smith Bros., and the 103-ton *Tre Soskende*, ex *General Wolseley*, built 1883 by the same firm, all three being registered at Lloyd's.

Mr. Charles Hillam, 15 years a foreman shipwright and apprenticed at the age of 13½ writes :—'' I myself served 7½ years at Furner & Leavers, who were Rye people, good builders.   Some of the smacks I helped to build as a lad were *Ashby*, *Croxly*, *Tenby*, *Pearl of Ocean* and several shrimpers for Cleethorpes.''

Ashby was built in 1892 as a cutter, from truck to keel measuring 100 ft., her entrance was very fine, length 72 ft., beam 17 ft. 6 in., moulded depth 9 ft., copper fastened.   Later re-rigged as a ketch she sailed out of Liverpool until after the first war, mainmast being 74 ft., deck to truck, with a 40 ft. boom, mizzen mast 42 ft. with a 20 ft. boom.

Mr. Hillam continues :—

'' I have living with me my father-in-law, William Foat.   As far back as 1869 at 11 years of age he went to sea as a Ramsgate boy, apprenticed under a man called Netherton in a smack *Rambler*, and sailed out of Grimsby all his sea-going days, as deck hand, third hand, mate, skipper and owner of two wooden fishing vessels, *Souvenir* (77 tons, built Grimsby 1878, and in Mr. Foat's ownership in 1884) and *Revival*, and well they looked.   In those early days the smacks were '' long boomers '', they mostly fished the west part of the Shoal about 80 miles from Spurn Head and the fish chiefly caught was plaice.   These were packed in boxes and put in the well which kept them alive until they arrived home, having been away 8, 9 or 10 days according to weather and quantity of fish caught.   My father-in-law was given 6d. per week for 5 years and 1s. per week for another 3 years, almost unbelievable isn't it ?   Deck hand, generally another apprentice with similar spending money, but if not an apprentice his wages were 16s. per week, plus keep.   Third hand £1, plus stocker, that is common fish and livers, that fetched little money.   The same fish now makes a good deal, such as skate, roker, lemon soles, dabs and others.   Mate and skipper were share fishermen, the nett earnings were divided into 8 shares the skipper receiving 1⅜ shares and the mate 1¼.   I knew one skipper who said the best he had in one series of trips was £80 in six weeks for himself and the worst when he was mate and earned 30s.   The average earnings for a 10 or 12-day trip was £50 to £60 gross.   The fleeting smacks were away for 8 to 10 weeks, the fleets were owned by Green, Morris, Moss, Guzzwell and others.   Mr. Foat has been both admiral and cutter for some of these firms.   Two brothers, Jack and Dick Powell were sailmakers here.

When I was a boy I can well remember seeing the Grimsby tugboats, *Honor*, *Rosamond*, *Gipsy King*, *Gipsy Queen* and others tow 6 to 9 smacks from the docks into the river Humber and while the tow was on the sails were being hoisted.   When about a mile from the lockpit the towropes were let go and what a lovely sight to see, perhaps 20 or more smacks with their barked canvas proudly sail towards Spurn and out to sea.

Many a time I remember smacks being towed in by other ships and how they looked, no masts or rigging. It was a common occurrence to see them coming up the Humber with flag struck, which denoted one or more of the crew had been washed overboard. I remember Mr. Foat telling the family that in one smack called *Lily* (59 tons, built Grimsby 1868) owner G. Jeff, almost everything had gone overboard, all bulwarks and stanchions, the small boat was hung up on the gaff end and practically everything that water could move had gone. The weather was so cold that when he went home his boot stockings could be stood up without collapsing.''

The tugs mentioned were all built of wood on the Tyne during the 1850's, with engines developing 18 to 26 h.p. and *Rambler*, 49 tons, was built at Wivenhoe in 1859. Mr. James Giles of Skegness wrote me in 1948, that her remains were again exposed on the sands there after being buried over 40 years, well heads, sternpost and some timbers being about 3 ft. above the surface.

Mr. C. Alp, whose experiences in a cod smack have already been quoted, writes me :—

" The life of a fishing apprentice was a very hard one. I was one of the lucky ones, I had my parents living in Grimsby as my father was a fisherman sailing out of the port. Usually nearly all the boys came from workhouses and homes in other towns. The wages of a boy cook were 1s. 6d. a week, the deck hand, a lad of about 18, 2s. 6d. to 3s. a week, the third hand was an all-round man getting from 18s. to £1 a week, but if an apprentice 5s. Mate and skipper were on shares, the mate got 7 per cent and the skipper 10 per cent of earnings after expenses had been deducted. They also used to get what they called stocker, that was liver and roe money, and old junk money. The fish livers were put in barrels holding about 40 gallons, and they used to get about 10s. a barrel. The cook got 4d., deck hand 8d., third hand 1s. 6d., mate and skipper the rest. The junk—old rope—was shared up about the same.

" Now the smack *Lizzie Thorpe* (85 tons, built Grimsby 1884) belonged to my employer, Mr. W. Toogood, to whom I was apprenticed. She was loaned to a firm to convert into a self-moving vessel. The patent tried was a kind of jet affair, two large holes were cut in the counter, one in each quarter, and an engine was fitted to eject water. When they got everything ready to try it out the smack moved ahead all right, but when they reversed the engine something went wrong and they nearly sank the vessel, so it was given up as a failure. Another smack, the *Leslie* (89 tons, built 1882 at Grimsby) was owned by Mr. Fred Rushworth, an old skipper. She was fitted with an engine that went with paraffin and it was a success, but it nearly ruined the owner, as he had to don his sea boots and oilskins and go to sea again till he got some of his creditors paid off.''

Mr. Alp is writing of a later period than Mr. Hillam, and his story throws an interesting light on the efforts of owners, who had recently built fine smacks, to equip them to compete with the steam trawlers which were carrying all before them.

Others took the plunge and scrapped brand-new vessels in favour of the rival, steam. Whole fleets were sold for " old rope " and many a bargain went to Danish and Scandinavian owners and in 1950, nineteen built at Grimsby, ten at Hull and three at Goole were still earning their living. A few were converted for trading.

Mr. James Giles tells me that Amos King, smackowner, who died at his farm at Conisholme in 1940, bought up the bulk of these smacks, reselling as opportunity offered. Accompanying his letter was a list of named vessels which were broken up, twenty-one at Skegness, seven at Chapel St. Leonards and ten at Sutton-on-Sea c 1901. He also loaned me a photograph taken in September, 1948, showing the mainmast of the 28-ton *Swan*, built at Grimsby in 1883, and wrecked on the Wainfleet Sands 17th July, 1915, the crew of four being rescued by the Skegness lifeboat. The mizzen mast disappeared many years ago, but the mainmast with shroud ends flapping in the wind still stands half-buried in the treacherous sand (Plate 110).

I have traced the loss of 243 smacks during the years 1879 to 1913. Of these 60 foundered, 87 sank after collision, 86 stranded and 10 were lost by fire.

Among them was *Rippling Wave*, G.Y.843, 82 tons, built at Galmpton in 1882, whose master and owner was H. W. Perry, an admiral of Grimsby fleets. A whole gale from the south-east was blowing when she sank after being in collision with another smack, *Samuel & Ann* of Hull, 90 miles N.E. by N. of Spurn.

Another was the 29-ton *Thomas Campbell*, built at Grimsby in 1880 for T. Campbell. She sank after collision with S.S. *Sampan* of Hull on the 1st April, 1913, three miles S.E. by S. of Spurn lightvessel, one of her crew of four being drowned.

A trading casualty was the 72-ton *Maid of Kent*, built in 1874 at Sandwich, which stranded on the 12th March, 1906 at Wilsthorpe Gap, Yorks in a N.N.W. storm, while bound for Rye with coal and potatoes and two passengers from St. Davids.

A few old smacks which stranded were *Admiral*, 57 tons, built 1841 at Barking, and lost on 18th September, 1880, half a mile east of Brinns Ness, Orkneys. *Alfred*, 57 tons, built 1846, at Barking, drove ashore 1¼ miles south of Saltfleet Haven, Lincs., on the 22nd December, 1886, and *Defence*, 46 tons, built 1835 at Gravesend, lost on Spurn Point 16th December, 1882, while *Emma*, 70 tons, built at Mistley, Essex in 1830, lost one of her crew on the 13th November, 1897, when the tiller rope broke. All these were probably cod smacks.

Grimsby is still one of the premier fishing ports in the world, having the largest ice factory which was making 1,100 tons a day in the 1930's, crushed and delivered into the trawlers at a few shillings a ton. In 1913, 625 steam fishing vessels were registered, over 500 were taken over by the Admiralty for war service, many never returning. The numbers rose again during the years between the wars, but 1939 saw the same story repeated.

New industries have risen, including one which fillets and cooks the fish which is attractively wrapped in cellophane for sale in shops throughout the country, and who will ever forget the ubiquitous fish cakes of the war years ?

114   BRIXHAM SLOOP, D.H.3
In Mount's Bay, c 1895.   Her topsail is diagonal-cut and sheet is fast to short jackyard at clew and leads down through single block on long pendant.

115   BRIXHAM SLOOP, D.H.855
In Mount's Bay. First reef lacing is in the eyelets and under foot of sail, topmast is reefed, topsail sheet reeves through block on long pendant at masthead below the standing end of the peak halyards.

116 BRIXHAM KETCHES AT LOWESTOFT
Both are converted sloops, mastheads are long, topmasts short. D.H.170
has a bonnet laced to the foot of foresail.

117 FOR SALE, AUGUST, 1936
Terminist, 37 tons, built 1912,
the last smack to be launched
from Jackman's yard at the
breakwater, Brixham. Converted into a yacht and still
afloat in 1952.

118 *VIGILANCE*, B.M.76 AT NEWLYN
39 tons, the last smack built by J. W. & A. Upham in 1926. Note
round stern, long run and skeg at heel of keel.

119 *ENCOURAGE*, B.M.63
40 tons, the last smack built by
R. Jackman in 1926, in his yard
next to Upham's The boat gangway is open as the punt is being
hoisted on board.

120 BRIXHAM SMACKS PUTTING TO SEA
A thunderstorm is brewing and all have one reef down. In centre is
B.M.326 *Sanspariel*, 24 tons, built at Brixham, 1912, fitted with a 30 h.p.
engine in 1931. The smack to leeward has just got the punt on board,
boat gangway is still open.

121 ON THE HARD, 5th AUGUST, 1933
Forseti, B.M.52, 43 tons, built by J. W. & A. Upham in 1926. The
bowsprit is run in and all spars are ashore.

122 SMACKS LAID UP FOR
SALE, OCTOBER, 1937
Inspire, B.M.13, 41 tons,
built at Brixham, 1924.

123 *BEST FRIEND*, EX-B.M.73
34 tons, built at Brixham in 1914, converted to a yacht with wheel
steering in early thirties.

124   A BRIXHAM MUMBLE BEE

White Violet, D.H.325, 25 tons, built at Brixham, 1891. The high-peaked mainsail combined with a short topmast gives a horizontal leech to topsail. Note length of masthead and the wooden horse athwartships just aft of tiller. This takes main sheet of winter boom.

125　A BRIXHAM MULE READY FOR LAUNCHING
We'll Try, B.M.338, 23 tons, built by J. W. & A. Upham, 1913.　Note the cradle
made of planks, the smack in frame in the background, the bunches of flowers and
greenery at bows and on truck of flagpole amidships.

126　SHIPWRIGHTS AT WORK, BRIXHAM HARBOUR, c 1882
D.H.199 is one of the big sloops with a 41 ft. rig, P.H.13 a Plymouth herring lugger
with a triangular watch mizzen sheeting on a long outrigger.　The ketch on which
the men are working looks like a conversion job.

127 THE FASTEST TRAWLER IN
THE WEST COUNTRY
Ibex, 42 tons, built by J. W. & A.
Upham in 1896. In her original
39½ ft. rig with mainsail from
D.H.416.

128 *REPLETE*, B.M.27
42 tons, built at Brix-
ham, 1924. Note
bowsprit run in, heel
rope, boat slide, fair-
leading post, iron horse
with traveller and single
blocks of fore sheet,
winch, hatch with cap
cover removed.

CHAPTER ELEVEN

DEVONSHIRE TRAWLING STATIONS

BRIXHAM

BRIXHAM, like Barking, has fishing traditions going back for centuries, but it is impossible to state with any accuracy when trawling commenced. Evidence that there were trawlers at the time of the Armada is very shaky and it appears probable that confusion between fishing vessels and armed ships arose in the minds of historians. Oldmixon, writing in 1739, stated that Sir Francis Drake captured a great galleon and sent her in to Dartmouth in charge of Sir Walter Raleigh's *Roebuck*, whereas Froude, *c* 1870, says that the Spanish vessel was taken into Torbay and left in the care of Brixham fishermen. On board the prize were several tons of gunpowder and this precious commodity was despatched to the English fleet in " *Roebuck*, the swiftest trawler in the harbour ".

Be that as it may. The first authentic documentary evidence I have traced appears in the Report of the 1833 Enquiry when Walter Smith, aged 70, stated he had been a fisherman for 47 years, " when I went to sea with father at 9 years of age only seven fishing vessels in the place, now 112, about twenty are left in port for trawling in winter, the rest go to the North Sea ". These 112 vessels were cutters of 30 to 40 tons, with one or two of 41 tons, in addition there were 70 of 4 to 18 tons engaged in long lining, etc.

Smith went on to say, " I was fishing near Dover before the French Revolution, to the west of Dungeness. 45 years back I was off the Kentish coast with two others, the first from Torbay to go so far east. Was often boarded by Revenue cutters to see if any tubs on board. 70 trawlers have been for the last 8 to 10 years to Ramsgate in the North Sea, fishing for the London market. In summer we had twelve go to Bristol Channel to the end of September, the rest at Brixham. Sixty to seventy go to Ramsgate in winter, leave here in November, some stay till Christmas, others mid-June, when they leave because too warm to send fish to London. I have fished from Sunderland, Durham and Hartlepool and all round the coast. I salt hake, whiting, conger, cod and ling, have the only curing house at Brixham, cured up to twenty tons when duty on salt, not so much since. Have salted thousands of ' buck-horn ', now families salt their own fish. Fishing is bad at Brixham now, many families on poor rate who earned a living. No trawling from Dartmouth, only a few hookers." "Buckhorn" were whiting salted and dried in the sun immediately after being caught.

Exeter, Bath and Salisbury were supplied by road, Bristol and Plymouth by water, and occasionally catches were landed at Portsmouth to be sent to Billingsgate in the fish waggons. Turbot caught in Torbay in December and January went to Exeter, but Bath was the principal market.

Torbaymen had been working on the Brown Bank in the North Sea for some six years, but were usually off Dover or Margate, a few had been fishing in Dublin Bay since 1818, starting the Irish trawling industry and about half-a-dozen worked over the grounds off Liverpool. Dover had been used since 1812 owing to the abundance of prime turbot found on the Varne and Ridge Banks, the fish being sent to London in light vans, but the harbour was poor, being partially blocked by a bar, tides were strong and in southerly winds craft were windbound. These conditions influenced the Devon men to sail out of Ramsgate, where a fine harbour had been built by Smeaton and the rise of the town as a popular watering place for wealthy visitors offered a local market. Other pioneers worked up the East Coast and the many Devonshire surnames still to be found in fishing ports bear testimony to settling by Brixham fishermen, who found there more profitable conditions than in their home waters.

Their smacks, called locally "sloops", were all cutter-rigged and in May, 1950, Mr. P. A. Upham courteously allowed me to take off the lines of the earliest half-model in their mould loft, D.H.79, believed to be *Charlie*, *c* 1838. Length of keel is 40 ft. 6 in., L.B.P. 42 ft. 10 in., L.O.A. 47 ft. 4 in., beam 16 ft. 10 in. The bows are bluff, floors flat and the lines cod's head and mackerel tail. I am more than delighted to have been able to take off the lines of both Brixham and Barking smacks of the same period (Plans 6, pages 321-2).

An excellent photograph of one of the early type smacks, D.H.60, was taken at Ramsgate by Frith in 1857 (Plate 11). For'ard is the handspike windlass with a small hatch below, then the winch used for bringing in the warp, abaft the mast is another hatch, then the pumphead or towpost and the companion giving access to the cabin aft. Writing in 1872, Holdsworth states that the warp room was abaft the mast, later practice was to have it for'ard and the warp has always led out over a roller at the stem head, not through a gangway on port side. The length of masthead, summer topmast and boom will be noticed, also the open framing at transom.

In 1852 about 70 smacks of 23 to 35 tons were regularly working on the Brixham grounds. Length of keel had increased to 46 feet in the sloop *Osprey*, built by J. W. Upham for R. N. Smith. Her keel was laid on the 25th October, 1855, the launch took place on the 9th January, 1856, and the "lump sum for hull, spars, boat, cabin and forecastle" was £400. In 1858 the keel of *Ajax*, measuring 50 ft., was laid in November, and the sloop was launched on the 16th April, 1859, her breadth being 17 ft. 6 in. and depth 9 ft., the "lump sum" again being £400.

It was stated at the 1863 Enquiry that the estimated value of smacks insured with the Fishing Club was £72,000, mostly not exceeding £500 a ship. In his evidence concerning the state of the trawling industry the President said :—" If they were to fish here for the same number of hours as they do in the North Sea it would pay them much better than to go there. They get more money in the North Sea but have to go out on Monday morning and remain at sea all week, coming in on Saturday morning. Expenses are heavier. Here the vessels come in almost every night." He went on to state that 95 smacks then belonged to Brixham men, 85 fished regularly from the port and the remainder during part of the year. 152 ships were insured in the Club, the only condition being that they belonged to Brixham men, but the owners of 57 had permanently settled at other ports.

Explaining the method of financing the building of smacks Mr. Webber, the magistrate's clerk said :—" A man may have £150 to £200, he has a new vessel built and finds people to put up the remainder. Tradesmen are ready to supply goods, if he is an industrious man, and give credit for everything he requires. He gives a mortgage on vessel, a great number of smacks are mortgaged because directly a man saves £100 he gets another smack. These mortgages are entirely on new vessels, tradesmen here know less of bankruptcies among themselves than almost any town in the neighbourhood."

The local fishing ground lay 3 to 8 miles off the land between Start Point and N.E. of Torbay, a distance of about 20 miles. In summer a few smacks landed fish at Tenby and in winter about a dozen went up to the North Sea, but most of the trawling was done on the home ground all the year round. Torbay has always been famous for soles, a large pair weighing up to 12 lbs. with a length of 22 inches. In April, 1872, a 42 lb. turbot 2 ft. 9 in. long, 2 ft. 5 in. wide and 4½ in. thick was landed.

Prior to the extension of the Great Western Railway into Brixham the smacks usually brought in their catches during the afternoon, the fish being sold in open market and sent away in light vans to Paignton or Torquay for forwarding by rail. In 1860 about 606 tons went from Paignton and 248 from Torquay. When the new station was opened on the hill above Brixham harbour it became the practice for trawlers to come in at all hours, mostly in the mornings, and the fish was despatched by fast passenger trains several times during the day, the freight to Billingsgate, a 5 to 6-hour journey, being £3 a ton, or £4 15s. by mail train. In 1861 some 512 tons were forwarded and just over 700 the three following years, while in 1877 it was over 2,000 tons.

Sales were by Dutch auction, women as well as men acting as auctioneers. Most of the fish went to Bristol for forwarding to inland towns according to instructions wired from Brixham. Ice was used in packing fish for rail transport but none was taken to sea as catches were landed fresh every day, except at weekends when it was the custom to remain in harbour from Saturday to Monday morning, the Devon men having a strict reverence for the Lord's Day.

A boom followed the opening of the railway and many outsiders invested in trawlers, but their prosperity was short-lived and trade soon returned to fishermen born and bred.

The size of smacks continued to increase. *I.C.U.*, launched from Upham's yard on 1st April, 1874, measured 50 $\frac{21}{100}$ tons and cost £440 for hull, spars and boat, but no ballast.

The sloop, named after a member of the Upham family had a 42 ft. rig and Mr. P. A. Upham told me her summer gaff was made of Norwegian spruce and measured 58 ft. After the smack was lost one winter with all hands, this immense spar was stored under a loft until the 1914 war when it was destroyed as dry rot had set in, the boom probably measured 65 ft.

In 1876 the sloop *Talisman*, 49 $\frac{8}{100}$ tons, was built for S. Tyrer as per agreement for £530, extras bringing up the total payment to £542 1s. 4½d. They included:

70 ft greenheart rail	£3.	10s	—
Extra for oak bulwark	1.	10	—
109 ft of 1½ in spruce for pound boards	2.	5.	10½
Labour for erecting same.		10.	—
Scraping and paying-up	1.	16.	—
To Customs for Board of Trade	1.	12.	—

The following year *Fish Girl* was built for F. Baddeley and launched on the 28th October. The agreement was £570, being at the rate of £10 per foot of keel which measured 57 ft. Extras included :

Making a winter topmast		6s	—
Cutting name in stern and making fenders		5s	—
73 ft of 1½ in pine for pound boards	£1.	7.	4
Fitting, nails etc.		5.	—
Oak sleepers.		5.	—
14 ft of 3½ in oak,. middle hatch	1.	0.	5
Oak for carling		4.	—
9 ft pine for hatch		2.	3
Labour, nails and bolts.		8.	6
Oak for dandy wink.		5.	—

A similar agreement was made for sloop *Bonny Lass*, built for R. Ellis, jun. Launched on the 19th March, 1878, the total cost for hull, spars, etc., was £588 0s. 4d., smith's work being £69 6s. 10d. Extras included :

Extra length of keel	£7.	10s	—
65 ft greenheart rail	3.	5.	—
Winter topmast	1.	0.	—
Making same.		7.	6d.
Winter boom 38 ft @ 2s 3d a ft.	4.	5.	6
Making same.		11.	6

These sloops were fastened with wooden trenails and had a stern horse for the main sheet and a rope horse for the fore sheet.

In 1872 there were 136 first-class smacks on the register at Dartmouth, practically all belonging to Brixham men, either living at home or settled at other stations. Six years later Eleazar Johnson, a trawler owner since 1834 when there were 70 smacks, said there were now 120 fishing out of the port and tonnage had increased from 30 to 50 to 60 tons. In 1834 the trawl beam was about 40 ft. long, now 43 to 47 ft., the mesh in the " purse " varying, " mine is 5 in. round, some are smaller, some bigger, but the take is about the same as in 1834. I have fished on all coasts but the best grounds lie 10 to 12 miles from Berry Head off Torbay. Here are turbot, soles, brill, John Dory, whiting and hake. I keep trawl down about 6 hours and prices are as good as ever they were. About May fish drop off and some boats go to the North Sea. Catch mullet from July to Christmas in 30 to 35 fathom on ground from Start Point to Portland among oozy weed ".

Silas Pine said that when trawling in Mount's Bay between Wolf Rock and Lizard he had caught 50 to 100 pairs of soles in a night, but only 2 to 3 pairs by day. In rough weather he went into the bay to haul his gear. William Lovell stated : " I fish for mullet in January, 23 miles off the Start or Berry Head. In March go to Penzance, North Sea or France, returning at end of July. Out of 120 smacks trawling only some 60 to 70 here now." (May, 1878.) There was no local sale for ray, or roker as it was called in London, it all went to France until about 1875 when the French Government stopped its sale. Mr. Smith told how he had caught 23 dozen in two days and sent the fish to Billingsgate where it sold for £6 14s. After paying rail and market charges he had £2 9s. left, out of which he had to pay for 19 pad baskets.

In 1882 according to J. W. Upham, shipbuilder, there were 154 cutters of 40 to 50 tons, and 50 to 60 small boats of 15 tons and less in the port. The large sloops were manned by a skipper, second and third hand and a boy, between 200 and 250 lads being apprenticed. The grounds lay within sight of land, " smacks go out to-day, work till to-morrow afternoon then make for Brixham. 300 of our men belong to Naval Reserve ".

In the early 19th century a natural harbour extended inland for a considerable distance and in 1950 I was told there was one old man, over 90, who as a very small boy remembered catching fish where Bolton Cross now stands, the lower part of the town being subsequently built over this area. The pier, opened by William IV in 1803, formed one side of the basin, the other being the hill extending to Berry Head. In 1863, the Magistrate's Clerk said the new pier was being built by the inhabitants who put in £500, £200 and so on. Brixham was only land-locked between Fishcombe Point and Berry Head and accommodation was insufficient for vessels using the port. The majority had to lie in the open roadstead, exposed to easterly gales and heavy seas rolling up Channel, the vessels being secured by extensive moorings laid down for each craft.

On the 11th January, 1866, a terrible gale caused unparalleled destruction, ships making for the harbour were unable to find their way in as the huge seas had carried away the lighthouse, but the women bravely made a mighty bonfire on the pier and kept it going with tar barrels, nets and anything they could lay hands on. Sixty vessels were wrecked, over one hundred lives lost and the coast was strewn with wreckage for miles around (Plate 111).

In 1883, Mr. Smith informed a conference that Brixham then had a population of about 7,000 and £90,000 was invested in 180 boats, but there was not harbour accommodation for all. He had been in one smack which was riding to moorings in the 1866 gale and every moment expected to get swamped. Mr. Saunders added that at spring tides there was accommodation for 40 to 60 vessels, at neaps only 20 to 30, the rest had to ride to moorings in outer roads. Six years before half-a-dozen smacks had been totally lost on the rocks, fourteen were undergoing extensive repairs for two months and some were driven right up into the main street. Photographs, c 1883, in my possession show that the hard sloped up in front of the houses on the Strand, the building of the quay wall being a later improvement. The bowsprits of the schooners almost poked into the bedroom windows, as one old chap humorously told me "the gals had to get up early in them days as there was keen competition for jobs on the end of jib-booms or yards !" (Plate 112.)

About 1,200 ft. of the breakwater had been built by the early nineties at a cost of some £23,000, affording shelter for 40 sloops, but the construction was not finally completed until a year or two before the outbreak of the 1914 war, having been largely financed by the fishermen themselves who voluntarily paid a levy of 3d. in the £ on all fish landed. There was now adequate shelter for the 300 large and small sail then registered at the port, except under extraordinary conditions in northerly gales and it was a fine sight to see the big ketches working in through the crowded harbour to pick up their moorings. These consisted of 30 fathom of heavy chain laid out to the N.E. and a similar length to the S.W., in the centre was a swing chain and swivel with a rope attached to a keg on the surface.

Collisions, etc., sometimes resulted as on the 27th January, 1900, when the cutter *Kingfisher* was sunk by *Floweret*, while the 50-ton *Superb* was lost on Fishcombe on the 23rd November, 1895, in a N.E. gale. Sharp-floored vessels lying in the inner harbour heeled considerably unless legs were used and on the 11th August, 1896, the 48-ton *Peto*, built at Brixham in 1876, fell over and sustained such damage that she was condemned.

Most of the trawlers were owned by men who had worked their way up from apprentices, and all worked on shares, the owner taking 3¾, master 1¼, and the two men one share each, seven shares in all, the apprentice getting "stocker money". There were no paid men (Plate 113).

Plates 114 and 115 show two of the big sloops working in Mount's Bay, c 1890. Note lead of topsail sheet and the short jackyard at clew in D.H.3. Although fine sea boats and very fast sailers, the ever-increasing length of main boom made them difficult to handle in a seaway, even though in winter a shorter boom and smaller mainsail were fitted, with the mainsheet working on a horse for'ard of the stern-post instead of on the taffrail. In the early eighties began the great change over to the dandy or ketch rig and Plate 116 depicts two converted cutters working out of Lowestoft.

In 1881 the ketch *Lizzie Grant* was built at Upham's yard for W. Grant and took the water on the 22nd November. Her length was 66 ft., breadth 18.1 ft. and depth 8.65 ft., tonnage 49 $\frac{60}{100}$ The agreement was £460, but an icebox was fitted at a cost of 10s. 6d. for labour and the material used was 178 ft. of 1½ in. pine costing £2 19s. 4d., 22 ft. of 2½ in. pine, 12s. 10d. and 60 ft. of pine at 5s., while cutting the name came to 1s. 6d. and the Custom's application £1. Ironwork was £65 2s. 11d. and anchors and chain £25 3s. 9d.

Magnificent ketches for Hull, Lowestoft and Ramsgate owners were now being built, many to the order of Charles and Robert Hellyer, who went from Brixham to Hull about 1854. Charles favoured names from Shakespeare for his vessels and I noticed *Orlando*, *Othello*, *Rosalind* and *Portia*. These " ships ", to use another local name, ran much larger than those built for Brixham owners. *Orlando* measured 81 $\frac{86}{100}$ tons on dimensions 74.5 by 20.8 by 10.3 and was launched on the 12th October, 1882, having cost £952 0s. 1d. for hull, spars and small boat, the agreement being £900. Extras included :—

8 tons of kentledge @ 61s	£24.	8s.	—
Landing dues on same		8	—
Cartage		6	—
Labour for stowing.		6.	6d.
50 tons of stone @ 1s 8d.	4.	3.	4

In 1883 the Lowestoft smack *Forget-me-not*, built to the order of W. Painter, cost £695 12s. 10d., Lamswood supplying all the blocks for £16 2s. 6d., and the ornamental mizzen cap was 8s. extra. In the following year *Othello*, built for C. Hellyer, cost £947 14s., her dimensions being 80.2 by 20.9 by 10.5, 88 $\frac{10}{100}$ tons. Another smack for Robert Hellyer had the following extras, mast hoops for main and mizzen £1 14s. and the iron castings for gangway, weighing 3 cwt. 1 qr., cost £2 5s., while the windlass casting of 5 cwt. 2 qr. 14 lb. for C. Hellyer's *Rosalind* cost £3 17s. and the lifting rods, levers and bolts £1 14s. 8d. This fine trawler measured 93 $\frac{28}{100}$ tons on dimensions 80.6 by 21.65 by 10.65, length of keel 71 ft., and cost £934 11s. 6d., being classed 12 years A1 at Lloyd's.

From yet another account for *Pilgrim*, launched 2nd August, 1886, for Hugh Perret of Ramsgate, I found that 60 fathom of $\frac{13}{16}$ short link chain cable, weighing 1 ton 3 cwt, 2 qr. @ 10s. 2d., came to £12 8s. 8d. and three anchors, weighing

3 cwt. 2 qr. 22 lb., 3 cwt. 2 qr. 25 lb. and 1 cwt. 3 qr. 25 lb. respectively @ 12s. were £6 2s. 4d., thimbles and shackles 12s. 10d. Her tonnage was 51 $\frac{82}{100}$, and dimensions 64.6 by 18.15 by 9, and total cost £667 7s. 10d.

In 1886 a winter topmast and its making cost £1 5s. for the 50-ton *Smiling Morn*, built for £465 7s. 6d., 6 ft. of oak @ 2s. 6d. for the towing post coming to 15s.

Striver, 20 $\frac{14}{100}$ tons, 52.5 by 12.9 by 6.75, built 1887 at a charge of £263, had two extra long shank anchors, weighing 4 cwt. 0 qr. 10 lb. @ 14s. 6d., £2 19s. 2d., and her wire rigging, costing £2 15s. 5d. extra, was 53 ft. of 2$\frac{3}{4}$ in., 11s. 1d., 173 ft. of 2$\frac{1}{4}$ in., £1 9s. 8d., 20 ft. of 1$\frac{3}{4}$ in., 2s. 2d., and 120 ft. of 1$\frac{1}{4}$ in., 9s.

The first steam capstan by Elliott & Garrood was fitted in *Ethel*, c 1887, and within a few years the hard work of hauling the trawl by hand was of the past.

The ketch *Ibex*, 50 $\frac{13}{100}$ G.T., designed and owned by Mr. Andrew Upham, was launched on the 8th November, 1896, and cost £490, including an extra bowsprit. She was destined to be the fastest trawler ever to sail out of Brixham and I shall have more to say about her later.

Other prices for ships of various sizes were :—

Doris May, launched 25th February, 1898. Agreement £530.

Silver Lining, launched 24th May, 1898. Agreement £515.

Gazelle, £550, plus £2 10s. for false keel.

Lynx, built for J. W. Upham in 1903, cost £560 including a summer topmast, tonnage 53 $\frac{28}{100}$ gross, 42 $\frac{67}{100}$ net. Dimensions 70.2 by 18.1 by 9.1. *Competitor*, built for P. A. Upham in 1904, cost £513, length of keel being 57 ft., tonnage 49 $\frac{43}{100}$, while *Vigilant*, built 1907, was £560, and dimensions 69.2 by 18.35 by 8.65. Many other smacks were built to similar measurements for the same agreement, £560, among them being *Floweret*, *Collie*, *Our Laddie* and *Prevalent*. After the 1914-18 war the usual agreement for hull, spars, etc., was £1,000 for such fine trawlers as *Compeer*, *Terpsichore*, *Forseti* and *Vigilance*, but *Replete* built in 1924, cost £1,080.

There were three classes of trawler, the ketches of over 40 tons, built for working in the Bristol Channel and still called by the older men " the big sloops ". The cutters were known as " Mumble bees ", a name derived from Mumbles at the head of the Bristol Channel, where very handy little smacks were used in the oyster dredging. Some were purchased by Brixham men as they were most suitable for inshore trawling, but many were later converted to ketch rig. The smaller ketches under 40 tons, were always " mules " and I inspected the half-model from which *William & Sam* and *Guess Again* were built by J. W. & A. Upham. The lines were taken off by the late P. J. Oke in 1938 (Plan 7, page 323).

Although built to approximately the same dimensions there was no rigid type, as each owner had his own ideas as to build, rig and how ship should be sailed. Prior to going to the Bristol Channel a 36 ft. rig was popular, but this was cut down to 34 to 35 ft. with a 10 ft. masthead, as being better suited to the conditions found there, with seas running in from the Atlantic.

Mr. F. A. Jackman, sail-maker, told me the quantities of canvas required for a typical sail plan for a Mumble bee.

Mainsail.	180 yards.
Foresail.	45 ,,
Storm jib	18 ,,
5 cloth jib	28 ,,
7 cloth jib	50 ,,
Big jib	70 ,,
Topsail	45 ,,

436 yards for full suit.

Dimensions varied, as did cut of sails, some men liked high-peaked mainsails, others low. The late P. J. Oke left some unfinished pencil plans of Mumble bees from which I made tracings (Plans 8 and 9, pages 324-7).

Plan 8 shows a Mumble bee with a 31 ft. rig and a high-peaked mainsail. The hull has a length overall of 60 ft., L.B.P., 54 ft. 8 in. and a keel of 46 ft. 6 in., moulded beam 14 ft., depth 7 ft. 6 in. The height of the stem above L.W.L. is 7 ft. 6 in. and the taffrail 4 ft. Draught aft is 8 ft. 6 in., for'ard 4 ft. 6 in.

The main sheet lower block is on a wooden horse, 6 in. thick, which goes across the deck over the rudder head. This can be seen in Plate 124 of *White Violet* which has a similar high-peaked mainsail. On the port side of the deck is the dandy wink for hauling in the aft end of the trawl beam, a steam capstan is fitted with the boiler in the cabin aft.

SCANTLINGS

Keel —	—	—	12 in. moulded.	7 in. sided.
Keelson	—	—	8 in. sq.	
Floors	—	—	9 in. moulded.	6 in. sided. Spaced 1 ft.
Frames (double)	—	—	4½ in. moulded.	3½ in. sided.
Beams	—	—	5 in. moulded.	4½ in. sided.
Shelf	—	—	6½ in. wide.	4 in. deep
Stanchions	—	—	5 in. by 4 in., spaced 2 ft. 3 in.	
Rail —	—	—	5 in. wide by 4 in. deep.	

PLANKING

Hull and deck	—		6 in. wide, 1½ in. thick.
Bilge planks	—		8 in. wide, 2½ in. thick.
Topsides	—	—	6 in. wide, 2 in. thick.

SAIL PLAN

Mainmast	—	—	L.O.A. 44 ft. 6 in. Dia. 11 in. to 8½ in.
Masthead	—	—	7 ft.
Rig —	—	—	31 ft.

Gaff –	–	–	28 ft. to jaws, 31 ft. L.O.A. Dia. 6 in.
Boom	–	–	39 ft. 6 in. to gooseneck. Dia. 8 in.
Bowsprit	–	–	L.O.A. 32 ft., outboard 22 ft. Dia. 10 in. to 6 in.
Topmast	–	–	L.O.A. 27 ft. 6 in. Dia. 6 in. to 5 in.
Crosstrees	–	–	10 ft.

Plan 9 is of *Nisha*, B.M.2, later re-rigged as a ketch and owned at one time by Emanuel Harris whom I had the pleasure of meeting in 1950. I saw the half-model in Mr. Upham's mould loft from which Mr. Oke took the lines in 1937, and I traced the plans from his unfinished draughts, now at the National Maritime Museum at Greenwich. Her dimensions were :—L.O.A. 59 ft. 3 in., L.B.P. 54 ft. 4 in., L.W.L. 53 ft., keel 46 ft. 3 in., moulded beam 14 ft., depth 7 ft. 6 in., draft for'ard 4 ft., aft 7 ft. 10 in.

SCANTLINGS

Keel –	–	–	7 in. sided, 10 in. moulded for'ard, 14 in. amidships and 9 in. aft.
Floors	–	–	8 in. sided, 9 in. moulded.
Frames	–	–	Double. 3½ in. sided, 6 in. to 3 in. moulded.
Room and space	–		18 in.
Keelson	–	–	8 in. sq.
Beams	–	–	4 in. sided.
Shelf	–	–	6 in. × 3½ in.
Planking	–	–	Deck, 1½ in. Ceiling, ¾ in. Hull, topsides 2 in. Bilge, 2½ in., remainder 1½ in.

SAIL PLAN

Rig –	–	–	25 ft.
Mast	–	–	Deck to cap. 31 ft., dia. 10 in. to 8 in., 6 ft. masthead.
Topmast	–	–	L.O.A. 30 ft., 5 in. dia., fid to sheave 28 ft.
Gaff –	–	–	27 ft. L.O.A.
Boom	–	–	37 ft. L.O.A. 6½ in. dia.
Bowsprit	–	–	L.O.A. 32 ft., dia., 8 in. to 6 in., 20 ft. outboard.

Nisha was built in 1907 by J. W. & A. Upham to the order of W. H. Robert, the agreement for hull, boat and spars being £250, with £5 extra for mizzen fittings, so evidently it was expected that later she would be converted to ketch rig.

The large trawlers were about 78 ft. L.O.A., 69 ft. L.B.P., 60 ft. on keel, and 18 ft. 4 in. beam, but sizes varied slightly in practically every ship. Other measurements were :—

Draught for'ard. 5 ft. 4 in. Aft. 10 ft. 8 in.

Bows. About 26 ft.

Freeboard. 2 ft.

Waterline to top of rail, for'ard. 7 ft. 10 in.

    do.   do.   amidships. 4 ft. 3 in.

    do.   do.   taffrail. 5 ft.

Smacks built by J. W. & A. Upham were 6 to 8 inches deeper in the moulded depth than those from Jackman's yard.

SCANTLINGS

Keel. Length 60 to 61 ft.	Elm.	8 in. sided.	13 in. moulded.
Keelson – – –	Oak.	10 in. sided.	10 in. moulded.
Stem – – –	Oak.	8 in. sided.	12 in. moulded.
Sternpost – – –	Oak.	8 in. sided.	10 in. moulded.
Floors – – –	Oak.	6 in. sided.	10 in. in middle.
Frames – – –	Oak.	5½ in. tapered 10 in. heel to 5 in. head.	
Deadwood, knees – –	Oak.	8 in. sided.	
Beams – – –	Oak.	6 in. sided.	8½ in. moulded.
Knees – – –	Oak.	5 in. sided.	
Shelf – – –	Oak.	4½ in. sided.	7 in. moulded.
Clamp – –	Pitch Pine.	2½ in. sided.	

PLANKING

Topsides – – –	Oak.	2½ in. × 8 in. Three strakes.	
Bilge – – –	Elm.	3 in.—3½ in. thick.	
Bottom – – –	Elm.	2 in. thick.	
Ceiling – – –	Pine.	1½ in. thick.	
Decks – – –	Pine.	2½ in. × 5 in.	
Covering board – –	Oak.	2½ in. thick.	
Rails – – –	Elm.	3 in. thick.	

SPARS

In early trawlers of pitch pine, later Oregon pine.

Rig – – –	34 ft. to 36 ft. mainmast. 26 ft. mizzen.	
Mainmast – – –	Deck to cap. 46 ft. 9 in.	
Mizzen – – –	Deck to truck. 43 ft.	
Bowsprit – – –	38 ft. to 39 ft.	
Topmast – – –	26 to 28 ft. in winter, 32 to 38 ft. in summer.	
Main boom – –	31 ft.	Main gaff 31 ft.
Mizzen boom – –	22 ft.	Mizzen gaff. 21 ft.
Mizzen topsail yard –	Average 27 ft. approx.	

The firm of J. W. & A. Upham was founded in 1838, by Mr. John William Upham, grandfather of one of the present directors, Mr. Percy Andrew Upham, who most kindly allowed me to make notes of costs from the building book. He told me they used to build three smacks at a time, each in various stages of construction, one just started, one half-built and the third nearly finished, six to eight shipwrights and about 25 apprentices being employed. The foreman Couch was with them some sixty years, while the blacksmith Elliott came into the yard at the age of 11 and was with the firm all his working life, 65 to 66 years, with never a day off through illness and when he retired they continued to pay his wages until he died. He made all the ironwork for the smacks, including the trawl heads. A complete trawl net, supplied by the Gourock Rope Co., cost £10, the warp was made locally, but French rope was the best as it was like wire, the after lay, being put in first, never came out, whereas in English rope it was put in afterwards and worked out in use.

In those days a 60 ft. mast cost £10 to £12 for material and the price for making was 1s. an inch on the diameter. A spar maker could shape up a topmast in a day and always built the small boat, while the shipwrights would lay the deck of a big Lowestoft smack in a day. In addition to building wooden vessels of all types J. W. & A. Upham owned seven to eight smacks.

Other builders were Mathews at Fishcombe and Jackman at the Breakwater, the last smack built in that yard being *Terminist*, in 1912 (Plate 117). He then opened a yard on a site next to Upham's, where now stands an ice factory. Several trawlers were constructed by Gibbs of Galmpton, and Philip & Son of Dartmouth, but the preference was Brixham built for Brixham men.

In 1906 there were 220 first-class smacks of 15 tons and over registered at Brixham, Dartmouth having ceased to be the port of registry some ten years earlier. In 1910 numbers were 223, and in 1913 there was a fleet of about 140 big ketches.

The ten years prior to the outbreak of war in 1914 were the most prosperous Brixham had known. In 1904 landings were 64,976 cwts., value £56,745, two years later they rose to 66,797, value £59,306, the lowest year was 1912 with 53,293 cwt. Practically every trawler was owned by fishermen and employment was given to a large number of shipwrights, riggers, blockmakers, etc.

Thirty-five smacks were sunk by U-boats in the course of the war, but during the early 1920's only 15 trawlers of 40 tons and over were built, *Vigilance* being the last from Upham's yard (Plate 118), and *Encourage* from Jackman's (Plate 119), both being launched in 1926.

In 1919 landings of fish rose to 90,637 cwt., and the following year 84,498 cwt., value £186,920, but there was a steady decline until 1928, with 43,310 cwt., value £77,585, a drop of over 51 per cent. The serious losses of gear, due to the numerous war wrecks in the Bristol Channel, led to few smacks working those once prolific grounds, while between Hope's Nose and Stoke Point, about 44 miles, lay 120 vessels, including an 18,000 ton liner five miles from Berry Head. Little wonder sailing trawlers were laid up, when a warp alone cost £40, and few lads choosing to go into fishing meant that the brunt of the hard work fell on the old men.

I shall never forget my first sight of a Brixham smack over a quarter of a century ago. I was lecturing in Torquay and my hotel bedroom overlooked the lovely Torbay, so I was up betimes and saw the lights of a sailing vessel working towards the harbour, for beautiful fresh fish was then landed on the quay to appear at breakfast if you were lucky, if not at that meal, it was barely 24 hours out of the water by dinner time. As dawn came up the russet sails of a trawler showed through the soft haze of a perfect autumn morning as she slowly crept into port. The mists cleared with the rising sun and the easterly breeze whipped up white horses on the deep blue-green seas. Soon the distant Berry Head stood out sharp against the sky with brown and red sails everywhere making for Brixham, for about a hundred sail were on the register. Red cliffs, green hills and wooded slopes made a beautiful setting as development had scarcely begun where houses and streets sprawled when next I visited Torbay in 1933. Alas, I found about 30 big ketches ekeing out a living, but they were an unending source of interest and many a day we enjoyed watching them trawling in the bay, entering and leaving port, drying sail, etc., the good clean smell of Stockholm tar, old rope and the tang of the sea mingling with that nostalgic smell one always associated with an old-world harbour, while many of the fish on sale were still alive (Plates 120 and 121).

In 1936 there were only 45 fishing vessels on the register, 29 sail and 16 motor. The end was in sight for none was earning a living and by 1938 most of the big ketches lay in the basin with sale notices pasted on their bows, among them many built in the 1920's, *Vigilance, Inspire, Torbay Lass, Resolute, Girl Lena, Wendew* and *Floweret* being a few of the names (Plate 122).

Some had been converted into fine cruising yachts, able to go anywhere in the world. The 45-ton *Terpsichore* was launched on New Year's Day, 1925, for Emanuel Harris, but as she seemed unlucky at fishing he changed her name to *Mannequin*, a play on his nickname " Manny ". Later she was sold to the novelist A. W. Mason and again renamed, this time *Muriel Stephens*. After wintering at Brixham she sailed in June, 1947, for Vancouver via Cape Town. *Vigilant*, 38 tons, built 1907, took out a party of treasure seekers to Cocos Island in the Pacific, but months of fruitless search saw the abandonment of the quest and on the return journey she became leaky and was sold at Panama.

Plate 123 shows *Best Friend*, 34 tons, built at Brixham in 1914, photographed in a blow in the Solent. Flying the White Ensign of the Royal Yacht Squadron is a change indeed for a humble fishing smack, but a pull on the jib halyards would not come amiss.

In 1946 I got into touch with Walter Barnes, born 1875, whose voice has been heard over the radio in many broadcasts from the West Country. He wrote me that he served his apprenticeship in the 44-ton *Rescue*, D.H.76, later B.M.76, built in 1885 as a dandy, the price for hull, boat and spars being £450, and cost ready for sea £875. No steam capstan was fitted, all hauling being done by hand winch, but in 1889 a capstan with a big boiler was installed for £105. He was in *Rescue* for about twelve years, taking his skipper's certificate No. 4905 in October, 1896. On one occasion she did the 101 miles from the Longships to Brixham in ten hours in a strong sou'wester, and in a N.W. gale she made the distance of about 220 miles from St. Anne's Light, Milford Haven, to Berry Head inside 24 hours.

I mentioned I had a photograph of *White Violet*, D.H.325, 25 tons, built at Brixham 1891, and afloat until 1912 (Plate 124), and Walter wrote me her story :—

" John Wesley travelled the S.W. of England and his revivalism hit the fishermen very hard, he made them a God-fearing race of men. Now until the late nineties it was a crime to be at sea on Sunday, but it was sacrilege to shoot a trawl. But the Bristol Channel was discovered, Dover soles were plentiful and made good money, larger and better equipped smacks were built, women ashore demanded a better deal than their mothers had had, compulsory education had seen to that, so a new type of man emerged, who went on his voyage and fished any day and every day, but there were plenty who were followers of John Wesley and there still are. William Rouse was one of them. He knew if he went to sea in the large smacks he would have to fish on a Sunday, so he had built a smaller type of craft with a lot of rig, spreading plenty of sail and generous in speed, to fish in the English Channel for six days when the weather was fine, and rest and thank his Maker on the seventh. So he had *White Violet* built, she was ketch-rigged afterwards and was the fore-runner of a type 30 to 35 tons which we called ' mules '."

Four more years were to pass before I was able to get down to Brixham in May, 1950, and meet those with whom I had corresponded. The harbour looked forlorn without the black or grey hulls and the tanned sails of the smacks, and the water in the basin was the colour of mud, a striking contrast to the clear greeny-blue of other times. The hull of *Valerian*, B.M.161, built 1923, and a King's Cup winner at regattas, lay on the hard awaiting a purchaser, while *Sanspareil*, 24 tons, ex B.M.326, built 1912, *Rulewater*, 25 tons, ex B.M.353, built 1907 and *Resolute*, 27 tons, ex B.M.261, built 1906, now converted into yachts, lay out at moorings. Gone was the bustle and interest of other days, the only fish I saw sold on the market was landed by an Ostend and a Dieppe trawler. Sail lofts were derelict, but on the doors of the old blacksmith's shops could still be deciphered the burnt-in names of smacks whose ironwork had been made in the forges. The site of one shipyard was an ice factory and in Upham's dry dock an ex-Fleetwood trawler, now a yacht, was undergoing extensive repairs. The disappearance of sail dealt Brixham a severe blow economically and the loss of the fine, independent fishermen is to be deplored, skilled as they were in handling craft in any weather.

But I enjoyed talking to the old men. One, Samuel John Crang, had been a shipwright 54 years, man and boy. At the age of 15 he was bound apprentice on the 5th March, 1894, to John William and Andrew Upham " to learn their art " to quote the words on his indentures. His father, Richard Crang, had been apprenticed to John Barter, shipbuilder of Brixham, on the 25th September, 1855, so the son carried on the family tradition. Richard had been paid 8s. a week for the first six years and 10s. in the final twelve months, finding his own tools, and his indentures were beautifully inscribed in flowing copperplate writing on parchment, duly signed and sealed, and still in excellent preservation. In Samuel's day tools were provided and wages were 3s. a week for the first two years, 4s. for another two, with 1s. a year rise until 7s. in the last twelve months, then £1 a week.

In his early years the hours worked were 6 a.m. to 6 p.m., with half a hour for breakfast and one hour for dinner, Saturdays 6 a.m. to 5 p.m., later 6 a.m. to 2 p.m. and after the war they finished at 12 o'clock.

When building a smack the elm keel was laid first, then the oak stem and stern-post set up, next, floors with futtocks erected, starting amidships at dead flat, the frames being numbered for'ard and lettered aft. All frames were natural-grown local oak, cut by steam saw, the old sawpit seldom being used after he started work. A '' span '' frame was erected at every 3 to 4 stations, then a ribband was nailed round and the intermediate frames made to fit. The double futtocks used to be dowelled, but in his time they butted square. The keelson was bolted through every floor, deadwood and knee, aft and for'ard, set up with apron on top of knee and all through-bolted, one shipwright and two apprentices taking about a month to frame a big trawler of 60 to 61 ft. keel.

Then followed oak shelf, 4½ in. by 7 in., and stanchions which were morticed through the covering board, clear of the frames, being a tight fit between planking and shelf, through-bolted to shelf and beam, usually with two, sometimes with three bolts (Fig. 19). The hull was planked from topsides to bilge, and garboards to bilge, 2½ in. oak for topsides, three strakes of 3½ in. elm at bilges, and the remainder 2 in. elm. The oak beams, 8½ in. by 6 in. were all kneed, the for'ard ones on the aft side, and the after beams on the for'ard side, with two hanging knees of iron, one at the main sheet beam, the other at the mast beam. Clamp strake 2½ in., ceiling 1½ in., deck 2½ in. by 5 in., were all pitch-pine, carlings and partners, oak. The out-side of the hull was now cleaned and caulked, the vessel being ready for launching within 10 to 11 weeks from the laying of the keel (Plate 125). It was the custom to string up some bunting and a bunch of flowers at the bows and the smack was

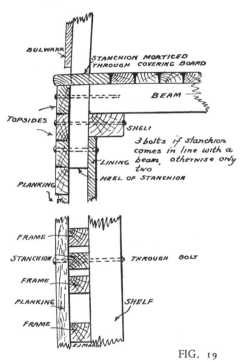

STANCHIONS AT BRIXHAM

FIG. 19

christened with a bottle of port or cider. Mr. Crang is standing by the forefoot of *We'll Try*, B.M.338, a 23-ton mule built in 1913, L.O.A. 56 ft., length of keel 50 ft. In the background is a smack in frame with stern timbers for a transom counter.

Masts and spars used to be pitch-pine, *Superb*, B.M.1, was the first Brixham smack to have Oregon pine which, however, proved soft for masts, although excellent for spars, as she pulled the peak halyards, bolts, washers, nuts and all, clean through the masthead, when rolling heavily at moorings in the outer harbour. Wire rigging had come in during the seventies.

Mr. Crang came out of his time in 1901, retaining any tools still good enough to use, and henceforward found his own, as was the custom. After three weeks lost time at 12s. a week he went to Devonport Dockyard for 3 years and 3 months at £1 14s. 6d. a week, being discharged on 5th August, 1904, through a reduction in the number of hands, next he worked for Philip & Son of Dartmouth for 5 years and 9 months, returning to Upham's in August, 1910, where he finished his working days.

It was good in these days to hear a man say how he had always been happy at his job, enjoying the work and seeing the results of his skill sailing out of the port or taking part in the regattas, while his 45 years with J. W. & A. Upham speak for themselves of relation between master and man.

I could not help thinking how much more pleasant to work sweet-smelling timber in a yard overlooking the waters of Torbay or the lovely Dart, than to be handling rusty steel plates in the clamour of a machine shop, but progress (?) has brought about the cessation of such work so far as sailing vessels for fishing and trading are concerned. However, I have yet to be convinced that it is to the ultimate good of a community to see skill, handed down from generation to generation, thrown on one side, and methods which brought prosperity to many a town and village around the coast, as well as a plentiful supply of fresh fish, discarded. But it is inevitable.

Plate 126 shows shipwrights working on a ketch c 1882, in the background is one of the big sloops, D.H.199.

Next I met Skipper John Henry Widger, who for eighteen years sailed the famous *Ibex* for Mr. Upham and he took me along to the yard where I had the pleasure of meeting Mr. Percy Andrew Upham. When he learned of my quest for data concerning the old days he brought along the building book, dating back to 1855 and still in use. The business was started in 1838, but the first book was no longer in existence, however, there was ample to satisfy even me, and I made notes of as many entries as possible, choosing those which gave cost of separate items. I much appreciated the privilege of going through this invaluable record and Mr. Upham's permission in allowing me to make use of this information enables a comparison to be made with prices ruling in other ports. He also showed me the half-models of a cutter, built 1838, or thereabouts, and the ketch *Ibex*, built 1896, and said I was welcome to take off the lines if I cared to do so. This caught me aback as, like the plumber, I had left my tools at home, never dreaming such an opportunity would come my way. All the time I was up in the mould loft looking at the many half-models I was puzzling out how best I could do the job, for I was determined to have a shot at it. It was most instructive to see the variations in underwater lines, the long, rather flat floors of trawlers built to work in the North Sea, the sharp ones of mules, Mumble bees,

129 *VALERIAN*, B.M.161 Detail of windlass showing pawl bitt and heel rope sheave.

130 *VALERIAN*, B.M.161
Detail of winch looking aft.

131 *VALERIAN*, B.M.161
Main sheet chock with bullseye to port, skylight and tiller.

132 *COMPEER*, B.M.21,
AT NEWLYN, 1929
40 tons, built at
Brixham, 1924. The
cleat for main sheet
is fore and aft, in
other smacks was
often at an angle, as
in plate 26.

133 *FERNLEAF*, B.M.317, 27th MARCH, 1926
24 tons, built at Galmpton, 1911. Detail at foot of mainmast showing parrel beads, leathering on gaff jaws, shoe, iron tumbler, topsail sheet block, mast hoops, gooseneck and cleats below. The left-hand rope is the trawl warp with a couple of turns round capstan. Note how lanyards are rove in deadeyes and light-board lashed to shrouds.

134 *T. H. E.*, B.M.275
25 tons, built at Brixham, 1908. Details of main masthead showing topping lift and downhaul, peak halyards with chain at standing end, main halyards and saddle, crosstrees, fore stay, shrouds and ratlines.

135 *WENDEW*, B.M.119
24 tons, built at Brixham, 1915. Detail of mizzen mast showing topping lift and downhaul, peak halyards, main halyards and saddle, shrouds shackled to eye lugs on iron collar at hounds, and upper block of aft fish tackle.

136 ON THE HARD, APRIL, 1938
Referee, B.M.369, 24 tons, built at Brixham, 1909. Note legs to keep hull upright, the rise of floors and rounded bilge, roller on port side of stem, and thick strakes of planking at bilge. M.112 is *Victoria II*.

137 *PREVALENT*, B.M.337

42 tons, built at Brixham, 1913. Winner at 1920 regatta. The mainsail has been borrowed from *Lynx*, B.M.317, the big tow foresail is set with sheet belayed well aft of main rigging, topsail sheet leads through block on pendant at masthead, not under jaws of gaff as was more usual practice. The mizzen topsail yard stands vertical and note that luff of jib is bar tight.

and finally those of the ketch *Ibex*, winner of 29 firsts in 33 races as Mr. Upham proudly told me.

As originally built she had a 39½ ft. rig, but dragged more than she could carry, so the mast was cut down to 38 ft. rig, a size only equalled by *Ella* and one other smack. The main boom measured 35 ft., summer topmast 41 ft. from fid to halyard sheave, with a 3 to 4 ft. pole above, on top of which flew the " weft ", Upham's red and blue flag, each a square, with the red next the spindle (Plate 127).

All that afternoon as my wife and I went up the beautiful Dart as far as Totnes, I was wondering how I could take off the lines. Finally I bought a large sheet of brown wrapping paper at Woolworth's and on the way kicked against a piece of flexible wire which I thought could be bent round to take off the moulds, but Mr. Upham suggested a strip of sheet lead when we met next morning and armed with these very unprofessional tools I spent the day taking off the lines. (Plans 10, pages 328-30). The registered dimensions as given in the building book do not quite agree with those of the half-model.

The lines are as taken from the half-model with a L.B.P. of 69.4 ft., but the deck plan and midship section are as built with a L.B.P. of 71.1 ft. L.W.L. was 69 ft. 9 in., draught aft 10 ft. 8 in., for'ard 5 ft. 4 in. L.O.A. 76 ft. 7 in. and G.T. $50\frac{13}{100}$.

Mr. P. A. Upham told me their usual practice was to use the same bow and stern moulds for every hull, putting in an extra frame or two amidships according to length required, but no other smack was ever built to the lines of the incomparable *Ibex*, appropriately named after the magnificent mountain goat which dwells in the high and inaccessible places of the earth and is of incredible speed and grace with a sleek, clean body.

A comparison of her dimensions with those of the crack Plymouth ketch *Erycina* as taken off by the late Mr. P. J. Oke show :

	Ibex	*Erycina*
L.O.A. — — —	76 ft. 7 in.	73 ft. 9 in.
L.B.P. — — —	71.1 ft.	68.75 ft.
Moulded beam — —	17.65 ft.	17.15 ft.
Depth — — —	9.1 ft.	9 ft.
Bow — — —	25 ft.	28 ft. 6 in.

The waterlines of *Ibex* were convex, those of *Erycina* concave, the floors in each were sharp but in the Plymouth smack were more hollow. *Ibex* drew 2 in. more water aft and 2 in. less for'ard than *Erycina*. Originally both had a 39½ ft. rig, *Ibex* was cut down to 38 ft. soon after her trials, but she carried a bigger topsail, and the sail plan shows what a press of canvas was set in summer weather.

SCANTLINGS

Keel	—	—	—	13 in. moulded.	8 in. sided.
Floors	—	—	—	10 in. moulded at throat.	
Keelson	—	—	—	10 in. sq.	
Beams	—	—	—	8½ in. moulded.	6 in. sided.

15

I had a long yarn with Skipper Widger, Jack to his friends as I hope I am, and he told me he came from a large family, being the oldest of 14 children. His father was a farm labourer and Jack went out to work part-time in a factory at the age of 10½, then to live in at a farmhouse for 9d. a week and his mother used to walk out 11 miles to collect his wages, see to his clothes and mending, and then walk home again. After farming for five years and earning 2s. 6d. a week at 16, the sight of the trawlers sailing past the fields and the lads jingling money in their pockets on Saturday night, made him decide to go to sea. At 17 he went in to Brixham to sail for a month on trial in *Escort*, D.H.105, 47 tons, built Brixham 1878. As soon as she got outside Jack was violently seasick and wished with all his heart that he was back again in the fields, but it soon passed and was forgotten and on 5th March, 1888, he was bound apprentice to Richard Mills, giving his age as 16 although actually 17. He served for five years, being found in food and clothes, " good clothes they were too," and as spending money he had the " stocker ", crabs, oysters and squid, but not to exceed 2s. 6d. a week. Being keen on his job Jack rose to third hand in 14 months, getting 5s. a week, and at the beginning of his fourth year got his Certificate of Competency, No. 4102, dated 5th September, 1893, taking charge of the smack when out of his time while the skipper was away for a month for his R.N.R. training. He then went as mate in *Melita* for a few weeks, acting as skipper from Christmas to Good Friday, then continuing as mate for two years until he broke a leg and fractured a knee when the smack fouled a wreck and he got caught up in the warp. As mate he was entitled to 1 share, as skipper 1¼.

On going back to sea Jack was mate of *Gladys* for 1½ years and then went skipper in a new smack *Dove* for two years. In 1899 he took over *Ibex* for Mr. Upham and sailed her for 18 years. In Jubilee year she had beaten the famous Plymouth smacks *Erycina* and *Vanduara* in their home waters and in 1901 *Ibex* again defeated the crack *Erycina*, which, ketch-rigged, had a 39½ ft. rig and a larger stay foresail but her mainsail was one cloth less than that of the Brixham vessel. In all Jack defeated *Erycina* three times out of four, winning one race by 15 minutes, but at one regatta *Ibex* came out after a refit with a new mast and the rigging stretched so much that the deadeyes were nearly on deck and *Erycina* won by 5½ minutes. Plymouth trawlers were at their best in light weather, Brixham in heavy.

It was easy to see what a love Jack had for his ship, " she went over the seas like a lifeboat, very rare to take water aboard, could walk about deck in carpet slippers." Her lifting bows enabled her to " go " in a lop, as she rose to the seas instead of crashing through them, while she was good in any weather, running or reaching and going to wind'ard " would cut wind in two halves ". Jack attributed her sea-keeping abilities to the fact that she had 39 tons of clean pig iron ballast under the fish room and no stone, and with 6 ft. clear headroom in the hold there was plenty of air for buoyancy. Good at laying-to under reefed mainsail and mizzen with one reef in the stay foresail, *Ibex* would eat up into the wind when hove-to. One night *Ella*, her local rival in lofty rig, could just be seen away in the distance in the moonlight, both ships laying-to, but by dawn *Ibex* had worked right up to her.

Being very handy, the smack handled like a yacht and her qualities can be judged from the following incidents. One Saturday, near Christmas time, Jack was to the west of Lundy in a hard nor'easter, around midnight the wind backed to the south'ard so he lay in for Trevose. About 3 a.m. the jib had just been taken in when the mast went by the board. "The night was as dark as a bag when I ran up on deck but I could see the mast had gone. We cut away to make her head come up, but left stay as a sea anchor, showed a flare, but no one about. As she lay all right head to wind I went below, got out my accordion and played 'A little ship lay on the sea'. At daylight wind westered, so fair for Padstow, got warp out aft and put a jib across deck to mizzen, hoisted two balls and a flag as a distress signal, and against ebb tide we worked ten miles under jury rig before we were seen from shore and a tug came out."

Another time they were on the St. Ives ground with gear down when the main-sail burst. The topsail was rigged aft of the mast as a trysail, the big stay foresail set and a 9-cloth jib run out. They beat against the wind, tack and tack, while another smack astern, seeing a chance of salvage money, tried to catch up, but was unable to get near. At 8 a.m. after rounding Land's End the wind freed and under jury rig, Brixham, 100 miles to east'ard, was reached twelve hours later.

The speed of *Ibex* was remarkable. At five o'clock one evening they left Trevose Head and landed the catch next morning at 8 a.m. on Plymouth quay, 140 miles away. One trip from Brixham earned £57, 400 pairs of soles were taken on the ground off St. Ives and although a dead beat back, the haul was landed at the home port four days after leaving it. A very smart performance. Another Saturday they were working on the ground off Milford Haven, at 2 p.m. St. Anne's Head was abeam. The wind was foul for working down the Bristol Channel so Jack kept *Ibex* off towards Ireland for six hours, then lay south on the other tack and the first light seen was the red flash from Round Is. Lighthouse on the Scillies. The wind came aft so they squared away for the run up Channel and Jack made fast to the pier at Brixham about Sunday dinner time. Another smack which sailed at the same time did not come in until the Wednesday.

With such sailing qualities it is not surprising that *Ibex* flew a string of winning flags from taffrail to topmast head and finally had to drop out of racing at the regattas as no one would sail against her, the result being a foregone conclusion. This did not suit Mr. Upham or Jack, so after a year or two's absence it was decided to reduce her sailplan. The mizzen mast was shifted two feet further for'ard and a correspond-ing length cut off the main boom, necessitating taking one cloth off the mainsail. When she came out again the wiseacres said she would do nothing now her wings were clipped, BUT SHE DID, romping home a winner by 15 minutes. The Committee then asked Mr. Upham not to race her again and she sailed no more at the regattas.

The war came and when U-boat sinkings began *Ibex* was laid-up for a while and

Jack was in *Gazelle* when his old command was sunk by gunfire, 14 miles S.E. by E. of Berry Head on the 29th January, 1918.   Other smacks put down that day were the 40-ton *Addax*, the 45-ton *General Leman* and the 40-ton *Perseverance*, Jack saw them being shelled and undoubtedly *Gazelle* would have shared the same fate, but luckily the submarine submerged and made off when a patrol boat came hurrying up.

I am more than pleased to have the privilege of recording the lines of this famous trawler and to have met her skipper.

Jack next sailed *Competitor* for Mr. Upham for two years, then had *Guess Again* for four years before going in *Elsie May* for a fisherman owner.   After trawling off the Scillies they left the ground early one Saturday to come home and Jack saw the lights of a steamer approaching, green to his green, so nothing to worry about, but she suddenly altered course and rammed the smack's starboard bow, cutting her right down.   The water was over the bulkheads inside five minutes, so the crew took to the boat and rowed from 11 p.m. until 6 a.m. Sunday morning when they reached the Cornish village of Cadgwith.   The culprit, believed to be a steam trawler, was never traced although £100 reward was offered by the Insurance Society, which sent agents into most of the likely ports to see if any sign of smack's paint could be found on the bows of a vessel.

Jack now went skipper in *Us Dree* for a couple of years, finally going back to Upham's to have *Silver Lining* for seven years until one day he went to scum out the boiler, had a black-out and fell, fracturing three ribs.   After a while the men came to look for him and found him lying unconscious, so put him in his bunk and headed for home and assistance.   Jack lay like a log for some hours and on coming-to went up on deck, and not knowing he had been out for so long told the mate it was time to put ship about, then he heard what had happened.   *Silver Lining* was sunk at moorings in 1940 when a German aeroplane dropped a bomb clean down the hatch and blew her to pieces.

Speaking of a salvage experience, Jack said one night they were hauling the trawl in a gale off the Wolf when they saw blue rockets shooting up.   '' Must be a vessel on Seven Stones,'' so *Ibex* sailed down under the stern of the light-vessel and Jack hailed to find out what was the matter.   They came about several times and eventually learned that the winch had broken, so impossible to pay out more cable and crew were in fear of dragging.   Asked if he wished it to be reported the master said yes, so Jack sailed into Penzance ഄ do so.   Trinity House awarded him £25 in appreciation of his services.

Jack also mentioned that the trawl once brought up a duffle coat from H.M.S. *Formidable*, sunk January, 1915, and he found it very useful on cold nights.

When he first went to sea the fleet fished off Ireland and the smack took 2½ tons of Norwegian block ice, it being the boy's job to break it up with a mallet and marlinspike, and catches were frequently landed at Brixham within 24 hours.   If fishing on the local grounds they made two trips a week, taking 10 cwt. of ice to sea each time, but were away for a week if working in the Bristol Channel and took 25 cwt. of ice, landing fish at Milford Haven or Swansea, if off the Cornish coast they put in to Padstow, Newlyn or Plymouth. His warp was three 50 fathom lengths spliced together, the whole weighing 12 to 13 cwt., but some manilla warps ran up to 14 cwt. The cost of a beam was about £3 10s., but £9 after the war. Jack preferred a square stern as with a round, or elliptical one the beam was not so snugly stowed.

In pre-war days to average £20 a week or £1,000 a year was good fishing, but in the war he once took £134 in a week and in *Competitor* grossed £4,000 a year. In *Dove*, fishing out of Plymouth, he took £80 in 48 hours in the Bristol Channel, landing the catch at Brixham after only a four day trip. In *Ibex* they were off St. Ives and had 130 pairs of fine soles in one haul, a gale came on and they had to lay-to under double-reefed main and mizzen and a storm jib. The wind fined down and they picked up the Godrevy light, put the trawl down for 3 hours and found another 100 pairs of soles, lay-to until 3 a.m. and shot again to take yet another 100 pairs, so with five trunks of big soles aboard they made sail for Brixham where these choice fish sold at £11 a trunk. On another trip they took eight trunks of soles and Jack reckoned that with the rest of the catch they would make £100, and he promised the mate a new suit of oilskins if they did, but when they got in there was a glut on the market. The soles only made £4 a trunk and there were no bids for much of the fine catch, so that instead of the £100 expected they only received £44. In calms they caught nothing.

Ibex was undoubtedly one of the finest smacks ever to sail out of Brixham, *Rose* and *Welcome* two of the unlucky ones, but *Bonny Lass* was far and away the most unfortunate, losing 31 sets of gear in 30 years owing to the warp parting.

Jack reckons his worst experience was in the hurricane of December, 1910. A fortnight before Christmas the fleet left Milford Haven for home, *Ibex* and two others came down from Neyland further up the river a few hours before the rest left the dock and so had more sea room when the gale came on.

" I think it was the hardest blow I have been in. When heaving down the second reef, a good sail, nearly new, gave out as the reef cringle went. We had to get the sail down and stow it on deck, and lay out the gale. The others that did not get so far to sea had a very bad time. Four vessels lost with all hands, besides others badly damaged, one ship losing skipper and mate. When the gale abated we ran before the wind which altered so we could fetch the land, and under mizzen, jib and staysail made Swansea."

Brixham trawlers always worked their warp over the bow, but the roller in the gangway was used if fast on a wreck. " We came by the head till clear, then passed aft on the capstan. Sometimes when towing on the port tack it was time we came around on the other tack. To do that, if staying, we would back off with the tiller hard up and have the mizzen sheet right out. Pass the bight of warp around the bow, bring it aft outside the rigging and on the dummy. Let go the stopper, hard down the helm, and pull in the mizzen sheet. But before that make sure to stop warp on the lee bow, so that it would not drop under the bottom. When around, let go this rope, then with the mizzen sheet out tight she would pay off fair with the tide if the wind was light. Instead of staying, we did not keep the warp on the bow, but dropped the bight under the bottom and then on to dummy, then let go the stopper and the warp coming tight we would gybe over. When working by hand in the old days we hauled by the bow until the dandy bridle came up and, when enough main bridles were in, passed it right aft outside rigging and in score aft on to what we called the ' dandy wink '. One man shipped a handle heaving in the slack, the others using fish tackle with a strop on fore bridle to sling it aft, taking it to capstan hand gear with two handles and two men, the boy hauling back the bridle and paying it down the main hatch. The slack of the after bridle was also pulled in. It took about two hours to get gear aboard.''

As at Lowestoft, all the heavy work in setting sails, reefing, warping out of harbour, etc., was done by steam capstan. The bowsprit was never fidded, except when racing and then a bobstay was often set up. In blowing weather this heavy spar was reefed as jibs were shifted, being held in place by a heelrope. The working foresail sheet consisted of two single blocks, the lower one traversing on an iron horse across the deck. On the lee side a rope, fast to an eyebolt in bulwarks, was passed round the sheet and belayed back to hold the sail a'weather when going about. The big tow foresail came outside the main rigging, sheeting home well aft. A gaff topsail, 6 cloths by the head, was often set in the early days, but a '' sharp-headed '' one was carried in later years, a handy-billy being used to set up the sheet. Masts and topmasts were varnished, gaffs and booms painted. Reef lacings were kept below until required, but the reef tackles were rove off round the booms. Trawling was generally done on the port tack, the warp being led for'ard over a roller at the bows with a bight made fast to the bitts and led in clear of main rigging over the gangway to the dummy or towpost, where it was made fast with a stopper. A becket slipped over the pumphead and the legs crossed over the warp which went out over the rail aft in the usual way.

Plates 128 to 135 show various details of typical Brixham smacks and the clean lines can be seen in Plates 118 and 136.

Generally speaking the main differences between the Devon and Lowestoft smacks were, finer lines, more rake to sternpost, deeper heel with corresponding increase in draught, longer bow, less forefoot, more rig and a partiality for a big balloon foresail which was later copied by the North Sea trawlers. The heavy hulls were very deceptive, giving little indication above water of the fine lines which gave them the speed for bringing catches to market in the shortest possible time.

Walter Barnes introduced me to Mr. J. H. Blackmore so that I could obtain some information concerning the Brixham Fishing Smack Mutual Insurance Society of which he is chairman. In 1834 the Friendly Society of Fishermen had been formed and about 150 members signed or made their marks on the deed which still exists.

No vessel was to be insured for more than £300, and could only take cargo from Brixham to another port, but not both ways. This latter clause was subsequently waived to allow owners and crews to convey their household goods to and from the N.E. coast. Any member entering a meeting in a state of intoxication, or interrupting business or using profane language was fined the sum of 1s., and if he or she continued to do so, or take God's most Holy Name in vain, a sum of 5s. was forfeit.

This Society later became the Brixham Fishing Smack Mutual Insurance Society and insured sailing vessels only. The chairman and directors, appointed annually, were paid only a small fee to keep expenses as low as possible. Practically every Brixham owner insured, about 250 being the average number, and ships were surveyed and valued before being accepted.

In 1898 Mr. Blackmore commenced his association with the Society and has been interested in it ever since. There were three classes, smacks over 40 G.T., under 40 G.T. and above 30, and 30 tons and under. The owner carried 25 per cent of the insurance, the Society the remaining 75 per cent, the maximum for a large ship was £800, but this was increased to £1,500 during the 1914-18 war. Losses were paid by calls during the current year, usually every three months according to needs and the average " premium " over ten years was 2½ per cent, a very low figure.

There was also The Steam Capstan & Iron Ballast Society, where the owner carried 10 per cent of valuation, but fishing gear was not insurable.

The worst year was in the 1914-18 war when six smacks were sunk in one week by U-boats, meaning a very heavy call on the owners, some of whom wanted the fleet laid up. Mr. Blackmore called a meeting and was sent to Plymouth to explain matters to owners of fishing vessels there, and try and get the M.P's interested so as to obtain their assistance in the matter. A deputation waited on the Lords of the Admiralty and the Minister of Agriculture and Fisheries, and as a result within a fortnight every Brixham owner joined the War Risk Association. The smacks were now organized into a fleet, Mr. Blackmore's *Prevalent* being admiral's ship with a naval lieutenant in charge. Prior to this innovation all fishing had been inside a line from Start to Portland, but under protection smacks were able to go to the better grounds outside, catching three times the quantity of fish, an important item in wartime. Some Lowestoft and Ramsgate men joined the fleet which was escorted by an armed steam trawler, and only one smack was subsequently sunk and she had strayed from the others.

In December, 1910, four Brixham smacks were lost with all hands during a heavy gale in the Bristol Channel. They were *Eva*, B.M.191, *Speedwell*, B.M.213, *Vigilance*, B.M.218, and *Marjorie*, B.M.246, while *Friendship*, B.M.244, had two men drowned. This disaster roused public sympathy and about £6,000 was collected for the dependants and from that fund the widows have received a weekly allowance ever since, also extras for sickness, etc., as need arises.

Mr. Blackmore told me he first went to sea in 1887, at the age of 13, going to the North Sea in the 42-ton sloop *Florinda*, built at Brixham in 1880 and owned by Wm. H. Blackmore. This was the last year a fleet went to the East Coast as the smacks afterwards went to the Bristol Channel where the fishing was very remunerative, earning more in three months than in nine elsewhere. A very good week's fishing brought in £50 to £60, but a low trip might not yield a fiver.

Hanging on the wall of the room in which we were talking was a splendid picture of his *Prevalent*, B.M.337, 42 tons, built by J. W. & A. Upham in 1913, and winner of the 1920 regatta. Mr. Blackmore was a keen contestant in many a hard-sailed race, his *Retriever* having won as far back as 1904, and he does not remember just how many prizes he won, but he showed me silver cups, trays and jugs galore, as well as one of two gold watches. Some were those given annually by Mr. Wallace of Vancouver, a Brixham shipwright who went to Canada and made good, but always remembered his Devon birthplace.

Prevalent was not a fast ship, but after the war Mr. Blackmore decided to race her so went down on the pier one day to see her come in and watch how she sat on the water. Some ballast was shifted, the position of the mast altered, new sails bent and the smack was winner of two prizes at her first attempt at racing (Plate 137).

His *Collie*, B.M.285, 52 tons, was launched from Upham's yard on 11th August, 1909, the first Brixham trawler to have an elliptical stern, and she also was a winner of several cups. Mr. Blackmore was sailing master on Mr. Upham's *Lynx* with E. Harris at the tiller on the never-to-be-forgotten occasion when she beat *Erycina* in her home waters. Both ships were on the starboard tack in the open sea when *Erycina* went about and tried to cross the bows of her rival, but could not clear. A collision was certain and *Lynx*, having the right of way, held on and the skipper refused to let her alter course so the bowsprit went through the mizzen and tore the sail. A protest was lodged by the Plymouth skipper and the Brixham owner, sailing master and skipper went to Plymouth with a chart and saw the chairman of the Regatta Committee, a barrister, who listened to their explanation and the result was that as *Erycina* failed to observe the rule of the road, *Lynx* was awarded the first prize.

Mr. E. Harris gave me a graphic description of an experience in his *Boy Denis* during a gale in 1914. A heavy sea struck the vessel N.N.W. of Start and hove her down, splitting the mainsail. All the gear was thrown about, the position of the ballast was reversed, the coal flung up on top of the boiler and so tightly wedged under the deck that it was almost impossible to shift it. The after trawl head was caught up on the mizzen boom and the for'ard one was amidships beyond the capstan. All the chain ran out of the locker, the gear in engine room was found up in the eyes of the ship, 150 fathom of 6 in. warp was turned upside down and landed back in the same place. The official recording of this S.W. blow was 130 m.p.h. at the Scillies, yet the smack sustained no damage.

Finally I had the good fortune to meet Mr. Frank Albert Jackman, aged 82, who has the reputation of having cut more sails that stood well than any other man in Brixham. He was apprenticed for seven years at the age of 14 to Mr. Dewdney who had as sailmaker a man named Crowte, the pay being 3s. a week for the first year, with one shilling a year rise and 8s. to 9s. in the final twelve months. Hours were 6.30 a.m. to 6 p.m., with half an hour for breakfast and one hour for dinner, Saturday 6.30 a.m. to 5 p.m., later they left off at 2 p.m. When out of his time he received £1 1s. a week and in all was fourteen years with Crowte, who allowed no one but himself to cut out sails. Mr. Jackman was offered a job at Lowestoft but was dubious about taking it as he knew nothing about cutting out, so he offered to pay Crowte if he would teach him, but he refused saying, " You take the job and when you get a suit to cut out let me know dimensions and I'll tell you how they should be cut." This did not suit the budding sail-maker for as he said he would then be working for two masters and if Crowte died where would he be. By keeping his eyes open and studying every book he was able to obtain, Mr. Jackman finally thought he had hit on the secret and as his uncle had just had a smack built he offered to make the sails. Agreement being reached, he ordered some bolts of canvas, cut them up and sewed the sails *in his spare time*. To his delight when the sails were bent they set well, so he asked Crowte for a shilling a week rise. He refused, so Mr. Jackman gave him a fortnight's notice and set up on his own, continuing in business for 44 years. " I never wanted for a day's work until I retired at the age of 72."

All sails were made of American or Manchester cotton, which came into favour when he was apprenticed, taking the place of flax. The usual rig was 36 ft., some had 35 ft. but only three 38 ft., *Ibex*, *Ella* and one other. About 1,000 yards were required to make an average suit and the time taken to make each sail single-handed was :—

	yds	10 hr. day
Mainsail	240	12 to 14 days
Summer topsail	84	4 days
Winter topsail	70	4 days
Mizzen	85	5 days
Mizzen topsail	40	2½ days
Stay foresail	65	3 to 3½
Big foresail	130	5 days
Mizzen staysail	85	5 days
Storm jib	25	1 day
5 cloth jib	40	2½ days
7 cloth jib	65	3 to 3½
10 cloth jib	90	4 to 4½

1019 yards.

For racing the big foresail was not allowed to exceed 17 cloths.

In the nineties the rate of pay for making-up was 2½d. a yard, £2 10s. being the charge for a mainsail, ten to twelve half-pound balls of twine being used. Later the price was 3d. a yard up to 1914. All sails were hand-sewn, with stitches 4 or 5 to the inch, double seams, and a man sewed 10 yards an hour or 100 yards in a ten-hour day. If rope and twine was found the price was 5d. a yard.

No. 1 canvas was 1s. a yard and there was a penny a yard drop per number, i.e., No. 2 was 11d., No. 3 was 10d., and so on. The big foresail, mizzen staysail and mizzen topsail were No. 9, and other sails Nos. 1, 2 and 3 canvas.

Mr. Jackman said with the pride of a true craftsman that it was a day's work for him to rope a mainsail, sewing through every strand and he never used a stitch mallet to tighten up the twine, except at the reefs. On the luff he had one seaming twine in the needle, on upper leech two roping twines and at clew two roping and one seaming twine. The luff rope was always put on tight, 3 inches in every yard tight, then when the sail stretched it came correct.

The bolt rope sizes for a mainsail were :—

Luff 2½ in. Head 2 in. Foot 2 in. Leech 3½ in. to reefs, 4½ in. reef to clew. For mizzen sail.

Luff 2¼ in. Head 1¾ in. Foot 1¾ in. Leech, upper 2¼ in., below reefs 3½ in.

Foresail. Luff 2½ in., foot and leech 2 in., with 2½ in. to 3 in. below reef to clew.

Big Foresail. Luff 2½ in., foot and leech 1½ in., with 2½ in. round clew.

Jibs. Luff 4 in., foot and leech 2 in., with 3 in. round clew.

Topsail. Luff 3 in., foot and leech 2 in., with 2½ in. round clew.

In the early days all the twine was white and the skeins were tarred with Stockholm tar by the boys, lasting far longer than that tarred in the factory, which came in later. Up to 1914 all grommets were hand-sewn and in a trawler's mainsail were 11 pairs, 22 holes in the luff, 18 in the head, 8 in the leech and 15, 13 and 12 in the reefs.

Sails were barked with oak, a half to one hundredweight being used for a suit, boiled in water overnight, poured hot into a tub and red or yellow ochre, or a mixture of both added, yellow and a little red making the best colour. A cwt. of tallow and a bucketful of Stockholm tar completed the mixture which was payed on hot with mops made of old canvas. Barking shrank the sails so up to 2½ ft. had to be allowed. This dressing came off when the sails were handled, but a mixture of salt water, ochre and linseed oil did not soil hands or clothes. Care had to be taken that it dried well in, otherwise a sail would catch fire through spontaneous combustion if rolled up while still damp.

Three weeks was the usual time allowed for a sail to stretch and if well looked after a mainsail would last 20 years, but it could be ruined so far as standing well was concerned if carelessly stretched the first time it was set.

Each trawler had a winter and a summer suit. The winter mainsail was one cloth less on the head but the same on the boom, otherwise it would have been necessary to alter the reef chocks. The summer mizzen was ten cloths by the head, the winter seven or eight, a change of gaff and boom being necessary. In summer a 36 to 38 ft. topmast was carried, in winter 26 ft., so two different sized topsails were required, but where smacks carried only one topmast, summer and winter, it measured 28 ft. These were in the palmy days, after the war the tendency was to have shorter spars.

The mizzen topsail yard was 18 to 25 ft. according to sail carried, some owners set it vertical but Mr. Jackman liked to see his at a slight angle as the sail stood better if the yard was slung with one-third of the length below the halyard strop and two-thirds above.

Mr. Jackman asked me if I knew the " art of a sailmaker ", the secret of making a sail stand and set well and on my saying no, he deliberated for a few minutes before deciding to tell me. Before cutting out a mainsail the first step was to draw a scale plan and run two perpendiculars from the leech to the throat and tack of the luff, which was 26 ft. in length for the big ketches, and add the peak and foot gores. Four feet slack had to be allowed in the 17 cloths, working in 10 in. on the first seam, 8 in. on second, 6 in. on third, 5 in. on fourth, 4 in. on fifth, 3 in. on sixth, 2 in. on seventh, and one inch on the remainder.

The first cloth cut was the tack cloth, and the four mast cloths each had a 7 ft. gore. There was a 5 in. seam in the tack cloth, running down to 3 in., then increasing again near the leech so as to form the curve or roach in the foot of the sail. Middle seams were 2 in., at head 3 in. These were for vertical-cut mainsails, for diagonal-cut Mr. Jackman treated them as two foresails, allowing 3 ft. to 3 ft. 2 in. gore in the diagonal. Making-up started from the leech inwards, the opposite to a vertical or parallel sail where work began from the mast outwards. The secret for making a diagonal sail stand was to put the last cloth at foot on tight, 18 in. tighter than the one above.

For a smart suit the gaff should be 2 ft. shorter than the boom, with one foot spare beyond the peak, and in cutting a mainsail an allowance for stretching of 2ft. was made on boom and gaff, 18 in. on a mizzen. There were reef bands in a diagonal sail, but none in a straight-cut one (Plate 138).

Linings on leech were one half-breadth to the upper reef cringle and two lots of two-foot breadth from the third reef down to the clew, on the luff was one cloth breadth, all sewn on the port side.

It usually took 8 to 10 weeks for Mr. Jackman to make a full suit of sails, every one being hand-sewn and in 1915 a rig-out for the 50-ton *Seaplane* with a 33 ft. boom, was mainsail and topsail, mizzen and topsail, stay foresail, big foresail, mizzen staysail, 4, 5, 7 and 10 cloth jibs, and the price complete was £85, a year or so later the cost of a new mainsail alone was £83.

Mr. Jackman told me he loved sewing sails: " I always enjoyed my work, never laid them out in a loft, always made them straight over my knee. I could make a suit here," he said, waving his hands round the small room in which we were talking.

Plate 139 shows men paying on the warm mixture which has been heated up in the brick coppers. The foresail and mizzen from a mule are being dressed, overhead hang the mainsail and topsail.

In a strong breeze the heavy ketches were very fast as was evidenced at the August regattas. In 1922 after racing over a course of some 40 miles, only 2 min. 7 sec. divided first and last, the winner being *Floweret*, 40 tons, built 1909, by Upham. The 1927 race was sailed in a hard blow, one smack carrying away her bowsprit, and the average speed of the winner was just over 12 knots, good going over a course set to test every point of sailing. A pleasing feature of these races was the sportsmanship displayed. If a man thought a sail from another smack set better than his own, it was freely loaned, in 1920 *Prevalent* set a mainsail belonging to Mr. Upham's *Lynx*, while Mr. Blackmore had loaned some of his sails to another man. Smacks sailed in working trim but the usual crew of four was increased to twelve, there being no lack of volunteers from ships not taking part in the regatta. Cracking-on was indulged in, sails or spars carrying away before anything was taken in, and a whole volume could be written about the many incidents when all were crowded together at the mark boats, etc. (Plates 140 and 141).

For seamanship the Brixham fishermen were unsurpassed. On 1st January, 1915, the battleship *Formidable* was torpedoed in the Channel by U.24, a gale was blowing and the *Provident* was lying hove-to off the Start when a deeply laden boat load of survivors drove past. By handling his smack magnificently, including a gybe, Skipper W. Pillar succeeded in effecting a rescue after a long struggle, earning him an award of £250 from the Admiralty, with a proportionate amount to the crew.

With the principal fishing grounds lying right across the shipping lanes many a trawler was lost with all hands in collision with sailing ships or steamers, the men often being left to their fate. *Morning Star*, 49 tons, built 1867, was a total loss on the 1st February, 1884, following a collision with the Russian barque *Alexandre I*, 23 miles S.E. of Start in a fresh sou'west breeze, 2 of the crew being drowned. On the 28th March, 1885, the 40-ton sloop *Emblem*, built 1858, was run down by *Loch Moidart*, a 2,000-ton full-rigged ship, 10 miles E.S.E. of Berry Head in a light S.S.W. wind. On the 6th January, 1883, the 51-ton sloop *Nimble*, built 1877, was sunk in collision with S.S. *Swansea* off Start Point, four of the crew of five being lost.

The increase in steamer traffic added to the perils of collision as it kept going in calms and so numerous were the sinkings that red flares were carried in smacks to be burnt immediately the lights of a steamship were sighted, so great was the fear of being run down. *I.C.U.* was sunk on Christmas Eve, 1884, by a liner going up Channel and the collision was not reported. By a coincidence a member of the Insurance Society was travelling in a railway carriage and a gentleman casually mentioned he had just come home in a liner which ran down a trawler. Having learned the day and time, and the destination, the insurance man went to the port, saw the steamer and found a piece of sail on her anchor. Result a Board of Trade Enquiry and compensation had to be paid to the widows and children of the drowned men and for the loss of the smack.

During a westerly gale on the 1st March, 1901, the 40-ton ketch *Wayfarer*, built 1896, was struck by lightning while fishing out of Milford Haven and becoming leaky she was abandoned 25 miles N.N.W. of Godrevy Head.

The ever present risk of sudden death was seen in November, 1912, in the smack *Our Bairns*, 38 tons, built 1910. While the third hand was passing the reef lacing the pendant carried away, causing the boom to drop and tighten the mainsail. This flung the unfortunate man overboard off Popton Point, Milford Haven. In March, 1922, a sudden gale blew up and *Majestic*, 39 tons, built Brixham in 1904, and *Love & Unity*, 39 tons, built Galmpton 1906, were lost with all hands, and serious damage was done to other smacks.

Between 1879 and 1913, I have traced the loss of 124 Brixham vessels, only 14 foundered, but 54 were lost in collision, 47 stranded and 9 were burned out.

On July 7th, 1934, the 42-ton *Replete*, built Brixham 1924, skipper and owner J. R. Bond, was trawling off Land's End when the gear fouled a wreck early on Sunday morning. Smoke was seen coming up from below and the crew rushed down and tried to put out the flames in the boiler room, but within ten minutes had to take to the punt. The smack burned to the water's edge and then sank. In January, 1937, the 24-ton *Girl Inez*, built at Brixham in 1917, was lost by fire off the Irish coast.

Before we left Brixham my wife and I walked down the cool, leafy lane to visit Gibb's old shipyard at Galmpton, where so many fine smacks were built for owners in every fishing port. We found a lovely site, quiet and deserted on that perfect May afternoon, birds were singing everywhere and cows grazed on the buttercup-covered slopes, overhead was a blue sky with fleecy white clouds and the soft S.W. wind was laden with the perfume of hawthorn. The peace was only broken by the sound of a distant tractor. The mud was gullied by the ebbing tide, but soon a small schooner yacht out in the stream swung head to the incoming flood and tiny trickles spread over the acres of ooze, where a Bermudian-rigged cutter lay, her decks and lower rigging covered with green, slimy weed, for she had seen many an ebb and flow to judge from her appearance. At the foot of the slip where she was built in 1906 lay the hull of *Seafarer*, B.M.258, listing to starboard with sides and deck green with marine growth (Plate 142).

Her port bulwarks had gone and ropes hung over the side. On the old stone quay lay rusty wire, broken timbers and lengths of chain, alongside was the faded blue hull of *William & Sam*, B.M.352, a mule built by Upham in 1917, and a winner at the regattas. Bulwarks had gone from the mast aft on the port side and from amidships on the starboard, the stanchions standing up gaunt. The covering board was breaking away, mizzen boom lay across the starboard rail, while the halyards hung against the mast which was still supported by the shrouds. The deck was littered with broken hatch coamings, etc., the main mast bare with the port deadeyes slatting against it and frayed rope ends swaying in the breeze from the crosstrees, but the forestay was taut (Plate 143).

To starboard lay the spritsail barge *Magnet*, 45 tons, built Milton 1899, converted to a yacht and awaiting a purchaser. Her torn mainsail stirred forlornly to the touch of the wind, while the mizzen sprit swung gently to and fro with a plaintive creak. Beyond lay the sheds with the slips running down to the water and the path was lined with hawthorn bushes in all their full beauty, screening the long wooden chest in which many a plank had been steamed in the days when the yard rang to the sound of adze and mallet (Plate 144).

An ancient steam yacht and two hulls of wartime craft lay heeled at various angles, but *Pride of Paignton* lived up to her name with freshly painted hull. Along the strand were the frames, closely spaced and solid, of what seemed to be a trading smack. A graveyard indeed, but what a beautiful spot, with the wooded slopes reflected in the cool, limpid water, lush fields and utter silence. A man working on a crane, the only sign of life, informed me that *William & Sam* had been converted into a yacht some years before and broke her back when being put on the blocks for refit, owing to insufficient water.

I spent some time wandering about this delightful backwater, thinking of the time when the name of Galmpton was written on many a ship's papers, of the lives of shipwrights and others who had spent their working days in idyllic, sylvan surroundings, a trifle remote perhaps, but what compensations. I brought away a few snapshots and a cringle from a scrap of sailcloth lying on the deck of *William & Sam*, thinking, well this is the end of an era, of red sails on the blue waters of Torbay, of smacks riding out bitter winter gales in the Bristol Channel where the seas run in unchecked from the North Atlantic to break in fury against the rocky coasts of Cornwall, North Devon and Wales, of men fighting to claw off a lee shore, and of sunlit regatta days with trawlers in a hard thrash to wind'ard and keen eyes anxiously watching to see if they would fetch the markboat. All gone for ever and fast fading into the mists of the past, but thanks to the kind co-operation of those I met and talked to, there will be some record of smacks and fishermen, both Devon built and bred.

PLYMOUTH

TRAWLING from this Devon port was always more localized than at Brixham, most of the fishing being on the ground about 21 miles in length and 9 in greatest breadth, inside the Eddystone and chiefly to the west of the lighthouse, which lies 8½ miles S.W.⅓S. from Penlee point at the entrance to Plymouth Sound. In the middle of the 19th century the usual practice was for the smacks to go out early in the morning and return in the afternoon, as all fishing was done by daylight, except when working for soles, whose nocturnal habits meant they could be caught only at night. Sometimes the trawlers worked in Bigbury and Whitesand bays, occasionally in Looe and Mevagissey bays, and Mount's Bay.

In the 1820's about thirty fishing vessels belonged to the port, in 1843 there were 62 trawlers, mostly sloops, but 5 or 6 were yawl-rigged. The larger smacks worked a 40 ft. beam, the smaller yawls a 30 ft. one, the cost of fishing gear being £40 to £50. By 1863 the number had risen to 64 of about double the tonnage and the average take of fish for each smack was half-a-ton. 1,092 tons were forwarded by rail in 1859, increasing to 1,912 tons three years later. In 1872 there were 66 first-class trawlers averaging 34 tons each, 6 years later Prosser German, a fisherman for 40 years, gave the number of big smacks as 40, equally divided between owners and masters. He told the Commissioners that he fished up to 40 miles off Plymouth, where the bottom was sand and shells, closer inshore was sand and mud. Catches included hake, conger, halibut, soles, turbot, red mullet, brill and skate. In summer it was usual to go outside the Eddystone, in the fall of the year to work between the rock and the land where hake was plentiful, and smacks sometimes went as far west as Looe. Inside the Eddystone depths ranged from 25 to 30 fathom, outside up to forty. Mr. Simms said he once helped to heave in 100 dozen hake in one bag, using a runner on the tackle, each weighed up to two stone, but he had known them 56 lb.

There was little sale for skate which was used as bait or manure, but some of the choicest were exported to France and Holland where the fish was considered a delicacy. Monks, a species of skate, were so worthless as marketable fish that they were allowed to the crews as perquisites, but fashions change in public taste, and in January, 1913, there was a strike of fishermen on several of the Plymouth trawlers owing to the decision by owners that only a proportion of the sum realized by the sale of monks was to go to the men, as there was now a ready sale to fried fish shops. Monks have flapper-like wings flying eagle-fashion through the water, and when at rest dig holes in the sand to lie concealed with only the eyes visible, awaiting their prey, which is attracted by the curious projection from the head that gives another name, "angler," to the species.

Plymouth trawlers carried a cloud of light canvas, especially when fishing for hake as it was necessary to keep the net well clear of the bottom. Hulls were designed for speed and a few fast cutters were the 40-ton *Coquette*, built 1868, *Wildfire*, 36 tons, built 1870, and *Excelsior*, 43 tons, built 1878. The fishing ground was exposed to the full force of S.W. gales, especially in winter, hence landings fluctuated considerably, and often days passed before the smacks were able to beat out to sea with their huge mainsails close-reefed.

The usual anchorage was in the Cattewater (Plate 145). On its shores were three building yards, two patent slips and a graving dock, while smacks could be put on the hard at Sutton Pool, a fishing settlement in Saxon times and the home of fishermen ever since. From the yard of W. H. Shilston came many fine cutters, designed by H. V. Prigg and registering up to 47 tons, the best known being *Erycina*, P.H.63, 46 tons, built 1882, and *Vanduara*, P.H.119, 46 tons, built 1880, both were later converted to ketch rig, *Erycina* changing about 1894.

Fortunately one of Mr. Prigg's original sail plans still exists and is now in the National Maritime Museum at Greenwich. From it I made a tracing in March, 1950 (Plan 11, page 331). It is for a cutter with a length overall of 71 ft., L.B.P. 63 ft., L.W.L. 60 ft. 6 in., 36 ft. 6 in. rig with a 9 ft. 6 in. masthead. The topmast is 32 ft., gaff 32 ft., boom 47 ft. 4 in., bowsprit 36 ft. overall, and sheer 1 ft. 7 in.

My tracing from a photostat of the original lines of *Erycina* shows the hollow floors and well-rounded bilges (Plan 12, page 332). The moulded breadth, 17 ft. 2 in., extreme beam 17 ft. 7 in., was rather more fine than that of the average trawler, but she was built for speed and it is interesting to compare her lines with those of the crack Brixham smack *Ibex*, as they sailed against each other in the local regattas many times.

Erycina had a 28 ft. 6 in. bow and when cutter-rigged swung a 49 ft. boom, but this heavy spar, swanging about in a light wind and an oily swell, was a severe strain on the rigging and when the conversion to ketch rig took place it was shortened to 31 ft. 6 in. The position of the mainmast remained the same, but the mizzen was much farther aft than in the later ships built at Brixham and Galmpton. The stern had a squat, rather ugly appearance as Plymouth-built counters were not so graceful as in the Brixham design.

When fishing for hake, two square sails were set on the weather side, the upper one had a 8 ft. yard, the lower 21 ft. with the foot boomed out with a 37 ft. spar (Plan 13, page 333). The bowsprit measured 40 ft. with 28 ft. outboard and in the palmy days her ketch rig was 39 ft. 6 in., but this was later cut down to 37 ft. 6 in.

After fishing for over fifty years *Erycina* was laid up and the late Mr. P. J. Oke took off her lines. I made tracings from his unfinished plans, now at Greenwich (Plans 14, pages 334-5). The depth of hull and fine lines can be seen in Plates 146 and 147. The moulded depth at stern was 12 ft., amidships 9 ft., draught aft 10 ft. 6 in., for'ard 6 ft. 6 in.

Oak keel	– –	60 ft. long, 9 in. sided, 12 in. moulded.
Frames	– –	Oak, doubled, 3 in. $\times$ 3$\frac{1}{2}$ in. moulded.
Fastenings	–	Trenails, split and caulked.
Beams	– –	10 in. sq., main beam 12 in. sq.
Planking	– –	2$\frac{1}{2}$ in. yellow pine.
Main sheet block	–	6 in. $\times$ 8 in., mizzen sheet block 6 in. $\times$ 5 in.
Main halyard block		6 in. $\times$ 8 in.
Deadeyes	– –	Main 9 in. dia. Mizzen 5 in. dia.
Ballast	– –	35 to 40 tons pig iron and scrap.

138 A WELL-CUT SUIT OF
SAILS
Doris May, B.M.46, 43
tons, built by J. W. & A.
Upham, 1899. For thirty
years her sails were cut
and hand-made by F. A.
Jackman.

139 DRESSING SAILS, BRIXHAM
C 1900.
this work, also called "barking,"
was usually done by the crew.

140 A BRIXHAM REGATTA
From left to right. B.M.346 *Guess Again*, 24 tons, built at Brixham, 1916.
B.M.275 *T.H.E.*, 25 tons, built at Brixham, 1908. B.M.48 *Boy Aubrey*, 41 tons,
built at Brixham, 1925. B.M.25 *Maid Honor*, 28 tons, built at Brixham, 1924.

141 *WILLIAM & SAM*, B.M.352
25 tons, built at Brixham, 1917. Winner of Mule class, 1928 Regatta.

2 *SEAFARER*, B.M.258 22 tons, built at Galmpton, 1906. Lying derelict at Galmpton, 20th May, 1950.

3 *WILLIAM & SAM*. B.M.352 Being broken up at Galmpton, May, 1950.

THE OLD STEAM CHEST AT GALMPTON, MAY, 1950.

145 PLYMOUTH TRAWLERS LYING IN THE CATTEWATER, 1931

146 *ERYCINA*, P.H.63
    31 tons, built at Coxside, Plymouth, 1882.

In 22 races at Plymouth regattas *Erycina* won 15 first, 4 second and 2 third prizes, while her local rival *Vanduara*, also designed by Mr. Prigg, took 3 first and 5 second places in eight races (Plate 148).

By 1874 from 60 to 100 Brixham and Plymouth smacks were working in Mount's Bay from mid-February to the end of April in depths of 30 fathom 12 to 14 miles offshore, landing catches at Newlyn where the last London train left at 3.50 p.m., but the G.W.R. would always put on a special if 20 and more tons were available. Many bitter complaints were raised by the local drift-net fishermen, who alleged that the trawlers frequently destroyed scores of mackerel nets in a night, and the antagonism ended in the Newlyn riots, when troops had to be sent from Plymouth to restore order.

Plate 149 shows *Coronet*, P.H.58, 46 tons, built Brixham 1887, leaving Penzance under single-reefed mainsail and small jib, but the bowsprit has not been reefed. By 1890 she was ketch rigged. Plate 150 is the Plymouth sloop, P.H.46. The craft flying the White Ensign may be a Revenue cutter, or she might be the yacht *Oimara*, built 1867, which had a 64 ft. rig calling for five shrouds a side, gaff measured 47 ft. 5 in., boom 72 ft., topmast 49 ft. 6 in. from fid to sheave, while the bowsprit had 49 ft. 6 in. outboard. The fishing smack has one reef down in the mainsail and a winter topmast. The topsail has a very horizontal leech and the halyards are bent to a short yard at head of sail, judging from the amount of spare spar at the peak of gaff the mainsail has not yet been stretched and it looks new.

The fishing grounds lying in the track of shipping passing up and down Channel meant many a Plymouth trawler was run down. On the 18th December, 1890, the 40-ton cutter *Coquette*, built 1868, was sunk in a light easterly wind after collision with S.S. *Fairway* of London, 10 miles S.S.E. of the Eddystone, four of the crew of five being lost. The 50-ton ketch *Delight*, built 1891, was fishing on the 21st March, 1895, when on a calm night she was run down by S.S. *Berlin* of Liverpool, 15 miles S.S.W. of Eddystone, two of the crew of four being drowned.

Vessels running into Plymouth Sound in a hard blow were liable to collide with the breakwater and the 46-ton *Irex*, built 1887 (Plate 151), stranded there on the 17th May, 1899, in a moderate S.S.W. gale. She was another of the smacks built by W. H. Shilston and in his ownership at the time of her loss.

Taking the ground in a sharp floored vessel was always risky and on the 21st March, 1889, the 36-ton cutter *Heroine*, built at Plymouth in 1847, stranded in Penzance harbour in a strong nor'easter and as the tide ebbed fell over, sustaining such damage that she was condemned after a life of 42 years.

A characteristic of Plymouth trawlers was the gypsy windlass many carried instead of the more normal pattern. This is seen in Plate 152 of the 32-ton *Lile* P.H.347, built at Plymouth in 1894. The condition of the starboard bitt tells of the years the bowsprit has been run in and out, likewise the deeply scored rail. The windlass of the Brixham smack *Valerian* is shown in Plate 129.

Lile was still fishing in the 1930's and Plate 153 shows her drying sail in Sutton Pool on the 31st July, 1933. Note the long, graceful bow and the shape of the stern.

In the eighties the Great Western Railway and the London and South Western charged 60s. a ton for mackerel, cod, etc., forwarded at owners' risk, but herring were conveyed at 45s.

Years ago the Barbican presented an animated scene when the quays were crowded with fishing vessels moored bows on—hookers discharging catches of silvery whiting and other line caught fish, trawlers unloading a bewildering variety of soles, plaice, skate, etc., with here and there a lugger or East Coast drifter. Sails and nets hanging in picturesque confusion added a splash of colour, along the stone setts rattled low lorries drawn by sturdy cobs, while buyers in stove pipe hats and bowlers bid against each other as the lots were rapidly disposed of, and fish-wives waited their turn for the remainders which would be hawked around the side streets. Everywhere seethed with activity, especially during the herring season when scores of drifters packed every available inch of space.

Then came the steam trawlers with their certainty of delivery. During the summer months their catches would often be sold long before the first of the smacks came slowly into sight with crews toiling at the long sweeps and vainly hoping that their hauls would make enough to pay expenses. In blowy weather however the sailing fleet could leave their rivals plodding far astern and so get the first of the market, but it was a losing battle. In 1910 there were 52 first-class fishing vessels on the register, in 1922 only 14 large trawlers were working. Now all have gone and to-day sail is just a memory.

CHAPTER TWELVE

RAMSGATE AND OTHER STATIONS

IT was not until the Brixham sloops began working out of Ramsgate in the early years of the 19th century that the Kentish fisherman took to trawling, as hitherto they had used drift nets and two and three-masted luggers. At the end of the Napoleonic wars it is doubtful if more than three or four trawlers of 28 to 30 tons were owned locally and these had been purchased from the Devon men, who fished out of the port during the winter months, returning to Brixham in the early summer. The fact that no mention is made of Ramsgate in the 1833 Enquiry into the state of the Channel fisheries suggests that local trawling was negligible. Sixty to seventy Brixham smacks were fishing in the southern part of the North Sea and landing their catches at Ramsgate, where a big business was done by Fowler's Posting House conveying choice fish to London in light spring vans with two horses driven at posting speed. The journey took seven to ten hours and the traffic paid well, posting masters being glad to forward it at all hours and the fish arrived in far finer condition than that sent by rail in later years.

About 1845, Hull was largely colonized by Ramsgate and Brixham fishermen. Many settled there and prospered. In 1878, John Gidley told how he had been a smack owner for 37 years and was one of the first men to fish in the North Sea from Ramsgate, but was not able to make a living. About 1833 he went to Scarborough and then to Hull, finally fishing out of Grimsby for 21 years. Another Ramsgate man, William Sudds, was reputed to have discovered the famous Silver Pits about 1837. George Fellows, president of the Grimsby Smackowners' Mutual Insurance Society, with £320,000 insured, said he was apprenticed in 1840, at Ramsgate, serving 5 years and 8 months. When out of his time he went to Hull and from 1847 was a master.

Plate 11 shows one of the Brixham sloops, D.H.60, in the Inner Basin in 1857, and Plate 154 is another photograph taken at the same time. In the background is R.E.25 with the old-fashioned curved stem and upright sternpost, and the hull is similar to that seen in the early Barking smacks and the plan of the Southampton fishing hoy of 1804. The trawlers in the foreground, R.E.184 and R.E.6 are of a much later type than D.H.60. The bluff bows have gone, the rig is lofty, with the boom well over the taffrail and the sails are not tanned. R.E.6 has a handspike windlass and a geared winch for'ard of the mast as was Brixham practice, but R.E.184 is fitted with a conical capstan amidships, Barking fashion, which rather suggests that the Thames men made use of the harbour in the early years of the 19th century as well as the Devon fishermen. The straight stem rakes slightly aft with no round to the forefoot, the hull is deep and the sternpost rakes aft. This design with deep heel and wide garboards, often as much as 15 in., was not suitable to local conditions as when the smacks took the ground on the mud bank in the outer harbour their hulls were very liable to wring and this led to narrow garboards and shorter sternposts. When the harbour was built by the Trustees in the second half of the 18th century the engineer, Smeaton, based his design of the quay walls on the shape of the trunk of an oak tree and the lower blocks curved outwards. With a straight stem the tendency was for the forefoot to pound against the stone foundations when there was any run of sea and so sustain damage. In later designs the round-up of the fore-foot was greatly increased as can be seen in Plate 155 of six smacks lying on the hard for hull cleaning and re-tarring. R.160, *Leonora*, 26 tons, built at Rye in 1897, has only a slight curve, but the others show an ever increasing round-up. R.15, *Peace*, 27 tons, built at Ramsgate in 1902, R.257, *Rhodora* and R.185, *Sweet Hope*, built at Porthleven in 1902, are not so extreme as R.152, *W.E.*, 25 tons, built at Ramsgate in 1909.

Plate 156 shows the Military Road which was built at the foot of the cliffs c 1808, to facilitate the embarkation of troops. In 1815 over ten thousand cavalry under Sir John Hill embarked on transports in the course of a few tides en route for Belgium just prior to the Battle of Waterloo. Moses & Deveson's sail loft can be seen under the tideball and the steps giving access from the top of the cliff are as described by Mr. Breach. All the smacks are converted sloops, on the left is *Armenia*, built at Ramsgate in 1861, for J. Macey who later settled at Lowestoft. In 1884 she was converted to ketch rig. R.57 is the 44-ton *William and Mary*, built at Barking, 1866, and fishing until 1901, she has a patent capstan worked with handles. R.244 has her boat gangway open. Yet another photo of the same vintage depicts R.173 with a roller gangway on the port side. At that time the registration letter was either R.E. or R., the latter subsequently becoming the standard.

The Ramsgate men trawled between the headlands of the North and South Forelands, catching quantities of choice fish, turbot, soles, dory and mullet in the bays, but in the winter several went into the North Sea to sail out of Lowestoft, where many owners settled and some of the largest smacks were based, as the numerous sandbanks in the neighbourhood of the Kentish harbour were a considerable danger in bad weather. The majority fished in the southern part of the North Sea and as far west as Rye Bay, but never in the Channel.

In 1863 about 50 trawlers of 45 to 55 tons were registered, practically all the property of fishermen, in 1872 there were 139, averaging 37 tons each, and in June the following year about 100 were fishing locally, the rest away. By 1882 the numbers had decreased to 120, as the period October, 1881, to October, 1882, had seen the loss of 15 smacks with all hands, but by 1887 there was an increase to 140, seven new vessels having been built that year and twelve transferred from other ports.

During the eighties skipper and mate were on shares and the three apprentices drew spending money in port, the cook receiving threepence a night, deckie sixpence and third hand a shilling, " over and above " the stockerbait which consisted of small fish, dogfish, weavers, crabs, etc., sold through the third hand when the smack came into harbour. A charge of 14s. a week was made to board a lad at the Fisher Home Institute, there being 220 apprentices in the port and in 1882 the collector of Customs said there were 52 first-class and 28 second-class trawlers on the register, only one being fitted with a steam capstan.

Block ice was brought over from Norway and stored in ice houses ashore. At first it came in Scandinavian brigs but later the Ramsgate Smack Owners' Ice Co. Ltd., owned the 150-ton schooner *Elizabeth Morton*, built at Ipswich in 1870, and the 190-ton schooner *Luz*, built Dartmouth 1869. Their storage place was situated at the west end of the basin, another company, The Isle of Thanet Ice Co. Ltd., occupied premises at the eastern end.

When the London, Chatham & Dover Railway came into the town surplus fish was sent to Billingsgate and in 1863, 73 tons 13 cwt. was forwarded and 585 tons 13 cwt. the following year. Within twenty years consignments had quadrupled, in 1880, 2,612 tons were despatched and quantities averaged around this figure for several years. Freight to Billingsgate was 40s. a ton for prime fish, 22s. 6d. for offal.

Until the eighties the majority of the smacks were cutter rigged—local name sloops or long-boomers—and even after the ketch rig became popular many cutters were retained to act as carriers, so long as fleet fishing under an admiral remained the practice. The cutters could sail within 4½ points of the wind against the five of the ketches, which trawled to within six points in moderate weather. Ramsgate now had a magnificient fleet and the fish trade was booming, when the smacks were closely packed in the basin, bows on to the quay, the effect was as of a forest of masts and spars (Plate 157). This photograph was taken about Whitsuntide when the trawlers fitted out with summer rig. In the background are a few with short top-masts aloft but the rest have their long spars and crosstrees, some have their foresails furled to the stay with stops, others have them dropped on the stemhead. *Aid* was a wooden tug, built at Blackwall in 1855, and owned by the Board of Trade who administered the harbour. Driven by paddles, her engines developed 50 h.p. and her length was 89.2 ft., beam 18 ft., depth 9.9 ft. Net tonnage 16, gross 112.

The building of the big ketches practically ceased after 1894, when an Act was passed prohibiting any trawler of 25 tons and upwards from going to sea, unless

229

both skipper and mate held certificates and no lad under 16 could sail unless bound apprentice. This did not suit either owners or skippers, many of whom, starting as smack boys, were splendid seamen and fishermen, but not "book larned" and a lad could not be taken to sea to find out if he cared for the life unless he was bound by indentures. The tendency now was to build smaller vessels, known as "toshers", just a fraction under 25 net tons, so avoiding the restrictions. An additional advantage was the fact that towing charges were halved.

The double-ended 120 h.p. steel paddle tug *Aid* had been built at Preston in 1889, to replace the old wooden one of the same name and she was always standing-by in the outer harbour, with banked fires at half-an-hour's notice for steam, as she took the lifeboat to sea on every rescue call and was therefore available to tow smacks in or out if her services were required, 5s. being the charge with a maximum of three at a time.

In the heyday of sail the trawlers carried long main topmasts in summer and set a big gaff topsail on both main and mizzen masts, the yards running up to 17 ft. in length. Jib topsails, set when making a passage or racing to market, were a frequent cause of broken spars if the skippers hung on to them just too long when it began to blow up. On the other hand this sail, being made of lighter canvas, frequently held a breeze when the lower sails hung lifeless. Mr. W. W. J. Cowell told me that once when he was in *Bonnie Belle*, R.447, they were caught in a calm near the Galloper while making for market. Working through the sands they could hear flaps aloft as the jib topsail filled to an air imperceptible on deck and a streak of phosphorescence at the bows showed that the smack was moving through the water. Ahead could be seen a cluster of lights from other vessels, partner fishing, and laying all lashed together as was the custom in a calm. Skipper Janes drew towards them and presently loud shouts told him that they feared being run down, but his reassuring hail was a surprise as the other skippers did not believe a smack could carry way under the conditions prevailing.

Some of the keener men would often set a staysail on the mizzen when in a hurry and for the most part everyone took a pride in his smack, paint being abundantly used to keep a vessel smart. In later years the fashion was for shorter spars, no crosstrees and a jib-headed topsail on the mainmast only, with a bigger gaff and boom sail on the mizzen. Main and mizzen had three reefs in each, using a lacing not points, and the stay foresail had one reef, jibs being set to suit the weather. In the modern smacks all the sails were diagonal-cut.

When the fleet fishing was abandoned, two or three owners would go "partner fishing", transferring catches at sea to any trawler returning home. These trips lasted eight weeks, but a single-boat one was seven days. The smacks took up to two tons of broken ice to sea and 10 to 15 cwt. of coal for use in the galley stove and capstan boiler. Apprentices were carried up to the outbreak of the 1914 war and Mrs. Cowell told me her father, Skipper Janes, had four to five. When his smack came in she went aboard to fetch the washing and cooked for the lads when ashore in her home. Often her dad gave her two shillings to buy chops and steaks for the boys' breakfasts, if they did not have bacon and eggs, and about three loaves would be cut up for each meal, with plenty of butter, no margarine in those days. Dinner was either a leg of mutton, a couple of rabbits or a stew, followed by big helpings of suet pudding, a fish tea or saveloys, etc., rounded off the day's meals to which the ever-hungry lads did full justice. She used to mend and wash their clothes which were provided by her father who paid all the boys' expenses, even haircuts, and gave them spending money. When out of his time an apprentice was given a suit of the best pilot cloth, a complete outfit of fearnought trousers, stockings, vests, jerseys and so on, long leather sea-boots costing £2 and more a pair, the whole rig-out coming to about £20.

Many a lad now went as skipper and soon had a smack "to work out", putting down so much and paying off the balance from his earnings as skipper, being well on the way to a decent living, maybe prosperity, if luck was with him and he was a trier.

Mr. A. H. Lanfear tells me his maternal grandfather, George Sparks, was a Brixham man who brought his wife and family to Ramsgate in a smack about 1861, following an incident when he and the Preventive men did not see eye to eye over some kegs sunk in the basin under his vessel which was confiscated and he saw the inside of Exeter gaol for a few months. His paternal grandfather, Alfred Lanfear, served his time in square-riggers, eventually coming to Ramsgate about 1846. Among his trawlers was the 38-ton sloop *Brave*, built at Sandwich in 1858, and he was the first salesman on the fish market. In the course of time his son, A. H. Lanfear, took over the business to be followed in turn by his son, who told me he started as a boy of 14 in the sail-making loft 54 years ago, when the four men, employed solely on his father's work, could make a suit of sails in a week to ten days, Haywards No. 2 canvas costing 1s. 2d. a yard. Twenty apprentices were indentured and the firm owned their own sail and rigging loft, as well as supplying all stores, etc., to their trawlers. Some of the nets were braided ashore, others purchased away, English warp was always used but another Ramsgate owner, W. Casely, preferred French. Their smacks usually went single boating, but occasionally partner fishing in the summer, taking a ton of ice for a week's trip in the southern half of the North Sea and off the Dutch coast, never going below the latitude of Lowestoft. Catches mainly consisted of choice fish, soles, plaice, brill and whiting, with skate becoming more valuable as demand increased in the fried fish shops. The fish was landed at Lowestoft or Ramsgate as the wind served. The outbreak of war in 1914 saw 43 smacks owned by the firm, one of the largest fleets in the port, and about a dozen fell victims to enemy attack. After the Armistice the remainder were sold, mostly to Lowestoft and West Country buyers, steam trawlers taking their place.

Mr. Fred Mynheer tells me that he went to sea in 1890, at the age of 12 years and 6 months, sailing in the 38-ton dandy *Young Tom*, built at Rye in 1879. Being the son of a fisherman and living in the town he was not apprenticed—after 1894 a lad could not go to sea in a smack unless bound by indentures—his skipper was Dick Curling of whom he speaks highly. As cook young Mynheer was paid 7s. a week and one day was told to boil a duff, having no idea how to set about the job the result looked like a stew, but all his skipper said was " never mind, boy, it's my fault, I should have shown you how to do it ", a striking contrast to the more usual oaths, a cuff round the head or a booting. He first went to the Bristol Channel as third hand in *William and Rose* (Plate 160), she was rammed by a Brixham smack off Godrevy, losing her bowsprit and had to put into Newlyn for repairs, on his return to Ramsgate he sailed as mate at the age of 19. In 1903 he went skipper in the 27-ton *Peace*, built at Ramsgate by Moses in 1902, next having the 26-ton *Patience*, R.159, built at Ramsgate in 1904, taking her " to work out ". After the 1914-18 war he went in steam trawlers, finishing up in 1934 with a record of never having lost a ship or a man, or being dismasted. Mr. Mynheer told me he thought sail was better than steam, especially in bad weather when laying-to, while the two drags in 24 hours contrasted with the seven in the power driven vessel.

Patience towed a 39 ft. beam with a 180 mesh trawl and the following grounds were worked during a twelve month. From Christmas to February, some seven weeks, they were in the vicinity of the North Hinder, about the middle of February they went away to the west'ard, working in the Bristol Channel until May, sometimes having an average of a hundredweight of soles a haul in Padstow Bay, Trevose and Lundy being other good grounds. By Whitsuntide they returned home to fit out for the summer fishing in the North Sea off Lowestoft and Smith's Knoll, each trip lasting eight weeks, four " settlings " in all, the catches being landed at Lowestoft or the home port to which they returned to fit out for another trip. September saw them working off the Dutch coast, where they fished until it was time to come home for Christmas.

Often catches realized very low prices, in January, 1907, fine whiting were sold in the fish market at sixpence a trunk, and plaice at ten a penny !

On the foreshore under the East Cliff was a shipyard and stores, here Messrs. Caught built the hull of *Majestic* in 1816, the first vessel to run under steam power between London and Margate and owned by a Margate Company sponsored by a Mr. Cheesewright, but the venture was not a success. The last ship was the 24-ton cutter *Prince Frederick William*, launched in 1858 and for many years a trader to French ports until she was used as a pleasure yacht, taking large numbers of trippers for cruises round the Goodwins until the early years of the 20th century. When the railway station was built the chalk excavated from the tunnel was dumped into the sea on the west side of the harbour and the shipyard was moved to this site. I recall the ships' figureheads which adorned the gables of the sheds. Here Mr. Moses built many smacks for local owners and Mr. W. H. L. Moses told me that his grandfather, in partnership with Mr. Deveson, owned the sail loft under the cliff.   The smacks were constructed of local elm and oak cut down in the woods around Canterbury and brought to Ramsgate on horse-drawn timber tugs.   He himself started in the yard in 1900, working on the 27-ton *Peace*.   A tosher took three months to build and the price for hull, spars and small boat was £600, cost ready for sea £1,000.   The last trawler to be built in this yard was *New Clipper* prior to the outbreak of war in 1914 and the site is now a car park.

Some came from the yard of Collar & Sons at Whitstable, J. W. Upham and R. Jackman built several at Brixham, while Gibbs of Galmpton, Hoad and G. & T. Smith of Rye were responsible for many a fine smack.   A few of those from Lowestoft had clinker-built hulls, one was *Edith*, R.109, laid down for Tucker in 1894, and the first smacks to be fitted with elliptical sterns came from the Suffolk port.   Hence there were many varieties in design to be seen in the harbour (Plate 159).   The brigantine discharging coal is *Gloriana*, 147 tons, built as a snow at Amble in 1860. Moses & Deveson's sail loft under the tideball has gone and the new Marine Drive sweeps up the face of the cliff.

Generally speaking, Ramsgate smacks had more beam and less draught than those at Brixham and the rig was never so lofty.   One feature which caught the eye was the fashion of having the weft on a short staff hoisted by halyards through a sheave in the cap and sagging away to leeward (Plate 158).   Some had long whip pendants, all had reeving bowsprits.   Bows were short, stems straight with slightly rounded fore-foot, but in many of the later boats the tendency was to round the forefoot more and more and increase the size of the rudder.   This made for easier handling and the smacks could sail round and round a buoy while waiting to leave harbour.   Brixham-built hulls always had a good sheer for'ard and a spring aft, other builders tended towards a low stern for ease in working the gear.   Steam capstans came in early in the eighties, the first smack being fitted out at Grimsby with one by Ransome Sims of Ipswich with engine and boiler below deck, but the Elliott & Garrood pattern with the engine on the top of the capstan soon superseded the other design.

Thanks to Mr. Don Paterson who loaned me the half model now in his possession I was able to take off the lines of one of the large smacks, c1880 (Plans 15, pages 336-7). L.O.A. is 74 ft., L.B.P. 67 ft. 6 in., keel 60 ft. 6 in., moulded beam 17 ft. 2 in., moulded depth of frames amidships, 9 ft. 6 in.

The curved stem rakes aft, entrance and waterlines are hollow, the run long and fine, no doubt fast but wet in a seaway.   I have a photograph of a model of *Patience*, R.249,. which was once in the Science Museum and her lines are very similar but the stem is straighter.

For the cost of one of the large smacks I am indebted to Mr. P. A. Upham for permission to quote from the building book.   In 1886 *Pilgrim* was built by J. W. Upham at Brixham for Hugh Perret and launched on the 2nd August.   Her L.B.P. was 64.6 ft., beam 18.15 ft., depth 9 ft. and tonnage 51 $\frac{82}{100}$.   The agreement for hull, spars and small boat was £620, but various extras brought the total paid up to £667 7s. 10d.   These items included :—

Extra thickness of planking	£17. 10s.
Mast hoops	£1. 14s.
Two galvanised water tanks.	£8.
60 fathom of 13/16 short link chain cable	£12 8s 8d.
Three anchors	£6 2s 4d.

The ice box and fish pounds in the hold took 900 ft. of 1½ in. pine and 120 ft. of deck planking for the platform. Labour was charged at 50s and nails used 7s 6d.

Masts and spars :—

Foremast.	*L.O.A.*		52 ft. 6 in.
Topmast	–	–	30 ft. rig.
Mizzen mast	–	23 ft. 6 in. with 13 ft. pole.
Bowsprit	–	–	34 ft.
Main boom	–	–	34 ft.
Main gaff –	–	30 ft.
Mizzen boom	–	20 ft.
Mizzen gaff	–	16 ft.

The plan of a typical tosher appears on page 338.   I measured up a very beautiful model belonging to the late Mr. Kerbey Cleveland of Margate when it was in my hands for repairs, following extensive damage from bomb blast in the recent war.   It was made by the master rigger at Moses' shipyard and as might be supposed the workmanship in spars, blocks and rigging was excellent, but the hull was not up to the same high standard and its beam was on the narrow side.   The name *Mildred & Jack* appears to be fictitious as R.1 was *Erycina* (Plan 16, page 338).

The measurements were :—

L.O.A.	–	–	57 ft.
L.B.P.	–	–	52 ft. 6 in.
Extreme beam	–	13 ft. 6 in.
Mainmast	–	–	34 ft. deck to cap. 27 ft. 6 in. rig.
Masthead	–	–	7 ft.
Topmast	–	–	27 ft.
Bowsprit	–	–	30 ft. L.O.A., 20 ft. outboard.
Main boom –	–	26 ft.
Main gaff –	–	25 ft.
Mizzen mast	–	34 ft. deck to truck.
Mizzen boom	–	20 ft.
Mizzen gaff	–	18 ft.
Main crosstrees	–	12 ft.
Trawl beam	–	34 ft.

These 24-ton smacks carried 10 tons of pig iron and 8 of iron dross, stowed amidships under the fish room. Shingle ballast was carried in many trawlers and Mr. Moses related how he once had a smack on the slip for repairs and found her planking worn thin with the constant scour as the vessel rolled.

In December, 1939, I met the late Mr. H. L. Summers who told me of his father's remarkable rise from smack boy to owner of a big fleet. Orphaned through the sudden death of his father in the 1850's, the lad was apprenticed at the age of 12½ by the Minster Guardians and had to make his own way in the world. Skipper before he was twenty, this ambitious young man had his first smack built at Ramsgate, the 33-ton cutter *Silent*, and in 1872 she was christened by his youthful son, who also sailed round from Rye in another vessel *Echo*, R.408, built at Rye in 1878. Smack after smack followed in rapid succession, no less than 59 being built to his order, many more were purchased second-hand and H. Summers was among the first owners to have suits of angulated, or diagonal-cut, sails. The 33-ton cutter *Godild*, built at Rye in 1876, was subsequently lengthened 15 ft. at Collar's yard, Whitstable and re-rigged as a dandy.

In 1896-98 he made a bold experiment when three trawlers, *Vie*, *Vis* and *Via*, were built with the spoon bows then fashionable for the big yachts, *Vie* was built at Lowestoft, *Vis* and *Via* by Collar at Whitstable (Plate 158). This " snib bow ", as it was called by fishermen, joined the keel just for'ard of the mast step, the vessels proved to be very handy and did not crush their forefoots if pounding against the quay foundations.

I had with me several photographs and Mr. H. L. Summers instantly identified *Spray*, *Vivid*, *Staghound*, *British Queen* and *Flora Isabella* as belonging to their fleet (Plate 159). He went on to give me the names, registered numbers and place of building of dozens of their smacks, a wonderful feat of memory, as I have since been able to check up most of them in various registers.

In 1877 the average length of keel was 50 ft., in the '80's 55 ft. and the cost of a 35 to 40-ton smack was £800, if fitted with a steam capstan £900, and he showed me a letter from Gibbs of Galmpton, dated June, 1887, stating that they could deliver within ten weeks from the placing of the order. He himself went down to Galmpton to supervise building and on one occasion combined pleasure with business by spending his honeymoon in that sylvan spot. In 1895 the 25-ton *Quartette*, R.164, the fourth built from the same lines, hence the name, did the trip from Dartmouth to Ramsgate, about 215 miles, in 25 hours, good sailing for a vessel fresh from the builders. Many of their large smacks were registered at Lowestoft and worked from the Suffolk station (Plates 35 and 42).

Mr. Summers showed me a fine model mounted in a gilt frame, with an oil painting of the entrance to Ramsgate harbour as a background and, after winding up a clockwork motor, the hull rolled and pitched in a most realistic manner. Unfortunately I had no further opportunity of chats with him as he left the district about the time of Dunkirk and when I enquired in 1946, I learned he had passed away.

In 1949 I met Mr. Shippam, once skipper of *Vie*, R.141 (Plate 158) and he told me she handled beautifully and with a five-cloth jib set and no foresail would work a lee tide, but the staysail was needed for a weather one. She towed with a touch of lee helm and in blowing weather would still work up into the wind. (*Vie*, built Lowestoft 1896, owner in 1907, G. T. Offen, 25 tons.)

In 1912 there were 175 fishing vessels on the register and I can remember the days when the inner basin was so crowded with smacks that it would have been possible to walk across their decks from one side to the other. What a picture they made as they rode in the outer harbour with cables hove short, mainsails hanging in creases, foresail just lifting and wisps of smoke rising from boiler funnel. All around would be the " cheep " of blocks as the great patched sails crept up the masts, the calm greenish water becoming patterned with russet and black shadows and an old Belle steamer coming in crowded with trippers would make the hulls rock gently with the swell from her paddles. Slowly the smacks swing their bows towards the entrance and pass out between the pier heads, Pegwell Bay sparkles with crushed emeralds and creamy lace, the soft sou'west breeze kisses the sails, hulls heel to its caress and pitching more and more the trawlers settle down to that heaving, scrunching battle with their old enemy, the sea.

Another day I recall it was blowing great guns from the east nor'east, glancing out of my window I saw the close-reefed sails of several smacks on the eastern horizon and guessed they were making for Ramsgate. I dashed up to the station and just caught a train which in those days took you right down to the harbour and as it emerged from the tunnel I saw I was in time. The seas were breaking right over the east pier in clouds of foam and spray, and pounding in on the foreshore in a deadly smother. I ran along to the western pier head as the first smack headed in for safety. Now Ramsgate harbour is not easy to enter, you cannot go straight in at right angles to a line between the pier heads, except when the ebb is running, and it was now about high water and the flood stream from the Channel sets strongly across the 208 ft. entrance from two hours before to four hours after H.W. Flying in from the nor'ard, the smacks stood well down into Pegwell Bay before shooting up into the tide and skirting along the western arm towards that narrow gap (Plate 160). A touch of helm and the first one was tearing through and it looked almost certain that she would crash against the wall, but no, carrying tremendous way she drove past the danger into the calmer water inside, rounded to and dropped her sails. I can hear now the hissing roar of the seas, the creak of spars and thunder of canvas. One by one the rest of the fleet made port, confidently handled by men who had probably done it scores of times in similar and worse conditions, but to me it was an incident that lives vividly in my mind's eye long years afterwards. I got soaked through but it was worth it !

Mr. W. W. J. Cowell mentioned an amusing instance when he was skipper of *L.S.D.*, R.150. It was blowing hard from the nor'ard and he was carrying a press of sail to try and save the tide. An outgoing smack hailed him that the gates into the basin were about to shut, so instead of going right down into Pegwell Bay and coming in by skirting the west wall, he slipped along the east pier, shoved the tiller hard down on clearing the head and shot in all ashake. The bollard warmers viewed this proceeding with amazement and thought the smack must be a Lo'sterman bound to the west'ard whose skipper did not know the local conditions. Meanwhile the lock-keeper delayed closing the gates until *L.S.D.* was safely inside the basin.

Many a vessel has missed that narrow entrance to crash against the stone wall and breaking off her bowsprit be rendered helpless to beat back against wind and tide, and so be driven remorselessly ashore on the sands beyond. Smacks could stand up to some hard knocks as the following incident shows. On the 22nd May, 1910, *Boy Will*, R.28, a tosher, registering 24 tons, built at Porthleven in 1897 and owned by H. L. Summers, was leaving harbour with all sail set when the tiller broke just as the east pier head was abeam. She struck the heavy wooden landing stage with a fearful crack, cutting through the thick covering beam and deck, but sustained no damage herself.

Splendidly built though the smacks were and superbly handled, at times disaster overwhelmed the best of them. Somewhere around the 14th October, 1881, seven well-found vessels went missing with all hands. They were the 44-ton *Coquet Water*, built 1862, the 38-ton *Will Watch*, built 1864, the 44-ton *Striver*, built 1870, the 35-ton *William and Mary*, built 1872, the 32-ton *Silvery Wave*, built 1875, the 45-ton *Silver Dart*, built 1877, and the 33-ton *Lily*, built 1876.

On the 29th April, 1882, the fleet was fishing off Schoniven when *Mayflower*, 39 tons, built 1866, *Industry*, 33 tons, built 1856, *Edwin & Mary*, 35 tons, built 1873, *Prince of Wales*, 22 tons, built 1874 and *Catherine*, 44 tons, built 1876, disappeared in a sudden gale. In the following October three more smacks went missing, the 44-ton *Young Rose*, built 1868, the 35-ton *Elisha*, built 1869 and the 33-ton *Regard*, built 1874.

The lives of 75 men out of a fishing population of 915 was a high price to pay for fish.

There was a curious accident in June, 1910, when *Invicta*, R.121, was fishing some 10 miles off Hastings. In a light wind and calm sea, she rolled the mainmast out and it crashed down on deck, breaking the spars and capstan. *Ianthe*, R.106, assisted the disabled smack into harbour.

Mr. Moses tells me he remembers an occasion when six smacks found a dismasted sailing ship in the Channel, all made their warps fast and succeeded in towing the valuable find into port, thereby earning a decent salvage award.

Collisions took their toll. On the 11th January, 1888, the 41-ton *Brilliant*, built at Rye in 1876, was sunk in a light westerly wind by an unknown steamer, 12 miles N.E. by N. of the North Foreland. On the 26th September, 1879, the 41-ton dandy *Racer*, built 1859, was in collision with S.S. *Pleiades*, 3 miles S.S.E. of the North Foreland and was a total loss.   The 41-ton cutter *Transit*, built at Galmpton in 1879, was lost with three of her crew on the 28th September, 1891, after colliding with the German barque *Columbus*, 45 miles E.S.E. of Lowestoft.

Iona, R.96, was run down by S.S. *Ethelwynne* on the 9th October, 1909, and on the 16th December the following year the 23-ton *Alpha*, built 1879, ran foul of the schooner *Nikita* of Plymouth, 4 miles E. by N. of the North Foreland.   The tragedy in so many instances was that the trawlers were within sight of home.

British Queen, R.427, 41 tons, built at Rye in 1879 (Plate 159), foundered 10 miles E. of Smith's Knoll Light Vessel on the 12th September, 1912.   *Valiant*, R.233 stranded on the Naze about 8 a.m. one Sunday morning in June, 1910, and was abandoned by her crew who were picked up by a yacht and landed at Walton-on-Naze.   The trawler refloated, was taken into Harwich and reboarded by her own crew.   On the 5th October, 1912, the 29-ton cutter *Excelsior*, built at Hull in 1857, was burnt out 15 miles S.S.E. of Hastings.

So far as I can trace the years 1879 to 1913 saw a total of 65 smacks lost, of these 30 foundered, 20 sank after collision, 13 stranded and two were lost by fire.

Speaking of the war years Mr. A. H. Lanfear said that *Rhodora*, R.257 ran ashore on the French coast and as no one was allowed to go over and salve her she became a total loss.   *Alessie*, R.189, built at Kingsbridge by Date Bros. in 1909, ran up on to the shingle at Dungeness as the usual light was not showing, but was refloated in a parlous condition and eventually sold to Brixham owners who repaired her and she fished out of the Devon port for many years until she was sold for conversion to a yacht c 1930.   *Reliable*, R.242, was found wrecked in a Cornish bay with all sail set and no trace of her crew.   It was believed that Skipper Ellison, second hand, Peel, and the deck hand, Holden, took to the small boat when the trawler was attacked by a German submarine, which was unable to complete the sinking, perhaps being forced to submerge before having time to place the bomb on board.   No trace of the missing men was ever found.

In 1906 the register contained the names of 168 fishing vessels, in 1910 there were 141, but the terrible years of the 1914-18 war brought about the end of the sailing fleet.   Several smacks were mined in the first few months, among them *Industry*, R.227, built at Galmpton in 1906, lost with all hands (Plate 161).   Close proximity to the Continent saw the harbour exposed to many a raid by Zeppelins and Gothas. Some owners sent their vessels to fish out of West country ports, others sold them for what they would fetch.   *Harry Martin*, R.156, built at Porthleven in 1907, was sold to Brixham owners for about £200 and re-named *Seacroft*, B.M.363.   It was heart-breaking for men who had struggled to save enough to buy a smack of their own to be forced to sell at a give-away price.   Skipper Janes had to part with his *Bonnie Belle*, R.447, as he could not afford to keep spending money on her upkeep when she was laid-up.   After the war he had to ship as a paid hand.

Following the cessation of fishing many of the younger men volunteered for service in minesweepers and the Dover Patrol. Among them was Mr. W. W. J. Cowell who told me that he first went to sea at the age of 16 on the 27th March, 1901, being apprenticed with Skipper George Janes of the smack *Bonnie Belle*, R. 447, 29 tons, built at Ramsgate, 1880. He received the usual spending money and the following salvage awards, should any come their way, as cook 5s., deck hand 10s., and third hand £1 for every £100 received by the vessel. On his return from the first trip he was told of his father's death and was then taken care of by the skipper, eventually marrying his daughter. Out of his time on the 5th April, 1905, he served in *Leonora*, R.160, 26 tons, built Rye 1897, sailing as third hand in summer, mate in winter. In Plate 155 he can be seen tarring down her hull. After eight years he went mate in *Lizzie*, 29 tons, built Galmpton 1899, until she was laid up early in the war, then he sailed as skipper in *L.S.D.*, a nearly new smack, but there was soon some feeling about this as another man thought he should have command. He took over and went to sea with a mate, a one-time fisherman, who had been ashore running a tea room for twenty-five years. The smack was never heard of again.

Mr. Cowell now applied for service in the Dover Patrol and whilst awaiting his call, shipped aboard S.S. *Tregarth* for a trip to Penarth for coal, sailing under sealed orders they later discharged at Chatham. Returning to Cardiff early in December, 1914, he found his papers to join up at Dover and was with the patrol until the end of the war, being principally engaged in sinking mines and laying anti-submarine nets, the usual routine being two nights in harbour, and four to five at sea. On the 11th June, 1917, they slipped about 5 a.m. and presently sighted two German seaplanes dropping bombs on the net buoys. Mr. Cowell, now a gunner, opened fire with a 6-pounder Hotchkiss and after three or four rounds hit the first plane which was flying towards them to attack. The engine blew up and the drifter *I.F.S.*, a Yarmouth boat, steamed through the falling pieces. Mr. Cowell now engaged the second seaplane, winging it after a few shots, it came down on the sea and the two Huns climbed out on the wings and were picked up. Presently the patrol yacht *Zenda* came up to enquire the reason for firing, took the prisoners aboard and started towing the wreck but it soon sank. For this fine exploit Mr. Cowell was awarded the D.S.M., and a D.S.O. went to the naval lieutenant in charge, who received his medal from King George V, but Mr. Cowell was then at Dunkirk teaching the French how to use mined nets and received his award later at the hands of Rear Admiral Bacon.

One night the patrol, anchored in the vicinity of the North Goodwin, saw smoke and flames coming from the funnels of approaching destroyers and they were taken for ours until fire was opened and seven drifters sunk, but luckily *I.F.S.* escaped damage. On another occasion off Zeebrugge they were attacked in daylight and one drifter was disabled owing to her engine running hot. The crew was taken prisoner but were later exchanged and the skipper was made master of *East Britain*, Captain Bird's special drifter, Mr. Cowell sometimes serving as mate when inspection trips were made round the mined nets, those automatically exploded when anything got entangled. One end was anchored and the line of nets paid out, each mine weighing 94 lb., the other end was buoyed, batteries connected up and events awaited. Once when hauling they discovered German naval caps and clothing in the nets, the far end was on the bottom with the battery riddled with bullets. The U-boat had evidently tried to free himself by firing at the battery when it was on the surface at slack water as buoys, etc., were submerged when the strong tides were running.

Later in the war seven or eight drifters lay head to tide, watching the lighted buoys, whose 2,000 C.P. flares burned for 20 minutes, lighting up the Straits with an unearthly glare but making the darkness more intense than ever when they burnt out. One Sunday a periscope was sighted at the back of the Varne but as they were only armed with rifles the submarine got away down Channel.

After the Armistice Mr. Cowell went mine sweeping and on demobilization in June, 1919, served in steam trawlers for 25 years, often finding queer hauls in the trawl. Once a piece of the U-boat from which Roger Casement landed in Ireland came up and I saw this relic in use as a door stop. In the recent war Mr. Cowell served for a time in the Milford Haven patrol boats and after hostilities ceased went trawling out of Margate in a small boat, finishing his sea going career as the last skipper of *Provider*, a Ramsgate steam trawler built at Appledore in 1907.

To return to the 1914-18 war. An annual loss of about £100,000 crippled owners and of the 155 smacks sailing out of the port in 1914, no less than 51 were lost by enemy action. One of the blackest days was the 24th March, 1917, when six were sunk 12 to 15 miles S.E. to S.W. of the Eddystone. They were R.126, *Endeavour*, 25 tons, built Galmpton 1894, *Enigma*, R.175, 24 tons, built Porthleven 1898, *H.C.G.*, R.253, *Qui Vive*, R.22, 22 tons, built Porthleven 1900, *Reindeer*, R.62, 28 tons, built Galmpton 1889, and *Satanita*, R.52, 30 tons, built Rye 1900. Three of these belonged to one owner, and in addition, *Alice*, L.T.962, *Boy Walter* and *Mavflower* were sunk, making nine in all. Mr. Albert A. Horne, who was in *Enigma*, spoke to me in moving tones of their feelings of horror and dread when that sinister grey shape rose up out of the sea in the midst of the fishing fleet and began sinking one vessel after another, of their relief when they saw that the small boats were being allowed to leave before the smacks were sunk, and finally when it came to their turn and they had to abandon everything. The wheel of fate indeed turned full circle during the life of this old fisherman—as a young man he was at Lowestoft that bitter winter day when a smacksman brought in the survivors of the German liner *Elbe*, now 22 years later the Huns were ruthlessly sinking unarmed and innocent fishermen and in the recent war he was twice in trawlers which were bombed and sunk, and in another which was machine gunned.

After the Great War the fishing at Ramsgate languished, as the few owners who contemplated replacing their losses were put off by the high prices asked for building new smacks. In 1922, Robert Jackman & Sons of Brixham submitted a tender of £1,225 for a vessel 50 ft. on keel, 17 ft. 2 in. beam and a depth of 7 ft.

147 *ERYCINA*, P.H.63
Note hollow floors and fine entry.

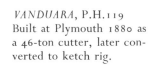

48 *VANDUARA*, P.H.119
Built at Plymouth 1880 as
a 46-ton cutter, later converted to ketch rig.

149 *CORONET*, P.H.58
Built at Brixham as a 46-ton cutter in 1887, converted to ketch 1890.
The mainsail has one reef down and small jib is set.   Topsail sheet leads
through block on pendant at masthead.   One sweep is out on starboard
side aft.

150 LEAVING PENZANCE, c 1895

P.H.46 has one reef down in mainsail, topsail has a very short yard at head, the boy is sculling the smack's boat, in foreground is a lug-rigged crabber.

152 *LILE*, P.H.347
32 tons, built at Plymouth, 1894.   Note gypsy windlass, winch, fore horse and bowsprit heel rope with its fall going to capstan.

151 *IREX*, P.H.200
46 tons, built 1887 at Plymouth by W. H. Shilston.

153 DRYING SAIL, SUTTON POOL, 31st JULY, 1933. *LILE*, P.H.347.

4 in.   By the time sails and fishing gear had been supplied there would have been little, if any, change out of £2,000.   The specification read :—

Keel of English elm.
Stem, sternpost, frames, keelson, shelves, beams, knees, covering boards and stanchions of English oak.
Floors 5 in., Frames 6 in. by 4 in. and 4 in. by 3½ in.
Plank 2¼ in. from gunwale to bilge, three strakes of 3 in. elm at bilges, 2 in. elm bottom.
Ceiling 1½ in. pitchpine.   Clamp 1¼ in. pitchpine to bilge, three strakes of 2¼ in. oak bilges.
Bottom 1¼ in. fir.
All outside and middle line fastenings to be galvanized iron.
Outside plank fastened with ⅝ in. galvanized bolts, bilges through-bolted and clenched, 2¼ in. pitchpine deck, dowelled.
One winch.
Oak chocks to capstan.   Gangway rollers.   Two tillers.
Cabin and engine room hatches with brass hinges and glass knobs.
Forecastle, platform, ice box and fish pounds.
One set of spars.   One boat with one pair of oars and boathook.
One set of blocks.   Mast hoops and deadeyes.
Ironwork to hull, spars and blocks, including castings, jib tack and topsail halyard chains.
Stem band and after shoe.
Cooking stove with galvanized iron funnel.
Oak tow post.
Wire standing rigging, forestay and hanks.   Gaff strops.
Vessel rigged and spars put in place.
Cement concrete.   Bolt holes cemented.
Vessel scraped and payed with one coat of tar and two coats of composition.
Name cut and gilded.
Bulwarks, deck work and spars three coats of paint.
Cabin and engine room grained and varnished.
Trucks gilded.
Ballast vessel with ten tons of iron, remainder limestone.
One trawl beam.   One pair of heads.
Pay the Board of Trade fees.

In 1923 only 26 sailing trawlers remained on the register and by 1931, *Quartette*, now R.361, was the sole survivor although a few auxiliaries were, and still are, fishing.   Sold during the war to a Devon owner and registered at Brixham, *Quartette* came back to Ramsgate ownership, sailed for a time out of Newhaven, then from her home port and I often used to see her working up and down the inshore ground opposite my house, together with *Volante*, R.110, which was built at Brightlingsea in 1893, measured 48.6 by 13.8 by 6.1, 20 G.T., 8 N.T., and was fitted with a 24 h.p. motor.   I photographed them in the inner basin at Ramsgate in October, 1932 (Plate 162).   *Volante* is on the inside berth, *Quartette* outside, and between them lies a cutter, R.47.

In 1935, *Quartette* was sold and went up to the E. India Dock to take in stores, etc., prior to sailing for Rio on the 12th April, forty years after her launch.

About midnight on Thursday the 12th October, 1950, *Volante*, then 57 years old, left Ramsgate for the fishing grounds near the Kentish Knock, about 13½ miles off Margate. The trawl was shot and the 62-year-old skipper, Peter Stupples, remained on deck whilst the mate, A. Bowers, aged 68, and the 50-year-old engineer, S. Harvey, went below. At 6.10 a.m. there was a tremendous explosion and the stern of the trawler was lifted right into the air and came down with a terrific bump, splitting open the whole of her bottom. The mine must have been 250 feet astern and about 13 fathom down. The men rushed up from below and with the skipper just had time to jump into the boat and row away, *Volante* disappearing within ten minutes. Fortunately the sea was fairly calm for the nine mile row to the Tongue Light vessel, which was reached about midday, the survivors being later taken ashore in the Ramsgate lifeboat.

Another link with the days of sail was broken.

SECONDARY TRAWLING STATIONS

DOVER

DOVER was never much of a trawling station although in the early 19th century 40 to 50 large sized sloops, mostly owned by Torbaymen, worked out of the port, but the poor harbour facilities, strong tides and danger of collision with the cross-channel packets prevented development. In the early sixties I find only 7 tons 7 cwt. and 7 tons 8 cwt. of fish forwarded by rail to Billingsgate in successive years, so one can hardly say the industry was flourishing, except perhaps for local sales. In 1872, there were 21 first-class fishing vessels, 20 in 1876, but two years later only 17 trawlers were registered, of 37 to 50 ft. length of keel and working with a 40 ft. beam and a net 2½ to 3 in. mesh in the cod end. The principal grounds lay on the Varne and Ridge banks, where turbot, brill, plaice and whiting were taken, the turbot varying from 8 to 20 lb. in weight.

An old photograph in my collection shows these early vessels were cutter-rigged, similar in design to the small sloops working out of Ramsgate, but *Surprise*, D.R.11, is a somewhat larger smack (Plate 13). Many of these cutters converted to ketch rig, the long boom being shortened and a mizzen mast stepped clear of the tiller (Plate 14). The true ketches never ran up to any size, the majority being toshers of under 25 tons, and to judge from other photos many and varied were the hulls. Some are half-decked with square boat transoms, others clinker-built with very short bowsprits and foresail tack well inboard, and one print shows a small ketch with a large jib set with its head to mizzen hounds, and tack boomed out on a pole, and she is actually trawling inside the harbour whilst one of the crew helps with a long sweep. *Mary Ann*, D.R.20, was built at Yarmouth in 1867 as a lugger and later converted to dandy rig with the bowsprit reeving through a gammon iron on the starboard side of the stem, to port she had a heavy sheave used when recovering lost anchors, a lucrative occupation in the days of sail, when vessels sheltering in the Downs often had to slip their cables in a hurry if the wind shifted suddenly. In the three years 1867 to 1869, over 600 anchors and cables were recovered and sold by auction at the Lord Warden Depot. The Board of Trade allowed salvage at the rate of £2 for every ton weight of anchor and chain. On one occasion two Margate luggers, *Secret* and *Enterprise*, landed 18 swept up between the Forelands, and anchors weighted 46 cwt. and more ! Often over 500 sail of ships would shelter in the roads and when they all got under weigh it was a sight indeed. A constant stream of traffic passed through the Straits, on one day alone in January, 1861, over 100 sailing vessels of all nationalities passed Dover, a glorious spectacle.

Mary Ann was still on the register in 1931 and I have already mentioned the long life of the little *Forget-me-not*, which is still fishing in South African waters.

In 1906 only ten fishing vessels sailed out of Dover and four years later numbers had fallen to five, but the " Gateway to England " will always be remembered in trawling history as being the first to be used by Brixham pioneers before the time of the French Revolution.

RYE

As befits one of the premier Cinque Ports, Rye has fishing traditions dating back for centuries, but little evidence is available as to the early history of trawling in Rye Bay where soles of the choicest quality have always been found. The complaint registered by the Mayor of Hythe in 1622, suggests that fishermen and others from Rochester and Stroud worked in that area. Although there is mention in the 1833 Report concerning the French poaching in Rye Bay there is nothing about any vessels belonging to the port, whose ancient harbour had by then lost much of its importance through silting-up. The very limited local market in the town and villages on Romney Marsh had been the reason for the landing of catches at Folkestone and Hastings. Rye has always been the port of registry for Hastings boats so it is difficult to trace how many actually fished from the Rother, but in 1878 John Miles stated there were 29 trawlers at Rye, mostly fishing in winter on the Diamonds, a ground 18 miles long and 9 broad, abreast of Dungeness, and in the bay itself in the summer months. William Hoad, smackowner, added some interesting facts about the gear used. The mesh was 19 to the yard in the upper part of the net, 27 in the cod, and the trawl was fitted with lines which were kept taut and the net slack, as the boat towed by the lines. This method was more expensive than a beam, but it enabled small fish to escape through the meshes as much of the fishing was done over the spawning grounds. Depths in Rye Bay varied from 3 to 6 fathom, but off Dungeness the water deepened to 16 and 18 fathom.

Rye smacks had their bowsprits to port and roller gangway to starboard as owing to the prevailing S.W. winds trawling was usually done on that side, thus keeping the bows to seaward, with the gear out to port they would always be working in towards the land.

In 1906 there were 33 sail on the Rye register, 29 in 1910, but several were the big luggers belonging to Hastings. In 1912 *Naomi & Lizzie*, R.X.74, a 27-ton cutter, built at Rye in 1881, was fishing in Rye Bay on the 9th September, when she was run down by the big four-masted barque *Lawhill*, 2 lives being lost.

The last sailing trawler of fish out of Rye was *Three Brothers*, R.X.153, built by G. & T. Smith and launched on the 15th July, 1896, from their yard on the Rother. Her lines were taken off by the late P. J. Oke in 1936, when she was laid up, with topmast struck and sails unbent (Plate 163). In August, 1946, I found her lying in a mud berth at Smith's yard and scrambling on board found that neglect and decay had played considerable havoc, but the following June my friend Mr. H. Oliver Hill took a snap of her down at the quay and it shows a big skylight fitted just aft of the mainmast and new strakes of planking in the bulwarks (Plate 164).

The Plans 17, pages 339-40, show her measurements to be :—

L.O.A.	— —	58 ft. 9 in.
L.B.P.	— —	51 ft. 5 in.
Moulded beam	—	15 ft.
Depth in hold	—	6.65 ft.
G.T.	— —	24.88.
N.T.	— —	19.18.

MASTS AND SPARS

Mainmast, deck to cap — —	36 ft. 6 in. Dia. 11 in. to 8 in.
Masthead — —	8 ft. Topmast. 26 ft. winter, 32 ft. summer. Dia. 6–3 in.
Main boom — —	26 ft. 2 in. Dia. 6 in. Gaff. 27 ft. 8 in. Dia. 5 in.
Mizzen mast, deck to truck — —	35 ft. 6 in. Dia. 7–3 in.
Mizzen boom —	16 ft. 3 in. Dia. 5½ in. Gaff. 17 ft. 6 in. Dia. 5–4 in.
Mizzen topsail yard	20 ft. Dia. 3 in.
Bowsprit. L.O.A. —	30 ft, outboard 20 ft. Dia. 8–5½ in.

The name of G. & T. Smith stood high as builders of repute, but the yard was about derelict when I was there, a half-finished hull for a Government fishing vessel lay on the stocks and was still there some years later. What did seem a shame was that many of the half models for ketches, sailing barges and smacks lay out in a bed of nettles, just cast on one side now their usefulness was done. I offered to give them a good home, but nothing came of it, as soon afterwards the place was in the hands of the Official Receiver. It had changed ownership some time previously.

FLEETWOOD AND LIVERPOOL

ON the north-west coast the fishing grounds in the Irish Sea were explored by the Brixham men in the first decade of the 19th century and one or two owners settled at Fleetwood and Liverpool, but little trawling appears to have been done as in the 1830's only two boats were fishing out of Fleetwood with small beam trawls.

The grounds in Liverpool Bay, between the coast and the Isle of Man, and More-cambe Bay yielded good hauls of soles, cod, plaice, haddock and roker and with the close proximity of large manufacturing towns offering markets, it was not long before the industry developed. In 1855 only eight trawlers were based at Fleetwood, but within four years the numbers had risen to 32 and in 1872 there were 53 first-class fishing vessels registered there and 35 at Liverpool, the port of registry for Hoylake. In 1876 Fleetwood had 70, Liverpool 41, and the years 1885 to 1895 were probably those of the greatest prosperity so far as sail was concerned.

When the size of the smacks increased a new ground was worked in Cardigan Bay where a bottom of sand and mud close inshore at Aberystwyth yielded fine hauls of turbot, brill, soles and ray. Thomas Cooper, a smackowner of Hoylake, said in 1878, that he used a 47 ft. beam and in his first season on this ground had 87 cod, averaging 20 lb. apiece, in one take on the 6th March. The ground was 20 miles long and two to six in breadth, but there being no harbour in the vicinity meant that a smack caught out in bad weather had to run for Holyhead, 60 miles to the nor'ard, or Pwllheli 38 miles away where the harbour dried out. The bigger ketches were usually away for 5 to 6 days, but the smaller cutters working inshore spent only a day at sea. They fished with a 26 ft. beam.

A typical ketch registered 38 to 40 tons, with a 48 ft. keel, and the majority were built in the Isle of Man, Whitehaven, Fleetwood, Freckleton and a few at Brixham. Floors were long and flat so that the smack could take the ground, lines were full for'ard, but finer aft.

Trawl beams ran up to 40 to 50 ft. in length and were generally of greenheart with the iron heads weighing 160 to 200 lbs., the nets were of hemp with meshes $4\frac{1}{2}$ to 7 in. and the 150 fathom manilla warp was hauled in by a hand winch at the bows and a dandy wink aft. Steam capstans were fitted in the early nineties.

Crew numbered four men and a boy and the earnings were divided into $6\frac{1}{2}$ shares, the owner taking $2\frac{1}{2}$ and the men one each. They gave the boy 1s. a week each, sometimes 1s. 6d. if they felt generous after a successful fishing. The lads went to sea at the age of 12 and after 3 years were entitled to a half share, rising to three-quarters and finally a full one at 17 or 18. The days were divided into four watches, two floods and two ebbs.

Plate 165 shows two Fleetwood smacks racing to market. F.D.51 is *Ida*, 32 tons, built at Brixham in 1869 and fishing up to 1915.

Plate 166 is of the Hoylake owned *Margaret Alice*, L.L.52, 51 tons, built 1875 at Port St. Mary, I.O.M. She is towing a weather tide in a light wind, the warp passing out right aft with a " breeching " fast to the taffrail, the lead-in over the bow roller to the winch can also be seen. The sail-maker has been busy judging from the numerous patches.

Milford Haven was frequently used by the Brixham fleet, but few trawlers were owned locally, in 1870 only thirteen being registered. The regular season on the Tenby ground was from April to September when the Devon men left for home and the local smacks laid up for the winter. One of them, M.18, is seen in Plate 167 making sail, with the crew about to sweat up the peak halyards. The topmast is housed and bowsprit run in, and the mizzen has new reef bands and linings.

ISLE OF MAN

TRAWLING was never on an extensive scale in the island, only a few smacks belonging to Douglas owners in the early seventies. Mr. Gawne writes that about 1882 the building of nickies for the herring fishing declined and some of the yards built a larger sized " lugger ", specially for trawling. These carried the original rig, dating back to the 1830's, of a gaff mainsail and a lug mizzen. They are fully described in my book " Sailing Drifters ". Josie Qualtrough laid down *Jane*, *Bonny Jane* and *Mary Magdalen*, each about 60 ft. overall, and many were built for Irish owners and fished away. About 1887 some of the so-called " luggers " converted to true ketch rig, with a gaff and boom mizzen sail, the long outriggers having proved a nuisance in a crowded harbour.

Alice, C.T.54, built 1886, is seen in Plate 168, just after her launch at Port St. Mary. She has a gaff mainsail and lug mizzen, and in Plate 169 her trawl net is hanging up to dry and the lugsail is stowed up and down the mast. The mainmast is stepped in a tabernacle and can be lowered by the forestay tackle consisting of two treble blocks. The hull in the foreground has the hauling winch for'ard and the dandy wink on the port side, and washstrakes are fitted on top of the rails. The men on the smack astern are wearing small, round sealskin caps.

Plate 170 shows three Ramsey trawlers putting to sea about fifty years ago. R.Y.42 is *Faithful* and the one to wind'ard is *Hearts of Oak*, R.Y.1, 24 tons, built at Peel in 1876, and fishing up to 1924.

Fourteen was the maximum number of smacks in Port St. Mary and their usual fishing ground lay off the Calf, the trawlers returning home when a good catch was on board, but they always reckoned to be in on Friday night for the weekend at home.

The trawlers also worked between the island and Liverpool. In September they were off Ramsey Light vessel, 15 miles E.N.E. of Douglas, in January off Douglas Bay Head, then to the Calf and round the Peel in summer, here the bottom was mud across to Ireland. William Proctor said he had 160 pairs of soles in one haul in 1878 from 38 to 50 fathom off the Calf, and the best grounds lay S.W. of the Calf in 50 fathom where soles were 8 to 10 lb. a pair.

The 1905 Olsen's shows only nine first-class fishing vessels registered at Ramsey and fifteen at Douglas and the name of *Alice* C.T.54 does not appear.

This brief reference to the secondary stations concludes the circuit of English waters as sailing trawlers were never owned in Scotland, except possibly in isolated instances. After such a prolonged lapse of time it has needed painstaking search to get into touch with men who knew the smacks in their prime, and to find photographs of every registration. Much has been lost for ever and as the years roll by it becomes more and more difficult to trace authentic information. The full story can never be told, but gleanings here and there have enabled me to piece together some sort of coherent record. Without the aid of those men I have mentioned it would have been almost impossible and I wish to express my warmest appreciation to those smacksmen, builders, shipwrights and sail-makers who placed information at my disposal and who alone can speak at first hand of those now far-off days.

CHAPTER THIRTEEN

MASTER HAND

WHEN I had completed my book " Spritsail Barges of Thames and Medway " with a full set of scale plans of the Whitstable barge *Kathleen*, which I measured up single-handed, I began to think of compiling a similar record of a sailing trawler. This was not going to be an easy job as no port lay within reach where I was likely to find a suitable hull. Lowestoft and Brixham were out of the question on account of distance, while Ramsgate had ceased to have anything worth while after the 1914-18 war. However, on Tuesday, 9th April, 1946, an anniversary day in our lives, my wife and I went over to Ramsgate to spend the afternoon and it proved to be another of my lucky days. One or two small auxiliaries lay alongside the cross-wall, but were not of sufficient interest to warrant measuring-up as I had in mind one of the big North Sea smacks, not a cut-down tosher.

Looking idly round the basin, I spotted a low, black hull with a Lowestoft registration lying by the tug *Doria* and I hastened off to see what she was, leaving my wife to go and look at the shops, the prime object or should I say the ostensible reason for our visit ! I soon picked out the letters L.T.1203, *Master Hand*, built Rye by G. & T. Smith in 1920, and wondered if this was to be the end of my quest. The hull looked in good condition, while the fact that masts and spars lay on deck promised a more simple measuring task than if they had been stepped. I at once hunted up the Assistant Harbour Master who informed me the hull had just been towed round for conversion to full power at Messrs. Claxton & Co's shipyard. I saw Mr. George Claxton, explained my wish to record the lines, etc., of one of the old sailing smacks, and he most courteously told me I could go on board at any time to take the necessary measurements. This was indeed a stroke of luck as here was what I had been seeking, almost on my doorstep and involving a cycle ride of only six miles each way.

On the Saturday I went over about 4 p.m. and found the hull alongside the old Military Road, but was unable to get on board, so contented myself with a few sketch plans and contemplated the task which lay ahead, to measure up every detail and record the lines on paper. Had I known then that this was going to mean dozens of hurried visits at all sorts of odd hours, for duty called for eight hours of my days, and the taking, single-handed, of over three thousand measurements, well, I might not have been so thrilled !

Monday saw me over about the same time, the basin had been drained and numerous objects lay in the thick mud, the kids having the time of their lives collecting souvenirs. I was thus able to inspect the underwater lines before meeting Mr. Joe Spicer, the master rigger who, having been in smacks himself, was most helpful when he learned the object of my visit. I went on board to see what lay before me, it was pretty dark below as only one cover could be removed, a capstan whelp or two lay on all the others to prevent any unauthorized access. Although the hull had been used throughout the war as an obstruction to prevent seaplanes landing on the Norfolk Broads, it was as tight as a bottle and the only water in the bilges was rain which had seeped in. The good Sussex oak was a golden yellow colour, sweet-smelling and hard as iron, as I soon discovered when I tried to get a gimlet in to hold the end of my tape measure. I worked away on deck until it was too dark to see the figures and decided to come over the next morning for as long as possible, luckily it was a leave day, as Mr. Claxton had told me they were going to lift off masts and spars if the crane was available.

After an early breakfast I was on board about half-past eight, the sun was hot and beat down on the glassy calm water slowly filling the basin. I had a torch with me as I knew all the sail lockers, fish pounds, ice-box, etc., would be gutted out as soon as the work of conversion began and I wanted to have as much recorded as possible before that happened. At 11.15 a.m. the men began to warp the hull under the crane, the mainmast was placed in slings and slowly the tackle took the strain as four men worked the handles. Inch by inch the two or more tons weight was raised from the deck to be swung out over the harbour, head towards the quay. How I regretted my inability to take photographs as it was impossible in those days to obtain film for my camera. Gradually the mast was steadied round by a couple of men hauling on ropes at the heel, a little more and it came in end-on, swung round and was lowered gently to the ground. I looked at my watch, five minutes past twelve. Shifting the main boom was a lighter job, the handles fairly flew round, Mr. Spicer had judged the centre of balance to a nicety and within five minutes the spar lay along-side the mast. Then the capstan was lifted, twisting slowly round and round as it swung over the rail to be lowered in a couple of minutes. Good going. The next job was to raise the boiler, weighing about 12 cwt., from its bed and through the small hatch directly above. A wire span was shackled round and at a word from Mr. Claxton lifting commenced. A quiet " go steady " and the top just entered the opening and scraped through, less than ten minutes work saw it ashore to be followed by the mizzen mast. The first lift showed the weight was not quite balanced. " Lower away," from Mr. Spicer " sling it a little more aft ". Then " try her again, boys ", but no, the spar was still unbalanced so another adjustment. " Now try her." "All right, Joe" and soon the three-quarter ton weight was lying on the quay. Eight minutes only had elapsed from start to finish.

The bowsprit was the next, first a rope sling was secured well aft, the crane took the weight and the spar was man-handled back, clear of the bitts. A wire sling was made fast and then "Take her up". A call from the crane men, "Now you can swing her aft, Arthur". "Hold her—all clear—heave—half a mo—lower away," something had fouled. "Try now—not too bad—swing down and push a lashing on." A rope was passed round the for'ard end for steadying purposes and out went the heavy spar over the harbour and in on to quay inside five minutes. The main gaff was slung, lowered for readjustment and ashore in three minutes, the mizzen boom and gaff went together in a couple of minutes, then the small boat and by ten minutes past one the deck was clear. The hull was warped to its old berth and I returned home, to be back once more the following afternoon to find the basin dried out and no means of getting on board, but the time was not wasted as I measured up some of the spars. Later Mr. Spicer fixed up a ladder and I went below to crawl about in semi-darkness recording all I could, on emerging at dusk rain was falling heavily so had a very wet ride home.

On my next visit I noticed the spacing of the beams varied in every instance so plenty of work to keep me occupied and when I went on deck I found to my horror that the ladder had been removed and a blank wall faced me. This was a blow, as I could see no means of escape, not a soul was about and it was almost dark, eventually I heard footsteps and my shouts brought a man who peered over to see what was the matter. He had fortunately been fishing off the end of the pier and was on his way home. I threw up the end of a rope I found lying on deck, told him how to belay it round a bollard and with my gear under my arm, my heart in my mouth, I climbed on to the rail, praying that the strands would take the strain. A deep breath and then hand over fist, a climb I learned at school over 35 years before. Phew ! I was jolly glad when I was able to scramble over the edge of the quay and let the keen east wind cool my fevered brow !

One notebook after another was filled with sketches and dimensions, each visit saw more and more of the fittings below gutted out, until the hull was open from bow to stern, but by then everything had been recorded. I crawled up into the counter to puzzle over the layout of the stern timbers and measure them by the light of a torch, while the air space left for ventilation between clamp and ceiling was the only means of inspecting the frames, allowing the insertion of a thin steel rule.

Then came the drawing out of the plans and gradually one thing after another checked up, but when I set out the deck plan against the below-deck one I was 8 inches out. Try as I could I was unable to make it different, my brain reeled with adding up dozens of measurements to fractions of an inch, time after time, but still that error remained. To cut a long story short it was not until I had the specification before me some weeks later that I traced the trouble. There were double bulkheads, with insulation between, at fore end of engine room. When working below from key points I had no idea that the bulkheads were other than normal thickness, but I was rather bucked to find everything had checked up so well.

One worry remained, the spacing of floors and frames, every one seemed to have a different scantling and space, while the distance between stanchions varied in nearly every case. Taking frames in pairs, 6 in. frame, 6 in. space, as at Lowestoft, brought confusion, stanchions were on top of frames or all over the place and bolt-heads showed that bolts would not go correctly through floors and keelson. I made several special journeys to check up, but always the same problem, floors and frames were not evenly spaced but just how did they go ?

In despair I decided to go over to Rye with my plans and see if I could pick up a clue, so I suggested to my wife that we celebrated her birthday by a trip to the Sussex town. Alas, the morning dawned hopeless with lowering skies and a south-west gale. A drizzle began to fall when we arrived at the coach, to be followed by a deluge. To counter a suggestion that we abandoned the day I staked my reputation as a weather prophet by announcing it would clear by noon or soon after. But did it ? It poured so persistently that the roof began to leak and Romney Marsh lived up to its name with disconsolate sheep huddled together in pools of water. On arrival we decided on a meal first, and I stoutly maintained the sun would come through. Just as we finished the sweet course, a watery gleam stole in through the window and by the time we left the cafe the sky had broken and great white sierras were piled up with patches of blue between. My name was no longer mud if the pathways were!

After making a few enquiries I went to an address but drew a blank, at last I ran the old gentleman to earth on his allotment and introduced myself, but his reply was a cold dollop. He had finished with smacks years before, did not want to have anything more to do with them, or see any plans, he had seen enough of them in fifty years or more. Now I hardly know the bow from the stern of a marrow, but I tried valiantly to keep my end up with a chat on allotments, edging in a word or two about my research. Then I tried to sound him on framing and drew the reply that frames went in pairs, " 6, 7½, 5½, 5, two foot spacing ". When I asked the reason for this curious fashion he simply said they always did it that way ! I hastily jotted down these cryptic figures on the brown paper wrapping round my despised plans and that was the sum total of my visit to Rye.

My wife joined me and we sat on a seat overlooking the Rother, drinking in the peaceful beauty of the old-world town of cobbled streets and mellow roofs. White clouds drove across the blue, below me lay the derelict yard and I pondered on the upsetting problems its closing must have made in many a home, when ship-wrights and craftsmen found their skill was no longer marketable.

On my return home about 10 p.m. I at once went to my drawing board and no Egyptian archaeologist, with the Rosetta-stone at hand to decipher some hieroglyphics, was ever more excited than I was when I set out the spacing and found everything fitted in perfectly.

I had hoped to find at Rye the half model from which *Master Hand* was built or a table of offsets, so that I could draw up her lines as they had yet to be done and it was difficult to see how they were to be taken off while the hull was afloat. Would I be able to find the time when she was hauled up for the fitting of the propeller ? A 'phone call from Mr. Claxton towards the end of August saw me in Ramsgate once again, the hull was on the patent slip, but it looked a task indeed to capture all those flowing curves on paper. I got into touch with my friend Mr. C. J. Greene, a fellow S.N.R. member, and he agreed to help, so one sunny morning we met on the slipway to think out the best way. Luckily the lattice uprights were plumb and it appeared that the upper line of the boot topping was horizontal, a check showed this to be the case and it made a datum line. All that remained was to mark off stations on the rail with a chalk, drop a plumb bob, erect a long batten marked in feet and inches and measure in to hull. This was a two-man job, so every time I had to scramble up ladder, move the line, secure it afresh, descend and work below. A breeze kept the plumb line swinging like a pendulum, while the long flexible batten swayed about in all directions, making it difficult to get true readings. The underside of keel was fairly straight so a datum line was fixed three inches above the bottom and we worked steadily aft, filling page after page with mystic figures which might, or might not, yield accurate results. Hoping for the best we carried on, refreshed from time to time with succulent plums my wife discovered. Then to the drawing board again to set out the stations, mark off the measurements and find the batten touching each point in a fair curve, a few checking dimensions on diagonals and the job was done.

Another speculative trip to Rye was a success as I met Mr. P. W. Jempson who kindly gave me the original contracts for the building of *Master Hand* and her sister ship *Helping Hand* (Plate 174), I also asked if I might have an old stock-taking book which he was about to consign to the waste paper basket, and it proved to be a gold mine from my point of view, with timber prices, fittings, etc., for the year 1908, that and a few excellent photographs rounded off a very worth-while journey.

During May I had received a letter " out of the blue " from Skipper J. T. Crouch of Lowestoft, who had heard I was interested in *Master Hand* and wrote to say he had been in charge of her fitting out at Rye. Correspondence followed, as this was yet another stroke of good fortune and in October we went up to the Suffolk town to spend a few days leave, and learn all I could about the smack. Any question was readily answered, the use of each pin, ringbolt, etc., was noted and on my return home I filled another book with the lead of every rope, method of working trawl and a host of other things, sent them to the skipper, who checked them over. Hence a very accurate and exhaustive collection of data is available and to my mind this is a better proposition than jumping from one smack to another, finding those many small items of difference between one port and another, and one ship and its neighbour.

The final problem was her sails as none were on board when I was working on the plans. Many enquiries at Lowestoft led me eventually to write to Mr. James Breach, part-owner and maker of her suit of canvas, and he replied by return offering to give any assistance. It is thanks to him and Mr. R. Bowles, his friend, that these particulars were made available, and I really think the name *Master Hand* to be appropriate in more ways than one, as it seems amazing that I have been able to trace up so much data concerning her. I am deeply grateful to all who assisted me to make an accurate record of a Rye-built Lowestoft trawler.

My last sight of the vessel on which I had spent so much time and energy was in November, 1946, now having full power below, gallows, wheelhouse and new fittings on deck, only the hull the same as in the days of sail. On the 10th she sailed for Brixham, taking 32 hours for the run, then the weather was so bad that only two nights fishing a week was possible, but the first three weeks' catches were £250, £300 and £280. In May 1950, I heard she was working out of Plymouth.

AGREEMENT.

Rock Channel Shipyard, Rye, November 15th, 1919.

IT is this day mutually agreed between Mr. James Breach, of 118 Clapham Road, Lowestoft ; and Mr. James F. Goffin, of 125 Clapham Road, Lowestoft in the County of Suffolk, smackowners, of the one part, and Geo & Thos Smith, Ltd., Ship and Barge Builders of Rye, in the County of Sussex, of the other part, that the said Geo & Thos Smith, Ltd., do build and fit a vessel of the dimensions and description, as under, for the said Messrs. James Breach, and James F. Goffin.

DIMENSIONS.

Length along Deck-line, from Fore-part Stem to After-part Stern-post .. .. } Seventy feet. (70 ft.)
Breadth of Beam .. .. .. Eighteen feet six inches. (18 ft. 6 in.)
Depth in Hold .. .. Nine feet. (9 ft.)

The Keel, Stem, Stern-post, Keelson and the whole of the frame to be of English Oak.

The whole of the outside planking from Keel to Planksheer, also the Planksheer to be of English Oak and fastened with galvanized Iron Bolts, Bolt heads outside covered with Cement and Varnish.

Pitch Pine Decks fastened with Galvanized Iron Spikes, and Dowelled over Spike heads ; Decks ends not to run to Stern Boards and Vessel to have Round Stern. Square (see letter 21-11-19). J. S.

Fitted with Windlass, Winch, with Bowsprit Roller at Foremast ; Two Pumps with Three Sets of Pump Gear ; Three Hatchways with necessary Hatches and Hatch Bars and Brass to Main Hatch ; Main Sheet Chock with revolving Block, Towpost, with Greenheart Chafing pieces ; Fair-leading post with Sheave, Steering Grating ; and carved Oak Tiller Brasses fitted.

Bulwarks to be of Pitch Pine, with the middle board rounded ; Greenheart

Capping on the Rails, half round Iron on Bow Rails, Chafing pieces, and Berthing for Trawlhead on Bulwark and on outside planking.

Deck frame, Shelves, Inside planking to Bilge, also the Bilge to be of English Oak ; Pitch Pine and English Oak below the Bilges, and five pairs Iron Hanging Knees to Beam Arms.

Builders to find Lightboards and Stanchions ; Gangway Roller, Iron Roller, and Iron Cletes on Bow, Angle Iron plate on each side of Stem ; Stem plate ; Iron Cletes on Taffrail and Dandy Score ; Galvanized half-round Iron on Planksheer on each side from Stem to Stern ; also stout Galvanized half-round Iron on Third Strake Topside from Stem to Mizzen Rigging on each side.

To provide Masts, and Bowsprit of Pitch Pine ; Spars, one Winter Topmast instead of a Boomer out ; Blocks, Lower Deadeyes, and Bullseyes, the necessary Ironwork fixed to the same, and Bowsprit Traveller, also one pair of Oars and Boathook, Purchasers to find their own Boat. Five Irons for Cavills on each side, and one Iron Heel Plate.

Cabin to be bright, of Pitch Pine and Teak ; the Stoves provided by the Builders ; Companion and Skylight. Deck lined in front of Companion ; Two Decklights over Cabin ; Two Galvanized Tanks fitted in Engine Room ; Two Ditto in the Hold, Glass Plate over Fireplace. Engine Room with Double Bulkhead and insulated Paper at Fore end and Carpenter's work fitting and supplying Capstan Chock. Antifouling Composition on bottom to Waterline.

Forecastle and Chain Box as usual for Lowestoft.

The Hull outside to have two coats of Tar ; Outside of Bulwarks three coats of Paint. Inside of Bulwarks, and necessary Deck fittings to be Bright and Varnished ; the Names on Bows and Stern Hawse, to be cut in and gilded ; the Streak round the Vessel's side to be gilded.

Ballast to be of Cement and Shingle between Timbers ; eight tons heavy Iron Ballast, and Iron Slag in the Hold ; Platform over the Ballast ; Ice Box to be of four thicknesses of Matchboard, lined with Insulating Paper, and Packed with compressed Cork Slabs.

The Vessel is to be built in a Workmanlike Manner with the necessary fittings as mentioned for the sum of Two thousand Four hundred Pounds (£2,400).

£	The payments to be as follows :—
50	On Agreement.
100	On December 15th, 1919. When keel is laid. (Pencil note.)
250	When in Frame.
250	When the Vessel is planked outside.
350	When Decks are laid.
350	When launched.
1,050	The Balance of One Thousand and Fifty Pounds on Completion ; the Builders shall then deliver their Certificate.

£2,400   Delivery of this Vessel to be on or before Augst 1st, 1920.

(Signed)   JAMES BREACH   GEO & THOS SMITH, LIMITED

           JAMES GOFFIN   Jno Smith . . . Secretary.

This most interesting document was not drawn up by a lawyer on parchment, it was a double sheet of ruled foolscap, written in longhand, with capital letters where shown and obviously no money was spent on frills, just a simple, straight-forward agreement, signed over a sixpenny stamp.

The agreement for the sister ship *Helping Hand* is a slightly more elaborate document in that the heading and dimensions are printed on ruled foolscap, leaving the details to be filled in, otherwise it is the same specification. Mr. Jempson told me they lost money on the building of *Master Hand*, so the price was increased to £2,900. The date of signature is 24th September, 1920, Mr. Leonard R. Tripp signs as the part-owner with Mr. James Breach, and Henry Jempson is now a director of G. & T. Smith Ltd., having been the foreman shipwright for many years. The vessel was to be delivered on or before 1st August, 1921, and once again Skipper J. T. Crouch went down to supervise the fitting out. He writes me that he knew Mr. Jempson quite well " he was the foreman shipwright and the one you mention, the young one, was the foreman ship's carpenter and good men they were ". He goes on to say :—

" *Master Hand* was built of the best Sussex oak, every bit of her, all the essential parts, as for her sea and sailing qualities she did not have much speed, but a good company keeper when pressed to it and she could stand it. A fine sea ship, no one wanted better, when it blew a gale you had something to trust to. I had seven months' successful fishing in her, then in the following July I went to Rye again to fit out her sister ship the *Helping Hand* for the same owners and was in her for a further 2 years and 9 months, which was again very successful. I think they were the last two vessels to be built for Lowestoft. I went to Rye after the *Master Hand* in November, 1920, her fit out was two sets of sails, consisting of two mainsails, two mizzens, five topsails, six jibs, one spinnaker, one staysail, three foresails (two stay foresails and one tow foresail). Two oak trawl beams, 48 ft. long, two pairs of trawl heads, two ground ropes, two pairs of bridles, two dandies, three trawls, one trawl rope of 110 fathom, all the running gear, one steam capstan and boiler, 75 fathom chain cable, three anchors, one pair sidelights, two masthead lights, one breakdown light, all cooking and eating utensils, clock, barometer, binoculars and other sundries too numerous to mention. This will give you a little idea of where £1,500 went. It took about a month to fit out at Rye, 48 hours to get to Lowestoft and another week to fit out for fishing gear, etc. We carried about 8 tons of fresh water, 2½ tons of coal, 3 tons of ice, that would fill us up and last for a week at sea. One of the owners, a master sail-maker, made the sails himself with two of his employees. We had two rigs, one for winter, the other for the summer, one fore topsail with a 14 ft. yard and the other a leg-of-mutton sail as we call it, and a 20 ft. yard mizzen topsail and a small leg-of-mutton one for the winter, the reason for the long pole on the mizzen mast. In her summer rig she looked the perfect type of sailing smack." Plate 171 shows her in winter rig.

Skipper Crouch was present at the launch of *Master Hand* and he sent me a photograph (Plate 172). He mentions that the earnings averaged about £2,000 a year, £6,600 in three years. A fair trip was 20 to 30 boxes in summer, 50 to 60 in winter. I wish to record once again my sincere appreciation of the invaluable help he gave me on all occasions in my efforts to ensure accuracy.

The Plans 18 appear on pages 341-7.

DIMENSIONS

L.B.P. – –	70 ft.	
L.O.A. – –	78 ft. 9 in.	
Length keel – –	62 ft. 6 in.	
Beam, moulded –	18 ft. 6 in. Extreme, 19 ft.	
Depth of hold –	9 ft. Reg. Tons. 45 $\frac{75}{100}$.	
Draught for'ard –	4 ft. 6 in. to 5 ft. Aft, 9 ft. 6 in.	
Official number –	No. 14001.	

SCANTLINGS

Keel – – –	8 in. sided, 12 in. moulded.
Stem – – –	8 in. sided, 12 in. moulded.
Apron – –	8 in. sided, 10 in. moulded.
Sternpost – –	8 in. sided, 15 in. moulded at heel, 10 in. at head.
Keelson – –	7 in. sided, 9 in. moulded.
Floors – –	6 and 5½ in. sided, 8 to 6½ in. moulded.
First futtocks –	6 and 5½ in. sided, 6½ to 5½ in. moulded.
Second do –	6 and 5½ in. sided, 5½ to 4½ in. moulded.
Beams – –	6 in. sided, 6½ to 7 in. moulded. At mast, 7 in. sq.
Carlings – –	5 in. sided, 3 to 5 in. moulded.
Hatch coamings –	3 in. sided, 11 in. moulded.

All these timbers are English oak, and most of them can be seen in Fig. 24 on page 268.

OUTSIDE PLANKING

Garboards – –	2½ in. thick. Oak.
Topsides and bilges	3 in. thick. Oak.
Covering board or planksheer –	2½ by 12 in. Oak.
Deck – –	5 by 2½ in. Pitch pine.
2 centre planks –	6½ by 2½ in. Pitch pine.

BULWARKS

Stanchions – –	5 by 5, tapering to 4 in. Oak
Rail – – –	6 by 3½ in. Oak.
Capping – –	6 by 1½ in. Greenheart.

154 INNER BASIN, RAMSGATE, 1857
R.E.25 in background has curved stem and straight sternpost, R.E.184
has straight stem, no round to fore foot, raking sternpost and hand
capstan amidships, R.E.6 is Brixham type with winch for'ard and horse
across deck to take main sheet of winter boom. Her mast is being
scraped down by shipwrights who work on a staging lashed to shrouds,
when job was done by crew they sat on gaff which was gradually lowered.

155 ON THE HARD, c 1911

R.15 *Peace*, 27 tons, built at Ramsgate, 1902. R.160 *Leonora*, 26 tons, built at Rye, 1897. R.257 *Rhodora*, 25 tons, built at Porthleven, 1908. R.185 *Sweet Hope*, 23 tons, built at Porthleven, 1902. R.152 *W.E.*, 25 tons, built at Ramsgate, 1909. Note the difference in the round-up of fore-foots, and the double-ended tug *Aid* in the background.

156 CONVERTED SLOOPS, c 1885

On the left is *Armenia*, built at Ramsgate as a sloop in 1861, converted to a 36-ton ketch in 1884. R.57 is *William & Mary*, 44 tons, built at Barking 1866.

157 FITTING OUT AT WHITSUNTIDE, c 1885
Winter topmasts are being removed and summer spars with cross-trees sent aloft.   Some of
the foresails are in stops, others are dropped on stem heads. *Aid* was a wooden paddle tug, 50
h.p., built at Blackwall, 1855, N.T. 16, G.T. 112, length 89.2 ft., beam 18 ft., depth 9.9 ft.

158   A SNIB-BOWED TRAWLER
Vie, R.141, 25 tons, built at Lowestoft, 1896.   The dredger is *Hope*, built of steel at
Paisley in 1901, and owned by the Board of Trade.

159   INNER BASIN, RAMSGATE, C 1899

R.212 *Pride of the Ocean*, built as a 34-ton cutter at Ramsgate, 1870, later converted to a 27-ton ketch. R.233 *Valiant*, built at Ramsgate as a 38-ton sloop, 1872. R.427 *British Queen*, 41 tons, built at Rye 1879, ahead is 95R., a tosher, then R.405 *Flora Isabella*, 42 tons, built at Rye, 1878. Against quay is a Rochester barge, then R.170 *Spray*, 27 tons, built at Galmpton, 1898, by Gibbs, R.172 *Vivid*, 20 tons, built at Porthleven, 1898 and R.80 *Staghound*, 20 tons, built at Whitstable, 1890, by Collar & Sons. The brigantine is *Gloriana*, 147 tons, built at Amble, 1870, then comes R.34 *Our Boys*, 18 tons, built at Rye, 1888, and R.109 *Edith*, 38 tons, built at Lowestoft, 1893, with a clench-built hull.

160 *WILLIAM & ROSE*, R.423
37 tons, built at Rye, 1879.   She is heading in for the harbour entrance
with a pair of reefs down.

161 *INDUSTRY*, R.227
28 tons, built at Galmpton,
1906.

162 INNER BASIN, RAMSGATE, OCTOBER, 1932
R.361 *Quartette*, 25 tons, built at Galmpton, 1895.
R.47 an auxiliary cutter. R.110 *Volante*, built at
Brightlingsea, 1893, 14 tons, reduced to 8 when
fitted with an engine, 1925. Mined 1950.

163 LAID UP AT RYE, 1936
Three Brothers, R.X.153, 19 tons,
built at Rye, 1896.

164 *THREE BROTHERS* AT RYE, JUNE, 1947

165 FLEETWOOD TRAWLERS
F.D.51 *Ida*, 32 tons, built at Brixham, 1869.

166　HOYLAKE TRAWLER WORKING A WEATHER TIDE
　　L.L.52 *Margaret Alice*, 51 tons, built at Port St. Mary, I.O.M., 1875.
　　The warp has a breeching fast to taffrail, foresail has a bonnet, note the
　　pole mast and wash strakes on the quarters.

167 MILFORD HAVEN TRAWLER, M.18
The crew are sweating up peak halyards, the topmast is housed.

168 PORT ST. MARY, ISLE OF MAN
C.T.54 is *Alice*, just after her launch in 1886, her pole mast has a gaff and boom sail, but mizzen has a standing lug. The schooner is *Kate* of Peel, 122 tons, built at Peel in 1872.

169   TRAWLERS AT PORT ST. MARY
C.T.25 is *Confidence*, C.T.54 *Alice*, the schooner is *Kate*.   Note wash
strakes and dandy wink aft on smack in foreground.

170   RAMSEY TRAWLERS
R.Y.42 *Faithful*, in centre is *Border Queen*, and to wind'ard is *Heart of
Oak*, R.Y.1, 24 tons, built at Peel, 1876 and fishing up to 1924.

Boards. Middle	—	9 by 1½ in., rounded.	Pitch pine.
Upper	—	7 by 1 in.	Pitch pine.
Lower	—	6 by 1 in.	Pitch pine.
Taffrail	— —	15 by 3½ in.	Oak.

INSIDE PLANKING, *etc.*

Shelf	— —	7 by 6 in.	Oak.
Clamp	— —	8 by 3 in.	Oak.
Bilge stringers	—	3 in. thick.	Oak.
Ceiling	— —	1½ in. thick.	Pitch pine.
Lining	— —	2 in. thick.	Oak.
Platform, sail room		1¼ in. thick.	Pitch pine.
remainder		1½ in. thick.	Pitch pine.
Bulkheads	— —	1½ in. thick.	Pitch pine.
Icebox	— —	Four thicknesses of matchboarding.	
Cabin	— —	Pitchpine and teak.	
Cabin stanchion	—	6 in. sq.	Oak.
Knees	— —	6 in. thick.	Oak.

WINDLASS

Pawl bitt	— —	8 in. sq.	Oak.
Starboard bitt	—	8 by 7 in.	Oak.
Side bitts	— —	12 by 4 in.	Oak.
Barrel	— —	10 in. dia.	Oak.
Ends, turned and morticed—	—	12 in.	Elm.

WINCH

Bitts —	— —	11 in. tapering to 9 in. × 4½ in.	Oak.
Towpost	— —	9½ in. sq., tapering to 7 in.	Oak.
Chafing pieces	—		Greenheart.
Bowsprit roller bitt		6½ × 4½ in.	Oak.
Fairleading post	—	9 × 8 in.	Oak.

Spalls (small beams below platform).

Warp room	4 × 3 in.
Boiler room	6 × 4 in.
Remainder	5 × 2 in. and 5 × 2½ in.

Iron knees	— —	3 × 1 in.	2 ft. 8 in. arms.
Pump boxes and plugs		Elm, turned.	
Trenails	— —	1¾ in. dia.	

MASTS AND SPARS
as measured

Mainmast –	–	Dia. 15 to 12 in. L.O.A. 53 ft. 7 in. Rig 36 ft.
Masthead –	–	9 ft.
Housing –	–	8 ft. 3 in.
Mizzen mast –		Dia. 12 in. L.O.A. 49 ft. 5 in. Rig 27 ft. 6 in.
Housing –	–	4 ft. 5 in.
Bowsprit L.O.A. –		36 ft. 8 in. Dia. at heel, 11 in., at end 9 in.
Main gaff –	–	Dia. 8 in. 31 ft. 2 in. to jaws.
Main boom –	–	Dia. 9¾ in.– 10 in. 33 ft. 7 in. to gooseneck.
Mizzen gaff	–	Dia. 6¾ in. 21 ft. 10 in. to jaws.
Mizzen boom	–	Dia. 8 in. 24 ft. 4 in. to gooseneck.

Topmast (not on board) 28 ft. winter.   34 ft. summer.

Deadeyes –	–	Elm. Main 7 × 4½ in. Mizzen 6 in. dia.
Chain plates	–	Iron. 5 ft. × 3 in. × 1 in.

Mast battens	–	Oak. 2 in. wide, ½ in. thick. To take chafe of jaws.
Tumblers –	–	Elm.
Reef clamps	–	Elm.
Cleats –	–	Elm. Mostly 12 in. long × 2 × 2 in. Some are oak.
Jib sheet bullseyes –		Applewood. 1 ft. 2 in. long.
Trucks –	–	Elm.
Mast cap –	–	Oak.
Cheeks –	–	Oak.
Mast hoops	–	Ash. 1¾ in. wide × 1 in. thick.
Forestay heart	–	Elm. 1 ft. × 8 in. × 5 in.
Jaws –	–	Oak.
Pump brakes	–	4 ft. 9 in. long, 2 in. sq. for 2 ft., then rounded.
Main parrels	–	2¼ in. × 2 in.

There were 21 strakes of planking amidships and 36 deck planks, the margin plank averaging 8½ in. in width.

COLOUR SCHEME

Green inside bulwarks and on sides of stanchions.
Rail and faces of stanchions.   Mast colour.
Arch board, blue, stern frames, green sides.   Blue round helmport.
Cavil rails.   Mast colour.
Hatch covers.   Blue.   Coamings inside, blue.   Outside, mast colour.
Boat, dark green inside and out.
Windlass barrel, blue, ironwork red.   Woodwork, mast colour.
Winch.   Similar to windlass.
Transit Rail across stern has name MASTER HAND in gilt with a star on either side
Capstan.   Green.

Carved on beam in sail room.

CERT^D 30 S^N STORE 3 TONS.   CERT SAILROOM 1 $\frac{41}{100}$ TONS

Draught marks in Roman figures 6 inches high.

Tiller has ornamental scroll work carved on both sides.

Anchor cable 60 fthm.   Links $4 \times 2\frac{1}{2}$ in.   Always two turns round windlass, passes down through chain pipe to locker on fore side of mast.

Bowsprit kept well greased, one pull and would run in by itself.
In foul weather, heel just for'ard of winch, in fair, up to stanchion of windlass. Set up with a heel rope, not fidded, run in by a pull on topmast stay.

FORE DECK

Fig. 20

STEM AND APRON	2 in. iron band round head carries S hook to go in the tack span of foresail.
IRON STRAP	3 in. wide. Extends 2 ft. 5 in. along each bulwark at 11 in. from deck.
HAWSE PIECES	2 ft. 6 in. long, 6 in. thick, hawse pipes 9×7 in.
FORE STAY	5 in. circ. weighs about 3 cwt., leads down face of stem in score 4 in. deep, then in through hole in stem and apron, 1 ft. 6 in. from deck, has a scored heart spliced in end and is set up with a lanyard to the hole in knee of pawl bitt.
ROLLER	7 in. dia., 8 in. long, to port of stem head.
BOWSPRIT	Reeves through hole 1 ft. by 2 ft. in starboard hawse piece.
LEAD-IN HOLES	Two on starboard side of stem, through rail.
FAIRLEADS	On either rail, 1 ft. 7 in. long, 4 in. high, with 4 in. dia. sheave, cleat on inner face of first stanchion.
DECK LIGHT	6 in. long, 5 in. wide, let in planking for'ard of windlass.
CAVIL RAIL	From aft side of stem to fore side of pawl bitt, 5 in. wide, $2\frac{1}{2}$ in. thick, carries three belaying pins 1 ft. long, $\frac{3}{4}$ in. dia.
ANCHOR	Shank 4 ft. long, 4 in. thick, fluke to fluke 3 ft. 10 in., palms, 9 in. long, crown 4 in. thick, ends 3 in. Folding stock, 5 ft. 3 in. long, one end turned down 1 ft. 3 in., ball at each end. Shackle, 1 ft. long, 9 in. wide. Shackle to cable, 7 in. long.
CABLE	Studded links, 4 in. long, $2\frac{1}{2}$ in. wide. 60 fthm. long.

WINDLASS

Fig. 21

PAWL BITT	8 in. sq., 3 ft. 7 in. above deck, total length 12 ft., morticed into keelson. Fair-leading sheave on head, $5\frac{3}{4} \times 1\frac{3}{4}$, knee 6 in. thick on fore side. Iron rubbing strakes, 2 ft. 3 in. $\times 2 \times \frac{1}{2}$ in. on port side. Sheave for heel rope on starboard side.

STARBOARD BITT	7 in. × 8 in., 3 ft. 7 in. high, goes down to floors, heavy cleat 15 in. long, 2 in. wide on starboard side, hole fore and aft for heel rope.
CHOCK	1 ft. 3 in. up from deck is shaped chock 4 in. thick for bowsprit, 13 in. above is 5 in. dia. wooden roller.
CHEEK OF BITT	On aft side of starboard bitt, 4 in. thick, extends 1 ft. 5 in. below deck and is through bolted to bitt and beam. 2 ft. 11 in. high above deck. Head forms belaying post 6 in. wide, 7 in. deep.
PORT BITT	12½ in. long, 4 in. thick, 2 ft. 7 in. above deck, is morticed into carling, 10 × 9½ in., below deck. Knee on fore side extends to covering board, head is formed into two belaying posts 4 in. high.
BARREL	9½ in. dia. on starboard side, iron pawl rim in centre, whelps on port side, making barrel 18 in. dia.
ENDS	1 ft. 2 in. long, 1 ft. dia. at inside, turned to shape with holes 3 in. sq. to take handspikes.

CAVIL RAILS
Fig. 22

RAIL	7 ft. 8in. long, 3 in. sq., on either side, bolted to stanchions, ends project 7 in. to form cleats.
BELAYING PINS	1 ft. 4 in. long by ¾ in., iron, two in each rail, one heavier one in each bulwark rail.
HALF-ROUND IRON	Two, 1½ in. wide, extend from stem to chock on cap.
BULLSEYES	Of applewood, 1 ft. 2 in. long, 6 in. wide, 2 in. thick, two in each middle strake, holes 8 in. centred, for'ard one takes knotted standing end, aft one fall of jib sheets, end knotted.
THUMB CLEAT	Heavy thumb cleat on stanchion, starboard side, under which topsail halyard goes before belaying on pin in rail above.
BELAYING PIN	1 ft. 8½ in. long, 6 in. above rail, head shaped.
BULLSEYE	Aft of stanchion, is lead-in for spinnaker sheet, 11 in. deep, 5 in. wide, 1½ in. thick.
RINGBOLT	On starboard side of deck, to take snatch block.
HATCHWAY	2 ft. sq. in centre of deck, coamings 6 in. × 3 in. above deck, guard coamings 3 ft. 4 in. long, on sides, 2½ in. from main coamings, fore one 3 ft. 2 in. Cap cover just fits over hatch, between coamings.

WINCH
Fig. 23

POSITION	Is off centred 4 in. to starboard to allow bowsprit to run in clear of bitt. Hatchway below between knees.
BITTS	11 in. × 4½ in., tapering to 9 in. × 4 in. at heel where they mortice into floors. 4 ft. 4 in. high above deck. On outer faces are two iron rubbing strakes and ringbolts where handles stow when not in use.

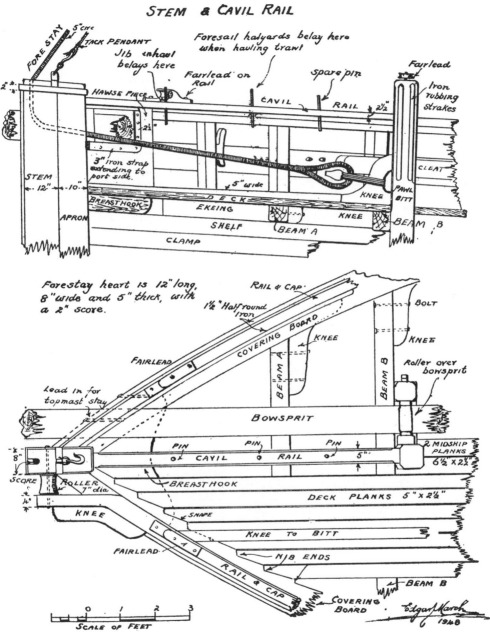

STEM & CAVIL RAIL

FORE STAY

5" circ

TACK PENDANT

Jib inhaul belays here

Foresail halyards belay here when hauling trawl

Fairlead on Rail

spare pin

Fairlead

2" 4"

HAWSE PIECE

CAVIL

RAIL

2½"

Iron rubbing Strakes

STEM — 12" — 10" —

2½"

3" Iron strap extending to port side.

5" wide

CLEAT

KNEE

PAWL BITT

BREASTHOOK

DECK

EKEING

KNEE

BEAM B

APRON

SHELF

BEAM A

CLAMP

Forestay heart is 12" long, 8" wide and 5" thick, with a 2" score.

RAIL & CAP

BOLT

1½" Half round Iron

COVERING BOARD

KNEE

KNEE

FAIRLEAD

BEAM A

BEAM B

Roller over bowsprit

Lead in for topmast stay

BOWSPRIT

2 MIDSHIP PLANKS
6½" x 2½"

8"

PIN

PIN

PIN

SCORE

CAVIL

RAIL

5"

ROLLER 7" dia

BREASTHOOK

DECK PLANKS 5" x 2½"

KNEE

SNAPE

KNEE TO BITT

FAIRLEAD

NIB ENDS

RAIL & CAP

BEAM B

COVERING BOARD

Edgar March 1948

0   1   2   3
SCALE OF FEET

FIG. 20

WINDLASS

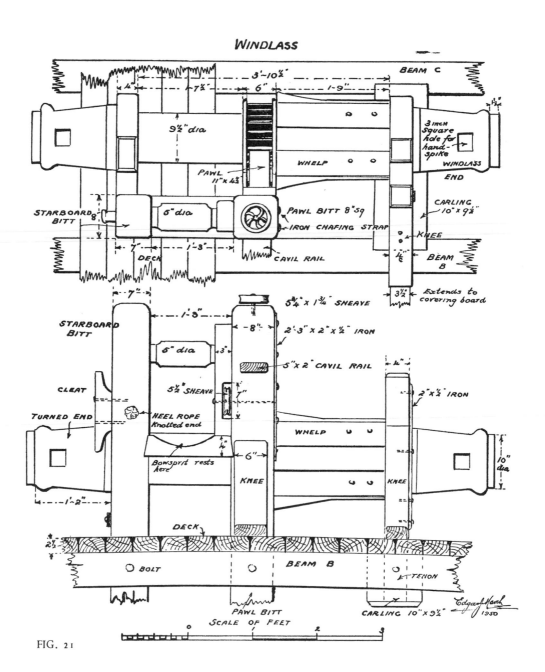

FIG. 21

WINDLASS
PORT BITT

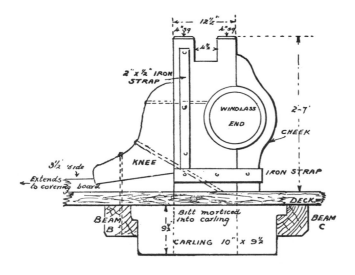

- 12½"
- 4"sq
- 4½"
- 2"x½" IRON STRAP
- WINDLASS END
- 2'-7"
- CHEEK
- 3½" side
- KNEE
- IRON STRAP
- Extends to covering board
- DECK
- Bitt morticed into carling
- BEAM B
- BEAM C
- 9½"
- CARLING 10" X 9½"

STARBOARD BITT

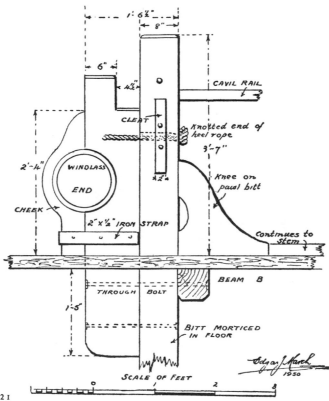

- 1'-6½"
- 8"
- 6"
- 4½"
- CAVIL RAIL
- CLEAT
- Knotted end of heel rope
- 3'-7"
- 2'-4"
- WINDLASS END
- Knee on pawl bitt
- CHEEK
- 2"x½" IRON STRAP
- Continues to stem
- BEAM B
- THROUGH BOLT
- 1'-5"
- BITT MORTICED IN FLOOR
- 4"
- SCALE OF FEET
- Edgar J. March 1950

0   1   2   3

FIG. 21

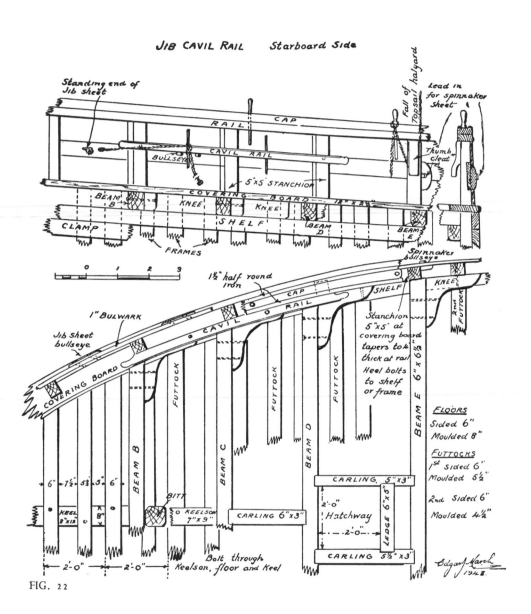

JIB CAVIL RAIL   Starboard Side

Standing end of Jib sheet

Fall of Topsail halyard

Lead in for spinnaker sheet

CAP

RAIL

CAVIL RAIL

BULLSEYE

Thumb cleat

5"x5" STANCHION

COVERING BOARD   12"x 2½"

BEAM B

KNEE

KNEE

BEAM D

BEAM E

CLAMP

SHELF

FRAMES

Spinnaker bullseye

1½" half round iron

SHELF

KNEE

1" BULWARK

CAVIL

CAP

RAIL

Stanchion 5"x5" at covering board tapers to 4" thick at rail Heel bolts to shelf or frame

2nd FUTTOCK

Jib Sheet bullseye

COVERING BOARD

FUTTOCK

FUTTOCK

FUTTOCK

BEAM B

BEAM C

BEAM D

BEAM E 6"x 6½"

FLOORS
Sided 6"
Moulded 8"

FUTTOCKS
1st Sided 6"
Moulded 5½"

2nd Sided 6"
Moulded 4½"

CARLING 5"x3"

CARLING 6"x3"

2'-0"
Hatchway
2'-0"

LEDGE 6"x3"

6" 7½" 5½" 5" 6"

BITT

KEEL 8"x12"

8"

KEELSON 7"x9"

2'-0"   2'-0"

Bolt through Keelson, floor and Keel

CARLING 5½"x3"

Edgar March 1948.

FIG. 22

CLEAT	14 in. oak cleat on inside face of starboard bitt, 1 ft. 3 in. from deck.
KNEES	1 ft. 6 in. high, throat 11 in., $4\frac{1}{2}$ in. thick. Ringbolts on upper face, one to port is for lashing anchor, one to starboard for spare anchor.
BARREL	3 ft. 6 in. long. 13 in. dia. at ends over whelps. To starboard is 2 ft. $\times$ $2\frac{1}{2}$ in. toothed wheel.
PAWLS	On inside faces of bitts. 9 in. dia., 2 in. wide cogs, on ends of spindle.
SLIDING BAR	Has 6 in. dia. $\times$ 3 in. toothed cog wheel, bar 2 in. dia., ends square to take handles. On fore side of bitts. (See Plate 129 for a similar pattern.)
CHAIN PIPE	5 in. inside dia., to port of centre line, just aft of windlass.
IRON HORSE	6 in. clear of deck, has iron traveller for fore sheet.

MAST PARTNERS, ETC.
Fig. 24

CARLINGS	Two oak carlings, one to starboard $13\frac{1}{2}\times 6$ in., to port 13×6 in., let into beams F and G.
PARTNER	On aft side of beam F, 13×6 in.
BOWSPRIT ROLLER (also Fig. 50)	To starboard, oak bitt $6\frac{1}{2} \times 4\frac{1}{2}$ in., bolted to carling below deck, 2 ft. 1 in. above deck, with thumb cleat on aft side. A 6 in. dia. roller, 1 ft. 3 in. long, turns on a spindle passing through bitt and mast heel.
FAIR-LEADING POST (also Fig. 25)	To port, post is 9×8 in., 1 ft. 10 in. above deck, bolted to beam and carling below, has 6 in. dia. sheave, port arm being 4 in. clear of deck. $1\frac{1}{4}$ in. iron band round head, on side next mast is a 13 in. oak cleat under which topsail sheet passes before belaying to cleat aft side of mast.
EYEBOLTS	Two on either side of mast, to take tackles if required, but seldom used in *Master Hand*. In some smacks topsail tack purchase and main truss hook here instead of on gooseneck band.
MAIN HATCHWAY	Aft of mast, 3 ft. sq., coamings 8 in. above deck, 3 in. thick, resting on carlings 5×3 in. Has two covers.
EYEBOLT	On aft coaming, takes mizzen staysail tack when that sail is set.
RINGBOLTS	In deck. To starboard for boat gripe, to port for stopper of warp.
BOAT SLIDE	Oak, 3 in. thick, at aft end of starboard coaming.

MAIN CAVIL RAIL. STARBOARD SIDE.
Fig. 26

CHOCK	3 ft. 3 in. long, 6 in. thick, 7 in. high fore end, on rail for'ard of shrouds. Has 3 eyebolts.
CAVIL RAIL	9 ft. 10 in. long, 6 in. wide, 3 in. thick, bolted to stanchions.
THUMB CLEATS	Three heavy wooden cleats on face of stanchions below cavil rail.
EYEBOLTS	Three on rail of bulwarks, three on chock.

BOAT GANGWAY	One was fitted originally, but was a solid bulwark in 1946. 6 ft. 6 in. wide between stanchions.
BULLSEYE	On inside of bulwark rail, for'ard of chock, takes bowline when foresail is held a'weather.
BELAYING PINS	Five in cavil rail, iron, 1 ft. long, $\frac{3}{4}$ in. dia.
IRON CAVIL	Through deck and beam below, with forelock, canvassed and kept well greased. Standing end of main halyard passes under before belaying on pin above. 6 in. high, 4 in. across.
DEADEYES	7 in. dia., $4\frac{1}{2}$ in. thick, with $1\frac{1}{2}$ in. score, centred 3 ft. 4 in.
CHAIN PLATES	3 in. × 1 in., mostly 5 ft. long.
SHROUDS	$3\frac{1}{2}$ in. circ. over serving, ends are 18 in. above top of deadeyes.
RATLINES	15 in. apart.

MAIN CAVIL RAIL. PORT SIDE
Fig. 27

CHOCK	3 ft. 2 in. long, 7 in. high for'ard end, 6 in. thick.
EYEBOLTS	Three on chock, three on bulwark rail.
SMALL CHOCK	Aft, by gate to gangway. 12 in. long, 5 in. high, 6 in. thick.
CAVIL RAIL	9 ft. 11 in. long, fore end shaped as cleat to take lantern halyards. 6 in. wide, 3 in. thick.
BELAYING PINS	Four in cavil rail, 1 ft. long, $\frac{3}{4}$ in. dia., iron.
THUMB CLEAT	One only under rail.
IRON CAVIL	In deck as on starboard side, fall of main halyards goes under before belaying to pin above.
RINGBOLT	In deck, takes hook of fish tackle purchase.
BERTHING	6 ft. long, 2 ft. 6 in. wide, 1 in. thick, to protect deck where trawl head berths, ringbolt in centre takes strop.
GANGWAY	1 ft. 4 in. wide between stanchions, iron guards on sides, a hinged gate covers gap in rails.
ROLLER	Iron, 8 in. dia., 1 ft. long.
BERTHING	On outside planking from covering board to bilge, 7 ft. 9 in. long, 1 ft. wide boards 1 in. thick, the two lowest being 10 ft. long. Vertical boards to rail.

CAPSTAN
Fig. 15, page 95

PATTERN	Steam capstan made by Elliott & Garrood, Beccles.
CARLINGS (Fig 24)	Starboard one $9\frac{3}{4}$ × 6 in., centre one, takes spindle, 7 × 6 in., port one $9\frac{1}{2}$ × 6 in., let in between beams H and I.
ICE BUNKER COVER	11 in. inside dia., $1\frac{1}{2}$ in. rim, to starboard of centre deck plank.
FISH HATCHWAY	Inside measurements 2 ft. long, 2 ft. 4 in. wide.
CARLINGS	5 in. wide, 3 in. thick.
COAMINGS	8 in. above deck, 3 in. thick.
CAP COVER	Close fit over coamings, has one ringbolt on each side and one on fore side.

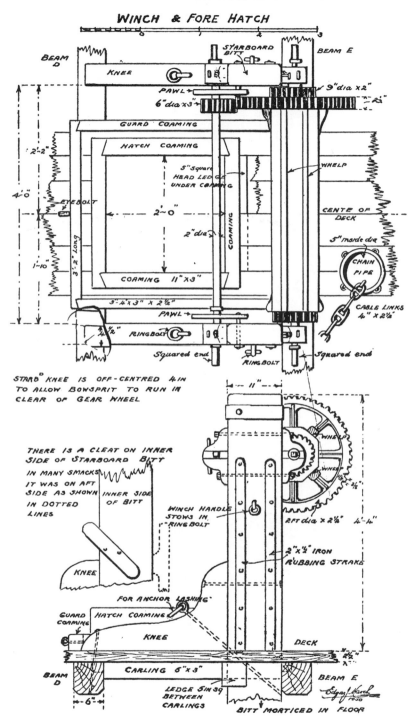

WINCH & FORE HATCH

STARB° KNEE IS OFF-CENTRED 4IN
TO ALLOW BOWSPRIT TO RUN IN
CLEAR OF GEAR WHEEL

THERE IS A CLEAT ON INNER
SIDE OF STARBOARD BITT
IN MANY SMACKS
IT WAS ON AFT
SIDE AS SHOWN
IN DOTTED
LINES

PORT BITT, LEDGE & CARLING

FIG. 23

267

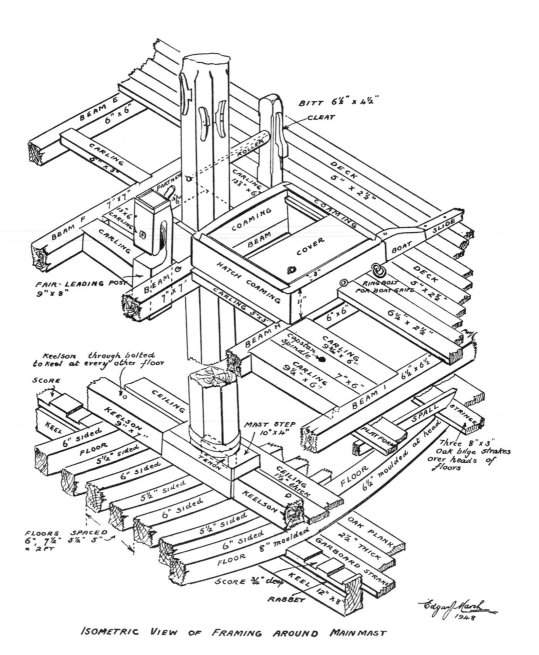

ISOMETRIC VIEW OF FRAMING AROUND MAINMAST

FIG. 24

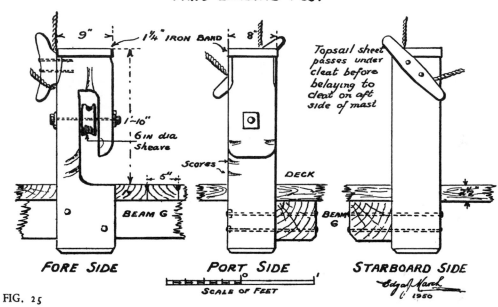

FAIR LEADING POST

9″   1¾″ IRON BAND   8″

Topsail sheet passes under cleat before belaying to cleat on aft side of mast

1′-10″

6 IN DIA SHEAVE

Scores

DECK

5″

BEAM G

BEAM G

2½″

FORE SIDE

PORT SIDE

SCALE OF FEET

STARBOARD SIDE

Edgar March 1950

FIG. 25

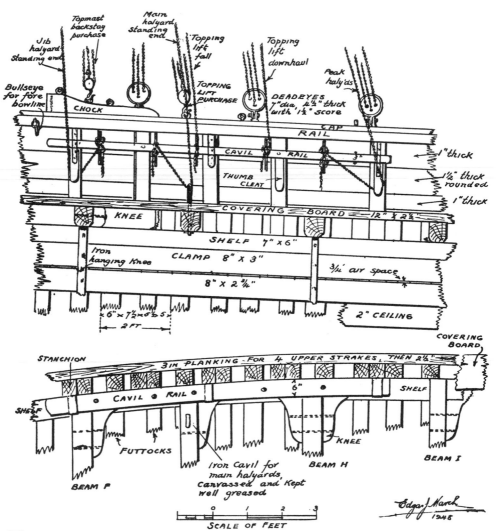

MAIN CAVIL RAIL Starboard Side

FIG. 26

TOWPOST OR DUMMY
Fig. 28

POST	Oak, 12 ft. long, 3 ft. 3 in. above deck, morticed into keelson, head shaped to take pump brake, 10 × 9 in., bolt passing through sides. 9½ in. sq. under deck, tapers to 7 in. sq.
CHAFING PIECES	Greenheart, shaped and fitted round post to height of 2 ft. 8 in. above deck.
BASE	3 ft. 6 in. long, 1 ft. 4 in. wide, 3 in. thick, ends rounded.
PUMPS	On either side of towpost. Elm plugs inserted when not in use. Discharge pipe on aft side of base, to starboard.
CHOCK	5½ in. thick, 1 ft. 9 in. long, shaped, on fore side of beam L, 2 in. wedge on aft side beam K.
LONG CLEAT	3 ft. 7 in. long bolted to stanchions on port bulwarks, aft of gangway.
BUNKER COVERS	Two covers on port side, one on starboard side, opposite dummy, over fresh water tanks.
BOILER PLATE	3 ft. 9 in. sq., 3 in. above deck, boiler funnel 7 in. dia., 4 ft. high, in centre, safety valve 11 in. dia. to starboard.
FAIRLEAD	On for'ard end, starboard side, 1 ft. 1 in. long, 5 in. wide, 4 in. dia. sheave, used when hauling in leech line of trawl.
COAL BUNKER	Cover 14 in. dia. on starboard side of deck.
RING BOLTS	Two on stanchions starboard side, for boat gripes.

COMPANION OR HOODWAY
Fig. 29

HATCHWAY	2 ft. 11 in. long, 1 ft. 11 in. wide.
CARLINGS	5 × 3 in. between beams N and O.
COAMINGS	8 in. × 3 in.
HOODWAY	Outside dimensions 3 ft. 5 in. long, 2 ft. 5 in. wide. Height 2 ft. 5 in. aft, 2 ft. 2 in. for'ard, sliding roof.
GRATING	2 ft. 4½ in. × 1 ft. 2½ in.
LIFEBUOY	On fore side behind brass rail.
FUNNEL and VENTILATOR	For stove, to starboard 6 in. dia., 4 ft. 3 in. high. 3 ft. 11 in. high, 14 in. dia. cowl, both on rounded wood bases 2 in. thick.
DECKLIGHTS	Two in deck to starboard, 6 in. long, 5 in. wide.
WATER BUNKER	Cover to starboard, in deck.
LONG CLEAT	3 ft. 9 in. long, 2 in. wide, 3 in. thick across stanchions on starboard side.

MAIN SHEET CHOCK
Fig. 30

BASE	3 ft. 6 in. long, 1 ft. 3 in. wide, 10 in. high, 3 in. thick bolted to beam Q through deck.
CLEAT	1 ft. 7 in. long on centre of aft side. 3½ in. thick.

BULLSEYE	$5\frac{1}{2}$ in. dia. on port side, for'ard.
BLOCK	12 in. × 9 in. × 6 in., iron strap $2\frac{1}{2}$ in. wide, revolves freely on bolt across chock, 6 in. dia. sheaves, 2 in. wide, side cheeks $1\frac{1}{2}$ in. thick.
RINGBOLTS	In deck. To port for stopper for fore bridle when shooting gear round stern. One on aft side of stanchion on port side.

SKYLIGHT
Fig. 31

HATCHWAY	2 ft. 4 in. long, 2 ft. wide.
CARLINGS	6 × 3 in., let down $1\frac{1}{2}$ in. into beams R and S.
COAMINGS	8 × 3 in., through bolted to carlings and beams.
ROOF	Aft end hinged to lift for ventilation, 2 ft. high.
EYEBOLT	In deck to starboard, used when working gear on the starboard side.

BULWARKS
Fig. 32

HEIGHT	2 ft. 7 in. for'ard, 2 ft. 4 in. amidships and aft.
STANCHIONS	5 in. × 5 in., tapering to 5 × 4.
RAIL	Oak, 5 in. wide, $3\frac{1}{2}$ in. thick.
CAPPING	Greenheart, $1\frac{1}{2}$ in. thick, 6 in. wide, edges rounded.
THOLE PINS	Ten holes in port rail, eight in starboard.
UPPER STRAKE	7 in. wide, 1 in. thick. Lower strake 6 in. wide.
MIDDLE STRAKE	Rounded. 9 in. wide, $1\frac{1}{2}$ in. thick.
SCUPPERS	1 in. high.

MIZZEN MAST
Fig. 33

CARLINGS	6 × 6 in. between beams S and T.
PARTNER	$7\frac{1}{2}$ × 6 in., wedges around mast, angle chocks in corners.
EYEBOLTS	Two on either side of mast, in deck.
GRATING	8 ft. long, 2 ft. wide, aft of mast.
BINNACLE	On aft side of mast, not on board when I measured up in 1946, can be seen in plate 173.
RINGBOLT	In deck to port, for snatch block.

CAVIL RAIL. STARBOARD SIDE
Fig. 34

CHOCK	On rail, 3 ft. 6 in. long, brass rubbing piece on face and rail.
SOCKETS and BASES	Two in rail to take light board stanchions, $1\frac{1}{2}$ in. dia. hole, 2 ft. 4 in. centred, plate 3 in. sq., 5 in. long, 2 in. high, on deck.
CAVIL RAIL	6 in. wide fore end, 8 in. aft, 4 in. thick, for'ard end shaped as cleat 9 in. long from stanchion, aft end is kneed into transit rail.
CLEAT	Oak, 2 ft. long, 4 in. wide, for mooring rope.

171　*MASTER HAND*, L.T.1203
46 tons, built at Rye, 1920.　In winter rig with short topmast.

172　LAUNCH OF *MASTER HAND*, 1920
Skipper J. T. Crouch is second from the stem, note the rough lopped trunks used for scaffold staging, the berthing on side of hull under and aft of gangway, and the small for'ard cradle.

173 DECK VIEW, *MASTER HAND*, JULY, 1934
Showing spare beam and snatch block, binnacle aft of mizzen, skylight, hoodway, boiler
plate and funnel, towpost, fair-lead for leech line, steam capstan and heel of bowsprit

174 *HELPING HAND*,
L.T.1239
46 tons, built at Rye, 1921

175 A TYPICAL RYE STERN. *MASTER HAND*, L.T.1203
Neither square, nor round as in smack alongside. Note name cut in
transit rail and dandy score to port.

176　*CHRYSOBERYL*, L.T.1089, JUNE, 1928
　　43 tons, built at Lowestoft, 1907.

177　*EAST DEAN*, L.T.1233, JUNE, 1928
　　42 tons, built at Lowestoft, 1921.　Showing how boat is lashed down
　　with gripes.

178 *SUNBEAM*, L.T.669, JUNE, 1928
59 tons, built at Lowestoft, 1905.

179 *MASTER HAND*, L.T.1203
Coming into Lowestoft with two reefs down, reefed foresail and small
jib.   Note seas breaking on the Newcome Sands.

180 DROPPING SAIL

Master Hand, L.T.1203. The bowsprit is being run in.

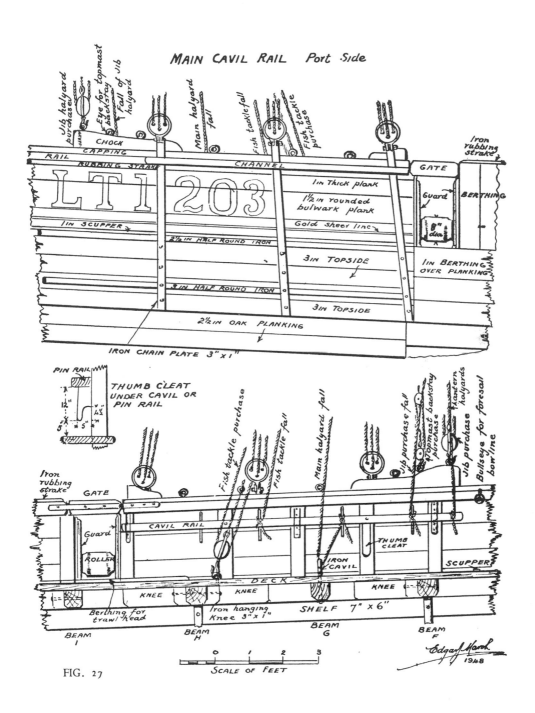

MAIN CAVIL RAIL   Port Side

FIG. 27

SCALE OF FEET

TOW POST
OR "DUMMY"

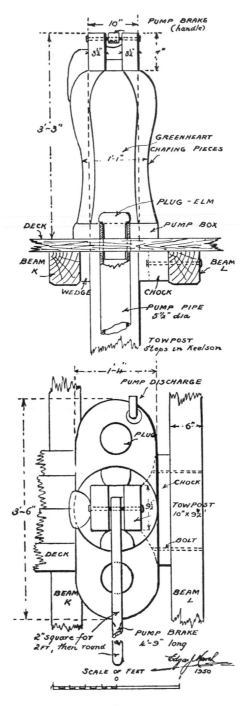

PUMP BRAKE
(handle)

10"

3½"   3½"

7"

3'-3"

GREENHEART
CHAFING PIECES

1'-1"

PLUG - ELM

PUMP BOX

DECK

BEAM
K

BEAM
L

WEDGE

CHOCK

PUMP PIPE
5½" dia

TOWPOST
Steps in Keelson

1'-4"

PUMP DISCHARGE

PLUG

6"

CHOCK

TOWPOST
10" x 9½"

9½"

BOLT

3'-6"

DECK

BEAM
K

BEAM
L

2" square for
2 ft, then round

PUMP BRAKE
4'-9" long

Edgar March
1950

SCALE OF FEET
0

FIG. 28

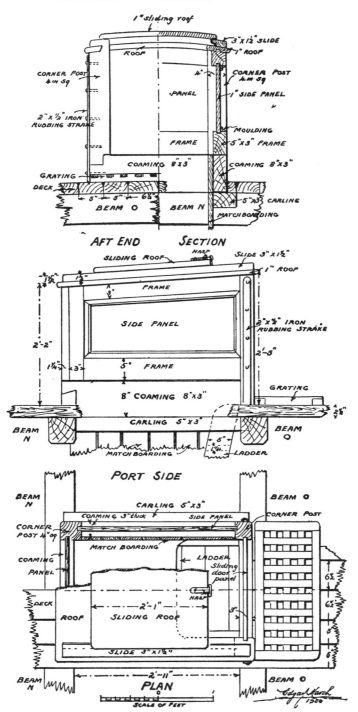

COMPANION or HOODWAY

FIG. 29

Main Sheet Chock

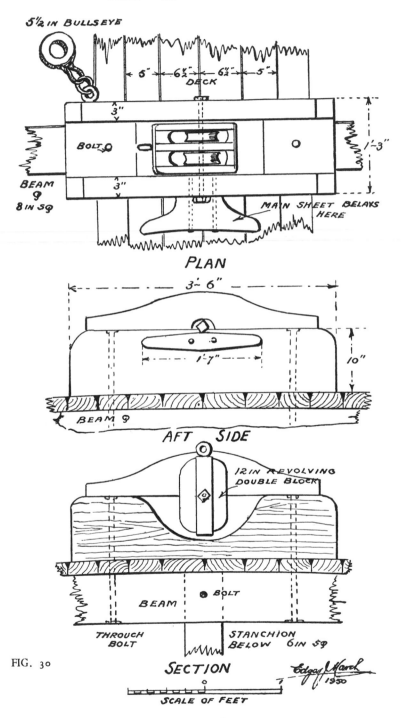

5½ IN BULLSEYE

5" 6½" 6½" 5"
DECK

3"

BOLT

1'-3"

BEAM
9
8 IN SQ

3"

MAIN SHEET BELAYS
HERE

PLAN

3'-6"

1'-7"

10"

BEAM 9

AFT SIDE

12 IN REVOLVING
DOUBLE BLOCK

BEAM

BOLT

THROUGH
BOLT

STANCHION
BELOW 6 IN SQ

FIG. 30

SECTION

Edgar March
1950

SCALE OF FEET

276

BELAYING PINS	Three of iron, 1 ft. long, ¾ in. dia.
EYEBOLTS	Two for'ard, one aft of cleat. One on inside of rail for relieving tackle.
DEADEYES	Two 6 in. dia., centred 2 ft. 8 in. on port side 2 ft. 6 in.

CAVIL RAIL. PORT SIDE
Fig. 35

RAIL etc.	Similar to starboard side.
EYEBOLT	On inner face of bulwark rail for relieving tackle.
CLEAT and EYEBOLT	Aft on cavil rail for quarter strop of beam, eyebolt aft for standing end of strop.
KNEES	In angles of cavil rail and transit rail, 4 in. thick, 1 ft. 11 in. and 1 ft. 7 in. arms. Rail and taffrail, 2 ft. 6 in. and 2 ft. 5 in., 8 in. throat, 3 in. thick.
BERTHING	1½ in. thick on top of cap.
DANDY SCORE (Fig. 37)	On upper side is 6 in. dia. roller, on side 4 in. dia., sides bolted to wooden base 2 ft. long, 4 in. thick.

TILLER
Fig. 36

TILLER	8 ft. long, 4 in. sq., to 4 × 3½ in. at end, morticed into rudder head, carved with scroll work, two brass-faced handgrips 3 ft. 6 in. above deck.
IRON STRAPS	2½ in. wide, ½ in. thick, 2 ft. 10½ in. long, bolted through 3 in. lug at back of rudder head. One on head of sternpost 2¾ in. wide for gudgeon.
HELM PORT	Faced with planks 6 in. wide, 2½ in. thick, carried up 2 in. above deck.
RUDDER	9 ft. 6 in. long, 4 in. thick, aft is natural grown timber 1 ft. 3 in. wide, 6 in. piece next, then 9 in., end piece is 8½ in. sq.
PINTLE and GUDGEONS	2 in. dia., gudgeons 2½ in. wide, ½ in. thick, through-bolted.
RUDDER HEAD	7½ in. by 8 in.

STERN
Figs. 37 and 38

TAFFRAIL	1 ft. 3½ in. wide, 3½ in. thick. Half-round iron on outer edge.
FAIRLEAD	Iron, on wood base 2 ft. 6 in. long, 1½ in. thick, on starboard side only.
SHEET PLATE	Iron, 2 ft. 3 in. long, 2¾ in. wide, in centre of taffrail with eye to take shackle of double block.
TRANSIT RAIL	11 in. wide, 4 in. thick, has two sockets for stern light stanchions, plate 3 in. sq., centred 4 ft.
CLEAT	4 ft. long, 3½ in. wide, 3 in. thick across horn timbers, mizzen sheet belays here.

STERN TIMBERS	All butt on fashion timbers, with filling timbers between, trenailed to arch board, the horns are 6 in. wide, the others $5\frac{1}{2}$ in.
ARCH BOARD	1 ft. 11 in. wide, in two boards, is the continuation of covering board.
EYEBOLT	To port, for standing end of mizzen boom guy.

OUTSIDE HULL

LETTERS	At bow, cut in rail, MASTER HAND, 3 in. high, with star.
REGISTRATION (Fig. 27)	L.T. 1203, 13 in. high, white on black ground.
CHAFING PIECES	Six pieces, 3 in. wide, on port side only.
IRON RUBBING STRAKES	3 in. $\times$ $1\frac{1}{2}$ in. on rail where shown in plans, $2\frac{1}{2}$ in. half-round, on covering board, 3 in. half-round on third strake of topsides.

DECK FRAMING

BEAMS (Plan 18, page 344)	All for'ard of 'midships have knees on aft side, those aft have them on fore side, beam H has them on fore side as well as aft, beam K has none, beam Q has one on aft port side as well. Spacing and size varies, round-up is $3\frac{1}{2}$ in. on beam G, which has official number 14001 and 45 $\frac{75}{100}$ reg. tons, cut in aft side.
CARLINGS	In addition to those forming hatches, etc., there are two on centre line, one between beams D and C is 6 $\times$ 3 in., the other between E and F is 5 in. $\times$ 3 in. From beams O to T on either side are $6\frac{1}{2}$ by 6 in. carlings.
HANGING KNEES	Of iron, arm under beam 2 ft. 8 in. long, extend down ceiling to bilges at beams C, F, H, J, L, and Q, one at C is extra to specification.
BREASTHOOK	Wood, 6 in. thick, throat 2 ft. 1 in., at stem under deck. Iron one with arms 3 ft. 6 in. long is 2 ft. 6 in. above platform for'ard.

The starboard side of plan shows the covering board and stanchions, the port side has the covering board removed to show the heads of futtocks.

BELOW DECK

FORE PEAK (Plan 18, page 345)	Extends 4 ft. from apron, has vertical slats 3 in. by 1 in., 3 in. apart, from shelf 3 ft. above platform.
SAIL ROOM	10 ft. long. Gangway 3 ft. 7 in. wide has 5 in. by 3 in. fore and afters from fore peak to bulkhead, 3 ft. up. Tenoned in them are 3 $\times$ 1 in. slats, 3 in. apart to form racks, sloping inwards and downwards. Similar slats are vertical at aft end of room. Small sails stow to port, big to starboard.
HEAD ROOM	5 ft. 5 in. average under beams.
TALLOW BOX	2 ft. 1 in. sq. and 2 ft. high on fore side of windlass bitts. 9 in. wide shelf at aft end, $2\frac{1}{4}$ in. sq. post at port fore end.

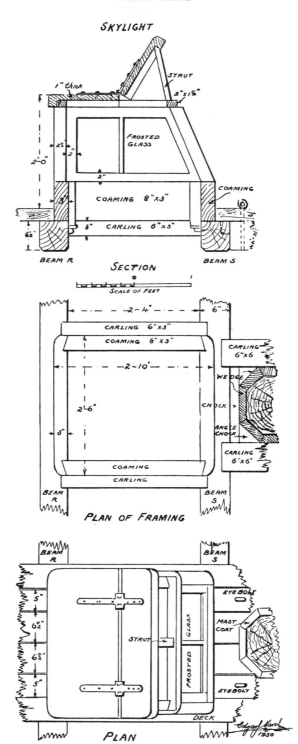

SKYLIGHT

1" thick

STRUT

2"x1⅛"

FROSTED GLASS

2⅜"
2

2'-0"

2"

COAMING 8"x3"

COAMING

3"

3"   CARLING 6"x3"

6½"

BEAM R   BEAM S

SECTION

SCALE OF FEET

2'-4"   6"

CARLING 6"x3"

COAMING 8"x3"

CARLING 6"x6

2'-10'

WEDGE

2'-6"

CHOCK

8"

ANGLE CHOCK

CARLING 6"x6'

COAMING

CARLING

BEAM R   BEAM S

PLAN OF FRAMING

BEAM R   BEAM S

5"

EYEBOLT

6½"

MAST COAT

STRUT

6½"

FROSTED GLASS

5"

EYEBOLT

FIG. 31

DECK

Edgar March
1950

PLAN

279

SECTION OF BULWARKS

SCALE OF FEET

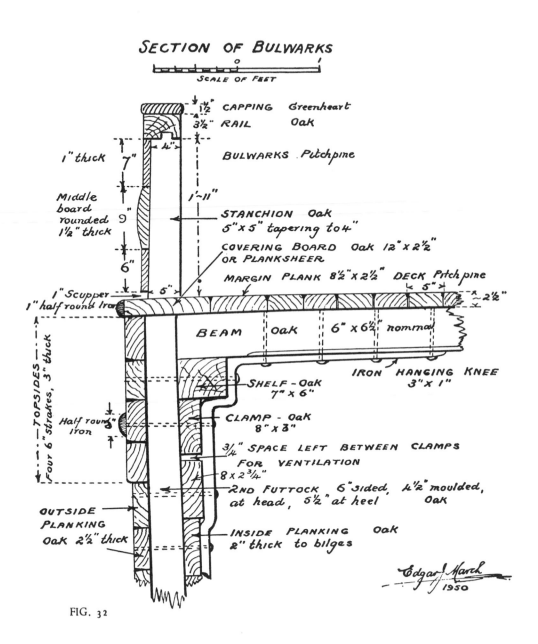

1½" CAPPING Greenheart

3½" RAIL Oak

1" thick 7"

BULWARKS Pitchpine

Middle board rounded 1½" thick 9"

1'~11"

STANCHION Oak 5"x 5" tapering to 4"

COVERING BOARD Oak 12"x 2½" OR PLANKSHEER

6"

MARGIN PLANK 8½"x 2½" DECK Pitchpine

1" Scupper

1" half round Iron

5"

5"

~ 2½"

BEAM Oak 6"x 6½" nominal

IRON HANGING KNEE 3"x 1"

SHELF - Oak 7"x 6"

CLAMP - Oak 8"x 3"

¾" SPACE LEFT BETWEEN CLAMPS FOR VENTILATION

8 x 2¾"

2ND FUTTOCK 6"sided, 4½" moulded, at head, 5½" at heel Oak

Half round Iron

- - TOPSIDES - - Four 6" strakes, 3" thick

OUTSIDE PLANKING Oak 2½" thick

INSIDE PLANKING Oak 2" thick to bilges

Edgar March 1950

FIG. 32

280

CARLINGS AT SKYLIGHT & MIZZEN MAST.

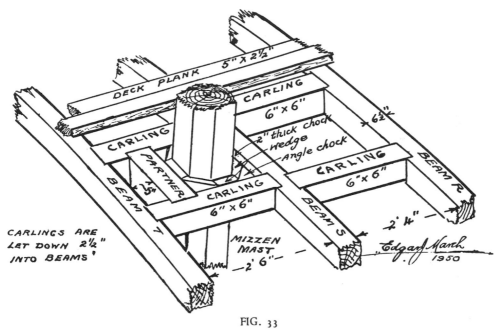

DECK PLANK 5" X 2½"

CARLING
6" X 6"

CARLING

2" thick chock
wedge
Angle chock

CARLING
6" X 6"

PARTNER

BEAM R

CARLING
6" X 6"

BEAM T

BEAM S

6½"

2' 4"

CARLINGS ARE
LET DOWN 2½"
INTO BEAMS'

MIZZEN
MAST
2' 6"

Edgar March
1950

FIG. 33

MIZZEN CAVIL RAIL Starboard Side

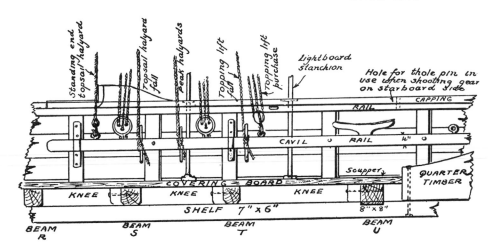

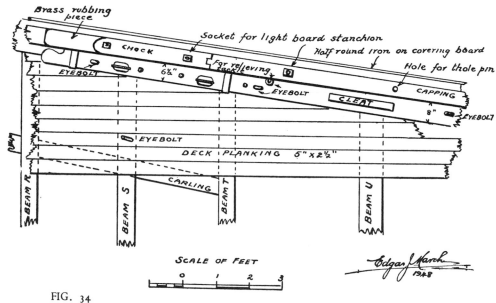

SCALE OF FEET

FIG. 34

MATCHBOARDING	1 in. thick on either side of gangway for 5 ft. for'ard of bulkhead, has two steps 2 ft. long, 3 in. wide and thick on starboard side under fore hatch, one step on port side. Winch bitts butt against back of boards.
STORE ROOMS	5 ft. long. To starboard for spare net, to port for small warp, 60 fthm. and hauling line. Access through 4 ft. wide opening in aft bulkhead, 2 ft. above platform.
CHAIN BOX	On aft side of bulkhead, 5 ft. long, with mast step in aft end, 18 in. high above platform, $1\frac{1}{2}$ in. thick sides, depth to ceiling 4 ft. 3 in.
WARP ROOM	8 ft. 6 in. long. To starboard is pound board 12 in. high, $1\frac{3}{4}$ in. thick, beyond is storage for 110 fthm. trawl warp. On port side of chain box are 2 in. $\times$ $2\frac{1}{2}$ in. uprights, between them drops a 2 ft. $\times$ $1\frac{1}{2}$ in. division board. On for'ard side is store for fenders, on aft side spares, blocks, bridles, etc.
BULKHEAD	On aft side of beam H. 1 in. thick. Two steps 2 ft. long under hatch.
DOORWAY	To port, 19 in. wide, leads into fish room.
FISH ROOM	11 ft. 1 in. long. 6 ft. 3 in. headroom between beams.
ICE BOX	6 ft. long, 5 ft. 3 in. wide, with door 2 ft. wide, 2 ft. 3 in. high, bunkering port in deck above.
PILLARS	Thirteen in all, 6 in. sq., on 3 in. wedge bases, under beams.
F. W. TANKS	Galvanised iron, to port and starboard, 5 ft. 7 in. long, 1 ft. 8 in. wide, 3 ft. 6 in. high.
TOWPOST	On centre of aft bulkhead. Box around 2 ft. 6 in. high, 2 ft. 7 in. long, 1 ft. 9 in. wide, $1\frac{1}{2}$ in. thick sides. Pumps on either side of post which has step on fore side 3 in. wide.
BULKHEADS	2 in. thick plank, 6 in. space between, insulated.
BOILER ROOM	7 ft. 10 in. long, 5 ft. 9 in. headroom under beams.
BOILER	Against for'ard bulkhead, directly under hatch.
LOCKER SEATS	On either side, 1 ft. 3 in. wide.
COAL BUNKER	On starboard side. 5 ft. 6 in. long, 3 ft. wide.
F. W. TANK	2 ft. long, 1 ft. 3 in. wide. On starboard side against aft bulkhead.
CUPBOARD	With three shelves for stores.
GALLEY	2 ft. 6 in. high in recess, 2 ft. 4 in. wide.
BULKHEAD	2 ft. long fore and aft, between beams N and O, 1 in. matchboarding.
COMPANION LADDER	1 ft. 8 in. wide, sides $1\frac{1}{4}$ in. thick, eight rungs 5 in. wide.
DOOR	1 ft. 9 in. wide, 5 ft. 4 in. high, leads into cabin, 6 in. step up.
CUPBOARDS	On port side. Aft one for cook's stores, middle for lamps and paraffin, then F. W. tank.

CABIN

HEADROOM	5 ft. 3 in. under beams, which are lined with $\frac{1}{4}$ in. boards, painted white.

283

BUNKS	6 ft. long, sliding panels 2 ft. 2 in. long. To starboard, for skipper, third hand aft bunk. To port, for mate with cook's bunk below, the deck hand aft bunk.
LOCKER SEATS	1 ft. 3½ in. from floor all round cabin.
PILLAR	6 in. sq., carved with conventional scroll design, is under beam Q which is moulded 9½ in., tenons into keelson with knee on fore side.
TABLE	3 ft. 9 in. long, 3 ft. 11 in. wide fore end, 2 ft. 5 in. aft, 2 ft. 4 in. high, has 2 in. fiddle, ½ in thick, all round, projecting 1 inch above top.
FORE BULKHEAD *(Fig. 39)*	Has stove against it with mirror and 1 ft. 9 in. shelf over, four lockers on starboard side, two on port side, by bunks. On port side of stove are two drawers and three lockers.
MIZZEN MAST	Goes through shelf into step on deadwood.
LOCKERS, AFT.	To port and starboard, for crockery, in the centre of panelling is door 2 ft. 2 in. high, 1 ft. 9½ in. wide, giving access to counter where spare rope, gear and reef lacings are stored.

HEEL OF MAINMAST

Fig. 40

HOUSING	8 ft. 3 in. long, mast is octagonal-sided for 12 ft, faces 6½ in. tapering to 5½ in. A 2½ in. iron band is driven on 2 in. above tenon, 3 ft. 4 in. circ.
TENON	1 ft. long, 4 in. deep, 3 in. thick.
MAST STEP	10 in. wide, 4 in. thick, mortice cut in to receive tenon, bolted to keelson.
MAST COAT	Local name "scoot", canvas cover at deck to prevent water getting below.
CLEATS	Six heavy oak cleats on faces. Aft one is 1 ft. 4 in. long, 2½ in. thick, for topsail sheet. Next on port side, 1 ft. 2 in. long, for topsail tack, third, 1 ft 4 in. long, for leader, others are 1 ft. 1 in. long.
GOOSENECK BAND	2½ in. wide, in two halves bolted together at sides, with a 6 in. long link on bolt. The one to port takes topsail tack purchase, to starboard the main truss tackle. Eye or "shaffle" to take gooseneck is 4 in. dia., 1 in. thick rim.
DIAMETER	At gooseneck and above is 15 in.
MAST HOOPS	Fourteen in all, 18 in. dia., 1 in. thick, 1¾ in. deep. Twelve in use, two spare.
COPPER PLATE	Takes chafe of jaws when third reef is down, 10 in. deep in middle, 5 in. fore ends, battens from trestle-trees end here.
RIG	36 ft.

MASTHEAD

Fig. 41

CHEEKS	2 ft. 6 in. long, 1 ft. 4 in. wide at head, tapering to 6 in. at foot. 3½ in. thick at head, 2 in. at foot.

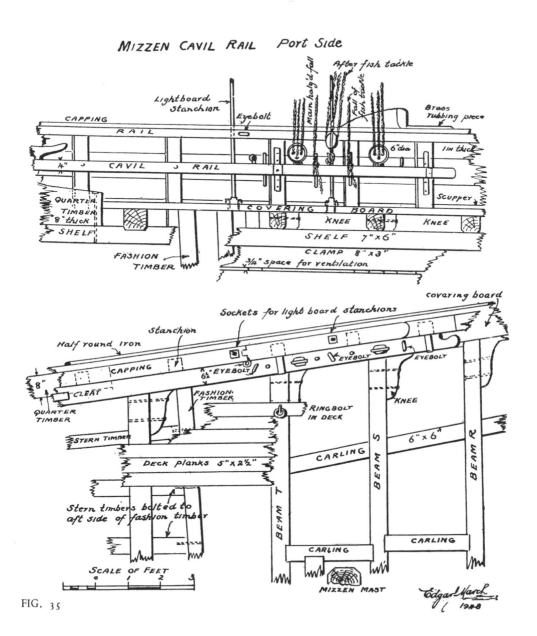

MIZZEN CAVIL RAIL   Port Side

FIG. 35

OAK TILLER.

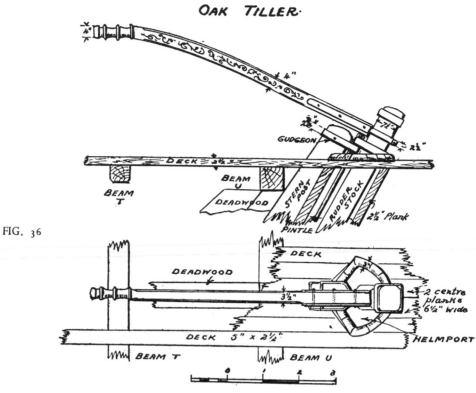

FIG. 36

DANDY SCORE & MIZZEN CAVIL RAIL

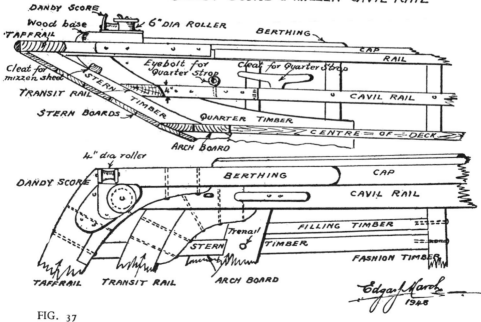

Edgar March
1948

FIG. 37

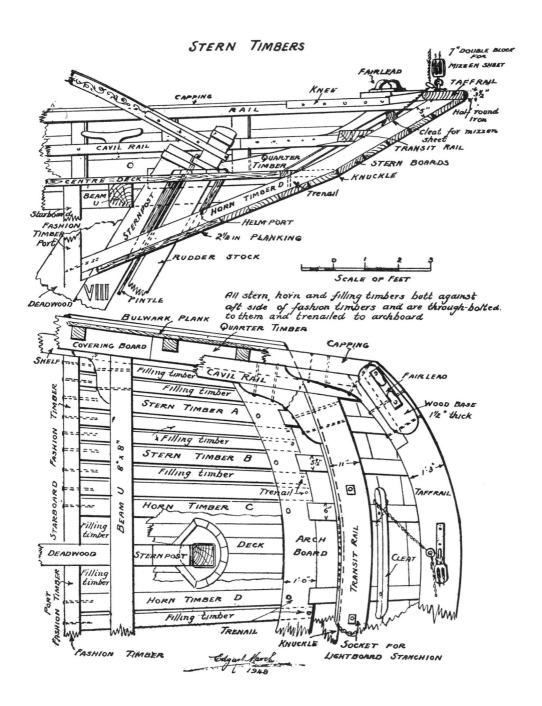

STERN TIMBERS

7" DOUBLE BLOCK
FOR
MIZZEN SHEET

FAIRLEAD

TAFFRAIL

KNEE

CAPPING

RAIL

Half round IRON

Cleat for mizzen
sheet

TRANSIT RAIL

CAVIL RAIL

QUARTER
TIMBER

STERN BOARDS

CENTRE DECK

KNUCKLE

BEAM
U

HORN TIMBER D

Trenail

Starboard
FASHION
TIMBER
Port

STERNPOST

HELM PORT

2½ in PLANKING

DEADWOOD

VIII

PINTLE

RUDDER STOCK

SCALE OF FEET

All stern, horn and filling timbers butt against
aft side of fashion timbers and are through-bolted
to them and trenailed to archboard

BULWARK PLANK

QUARTER TIMBER

COVERING BOARD

Quarter Timber

CAPPING

Shelf

Filling timber

CAVIL RAIL

FAIRLEAD

Filling timber

STERN TIMBER A

WOOD BASE
1½" thick

Filling timber

STERN TIMBER B

Filling timber

Trenail

HORN TIMBER C

TAFFRAIL

DECK

ARCH
BOARD

STERNPOST

DEADWOOD

CLEAT

Filling
timber

HORN TIMBER D

Filling timber

Trenail

FASHION TIMBER

Edgar March
1948

KNUCKLE

SOCKET FOR
LIGHTBOARD STANCHION

FIG. 38

287

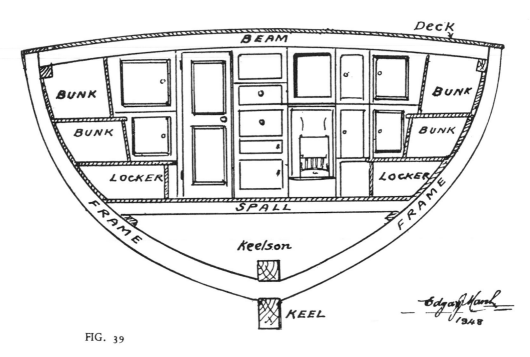

CABIN BULKHEAD

FIG. 39

EYE PLATES	Through-bolted diagonally on cheeks, 7 in. long, 3 in. wide, eye to port takes shackle of fish tackle pendant, to starboard takes hook of single block for topping lift.
TRESTLE-TREES	Wood, 3 ft. long, 4 in. deep, 3½ in. wide.
IRON BOLT	¾ in. sq., at aft end, against mast.
BOLSTERS	Wood, 1 ft. 6 in. long, 4 in. deep, 1½ in. wide at top.
WINTER CROSSTREE	Halved into fore ends of bolsters, 3 in. by 2½ in., 2 ft. 6 in. long, 1 ft. 2 in. from fore end of trestle trees.
SUMMER CROSSTREE	18 ft. long, 4 in. by 3 in. Bolt holes are on fore side of yoke, with iron plate below.
YOKE or LOWER CAP	4 in. thick, wood. 9 in. sq. opening for heel of topmast.
IRON BAND	¼ in. thick, 4 in. wide, bolted all round yoke and trestle trees.
EYEBOLTS	Under fore end of yoke, for foresail halyards.
FAIRLEADS	For jib halyards, which lead through eye at outer end, 9 in. long.
BATTENS	2 in. wide, ½ in. thick, extend from lower end of cheeks for about 16 ft. to copper chafing piece. 1 in. iron strap round mast just under foot of cheeks.
HEEL of TOPMAST	Has diagonal sheave for mast rope and fid hole. Winter mast 28 ft. long.
TRUCK (Fig. 42)	6 in. dia., 3 in. thick, with gilded arrow vane and red or green flag on wire frame.
MASTHEAD	9 ft. long, 3 ft. 1 in. circ. at yoke. Head is shaped 9½ in. by 9 in. to fit in iron cap.
CAP	Iron, shaped as shown, 4 in. deep, ring for the topmast had 9 in. dia. inside, arms 2¼ in. deep.
LANTERN ARM	On fore side of ring, 1 ft. 4 in. long, eye at end to take shackle of small single block for halyards.
SADDLE or HORSE	3½ in. iron band bolted round masthead, carries 1 ft. 6 in. shaped arm, with hole at lower end to take shackle of treble block for main halyards, which is 1 ft. by 10 in. by 8 in. Arm rests in groove on plate 1 ft. 4 in. long, 1½ in. thick, bolted to aft side of masthead.
EYEBOLTS	Three on aft side, lower one takes standing end of peak halyards, the two upper ones the hooks of the single blocks.
JIB BAND	Iron, 2½ in. wide, bolted round masthead between lower and middle eyebolts, has eyes on either side to take single blocks of jib halyards.
CHEEK BLOCK	For topmast mast rope, bolted to starboard side of masthead under upper eyebolt. 4 in. sheave. Iron case 1 ft. 3 in. long 4½ in. wide, 3 in. thick.
FORESTAY	Collar 6 ft. long rests on upper aft side of band for main halyard horse. Wire is 5 inches circumference over serving. Weight approx. 3 cwt.
SHROUDS	Wire, 3½ in. circ.

MAIN BOOM
Fig. 43

LENGTH	33 ft. 7 in., 2 ft. 4½ in. circ. at gooseneck, 2 ft. 9 in. at main sheet strop. Approx. 9¾ to 10 in. dia.
GOOSENECK	18 in. long, 6 in. wide, 2 in. dia., hole 3½ in. from end takes forelock which prevents boom being unshipped.
IRON BANDS	Driven on end, inner one 1½ in. wide, others ½ in.
EYE PLATES	For reef tackles, 11½ in. long, 2½ in. wide, through-bolted.
CLEAT	13½ in. long on upper side of boom, 2 ft. 11 in. from end.
CLAMPS	Two on either side, 1 ft. 9 in. long, 4 in. thick, 4 in. wide. 3½ in. dia. sheaves, end of axle bolt formed into eye, 3 in. outside dia., for reef pendants, 6 in. by 2½ in. plate under.
STROP BAND	Iron, 3½ in. wide, carries 2 in. strop for main sheet block.
IRON PLATES	One on either side 12 in. long by ¾ in., with holes 2 in. by 1 in. oval shape, 8 in. centred, for clew earing.
END IRON	2¼ in. wide, driven on, 3 in. eye lug on upper side to take shackle of topping lift.

MAIN GAFF
Fig. 44

LENGTH	31 ft. 2 in., 2 ft. 1 in. circ. at jaws, 1 ft. 9 in. at peak. Approx. 8 in. dia. to 6¾ in.
IRON BAND	1½ in. wide driven on inner end.
EYEBOLT	On underside of gaff to take shackle at throat of mainsail.
SLOT	4 in. long at bottom, 9 in. on upper side, 2 in. wide, iron tumbler works in this slot.
IRON TUMBLER	4 in. wide, 1 in. thick, 5 in. above gaff with hole to take shackle of 12 in. double block of main halyards. Lower end 2¾ in. wide, pivots on 1 in. dia. bar bolted to underside of horns.
HORNS or JAWS	5 ft. 9 in. long, 5 in. thick, shaped as shown, 7 in. wide at tumbler, 4 in. at tips, through-bolted to sides of gaff.
IRON BANDS	Two 2 in. wide, driven on over inner ends.
EYEBOLT	On under side of port horn to take topsail sheet block, a 7 in. × 5 in. single one.
WOOD TUMBLER	1 ft. 11 in. long, 7 in. thick at centre tapering to 3 in., pivots on through-bolt across inside of jaws, and slides on mast battens.
PARREL HOLES	Vertical hole in end of each horn to take the rope holding the 2¼ in. × 2 in. wood trucks.

PEAK OF GAFF
Fig. 45

FISH BATTEN	9 ft. 6 in. long, 3 in. sq., lashed on upper side to strengthen spar in way of strops. Lashings 6 in. wide.

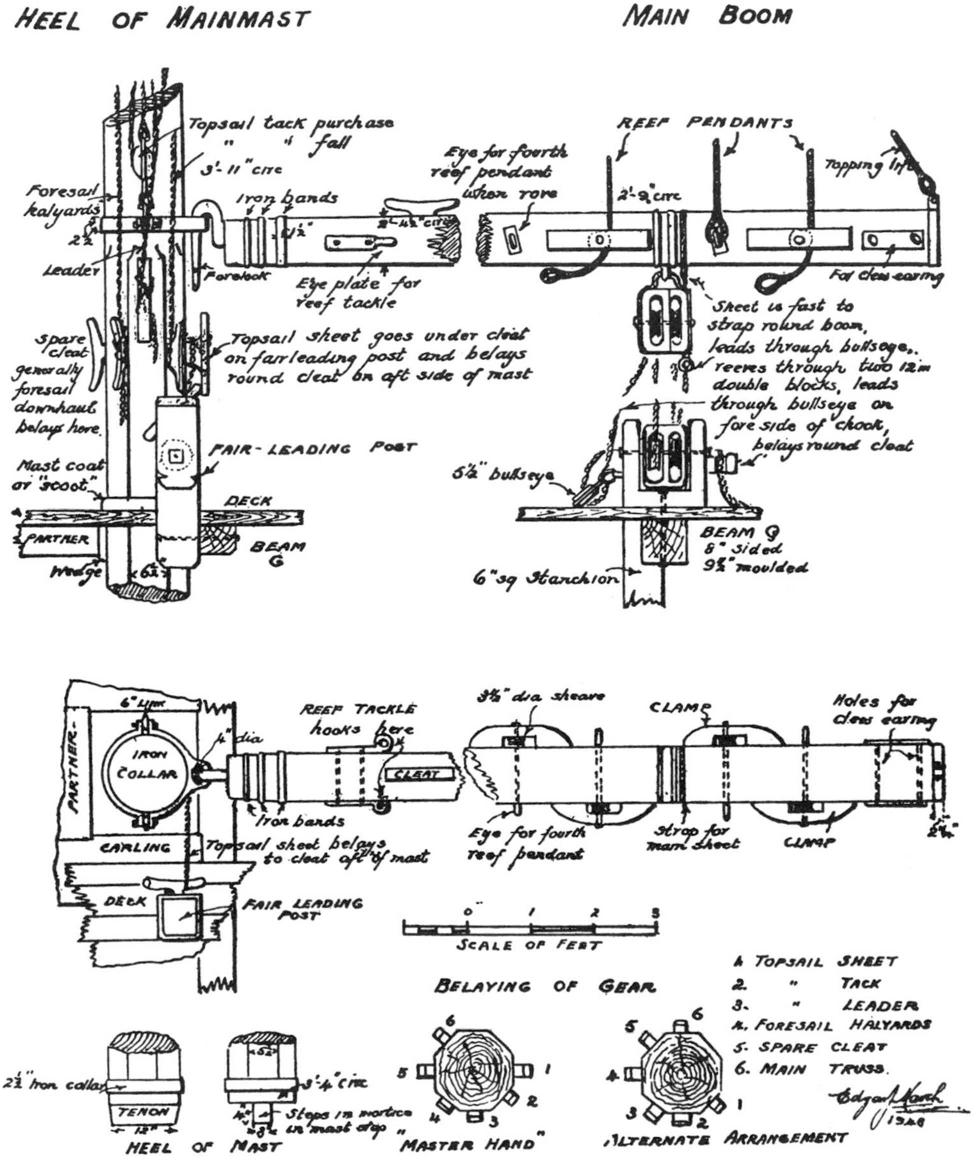

HEEL OF MAINMAST

MAIN BOOM

REEF PENDANTS

Topsail tack purchase
"   "   "   fall
3'-11" circ

Foresail
kalyards

Iron bands

Eye for fourth
reef pendant
when rove

Topping lift

2'-2" circ

Leader

Forelock

Eye plate for
reef tackle

2½-4" circ

Fol clew earing

Spare
cleat
generally
foresail
downhaul
belays here

Topsail sheet goes under cleat
on fairleading post and belays
round cleat on aft side of mast

Sheet is fast to
strap round boom,
leads through bullseye,
reeves through two 12 in
double blocks, leads
through bullseye on
fore side of chock,
belays round cleat

FAIR-LEADING POST

Mast coat
or 'scoot.'

5½" bullseye

DECK

PARTNER

BEAM
G

Wedge

6½"

BEAM G
8" sided
9½" moulded

6" sq Stanchion

REEF TACKLE
hooks here

3½" dia sheave

CLAMP

Holes for
clew earing

6" thick

IRON
COLLAR

CLEAT

PARTNER

Iron bands

Eye for fourth
reef pendant

Strap for
main sheet

CLAMP

CARLING

Topsail sheet belays
to cleat aft of mast

DECK

FAIR LEADING
POST

SCALE OF FEET

0   1   2   3

BELAYING OF GEAR

1. TOPSAIL SHEET
2.   "   TACK
3.   "   LEADER
4. FORESAIL HALYARDS
5. SPARE CLEAT
6. MAIN TRUSS.

2½" iron collar

TENON

Steps in mortice
in mast step

3'-4" circ

HEEL OF MAST

"MASTER HAND"

ALTERNATE ARRANGEMENT

FIG. 40

FIG. 43

MAIN MASTHEAD

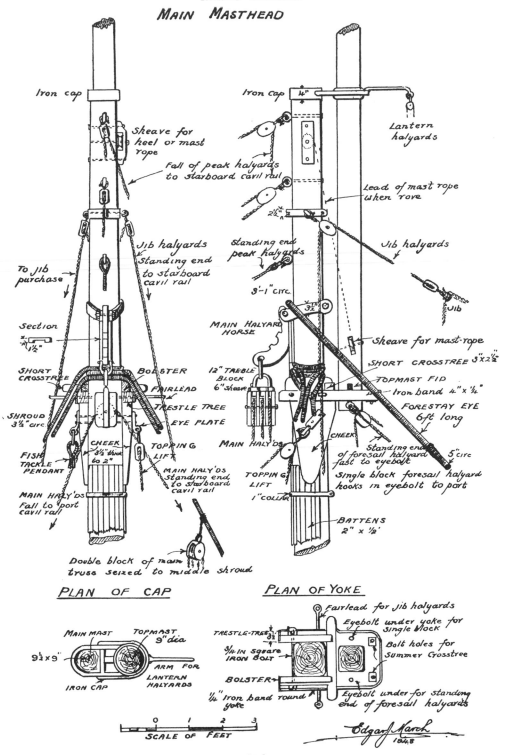

Iron cap

Sheave for heel or mast rope

Fall of peak halyards to starboard cavil rail

Jib halyards Standing end to starboard cavil rail

To jib purchase

Section $1\frac{1}{2}$"

SHORT CROSSTREE

BOLSTER

FAIRLEAD

SHROUD $3\frac{1}{2}$" circ

TRESTLE TREE

EYE PLATE

CHEEK $3\frac{1}{2}$" thick to 2"

TOPPING LIFT

FISH TACKLE PENDANT

MAIN HALY'DS Standing end to starboard cavil rail

MAIN HALY'DS Fall to port cavil rail

Double block of main truss seized to middle shroud

Iron Cap 4"

Lantern halyards

Fall of peak halyards to starboard cavil rail

Lead of mast rope when rove

$2\frac{1}{2}$" ʌ

Standing end peak halyards

Jib halyards

$3'-1"$ CIRC

Jib

MAIN HALYARD HORSE

$\frac{1}{32}$" $3\frac{1}{2}$

Sheave for mast-rope

SHORT CROSSTREE $3"\times2\frac{1}{2}"$

12" TREBLE BLOCK 6" sheave

TOPMAST FID Iron band 4" x $\frac{1}{4}$"

FORESTAY EYE 6ft long

MAIN HALY'DS

CHEEK

Standing end of foresail halyard fast to eyebolt

5" circ

TOPPING LIFT 1" collar

Single block foresail halyard hooks in eyebolt to port

BATTENS 2" x $\frac{1}{2}$"

PLAN OF CAP

MAIN MAST

TOPMAST 9" dia

$9\frac{1}{2}$" x 9"

ARM FOR LANTERN HALYARDS

IRON CAP

PLAN OF YOKE

Fairlead for jib halyards

Eyebolt under yoke for single block

TRESTLE-TREE $3\frac{1}{2}$

$\frac{3}{4}$ IN square IRON BOLT

Bolt holes for summer crosstree

BOLSTER

$\frac{1}{4}$" iron band round yoke

Eyebolt under for standing end of foresail halyards

0 1 2 3

SCALE OF FEET

Edgar March 1948

FIG. 41

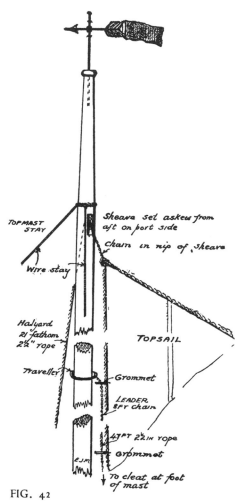

TOPMAST HEAD & LEADER

FIG. 42

MAIN GAFF

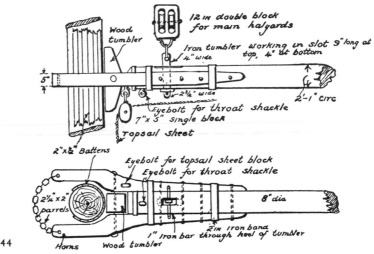

Wood tumbler

12 in double block for main halyards

Iron tumbler working in slot 9" long at top, 4" at bottom

4" wide

2¼" wide

2'-1" circ

Eyebolt for throat shackle

7"x 5" single block

Topsail sheet

2"x ½" Battens

Eyebolt for topsail sheet block
Eyebolt for throat shackle

2¼ x2 parrels

8" dia

FIG. 44

Horns

Wood tumbler

1" Iron bar through heel of tumbler

2 in Iron band

UNDER SIDE OF JAWS

0   1   2   3

SCALE OF FEET

MAIN PEAK

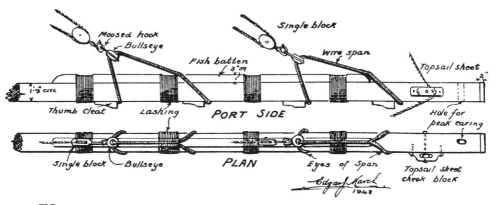

Moused hook
Bullseye

Single block

Wire span

Fish batten 3" sq

Topsail sheet

1'-9 circ

Thumb Cleat   Lashing   **PORT SIDE**

Hole for peak earing

Single block   Bullseye   **PLAN**   Eyes of Span

Topsail sheet cheek block

Edgar March 1948

FIG. 45

THUMB CLEATS	Four on under side of spar, 8 in. long, 2½ in. thick, hold **wire** spans in position.
SPANS *or* STROPS	Wire, parcelled and served, eye splice in each end slips along gaff, bullseye takes hook of single block of peak halyards.
CHEEK BLOCK	On port side for topsail sheet. 2½ in. sheave in iron case, 4 in. deep, 1 ft. long and 3 in wide.
EARING HOLE	Vertical hole 9 in. from end takes peak earing of mainsail.
END IRON	Iron, 2 in. wide, driven on end of gaff.

MIZZEN MAST
Figs. 46 & 49

LENGTH	49 ft. 5 in. with ornamental cap 1 ft. high on head. 1 ft. 8 in. circ. at top, 1 ft. 10 in. at eyebolts, 2 ft. 6 in. at hounds, 3 ft. 2 in. at gooseneck band.
HOUSING	Lower end 11 in. sq. for 4 ft., octagonal-sided for 4 ft.
TENON	10 in. long, 3 in. deep, 3 in. thick, 2 in. iron band driven on heel of mast.
GOOSENECK BAND	3 in. wide, mast here about 12 in. dia. As on mainmast.
CLEATS.	Six, 1 ft. 2 in. long, as on main mast.
BINNACLE	Secured with two iron bands on aft side of mast.
BATTENS and COPPER CHAFING PIECE	2 in. × ½ in., extend from hounds for a distance of 9 ft. 4 in., at foot is copper band 8 in. deep at centre as on main mast.
RIG	27 ft. 6 in.
MAST HOOPS	Ten in number. One spare always ready for use.
HOUNDS	3 in. iron collar, two eyes on each side to take shackles of mizzen shrouds, one on fore side for shackle of 7 in. double block of aft fish tackle.
SADDLE	Plate 15 in. long, through-bolted, projects 10 in. aft of mast, arms 1½ in. wide, 1 in. thick. Eye in centre takes the 6 in. shackle of the 7½ × 5½ × 5 in. double block of main halyards, 4 in. sheaves. Mast dia. is about 9½ in.
EYEBOLTS	Three on aft side, 2 ft. apart, for single blocks and standing end of peak halyards. One on starboard side originally took topping lift, one on foreside for 7 in. double block, staysail halyards.
CHAFING PIECE	Zinc, 1 ft. 4 in. deep under topsail halyard sheave to take chafe of yard off the mast.
HALYARD SHEAVE	5 in. dia. sheave, 11 in. × 1 in. plate on port side of mast, 3½ in. wide slot, cut athwartships.
TRUCK	1 ft. high, ornamental turned.

MIZZEN GAFF
Fig. 47

LENGTH	21 ft. 10 in. Circ. at jaws 1 ft. 9 in., peak 1 ft. 5 in. or approximately 6¾ in. to 5 in. dia.

EYEBOLT	On under side for throat shackle of sail.
SLOT	3½ in. long at bottom, 8 in. at top, fittings as on main gaff.
HORNS	6 ft. long, 3½ in. thick, shaped as shown. 6 in. wide at tumbler, 3 in. at tips. Four through-bolts.
EYEBOLT	On underside of port horn to take topsail sheet block, single, 5 in. × 4 in. × 2½ in.
WOOD TUMBLER	1 ft. 6 in. long, 6 in. thick, 6 in. wide at centre tapering to 2 in. Pivots on bolt through horns.
PARRELS	As for mainmast.

MIZZEN PEAK
Fig. 48

THUMB CLEATS	Four in all. The two outer ones are on underside of spar, the two inner ones are off-centred. Aft cleat 6 in. × 1½ in., middle ones 8 in. × 1½ in., fore cleat 9 in. × 1½ in.
WIRE SPANS	As on main gaff.
CHEEK BLOCK	For topsail sheet. Wood clamp 1 ft. long on port side, 3 in. wide, 2 in. thick, 2½ in. sheave.
EARING HOLE	11 in. from end of gaff, 1 in. dia. vertical hole to take peak earing of mizzen sail.
IRON BAND	2 in. wide driven on end of spar.

MIZZEN BOOM
Fig. 49

LENGTH	24 ft. 7 in. Circ. 1 ft. 11 in. at inner end, 2 ft. 1 in. at sheet strop. Approx. 7¼ in. dia. to 8 in.
GOOSENECK	11 in. long, 5 in. wide, 1½ in. dia.
IRON BANDS	3 in. wide on end, second one, 8 in. from end, is 2 in.
CLEAT	1 ft. 2 in. long, 3 in. high, on upper side of spar.
EYE PLATES	For reef tackles. 8 in. × 2 in., with 2 in. dia. eyes, through-bolted.
THUMB CLEAT	On upper side, 9 ft. from end of spar, 9 in. × 2 in.
IRON BAND	8 ft. from end of spar, 3 in. wide, carries 2 in. wide strop for sheet block, double, 7 in. × 6 in. × 5 in., with 4 in. sheaves.
CLAMPS	4 ft. 8 in. long. 3½ in. wide. 3 in. thick, shaped as shown. Two 2½ in. dia. sheaves in 1½ in. wide slots on port side, one in centre clamp on starboard side. Slots 4 in. long.
HOLES	One in centre clamp to port, two in outer ones to starboard, to take standing ends of reef pendants. 1½ in. dia.
EARING HOLE	1¼ in. vertical hole, oval shaped, 4 in. from end.
END IRON	2 in. wide driven on end of spar, 2½ in. eye lug on upper side to take shackle of topping lift.

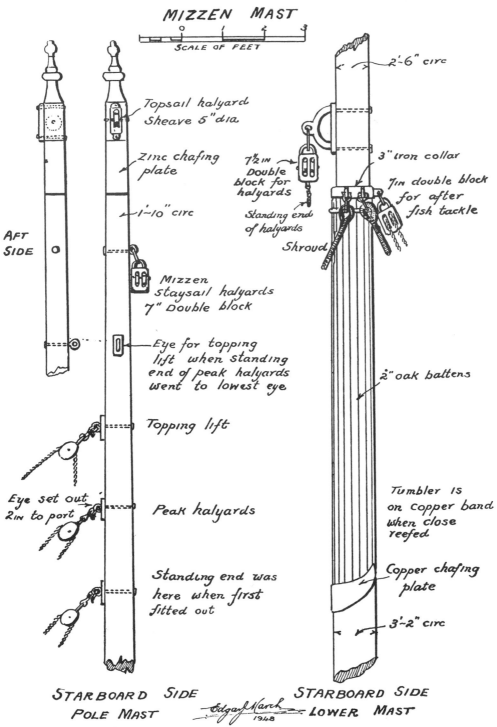

MIZZEN MAST

SCALE OF FEET

Topsail halyard
Sheave 5" dia.

Zinc chafing
plate

7½ in
Double
block for
halyards

1'-10" circ

Standing end
of halyards

AFT
SIDE

Mizzen
staysail halyards
7" Double block

Eye for topping
lift when standing
end of peak halyards
went to lowest eye

Topping lift

Eye set out
2 in to port

Peak halyards

Standing end was
here when first
fitted out

2'-6" circ

3" iron collar

7 in double block
for after
fish tackle

Shroud

2" oak battens

Tumbler is
on copper band
when close
reefed

Copper chafing
plate

3'-2" circ

STARBOARD SIDE
POLE MAST

Edgar March
1948

STARBOARD SIDE
LOWER MAST

FIG. 46

297

MIZZEN GAFF

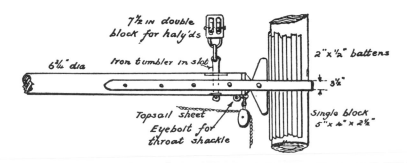

7½ in double
block for haly'ds

6¾" dia

Iron tumbler in slot

2"x½" battens

3½"

Topsail sheet

Single block
5"x 4"x 2½"

Eyebolt for
throat shackle

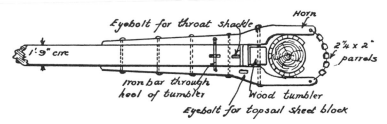

Eyebolt for throat shackle

Horn

1'9" circ

2¼ x 2"
parrels

Iron bar through
heel of tumbler

Wood tumbler

Eyebolt for topsail sheet block

FIG. 47

UNDER SIDE OF JAWS
PEAK

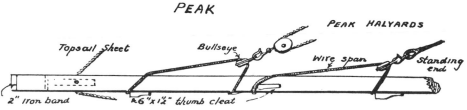

PEAK HALYARDS

Topsail Sheet

Bullseye

Wire span

Standing
end

2" iron band

26"x 1½" thumb cleat

STARBOARD SIDE OF PEAK

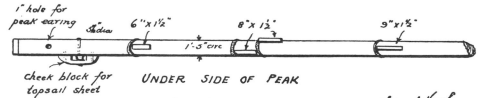

1" hole for
peak earing

Radius

6"x 1½"

8"x 1½"

9"x1½"

1'5" circ

Cheek block for
topsail sheet

UNDER SIDE OF PEAK

0   1   2   3   4
SCALE OF FEET

Edgar March
1948

FIG. 48

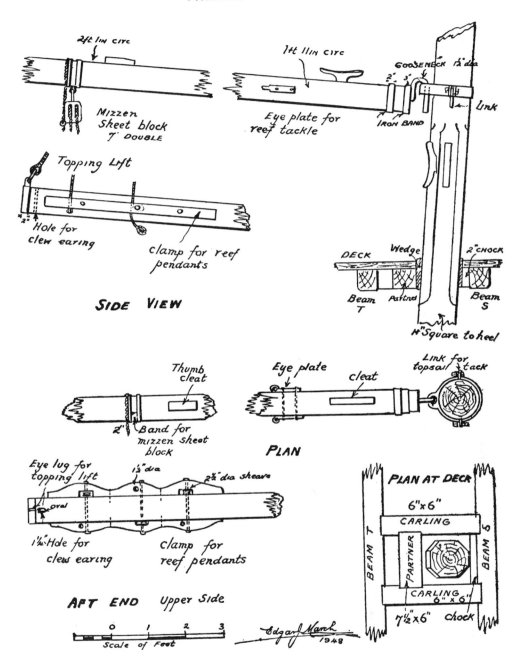

MIZZEN BOOM

2ft 1in circ

1ft 11in circ

GOOSENECK 1½" dia

Mizzen Sheet block 7" DOUBLE

Eye plate for reef tackle

IRON BAND

Link

Topping Lift

Hole for clew earing

clamp for reef pendants

SIDE VIEW

DECK

Wedge

2" CHOCK

Beam T

Partner

Beam S

N" Square to heel

Thumb cleat

Eye plate

cleat

Link for topsail tack

2" Band for mizzen sheet block

PLAN

Eye lug for topping lift

1½" dia

2½" dia sheave

oval

1¼" Hole for clew earing

clamp for reef pendants

AFT END   Upper Side

Edgar J March 1948

0   1   2   3
Scale of Feet

PLAN AT DECK

6" x 6"

CARLING

BEAM T

PARTNER

BEAM S

CARLING 6" x 6"

7½" x 6"   Chock

FIG. 49

BOWSPRIT

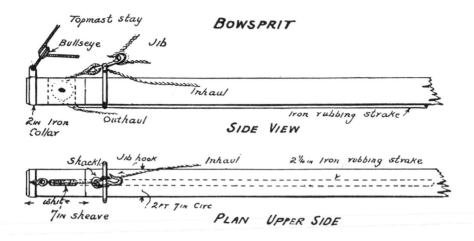

Topmast stay

Bullseye   Jib

Inhaul

2in Iron Collar   Outhaul   Iron rubbing strake

SIDE VIEW

Shackle   Jib hook   Inhaul   2¼in Iron rubbing strake

white

7in sheave   2FT 7in Circ

PLAN UPPER SIDE

PLAN AT HEEL

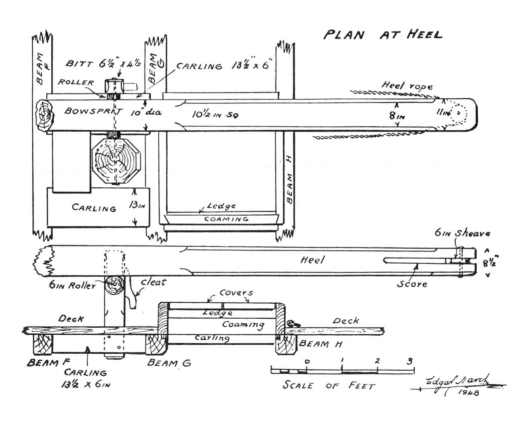

BEAM F   BITT 6½" x 4½"   BEAM G   CARLING 13½" x 6"

ROLLER

BOWSPRIT 10" dia   10½ in SQ   Heel rope

8in   11in

BEAM H

CARLING   13in   Ledge   COAMING

6in Sheave

6in Roller   cleat   Heel   8½"

Score

Covers

Ledge   Coaming

Deck   Carling   Deck

BEAM F   BEAM G   BEAM H

CARLING 13½ x 6in

SCALE OF FEET   0 1 2 3

Edgar March
1948

FIG. 50

BOWSPRIT
Fig. 50

LENGTH	36 ft. 8 in. 2 ft. 7 in. circ. at end, approx. 9 in. dia.
END IRON	2 in. wide driven on end of spar, on upper side is eye lug, 3 in. high, to take shackle of bullseye for topmast stay.
SHEAVE	7 in. dia. sheave in slot 9 in. long, 1¾ in. wide.
TRAVELLER	Dia. 1 ft. 3 in., with hook and shackle a loose fit on ring. Hook goes into jib tack cringle, shackle has outhaul spliced to it. Inhaul is seized to ring.
RUBBING STRAKE	Iron. 9 ft. 11 in. long, 2¼ in. wide, on under side of spar to take chafe when bowsprit is run in.
HEEL	10 in. dia., 10½ in. sq. for 8 ft. 2 in., edges chamfered, tapering on upper side only to 8½ in. thick and 11 in. wide on upper and lower faces. 10 in. long slot, 2 in. wide, takes 6 in. dia. sheave for heel rope, scores 1 ft. 9 in. long on side faces.

All these details are as in *Master Hand*, L.T.1203, when I measured her up in 1946 and in many instances are peculiar to her. For example, the iron arm to take the main halyard block at masthead was also fitted in *Helping Hand*, but in most smacks the horse or saddle is similar to that seen on the mizzen mast, while the fish batten on peak of gaff was unusual, the placing of chocks at main rigging prevented any damage to fore shrouds should a mooring warp slip, the positioning of certain eyebolts was individual, and belaying of gear at mast cleats differed from Brixham practice. I was a little doubtful if I had taken down the lead of the main topsail sheet correctly, but a letter reassured me : "The sketch of the topsail fairlead is quite correct. I had it put there myself. The first one was on the heel of the mast but was not a very true lead when the capstan was going one way so I had it put on the inside of the post. When it was on the mast it was a bit of a cross lead, used to cut across the bottom of cleat and chafe the sheet. It was the only one that I saw, as most of the smacks used to work the sheet in the post itself (Plate 61). Having the lead on the post was just a little matter of convenience I thought, as then the sheave was all clear if you wanted it for any other purpose."

Every item has been discussed with and checked by Skipper J. T. Crouch who has always been a willing and authentic source of information.

SAIL PLAN.

Data supplied by Mr. James Breach and Mr. R. Bowles, Sailmakers.

Sail	Yards	No.	Luff	Leech	Head	Foot
Mainsail	230	1	25 ft.	49 ft.	30 ft.	33 ft.
Boltrope			2½ in.	4 in.	2¼ in.	2 in., 3 ft. at clew 4 in.
Mizzen sail	115	3	18 ft.	34 ft.	21 ft.	23 ft.
Boltrope			2¼ in.	3–2¼.	2 in.	2 in., 3 ft. at clew 3 in.
Main topsail	60	3	31 ft.	23 ft.		31 ft. Jib headed.
Boltrope			3 in.	2 in.		2 in.
Mizzen t'sle	44	6	14 ft.	17 ft.	15 ft.	20 ft.
Boltrope			2½ in.	1½ in.	2 in.	1½ in. Gaff topsail

Reefs   Three reefs, 4 ft. deep, in mainsail.
Three reefs, 3 ft. deep in mizzen sail.
Two reefs, 3 ft. deep in foresail.

	Yards	No.	Luff	Leech	Foot
Foresail	50	2	34 ft.	29 ft.	21 ft.
Boltrope			2½–2¼ in.	2½–2¼ in.	2 in.
Tow foresail	90	6	34 ft.	32 ft.	34 ft.
Boltrope			2½–2 in.	2½–2 in.	2 in.
Jib	100	6	49 ft.	33 ft.	25 ft.
Boltrope			3½ in.	1½ in.	1½ in.
9 cloth jib	75	4	48 ft.	32 ft.	22 ft. 6 in.
Boltrope			3½ in.	2 in.	2½ in., 3 in. for 3 ft. each side of clew.
7 cloth jib	55	3	33 ft.	28 ft.	15 ft.
Boltrope			3½ in.	2 in.	2 in., 2½ in. at clew.
5 cloth jib	33	2	28 ft.	24 ft.	11 ft. 6 in.
Boltrope			3½ in.	2 in.	2 in., 2½ in. at clew.
Storm jib	18	1	23 ft.	18 ft. 6 in.	9 ft.
Boltrope			3½ in.	2½ in.	2½ in.
Staysail	50	6	31 ft.	29 ft.	25 ft.
Boltrope			2½ in.	1½ in.	1½ in.

All sails are diagonal cut.

Yardage, including linings, pieces, bands, etc., approximately 920 yards. With extra foresail, 50 yards, a total of 970 yards for a full suit.

Labour.   2s. 3d. a yard.
Rope.   4 strand white manilla.

RUNNING GEAR

	fathom	inch
Main halyards	24	3
Purchase	15	2¼
Main peak halyards	36	3
Main sheet	20	3½ cable laid warp.
Mizzen main halyards	15	2½
peak do	23	2¼
Mizzen sheet	20	2¼
Jib halyards	22	3
Purchase	15	2¼
Sheets	14	2½ 7 fthm. on each bow.
Foresail halyards	16	2

	fathom	inch	
Fore topsail halyards	23	$2\frac{1}{2}$	
Sheet	20	$2\frac{1}{2}$	
Tack	2	3 strop and tackle	
Leader	8	$2\frac{1}{2}$ and 8 ft. chain	
Mizzen topsail halyards	16	$2\frac{1}{4}$	
Sheet	14	$2\frac{1}{4}$	
Tack	2	3 strop and tackle	
Main topping lift	12	$1\frac{1}{2}$ wire, tackle & downhaul	
Mizzen topping lift	8	2 rope, and purchase	
Main double reef tackle	20	$2\frac{1}{2}$	
1st reef tackle	$12\frac{1}{2}$	$1\frac{1}{2}$ wire and rope combined	
Reef lacings	7	$1\frac{1}{2}$ three required	
Mizzen reef lacing	$5\frac{1}{2}$	$1\frac{1}{4}$ three required	
Reef tackle	8	2	

LEAD OF RUNNING GEAR, ETC.

TOPMAST STAY
(Figs. 42, 50, 20)

Eye over shoulder at topmast head or thimble is shackled to eye on iron band, leads down through bullseye on bowsprit end-iron, reeves through inner hole in starboard rail and belays round starboard windlass bitt. 66 ft. $1\frac{3}{4}$ in. wire.

JIB OUTHAUL
(Fig. 50)

Spliced to shackle freely working on iron traveller, leads through sheave in end of bowsprit, back over top of starboard rail to belay round inner head on starboard bitt.

INHAUL
(Figs. 50, 20)

Seized to traveller, belays round first pin, next stem, on cavil rail.

SHEETS
(Fig. 22)

Double. Standing end is knotted on inside of for'ard hole in bullseye, leads through bullseye hooked in clew of jib, back through aft hole and belays round pin in cavil rail, or on heavy pin on bulwark rail, end is knotted.

HALYARDS
(Figs. 26, 41, 27)

Standing end belayed round first pin, for'ard end starboard cavil rail, leads down under thumb cleat, up through fairlead to single block hooked to eye on band, down to reeve through single block hooked in head of sail, back through fairlead and single block on port side of band, and down to luff purchase. Double block on end of pendant, single block hooks in for'ard eyebolt on chock, fall belays round first pin in port cavil rail.

FORESAIL

Hanked to fore stay with eleven 5 in. hanks.

TACK
(Fig. 20)

Short wire span, thimble each end, upper one shackles or is lashed to tack cringle, lower goes over hook at stemhead.

SHEET

Upper deadeye has long bent hook to go in clew cringle, lower one is shackled to traveller on horse. Lanyard reeves through holes in deadeyes, belays round itself.

HALYARDS
(Figs. 41, 40)

Standing end fast to eyebolt under starboard side of yoke, reeves through single block hooked to head cringle, up to single block hooked to eyebolt, port side, fall belays round cleat on port for'ard face of mast heel.

DOWNHAUL
(Fig. 40)

Fast on tail of block in head cringle, usually belays to cleat on fore side of mast.

MAIN HALYARDS
(Figs. 26, 41, 44, 27)

Standing end is belayed round second pin in starboard cavil rail, leads under iron cavil in deck, up to treble block on horse, down through double block of tumbler of gaff, reeving with the sun, fall goes under iron cavil in port side of deck and belays to second pin in cavil rail. Mainsail hoisted by steam capstan.

PEAK HALYARDS
(Figs. 41, 45, 26)

Standing end fast to lowest eyebolt in masthead, reeves through single block of inner span on peak of gaff, back to single block hooked to centre eyebolt, on to second span block, up to single block hooked in upper eyebolt, down under thumb cleat aft end of starboard cavil rail and fall belays on aft pin.

SHEET
(Figs. 43, 30)

Always left-handed or cable-laid rope, this being softer and more flexible than right-handed. The standing end is fast round strop on boom, aft of block, leads through bullseye on tail of upper block, reeves through lower block, fall is taken through bullseye on fore side of chock and belays round cleat on aft side. Skipper Crouch preferred this lead as taking standing end from tail of upper block, the common practice, increases the strain on block.

TOPPING LIFT
(Figs. 43, 41, 26)

Pendant of $1\frac{1}{2}$ in. wire, standing end shackled to end-iron on boom, leads up to single block hooked to eyeplate on starboard cheek, down to luff purchase, single block of which hooks in eyebolt on starboard rail between fore and middle shrouds, fall belays on third pin in cavil rail.

DOWNHAUL
(Fig. 26)

Small single block seized well up wire pendant. Standing end of rope seized to middle starboard shroud, leads up through single block, fall belays round fourth pin in cavil rail.

MAIN TRUSS
(Figs. 41, 40)

Used when reefing, also as boat hoist when required. Large double block seized well up starboard middle shroud, single block hooks in link on starboard side of gooseneck band, fall belays on wood cleat on starboard for'ard face of mast heel.

TOPSAIL LEADER
(Figs. 42, 40)

8 ft. length of small chain, fast to iron traveller sliding freely on topmast, takes chafe of three grommets on luff of topsail, 47 ft. of $2\frac{1}{2}$. in rope at lower end of chain, belays round cleat on centre face, port side heel of mast.

HALYARDS
(Figs. 42, 22)

Reeve diagonally from port to starboard through sheave in topmast head, fall passes under thumb cleat on stanchion and belays on pin in starboard bulwark rail. Usually chain in nip of sheave, and sail mostly hoisted by steam.

SHEET
(Figs. 45, 44, 40)

Chain in nip of sheave on port side of peak of gaff, then rope reeves through single block hooked to eyebolt under side of port horn, down under heavy cleat on inside face of fair-leading post and belays round cleat on aft face of mast.

TACK
(Fig. 40)

Wire pendant spliced to tack of sail, lower end has double block of luff purchase, the single block hooks in link on port side of gooseneck band, and fall belays to cleat on aft port face of mast heel.

MIZZEN HALYARDS
(Figs. 46, 47, 35)

Standing end fast to tail of upper double block, reeves through lower double block and fall belays to centre pin in port cavil rail.

PEAK HALYARDS
(Figs. 46, 48, 34)

Originally standing end was fast to lowest eyebolt above hounds, and fall rove through two single blocks on spans and two on mast, but Skipper Crouch found this was too much purchase and gaff would not come down quickly, so lead was altered and standing end made fast to the bullseye on inner span and all blocks, including topping lift, came down one eyebolt on mast. Fall belays on centre pin in starboard cavil rail.

SHEET
(Figs. 49, 38)

Originally upper block shackled to bullseye on wire span on boom, later the standing end was fast round boom and double block was on strop, with bullseye on tail for fairlead, fall reeves through lower double block, on through bullseye at lower end and fall belays round long cleat across horn timbers.

TOPPING LIFT
(Figs. 49, 46, 34)

Standing end of pendant shackled to end-iron on boom, reeves through single block hooked in upper eyebolt above hounds, originally in eyebolt on starboard side higher up, leads down starboard side to luff purchase, single block hooks to eyebolt in cavil rail aft of shrouds and fall belays to third pin.

DOWNHAUL
(Fig. 34)

Is seized to upper part of pendant and belays round starboard cavil rail.

TOPSAIL LEADER

As main mast.

HALYARDS
(Figs. 46, 34)

Lead from port to starboard through sheave in pole mast, down to whip purchase, standing end is hooked to eyebolt for'ard end of starboard cavil rail, leads up through single block on lower end of halyard, and fall belays on leading pin in cavil rail.

SHEET
(Figs. 48, 47)

Chain in nip of sheave on port side of gaff, rope leads through single block hooked to eyebolt under port horn, and belays on cleat foot of mast.

TACK
(Fig. 49)

Rope pendant spliced to tack cringle with luff purchase at lower end, single block of which hooks in link on port side of gooseneck boom and fall belays on cleat below.

STAYSAIL HALYARDS
(Fig. 46)

Double block hooks to eyebolt on foreside of pole mast, tack of sail in eyebolt on aft coaming of main hatch. When not in use the single block hooks in eyebolt in starboard cavil rail.

AFTER FISH TACKLE
(Figs. 46, 35)

Double block hooks in fore eye on collar at hounds, single block hooks in eyebolt in port cavil and fall belays on leading pin. Also used as boat hoist when required.

FOR'ARD FISH TACKLE
(Figs. 41, 27)

Wire pendant is shackled to eyeplate on port cheek of main mast, at lower end is a 10 in double block of luff tackle, single block hooks in eyebolt in deck, for'ard of trawl head berthing and fall belays round third pin in port cavil rail.

MAIN TOPMAST *MAST ROPE* (Fig. 41)	Only rove when required, then standing end was made fast to iron bar abaft yoke, rope rove through sheave set diagonally in heel of topmast from port to starboard, led up through sheave on starboard side of masthead and fall was led to capstan through snatch block hooked to ringbolt in deck.
BOWSPRIT HEEL *ROPE* (Figs. 21, 50)	Standing end was knotted, then rope led through fore and aft hole in starboard windlass bitt, round sheave in heel of spar, back through sheave on starboard side of pawl bitt, and through snatch blocks to capstan when in use. When bowsprit was out the fall was passed back round into heel of spar and led for'ard to belay to cleat on starboard bitt.
LANTERN HALYARDS (Figs. 41, 27)	Rove through small single block on arm at mast cap and belayed round fore end of port cavil rail.

A general view of deck, taken in July, 1934, is seen in Plate 173, with binnacle just abaft mizzen mast, skylight, hoodway, boiler plate with fair-lead for leech line, towpost, hatch, heel of bowsprit, steam capstan, fair-leading post, fish battens on peak of gaff, reef cringles and pendants.

The stern with name MASTER HAND cut in transit rail is seen in Plate 175. Although much is covered with snow it is possible to pick out the roller cleat on starboard side of taffrail for the mooring warp, to port is the dandy score and boom guy, in foreground is helm port with rudder head and head of sternpost, part of ground rope and net lie over port rail. Compare the Rye type of round stern with the elliptical one alongside, where stern boards run diagonally, and the method of stowing mizzen sail repays careful study as practically everything in the way of gear, robands, etc., can be distinguished. The outside of the stern is similar to that of her sister ship *Helping Hand* (Plate 174). The stern boards go athwartships and from taffrail to knuckle measure 11, 10, 9, 10, and 10 inches respectively. Below knuckle are four 1 ft. boards, the ends of main planking butting against the lower one.

Close-ups of typical Lowestoft main rigging are seen in Plate 176 of *Chrysoberyl*, L.T.1089, 43 tons, built at Lowestoft in 1907, while Plate 177 of *East Dean*, L.T. 1233, 42 tons, also Lowestoft built in 1921, shows how the boat was secured, the for'ard gripe goes to eyebolt aft of shrouds with a deadeye at other end, a similar gripe is fast to eyebolt in deck and a lanyard rove off between the deadeyes tightens everything up. Plate 178 is a bow view of *Sunbeam*, L.T.669, 59 tons, built 1905.

For photographs of *Master Hand* under sail I am indebted to Mr. J. M. Mitchley who sent me a number of negatives as before the war he was making a praiseworthy effort to take a snap of every Lowestoft smack still working. He wrote " I had other material at one time but much of it was destroyed by a bomb early in the war and to blame for the bad state of some of the prints and negatives. I spent over a week digging in the ruins to salvage what I could ".

Plate 179 shows the smack making for Lowestoft with two reefs down and a storm jib set, in the background are seas breaking on the sandbanks. The negative was badly damaged but enough remained to make a reasonable enlargement.

Plate 180 makes a fine concluding picture. Sail is being dropped at the end of a trip and never shall we see the like again.

Progress in the development of steam and diesel-engined trawlers has brought about the end of the sailing smack some sixty years after steam first became a serious competitor. The winds, blowing free to all, have been supplanted by engines powered by foreign fuel, costly to buy and dependent upon national caprice for supply. To-day—1952—I was reading a company report wherein it was stated that costs continued to rise in an ever-increasing spiral and that £260 a day was the running expense of the latest type of fishing vessel, against £225 in 1946. Fantastic when one considers the outlay for a sailing smack. The lovely *Ibex* was built for only £490, less than two days expenditure on a modern vessel, or in other words the *increase* in six years—£35 a day—would cover her price in a fortnight ! Fish cost nothing to produce, but their capture becomes more and more expensive every year.

Sad as it is to see the disappearance of the picturesque sailing smacks, still sadder is it to realise that the splendid men who manned them are going fast, never to be replaced in our generation. Many were of that cheerful, happy disposition, so missing in the world to-day. I recall a chat with a fine old trawlerman who gazed out across the well-nigh derelict harbour, once crowded with sail, and commented regretfully, " In the old days there was always laughter when the men were working, you don't hear it nowadays ".

The smacksmen who survive are nearing the end of their life's voyage and I am indeed glad to have had the privilege of meeting those who have been so helpful in assisting me to record something of a way of life gone for ever. We shall not see such men again. ´ To one and all I say a very heartful THANK YOU.

PLAN SECTION

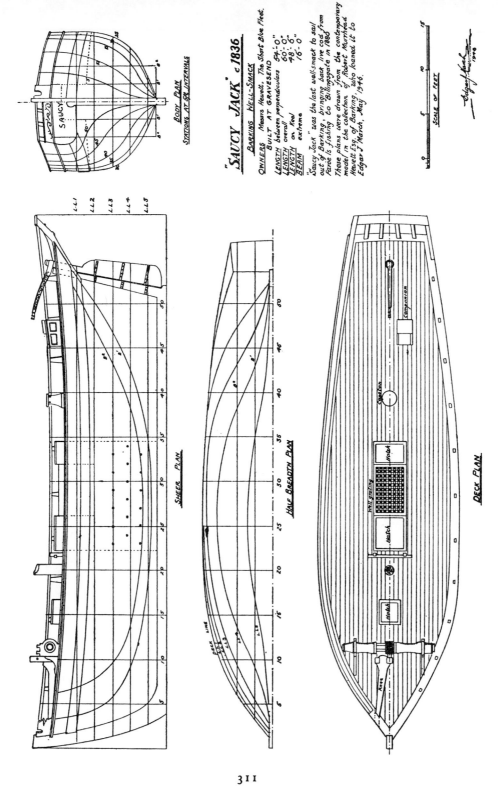

PLAN 1. Barking well-smack *Saucy Jack, c* 1836

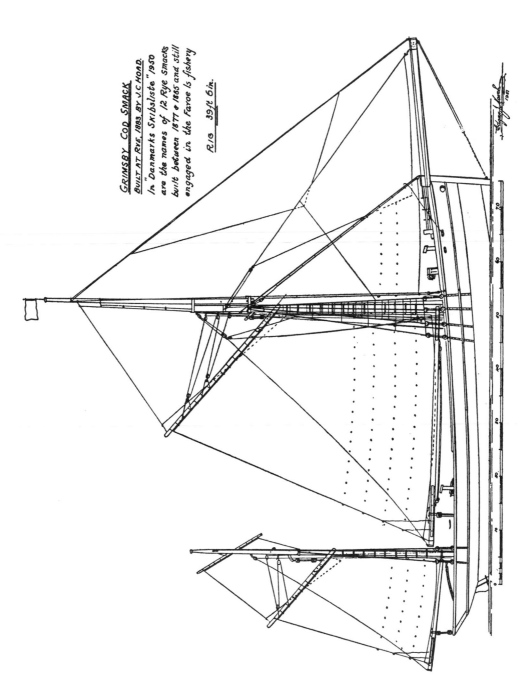

GRIMSBY COD SMACK

BUILT AT RYE, 1883, BY J.C.HOAD.

In Danmarks Skibsliste "1930 are the names of 12 Rye smacks built between 1877 & 1885 and still engaged in the Faroe Is fishery

R.13   39ft 6in.

PLAN 2.   Grimsby cod smack, c 1883

312

WELL

FOR ICELANDIC
BUILT AT RYE, 188
MODEL CONSTRUCTED BY B
LINES TAKEN OFF MODEL BY EDGA
BY PERMISSION OF THE DIRECTOR,
ALL MEASUREMENTS TAKE
REG

LENGTH OVERALL 85FT   L&P 77.3FT   LENG

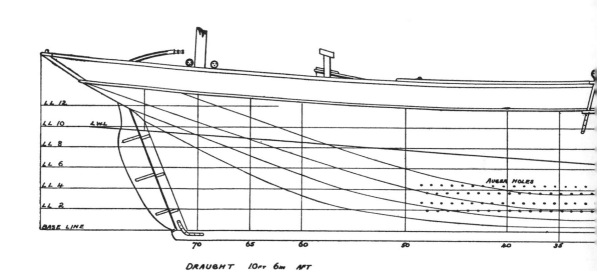

LL 12
LL 10   LWL
LL 8
LL 6
LL 4
LL 2
BASE LINE

70   65   60   50   40   35

AUGER HOLES

DRAUGHT   10FT 6IN   AFT

SCALE OF FEET

10   20   30

IN 1883 THE 76 TON "WILLIAM MARTIN" WAS BUILT AT RYE FO
IN 1950 SHE WAS REG⁰ AT RIDEVIG & IN

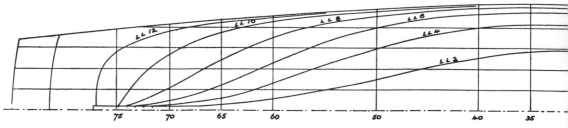

LL 12   LL 10   LL 8   LL 6
LL 4
LL 2

75   70   65   60   50   40   35

PLAN 2.   Grim

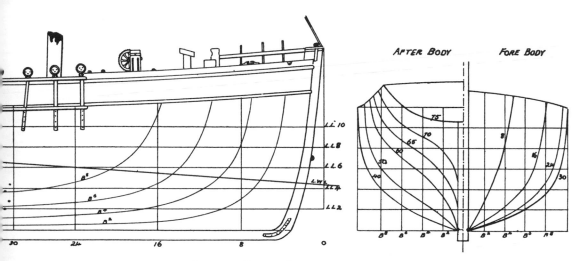

SMACK
COD FISHERIES
by J C HOAD
ILDER FOR FISHERIES EXHIBITION 1883
J MARCH of WESTGATE-ON-SEA, 28 JULY 1948
SCIENCE MUSEUM, SOUTH KENSINGTON
TO OUTSIDE OF PLANKING
NS 88

KEEL 70FT   MOULDED BEAM 20·3 FT   DEPTH 12·2 FT

AFTER BODY   FORE BODY

L L 10
L L 8
L L 6
L W L
L L 4
L L 2

B⁸   B⁶   B⁴   B²   B²   B⁴   B⁶   B⁸

DRAUGHT 5м·6м FOR'ARD

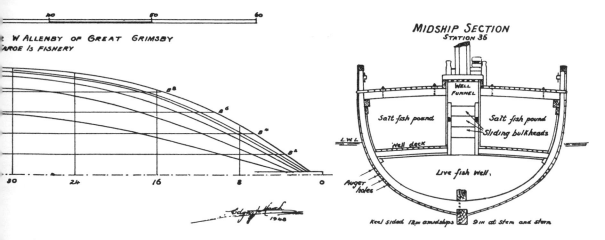

W ALLENBY OF GREAT GRIMSBY
AROE Is FISHERY

MIDSHIP SECTION
STATION 36

WELL
FUNNEL

Salt fish pound   Salt fish pound
                    Sliding bulkheads
L.W.L.   Well deck

Live fish Well.

Auger
holes

Keel sided 12м amidships   9 in at Stem and stern

by cod smack, c 1883

314

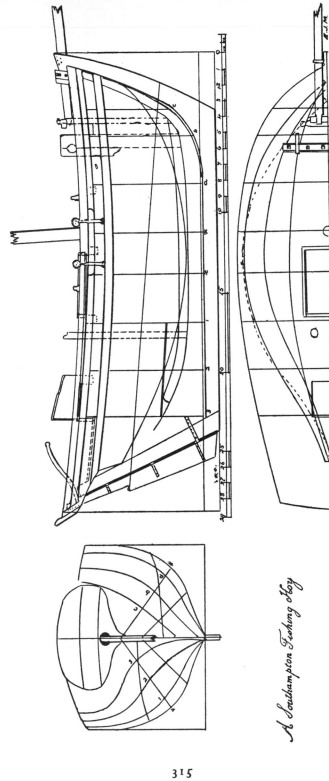

A Southampton Fishing Hoy

PLAN 3. Southampton fishing hoy, c 1804
Traced by author from photostat in Science Museum, S.W.

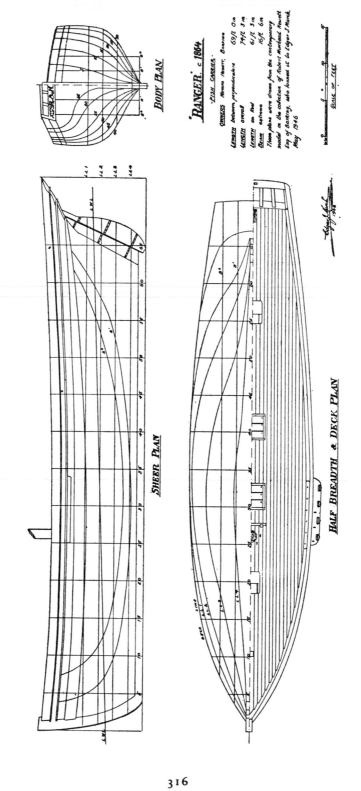

BODY PLAN

"RANGER." c 1864

- FISH CARRIER-

OWNERS   Messrs Hewett, Barking

LENGTH between perpendiculars   69ft 0in
LENGTH overall   74½ ft 3 in
LENGTH on keel   61 ft 3 in
BEAM extreme   16 ft 6in

These plans were drawn from the contemporary
model in the collection of Robert Morland Hewett
Esq of Barking, who loaned it to Edgar J March,
May 1946

SCALE OF FEET

SHEER PLAN

HALF BREADTH & DECK PLAN

PLAN 4.   Barking fish carrier *Ranger*, c 1864

316

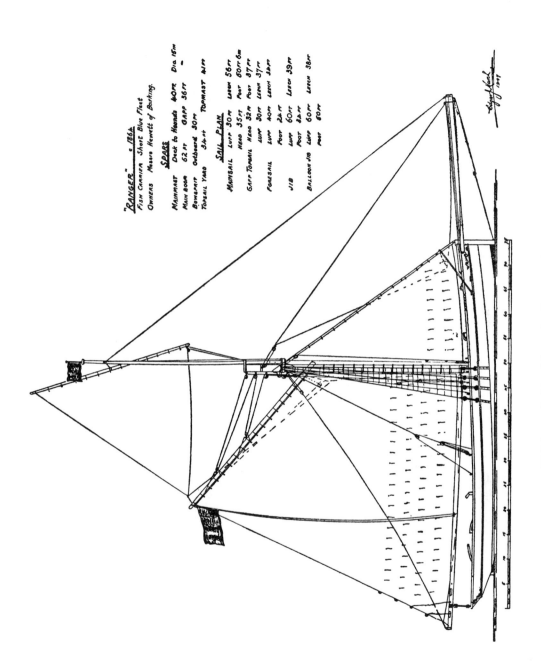

"RANGER" c 1864
FISH CARRIER SHORT BLUE FLEET
OWNERS Messrs Hewett of Barking.

SPARS

MAINMAST	Deck to Hounds	40FT	DIA 15in
MAIN BOOM	62 FT	GAFF 36FT	—
BOWSPRIT	Outboard 30FT		
TOPSAIL YARD	34 FT	TOPMAST 41FT	

SAIL PLAN

MAINSAIL	LUFF 30FT	LEECH 56FT
	HEAD 35FT	FOOT 60FT 6in
GAFF TOPSAIL	HEAD 32FT	FOOT 37FT
	LUFF 30FT	LEECH 37FT
FORESAIL	LUFF 40FT	LEECH 38FT
	FOOT 24FT	
JIB	LUFF 60FT	LEECH 39FT
	FOOT 8¼FT	
BALLOON JIB	LUFF 60FT	LEECH 36FT
	FOOT 60FT	

PLAN 4.   Barking fish carrier *Ranger*, c 1864

317

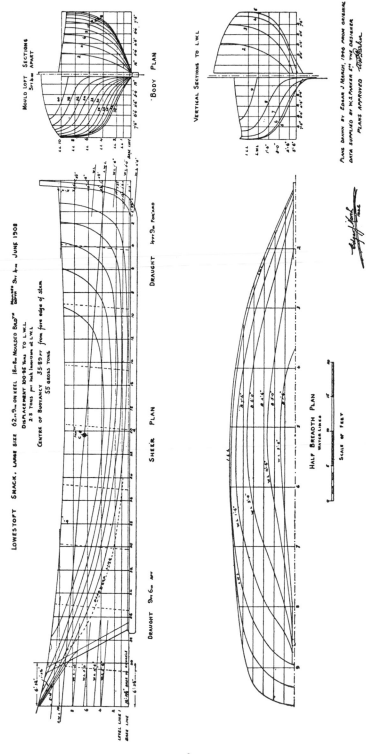

PLAN 5. Large Lowestoft smack, c 1908

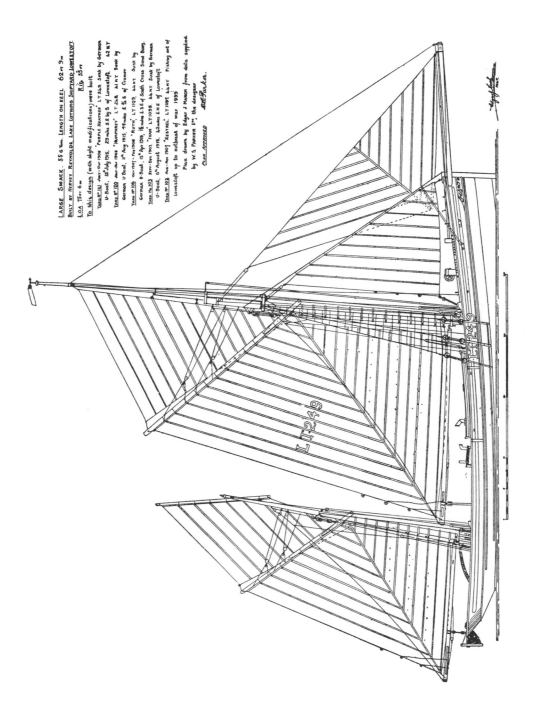

LARGE SMACK. 55.6 TONS. LENGTH ON KEEL 62 ft 9 in
BUILT BY HARVEY REYNOLDS. LAKE LOTHING SHIPYARD LOWESTOFT.
LOA 75 ft 6 in
Rig 35 ft

To this design (with slight modifications) were built

Yard N° 141 June–Oct 1904 "Purple Heather" LT 243 Sunk by German
U-Boat, 12th July 1915. 23 miles SE by S of Lowestoft. 42 RT
Yard N° 150 Nov–Dec 1904 "Humphrey" LT 248 Also Sunk by
German U-Boat, 1st Aug 1915, 49 miles E ½ S of Cromer.
Yard N° 108 Dec 1907–Feb 1908 "Ruth", LT 1109, Also Sunk by
German B-Boat, 15th Apr 1918, 1½ miles E.S.E of South Cross Sand Buoy,
Yard N° 109 Sept–Dec 1907, "Ivan" LT 1098. Also Sunk by German
U-Boat, 6th August 1915, 42 miles E.N.E of Lowestoft.
Yard N° 103 Aug–Nov 1907 "Kestrel" LT 1097 Also Fishing out of
Lowestoft up to outbreak of war 1939

Plan drawn by Edgar J Manson from data supplied
by W.S. Parker Jnr, the designer
Plan Approved [signature]

[signature]

PLAN 5. Large Lowestoft smack, c 1908

319

SMALL TRAWLER ABOUT 40 TONS REG, c 1907

LENGTH ON KEEL 52 FT

BUILT AT HERVEY REYNOLD'S SHIPYARD, LAKE LOTHING, LOWESTOFT

SPAR PLAN

MAIN MAST	Deck to Shoulder	30ft 6in
TOPMAST	Pole Extreme	8ft
MAIN BOOM	Heel to Shoulder	26ft 3in
MAIN GAFF	Throat to Earing hole	28ft 9in
BOWSPRIT	Outside Stem	27ft
MAIN TOPSAIL YARD	Hole to hole	19ft
MIZZEN MAST	Deck to hole	18ft
	Deck to Shoulder	25ft
MIZZEN BOOM	Shoulder to pin of Sheave	10ft 6in
MIZZEN GAFF	Mast to Earing hole	19ft 3in
TOPSAIL YARD	Throat to Earing hole	17ft
	Hole to hole	16ft

TO THIS DESIGN WERE BUILT WITH SLIGHT MODIFICATIONS:-

"MASKADA" LT 374, 37 TONS, LAID DOWN, AUG 1907 FOR J.A. SWAN,

"OLEANDER" LT 1116, 36 TONS, LAID DOWN, JULY 1907 FOR MESSRS

PAINTER 8th SUNK BY U-BOAT, 8th FEB 1916, 48 MILES SE OF LOWESTOFT,

CONTRACT PRICE, £650 for hull spars & mast head

SMACKS IN 1904 HAD A 45ft-0in KEEL AND A MOULDED BREADTH

OF 16ft-3in. THOSE BUILT WITHOUT MIZZEN WERE LENGTHENED 3ft-0in IN CENTRE

DRAWN BY EDGAR J MARCH FROM DATA SUPPLIED BY M? PARKER

PLAN APPROVED,

L.T.374

PLAN 5. Small Lowestoft smack, c 1907

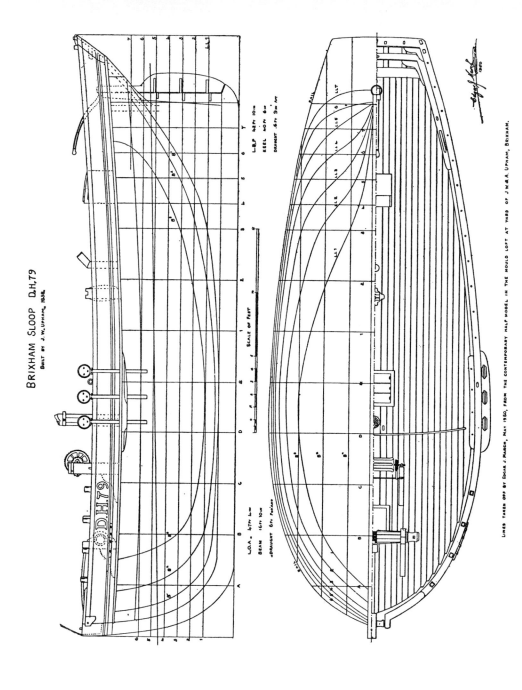

BRIXHAM SLOOP D.H.79

BUILT BY J. W. UPHAM, 1838.

L.O.A. 47ᶠᵗ 6ᴵᴺ
BEAM 16ᶠᵗ 10ᴵᴺ
DRAUGHT 8ᶠᵗ FOR'ARD

SCALE OF FEET

L.B.P 42ᶠᵗ 10ᴵᴺ
KEEL 40ᶠᵗ 6ᴵᴺ
DRAUGHT 6ᶠᵗ 3ᴵᴺ AFT

LINES TAKEN OFF BY EDGAR J. MARCH, MAY 1950, FROM THE CONTEMPORARY HALF MODEL IN THE MOULD LOFT AT YARD OF J.W.& A. UPHAM, BRIXHAM.

PLAN 6.   Brixham sloop *Charlie, c* 1838

321

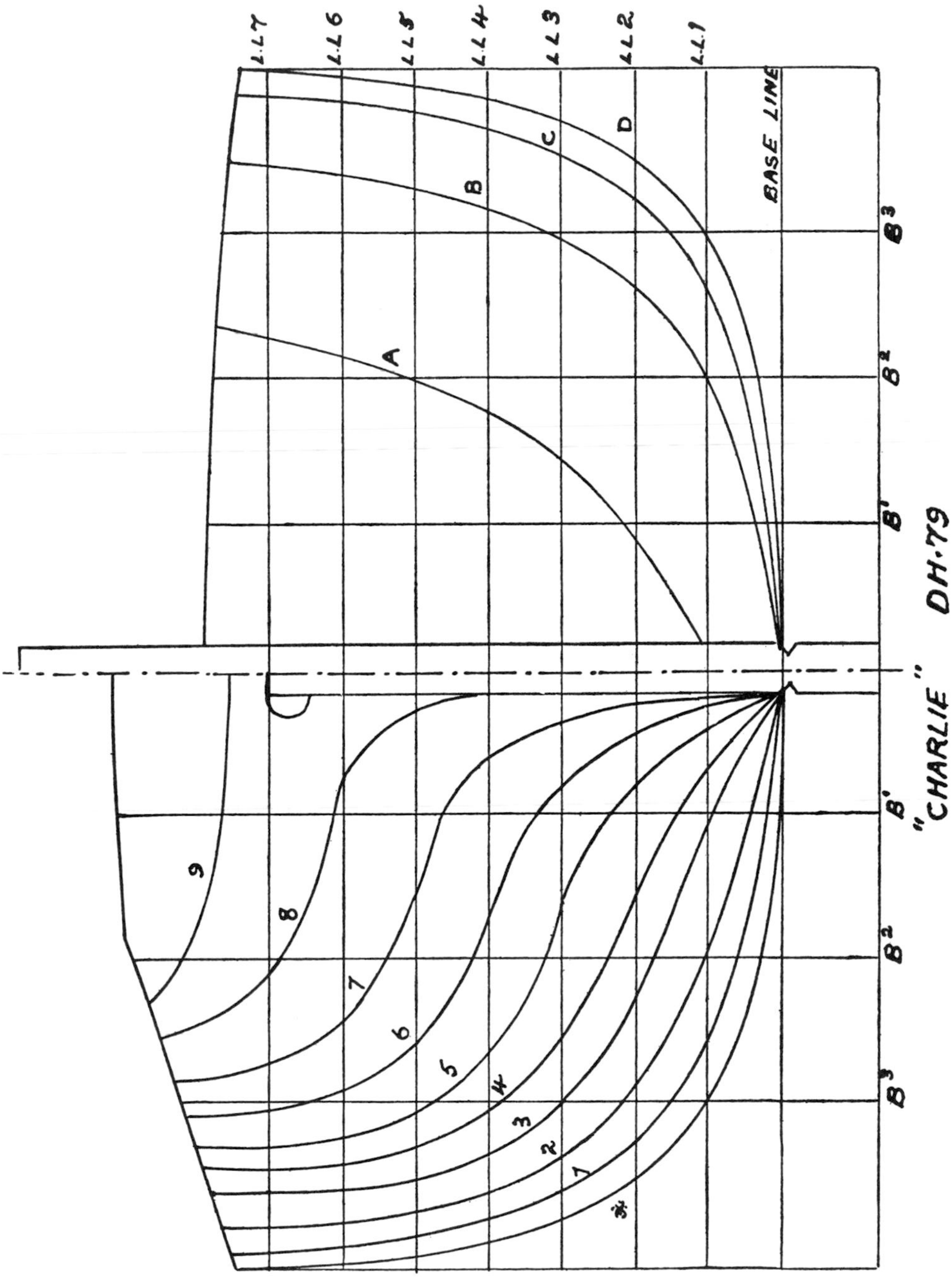

"CHARLIE" DH·79

LL 7
LL 6
LL 5
LL 4
LL 3
LL 2
LL 1

A
B
C
D

BASE LINE

B^3
B^2
B^1
B^1
B^2
B^3

9
8
7
6
5
4
3
2
1
½

PLAN 6. Brixham sloop *Charlie*, c 1838

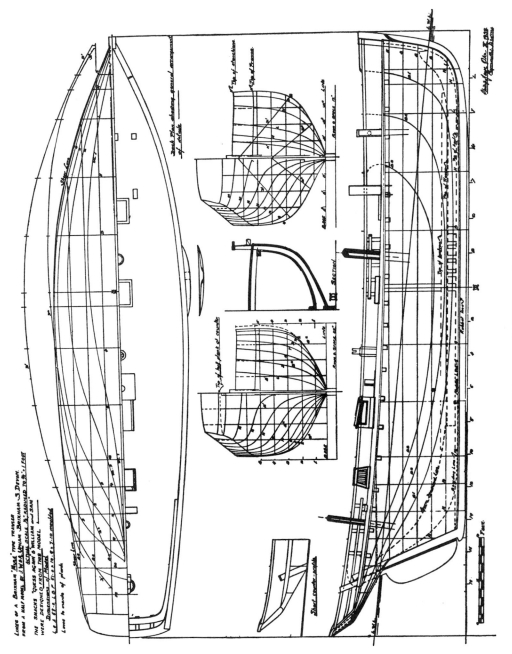

PLAN 7. Brixham mule *William & Sam*, 1917

PLAN 8. Brixham Mumble bee, 31 ft. rig

324

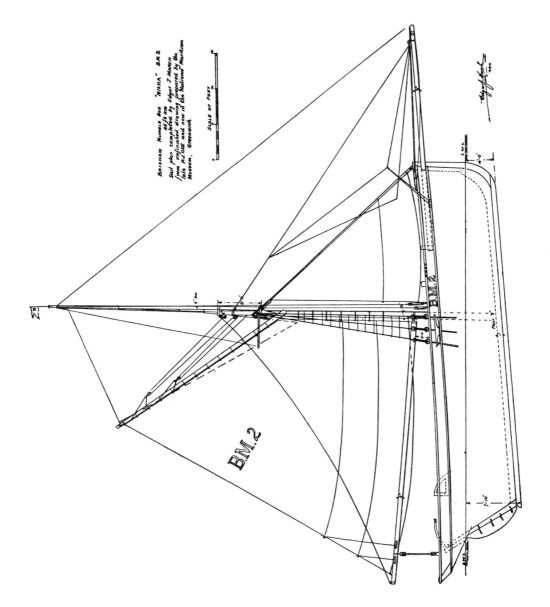

Brixham Mumble bee "NISHA" BM 2
25/8 rig
Sail plan completed by Edgar J. March
from unfinished drawing prepared by the
late J. R. ORE and now in the National Maritime
Museum, Greenwich.

Scale of Feet

BM.2

BM.2

PLAN 9. Brixham Mumble bee *Nisha*, 1907, 25 ft. rig

325

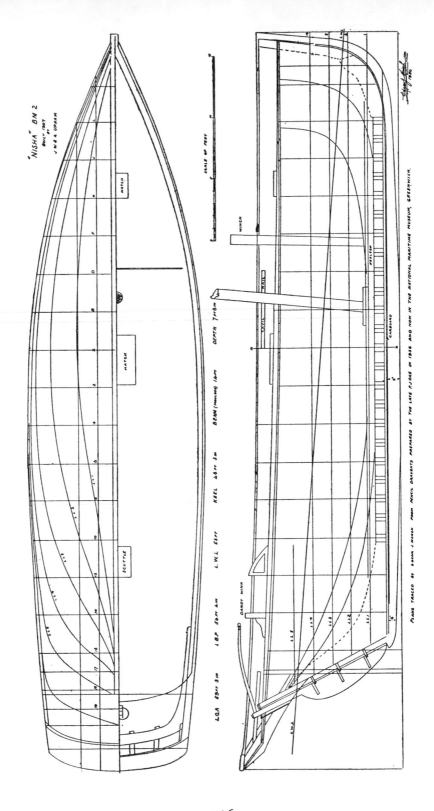

'NISHA' BN 2
BUILT 1907
BY
J.W.& A. UPHAM

SCALE OF FEET

DEPTH 7ft 6in

BEAM (moulded) 16ft

KEEL 66ft 3in

L.W.L. 53ft

L.B.P. 58ft 6in

L.O.A. 68ft 3in

PLANS TRACED BY BROOK J.MARSH FROM PENCIL DRAUGHTS PREPARED BY THE LATE F.JOKE IN 1936 AND NOW IN THE NATIONAL MARITIME MUSEUM, GREENWICH.

PLAN 9. Brixham Mumble bee *Nisha*, 1907

326

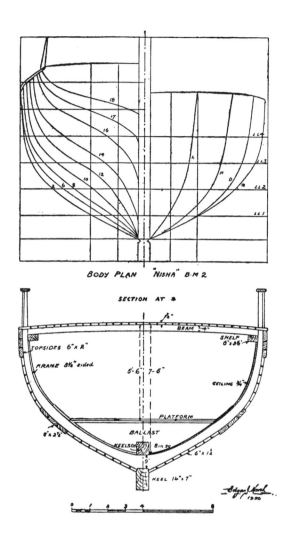

BODY PLAN "NISHA" B·M 2

SECTION AT ℄

BEAM 5"×4"

TOPSIDES 6"×2"

SHELF 6"×3½"

FRAME 3½" sided.

CEILING ⅜"

5'-6" 7'-6"

PLATFORM

BALLAST

6"×2½"

KEELSON 8in 5o

6"×1¼"

KEEL 16"×7"

PLAN 9. Brixham Mumble bee *Nisha*, 1907

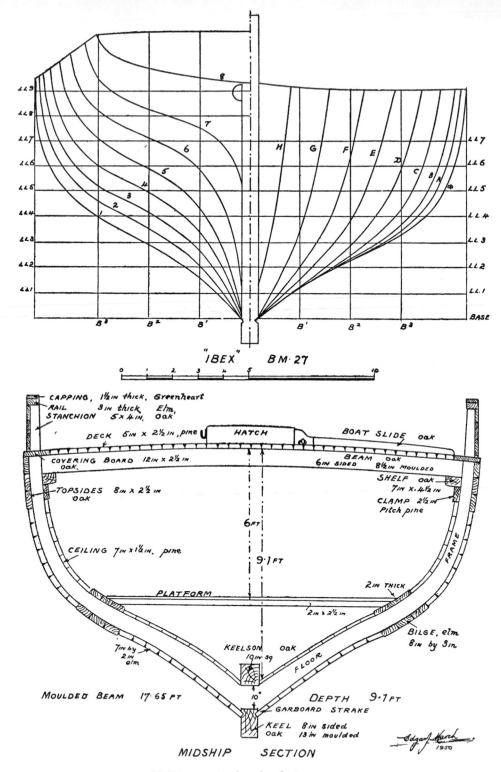

"IBEX" B.M. 27

CAPPING, 1½ IN thick, Greenheart
RAIL 3 IN thick Elm.
STANCHION 5 × 4 IN. Oak

DECK 6 IN × 2½ IN. pine HATCH BOAT SLIDE Oak

COVERING BOARD 12 IN × 2½ IN
Oak.
BEAM Oak
6 IN SIDED 8½ IN MOULDED

TOPSIDES 8 IN × 2½ IN
Oak
SHELF Oak
7 IN × 4½ IN
CLAMP 2½ IN
Pitch pine

6 FT

CEILING 7 IN × 1½ IN. pine

9·1 FT

PLATFORM
2 IN THICK

2 IN × 2½ IN

BILGE, elm
8 IN by 3 IN

KEELSON Oak
10 IN SQ

FLOOR
7 IN by
2 IN
elm

MOULDED BEAM 17·65 FT

DEPTH 9·1 FT

GARBOARD STRAKE

10"

KEEL 8 IN Sided
Oak 13 IN moulded

Edgar March
1950

MIDSHIP SECTION

PLAN 10. Brixham ketch *Ibex*, 1896

328

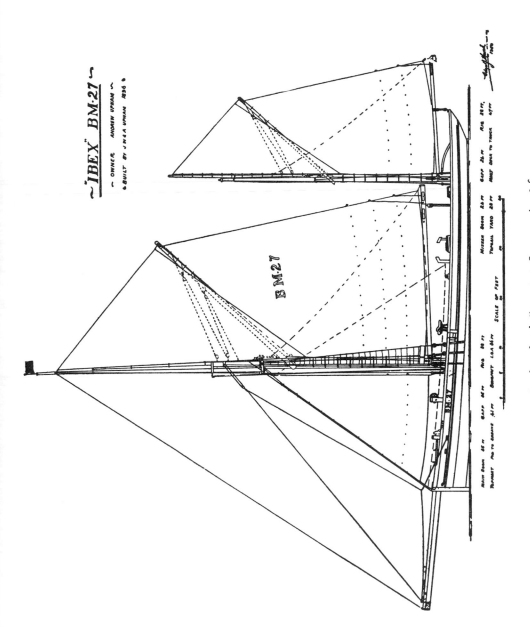

PLAN 10. Brixham ketch *Ibex*, 1896, Summer rig 38 ft.

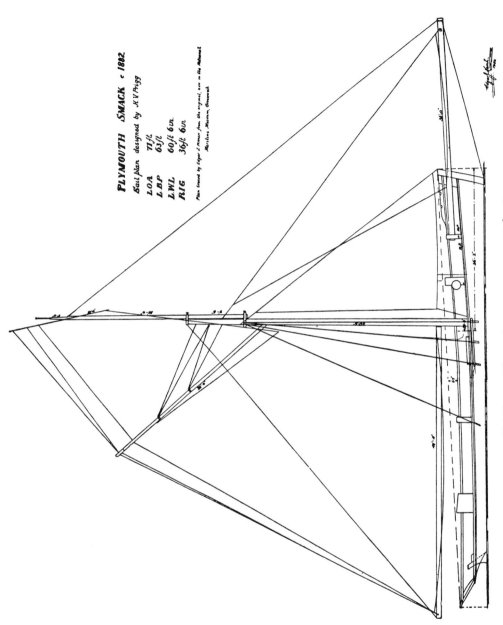

PLYMOUTH SMACK c 1882

Sail plan designed by J.V.Pigg

LOA   71 ft
LBP   63 ft
LWL   60 ft 6 in.
RIG   36 ft 6 in.

Plan traced by Edgar J March from the original, now in the National Maritime Museum, Greenwich

PLAN 11. Plymouth cutter, c 1882, 36½ ft. rig
Traced by Author from original plan now in National Maritime Museum

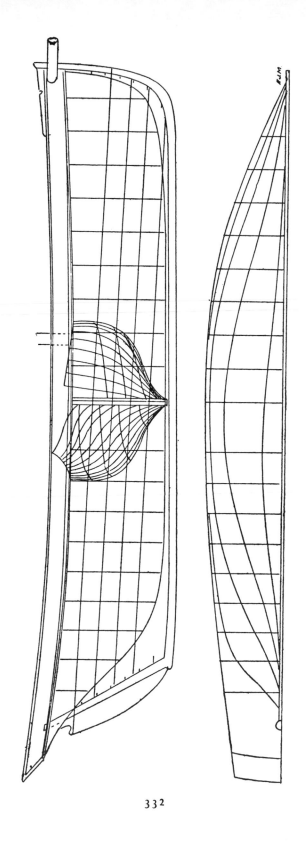

PLAN 12. Plymouth cutter *Erycina*, 1882

Traced by author from photostat of original lines in Science Museum, S.W.

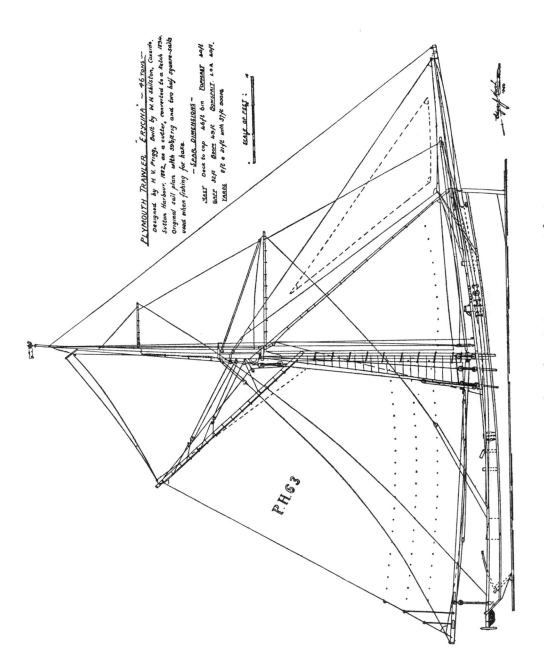

PLYMOUTH TRAWLER "ERYCINA" — 46 TONS —
designed by H. V. Prigg. Built by W. H. Shilston, Cawsand.
Sutton Harbour, 1882, as a cutter, converted to a ketch 1894.
Original sail plan with 39½ft rig and two half square-sails
used when fishing for hake.

— SPAR DIMENSIONS —

MAST   Deck to cap   46 ft 6 in   TOPMAST   20 ft
GAFF   32 ft   BOOM   49 ft   BOWSPRIT   LOA   40 ft.
YARDS   8/c & 21 ft with 37 ft booms

SCALE OF FEET:

P.H.63

PLAN 13.   Plymouth cutter *Erycina*, 1882, 39½ ft. rig

333

~ ÉRYCINA ~

L.O.A 73ft 3in   L.B.P 66ft 9in   KEEL 60ft   BEAM (extreme) 17ft 7in

SCALE OF FEET

PLANS TRACED BY EDGAR J. MARCH FROM PENCIL DRAUGHTS PREPARED BY THE LATE P.J.OKE IN 1934 AND NOW IN THE NATIONAL MARITIME MUSEUM, GREENWICH.

PLAN 14.   Plymouth ketch *Erycina*, 1934 plan

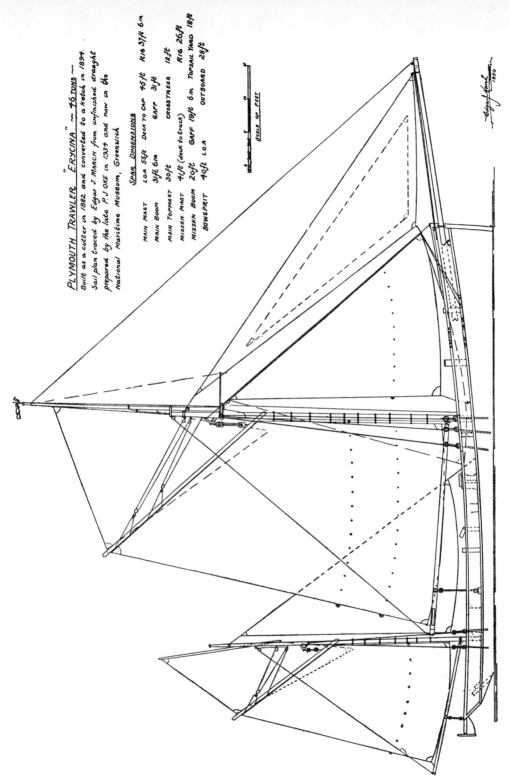

PLYMOUTH TRAWLER "ERYCINA" ~ 46 TONS ~

Built as a cutter in 1882 and converted to a ketch in 1894.
Sail plan traced by Edgar J. March from unfinished draught
prepared by the late P. J OKE in 1937 and now in the
National Maritime Museum, Greenwich.

SPAR DIMENSIONS

MAIN MAST	LOA 55ft	DECK TO CAP 45ft	RIG 37½ft 6in	
MAIN BOOM	31½ft 6in	GAFF 31ft		
MAIN TOPMAST	30ft	CROSSTREES	12ft	
MIZZEN MAST	41ft (deck to truck)		RIG 26ft	
MIZZEN BOOM	20ft	GAFF 19ft 6in 6in	TOPSAIL YARD 18ft	
BOWSPRIT	40ft L.O.A	OUTBOARD 28ft		

SCALE OF FEET

Edgar March
1950

PLAN 14.   Plymouth ketch *Erycina*, 37½ ft. rig, 1934

335

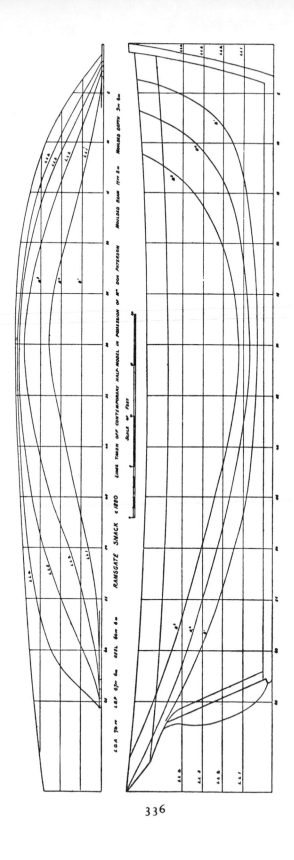

PLAN 15. Large Ramsgate smack, c 1880

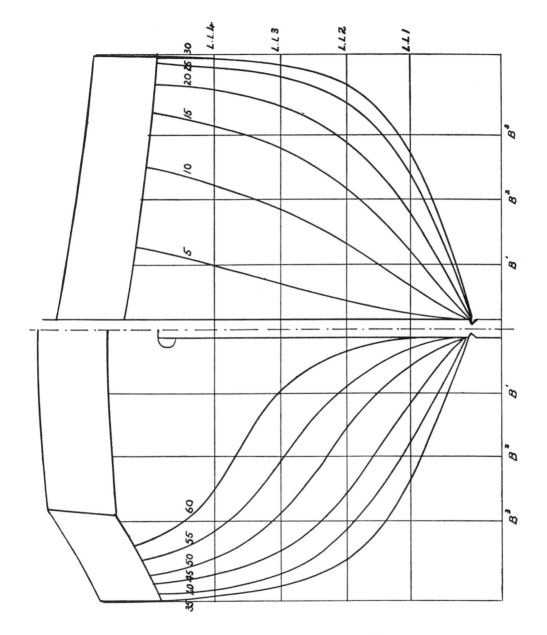

PLAN 15. Large Ramsgate smack, c 1880

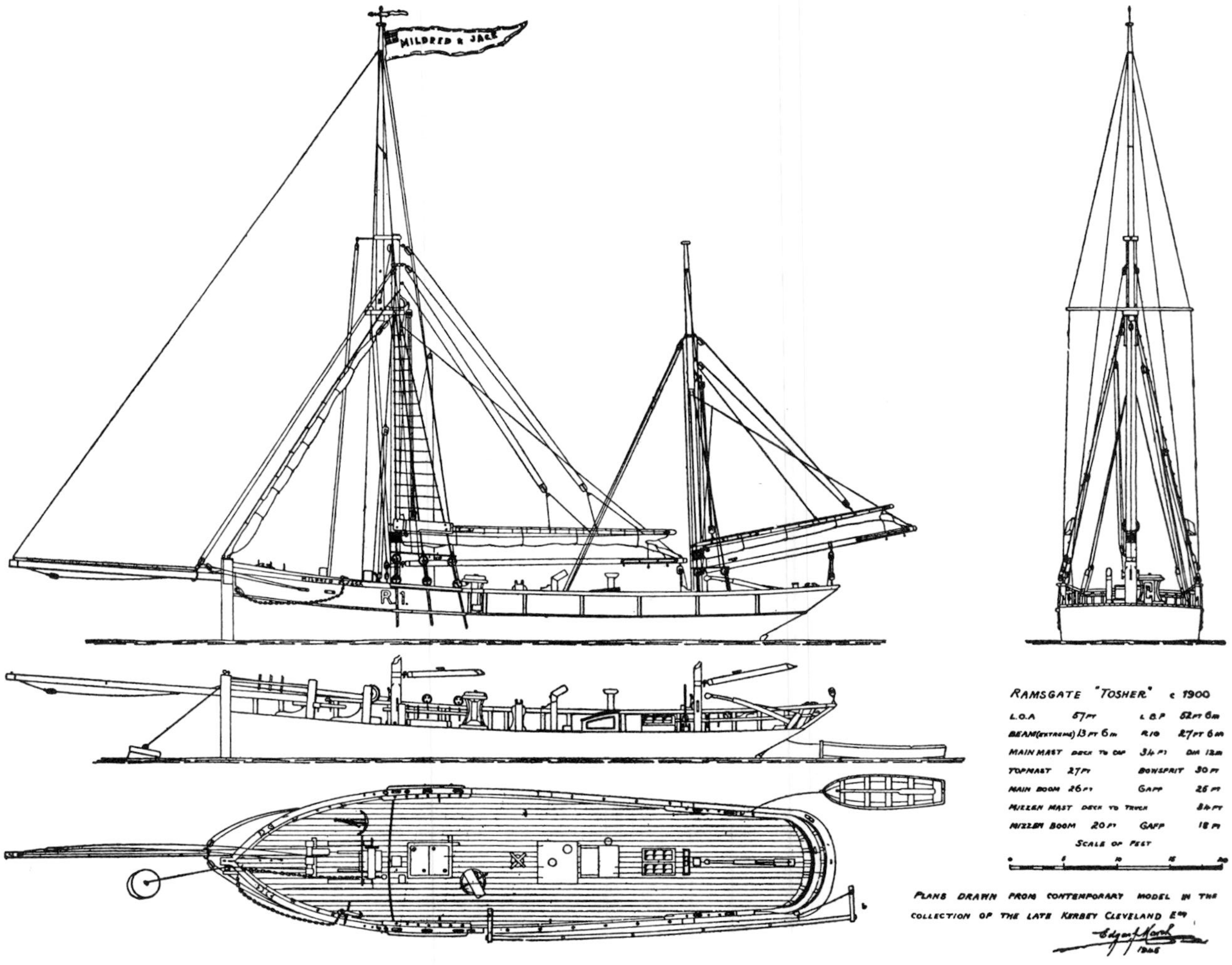

MILDRED & JACK
R 1.
RAMSGATE "TOSHER" c 1900
L.O.A 57 FT L.B.P 52 FT 6 IN
BEAM (EXTREME) 13 FT 6 IN R.10 27 FT 6 IN
MAIN MAST DECK TO CAP 34 FT DIA 12 IN
TOPMAST 27 FT BOWSPRIT 30 FT
MAIN BOOM 26 FT GAFF 25 FT
MIZZEN MAST DECK TO TRUCK 34 FT
MIZZEN BOOM 20 FT GAFF 18 FT
SCALE OF FEET
0 5 10 15 20
PLANS DRAWN FROM CONTEMPORARY MODEL IN THE
COLLECTION OF THE LATE KERBEY CLEVELAND ESQ
Edgar J. March
1946

PLAN 16. Small Ramsgate smack, $27\frac{1}{2}$ ft. rig, *c* 1900

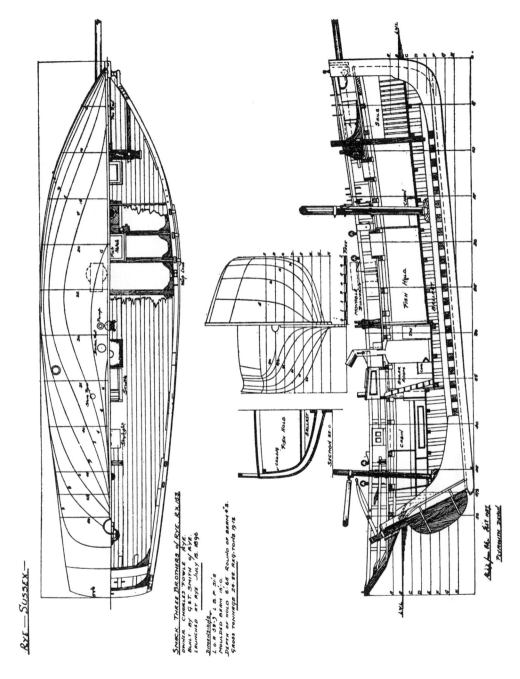

RYE — SUSSEX —

SMACK THREE BROTHERS of RYE. RX.63.
OWNER CHARLES TOWLE of RYE.
BUILT BY G&T SMITH of RYE.
LAUNCHED AT RYE JULY 16. 1896

DIMENSIONS
L.O.R 38·3) L.B.P. 31·6
MOULDED BEAM 13·0.
DEPTH OF HOLD 6·65 ROUND OF BEAM 4¾.
GROSS TONNAGE 24·25 REG·TONS 19·12.

PLAN 17. Rye smack *Three Brothers*, 1896

PLAN 17. Rye smack *Three Brothers*, 1896

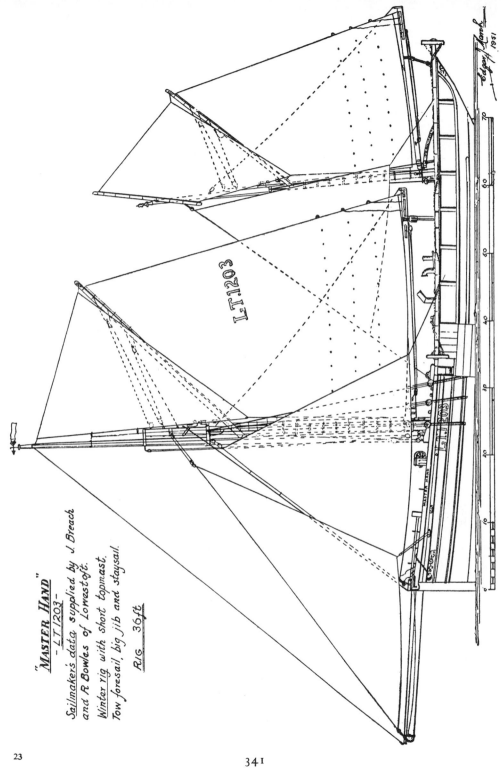

"MASTER HAND"
— LT. 1203 —
Sailmaker's data supplied by J. Breach
and R. Bowles of Lowestoft.
Winter rig with short topmast.
Tow foresail, big jib and staysail.
RIG 36ft

L.T.1203

Edgar March
1951

PLAN 18. Lowestoft trawler *Master Hand*, 1920, 36 ft. rig

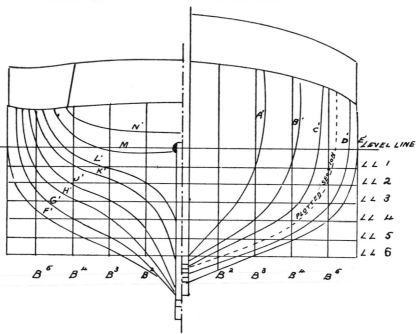

BODY PLAN
To outside of planking

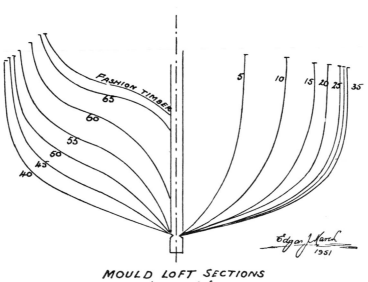

MOULD LOFT SECTIONS
To outside of frames

PLAN 18. Lowestoft trawler *Master Hand*, 1920

342

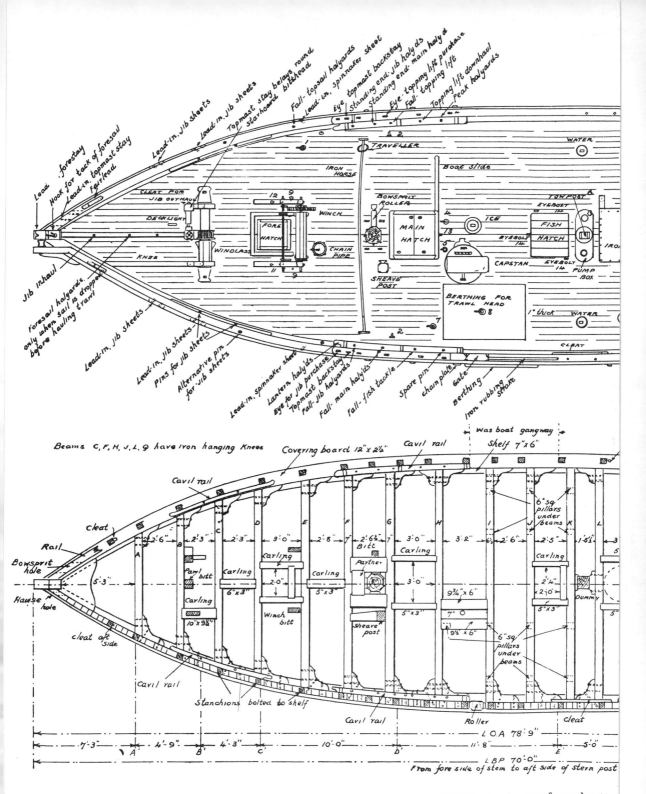

Beams C, F, H, J, L, 9 have iron hanging Knees   Covering board 12"x 2½"

PLAN 18.   Lowestoft trawler *Mast*

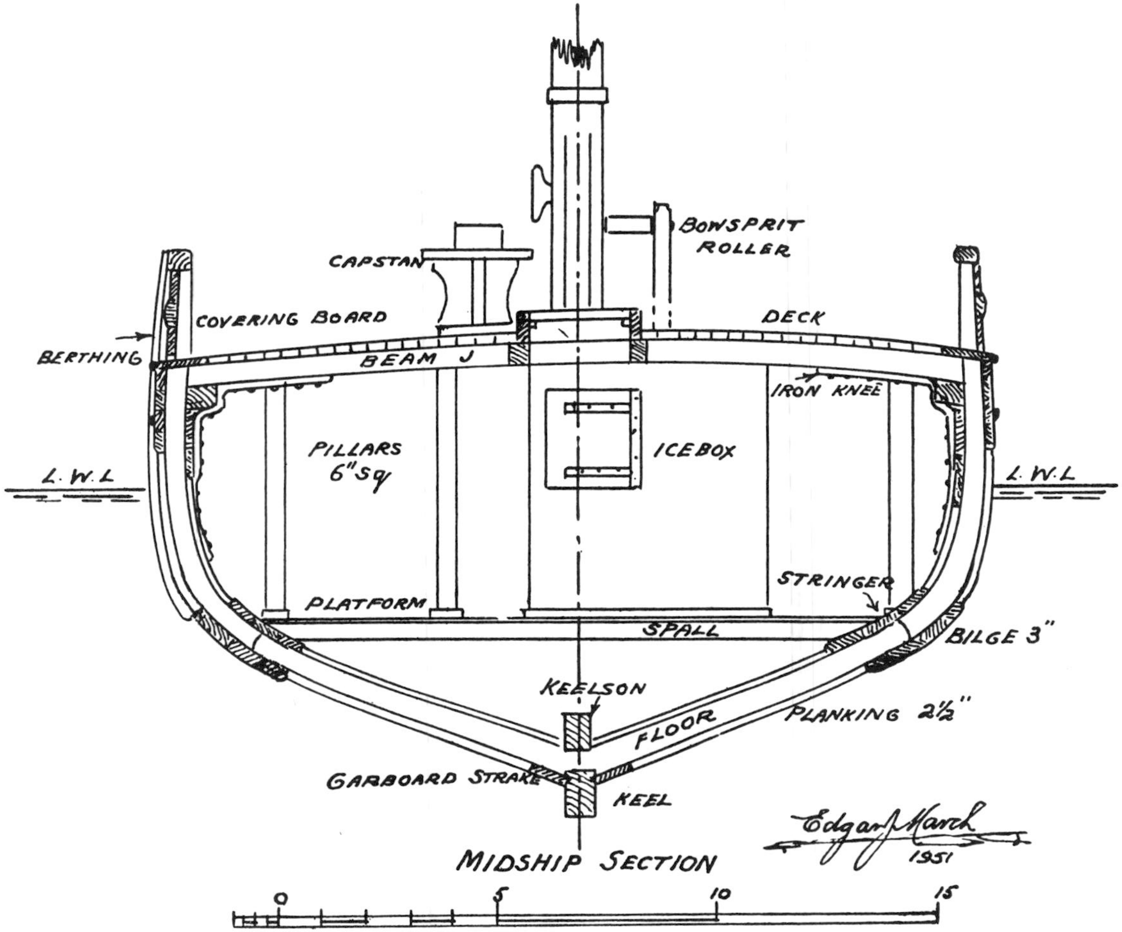
BOWSPRIT
ROLLER
CAPSTAN
COVERING BOARD
DECK
BERTHING
BEAM J
IRON KNEE
PILLARS
6"Sq
ICEBOX
L.W.L
L.W.L
STRINGER
PLATFORM
SPALL
BILGE 3"
KEELSON
FLOOR
PLANKING 2½"
GARBOARD STRAKE
KEEL
Edgar J March
1951
MIDSHIP SECTION
0
5
10
15

PLAN 18. Lowestoft trawler *Master Hand*, 1920

Yellow deal plank	1¼″ to 1½″ @ 2½d ft super, 3in @ 1s 4d c.f.	
Pitch pine plank.	1st class 1s 3d and 1s 6d c.f.	
	1½in @ 3¾d ft super, 3in @ 7d. ft super.	
Deck plank	1,460 ft run 5×2½ @ 2s	£12 13s 6d
Oregon pine, plank	2s 6d c.f.	
Yellow pine	3s 0d c.f.	
Red pine	2s 0d c.f.	
Walnut	2s 6d c.f.	
Oak tops for knees	1s 5d c.f.	
Large Scotch fir knee		1s 6d
Oak sidings for knees	4¾in thick @ 3s 6d c.f.	
121 oak knee crooks	@ 8d each	£4 0s 8d
Oak boat slides	4ft×4in×1in. @ 3d each	
Elm do do	4ft×4in×1¼in. @ 2d each	
Ash wedges	1,950 @ 1d each	
Trenails, oak	4,250, 15in long @ 4s 3d a hundred, or ½d each	
Stern horse	13½ ft super, market oak @ 1s 4d ft run	18s
Aft beam	12½ ft super, circular oak, sq edge @ 1s 11d	
Stern post	14½ ft super, 15in×8in @ 4s c.f.	£2. 18s 1d
Windlass	One 4ft oak barrel, 8 squared	9s 6d
Match board	1s 9d c.f, prepared	
Stern board, oak	10″×1½″ and 13″×1½″ @ 3s 9d c.f.	
Hatch carling, oak	2¾″×2¾″ @ 3s 9d c.f.	
Oak tiller	Cut out @ 6s 6d each, 7ft pieces @ 1s 6d each, rough	
Bulwarks	Pitch pine @ 2s 9d c.f.	
Platform	Pitch pine, 1½in @ 1s 10d ft super	
Boat boards	E.Elm. 6″×⅜″ @ 8s. per 100ft 7×½in @ 10s 6d	
	8″×⅝″ 14s per 100ft	
Fir sweeps	30ft cut out. 10s each	
Mast battens	Greenheart 2″×¾″ @ ¾d ft run	
	Oak 2″×¾″ ½d ft run	
Cross trees	Oak @ 3s 6d each. Ash @ 3s 3d each	
Horns for jaws	4ft × 3in @ 1s 9d. 5ft×4¼in @ 3s. each	
	6ft × 4½ @ 3s 9d.	
Tumblers	E.Elm. 32in×5″×3½″	@ 10d each
	21in×4″×4¼″	7d each
	22in×9″×5″	1s 5d each
Cleats	12″×2″×2in	½d each
Fendoffs	3s each	
Clamps E.Elm	12×3¾×1in, cut out	@ 3d each
Mainmast	21×4 ×1¼in, cut out	8d each
	21×4½×2in, cut out	1s each
Mizzen mast	4ft×2½in.	5d each
	2ft×3in	4d each

Boat hook staves.	16ft worked up	@ 1s 6d each	
	Gal'd hooks, 12in	10d each	
Oars	Fir	13ft	2s 6d each
		14ft	3s each
	Ash	15ft	4s each
Windlass ends. E.Elm	15in turned & morticed	6s 8d each	13in dia.
Deadeyes.	E.Elm	$5\frac{1}{2} \times 3\frac{1}{2}$in	1s each
		6×4in	1s 3d each
	Lignum vitae	$4 \times 3\frac{1}{2}$in	1s 4d each
Bullseyes.	L.V.	$6 \times 3\frac{1}{2}$in	2s each
		$5\frac{1}{2} \times 3\frac{1}{2}$ in	1s 10d each
		4×2 in	8d each
Hearts. L.V.	$6 \times 5 \times \frac{3}{4}$in thick	1s 4d each	
Fairleaders	$4'' \times 2\frac{3}{4}''$. L.V.	1s 3d each	
Oval elm	$12'' \times 8'' \times 5''$, worked up	2s 6d each	
Apple wood, jib sheet bullseyes, worked up		$4\frac{1}{2}$d each	
Trucks.	E.Elm. main topmast, turned up		
	with gal sheave, $6 \times 3\frac{1}{2}$in	@ 1s 2d each	
	$12'' \times 6''$, mizzen, with iron pins	1s 4d each	
Handspike Am. Elm.	5ft worked up	1s 3d each	
Pump boxes. E.Elm.	Turned up & morticed		
	5in lower	@ 9d each	
	5in upper	10d each	

Leathered complete, 1s 3d & 1s 8d

Plugs	$8'' \times 5''$, and $7\frac{1}{4}'' \times 2\frac{1}{4}''$ thick	@ 1s each	
Wedges	Ash. Hatch batten	$\frac{1}{2}$d each	
Pump brakes	Oak 4ft $\times 3\frac{1}{4} \times 2\frac{1}{4}$in	8d each	
Cleats, Oak	$12'' \times 2\frac{1}{2}'' \times 2\frac{1}{4}$in	3d each	
	$24'' \times 4'' \times 4''$, worked up	1s 3d each	
Cleats, thumb	$12 \times 3\frac{1}{4} \times 3\frac{1}{4}$in	7d each	
Mast Cap. Oak	3ft $\times 5\frac{1}{2} \times 3\frac{1}{2}$in	4s each	
Belaying pins, Greenheart.	19in long	4d each	
Parrels. E.Elm.	Turned up	$1\frac{1}{4}$d each	
Thimbles, galvanised	$2\frac{1}{2} \times 2 \times \frac{3}{4}$in	$\frac{3}{4}$d each	
Snatch block	Stropped complete	16s each	
Wood blocks	4in single with L.V. sheave	6d each	
with rope strops	7in do do do	$10\frac{1}{2}$d each	
	8in do do do	1s each	
Internal iron	6in do do do	2s 7d each	
bindings, fixed	12in do do do	6s 7d each	
hook	$7\frac{1}{2}$in single with gal iron sheave	2s 11d each	
Wood blocks	11in double, L.V sheaves, fixed hook, (patent)	@ £1. 5s each	

Snatch block	12in single, inside iron		
	strap	@ 10s each	
Main sheet blocks	11in		13s 4d each
Mast hoops	12in @ 5d	14in @ 7d	
	16in 8d	20in 11d	
Ship's axes	2s each		
Iron washers	16s a cwt		
Paint	7lbs for 2s		
Rooves. Copper	1s a lb		
Lead	1½d lb	Old lead 10s cwt	
Spikes	12s cwt		
Eyebolts ⅝in	18s cwt		
Bolts 5¾in	1½d a lb		
Dowells	14s per 1000, wood deck		
Varnish. Oak	2s a quart, pine 2s 1½d a gallon		
Water Tank	Galvanised for port side E.M.W.	£3. 6s 0d	
Bolts, gal.	16s cwt		
Rigging chain	16s 6d to 18s cwt		
Main sheet posts	9s each		
White Oakum	24s cwt	Hair 15s cwt	
Marine glue	37s 6d cwt		
Traveller 18lb	4s 6d for Ramsgate smack		
Iron knees	5s cwt		
Iron ballast	2s cwt		

Every item in the yard, numbering thousands, is priced and entered up, but the above are the main materials used in building a smack. Taken in conjunction with the complete costs for building at Lowestoft and Brixham it gives a very good idea of prices ruling before the 1914–18 war.

BLACKSMITH'S SHOP. NEW IRONWORK TO
E.M.W. L.T. 314. 47 tons, sunk by U-boat on
13th August 1915, 29 miles NE by N of Cromer.

	cwt	qr	lbs
Winch handles, two		1	7
Goose necks, three		3	2
Anchor shackles, three		1	7
Peak halyard hooks, three			19
Two feet and ring for fore horse		2	17
Main sheet and block strops, two		1	4
After shoe, one		2	7
Dove tail plates, two			24
Main halyard bolt and plate		1	7
Bands for main boom, two			22
Carried forward	3	3	4

	cwt	qr	lbs	
Brought forward	3	3	4	
Peak halyard eye bolts and plates, three			26	
Iron for mizzen sheet horse			7	
Irons and bolts for main sheet		1	13	
Bar and Plate for Togel			7	
Band for bowsprit			10	
Eye plates for main boom			7	
Two windlass bearings			9	
Mizzen slide band			24	
	4	3	23	@ 1 0s
Forms for rudder irons	1	3	7	@ 1 0s
$\frac{1}{2}$in eye bolts			19	
$\frac{5}{8}$in eye bolts			1 5	
$\frac{3}{4}$in eye bolts		2	14	
$\frac{7}{8}$in eye bolts			13	

Total 1cwt 0qr 5lbs @ 9s.

		cwt	qr	lbs	
$\frac{1}{2}$in rail bolts			1	1 2	@ 9s
$\frac{5}{8}$in Ring bolts				14	
$\frac{7}{8}$in Ring bolts				1 2	
$\frac{1}{2}$in Nuts	1 2lbs				
$\frac{5}{8}$in Nuts	7lbs				
1 in Nuts	5lbs				
1$\frac{1}{4}$in nuts	7lbs		1	3	@ 1 8s
Gangway Joint	24lbs @ 9s				
Bowsprit traveller	24lbs 9s				
Main halyard bolt, patent			1	10	@ 1 0s
Topping lift Band	@ 1 0s			14	
1 slide band (stock)				2 2	
1 main slide band	@ 1 0s		1	1 2	
Masthead Cap	1 0s		2	10	
Togel	1 0s			13	
Thimble & Plate for patent Main Halyard Bolt				14	
Form for mizzen gooseneck band	@ 4$\frac{1}{2}$d lb			18	
Five eye bands	1 0s			25	
Block hook	1 0s			26	
$\frac{9}{18}$ shackles				1 2	
Main sheet bullseyes	1 0s			10	
Gal. belaying pins	1 6s			14	
one Gal Damp	1 6s			5	
Bolts for winch	1 0s		1	21	
Cant bolts	9s 4d			8	
Dogs	9s 4d			3	

		cwt	qr	lbs
Two crosstree bolts and plate	@ 9s 4d			3
New tarred chain	9s		3	12
$\frac{5}{16}$ Blue chain	18s		3	16
One pair trawl heads	2¾d	168lbs		

Total for Blacksmith's iron work.   £10.   0s   0½d.

OUTFIT FOR A GRIMSBY SMACK
80 tons. c 1884

SPARS

	Length ft.	Diameter in.
Bowsprit	36	11½
Mainmast	57	17
Main topmast	33	9
Main boom	42	10¼
Main gaff	36	8½
Main topsail yard (large)	20	6
do (small)	10	6
Main cross trees	18	4
Square sail yard	45	7
Outrigger	34	6
Mainmast hoops		18
Mizzen mast	48	13
Mizzen boom	24	7
Mizzen gaff	20	5
Mizzen topsail yard	10	4½
Mizzen mast hoops		15
One boat.	16	
6 oars	14	

24 thole pins for ship's rail and 24 for boat.

36 belaying pins, mostly iron.

 4 handspikes.   2 boat hook staffs.   1 lavenet staff.

14 cleats   2 side light boards.   2 trucks.

SAILS

	Yards	Number
1 mainsail	264	0
1 large topsail	84	4
1 small topsail	59	1
1 jib topsail	72	7
Carried forward	479	

		Yards	Number
	Brought forward	479	
1 large foresail		98	4
1 working foresail		65	1
1 storm foresail		48	1
5 jibs, viz:—			
1 eleven cloth		95	5
1 nine cloth		70	2
1 seven cloth		48	1
1 five cloth		29	1
1 four cloth		19	1
1 mizzen sail		90	2
1 mizzen topsail		26	4
1 mizzen staysail		78	6

Total 1,145

2 main hatch tarpaulins	12	
1 skylight cover	2	
2 mast coats	4	

STANDING RIGGING

		Length ft.	Size in.
1 fore stay		63	5½ Wire
4 pairs main shrouds	42ft each	336	3¼ ,,
4 back stays.	67ft each	268	1¾ ,,
1 topmast stay		66	1¾ ,,
1 fish strop pendant		20	3 ,,
1 large fore halyard pendant,		17	3 ,,
1 boat tackle pendant		15	3 ,,
1 jumper stay for mizzen mast.		13	3 ,,
2 pairs mizzen shrouds.		31	2¾ ,,
2 main gaff strops 8½ ft each		17	2½ ,,
8 main lanyards each about 24 ft		192	3¼ Rope
1 fore stay lanyard		30	3¼ ,,
4 mizzen lanyards each about 20ft		80	2¼ ,,
1 mizzen jumper stay lanyard		20	2¼ ,,
1 strop in the rigging for bag rope		12	2½ ,,
16 deadeyes for main rigging			8in dia.
8 deadeyes for mizzen rigging			5 ,,
2 bullseyes for fore bowline			5 ,,
1 bullseye for main sheet			6 ,,
1 bullseye for mizzen sheet			4 ,,
2 bullseyes for jib sheets			4 ,,
2 bullseyes for gaff strop			6 ,,
12 parrels for main gaff, 8 for mizzen gaff.			

Total length of standing rigging.　　1,180 ft

RUNNING RIGGING

	Fathoms	Circ. in.
1 *main throat halyard*	30	3¼
1 *main peak halyard (length without)*	45	3¼
1 *main peak halyard (with purchase)*	36	3¼
1 *main peak purchase*	21	2¼
1 *main topping lift*	8½	4
1 *main topping lift runner*	7	3¼
1 *main topping lift purchase*	17	2¼
1 *main topping lift downhaul*	9	1½
1 *fish tackle fall*	37	3
1 *large fore halyard*	26	3
1 *small fore halyard, with single blocks*	18	2½
(*or fore halyard, double and single*)	25	2½
1 *small fore halyard purchase*	15	1½
1 *topsail halyard*	20	3¼
1 *jib halyard*	20	4
1 *jib halyard purchase*	20	2¼
1 *jib staysail halyard*	22	2½
1 *main sheet*	15	4
1 *main tack fall*	16	2
1 *starboard boat tackle*	25	2½
1 *topsail sheet*	19	3
1 *topsail tack*	3	3½
1 *topsail tack runner*	5	2½
1 *topsail tack fall*	8	2
4 *backstay tackle falls, each 5 fathom*	20	2
1 *watch tackle fall*	7	2
1 *reef tackle (main) fall*	20	3
1 *boom guy fall*	14	3¼
1 *jib topsail tack*	15	2½
1 *pair jib sheets*	8	3
1 *pair jib topsail sheets*	18	1¾
1 *1st main reef pendant (fitted)*	3½	4
1 *2nd main reef pendant (fitted)*	4	4
1 *3rd reef pendant (fitted)*	6	4
3 *reef lacings, each 8 fathom*	24	1
2 *fore bowlines, each 2½ fathom*	5	3
1 *pair flag halyards*	24	
2 *pair lantern halyards, each 12 fathom*	24	1
1 *jib tack fall*	11	2½
1 *bowsprit heel rope*	12	3
1 *jib inhaul*	6	2
1 *bobstay fall*	12	3

	Fathoms	Circ. in.
1 *bobstay uphaul*	4	1½
1 *topmast heel rope*	15	3
3 *reef pendant rackings, main, each* 3½	10½	2
1 *main boom earing*	5	2½
1 *main gaff earing*	4	2½
12 *mainsail hoop seizings, each* 1½ *fathom*	18	1
1 *mizzen throat halyard*	16	2¼
1 *mizzen peak halyard*	18	2¼
1 *mizzen topping lift*	8	2¾
1 *main topping lift fall*	17	1¼
1 *mizzen boat tackle fall*	24	2½
1 *mizzen sheet, for double and single*	10	2½
or two double	13	2½
1 *mizzen topsail halyard*	12	2¼
1 *mizzen topsail sheet*	11	1½
1 *mizzen reef tackle*	10	2
2 *tiller ropes, each* 2½ *fathom*	5	2
1 *mizzen topsail tack*	2½	2½
1 *mizzen topsail tack fall*	7	1½
3 *mizzen lacings, each* 6 *fathom*	18	1
3 *mizzen rackings, each* 2½ *fathom*	7½	1
1 *mizzen boom earing*	2½	2
1 *mizzen gaff earing*	2½	2
1 *mizzen* 1st *reef pendant*	3	2½
1 *mizzen* 2nd *reef pendant*	4	2½
1 *mizzen* 3rd *reef pendant*	5	2½
1 *coil twelve thread ratline line*	120	
1 *lead line*	60	
1 *log line*	40	
2 *balls spun yarn, three yarn*		
1 *ball spun yarn, two yarn*		
3 *balls marline*		
2 *balls amber line.*		
1 *small warp*	60	5½
1 *hauling line*	60	3¾
1 *tow rope*	25	6

Total length of running gear. 953½ *fathom, or* 1 *mile,* 147 *yards.*

CHAINS AND GROUND GEAR

1 *jib tack chain*	28ft
1 *bobstay chain, large link for bullseye* 6ft *up*	10ft
1 *topsail halyard*	14ft

1 *fore sheet, a large link in and out*	15ft
1 *fore stopper*	18ft
1 *mizzen topsail halyard chain*	9 ft
2 *boom guys, each 15ft*	30ft
1 *anchor chain*	60 fathom
1 *best bower anchor*	5½cwt
1 *second bower*	4½cwt
1 *kedge anchor*	3cwt
1 *bowsprit traveller*	15ft

4 *sheer poles or spreaders*
4 *hatch battens*
2 *pairs side light stanchions*
12 *hooks and thimbles, various sizes.*
15 *shackles, various sizes.*
12 *false links, various sizes.*

TRAWL AND FISHING GEAR

2 *trawl beams, 40 to 50ft*	*Rubbers for cod end*
2 *pair trawl heads, 360 to 400lb*	1 *trawl warp 150 fathom*
12 *iron wedges*	1 *pair bridles, 20 fathom each*
6 *thimbles*	1 *dandy bridle, 20 fathom*
2 *trawl warp shackles*	2 *head lines, 9 fathom each*
4 *bridle shackles*	2 *cod lines, 15 fathom each*
1 *dandy bridle chain & shackles*	2 *cod end lines, 3 fathom each*
2 *ground ropes, 16 fathom each*	2 *flappers*
2 *trawls*	2 *bolch lines, 20 fathom each*

Name and port of registry in letters not less than 4in high on stern.
Numbers on each bow and initials of port. 18in high. 2½in breadth.
Same in mainsail 24in high, 3½in breadth, on both sides of sail, above the close reef.
Boat to be numbered and lettered as vessel, 3in high, ½in breadth placed on outside of stern.

BLOCKS
76 in all

		Size
2 *main throat halyard*	1 *double,* 1 *treble.*	11in
5 *main peak halyard*	5 *single*	11in
1 *main peak halyard* (spare) *generally used for bowsprit heel rope*		
2 *main peak purchase*	1 *single,* 1 *double*	8in
2 *main sheet*	2 *double.*	13in
3 *main topsail tack.*	2 *single,* 1 *double*	8in
1 *main topsail sheet*	1 *single*	8in
2 *main tack*	1 *single,* 1 *double*	5in
2 *main topping lift*	2 *single*	10in

2 *main topping lift purchase*	1 *single*, 1 *double*	8*in*
2 *main topping lift downhaul*	2 *single*	5*in*
2 *fore halyards, large*	1 *single*, 1 *double*	11*in*
2 *fore halyards, small*	1 *single*, 1 *double*	8*in*
3 *jib halyards*	3 *single*	9*in*
2 *jib purchase*	1 *single*, 1 *double*	7*in*
4 *jib topsail gear*	3 *single*, 1 *double*	6*in*
1 *jib tack*	1 *single*,	6*in*
2 *fish tackle*	1 *double*, 1 *treble*	13*in*
2 *bobstays*	2 *single*	9*in*
1 *bowsprit heel rope*	1 *single*	11*in*
2 *starboard boat tackle*	1 *single*, 1 *double*	10*in*
2 *reef tackle*	1 *single*, 1 *double*	8*in*
2 *main boom guy*	1 *single*, 1 *double*	10*in*
2 *watch tackle, or handy billy*	1 *single*, 1 *double*	7*in*
8 *backstays*	4 *single*, 4 *double*	6*in*
2 *mizzen throat halyards*	1 *single*, 1 *double*	8*in*
3 *mizzen peak halyards*	3 *single*,	8*in*
1 *mizzen topping lift*	1 *single*,	8*in*
2 *mizzen topping lift purchase*	1 *single*, 1 *double*	5*in*
2 *mizzen sheet blocks*	2 *double.*	8*in*
2 *mizzen topsail tack*	1 *single*, 1 *double*	5*in*
1 *mizzen topsail sheet*	1 *single*	5*in*
2 *mizzen staysail*	1 *single*, 1 *double*	8*in*
2 *mizzen reef tackle*	1 *single*, 1 *double*	7*in*

FITTINGS AND GENERAL STORES

1 *windlass*	1 *mechanical foghorn*
1 *double winch*	2 *compasses*
1 *dandy winch*	1 *clock*
1 *capstan or* 1 *steam do*	1 *aneroid barometer*
1 *gangway roller*	1 *patent log*
1 *taffrail roller*	1 *deep sea lead,* 18*lbs*
1 *patent main sheet chock*	1 *hand lead,* 12 *lbs*
2 *iron pumps*	1 *vane*
1 *slush pump*	2 *cork fenders*
4 *complete sets of pump gear*	2 *life buoys*
2 *complete sets of slush pump gear*	3 *life jackets*
2 *water tanks*	2 *wood buckets*
1 *norman*	2 *galvanised buckets*
2 *spare winch handles*	1 *tub*
2 *spare capstan handles*	1 *beef cask*
2 *side lanterns, red and green*	1 *pork cask*
2 *masthead lanterns*	1 *lavenet*

1 *deck lantern*	4 *marline spikes*
2 *binnacle lamps*	2 *fids*
1 *cabin lamp*	1 *serving board and mallet*
1 *engine room lamp*	1 *flare can*
1 *forecastle lamp*	2 *turpentine cans*
1 *fog bell, 8in.*	2 *paraffin cans*
1 *boiler*	1 *cooking stove, complete*
1 *tar bucket*	1 *tin box for ship's papers*
1 *grease bucket*	2 *cold chisels*
Nails, various sizes	*Sail needles*
Sail palm	*Sail hook*
1 2 *braiding needles*	*Belly twine*
Roping twine	*Back twine*
Seaming twine	1 *axe*
1 *saw*	2 *hammers*

Knives, forks, platters, dishes, mugs, saucepans, kettles, and cabin utensils. Oil cans, poker and shovel, canisters for stores, jars for treacle, lard and butter. Boxes for salt and pepper. Flags and ensigns. Compasses and parallel rule. Charts.

GLOSSARY

ADMIRAL. A highly skilled fisherman in charge of a fleet of trawlers.

ARMING. A piece of tallow put into the cavity and over the bottom of the lead to bring up a sample of the seabed.

BARKING. A dressing applied to sails as a preservative. Originally produced from oak bark, later cutch obtained from East Indian trees.

BECKET. An eye in a rope, made in the form of a circle.

BEND. To make fast, to secure a sail to its spar.

BILGE. The round in a vessel's timbers where they begin to approach a vertical direction.

BINNS. An old word for the bends or wales.

BITTS. Upright timbers to secure the windlass and winch, which pass through the deck and mortice into floors or keelson.

BOARDING. Taking fish from a trawler to the fish carrier. Also known as trunking and ferrying.

BOLCH LINE. The rope to which a trawl net is bent before being attached to the ground rope.

BRAIDING. Making the meshes of a net.

BRAKE. The handle of a ship's pump.

BRASH. Rubbish brought up in a trawl net.

BRIDLES. Spans of rope or wire connecting the ends of the beam to the warp.

BULLSEYE. An oval piece of wood with a hole in the centre for a rope to reeve through, and a groove round the outside for the strop. Also oblong with two holes for the jib sheets.

CARLINGS. Pieces of oak fitted between the beams in a fore and aft direction.

CARVEL BUILD. A method of building where the planks are laid edge to edge, thus presenting a smooth surface.

CAVIL RAIL. Stout pieces of timber bolted horizontally to the stanchions to carry belaying pins. East Anglian name.

CEILING. The inside planking of the hull.

CHAIN PLATES. Iron bars bolted to the sides of hull to which the lower deadeyes are connected.

CLAMP. A special cleat at after end of boom through which the reef pendants pass. Also the strake of planking immediately under the shelves on which the beams rest.

CLENCH BUILD. A method of building where the strakes of planking overlap, forming "lands". Also known as clencher, clincher, clinker and lapstrake.

CLEW. The lower, after corner in a fore and aft sail.

COD. The long, narrow bag at the end of a trawl net in which the fish are finally contained. From the Anglo-Saxon "codd" a small bag.

CONVERTER SMACK. Vessels used for both trawling and drifting, chiefly found at Yarmouth.

COPER. A foreigner who supplied tobacco and drink on the high seas at cheap prices.

COVERING BOARD. The outside deck plank fitted over the timber heads. Also called the planksheer.

CRINGLE. A short piece of rope with each end spliced into the boltrope of a sail and enclosing an iron ring or thimble.

CUTTER. A single-masted fore and aft rigged sailing vessel. Also the name given to the steam fish carriers which brought the catches to market.

DANDY BRIDLE. The wire or rope used to bring the aft end of the trawl beam alongside when hauling.

DANDY RIGGED. Originally a cutter-rigged vessel with a lug mizzen, later fisherman's parlance for the ketch rig.

DANDY SCORE. The fairlead and rollers on the port side of taffrail.

DANDY WINCH. The small winch aft used when bringing the trawl beam alongside, usually known as the dandy wink.

DEADRISE. The approach the floor timbers make to the perpendicular.

DEADWOOD. Solid timbers bolted on the top of the keel, for'ard and aft, to receive the heels of frames which do not cross the keel.

DEMERSAL. Fish swimming near the bottom of the sea.

DRIFT. The distance between two blocks of a tackle.

DUMMY. The towpost or pumphead amidship to which the warp is attached by a stopper when towing the trawl is in progress.

DUTCH AUCTION. Where a salesman starts at a high price and comes down until he finds a bidder.

EARING. A rope attached to a cringle of a sail to bend it to its spar.

FALL. The hauling part of a tackle.

FASHION TIMBERS. The aftermost frames to which the transoms are bolted, thus forming the shape of the stern.

FAST, TO COME. When the trawl fouls an obstruction on the seabed.

FERRYING. Taking the fish from the smack to the fish carrier. Also known as boarding and trunking.

FLASKETS. Wicker baskets in which fish were packed.

FLEETING. The system of working trawlers in fleets, not individually, and boarding the fish every day.

FLOORS. The lowermost of the various pieces making up a "frame", and crossing the keel. The siding being the thickness in a fore and aft direction, the moulding, the depth or perpendicular dimension.

FORELOCK. A flat piece of iron driven through a hole in the end of a bolt to prevent its drawing.

FRAME. One of the ribs of a vessel, made up of floor timbers, futtocks, and top timbers. The siding being the thickness in a fore and aft direction, the moulding the depth athwartships, i.e., between inside and outside planking.

FUTTOCKS. One of the timbers making up a frame, the others being the floor and top timber.

GARBOARD. The strake of outside planking next to the keel into which it is rabbetted and fastened.

GOOSENECK. The hook fitted to the end of a boom to secure it to the shaffle round the mast.

GORES. The angle at one or both ends of such cloths as increase the breadth or depth of a sail.

GRIPES. Ropes used to secure a boat on deck.

GUNTACKLE PURCHASE. A tackle composed of two single blocks.

GUY. A rope attached to anything for steadying purposes.

HATCH BOATS. Small clinker-built craft, often fitted with wells, in which live cod were conveyed from Gravesend to Billingsgate.

HEAD IRONS. Iron frames on each end of trawl beam to raise it about 3 ft. clear of the seabed. Also called trawl heads.

HEART. A peculiar type of deadeye having only one eye. the lower edge of which is scored so as to grip the lanyard. Also the centre strand in a four-stranded rope.

HEEL ROPE. The rope by which a bowsprit is run in or out.

HOLLOW LINES. The horizontal lines of a vessel that have inflections, being concave instead of convex.

HOODWAY. East Anglian name for the companion leading to the cabin.

HORNS. The curved pieces of timber making up the jaws of a gaff.

HORN TIMBERS. The stern timbers at the middle of a square stern.

JUMP STAY. The fore stay to the mizzen mast.

KENTLEDGE. Pig iron ballast.

KNITTLES. Fisherman's name for reef points.

LACINGS. Thin ropes passed through eyelets in seams and round the foot of a sail when reefing down.

LADE-NET. A long handled net on an iron hoop in which live fish were taken out of the sea or the well.

LEADER. A chain and rope jackstay on which the grommets on the luff of a topsail run.

LEECH. The lee edge of a sail.

LEECH LINE. The rope used to haul inboard the ground rope of a trawl net.

LINER. Name given to smacks which fished with long lines.

LININGS. Strengthening pieces sewn on sails where extra wear or strain is expected. Also another name for the inside planking.

LUFF. The weather edge of a sail.

LUFF PURCHASE. A tackle composed of a single and double block, the standing end of the rope being fast to the tail of the single block.

MAST ROPE. The rope by which a topmast is sent up or lowered, sometimes called a heel rope, but this properly applies to a bowsprit only.

MOULDING. The depth of a timber, the side to which the mould is applied.

OFFAL. Coarser types of fish, as distinct from choice or "prime".

PAD. A wicker basket used as a fish measure.

PARCEL. To wind tarred canvas—parcelling—round a rope.

PARREL. The rope upon which is strung the hard wooden balls—the trucks or beads—which encircle the mast with the ends attached to the jaws of a gaff.

PAWL. A short bar of iron which prevents a capstan or windlass etc. from turning back.

PENDANT. A rope to which a tackle is attached. The rope rove through the reef cringles.

PLATFORM. The floor boards over the ballast, etc.

POUNDS. The space below deck where the fish trunks were packed.

PREVENTER. An extra rope rove as a support in case the original one carried away.

PRICKING. To pierce the bladders—the "sounds"—of deep-water fish, especially cod, before placing the fish in the well.

PRIME. Choice fish, the more expensive kinds.

QUARTER STROP. The rope used for squaring the trawl beam across the stern, and to secure it when along the rail.

RABBET. The groove cut in stem, keel and sternpost to receive edges or ends of planks.

RACK TO. To rack a tackle is to seize the two running ends together so as to prevent them from running out of the blocks even if the fall is let go.

RICKERS. The stems of young trees cut up for spars, stronger and more springy than hewn spars. Can be recognised by their knots.

RIG. The distance from deck to hounds, i.e., 34ft. rig, 36ft. rig.

RISING FLOOR. Sharp bottomed or V shaped.

ROACH. The curve on the foot or leech of a sail.

ROBANDS. Short lines by which the head of a sail is attached to its yard or spar.

RUNNER. A rope passed through a single block on a pendant, with a purchase at one end, the other being made fast.

SCANTLING. The finished dimensions of a piece of timber.

SCARPH. A joint uniting two timbers longitudinally.

SCUTTLE. An opening cut through a deck, framed up similar to a hatchway, usually covered with cap cover if the coamings are raised.

SENNET or SENNIT. A flat braid formed by plaiting ropeyarns or spunyarn together.

SHAFFLE. The split collar at foot of a mast to take the gooseneck of a boom.

SIDING or SIDED. The thickness of a timber between the flat surfaces.

SHEET. The rope by which the lower after corner—the clew—of a sail is controlled.

SHELF. The longitudinal timber on which the ends of the beams rest, also called a clamp, but properly speaking this is the strake of planking immediately below the shelf.

SINGLE BOATING. When a smack worked on her own and not with a fleet.

SKEG. The heel or extreme after end of the keel, sometimes projecting slightly abaft the sternpost.

SNOODS. Short lengths of line carrying baited hooks, attached to a long line.

SPALLS. Light beams carrying the platform. Also temporary beams to hold framing together until the main beams are crossed.

SPAN. A wire or rope with both ends made fast and a bullseye in the bight to which a purchase can be hooked.

SPRING. A rope temporarily attached to another rope, bollard, etc., by which a change of direction can be affected.

STEP. A heavy piece of timber bolted to keelson and floors with a mortice cut in it to receive the tenon in heel of mast.

STOCKER or STOCKERBAIT. Small or unmarketable fish, usually the perquisite of the crew.

STOCKFISH. Cod or ling split open, salted and dried in the sun.

STOPPER. A rope of less breaking strain than the warp on which the final strain of towing a trawl is taken. Sometimes called the "legs". Also a rope, fast at one end, and used to secure anything.

STRINGERS. Strengthening timbers running longitudinally inside a hull. Usually a thicker strake of planking.

SWIG, TO. When the fall of a tackle is put under a cleat and held firmly by some of crew, another man takes hold of that part of fall between cleat and block and throws his whole weight on it, the others taking in the slack obtained. By swigging, that little extra can be obtained when by steady hauling the blocks cannot be moved an inch.

TABLING. The broad hem or border round a sail to which the boltrope is sewed.

TACK. The lower fore corner of a sail.

THIMBLE. An iron ring, more or less triangular shaped, concave on the outside so that a rope can be spliced round it.

TRANSOMS. Timbers lying horizontally across the sternpost and bolted to the fashion timbers.

TRAVELLER. An iron ring travelling freely on a mast or spar.

TRENAILS. Long oak pins, one inch and over in diameter, driven through planks and timbers as fastenings, ends being wedged. The best form of fastening in a wooden vessel as the wood swells in water, no corrosive action takes place, and weight is less than that of iron bolts.

TRUCKS. The wooden balls threaded on a rope to form a parrel. Also the flat, circular wooden cap at head of a pole or topmast, usually with a small sheave to take the flag halyards.

TRUNKS. Oblong wooden boxes in which fish were packed.

TRUNKING. Taking fish from smack to fish carrier.

TYE. A chain, rope or wire attached to a yard and reeving through sheave at masthead with a tackle at lower end.

WALES. Thick plank on outside of hull below the covering board, also called the bends, or binns.

WARP. A heavy left-handed rope, 110 to 150 fathom in length, 6 in. to 8 in. circ., by which the trawl net is dragged through the water.

WASH. A measure of 21 quarts and one pint of water.

WELL. A watertight compartment to which sea had free access through auger holes and fitted in certain smacks called welled smacks, in which fish could be kept alive for a considerable time.

WHIP. A purchase consisting of one single block.

YOKE. The lower cap at masthead, usually made of wood. Also the horizontal piece of wood on rudder head to which the rudder or yoke lines are attached.

LIST OF PLATES

★

LIST OF PLATES

PHOTOGRAPHS SUPPLIED BY

Margate Library
11, 154.

Mr. J. W. Mitchley
41, 49, 50, 179, 180.

Mr. L. W. Moore
138, 171.

Skipper F. W. Moxey
77.

National Maritime Museum
98, 112, 113, 126, 139.

Nautical Photo Agency
8, 43, 44, 55, 58, 59, 60, 61, 62, 62a,
66, 68, 69, 71, 73, 76, 83, 86, 99, 111,
118, 119, 121, 128, 148, 151, 165,
166, 167, 168, 169.

Mr. D. Paterson
5, 64.

Mr. T. Peek
52, 53.

Ramsgate Library
12, 155, 156, 157.

Royal National Lifeboat Institution
56.

Mr. J. D. Rattar, Lerwick
3, 4.

Science Museum, Director of
2, 31.

Mr. R. Stimson
Frontispiece, 27, 30, 34, 173, 176, 177,
178.

Mr. G. W. Stone
45.

The Times
16, 120.

Mr. P. A. Upham
127.

Mr. & Mrs. G. E. Wilson
100, 101, 102.

Messrs. A. & S. Yallop
65, 72, 84.

LIST OF SCALE PLANS